Effective Computer Science Education in K-12 Classrooms

Serhat Bahadır Kert
Yıldız Teknik Üniversitesi, Turkey

IGI Global
Scientific Publishing
Publishing Tomorrow's Research Today

Vice President of Editorial	Melissa Wagner
Managing Editor of Acquisitions	Mikaela Felty
Managing Editor of Book Development	Jocelynn Hessler
Production Manager	Mike Brehm
Cover Design	Phillip Shickler

Published in the United States of America by
IGI Global Scientific Publishing
701 East Chocolate Avenue
Hershey, PA, 17033, USA
Tel: 717-533-8845
Fax: 717-533-8661
E-mail: cust@igi-global.com
Website: https://www.igi-global.com

Library of Congress Cataloging-in-Publication Data

Names: Kert, Serhat, 1978- editor
Title: Effective computer science education in K-12 classrooms / Edited by Serhat Kert.
Description: Hershey, PA : IGI Global, [2025] | Includes bibliographical references and index. | Summary: "The main objective of this book is to be a pedagogical reference for computer science educators, especially at the k-12 level. The book includes theoretical details for designing computer science education, practical applications for analysis, design, development, implementation and evaluation processes, and more"-- Provided by publisher.
Identifiers: LCCN 2024048711 (print) | LCCN 2024048712 (ebook) | ISBN 9798369345429 hardcover | ISBN 9798369345436 paperback | ISBN 9798369345443 ebook
Subjects: LCSH: Computer science--Study and teaching | Curriculum planning
Classification: LCC QA76.27 .E34 2025 (print) | LCC QA76.27 (ebook)
LC record available at https://lccn.loc.gov/2024048711
LC ebook record available at https://lccn.loc.gov/2024048712

British Cataloguing in Publication Data
A Cataloguing in Publication record for this book is available from the British Library.

Table of Contents

Preface xiii

Chapter 1
Coding Activity Implementations for K-12 Level Teachers 1
Ayşin Gaye Üstün, Sinop University, Turkey
Memnüne Kokoç, Karadeniz Technical University, Turkey

Chapter 2
Computational Thinking: Exploring Approaches in Early Childhood Education 27
Leonard Busuttil, Faculty of Education, Msida, Malta
Diane Vassallo, Faculty of Education, Msida, Malta
Patrick Schembri, Faculty of Education, Msida, Malta

Chapter 3
Effective Information Technology Education in Grade 10-12 Classrooms, South Africa: In the Further Education and Training Phase 55
Leila Goosen, University of South Africa, South Africa

Chapter 4
Information Security Awareness in K12 Computer Science Education 73
Tuba Kaynarca İdil, Anadolu University, Turkey

Chapter 5
Innovations Focusing on Artificial Intelligence in Computer Science Education 111
Ertürk Erdağı, Republic of Türkiye Ministry of National Education, Turkey

Chapter 6
Low-Code Programming for K-12 Education 145
İbrahim Halil Özdemir, Ege University, Turkey
Fırat Sarsar, Ege University, Turkey
Brendan Calandra, Georgia State University, USA

Chapter 7
Mapping the Anatomy of Novice-Generated Mistakes in Learning Programming 171
Fatih Erdoğdu, Zonguldak Bülent Ecevit University, Turkey
Seyfullah Gökoğlu, Bartın University, Turkey

Chapter 8
Methods for Accessible Computer Science and Computer Programming Education for Visually Impaired and Blind Students 193
Habibe Güneş, Firat University, Turkey

Chapter 9
Online Assessment in K12 Computer Science Education 223
Betül Tonbuloğlu, Distance Education Application and Research Center, Yildiz Technical University, Turkey

Chapter 10
Professional Development for K-12 Educators 263
Veysel Bilal Arslankara, T.C. Millî Eğitim Bakanlığı, Turkey
Elif Arslankara, T.C. Millî Eğitim Bakanlığı, Turkey
İlyas Asan, MONE, Turkey
Mehmet Külekçi, MONE, Turkey
Süleyman Sadi Seferoğlu, Hacettepe University, Turkey

Chapter 11
Teaching Machine Learning Through Educational Robotics 293
Gamze Mercan, Hacettepe University, Turkey
Zümrüt Varol Selçuk, Ordu University, Turkey

Chapter 12
Teaching Programming Through Metaphors 319
Erkan Geçitli, Ministry of National Education, Turkey
Bünyamin Yurdakul, Ege University, Turkey

Chapter 13
Tools and Resources for K-12 Computer Science Education 349
İsmail Tonbuloğlu, Marmara University, Turkey

Compilation of References 373

About the Contributors 467

Index 473

Detailed Table of Contents

Preface xiii

Chapter 1
Coding Activity Implementations for K-12 Level Teachers 1
Ayşin Gaye Üstün, Sinop University, Turkey
Memnüne Kokoç, Karadeniz Technical University, Turkey

Coding and robotics activities are vital for developing K-12 students' 21st-century skills, including problem-solving, algorithmic, logical, mathematical, critical, and computational thinking. Teachers play a key role by providing the right tools, designing level-appropriate activities, monitoring progress, offering immediate feedback, and adjusting teaching strategies as needed. This section outlines theoretical frameworks supporting these activities, fostering cognitive and social development. Vygotsky's Social Learning Theory aids skill acquisition through interaction, Piaget's Cognitive Development Theory ensures suitable activities, Bruner's Constructivist Learning Theory supports meaningful knowledge construction, Havighurst's Activity Theory helps complete developmental tasks, and the TPACK Model integrates technology with teaching strategies. These frameworks provide a structured approach to instructional design, promoting student-centered and interactive learning in coding and robotics education.

Chapter 2
Computational Thinking: Exploring Approaches in Early Childhood Education 27
Leonard Busuttil, Faculty of Education, Msida, Malta
Diane Vassallo, Faculty of Education, Msida, Malta
Patrick Schembri, Faculty of Education, Msida, Malta

This chapter reviews research on integrating computational thinking (CT) in early childhood education (ECE) over the past decade, emphasizing its growing importance as a crucial skill for the technological world. It explores how CT is taught in early years, the characteristics of CT activities, and their learning outcomes. The review identifies three methodologies: unplugged, coding, and robotics. Unplugged methods use tangible materials like games to teach CT without digital devices. Coding activities foster problem-solving and creativity, while robotics offer interactive learning with programmable robots. Learning outcomes include foundational CT skills, creative problem-solving, technical proficiency, cognitive and language development, and, with robotics, positive emotions, prosocial values, and environmental awareness. Integrating CT in ECE through these methodologies provides valuable learning experiences, fostering critical thinking and preparing young learners to be creative, analytical thinkers in a technologically advanced future.

Chapter 3
Effective Information Technology Education in Grade 10-12 Classrooms, South Africa: In the Further Education and Training Phase................................ 55
Leila Goosen, University of South Africa, South Africa

Against the background of effective Computer Science Education (CSE) in Kindergarten/Grade R-12 classrooms, the purpose of this chapter is to specifically investigate effective Information Technology (IT) education in grade 10-12 classrooms in South Africa, where the subject IT is offered in the Further Education and Training (FET) phase. As such, the chapter will e.g., provide an introduction to Computer Science in R-12 education, as well as effective teaching approaches and strategies in the South African context.

Chapter 4
Information Security Awareness in K12 Computer Science Education 73
Tuba Kaynarca İdil, Anadolu University, Turkey

Today's world is developing in many aspects like health, transport, communication. The area of technology is a kind of locomotive of the train because it affects the whole advancing arenas. Although shining development facilitates our lives and increases the life quality, it also causes some technologic threads. According to International Telecommunication Union (ITU) statistics, an estimated 5.3 billion people, or 66 per cent of the world's population, use the Internet. How nice to reach each other rapidly even though we are far away from each other, but what about hackers, malicious people? This chapter focuses on the importance of information security and cybersecurity education at K12 Level.

Chapter 5
Innovations Focusing on Artificial Intelligence in Computer Science Education 111
Ertürk Erdağı, Republic of Türkiye Ministry of National Education, Turkey

Computer science education is a field that needs constant development due to technological developments. Especially in recent years, the widespread use of the concept of artificial intelligence in all scientific fields has affected the field of computer science education. Today, the concept of artificial intelligence is used on a very large scale in many fields other than technical fields. This has enabled the integration of the artificial intelligence universe with all fields with an interdisciplinary approach. Artificial intelligence is capable of directing the entire educational process rather than being a stand-alone educational content during computer science education. Students can use this field to solve all problems in their field of expertise during and after their education. In this section, artificial intelligence techniques and subfields used in computer science education, artificial intelligence trends, challenges related to artificial intelligence, and the interaction of the curriculum with artificial intelligence are discussed.

Chapter 6
Low-Code Programming for K-12 Education 145
İbrahim Halil Özdemir, Ege University, Turkey
Fırat Sarsar, Ege University, Turkey
Brendan Calandra, Georgia State University, USA

Computer science is crucial in the information age, driving an international movement towards digital literacy. The rapid development of digital technologies, especially data science and AI, necessitates a deeper understanding of human-machine interactions. CS literacy is essential for individual and societal success, leading to increased research on programming instruction from an early age. Programming is now integral to K-12 curricula worldwide. To enhance computer programming education, strategies must address both cognitive and affective aspects. Low-code programming, which enables application creation with minimal manual coding, is a promising approach. This book chapter introduces low-code programming as a valuable toolset for K-12 Computer Science Education.

Chapter 7
Mapping the Anatomy of Novice-Generated Mistakes in Learning Programming 171
Fatih Erdoğdu, Zonguldak Bülent Ecevit University, Turkey
Seyfullah Gökoğlu, Bartın University, Turkey

Programming has become very important in modern education. Research shows that exposing students to coding at a young age positively contributes to their academic, cognitive and professional development. However, students may make some mistakes during the programming process, which are considered a natural part of programming. In this context, the aim of this study is to classify various mistakes encountered by novice programmers while learning programming. For this purpose, a literature review was conducted, and it was found that there are basically two types of mistakes: strategic mistakes and knowledge-based mistakes. It was found that these mistakes are divided into groups within themselves. This book chapter recommends that researchers and practitioners conduct practical studies of the mistakes uncovered and conduct qualitative research in which the mistakes can be examined in greater depth.

Chapter 8
Methods for Accessible Computer Science and Computer Programming Education for Visually Impaired and Blind Students 193
Habibe Güneş, Firat University, Turkey

Just like our fingerprints, we are born different from each other with many characteristics. What is expected from education is to respect these differences, to highlight individuals' unique and special characteristics, and to create experiences that will enable them to maximize their talents. However, when structuring education for individuals with special needs, it should be tailored to their individual needs and provide accessibility that allows them to develop skills relevant to the current technological age. In this book chapter, suggestions are presented for developing the basic skills of visually impaired individuals in computer science and coding education.

Chapter 9
Online Assessment in K12 Computer Science Education 223
Betül Tonbuloğlu, Distance Education Application and Research Center, Yildiz Technical University, Turkey

The use of online assessment methods in K12 computer science education, which allow students to be assessed via networked computers, increases efficiency and accuracy by facilitating data collection, analysis and reporting, and enables large-scale tests to be implemented easily and at low costs. Online assessment, which can be applied in different types such as diagnostic, formative and summative performance-based, criterion-referenced, self-assessment and peer assessment, can also be applied for different purposes such as online skills assessment, online aptitude assessment, online coding assessment, psychometric assessment. Traditional assessment tools such as online exams and standardized tests can be used for online assessment of K12 computer science education, while alternative assessment methods such as e-portfolios, digital rubrics, self-assessment and peer assessment can be preferred. Online exams, which are considered traditional assessment tools, stand out with different advantages such as the use of many question types in their structure, so that CS subjects with different content can be measured with question types suitable for their own dynamics, and the automatic evaluation and reporting of measurement results. In addition, online exams can be assigned as tasks to classes created in a virtual environment, their completion can be tracked, collective feedback can be provided and students' progress can be monitored. Standardized tests, which are generally used to assess cognitive skills, stand out with their features such as taking into account basic competence areas and being valid and reliable tools. Automated Assessment Tools, one of the alternative online assessment methods, are widely used for purposes such as the assessment of programming skills and code analysis, and provide many advantages such as making the quality of the assessment independent from the teacher and providing more qualified feedback to students, as well as saving educators from a significant workload. E-portfolios are more than just a space for students to accumulate their individual work, they can also be used for accreditation, application, graduate employability, evidence of professional competence, material repository, and many other purposes. Peer assessment makes important contributions to process assessment in CS education by using different types of assessment such as written assessment, evaluation of coding projects, debugging and algorithm analysis. Digital rubrics, on the other hand, are one of the alternative assessment tools frequently used in computer science education in order to understand at what level of expertise a learning outcome is acquired by students for which subheadings. Many different online assessment applications such as Rubric-Maker, Project Quantum, Computational Thinking Test, Bebras, LeetCode, Codetester, Mahara, etc. can be used in the assessment of K12 Computer Science education, which includes basic topics such as information technologies and information processing systems, computer networks, media creation and editing, data and analysis, algorithms and programming, ethics and cyber security. In this way, assessment designs can be created effectively and easily, ease of access can be provided, time and cost savings can be made, participation can be increased, and fast and advanced feedback can be provided. However, extra security measures such as authentication, plagiarism control, and proctored exams are needed to ensure the reliability of online assessment practices. Different types of proctored online exams such as live proctoring, recorded proctoring, and automated proctoring can be implemented; in addition, measures such as limiting the exam time, randomizing questions, locking internet browsers, voice recognition, face recognition, monitoring keyboard dynamics, and tracking typing style also positively affect the reliability of online exams. Online assessment methods have the potential to provide significant gains in terms of making a comprehensive assessment of students' knowledge, skills and competencies when applied in a contextually appropriate manner with strategies and tools appropriate to the outcomes in the K12 CS education content

Chapter 10
Professional Development for K-12 Educators 263
Veysel Bilal Arslankara, T.C. Millî Eğitim Bakanlığı, Turkey
Elif Arslankara, T.C. Millî Eğitim Bakanlığı, Turkey
İlyas Asan, MONE, Turkey
Mehmet Külekçi, MONE, Turkey
Süleyman Sadi Seferoğlu, Hacettepe University, Turkey

This chapter covers professional development and literacy in K-12 education, focusing on technology integration and leadership. It emphasizes the need for continuous education and support for teachers, highlighting personalized, collaborative, and sustained development. Key areas include: Data and information literacy: critical evaluation and use of information through inquiry-based and project-based learning.

Digital literacy: integrating technology, teaching responsible use of digital tools, and digital citizenship. Research-oriented teaching: fostering curiosity and critical thinking, enhancing students' research skills. Leadership: teacher leaders creating positive environments through vision, collaboration, and resilience. Overall, the chapter presents a holistic approach to prepare students for the 21st century.

Chapter 11
Teaching Machine Learning Through Educational Robotics 293
Gamze Mercan, Hacettepe University, Turkey
Zümrüt Varol Selçuk, Ordu University, Turkey

This study explores the pivotal role of educational robotics (ER) in enriching K–12 curriculums with machine learning (ML) and artificial intelligence (AI) concepts, highlighting the necessity of demystifying these advanced technologies for the younger generation. With the integration of AI into everyday devices, the urgency to familiarize students with AI and ML has escalated, making it essential for educational systems to adapt. Our research delves into the impact of ER as a practical tool for imparting complex AI and ML principles, fostering not only a deeper understanding but also stimulating interest in STEM fields. This investigation is grounded in the exploration of current ER applications and their potential to transform traditional learning environments into hubs of innovation and critical thinking. By analyzing various ER platforms and their effectiveness in teaching ML concepts, this study aims to offer insights into developing a comprehensive framework that can be utilized by educators to integrate AI and ML into the classroom dynamically and interactively.

Chapter 12
Teaching Programming Through Metaphors 319
Erkan Geçitli, Ministry of National Education, Turkey
Bünyamin Yurdakul, Ege University, Turkey

This chapter aims to provide computer science stakeholders with a perspective on teaching programming through metaphors. The chapter emphasises that the difficulties encountered in learning programming stem from the structure of programming as a learning task, individual traits, and many factors, including curriculum and teaching approaches as interactional setting variables. First, the need for pedagogical approach to teaching programming is emphasized, briefly introducing the teaching approaches used in programming. Teaching programming through metaphor is introduced as an alternative approach to teaching programming concepts. It explains metaphor as a concept, conceptual metaphor theory, and the use of metaphor in teaching programming concepts. Then, the need to reveal the pattern of the teaching process through in-depth qualitative studies is highlighted as a future research direction. Finally, it is argued that using metaphor is not limited to teaching of concepts, but can also improve thinking skills, differentiate teaching and support teachers' professional development.

Chapter 13
Tools and Resources for K-12 Computer Science Education 349
İsmail Tonbuloğlu, Marmara University, Turkey

K-12 computer science education utilizes a variety of tools and resources that make significant contributions. Tools such as unplugged computer science tools, block-based computer science tools, text-based computer science tools, physical computer science tools, robotic kits, artificial intelligence, etc. have an important place in K-12 computer science education. It is crucial to incorporate computer science instruction into the basic courses of K-12 students, as well as to incorporate these tools into the curriculum. Worldwide resources have a significant impact on the enrichment and dissemination of K-12 computer science education. The content and resources created by platforms like Computer Science Teachers Association (CSTA), International Society for Technology in Education (ISTE), National Centre for Computing Education (NCCE), etc. contribute significantly to K-12 computer science education. Websites such as K-12 Computer Science, CS for ALL, Teach Computing, Code.org, Scratch, etc. are also important platforms that have become learning communities in computer science education.

Compilation of References 373

About the Contributors 467

Index 473

Preface

In recent years, computer science education has emerged as an indispensable component of modern education, especially at the K-12 level. Its interdisciplinary nature, which blends logical thinking, creativity, and problem-solving, is proving essential for preparing students for an increasingly digital world. As the field of artificial intelligence advances and information technology continues to transform societies, the importance of digital literacy and computational skills cannot be overstated. These competencies are no longer optional; they are critical skills for every individual to thrive in a knowledge-based economy.

In this context, computer science education plays a pivotal role in not just enabling students to use technology, but in helping them to become innovative creators of technology. Digital tools and applications, while important, must be paired with an education that fosters critical thinking, creativity, and the ability to tackle complex problems. This is where effective computer science education comes into play—one that is not merely focused on tools but grounded in pedagogy.

Effective pedagogy in computer science requires moving beyond a tool-oriented mindset. The most significant challenges in the current landscape stem from an overemphasis on technology, often at the expense of a deeper pedagogical understanding. A technology-first approach can hinder the development of essential skills such as computational thinking, which encompasses abstraction, decomposition, pattern recognition, debugging, and algorithm creation. These skills, when taught through carefully designed programming applications, hold value not only within the field of computer science but across multiple disciplines.

This book, *Effective Computer Science Education in K-12 Classrooms,* aims to serve as a pedagogical guide for educators, researchers, and practitioners dedicated to advancing computer science education at the K-12 level. The primary objective of this volume is to emphasize the need for a pedagogy-first approach, ensuring that students not only learn how to use technology but also develop the thinking and problem-solving skills necessary for the future.

This collection of chapters is intended for K-12 educators, university students, researchers, policymakers, and academics who are involved in computer science education.

Chapter 1 emphasizes the critical role that coding and robotics activities play in developing K-12 students' 21st-century skills, including computational, algorithmic, and critical thinking. It outlines the theoretical frameworks that guide effective instructional design, such as Vygotsky's Social Learning Theory and the TPACK Model, which help integrate technology with pedagogy. These frameworks support a student-centered approach to learning that promotes cognitive and social development through well-structured, interactive activities.

Chapter 2 reviews a decade of research on integrating computational thinking (CT) in early childhood education (ECE). It highlights how unplugged activities, coding, and robotics foster foundational CT skills and creativity in young learners. These methodologies contribute to cognitive and language development, problem-solving abilities, and positive social-emotional outcomes, setting the stage for preparing young children to thrive in a technology-driven world.

Chapter 3 delves into the specific context of Information Technology (IT) education in South African Grade 10-12 classrooms, focusing on the Further Education and Training (FET) phase. This chapter introduces effective teaching strategies and approaches for IT education, providing a comprehensive understanding of computer science instruction in the South African educational landscape.

Chapter 4 addresses the growing importance of cybersecurity education at the K-12 level. With the increasing use of the internet worldwide, this chapter explores the need to educate students on information security and cybersecurity practices to safeguard against digital threats. It underscores the importance of integrating cybersecurity awareness into early education.

Chapter 5 explores the influence of artificial intelligence (AI) on computer science education. AI has become an interdisciplinary field with the potential to shape educational processes and problem-solving approaches. This chapter discusses AI's role in computer science education, the challenges it presents, and how educators can integrate AI into their teaching to enhance student learning outcomes.

Chapter 6 introduces low-code programming as a valuable tool for K-12 computer science education. As digital literacy becomes essential in today's world, low-code programming provides an accessible approach to teaching students how to create applications with minimal coding effort. This chapter highlights its potential in fostering both cognitive and affective skills in students.

Chapter 7 examines common mistakes made by novice programmers, classifying these errors into strategic and knowledge-based categories. Through a literature review, the chapter provides insights into how educators can better understand and address these mistakes, ultimately improving students' programming skills. Practical and qualitative studies are encouraged for a deeper exploration of the learning process.

Chapter 8 offers suggestions for adapting computer science and coding education to meet the needs of visually impaired individuals. It stresses the importance of accessibility and tailoring educational experiences to empower students with special needs to develop crucial skills for the technological era.

Chapter 9 focuses on the benefits and challenges of using online assessment methods in K-12 computer science education. By facilitating efficient data collection, analysis, and reporting, online assessments can enhance the evaluation process. However, it emphasizes the need for security measures to ensure the reliability of these practices while highlighting the potential gains in assessing students' knowledge and skills.

Chapter 10 emphasizes the importance of professional development and digital literacy in K-12 education. It stresses continuous support for teachers in integrating technology into classrooms and highlights key areas such as data literacy, responsible technology use, and leadership. This chapter presents a holistic approach to preparing educators and students for the digital age.

Chapter 11 explores how educational robotics (ER) can enhance K-12 curriculums by introducing students to machine learning (ML) and artificial intelligence (AI) concepts. By analyzing current ER platforms, this chapter demonstrates the potential of robotics to foster interest in STEM fields, stimulate critical thinking, and offer practical, interactive experiences in teaching advanced technologies.

Chapter 12 introduces the concept of teaching programming through metaphors as an innovative pedagogical approach. It emphasizes how metaphors can make complex programming concepts more relatable and easier to understand. The chapter encourages further research on metaphor-based teaching strategies to enhance conceptual understanding and improve students' problem-solving skills.

Chapter 13 examines various tools and resources that play a vital role in K-12 computer science education. From unplugged methods and block-based tools to robotic kits and artificial intelligence platforms, these resources contribute significantly to enriching students' learning experiences. The chapter highlights the global impact of organizations like CSTA and ISTE, and the importance of integrating these tools into K-12 curricula to expand computer science education.

The book explores key topics that support the design, implementation, and evaluation of computer science education, with a focus on the K-12 context. These topics include theoretical frameworks, practical applications for curriculum development, instructional strategies, assessment techniques suitable for various age groups, and the integration of programming and computational thinking into classroom practices. The volume also delves into the use of instructional technologies, approaches for teaching specialized subjects like artificial intelligence, and recommendations for computer science educators.

Moreover, this book provides insights into the evolving landscape of computer science education, offering a future-oriented perspective that will help educators adapt to ongoing changes. By offering guidance that is grounded in research and best practices, this reference aims to fill the current gap in pedagogical resources, empowering educators to provide effective and meaningful computer science education.

Whether you are designing curricula, teaching a classroom of budding programmers, or developing policy frameworks, we hope this book serves as a comprehensive and valuable resource for promoting effective computer science education in K-12 classrooms.

Serhat Bahadır Kert
Yildiz Technical University, Turkey

Chapter 1
Coding Activity Implementations for K-12 Level Teachers

Ayşin Gaye Üstün
https://orcid.org/0000-0001-9564-0761
Sinop University, Turkey

Memnüne Kokoç
https://orcid.org/0000-0003-3740-7341
Karadeniz Technical University, Turkey

ABSTRACT

Coding and robotics activities are vital for developing K-12 students' 21st-century skills, including problem-solving, algorithmic, logical, mathematical, critical, and computational thinking. Teachers play a key role by providing the right tools, designing level-appropriate activities, monitoring progress, offering immediate feedback, and adjusting teaching strategies as needed. This section outlines theoretical frameworks supporting these activities, fostering cognitive and social development. Vygotsky's Social Learning Theory aids skill acquisition through interaction, Piaget's Cognitive Development Theory ensures suitable activities, Bruner's Constructivist Learning Theory supports meaningful knowledge construction, Havighurst's Activity Theory helps complete developmental tasks, and the TPACK Model integrates technology with teaching strategies. These frameworks provide a structured approach to instructional design, promoting student-centered and interactive learning in coding and robotics education.

DOI: 10.4018/979-8-3693-4542-9.ch001

INTRODUCTION

In the 21st century, where technology is advancing rapidly, the development of skills not only determines the future professions of individuals and their place in society, but also the workforce, industrialization, and prestige level of countries on the international platform. Countries that develop and update their education policies not only contribute to education but also have a voice in the international community by pioneering in every field from economy to science. Of course, societies can reach this level of development by organizing educational environments and materials for individuals from school age and integrating learning scenarios that support high-level learning skills into learning environments.

In today's world, "coding" skills are one of the most important skills for the personal and professional development of countries for technological, scientific, and economic progress. In recent years, coding has attracted great attention all over the world and has become an important skill that students of all ages should learn (Arslan & Arçelik, 2019). As Bers (2019) points out, given the increasing impact of technology in education, coding competency is being promoted as a new literacy for all levels of education, including children in younger age groups. According to Seymour Papert (1980), coding helps children acquire a cognitive structure that is generalizable and important for lifelong learning and development. In a rapidly changing digital society, coding supports children's problem-solving (Hufad et al., 2021), algorithmic thinking (Metin, 2022; Saxena et al., 2020), logical thinking (Lin et al., 2023), mathematical thinking (Goldenberg & Carter, 2021), critical thinking (Tsarava et al., 2019), literacy (Hassenfeld et al., 2020) and computational thinking (Bers et al., 2014; Chou, 2020).

Coding is defined as "the process of problem-solving through commands given in a language that the computer can understand" (Van-Roy & Haridi, 2004). An algorithm is a set of step-by-step instructions that enable a machine to achieve a specific goal; these instructions need to be carefully prepared during the coding process. Developing algorithm skills in children contributes to their ability to understand, use, apply, develop, and complete algorithms in daily life (Voronina et al., 2016). In addition, algorithm education has an important role in the development of children's skills such as exploring, using systematic solution methods, planning, organizing, collaborating, and discussing (Kalelioğlu, 2015). Coding-based systems are an important component of society and children's daily lives. Children often use and experience these systems unknowingly through technologies such as cell phones, automatic doors, and robot vacuum cleaners (Lee, 2020).

At the K-12 level, depending on the coding platform used, there are three main types of coding: robotic, computerized, and computerless coding. Coding activities in which children interact with concrete robots while learning coding are called robotic coding (Su et al., 2023). For example, Bers et al.'s (2014) study shows that children learn basic coding concepts such as debugging, correspondence, sequencing, and control flow through the programming interface, hands-on use of the robot, movement games, and songs. The second type of coding is computer-based coding. For example, ScratchJr is the most common computer-based platform and programming language for children in this age group (Bers, 2018). With ScratchJr, children put together graphical programming blocks to make characters move, jump, dance, and sing (Kaplancalı & Demirkol, 2017). Other platforms that can enable children to code include Code.org, Daisy the Dinosaur, Kodable, and Move the Turtle (Pila et al., 2019).

Learning computerized coding in the first years of school can have different challenges. Research shows that introducing non-computerized coding activities before computerized coding increases children's motivation to learn coding (Akçay et al., 2019). When introducing coding to young children, it is necessary to start with non-computerized and concrete applications that allow children to physically move objects and experience game-based digital learning without requiring abstract coding (e.g. C language) (Campbell & Walsh, 2017). The use of embodiment makes children's coding experiences more concrete and relevant, thus further developing children's coding skills (Sung et al., 2017). Coding without a computer provides children with the opportunity to engage in activities related to coding concepts such as algorithms, loops, and conditions (Canbeldek, 2020). These activities focus on developing children's basic skills such as problem-solving, logical thinking, algorithmic thinking, and sequencing (Hufad et al., 2021; Lee & Junoh, 2019; Lin et al., 2023; Saxena et al., 2020).

Coding Education at K-12 Level

It is very important to integrate coding programs into education and classroom materials to use technology effectively in the field of education and to provide children with the ability to use computers in a useful way (Timur et al., 2021). Coding education is an important educational environment that ensures the continuity of the software field, which is the basis of information technologies (Kert & Uğraş, 2009). Saygıner and Tüzün (2017) state that the importance of coding education has been recognized and coding courses are included in the education curricula of many countries.

There is an increasing emphasis on teaching coding and robotics skills to students in K-12 education. With the increasing demand for technology skills in the workforce, it has become crucial for schools to provide students with the opportunity to develop these skills (Miani et al., 2021). As technology continues to evolve, the role of coding and robotics in education is becoming increasingly important.

By incorporating coding and robotics activities into K12 education, students can develop essential skills that will prepare them for future success.

Coding and robotics activities can be incorporated into the K-12 curriculum in a variety of ways (Mistretta, 2022). One of these approaches is to use coding as a problem-solving tool. Students can learn how to break down complex problems into smaller, more manageable pieces and then use code to create a solution. This approach not only teaches students basic coding skills but also helps them develop critical thinking and analytical skills (Moraiti et al., 2022). Another approach is to use robotics as a tool for hands-on learning. Students can design and build robots and learn about engineering, physics, and electronics in the process. By combining coding and robotics, students can create robots that can perform specific tasks, such as following a line or avoiding obstacles. This approach not only teaches students about robotics but also helps them develop collaboration and teamwork skills (Amri et al., 2022).

However, research shows that very few teachers have the experience and skills to manage such activities (Kong & Wong, 2017; Rich et al., 2019; Yadav et al., 2016). Faced with the challenge of using computers in the classroom, teachers prefer to return to traditional teaching methods (Negrini, 2020). Basic coding education makes teachers competent in technology and offers a vision that enables teachers to see themselves as designers of technology-enhanced curricula. Therefore, teachers teaching at the K-12 level need to learn coding techniques to contribute to the education of children in these age groups.

The Role of the Teacher in Coding Education at K-12 Level

Teachers can use online coding resources such as Code.org and Scratch (Block and Text Based Coding) to introduce students to coding concepts. These resources offer engaging and interactive activities that help students develop coding skills at their own pace. Teachers can also use robotics kits such as Lego Mindstorms, VEX Robotics or Arduino to teach students about robotics and engineering (Zhong et al., 2022). These kits come with various sensors, motors and other components that students can use to build their robots. In-class and out-of-class learning environments also provide opportunities for students to work on coding and robotics projects independently or in small groups (Ceylan & Kesici, 2017; Sun et al., 2022). For example, students can work on coding challenges or robotics projects as part of a self-paced learning module. Furthermore, teachers can assign coding or robotics projects as homework and give students the opportunity to work on these activities outside the classroom.

Teacher guidance is critical to the success of coding and robotics activities. Teachers play an important role in guiding and supporting students' learning processes. Their guidance increases students' motivation, encourages deeper learning and helps them overcome challenges. The immediate feedback and support provided by teachers during activities enables students to correct their mistakes and optimize their learning process (Graham et al., 2014). This guidance contributes to students becoming more independent learners by increasing their self-efficacy.

An advantage of using coding and robotics activities in an interdisciplinary learning environment is that they can be adapted to meet the needs of different learners (Horn & Staker, 2011; Graham et al., 2014; Bhakti et al., 2022). For example, students who struggle in math or science can benefit from hands-on learning experiences in robotics. Similarly, students who struggle with language arts can benefit from coding activities that help them develop logical thinking and problem-solving skills.

Theoretical Frameworks for Implementing Coding and Robotics Interventions at the K-12 Level

Coding and robotics applications in education are defined as the literacy of the future in the 21st century. These skills prepare future citizens by developing the ability to think computationally, analytically, critically, creatively, solve problems algorithmically, develop a sense of technological fluency and integrate innovative technologies into the educational environment. Internationally, many countries have aimed to develop innovative practices in primary education and have started to transform their national curricula. In this context, it is important to address pedagogical practices specific to the primary school period. In this context, the following theoretical frameworks are presented for the implementation of coding and robotics interventions at the K-12 level:

Vygotsky's Social Learning Theory: Vygotsky's Social Learning Theory argues that learning occurs largely through social interactions and that these interactions play a central role in the cognitive development of individuals. In coding and robotics education at the K-12 level, this theory provides an effective guide for students to acquire higher-level skills. Vygotsky's concept of "Zone of Proximal Development" (ZPD) refers to tasks that students cannot do on their own but can accomplish with the help of a teacher or a more competent peer (Vygotsky, 1978). In coding and robotics projects, students are often faced with complex problem-solving tasks. When teachers identify students' ZPDs in this process and provide them with appropriate support, students can learn complex coding languages and robotic systems more easily (Kozulin, 2003).

Teachers guide students' learning processes using Vygotsky's concept of "scaffolding". This technique involves providing students with intensive support at the beginning and gradually reducing this support as students acquire skills (Wood et al., 1976). For example, a teacher may help a student by providing step-by-step instructions when he or she encounters a specific coding problem in a robotics project but withdraw support when the student starts solving similar problems on his or her own. Furthermore, peer interactions and collaborative learning environments support students' cognitive development according to Vygotsky's theory. By working together in group projects, students learn from each other and build collective knowledge (Mercer & Littleton, 2007).

The use of concrete materials in coding and robotics education is also in line with Vygotsky's theory. Robots and programming tools help students understand abstract coding concepts through concrete experiences. Such practices support Vygotsky's view that learning is an active and social process (Blikstein, 2013). Students produce creative solutions by combining the physical and digital worlds in robotic projects and learn through social interactions in this process. In conclusion, Vygotsky's Social Learning Theory supports students' cognitive and social development holistically by emphasizing the critical role of teachers and peers in coding and robotics education.

Piaget's Theory of Cognitive Development: Piaget's Theory of Cognitive Development argues that children's cognitive abilities develop through certain stages and that different thinking processes come to the fore in each of these stages. In coding and robotics education at the K-12 level, this theory guides in designing activities appropriate to students' cognitive development levels. According to Piaget's theory, children go through four main stages of development: sensory motor (0-2 years), preoperational (2-7 years), concrete operations (7-11 years), and abstract operations (11 years and above) (Piaget, 1952). Coding and robotics education can be effectively implemented especially in the concrete operations and abstract operations stages. Students in the concrete operations stage learn by working with physical objects and concrete data. For students in this age group, concrete materials such as robotic tools and programming blocks are effective in developing problem-solving and logical thinking skills (Papert, 1980).

Students who reach the abstract operations stage have more complex and abstract thinking skills. During this period, students begin to understand more complex coding concepts such as algorithmic thinking, variables, and loops. According to Piaget's theory, these students can more easily understand abstract concepts and work with more complex programming languages (Inhelder & Piaget, 1958). Coding and robotics projects develop these students' creative problem-solving abilities and provide them with real-world applications. Moreover, students learn by experimenting and exploring in this process, which is in line with Piaget's theory emphasizing children's active learning process (Ackermann, 2001).

Piaget's stages of cognitive development guide teachers in assessing students' current cognitive capacities and providing them with appropriate learning experiences. For example, students in the concrete operations stage can be introduced to simple robotic kits and visual programming tools, while students in the abstract operations stage can be introduced to more complex robotic projects and textual programming languages. In this way, coding and robotics education is designed by students' cognitive developmental levels, supporting and contributing to their learning processes (Clements & Sarama, 2003).

Bruner's Constructivist Learning Theory: Jerome Bruner's Constructivist Learning Theory emphasizes that learning is an active and dynamic process and that individuals construct meaning by structuring knowledge. This theory plays an important role in the implementation of coding and robotics interventions at the K-12 level. Bruner (1966) states that students construct meaning by connecting new information to prior knowledge. Coding and robotics education offers students the opportunity to make these connections. When programming robots or working on coding projects, students use their prior knowledge and experiences to construct new concepts and skills (Papert, 1980). This process makes students' learning more in-depth and permanent.

According to Bruner's theory, learning takes place in three stages: enactive, iconic, and symbolic. In coding and robotics education at the K-12 level, these stages can be applied according to students' developmental levels. In the enactive stage, students learn by interacting with concrete materials and physical robots. In the iconographic stage, they understand concepts using visual representations and graphics. In the symbolic stage, they learn complex concepts through abstract symbols and language (Bruner, 1966). These stages help students learn by constructing knowledge and skills in coding and robotics projects.

Bruner also emphasizes the importance of discovery learning and advocates that students actively seek knowledge. Coding and robotics projects encourage the process of discovery by developing students' problem-solving and creative thinking skills (Sawyer, 2006). Students learn through trial and error to solve the problems they encounter in coding and robotics activities and have meaningful learning experiences in this process (Ackermann, 2001). Bruner's "spiral curriculum" approach suggests that knowledge should be processed repeatedly, each time in a deeper and more complex way (Bruner, 1966). In coding and robotics education, students continuously expand and deepen their knowledge by starting with simple projects in the beginning and moving on to more complex projects in the following years.

In conclusion, Bruner's Constructivist Learning Theory provides a framework for coding and robotics education at the K-12 level that encourages students' active participation, learning by discovery, and constructing meaning by structuring knowledge. This approach develops students' cognitive and creative skills and makes learning processes more effective and permanent.

Havighurst's Activity Theory: Robert Havighurst's Activity Theory argues that the developmental tasks that individuals must accomplish during certain life stages contribute significantly to their physical, cognitive, and social development. Coding and robotics interventions at the K-12 level play an effective role in the successful completion of these developmental tasks. Havighurst (1952) states that the skills and knowledge that need to be acquired during childhood and adolescence form the basis for individuals to be successful in later life. Coding and robotics education help students acquire basic skills such as problem-solving, analytical thinking, and technological literacy, which in turn supports their cognitive and social development (Gee, 2003).

According to Havighurst's theory, the successful fulfillment of developmental tasks increases individuals' self-confidence and adaptability. Coding and robotics projects offer students the opportunity to achieve tangible successes. When students accomplish a specific task by programming a robot or solving a problem by developing software, this sense of accomplishment increases their self-confidence and reinforces their belief in themselves (Papert, 1980). Moreover, since such projects often require collaborative and group work, they also develop students' social skills. In group projects, students communicate, cooperate, and learn the importance of teamwork to work together to achieve common goals (Johnson & Johnson, 1999).

Coding and robotics education not only develops students' ability to use technology effectively but also encourages their creative thinking and innovative problem-solving skills. Havighurst argues that such activities support individuals to adapt to their environment and become active and productive members of society (Havighurst, 1952). The challenges encountered in coding and robotics projects and the process of overcoming these challenges develop students' resilience and critical thinking skills. These skills contribute to their success both in their educational lives and in their future careers (Resnick, 2007).

In conclusion, Havighurst's Activity Theory emphasizes that coding and robotics education at the K-12 level are activities that contribute significantly to students' cognitive, social, and emotional development, increase their self-confidence, and support their lifelong learning skills. These trainings are an essential tool to help students complete developmental tasks, preparing them for future challenges.

TPACK Model: The TPACK (Technological, Pedagogical, Content Knowledge) Model enables teachers to develop effective teaching strategies by integrating technology with pedagogical and subject matter knowledge. In implementing coding and robotics interventions at the K-12 level, the TPACK Model provides a framework that enables teachers to use these innovative educational tools effectively. The TPACK Model developed by Mishra and Koehler (2006) emphasizes the integration of three core knowledge domains (technological knowledge, pedagogical knowledge, and content knowledge). Coding and robotics education require these three components to come together harmoniously.

Technological Knowledge (TK): Technological knowledge is one of the key components of this model and encompasses teachers' ability to use digital tools, software, and hardware effectively. In coding and robotics education, this technological knowledge is particularly focused on programming languages and robotic kits. Teachers' in-depth knowledge of programming languages (e.g., Python, Java, Scratch) and robotic kits (e.g., LEGO Mindstorms, VEX Robotics) enables them to provide students with an effective learning experience (Mishra & Koehler, 2006). Knowledge of programming languages allows teachers to teach their students algorithmic thinking, problem-solving, and coding skills. For example, visual programming languages such as Scratch are suitable for teaching basic programming concepts to younger age groups. At more advanced levels, text-based programming languages such as Python or Java can be used to help students develop more complex projects (Resnick et al., 2009). Teachers should know how these languages work, for which educational purposes they are suitable, and how to teach them. By combining technological knowledge with pedagogical knowledge, teachers can design appropriate projects for students and ensure that these projects achieve educational goals (Harris et al., 2009).

Knowledge of robotics kits enables teachers to teach students programming and engineering skills through physical devices and robots. Kits like LEGO Mindstorms or VEX Robotics help students embody their coding knowledge to create projects that can be implemented in the physical world. Teachers should know how to use these kits, the assembly and programming processes, and possible problem-solving methods. This knowledge allows teachers to integrate robotic projects into their lessons and students to have hands-on learning experiences (Bers, 2018). Teachers can support students' learning processes by selecting appropriate robotic kits according to their age and knowledge level (Angeli & Valanides, 2009).

Pedagogical Knowledge (PK): Pedagogical knowledge is one of the core components of this model and includes teachers' engagement with topics such as student-centered learning strategies and problem-solving techniques. By integrating this pedagogical knowledge with technological and content knowledge, teachers enable students to use technology effectively (Mishra & Koehler, 2006). Coding and robotics education offers a dynamic learning environment with the potential to provide students with cognitive, social, and emotional skills. Teachers' pedagogical knowledge enables them to guide effectively in this environment (Mishra & Koehler, 2006). Pedagogical knowledge enables teachers to adopt student-centered approaches in coding and robotics education. Student-centered learning customizes learning experiences to students' interests and learning styles. Coding and robotics projects encourage students' active participation and allow students to manage their learning process. Teachers use their pedagogical knowledge to design coding and robotics projects for students and align these projects with student-centered learning goals (Papert, 1980).

Furthermore, pedagogical knowledge improves teachers' ability to support students, considering different student needs and learning levels. Coding and robotics education presents students with tasks at various levels of difficulty. Using their pedagogical knowledge, teachers adapt these tasks to the individual needs and abilities of students. Thus, they provide an appropriate learning experience for each student and create an environment where everyone can succeed (Resnick, 2007). In conclusion, the TPACK model enables teachers to effectively guide coding and robotics education using their pedagogical knowledge. Pedagogical knowledge supports student-centered approaches, considers different student needs, and emphasizes the ability to adapt teaching strategies to students' characteristics. This approach allows students to develop their coding and robotics skills and get the most out of their learning experience.

Content Knowledge: Content knowledge refers to teachers' in-depth knowledge and understanding of the teaching domain. In coding and robotics education, teachers' content knowledge with mathematical and scientific concepts enables students to acquire basic skills and concretize concepts (Mishra & Koehler, 2006). Mathematical concepts play an important role in coding and robotics education because programming is fundamentally based on logical thinking and problem-solving skills. To develop students' algorithmic thinking skills, teachers can relate mathematical concepts to programming languages and robotics projects. For example, mathematical concepts such as loops, conditional statements, and variables can be like coding structures in a programming language. When teaching these concepts to students, teachers also strengthen their mathematical thinking skills and problem-solving abilities (Brennan & Resnick, 2012).

Scientific concepts are also important in coding and robotics education because these areas can be used to explore the basic principles of science and science phenomena. Students apply scientific methods in their robotics projects, making hypotheses, conducting experiments, and analyzing the results (Bers, 2019). For example, when a student uses sensors to control the movement of a robot, they must understand the basic principles of physical forces and energy in the process (Resnick et al., 2009). By integrating scientific concepts into coding and robotics projects, teachers increase students' interest in science and develop their scientific thinking skills (Brennan & Resnick, 2012). Teachers' content knowledge allows them to understand and integrate the relationship between mathematical and scientific concepts and coding and robotics (Papert, 1980). This approach helps students concretize abstract concepts and relate them to real-world applications. By applying mathematical and scientific concepts in coding and robotics projects, students increase their interest in these fields while strengthening their basic skills (Wing, 2006).

Technology, Pedagogy, and Content Knowledge (TPACK): TPACK (Technological Pedagogical Content Knowledge) is a framework that integrates the above three components (Technology Knowledge (TK), Pedagogical Knowledge (PK), and Content Knowledge (CK)) and emphasizes the interaction between these components. TPACK enables teachers to plan and implement their lessons effectively by bringing technology, pedagogy, and content together (Mishra & Koehler, 2006). The TPACK Model encourages teachers to integrate technology into their pedagogical content and make their learning processes more effective. This model enriches learning experiences by enabling teachers to integrate not only their technology use skills but also their pedagogical and content knowledge (Koehler & Mishra, 2009).

Instructional Design Plan Stages for Coding and Robotics Activities at K-12 Level

Coding and robotics activities at the K-12 level are important educational tools for developing students' problem-solving, critical thinking, and creative skills. Effective planning and implementation of these activities require a systematic and comprehensive approach to instructional design. The ADDIE Model (Analysis, Design, Development, Implementation, Evaluation) is a framework that is widely used in instructional design processes and consists of five basic stages (Molenda, 2003). This model guides the construction and evaluation of instructional materials and strategies. Each stage of the ADDIE Model will be discussed in the context of how it can be applied to coding and robotics activities at the K-12 level. These stages aim to provide teachers with a comprehensive instructional design guide by covering the processes of identifying student needs, creating instructional design, developing instructional materials, implementing activities, and evaluating activities.

Analysis Phase:

Identifying the Target Audience: In the target audience identification phase, teachers first identify the student groups that will implement the coding and robotics activity. The characteristics of these groups such as age, academic level, interests, learning styles, and experience with technology are taken into consideration (Gagné, 1985; Felder & Silverman, 1988). Considering students' differences increases the effectiveness of instructional design and optimizes learning experiences (Tomlinson,

2001). Assessing experiences with technology can also positively influence student motivation and engagement (Mishra & Koehler, 2006).

Needs Analysis: In the needs analysis phase, teachers assess students' strengths and weaknesses, learning needs, and goals. This helps them understand what coding skills students need, what subjects they need more guidance in, and what technology tools they need more use of (Dick & Carey, 1996). Accurate identification of student needs is critical for effective instructional design and successful learning outcomes (Gagné et al., 2005). Furthermore, by assessing students' current technology knowledge and skills, appropriate instructional strategies can be developed to increase their motivation and engagement (Mishra & Koehler, 2006).

Setting Goals: In the goal-setting phase, teachers clarify what they want to achieve from the coding and robotics activity. These goals may include students understanding specific coding concepts, developing specific robotics skills, or completing a specific project. Goals should meet SMART (Specific, Measurable, Achievable, Relevant, Time-bound) criteria, i.e. they should be specific, measurable, achievable, relevant, and time-bound (Locke & Latham, 2002). Setting SMART goals helps teachers plan the teaching process more effectively and assess students' achievement more accurately (Miller, 2012).

Design Phase:

Structuring the Program: In the structuring phase, teachers plan the overall structure and flow of the coding and robotics activity. This stage determines the beginning, development, and outcome of the activity. Teachers determine the duration, general aims, objectives, and sequence of the activity (Gagné et al., 2005). The structuring of the program should also be appropriate to the needs of the student groups, the resources available, and the context of the activity (Dick et al., 2005). For example, the structuring of a coding activity may include the introduction, teaching of key concepts, implementation, and evaluation (Morrison et al., 2010). This process is critical to improve the effectiveness of instructional design and optimize student learning experiences (Reigeluth, 1999).

Content Design: In the content design phase, teachers plan the materials and content they will present to students in the coding and robotics activity. This content may include coding concepts, robotics principles, projects, and tasks. When designing content, teachers consider students' learning needs, goals, and interests (Morrison et al., 2010). In addition, during the content design process, attention is paid to ensuring that the materials to be presented to students are effective, engaging, and stimulating for learning (Reigeluth, 1999). For example, visual programming tools such as Scratch or robotic sets such as LEGO Mindstorms can be used in content design (Resnick et al., 2009)

Technology Integration: In the technology integration phase, teachers integrate technological tools and resources into the content of the activity. This includes selecting the software and applications used to teach programming languages to students, identifying the hardware needed for robotics projects, and using digital tools effectively. Technology integration enables students to use technology effectively and develop their coding and robotics skills (Hughes et al., 2006). For example, appropriate software can be selected to teach students various coding platforms and programming languages, and the necessary hardware and software resources can be provided for robotics projects (Ertmer & Ottenbreit-Leftwich, 2010).

Implementation Phase

Education Sessions: These are the periods in which teachers interact directly with students during the implementation process of coding and robotics activities. These sessions can take the form of structured lectures, workshops, or laboratory sessions where teachers transfer specific topics, skills, and projects to students. During training sessions, teachers deliver an effective teaching experience by bringing together the three components of the TPACK model (technology, pedagogy, and content knowledge). For example, in a training session, the teacher teaches students basic programming concepts using Scratch while explaining the mathematical and scientific contexts of these concepts. In these sessions, teachers blend technology with pedagogical and content knowledge to provide meaningful learning experiences for students (Mishra & Koehler, 2006).

Teaching Strategies: These are the methods and techniques that teachers use to effectively teach coding and robotics activities. These strategies can be differentiated to suit students' individual learning needs and can include student-centered approaches. The Project-Based Learning strategy encourages students to work on projects with a specific goal. Students develop their coding and robotics skills by solving real-world problems (Blumenfeld et al., 1991). The Cooperative Learning strategy enables students to learn together through group work. Cooperative learning develops students' social skills and encourages learning through collaboration (Johnson & Johnson, 1999). With Differentiated Instruction, teachers personalize learning by using teaching methods appropriate to students' different ability levels and learning styles (Tomlinson, 2001). For example, some students may be more prone to visual learning, while others may learn better through kinesthetic learning. The teacher optimizes learning experiences by providing different resources and materials to different students. A direct instruction strategy involves the teacher directly teaching a particular topic or skill. Direct instruction can be particularly effective in teaching complex or critical concepts (Rosenshine, 1986).

Evaluation Phase:

Formative Assessment: This is a continuous type of assessment used to monitor students' learning, provide feedback, and adjust instructional strategies as needed. This type of assessment provides teachers with important information to understand and guide students' progress in coding and robotics activities. During formative assessment, teachers observe students' learning process, give them immediate feedback, and adjust instructional strategies as needed. This process encourages students' active participation in their learning and helps them identify their strengths and weaknesses (Black & Wiliam, 1998).

Summative Assessment: A type of assessment used to measure the extent to which students have achieved specific learning objectives at the end of a given learning period. This assessment is usually used for grading purposes and assesses students' learning outcomes. Summative assessment can be used in coding and robotics activities to measure students' level of completion of a specific project, acquisition of specific skills, or understanding of specific concepts (Garrison & Ehringhaus, 2007).

Steps to Plan Coding Activities in K-12 Using Activity Theory Framework

1. Research and Preparation

- Research is conducted on coding activities suitable for the level and needs of K-12 students.
- Appropriate tools and resources that can be used to teach coding skills are identified.
- The physical and technological requirements of the environment (classroom, computer lab, etc.) where the activities will be implemented are reviewed.

2. Goal Setting and Design:

- The objectives of the activities are set; for example, learning basic programming concepts, developing algorithmic thinking skills, or increasing problem-solving skills.
- Activities are designed according to student's age and level groups.
- Tools and materials to be used in the activities are determined.

3. Implementation of the Activity:

- Activities are carried out in the classroom or in out-of-class educational environments.
- The teacher introduces the activity to the students and explains its purpose.
- Students participate in coding activities and work to achieve the set goals.
- Students are guided and supported when necessary.

4. Evaluation of the Activity:

- After the activity, students' performance and achievements are evaluated.
- Students' coding skills, problem-solving skills, and cooperation skills are observed.
- Students' feedback is taken and included in the evaluation process.

5. Correction and Improvement:

- Based on the evaluation results, adjustments are made to improve the effectiveness of activities and student achievement.
- The design and implementation methods of the activities are improved.
- Planning is made for future coding activities considering student feedback.

The Activity Theory framework allows us to consider students' interactions, learning processes, and social dynamics when following these steps. In this way, coding activities in primary school can be made more effective and efficient. Sample Coding and Robotics Lesson Modules for teachers are presented in Table 1.

Table 1. Coding and robotics course modules flow

Module 1. Unplugged Coding Activity Worksheets	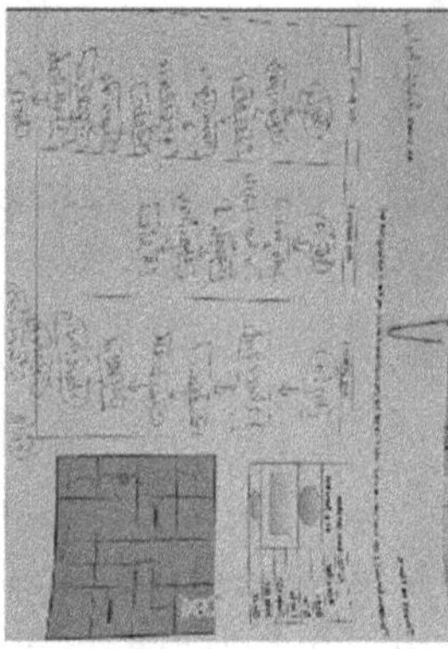 Figure 1. 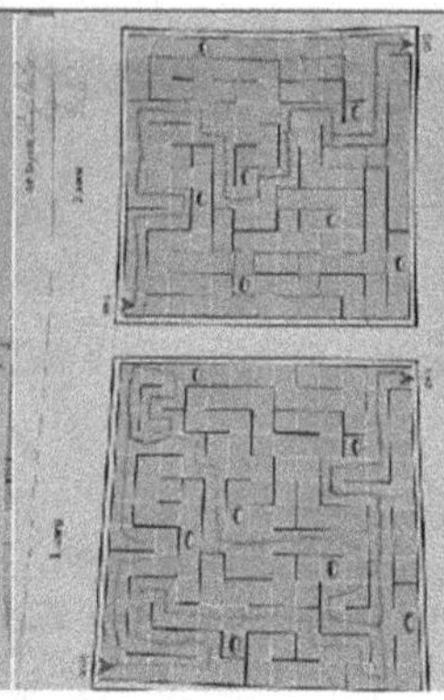 Figure 2. 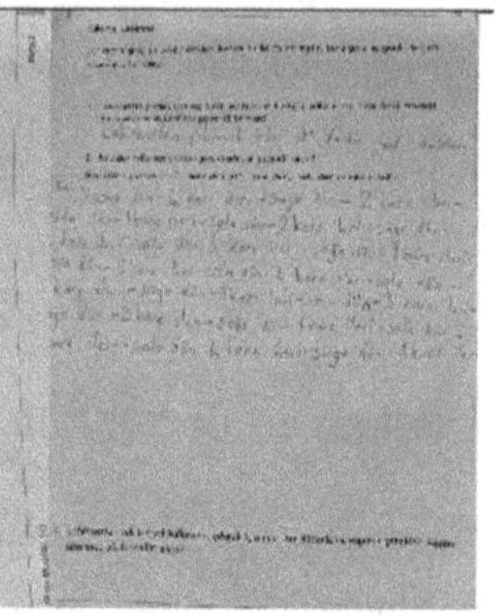 Figure 3. **Step 1.** Worksheets are prepared and tasks involving scenario-based problems are given to students. **Step 2.** Students perform the task by creating the correct algorithms and flowcharts. **Step 3.** Students are asked verbal and/or written reflective questions to evaluate the tasks. **Step 4.** Feedback corrections and evaluations are made about the programming concepts that are aimed to be gained.
Module 2. Plugged Coding Activity Worksheets	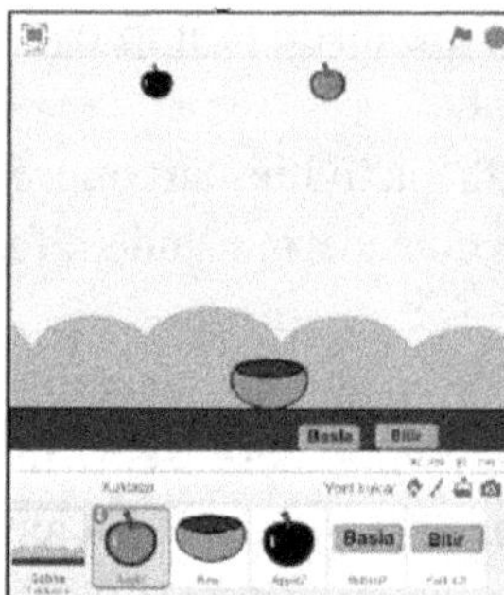 Figure 4. 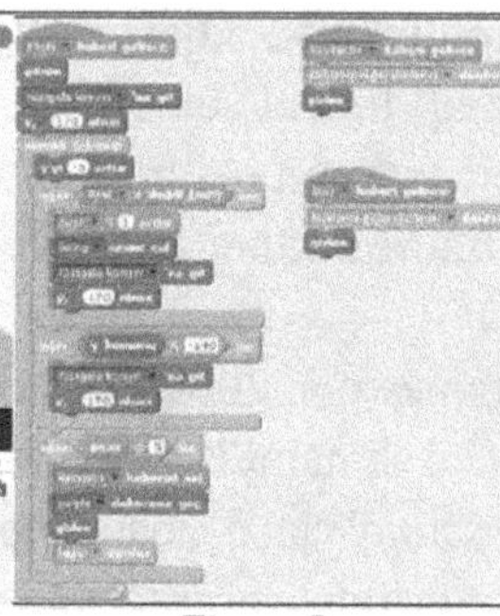 Figure 5. Activity: Scratch Apple Catching Game Rule: When you catch the red apple, you earn 1 point, when you catch the black apple, you die. Whoever catches 10 apples wins. You lose if you have 0 health left and/or time runs out -At the end of the activity, an evaluation was made with reflective questions (Appendix 2). **Step 1.** Interface Design is done **Step 2.** Game dynamics are designed (add points, health and time features to the game) **Step 3.** Coding the added objects and designing the animations **Step 4.** Running the game

continued on following page

Table 1. Continued

Module 3. Robotic Coding Activity Worksheets	 Figure 6. 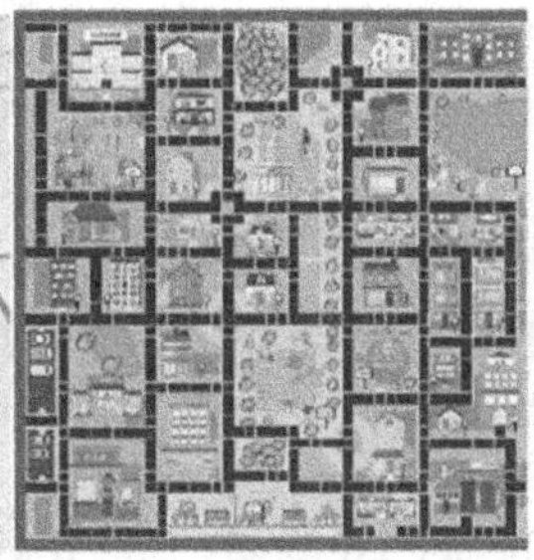 Figure 7. Activity: Map Location Puzzle Rule: Getting from place to place with the shortest path (number of steps/frames) and the fewest steps (lines of code) You live at number 18. Mission - 1: Leave the house and go to the zoo. Mission - 2: Go from the zoo to the park. **Step 1.** Algorithm and flow chart are prepared for the task to be performed by the robot. **Step 2.** Robot design is done. **Step 3.** The code is written and uploaded to the robot (the maze gaps and walls are calculated, and the robot finds its way out of the maze). **Step 4.** Students enable the robot to progress and reach the goal with different tasks on scenario-based maps.

The modules including the coding and robotics activity worksheets presented above are implemented as unplugged, plugged, and robotic coding, respectively, and follow a flow from simple to difficult. With unplugged coding, programming concepts are taught without a computer, with paper, pencil, and other physical objects. Basic coding concepts such as "sequence, condition, loop" can be learned and experienced offline without a computer and then the next step can be online coding. Thus, more complex applications and computer programs can be designed. Scenario-based work is done to do visual programming with the block and text-based Scratch program. Students can activate their imagination by designing animations and games according to the given tasks. For students to gain knowledge and skills in block-based coding studies, online exercises can be done with block-based coding programs (https://blockly.games/, https://www.code.org, https://studio.code.org/courses) before starting the lesson. With robotic coding, coding and robotic design are combined and the control of a physical environment with software is observed with a cause-effect relationship. Thus, students can take their coding skills to the next level.

DISCUSSION AND CONCLUSION

In this section, it is emphasized that the teacher is critical to the success of coding and robotics activities. Theories that teachers can use when designing coding and robotics activities at K-12 level are discussed. The effects of coding and robotics education at the K-12 level were examined within the framework of Vygotsky's Social

Learning Theory, Piaget's Cognitive Development Theory, Bruner's Constructivist Learning Theory and Havighurst's Activity Theory. These theories show that coding and robotics activities improve students' cognitive and social skills. Students' problem solving and algorithmic thinking skills increased through group work and collaborative projects, and their creative thinking and analytical skills improved (Blumenfeld et al., 1991; Johnson & Johnson, 1999; Papert, 1980; Sawyer, 2006).

However, there are some differences between these theories. While Piaget's Theory of Cognitive Development argues that students in the concrete operations stage may have difficulty in understanding abstract concepts (Piaget, 1952), Bruner's Constructivist Learning Theory suggests that these students can develop abstract thinking skills (Bruner, 1966). Furthermore, Havighurst's Activity Theory emphasizes the importance of individual achievement, while Vygotsky's Social Learning Theory emphasizes the importance of social interactions and cooperation (Vygotsky, 1978; Havighurst, 1952). These differences require teachers to balance between individual and group work when planning coding and robotics activities.

In conclusion, coding and robotics education is effective in developing students' problem solving, analytical thinking and social skills. At this point, educational approaches should be carefully selected according to the developmental characteristics and needs of student groups. At this point, it is important for teachers to develop strategies suitable for students' cognitive development levels and social interaction needs.

REFERENCES

Ackermann, E. (2001). Piaget's constructivism, Papert's constructionism: What's the difference. *Future of Learning Group Publication*, 5(3), 438.

Akçay, A. O., Karahan, E., & Türk, S. (2019). Bilgi işlemsel düşünme becerileri odaklı okul sonrası kodlama sürecinde ilkokul öğrencilerinin deneyimlerinin incelenmesi. *Eskişehir Osmangazi Üniversitesi Türk Dünyası Uygulama ve Araştırma Merkezi Eğitim Dergisi*, 4(2), 38–50.

Amri, S., Budiyanto, C. W., Fenyvesi, K., Yuana, R. A., & Widiastuti, I. (2022). Educational robotics: Evaluating the role of computational thinking in attaining 21st-century skills. *Open Education Studies*, 4(1), 322–338. DOI: 10.1515/edu-2022-0174

Angeli, C., & Valanides, N. (2009). Epistemological and methodological issues for the conceptualization, development, and assessment of ICT-TPCK: Advances in technological pedagogical content knowledge (TPCK). *Computers & Education*, 52(1), 154–168. DOI: 10.1016/j.compedu.2008.07.006

Arslan, K., & Akçelik, M. (2019). Programlama eğitiminde Scratch'in kullanılması: Öğretmen adaylarının tutum ve algıları. *Ulusal Eğitim Akademisi Dergisi*, 3(1), 41–61. DOI: 10.32960/uead.455502

Bers, M. U. (2018). Coding and computational thinking in early childhood: The impact of ScratchJr in Europe. *European Journal of STEM Education*, 3(3), 8. DOI: 10.20897/ejsteme/3868

Bers, M. U. (2019). Coding as another language: A pedagogical approach for teaching computer science in early childhood. *Journal of Computers in Education*, 6(4), 499–528. DOI: 10.1007/s40692-019-00147-3

Bers, M. U., Flannery, L., Kazakoff, E. R., & Sullivan, A. (2014). Computational thinking and tinkering: Exploration of an early childhood robotics curriculum. *Computers & Education*, 72, 145–157. DOI: 10.1016/j.compedu.2013.10.020

Bhakti, C., Farozin, M., & Suwarjo, S. (2022, July). A Design of Blended Learning Core Curriculum based on Personalized Learning for Career Readiness. In *Proceedings of the 1st International Conference on Social, Science, and Technology, ICSST 2021*, 25 November 2021, Tangerang, Indonesia. DOI: 10.4108/eai.25-11-2021.2318804

Black, P., & Wiliam, D. (1998). Assessment and classroom learning. *Assessment in Education: Principles, Policy & Practice*, 5(1), 7–74. DOI: 10.1080/0969595980050102

Blikstein, P. (2013). Digital fabrication and 'making'in education: The democratization of invention. In Walter-Herrmann, J., & Büching, C. (Eds.), *FabLabs: Of machines, makers and inventors* (pp. 203–222). Transcript Publishers. DOI: 10.14361/transcript.9783839423820.203

Blumenfeld, P. C., Soloway, E., Marx, R. W., Krajcik, J. S., Guzdial, M., & Palincsar, A. (1991). Motivating project-based learning: Sustaining the doing, supporting the learning. *Educational Psychologist*, 26(3-4), 369–398. DOI: 10.1080/00461520.1991.9653139

Brennan, K., & Resnick, M. (2012, April). New frameworks for studying and assessing the development of computational thinking. In *Proceedings of the 2012 annual meeting of the American Educational Research Association*, Vancouver, Canada (*1*, p. 25)

Bruner, J. S. (1966). *Toward a Theory of Instruction*. Belkapp Press.

Campbell, C., & Walsh, C. (2017). Introducing the new digital literacy of coding in the early years. *Practical Literacy*, 22(3), 10–12.

Canbeldek, M. (2020). *Erken çocukluk eğitiminde üreten çocuklar kodlama ve robotik eğitim programının etkilerinin incelenmesi* [Yayınlanmamış Doktora Tezi]. Pamukkale Üniversitesi.

Ceylan, V. K., & Kesici, A. E. (2017). Effect of blended learning to academic achievement. *International Journal of Human Sciences*, 14(1), 308–320. DOI: 10.14687/jhs.v14i1.4141

Chou, P. N. (2020). Using ScratchJr to foster young children's computational thinking competence: A case study in a third-grade computer class. *Journal of Educational Computing Research*, 58(3), 570–595. DOI: 10.1177/0735633119872908

Clements, D. H., & Sarama, J. (2003). Young children and technology: What does the research say? *Young Children*, 58(6), 34–40.

Dick, W., & Carey, L. (1996). *The systematic design of instruction* (4th ed.). HarperCollins College Publishers.

Dick, W., Carey, L., & Carey, J. O. (2005). *The systematic design of instruction* (6th ed.). Pearson.

Ertmer, P. A., & Ottenbreit-Leftwich, A. T. (2010). Teacher technology change: How knowledge, confidence, beliefs, and culture intersect. *Journal of Research on Technology in Education*, 42(3), 255–284. DOI: 10.1080/15391523.2010.10782551

Felder, R. M., & Silverman, L. K. (1988). Learning and teaching styles in engineering education. *Engineering Education*, 78(7), 674–681.

Gagné, R. M. (1985). *The conditions of learning* (4th ed.). Holt, Rinehart & Winston.

Gagne, R. M., Wager, W. W., Golas, K. C., Keller, J. M., & Russell, J. D. (2005). Principles of instructional design. *Performance Improvement*, 44(2), 44–46. DOI: 10.1002/pfi.4140440211

Garrison, C., & Ehringhaus, M. (2007). *Formative and summative assessments in the classroom.* Retrieved from https://www.nwea.org/blog/2017/formative-vs-summative-assessments-whats-difference/

Gee, J. P. (2003). What video games have to teach us about learning and literacy. [CIE]. *Computers in Entertainment*, 1(1), 20–20. DOI: 10.1145/950566.950595

Goldenberg, E. P., & Carter, C. J. (2021). Programming as a language for young children to express and explore mathematics in school. *British Journal of Educational Technology*, 52(3), 969–985. DOI: 10.1111/bjet.13080

Graham, C. R., Henrie, C. R., & Gibbons, A. S. (2014). Developing models and theory for blended learning research. In Spector, J. M., Merrill, M. D., Elen, J., & Bishop, M. J. (Eds.), *Handbook of Research on Educational Communications and Technology* (4th ed., pp. 485–495). Springer., DOI: 10.1007/978-1-4614-3185-5_38

Harris, J., Mishra, P., & Koehler, M. (2009). Teachers' technological pedagogical content knowledge and learning activity types: Curriculum-based technology integration reframed. *Journal of Research on Technology in Education*, 41(4), 393–416. DOI: 10.1080/15391523.2009.10782536

Hassenfeld, Z. R., & Bers, M. U. (2020). Debugging the writing process: Lessons from a comparison of students' coding and writing practices. *The Reading Teacher*, 73(6), 735–746. DOI: 10.1002/trtr.1885

Havighurst, R. J. (1952). Social and psychological needs of the aging. *The Annals of the American Academy of Political and Social Science*, 279(1), 11–17. DOI: 10.1177/000271625227900102

Horn, M. B., & Staker, H. (2011). The rise of K-12 blended learning. *Innosight institute, 5*(1), 1-17.

Hufad, A., Faturrohman, M., & Rusdiyani, I. (2021). Unplugged coding activities for early childhood problem-solving skills. *Jurnal Pendidikan Usia Dini*, 15(1), 121–140. DOI: 10.21009/JPUD.151.07

Hughes, J., Thomas, R., & Scharber, C. (2006). Assessing technology integration: The RAT - Replacement, Amplification, and Transformation framework. *Technology and Teacher Education Annual*, 1616-1620.

Inhelder, B., & Piaget, J. (1958). *The growth of logical thinking from childhood to adolescence: An essay on the construction of formal operational structures*. Psychology Press. DOI: 10.1037/10034-000

Johnson, D. W., & Johnson, R. J. (1999). Making cooperative learning work. *Theory into Practice*, 38(2), 67–73. DOI: 10.1080/00405849909543834

Kalelioğlu, F. (2015). A new way of teaching programming skills to K-12 students: Code. org. *Computers in Human Behavior*, 52, 200–210. DOI: 10.1016/j.chb.2015.05.047

Kaplancalı, U. T., & Demirkol, Z. (2017). Teaching coding to children: A methodology for kids 5+. *International Journal of Elementary Education*, 6(4), 32–37. DOI: 10.11648/j.ijeedu.20170604.11

Kert, S. B., & Uğraş, T. (2009, May). Programlama eğitiminde sadelik ve eğlence: Scratch örneği. *InThe First International Congress of Educational Research,* Çanakkale, Turkey.

Koehler, M., & Mishra, P. (2009). What is technological pedagogical content knowledge (TPACK)? *Contemporary Issues in Technology & Teacher Education*, 9(1), 60–70.

Kong, R., & Wong, G. K. (2017). Teachers' perception of professional development in coding education. *In 2017 IEEE 6th International Conference on Teaching, Assessment, and Learning for Engineering (TALE)*, 377-380.

Kozulin, A. (2003). *Vygotsky's educational theory in cultural context*. Cambridge University Press. DOI: 10.1017/CBO9780511840975

Lee, J. (2020). Coding in early childhood. *Contemporary Issues in Early Childhood*, 21(3), 266–269. DOI: 10.1177/1463949119846541

Lee, J., & Junoh, J. (2019). Implementing unplugged coding activities in early childhood classrooms. *Early Childhood Education Journal*, 47(6), 709–716. DOI: 10.1007/s10643-019-00967-z

Lin, Y., Liao, H., Weng, S., & Dong, W. (2023). Comparing the effects of plugged-in and unplugged activities on computational thinking development in young children. *Education and Information Technologies*, •••, 1–34. DOI: 10.1007/s10639-023-12181-x PMID: 37361760

Locke, E. A., & Latham, G. P. (2002). Building a practically useful theory of goal setting and task motivation: A 35-year odyssey. *The American Psychologist*, 57(9), 705–717. https://psycnet.apa.org/doi/10.1037/0003-066X.57.9.705. DOI: 10.1037/0003-066X.57.9.705 PMID: 12237980

Mercer, N., & Littleton, K. (2007). *Dialogue and the development of children's thinking: A sociocultural approach*. Routledge. DOI: 10.4324/9780203946657

Metin, S. (2022). Activity-based unplugged coding during the preschool period. *International Journal of Technology and Design Education*, 32(1), 149–165. DOI: 10.1007/s10798-020-09616-8

Miani, P., Kille, T., Lee, S. Y., Zhang, Y., & Bates, P. R. (2021). The impact of the COVID-19 pandemic on current tertiary aviation education and future careers: Students' perspective. *Journal of Air Transport Management*, 94, 102081. DOI: 10.1016/j.jairtraman.2021.102081 PMID: 36569599

Miller, P. H. (2012). *Theories of developmental psychology* (5th ed.). Worth Publishers.

Mishra, P., & Koehler, M. J. (2006). Technological pedagogical content knowledge: A framework for teacher knowledge. *Teachers College Record*, 108(6), 1017–1054. DOI: 10.1111/j.1467-9620.2006.00684.x

Mistretta, S. (2022). Virtual robotics in hybrid teaching and learning. *New Updates in E-Learning*, 145-156.

Molenda, M. (2003). In search of the elusive ADDIE model. *Performance Improvement*, 42(5), 34–37. DOI: 10.1002/pfi.4930420508

Moraiti, I., Fotoglou, A., & Drigas, A. (2022). Coding with block programming languages in educational robotics and mobiles, improve problem solving, creativity & critical thinking skills. *International Journal of Interactive Mobile Technologies*, 16(20), 59–78. Advance online publication. DOI: 10.3991/ijim.v16i20.34247

Morrison, G. R., Ross, S. M., Kalman, H. K., & Kemp, J. E. (2010). *Designing effective instruction* (6th ed.). Wiley.

Negrini, L. (2020). Teachers' attitudes towards educational robotics in compulsory school. *Italian Journal of Educational Technology*, 28(1), 77–90. DOI: 10.17471/2499-4324/1136

Papert, S. (1980). *Mindstorms: Children, computers, and powerful ideas*. Basic Books.

Piaget, J. (1952). *The origins of intelligence in children*. International Universities Press. DOI: 10.1037/11494-000

Pila, S., Aladé, F., Sheehan, K. J., Lauricella, A. R., & Wartella, E. A. (2019). Learning to code via tablet applications: An evaluation of Daisy the Dinosaur and Kodable as learning tools for young children. *Computers & Education*, 128, 52–62. DOI: 10.1016/j.compedu.2018.09.006

Reigeluth, C. M. (Ed.). (1999). *Instructional-design theories and models: A new paradigm of instructional theory* (Vol. II). Routledge.

Resnick, M. (2007). Sowing the seeds for a more creative society. *Learning and Leading with Technology*, 35(4), 18–22.

Resnick, M., Maloney, J., Monroy-Hernández, A., Rusk, N., Eastmond, E., Brennan, K., Millner, A., Rosenbaum, E., Silver, J., Silverman, B., & Kafai, Y. (2009). Scratch: Programming for all. *Communications of the ACM*, 52(11), 60–67. DOI: 10.1145/1592761.1592779

Rich, P. J., Browning, S. F., Perkins, M., Shoop, T., Yoshikawa, E., & Belikov, O. M. (2019). Coding in K-8: International trends in teaching elementary/primary computing. *TechTrends*, 63(3), 311–329. DOI: 10.1007/s11528-018-0295-4

Rosenshine, B. (1986). Synthesis of research on explicit teaching. *Educational Leadership*, 43(7), 60–69.

Sawyer, R. K. (2006). *The Cambridge handbook of the learning sciences*. Cambridge University Press.

Saxena, A., Lo, C. K., Hew, K. F., & Wong, G. K. W. (2020). Designing unplugged and plugged activities to cultivate computational thinking: An exploratory study in early childhood education. *The Asia-Pacific Education Researcher*, 29(1), 55–66. DOI: 10.1007/s40299-019-00478-w

Saygıner, Ş., & Tüzün, H. (2017). İlköğretim düzeyinde programlama eğitimi: Yurt dışı ve yurt içi perspektifinden bir bakış. *Akademik Bilişim Konferansı*, 1-5.

Su, J., Yang, W., & Li, H. (2023). A scoping review of studies on coding curriculum in early childhood: Investigating its design, implementation, and evaluation. *Journal of Research in Childhood Education*, 37(2), 341–361. DOI: 10.1080/02568543.2022.2097349

Sun, L., Guo, Z., & Zhou, D. (2022). Developing programming skills in K-12 students: A systematic literature review. *Education and Information Technologies*, 27(5), 7059–7097. DOI: 10.1007/s10639-022-10891-2

Sung, W., Ahn, J., & Black, J. B. (2017). Introducing computational thinking to young learners: Practicing computational perspectives through embodiment in mathematics education. *Technology. Knowledge and Learning*, 22(3), 443–463. DOI: 10.1007/s10758-017-9328-x

Timur, S., Timur, B., Güvenç, E., Us, I., & Yalçinkaya-Önder, E. (2021). Pre-service pre-school teachers' opinions about using block-based coding/SCRATCH. *Acta Didactica Napocensia*, 14(2), 299–317. DOI: 10.24193/adn.14.2.22

Tomlinson, C. A. (2001). *How to differentiate instruction in mixed-ability classrooms*. ASCD.

Tsarava, K., Leifheit, L., Ninaus, M., Román-González, M., Butz, M. V., Golle, J., & Moeller, K. (2019, October). Cognitive correlates of computational thinking: Evaluation of a blended unplugged/plugged-in course. In *Proceedings of the 14th Workshop in Primary and Secondary Computing Education*, 1-9. https://doi.org/ DOI: 10.1145/3361721.3361729

Van Roy, P., & Haridi, S. (2004). *Concepts, techniques, and models of computer programming*. MIT Press.

Voronina, L. V., Sergeeva, N. N., & Utyumova, A. (2016). Development of algorithm skills in preschool children. *Procedia: Social and Behavioral Sciences*, 233, 155–159. DOI: 10.1016/j.sbspro.2016.10.176

Vygotsky, L. S. (1978). *Mind in society: The development of higher psychological processes*. Harvard University Press.

Wing, J. M. (2006). Computational thinking. *Communications of the ACM*, 49(3), 33–35. DOI: 10.1145/1118178.1118215

Wood, D., Bruner, J. S., & Ross, G. (1976). The role of tutoring in problem solving. *Journal of Child Psychology and Psychiatry, and Allied Disciplines*, 17(2), 89–100. DOI: 10.1111/j.1469-7610.1976.tb00381.x PMID: 932126

Yadav, A., Hong, H., & Stephenson, C. (2016). Computational thinking for all: Pedagogical approaches to embedding 21st century problem solving in K-12 classrooms. *TechTrends*, 60(6), 565–568. DOI: 10.1007/s11528-016-0087-7

Zhong, B., Liu, X., Xia, L., & Sun, W. (2022). A proposed taxonomy for instructional models in STEM education: The case of robotics. *SAGE Open*, 12(2), 21582440221099525. DOI: 10.1177/21582440221099525

Chapter 2
Computational Thinking:
Exploring Approaches in Early Childhood Education

Leonard Busuttil
https://orcid.org/0000-0003-3779-891X
Faculty of Education, Msida, Malta

Diane Vassallo
https://orcid.org/0000-0002-9062-2297
Faculty of Education, Msida, Malta

Patrick Schembri
https://orcid.org/0000-0002-7808-5871
Faculty of Education, Msida, Malta

ABSTRACT

This chapter reviews research on integrating computational thinking (CT) in early childhood education (ECE) over the past decade, emphasizing its growing importance as a crucial skill for the technological world. It explores how CT is taught in early years, the characteristics of CT activities, and their learning outcomes. The review identifies three methodologies: unplugged, coding, and robotics. Unplugged methods use tangible materials like games to teach CT without digital devices. Coding activities foster problem-solving and creativity, while robotics offer interactive learning with programmable robots. Learning outcomes include foundational CT skills, creative problem-solving, technical proficiency, cognitive and language development, and, with robotics, positive emotions, prosocial values, and environmental awareness. Integrating CT in ECE through these methodologies provides valuable learning experiences, fostering critical thinking and preparing young learners to be creative, analytical thinkers in a technologically advanced future.

DOI: 10.4018/979-8-3693-4542-9.ch002

INTRODUCTION

Computational thinking (CT) refers to a specific set of mental skills used to formulate solutions to problems by converting given inputs to produce appropriate outputs while following detailed algorithms to perform this process (Denning, 2009). Essentially, CT is broadly defined as a combination of thinking processes that include abstraction, algorithm design, decomposition, pattern recognition, and data representation (Wing, 2006). What sets CT apart from other thinking skills is this focus on solving problems in ways that draw on concepts from computer science to produce solutions that can be represented in a form that a computer can execute (Cuny et al., 2010).

The prominence of CT in education has been steadily increasing, with some touting it as the "new literacy of the 21st century" (Wing, 2006). This is very much warranted given the rising prevalence of technology and its infiltration into the many facets of our daily lives since the set of competencies offered by CT is seen to be critical for success in today's rapidly changing world (Barr & Stephenson, 2011; Grover & Pea, 2013; Mishra et al., 2013). In the same way that language proficiency supports communication, being eloquent in CT is seen to provide a systematic and efficient scaffold when dealing with complex problems (Lu & Fletcher, 2009). This has led to the conviction that CT skills represent a "universally applicable attitude and skill set" (Wing, 2006, p. 33) that should be part of the repertoire of every child's analytical ability and thus should constitute a vital part of school learning.

In discussing the need for CT to be integrated into classroom practice and the different ways in which this could be achieved, many proponents of CT seem to agree that early childhood is the ideal time to start integrating CT into education (e.g. Manches & Plowman, 2017; Wing, 2008). Early childhood is considered a critical stage for the development of skills in the cognitive, social and emotional domains. The initial school class (K-2) is an ideal time to begin introducing CT concepts because it is the stage where children transition between concrete and abstract processes, thus, providing active experiences that stimulate their thought processes is seen to bear the potential to support this transition (Piaget, 1977). The methods through which this is done vary and include plugged (using some sort of digital device) or unplugged activities. Through CT and also age-appropriate device programming, children start becoming aware of the process of automation and the fact that it is a clearly defined set of instructions that drive a computer and not some kind of magic. This has the potential to lead children to begin solving problems in the concrete world through systemic steps and ultimately become designers of technology rather than just passive users (Wyeth & Wyeth, 2008).

In recent years, there has been a growing number of institutions across the world that have formally recognised the introduction of CT concepts and practices (Bocconi et al., 2018; Fowler & Vegas, 2021). This has marked an increasing emphasis on incorporating CT into ECE programs globally. This chapter aims to provide a systematic review of evidence-based research and initiatives to try and define the kinds of CT-related activities being conducted in the ECE stage of education.

This chapter presents the range of different approaches to CT that have been adopted in recent years in ECE. The main focus of this document is on answering the following research questions:

1. How is CT being taught in the early years?
2. What are the main characteristics of CT activities?
3. What are the learning outcomes that these activities aim to achieve?

To answer these questions, a systematic review of evidence-based research and initiatives that have been carried out with CT in ECE in the past decade has been conducted. This aims to provide a clear snapshot of the practices and experiences that characterise CT in ECE.

Exploring Definitions of CT

CT has gained significant attention as a crucial skill set for the 21st century. However, the absence of a universally accepted definition has made it challenging to grasp its comprehensive nature. A systematic review by Haseski et al. (2018) uncovered 59 different definitions that highlight problem-solving, technology, thinking, and individual and social qualities. CT finds its roots in Papert's Constructionism, where learning occurs through active engagement in constructing tangible outcomes using digital tools (Papert, 1980). Wing (2006) defines CT as the processes of abstraction, algorithmic thinking, and decomposition in problem-solving.

Resnick (2017) emphasises the creative and expressive aspects of using digital tools in designing and creating processes. Barr and Stephenson (2011) stress the importance of modelling, simulation, and data analysis in problem-solving using digital tools. These skills align with Papert's concept of the "computer as material" (Papert, 1980).

While programming plays a pivotal role in developing procedural thinking and CT the literature acknowledges that CT transcends programming (Voogt et al., 2015). Wing (2006) expanded the definition of CT to include framing problems and solutions in ways computers can understand and execute (Wing, 2010). Lu and Fletcher (2009) liken proficiency in CT to the ability to process information and tasks systematically, correctly, and efficiently.

Various skills, strategies, and dispositions constitute CT. Wing (2006) identifies thinking processes such as abstraction, algorithm design, decomposition, pattern recognition, and data representation. Similarly, Kalelioglu et al. (2016) propose a framework focusing on abstracting, decomposing, analysing data, recognising patterns, algorithmic thinking, implementation, and evaluation.

Certain elements, such as abstraction, decomposition, algorithmic thinking, and generalisation, have gained universal acceptance (Angeli et al., 2016; Grover & Pea, 2013; Lee et al., 2011; Selby & Woollard, 2013). The "big ideas" of computing summarise CT's characteristics, including creativity, innovation, abstraction, data, algorithms, programming, and networking (CollegeBoard, 2017; Grover & Pea, 2013).

Defining CT holds promise for understanding its integration in education, including the choice of topics, depth, order, and meaningful implementation. While a common definition remains elusive (Grover & Pea, 2013; Rich et al., 2020), considering similarities and relationships surrounding the CT discussion can inform its importance and guide integration efforts (Voogt et al., 2015).

METHODOLOGY

To answer the research questions raised in the introduction section, a systematic review of the literature was conducted to identify what research has been carried out in this area around the field of CT.

Literature Search Process

The search strategy employed for this study aimed to identify relevant research articles in the ACM digital library, IEEE Xplore, and SCOPUS databases. The search string included a combination of keywords and phrases related to the study's research topic, which was focused on exploring the use of unplugged and plugged activities to promote CT skills in young children.

This search string was designed to identify articles with relevant titles and abstracts that contained any of the following keywords: "plugged," "unplugged," "Computational Thinking," "robot," "coding," "robotics," "programming" (about early childhood), "young child*," "preschool," "kindergarten*," "pre-k*," "childcare," "child care," or "daycare." Papers published between January 2012 and March 23 were considered for this exercise.

The search strategy was designed to be comprehensive and minimise the risk of missing any relevant studies however no search strategy can be completely exhaustive, and some relevant studies may have been missed (Zawacki-Richter et al., 2020).

Eligibility Criteria

Eligibility criteria were established to ensure that only relevant studies were included in this systematic review. The eligibility criteria included the following:

1. Study design: Only peer-reviewed empirical research articles and conference papers published in conference proceedings were included in this review. Other forms of grey literature were excluded.
2. Participants: Studies that involved young children aged 2 to 8 years old were included. Studies that focused on older children, adolescents, or adults were excluded.
3. Interventions: Studies that investigated using unplugged or plugged activities to promote CT skills in young children were included. Studies that did not have an intervention or investigated other interventions unrelated to CT skills were excluded.
4. Outcomes: Studies that measured the effects of the intervention on CT skills or related outcomes (such as problem-solving, logic, or reasoning skills) were included. Studies that did not measure any relevant outcomes were excluded.
5. Language: Only studies published in English were included in this review.
6. Publication date: Studies published from January 1st, 2012, were included.

The eligibility criteria above were designed to identify studies that were relevant to the research questions while minimising the risk of bias. Limiting the age range of participants and intervention types ensured that the studies were directly relevant to the research question. Including only studies published in English ensured that the review was feasible within the available resources. Overall, these criteria were designed to ensure that the studies included in this review were of high quality and directly relevant to the research questions.

Data Extraction

The data extraction procedure was designed to extract relevant information from the included studies in a consistent and systematic manner. A standardised data extraction form was developed to collect information on the following variables:

- Study characteristics: Author(s), year of publication, title of the study, and journal in which the study was published.
- Participants: Sample size, age, gender, ethnicity, and any other relevant demographic characteristics.

- Intervention: Type of intervention (plugged or unplugged), duration, frequency, and any other relevant details.
- Outcomes: Primary and secondary outcomes measured, assessment tools used, and any relevant findings.
- Study quality: Quality assessment criteria and results of quality assessment.

The data extraction form was pilot-tested on a sample of included studies to ensure that it captured all relevant information and was easy to use. Two reviewers independently extracted data from each included study, and any discrepancies were resolved through discussion and consensus. Data were entered into a database for analysis.

The data extraction procedure was designed to ensure that relevant information was extracted from each study consistently and systematically. By using a standardised data extraction form, the risk of errors or bias was minimised. The use of independent reviewers and consensus-building ensured that the data extracted were reliable and valid. Overall, the data extraction procedure was designed to ensure that the data analysed in this review were of high quality and directly relevant to the research question.

The literature search process resulted in over 3000 entries located in the three databases. These entries were reduced to 85 potential papers after reviewing the title and abstract of all entries in the searches and removing duplicate entries.

APPROACHES TO CT IN THE EARLY YEARS

After conducting a comprehensive analysis of the literature derived from the search process, three primary approaches to the integration of computational thinking in early years education have been identified.

Unplugged Approaches to CT

Educators have been exploring innovative ways to integrate CT into early childhood education. One popular approach is the use of unplugged activities, which involve tangible or non-digital materials like games, puzzles, crafts, and manipulatives to teach CT concepts without relying on computers or digital devices (Battal et al., 2021; Bell & Vahrenhold, 2018; Busuttil & Formosa, 2020). This section reviews

18 papers on unplugged approaches to CT, exploring how unplugged activities are utilised in early childhood education to introduce CT.

Out of the 27 papers involving unplugged activities related to CT, only ten exclusively focus on unplugged CT implementations. The majority of the papers (17) explore a combination of robotics, coding, and unplugged activities.

There is a clear link between CT and the STEM (Science, Technology, Engineering, and Mathematics) field. The teaching of Computing drew heavily from STEM methodologies, explaining the current connection between STEM and CT (Bers, Strawhacker, et al., 2022). For instance, Storjak et al. (2020) incorporated unplugged programming and hands-on robot play in STEM workshops for young children.

The benefits of coding and robotics are further confirmed by Sung et al.(2022), who investigated the effects of embodied instruction on soft skills like problem-solving, debugging, programming proficiency, self-determination, and self-efficacy. Similarly, Lee et al. (2020) and Metin (2020) utilised unplugged and robotics activities to develop coding skills effectively in young children. Gartig-Daugs et al. (2016) successfully combined Froebel and Montessori ideas with computer science to explain computational concepts to children, encouraging meaningful experiences and constructivist learning. Additionally, Leung, Wu, & Li (2024) examined young children's computational thinking skills using unplugged activities, highlighting the benefits of knowledge construction in early childhood.

Some papers within the STEM framework use CT not as a basis for further programming but to achieve outcomes beyond CT and programming. For instance, Ioannou and Bratitsis (2017) employed unplugged activities and robot programming to teach the concept of speed in kindergarten. Canbeldek and Isikoglu (2023) integrated a Coding and Robotics Education Program into early childhood education to positively affect cognitive and language development and creativity. Barragan-Sanchez et al. (2023) used unplugged and robot-based CT activities to modify problematic behaviours, stimulating students' participation and creativity. Hu et al. (2024) explored young children's experiences in unplugged activities, finding significant benefits for early learning.

Studies by Luo et al. (2022), Perez-Marin et al. (2022), and Somuncu and Aslan (2021) focused on applying CT in problem-solving activities and improving skills such as sequencing, plotting routes, and mathematical reasoning. Additionally, Kandlhofer et al. (2016) included Artificial Intelligence concepts in a playful, constructionist module. Ş. Metin et al. (2024) adapted computational thinking skill scales for young children, providing a valuable tool for assessing CT development in early education contexts. Lin et al. (2024) compared the effects of unplugged and plugged-in activities, finding that both approaches effectively enhanced computational thinking in young children. Masarwa et al. (2024) demonstrated the effectiveness of the "Sorting Like a Computer" learning unit in teaching computational thinking to kindergarten children.

A common theme in these studies is the use of creativity, play, and playful practice to integrate CT. Noma et al. (2003) used hands-on playing experiences with toys to teach computation and programming, while Meyer-Baron et al. (2022) employed themed physical boxes with CT tasks in an escape-room style. Critten et al. (2022) scaffolded coding clubs to encourage logical thinking, problem-solving, and debugging through guided play activities. Yang et al(2023) utilised digital storytelling as a culturally responsive approach to CT learning, while others (Benetti & Mazzini, 2020; Pérez-Marin et al., 2022) integrated stories to motivate coding experiences. Leung, Wu, Li, et al. (2024) highlighted the role of scaffolding and guided play in fostering young children's computational thinking through animation art. Fridberg & Redfors (2024) explored the use of words during early childhood STEM teaching supported by robotics, emphasising the importance of language in computational thinking educationBusuttil et al. (2023) introduced a novel board game design, "Mystery at the Museum," which promotes CT skills through collaborative and engaging gameplay for young children. Bratitsis et al. (2023) discussed the CThink.IT approach, using board games to cultivate CT skills in early childhood, emphasising the value of structured game design and active participation in learning.

Unplugged approaches provide a suitable starting point for introducing CT to very young students, laying the foundation for more complex programming and problem-solving tasks involving robotics and coding. Unplugged activities offer embodied cognition, enabling the physical enactment of abstract CT concepts, which proves effective for young children. Furthermore, these approaches have demonstrated benefits for diverse student groups, including those from disadvantaged backgrounds and with special needs. However, there is a lack of unplugged resources for CT in early childhood education, necessitating further research and development in this area to support the acquisition of CT skills in young learners.

Coding

Scholarly literature offers numerous examples of coding implementations in early childhood education, ranging from coding games to open-ended coding environments like Scratch Junior or Viscuit. Additionally, some approaches involve programming tangible objects.

This systematic review identified 19 relevant papers on coding in early childhood education. Among these, 10 papers focused on open-ended coding and programming environments, 7 on programming with tangible objects, and 2 on coding games.

Flannery et al. (2013) discussed the design and development of ScratchJr, a programming language for children in grades K-2. ScratchJr enables interactive and animated story creation and provides curricula and online resources for educators. Portelance and Bers (2015) conducted a study with second-grade students using ScratchJr to create animated stories and games on tablet devices, emphasising skills related to CT such as debugging and modularisation. Kyza et al. (2022) used ScratchJr to teach coding practices and CT to primary school children, observing differences in coding practices and CT concepts between age cohorts. Additionally Leung, Wu, & Li (2024), found that children's knowledge construction of computational thinking (CT) through ScratchJr significantly enhanced their problem-solving and critical thinking skills.

Storytelling is a popular approach to introduce CT in early years education. Yang et al. (2023) explored using story-inspired programming with robots and tablets, resulting in improved CT scores. Canbeldek and Isikoglu (2023) researched a program integrating unplugged, coding, and robotic kits to enhance cognitive development, language, and creativity in young children. Similarly, Fridberg & Redfors (2024) investigated the use of words during early programming and coding activities, emphasising the role of verbal interactions in enhancing CT skills. Levinson & Bers (2024) also highlighted the impact of storytelling in CT development through the use of narrative-based programming activities.

Viscuit, an open-ended coding environment, was discussed by Watanabe et al. (2019, 2020). The study demonstrated that young children effectively created valid programs and utilised multiple programming techniques with Viscuit. Falloon (2024) further supported the effectiveness of open-ended environments like Viscuit, noting that they advanced young students' computational thinking by encouraging exploration and experimentation.

Tangible programming toys, combining physical and digital components, provide a unique learning experience. Liu and Iversen (2022) studied the interactions of a child with an Osmo Coding Awbie game, highlighting the benefits of dialogues during gameplay for CT education. Wu et al. (2024) similarly examined the impact of robotic kits in early education, finding that these tools significantly improved children's engagement and understanding of coding concepts. Yang (2024) also emphasised the benefits of using tangible programming toys to support CT and problem-solving skills.

Coding games are another avenue to introduce CT to young children. Lennon et al. (2022) investigated the impact of game features on children's learning and engagement, finding that open-structure games supported independent learning. Montuori et al. (2022) explored gender differences in coding, discovering that boys showed an advantage in coding skills after an introductory course. Chen et al. (2024) introduced ChatScratch, an AI-augmented system that significantly enhanced young learners' coding abilities by providing real-time assistance and feedback during game-based learning activities.

Kim (2020) investigated how hands-on robot activities improved problem-solving skills in young children, highlighting the potential of such activities to promote creative problem-solving. Wu et al. (2024) reinforced this by demonstrating that combining hands-on activities with coding instruction led to substantial improvements in both cognitive and motor skills.

Coding in early childhood education offers diverse and valuable learning opportunities, contributing to the development of CT skills and creative problem-solving abilities in young learners.

Robotics

Robotics is another approach that educators have undertaken to incorporate CT competencies into early childhood education. 57 papers on robotics approaches to CT were identified in this systematic review, which highlights the growing popularity of using robotics to teach CT. Out of these 57 papers, 38 papers exclusively focus on robotics implementations of CT, 11 papers combine robotics with unplugged activities, 5 papers combine robotics with programming, and only 3 papers explore the combination of all three methods.

Robotics, Unplugged and Programming

A detailed examination of the two articles (Canbeldek & Isikoglu, 2023; Yang et al., 2023) that delve into the integration of all three methods, it was found that these interventions were particularly effective. The studies highlight the favourable outcomes of incorporating technology (coding, robotics, unplugged) and pedagogical approaches (e.g., storytelling) into early childhood education activities, which improve children's cognitive development, language skills, and creativity. Furthermore, Yang et al. (2023) specifically point out the efficacy of Story Inspired Programming (SIP) interventions in enhancing young children's CT skills, in comparison to unplugged CT education. Alonso-García et al. (2024) further support these findings by demonstrating that combining unplugged activities with robotics enhances computational thinking (CT) skills and overall cognitive development in young children.

Robotics and Programming

Kim (2020) compares the effectiveness of hands-on robot activities with EPL activities, while Bers (2010) contrasts screen-based activities, namely ScratchJr and the tangible robotic kit KIBO. It is noteworthy that although Gordon et al. (2015) and

Bers (2018) share a common focus on exploring technology to foster computational literacy, they differ in their approach and emphasis. Gordon et al. (2015) assess the efficacy of the SoRo Toolkit, a programming tool, while Bers (2018) highlights the importance of developmentally appropriate programming languages and robotics systems, such as ScratchJr and KIBO. Nonetheless, all three papers underscore the potential benefits of introducing programming and CT skills to young children. Kim (2020) reports a positive impact on children's problem-solving and creative thinking skills, Bers (2018) demonstrates that preschool children can grasp programming concepts, and Gordon et al. (2015) stress the significance of computational literacy in today's world and the potential for programming to empower children as digital producers. Wu et al. (2024) add to this discussion by exploring a robotic intervention aimed at teaching coding to young children, showing significant improvements in their programming and problem-solving skills.

Robotics and Unplugged Activities

The examination of the 11 papers that combine robotics with unplugged activities revealed that the latter focuses on nurturing CT skills, such as algorithmic thinking, abstraction, decomposition, pattern recognition, and logical reasoning. On the other hand, robotics activities aim to provide hands-on experiences with coding and robotics that support the development of CT skills such as sequencing, debugging, conditional logic, and iteration. This is demonstrated by several papers, including Sung (2022), Metin (2020), and Sung et al. (2022). Furthermore, Somuncu and Aslan (2021) developed a coding education program that utilises a build-up approach, where the initial four activities employ unplugged coding methods to teach the basic components of programming, such as "Hop Scotch Coding," which consists of cards resembling code blocks with movement command cards. Subsequently, the remaining activities entail working with the Bee-Bot programmable toy. Similarly, Storjak et al. (2020) employed the same concept of introducing programming through unplugged methods, specifically graph paper programming worksheets, while in the second learning scenario, pupils were introduced to two educational robots: Codey Rocky, controlled using the Makeblock application on a tablet, and Thymio, controlled using the on-robot buttons. Storjak et al. (2020) suggest that combining unplugged activities with robots helps bridge the gap between imagination and reality, thus enhancing learning. Several other papers have also utilised this approach. Fridberg & Redfors (2024) emphasise the importance of integrating both unplugged and robotic activities in early childhood education, finding that this combination effectively nurtures algorithmic thinking and logical reasoning among young learners.

Additional papers focus on curriculum design, such as Barragán-Sánchez et al. (2023), who describe an intervention program aimed at modifying problematic behaviours using a tale and activities of increasing difficulty. The study employed several unplugged activities, such as following instructions with one's own body, along with a robotics activity using the Mouse Activity floor robot. Results indicate that students achieved better cognitive outcomes and showed greater interest in learning challenging abstract concepts. Similarly, Critten et al. (2022) designed a set of guided activities suitable for coding clubs attended by preschool children, combining unplugged activities with the use of Bee-Bot robots.

Robotics

Among the 35 papers focusing on robotics, various themes emerge, including curriculum design and educational activities aimed at enhancing learning outcomes.

One of the studies (Christidi & Christopoulou, 2022) focused on activities about water pollution using the programmable Blue Bot robot. The research findings indicated that the use of educational robots allowed young students to acquire programming and algorithmic thinking skills playfully while enhancing their cognitive and communication abilities. Similarly in another study (Bers, Govind, et al., 2022), a curriculum called Coding as Another Language (CAL) was created, utilising KIBO robotics. Children engaged in activities such as arts and crafts, reading and writing exercises, open-ended projects, songs, and games, while CAL-KIBO integrated coding. The researcher's analysis suggests that baseline literacy skills were related to students' acquisition of CT skills, and participation in the curriculum showed improvement in coding and unplugged CT skills.

Another study that introduced educational robotics to children through the Bee-Bot educational robotics kit (González & Muñoz-Repiso, 2017) aimed at developing teaching activities and achieving curricular objectives. The students practised various movements and displacements that could be made with the robot, using a mat or rug specifically designed for Bee-Bot. The teachers expressed a positive attitude towards the application, and most of the students agreed that they enjoyed learning with Bee-Bot. In another study, the same authors developed a framework for designing and integrating learning activities with robotics to foster programming skills and CT in early childhood classrooms (González & Muñoz-Repiso, 2018). The findings demonstrated that utilising programming and robotics challenges for educational purposes has the potential to offer significant benefits and opportunities for enhancing CT skills among young learners.

Several other papers centred around the same theme explore the impact of robotics on children's values. For instance, one such research explores the benefits of robotics in early childhood education, specifically focusing on prosocial values (Zilinskiene, 2022). The research concludes that learning with robots fosters positive emotions and prosocial values while decreasing negative emotions. In a similar study, Silvis et al. (2022) focused on the affective dimensions of child-computer interaction and analysed children's natural conversations with robots during coding lessons, intending to explore broader contexts for CT in collaboration with others.

In their study, Yang et al. (2022) focus on education within low-income communities by examining the affordances and challenges of robot programming (RP) in early childhood education in a low-income public housing estate. The research made use of a Matatalab, a programmable robot kit that operates without a screen, as the programming platform.

Silvis et al. (2022) investigate how children develop technical knowledge in tangible programming environments while utilising robots such as Botley and Cubetto. The researchers aim to teach the technical skills necessary for operating and fixing technological tools. The students are given the task of moving the robot from one location to another by arranging physical tiles or buttons to create directional codes. The authors observe that as the children fix errors in the program and physical apparatus, they demonstrate crucial technical knowledge. Similarly, Flood et al. (2022) focus on tangible programming toys that support body synchronicity, where children use knowledge of their bodies to solve problems computationally, and how teachers respond to preschoolers' body syntonic problem-solving. In this study, the children spontaneously used their bodies to take the perspective of the Code-a-pillar to complete each programming challenge, while the teacher was responsive to the children's use of body synchronicity. The authors show how a teacher attended and responded to the productive beginnings of problem decomposition, debugging, and abstraction present in children's embodied problem-solving. Zhang et al. (2024) introduce a metaphor-based robot programming approach that effectively enhances young children's understanding and application of computational concepts.

Burleson et al. (2018) present the results of an educational human-robot interaction (HRI) comparative case study involving 6-year-old students in the use of Active Learning Environments with Robotic Tangibles (ALERT) robot, a tangible interface for spatial programming. The researchers engaged children in interactions with both the physical ALERT and digital Robopad robots and compared their engagement in spatial programming using the physical space of the room or the digital space of the computer screen. This study demonstrates innovative opportunities for advancing mixed reality spatial programming activities as a form of HRI. Additionally, Yildiz and Çengel (2022) conducted a study to assess the fundamental robotic coding abilities of preschool students with intellectual disabilities.

A study by Samuelsson (2022) introduces programming for children by using programmable robots and storytelling using the Ukrainian folk tale Rukavitjka (The Mitten). Moreover, Brainin et al. (2022) examine the contribution of robot programming to an intervention aimed at promoting spatial language (spatial vocabulary) and spatial ability (mental rotation, visual-spatial memory) among 84 preschool children, while utilising Bee-Bot. The results show that the children who received the robot-based intervention demonstrated the most significant improvement in spatial vocabulary and mental rotation test scores compared to the children who only participated in the control group.

Nacher et al. (2016) evaluated the usability of a tangible-mediated robot in collaborative kindergarten activities breaking down the task of controlling a robot into four simple actions (move forward, stop, turn left, and turn right) and using tangible sticks to represent the robot's actions. In a similar vein, a study by Hall and McCormick (2022) examined preschool children's CT experiences when using button-operated robots (Bee-Bot) during guided play, focusing on movement and direction, algorithm design, and debugging. Finally, Terroba et al. (2022) characterised CT while resolving seven problems of increasing difficulty while using a ground robot with programmed directionality controls. Bui et al. (2024) conducted research on STEM in early childhood education, emphasiSing the integration of robotics to improve cognitive development and problem-solving skills.

The papers analysed throughout this exercise used various robotic kits, with the Bee-Bot and Kibo being the most popular kits explored in literature.

CHALLENGES AND BARRIERS INTEGRATING COMPUTATIONAL THINKING IN EARLY CHILDHOOD EDUCATION

Integrating computational thinking in early childhood education encounters several significant challenges and barriers. These challenges can be categorised into distinct themes: accessibility, complexity and cognitive load, development and appropriateness, equity and inclusion, teacher preparation and professional development, logistical and practical challenges, and family and community engagement.

Accessibility

Ensuring accessibility for all children, particularly those with disabilities, is a significant challenge. Accessibility issues can limit the participation and learning opportunities for children with physical, sensory, or cognitive disabilities, thereby hindering the creation of an inclusive learning environment (Silva et al., 2023).

Addressing these barriers requires the development of tools and materials that are adaptable to the diverse needs of all learners (Bers, Strawhacker, et al., 2022).

Complexity and Cognitive Load

The complexity of computational tools and concepts poses another significant barrier. Young children may struggle with the cognitive load imposed by certain tools, which can hinder their ability to engage with computational thinking activities (Bati, 2022). Ensuring that the tools are age-appropriate and manageable for young learners is essential for effective integration (Silva et al., 2023).

Development and Appropriateness

The development of appropriate tools and practices that align with the developmental stages of young children is crucial. Developmentally inappropriate tools can lead to frustration and disengagement among children (Bers, Strawhacker, et al., 2022). Therefore, it is important to create resources that are tailored to the cognitive and motor skills of early learners (Bati, 2022).

Equity and Inclusion

Equity and inclusion remain critical concerns. There are significant disparities in access to computational thinking education based on socio-economic status, gender, and other demographic factors. For instance, girls and children from lower socio-economic backgrounds are often underrepresented in computational thinking activities (Bati, 2022). Promoting equity requires intentional efforts to ensure that all children have equal opportunities to participate and succeed (Silva et al., 2023).

Teacher Preparation and Professional Development

Teachers play a vital role in the successful integration of computational thinking. However, gaps in teacher knowledge and preparation can impede this process (Bers, Strawhacker, et al., 2022). Effective professional development programs are necessary to equip teachers with the skills and confidence needed to teach computational thinking to young children (Bati, 2022).

Logistical and Practical Challenges

Logistical challenges, such as limited time and resources, also affect the integration of computational thinking in early childhood education. Practical issues, including the availability of appropriate technology and materials, can hinder the implementation of these programs (Bers, Strawhacker, et al., 2022).

Family and Community Engagement

Family and community engagement is essential for the success of computational thinking initiatives. Parents and caregivers often lack awareness or understanding of computational thinking, which can limit their ability to support their children's learning at home (Silva et al., 2023) . Building strong partnerships with families and communities can enhance the effectiveness of computational thinking education (Bers, Strawhacker, et al., 2022).

CONCLUSION

This chapter presented various approaches to integrating CT in early childhood education in the last decade. This chapter aims to explore how CT has been taught in the early years, identify the main characteristics of CT activities, and understand the learning outcomes these activities aim to achieve. A systematic review of evidence-based research and initiatives carried out with CT in ECE over the past decade has been done to accomplish this. Through this review, the chapter aimed to provide a comprehensive and informative snapshot of the practices and experiences that have characterised the integration of CT in ECE during this timeframe.

Approaches to CT in the early years revolve around three primary methodologies. These methodologies aim to integrate computational thinking into early childhood education and foster the development of essential cognitive skills in young learners. The main three approaches identified include unplugged methodologies, coding, and robotics approaches.

Unplugged approaches in early childhood education involve the use of tangible or non-digital materials, such as games, puzzles, crafts, and manipulatives, to teach fundamental computational thinking concepts. Educators leverage these hands-on activities to introduce young children to algorithmic thinking, pattern recognition, logical reasoning, and abstraction, without relying on digital devices. These unplugged activities provide an effective foundation for teaching CT to very young students and promote embodied cognition, enabling the physical enactment of abstract concepts, which is particularly beneficial for their learning process. Furthermore, unplugged activities have proven to be inclusive and supportive of diverse student groups, including those from disadvantaged backgrounds and with special needs.

Coding in early childhood education encompasses many practices, from open-ended coding environments like Scratch Junior or Viscuit to programming tangible objects. Children engage in problem-solving exercises through coding activities that encourage creativity and logical thinking. By exploring age-appropriate programming environments, young learners acquire technical proficiency and a deeper understanding of computational concepts. These coding activities facilitate independent learning and creative expression, nurturing children's creative problem-solving abilities and computational literacy.

Robotics approaches have garnered significant attention in early years education as an effective means of fostering computational thinking skills. The integration of programmable robots in educational activities provides young learners with interactive and experiential learning opportunities. Robotics activities enable children to engage in hands-on programming and interactions with tangible robotic kits. These activities bridge the gap between imagination and reality, facilitating cognitive and language development, creative problem-solving, and environmental awareness. Through robotics, children acquire technical knowledge and develop a broad range of skills, including cognitive development, language skills, creativity, and problem-solving abilities.

The learning outcomes of these CT activities in the early years are diverse and significant. They aim to equip young learners with essential skills for their intellectual and emotional development. Core learning outcomes include the development of foundational CT skills such as algorithmic thinking, sequencing, logical reasoning, and problem decomposition. Additionally, CT activities foster creative problem-solving abilities, encouraging children to approach challenges with innovative solutions. Technical proficiency is another key learning outcome, as children acquire programming skills essential in today's technologically advanced society.

Moreover, these activities contribute to cognitive and language development, with robotics activities, in particular, offering interactive and engaging experiences that promote cognitive growth. Some studies suggest that learning with robots fosters positive emotions and prosocial values, emphasising collaboration and empathy among young learners. Furthermore, specific robotics activities centred on environmental themes contribute to raising awareness about ecological issues, nurturing a sense of environmental responsibility.

Despite the promising benefits of integrating CT into early childhood education, several barriers and challenges must be addressed to ensure successful implementation. Accessibility remains a critical issue, particularly for children with disabilities, requiring the development of adaptable tools and materials. The complexity of computational tools and concepts can impose a significant cognitive load on young children, necessitating age-appropriate and manageable tools. Developmentally appropriate resources are crucial to avoid frustration and disengagement among children.

Equity and inclusion are vital concerns, as disparities in access to CT education based on socio-economic status, gender, and other demographic factors persist. Promoting equity requires intentional efforts to ensure all children have equal opportunities to participate and succeed. Teacher preparation and professional development are essential, as gaps in teacher knowledge and preparation can impede the integration of CT. Effective professional development programs are necessary to equip teachers with the skills and confidence needed to teach CT to young children.

Logistical challenges, such as limited time and resources, also affect the integration of CT in early childhood education. Practical issues, including the availability of appropriate technology and materials, can hinder the implementation of these programs. Finally, family and community engagement is crucial for the success of CT initiatives. Building strong partnerships with families and communities can enhance the effectiveness of CT education.

Integrating computational thinking in early childhood education through unplugged methodologies, coding implementations, and robotics approaches offers valuable and diverse learning opportunities for young learners. These activities prepare children with essential skills and knowledge for their future, facilitating their growth as creative and analytical thinkers in an ever-evolving technological landscape.

REFERENCES

Alonso-García, S., Rodríguez Fuentes, A.-V., Ramos Navas-Parejo, M., & Victoria-Maldonado, J.-J. (2024). Enhancing computational thinking in early childhood education with educational robotics: A meta-analysis. *Heliyon*, 10(13), e33249. DOI: 10.1016/j.heliyon.2024.e33249 PMID: 39035481

Angeli, C., Voogt, J., Fluck, A., Webb, M., Cox, M., Malyn-Smith, J., & Zagami, J. (2016). A K-6 computational thinking curriculum framework: Implications for teacher knowledge. *Journal of Educational Technology & Society*, 19(3), 47–57.

Barr, D., Harrison, J., & Conery, L. (2011). Computational Thinking: A Digital Age Skill for Everyone. *Learning and Leading with Technology*, 38(6), 20–23.

Barr, V., & Stephenson, C. (2011). Bringing computational thinking to K-12: What is involved and what is the role of the computer science education community? *ACM Inroads*, 2(1), 48–54. DOI: 10.1145/1929887.1929905

Barragán-Sánchez, R., Romero-Tena, R., & García-López, M. (2023). Educational Robotics to Address Behavioral Problems in Early Childhood. *Education Sciences*, 13(1), 22. Advance online publication. DOI: 10.3390/educsci13010022

Bati, K. (2022). A systematic literature review regarding computational thinking and programming in early childhood education. *Education and Information Technologies*, 27(2), 2059–2082. Advance online publication. DOI: 10.1007/s10639-021-10700-2

Battal, A., Afacan Adanr, G., & Gülbahar, Y. (2021). Computer science unplugged: A systematic literature review. *Journal of Educational Technology Systems*, 50(1), 24–47. DOI: 10.1177/00472395211018801

Bell, T., & Vahrenhold, J. (2018). CS Unplugged How Is It Used, and Does It Work? In *Adventures Between Lower Bounds and Higher Altitudes* (pp. 497–521). Springer. DOI: 10.1007/978-3-319-98355-4_29

Benetti, E., & Mazzini, G. (2020). Coding Training Proposal for Kindergarten. *2020 International Conference on Software, Telecommunications and Computer Networks (SoftCOM)*, 1–5. DOI: 10.23919/SoftCOM50211.2020.9238207

Bers, M. U. (2010). The TangibleK Robotics Program: Applied Computational Thinking for Young Children. *Early Childhood Research & Practice*, 12(2), 2.

Bers, M. U., Govind, M., & Relkin, E. (2022). Coding as Another Language: Computational Thinking, Robotics and Literacy in First and Second Grade. In *Computational Thinking in PreK-5: Empirical Evidence for Integration and Future Directions* (p. 30-38). Association for Computing Machinery. DOI: 10.1145/3507951.3519285

Bers, M. U., Strawhacker, A., & Sullivan, A. (2022). *The state of the field of computational thinking in early childhood education.*

Bocconi, S., Chioccariello, A., & Earp, J. (2018). The Nordic Approach To Introducing Computational Thinking And Programming In Compulsary Education. *Report Prepared for the Nordic@BETT2018 Steering Group.*

Brainin, E., Shamir, A., & Eden, S. (2022). Promoting Spatial Language and Ability Among SLD Children: Can Robot Programming Make a Difference? *Journal of Educational Computing Research*, 60(7), 1742–1762. DOI: 10.1177/07356331221083224

Bratitsis, T., Tsapara, M., Melliou, K., Busuttil, L., Vassallo, D., Callus, J., Meireles, G., Koliakou, I., Kojok, T., & Sousa, S. (2023). Cultivating Computational Thinking in Early Years Through Board Games. The Cthink.it Approach. *IMCL2023 – 15th International Conference on Interactive Mobile Communication, Technologies and Learning*, 158–161.

Bui, T.-L., Tran, T.-T., Dang, U. P., Nguyen, T.-H., Nguyen, T.-L., Vu, C.-T., Nguyen, M.-T., Tran, V.-N., & Hoang, A.-D. (2024). Research on STEM in Early Childhood Education from 1992 to 2022: A Bibliometric Analysis from the Web of Science Database. *European Journal of Educational Research*, 13(3), 1057–1075. DOI: 10.12973/eu-jer.13.3.1057

Burleson, W. S., Harlow, D. B., Nilsen, K. J., Perlin, K., Freed, N., Jensen, C. N., Lahey, B., Lu, P., & Muldner, K. (2018). Active Learning Environments with Robotic Tangibles: Children's Physical and Virtual Spatial Programming Experiences. *IEEE Transactions on Learning Technologies*, 11(1), 96–106. DOI: 10.1109/TLT.2017.2724031

Busuttil, L., & Formosa, M. (2020). Teaching Computing without Computers: Unplugged Computing as a Pedagogical Strategy. *Informatics in Education*, 19(4), 569–587. DOI: 10.15388/infedu.2020.25

Busuttil, L., Vassallo, D., Callus, J., Bratitsis, T., Tsapara, M., Melliou, K., Meireles, G., Tarraf Kojok, N., Koliakou, I., & Sousa, S. (2023). Promoting Computational Thinking in Early Childhood: A Novel Board Game Design. *ICERI Proceedings.*

Canbeldek, M., & Isikoglu, N. (2023). Exploring the effects of "productive children: Coding and robotics education program" in early childhood education. *Education and Information Technologies*, 28(3), 3359–3379. DOI: 10.1007/s10639-022-11315-x

Chen, L., Xiao, S., Chen, Y., Song, Y., Wu, R., & Sun, L. (2024). ChatScratch: An AI-Augmented System Toward Autonomous Visual Programming Learning for Children Aged 6-12. *Conference on Human Factors in Computing Systems - Proceedings*. DOI: 10.1145/3613904.3642229

Christidi, Z., & Christopoulou, E. (2022). Environmental Awareness in Preschool Education via Educational Robotics and STEAM Education. *2022 7th South-East Europe Design Automation, Computer Engineering,Computer Networks and Social Media Conference (SEEDA-CECNSM)*, 1–8. DOI: 10.1109/SEEDA-CECNSM57760.2022.9932911

CollegeBoard. (2017). *AP computer science A: Course and exam description*. AP Central.

Critten, V., Hagon, H., & Messer, D. (2022). Can pre-school children learn programming and coding through guided play activities? A case study in computational thinking. *Early Childhood Education Journal*, 50(6), 969–981. DOI: 10.1007/s10643-021-01236-8

Cuny, J., Snyder, L., & Wing, J. M. (2010, November 17). (Manuscript submitted for publication). Demystifying computational thinking for noncomputer scientists. *Work (Reading, Mass.)*.

Denning, P. J. (2009). The profession of IT Beyond computational thinking. *Communications of the ACM*, 52(6), 28–30. DOI: 10.1145/1516046.1516054

Falloon, G. (2024). Advancing young students' computational thinking: An investigation of structured curriculum in early years primary schooling. *Computers and Education, 216.0*. DOI: 10.1016/j.compedu.2024.105045

Flannery, L. P., Silverman, B., Kazakoff, E. R., Bers, M. U., Bontá, P., & Resnick, M. (2013). Designing ScratchJr: support for early childhood learning through computer programming. *Proceedings of the 12th International Conference on Interaction Design and Children*, 1–10. DOI: 10.1145/2485760.2485785

Flood, V. J., Wang, X. C., & Sheridan, M. (2022). Embodied responsive teaching for supporting computational thinking in early childhood. *Proceedings of International Conference of the Learning Sciences, ICLS*, 855 - 862. https://www.scopus.com/inward/record.uri?eid=2-s2.0-85145770444&partnerID=40&md5=60994482aacf819ed93b47195152cee6

Fowler, B., & Vegas, E. (2021). *How England Implemented Its Computer Science Education Program*. Center for Universal Education at The Brookings Institution.

Fridberg, M., & Redfors, A. (2024). Teachers' and children's use of words during early childhood STEM teaching supported by robotics. *International Journal of Early Years Education*, 32(2), 405–419. DOI: 10.1080/09669760.2021.1892599

Gärtig-Daugs, A., Weitz, K., Wolking, M., & Schmid, U. (2016, October). Computer science experimenters kit for use in preschool and primary school. *Proceedings of the 11th Workshop in Primary and Secondary Computing Education*. DOI: 10.1145/2978249.2978258

González, Y. A. C., & Muñoz-Repiso, A. G.-V. (2017). Educational robotics for the formation of programming skills and computational thinking in childish. *2017 International Symposium on Computers in Education (SIIE)*, 1–5. DOI: 10.1109/SIIE.2017.8259652

González, Y. A. C., & Muñoz-Repiso, A. G.-V. (2018, October). A robotics-based approach to foster programming skills and computational thinking. *Proceedings of the Sixth International Conference on Technological Ecosystems for Enhancing Multiculturality*. DOI: 10.1145/3284179.3284188

Gordon, M., Rivera, E., Ackermann, E., & Breazeal, C. (2015). Designing a relational social robot toolkit for preschool children to explore computational concepts. *Proceedings of IDC 2015: The 14th International Conference on Interaction Design and Children*, 355–358. DOI: 10.1145/2771839.2771915

Grover, S., & Pea, R. (2013). Computational Thinking in K-12: A Review of the State of the Field. *Educational Researcher*, 42(1), 38–43. Advance online publication. DOI: 10.3102/0013189X12463051

Hall, J. A., & McCormick, K. I. (2022). My Cars don't Drive Themselves: Preschoolers' Guided Play Experiences with Button-Operated Robots. *TechTrends*, 66(3), 510–526. DOI: 10.1007/s11528-022-00727-8

Haseski, H., Ilic, U., & Tugtekin, U. (2018). Defining a New 21st Century Skill-Computational Thinking: Concepts and Trends. *International Education Studies*, 11(4), 29–42. DOI: 10.5539/ies.v11n4p29

Hu, W., Huang, R., & Li, Y. (2024). Young children's experience in unplugged activities about computational thinking: From an embodied cognition perspective. *Early Childhood Education Journal*, 52(4), 769–782. DOI: 10.1007/s10643-023-01475-x

Ioannou, M., & Bratitsis, T. (2017). Teaching the Notion of Speed in Kindergarten Using the Sphero SPRK Robot. *2017 IEEE 17th International Conference on Advanced Learning Technologies (ICALT)*, 311–312. DOI: 10.1109/ICALT.2017.70

Kalelioglu, F., Gulbahar, Y., & Kukul, V. (2016). *A framework for computational thinking based on a systematic research review.*

Kandlhofer, M., Steinbauer, G., Hirschmugl-Gaisch, S., & Huber, P. (2016). Artificial intelligence and computer science in education: From kindergarten to university. *2016 IEEE Frontiers in Education Conference (FIE)*, 1–9. DOI: 10.1109/FIE.2016.7757570

Kim, S. U. (2020). A Comparative Study on the Effects of Hands-on Robot and EPL Programming Activities on Creative Problem-Solving Ability in Children. *ACM International Conference Proceeding Series*, 49–53. DOI: 10.1145/3401861.3401866

Kyza, E. A., Georgiou, Y., Agesilaou, A., & Souropetsis, M. (2022). A Cross-Sectional Study Investigating Primary School Children's Coding Practices and Computational Thinking Using ScratchJr. *Journal of Educational Computing Research*, 60(1), 220–257. DOI: 10.1177/07356331211027387

Lee, I., Martin, F., Denner, J., Coulter, B., Allan, W., Erickson, J., Malyn-Smith, J., & Werner, L. (2011). Computational thinking for youth in practice. *ACM Inroads*, 2(1), 32–37. DOI: 10.1145/1929887.1929902

Lee, V. R., Poole, F., Clarke-Midura, J., Recker, M., & Rasmussen, M. (2020). Introducing Coding through Tabletop Board Games and Their Digital Instantiations across Elementary Classrooms and School Libraries. *Proceedings of the 51st ACM Technical Symposium on Computer Science Education*, 787–793. DOI: 10.1145/3328778.3366917

Lennon, M., Pila, S., Flynn, R., & Wartella, E. A. (2022). Young children's social and independent behavior during play with a coding app: Digital game features matter in a 1:1 child to tablet setting. *Computers & Education*, 190, 104608. Advance online publication. DOI: 10.1016/j.compedu.2022.104608

Leung, S. K. Y., Wu, J., & Li, J. W. (2024). Children's knowledge construction of computational thinking in a play-based classroom. *Early Child Development and Care*, 194(2), 208–229. DOI: 10.1080/03004430.2023.2299405

Leung, S. K. Y., Wu, J., Li, J. W., Lam, Y., & Ng, O. L. (2024). Examining young children's computational thinking through animation art. *Early Childhood Education Journal*. Advance online publication. DOI: 10.1007/s10643-024-01694-w

Levinson, T., & Bers, M. (2024). Robotics in universal prekindergarten classrooms. *International Journal of Technology and Design Education*. Advance online publication. DOI: 10.1007/s10798-024-09905-6

Lin, Y., Liao, H., Weng, S., & Dong, W. (2024). Comparing the effects of plugged-in and unplugged activities on computational thinking development in young children. *Education and Information Technologies*, 29(8), 9541–9574. DOI: 10.1007/s10639-023-12181-x

Liu, Y. Y., & Iversen, O. S. (2022). Computational Thinking through Tangible Play: Understanding Social Dialogues in Children's Learning. *Proceedings of Interaction Design and Children, IDC*, 2022, 596–603. DOI: 10.1145/3501712.3535288

Lu, J. J., & Fletcher, G. H. L. (2009). Thinking about computational thinking. *SIGCSE Bulletin*, 41(1), 260–264. Advance online publication. DOI: 10.1145/1539024.1508959

Luo, F., Israel, M., & Gane, B. (2022). Elementary computational thinking instruction and assessment: A learning trajectory perspective. [TOCE]. *ACM Transactions on Computing Education*, 22(2), 1–26. DOI: 10.1145/3494579

Manches, A., & Plowman, L. (2017). Computing education in children's early years: A call for debate. *British Journal of Educational Technology*, 48(1), 191–201. DOI: 10.1111/bjet.12355

Masarwa, B., Hel-Or, H., & Levy, S. T. (2024). Kindergarten children's learning of computational thinking with the "Sorting Like a Computer" learning unit. *Journal of Research in Childhood Education*, 38(2), 165–188. DOI: 10.1080/02568543.2023.2221319

Metin, S. (2020). Activity-based unplugged coding during the preschool period. *International Journal of Technology and Design Education*, 32(1), 149–165. DOI: 10.1007/s10798-020-09616-8

Metin, Ş., Başaran, M., Seheryeli, M. Y., Relkin, E., & Kalyenci, D. (2024). Adaptation of the Computational Thinking Skills Assessment Tool (TechCheck-K) in Early Childhood. *Journal of Science Education and Technology*, 33(3), 365–382. DOI: 10.1007/s10956-023-10089-2

Meyer-Baron, L., Stieger, R., Waldvogel, B., Schumann, N., Ruedisueli, C., & Mayr, F. (2022). Observing Computational Thinking Skills of Kindergarten Children. *Proceedings of the 17th Workshop in Primary and Secondary Computing Education*, 1–4. DOI: 10.1145/3556787.3556867

Mishra, P., Yadav, A., Henriksen, D., Kereluik, K., Terry, L., Fahnoe, C., & Terry, C. (2013). Rethinking Technology & Creativity in the 21st Century. In *TechTrends* (Vol. 57, Issue 3). DOI: 10.1007/s11528-013-0655-z

Montuori, C., Ronconi, L., Vardanega, T., & Arfé, B. (2022). Exploring Gender Differences in Coding at the Beginning of Primary School. *Frontiers in Psychology*, 13, 887280. Advance online publication. DOI: 10.3389/fpsyg.2022.887280 PMID: 36211854

Nacher, V., Garcia-Sanjuan, F., & Jaen, J. (2016). Evaluating the Usability of a Tangible-Mediated Robot for Kindergarten Children Instruction. *2016 IEEE 16th International Conference on Advanced Learning Technologies (ICALT)*, 130–132. DOI: 10.1109/ICALT.2016.59

Noma, H., Sasamoto, H., Itoh, Y., Kitamura, Y., Kishino, F., & Tetsutani, N. (2003). Computer learning system for pre-school-age children based on a haptized model railway. *First Conference on Creating, Connecting and Collaborating Through Computing, 2003. C5 2003. Proceedings.*, 118–119. DOI: 10.1109/C5.2003.1222343

Papert, S. (1980). Mindstorms Children, Computers, and Powerful Ideas (Second edition). In *BasicBooks* (Vol. 1).

Pérez-Marin, D., Hijón-Neira, R., & Pizarro, C. (2022). Coding in early years education: Which factors influence the skills of sequencing and plotting a route, and to what extent? *International Journal of Early Years Education*, 30(4), 969–985. DOI: 10.1080/09669760.2022.2037076

Piaget, J. (1977). *The development of thought: Equilibrium of cognitive structures.*

Resnick, L. B. (2017). Toward a cognitive theory of instruction. In *Learning and motivation in the classroom* (pp. 5–38). Routledge. DOI: 10.4324/9781315188522-2

Rich, K. M., Yadav, A., & Larimore, R. A. (2020). Teacher implementation profiles for integrating computational thinking into elementary mathematics and science instruction. *Education and Information Technologies*, 25(4), 3161–3188. DOI: 10.1007/s10639-020-10115-5

Samuelsson, R. (2022). Cultural Heritage Through Educational Robots: Using a Ukrainian Folk Tale with a Programmable Robot in Early Childhood Education. *HCI International 2022–Late Breaking Posters: 24th International Conference on Human-Computer Interaction, HCII 2022, Virtual Event, June 26–July 1, 2022, Proceedings, Part I*, 336–343.

Selby, C., & Woollard, J. (2013). Computational Thinking : The Developing Definition. *ITiCSE Conference 2013.*

Silva, E. F., Dembogurski, B. J., & Semaan, G. S. (2023). A literature review of computational thinking in early ages. In *International Journal of Early Years Education* (Vol. 31, Issue 3). DOI: 10.1080/09669760.2022.2107491

Silvis, D., Clarke-Midura, J., Shumway, J. F., Lee, V. R., & Mullen, S. (2022). Children caring for robots: Expanding computational thinking frameworks to include a technological ethic of care. *International Journal of Child-Computer Interaction*, 33, 100491. DOI: 10.1016/j.ijcci.2022.100491

Silvis, D., Lee, V. R., Clarke-Midura, J., & Shumway, J. F. (2022). The technical matters: young children debugging (with) tangible coding toys. *Information and Learning Sciences, ahead-of-print.*

Somuncu, B., & Aslan, D. (2021). Effect of coding activities on preschool children's mathematical reasoning skills. *Education and Information Technologies*, 27(1), 877–890. DOI: 10.1007/s10639-021-10618-9 PMID: 34226819

Storjak, I., Pushkar, L., Jagust, T., & Krzic, A. S. (2020). First steps into STEM for young pupils through informal workshops. *2020 IEEE Frontiers in Education Conference (FIE)*, 1–5. DOI: 10.1109/FIE44824.2020.9274139

Sung, J. (2022). Assessing young Korean children's computational thinking: A validation study of two measurements. *Education and Information Technologies*, 27(9), 1–29. DOI: 10.1007/s10639-022-11137-x

Sung, W., Ahn, J., & Black, J. B. (2022). Elementary Students' Performance and Perceptions of Robot Coding and Debugging: Embodied Approach in Practice. *Journal of Research in Childhood Education*, 36(4), 681–696. DOI: 10.1080/02568543.2022.2045399

Terroba, M., Ribera, J. M., Lapresa, D., & Anguera, M. T. (2022). Observational analysis of the development of computational thinking in Early Childhood Education (5 years old) through an intervention proposal with a ground robot of programmed directionality. *European Early Childhood Education Research Journal*, 30(3), 437–455. DOI: 10.1080/1350293X.2022.2055102

Voogt, J., Fisser, P., Good, J., Mishra, P., & Yadav, A. (2015). Computational thinking in compulsory education: Towards an agenda for research and practice. *Education and Information Technologies*, 20(4), 715–728. DOI: 10.1007/s10639-015-9412-6

Watanabe, T., Nakayama, Y., Harada, Y., & Kuno, Y. (2020). Analyzing Viscuit Programs Crafted by Kindergarten Children. *ICER 2020 - Proceedings of the 2020 ACM Conference on International Computing Education Research*, 238–247. DOI: 10.1145/3372782.3406253

Watanabe, T., Nakayama Kagawa-Fujimigaoka, Y., Kanagawa, K., Yasunori, J., Digitalpocket, H., Kanagawa, L., Kuno, J. Y., Nakayama, Y., Harada, Y., & Kuno, Y. (2019). *How Can Children Express Their Intentions Through Coding?-Anal-ysis of Viscuit Programs in Kindergarten.* https://doi.org/DOI: 10.1145/3304221

Wing, J. M. (2006). Computational thinking. *Communications of the ACM*, 49(3), 33–35. DOI: 10.1145/1118178.1118215

Wing, J. M. (2008). Computational thinking and thinking about computing. *Philosophical Transactions.Series A, Mathematical, Physical, and Engineering Sciences, 366*(1881), 3717–3725. [doi]DOI: 10.1098/rsta.2008.0118

Wing, J. M. (2010). Computational Thinking: What and Why? *Thelink - The Magaizne of the Varnegie Mellon University School of Computer Science, March 2006.*

Wu, Z., Zheng, L., & Huang, L. (2024). Learning to code and coding to learn: A robotics curriculum integrating tangible programming and road safety education for young children. *Education and Information Technologies*. Advance online publication. DOI: 10.1007/s10639-024-12757-1

Wyeth, P., & Wyeth, G. (2008). Robot building for preschoolers. *RoboCup 2007. Robot Soccer World Cup XI*, 11, 124–135.

Yang, W. (2024). Coding With Robots or Tablets? Effects of Technology-Enhanced Embodied Learning on Preschoolers' Computational Thinking and Social-Emotional Competence. *Journal of Educational Computing Research, 62.0*(4.0), 938–960. DOI: 10.1177/07356331241226459

Yang, W., Luo, H., & Su, J. (2022). Towards inclusiveness and sustainability of robot programming in early childhood: Child engagement, learning outcomes and teacher perception. *British Journal of Educational Technology*, 53(6), 1486–1510. DOI: 10.1111/bjet.13266

Yang, W., Ng, D. T. K., & Su, J. (2023). The impact of story-inspired programming on preschool children's computational thinking: A multi-group experiment. *Thinking Skills and Creativity*, 47, 101218. Advance online publication. DOI: 10.1016/j.tsc.2022.101218

Yildiz, E. P., & Çengel, M. (2022). An Experimental Study in Determining Basic Robotic Coding Skills of Pre-School Students with Intellectual Disabilities. [IJIM]. *International Journal of Interactive Mobile Technologies*, 16(23), 84–98. DOI: 10.3991/ijim.v16i23.36077

Zawacki-Richter, O., Kerres, M., Bedenlier, S., Bond, M., & Buntins, K. (2020). *Systematic reviews in educational research: Methodology, perspectives and application*. Springer Nature. DOI: 10.1007/978-3-658-27602-7

Zhang, X., Chen, Y., Hu, L., Bao, Y., Tu, Y.-F., & Hwang, G.-J. (2024). A metaphor-based robot programming approach to facilitating young children's computational thinking and positive learning behaviors. *Computers & Education*, 215, 215. DOI: 10.1016/j.compedu.2024.105039

Zilinskiene, I. (2022). Insights from Empirical Results on Robotics in Early Childhood Education: Lithuanian Case. *TEM Journal*, 11(3), 1103–1107. DOI: 10.18421/TEM113-15

Chapter 3
Effective Information Technology Education in Grade 10–12 Classrooms, South Africa:
In the Further Education and Training Phase

Leila Goosen
https://orcid.org/0000-0003-4948-2699
University of South Africa, South Africa

ABSTRACT

Against the background of effective Computer Science Education (CSE) in Kindergarten/Grade R-12 classrooms, the purpose of this chapter is to specifically investigate effective Information Technology (IT) education in grade 10-12 classrooms in South Africa, where the subject IT is offered in the Further Education and Training (FET) phase. As such, the chapter will e.g., provide an introduction to Computer Science in R-12 education, as well as effective teaching approaches and strategies in the South African context.

INTRODUCTION

This section will describe the general perspective of the chapter and end by specifically stating the objectives.

DOI: 10.4018/979-8-3693-4542-9.ch003

Effective Computer Science Education in K-12 Classrooms

Introduction to Computer Science in K-12 Education

The Role of Parents and Community in Computer Science Education

"The *introduction of computer science education* (CSE) *in*" *K-12 education* is an emerging trend around the world. Gouws and Lotriet (2024, p. 187) were therefore introducing computer science education through robotics education in *community*-engaged contexts and reflecting on good practice in this regard.

Today, computer science draws attention as an increasingly important field in education with its interdisciplinary characteristics.

Curriculum Development for K-12 Computer Science

An interdisciplinary approach to computer science formed part of the development of a "Brain-based learning, Inquiry-based approach and Computational thinking (BIC) Science" module as described in a paper in the *proceedings of the international conference on computational thinking education* (Mensan & Osman, 2018, p. 93). Since the latter authors were of the opinion that "every student from Primary One to Form Five should be taught CT and coding", CT and computer science were "added to the curriculum of primary and secondary" Science education.

The effects of information technologies on social development had reached significant dimensions with the progress of Artificial Intelligence (AI) research. In this context, digital literacy had become an important skill that must be learned by every individual. In addition to the use of information tools in accordance with goals, the development of individual productivity is made possible by effective computer science education. In addition, the development of thinking and problem-solving skills is among the important achievements of computer science education. In particular, computational thinking skills, which include sub-skill areas such as abstraction, decomposition, pattern recognition, debugging and algorithm creation, are interdisciplinary skill areas that can be developed through programming *applications*.

Özcan and Kert (2020, p. 1176), in a Cypriot journal article on educational sciences, discussed "the importance of vocabulary knowledge in language education and the use of mobile" *applications* ('apps') in collocation teaching.

Professional Development for K-12 Educators

The purpose of the chapter by Bai (2024, p. 170) was to report on a study that provided teacher education students with an *introduction to* "computational thinking (CT) knowledge and coding skills in a graduate educational technology class"

Supporting the development of these skills requires a new perspective on computer science education. Tool-oriented educational approaches stand out as the biggest obstacle to focusing on the pedagogical dimensions of the learning process. Effective computer science education, as in all educational processes, requires moving from pedagogy to technology. A pedagogy-based approach to computer science education involves a detailed and scientifically grounded examination of all instructional design components. In this context, learner and content analysis, efficient use of learning resources, proper organization of classrooms and laboratories, effective design of instructional tools and materials, implementation of teaching strategies appropriate for the target audience, design of practices in accordance with learning outcomes, and correct assessment approaches that include all objectives, can be listed. When considered in all its dimensions, the use of the right pedagogical approaches in Computer Science education is an area of study that needs to be examined in detail. The lack of resources in this context can negatively affect all computer science education processes. In particular, it is seen that there is a need for scientific reference sources that can be a road map in computer science education starting from K-12 level.

Recommended Topics

This chapter will address all of the recommended topics suggested for the book:

- Introduction to Computer Science in K-12 Education
- Curriculum Development for K-12 Computer Science
- Teaching Approaches and Strategies
- Inclusive Practices in Computer Science Education
- Professional Development for K-12 Educators
- Tools and Resources for K-12 Computer Science Education
- Assessment and Evaluation in Computer Science Education
- Overcoming Challenges in K-12 Computer Science Education
- The Role of Parents and Community in Computer Science Education
- Case Studies of Successful K-12 Computer Science Programs
- Future Trends and Innovations in K-12 Computer Science Education

Apart from these recommended topics, other topics that can contribute to the provision of effective computer science education at the K-12 level were also considered as part of this chapter in the book.

Target Audience

Like the target audience of the book, that of this chapter includes K-12 computer science educators, university students, researchers, educational policy makers, practitioners and academics.

Objectives

Similar to the objective of this book, that of the chapter is to act as a pedagogical reference for computer science educators, especially in grades 10-12. This chapter also share some of the objectives in the Masters of Education dissertation of Goosen (1999) of this chapter, related to the effective teaching of Computer Science, in the secondary school and with specific reference to Outcomes Based Education (OBE).

The purpose of the research previously reported on by Goosen (2020a, p. 212) in the proceedings of the South Africa International Conference on Education (SAICEd) related "to the topic of developing a theoretical model for the effective teaching of Information Technology (IT) for meaningful change in secondary education."

As part of the book, this chapter includes theoretical details for designing computer science education, practical *applications* for analysis, design, development, implementation and evaluation processes, perspectives that combine theory and practice in computer science teaching, guiding teaching strategies, assessment approaches that can be used in different age groups, thematic programming teaching examples, instructional technologies that can be used in computer science education, suggestions for computer science teachers, computer science education curricula at K-12 level, teaching methodologies for special subject areas such as artificial intelligence, and perspectives on the future of computer science education.

BACKGROUND

This section of the chapter will provide broad definitions and discussions of the topic on Effective Information Technology Education in Grade 10-12 Classrooms, South Africa in the Further Education and Training Phase and incorporate the views of others (in the form of a literature review) into the discussion to support, refute, or demonstrate the authors' position on the topic.

In line with two of the references cited in the previous section of this chapter, the effect of robotics on six graders' academic achievement, computational thinking skills and conceptual knowledge levels was discussed in a journal article on *thinking skills and creativity* by Kert, ErkoÇ and Yeni (2020, p. 1). The latter "study compared the pedagogical effects of educational robot development and the block-based programming perspectives, which are used in programming education".

The study reported on by Işik Arslanoğlu, Kert and Tonbuloğlu (2023, p. 1) in an *Education and Information Technologies* journal article aimed "to examine the effect of" augmented reality-assisted programming education activity "supported by participatory design on the basic and computational thinking skills of" children who think together, design together, and code together.

The preliminary work reported on by Prickett, Crick, Harvey, Walters and Yang (2020, p. 2) investigated the relationships between effective learning in computer science education and exploring the role of resilience in the success of "first-year undergraduate computer science to provide insight into the factors" applicable.

Teaching Approaches and Strategies

The study reported on by Ibrahim, Callaway, Kert and Erkoç (2021, p. 185) in the proceedings of the *Society for Information Technology* and *Teacher Education International Conference* examined the effective use of college "students' discussion reflections on their course scores in an online learning environment regarding" enhancing their *self-regulated learning* strategies.

The *advances in intelligent systems and computing* journal article by Goosen (2020b, p. 357) "related to developing a theoretical model for the" effective teaching of Information Technology, including "which adjustments needed to be made with regard to the teaching strategies and methods of IT, and what the implications of these adjustments would be for the" professional development "of IT teachers. The use of direct and problem-based instruction, as well as discovery and cooperative learning, was explored theoretically towards the development of the model for the effective teaching of" IT.

Tools and Resources for K-12 Computer Science Education

As part of the *proceedings of the Conference on Innovation and Technology in Computer Science Education*, Ibeto and Baghban Karimi (2023, p. 666) indicated that "Open Educational Resources (OER) are changing how" *computing* science is taught and learnt. The latter study aimed to report on a query "to inform open text-book development for a *computing* science course" and the effective use of OERs.

Based on their experience, the paper by Goodfellow and Liaskos (2023, p. 589) in the same *proceedings* presented tips for effectively "implementing blended learning in computer science education".

In their chapter, Ngugi and Goosen (2021) studied *innovation*, entrepreneurship, and sustainability for Information and Communication Technology (ICT) students towards the post-COVID-19 era.

Professional Development for K-12 Educators

An *International Conference on Computational Science and Computational Intelligence (CSCI)* paper by Allison (2020, p. 898) presented a framework for effective Continuing Professional Development (CPD) in the FE sector in the case of computer science educators from further education colleges in terms of "what is required for effective teacher CPD."

Curriculum Development for K-12 Computer Science

A correlation model reported on by Kovač and Eret (2012, p. 1393) in the *proceedings of the 35th International Convention (MIPRO)* showed "the way in which the related areas of computer science and mathematics" could be supplemented, if it is to be transformed in terms of the way in which the primary education curriculum of mathematics and computer science were taught and created.

Assessment and Evaluation in Computer Science Education

The *Transactions on Computing Education* journal article by Paiva, Leal and Figueira (2022, p. 1) surveyed the state of the art in a review of "the automated assessment of CS" education assignments, focusing on a "new era of automated assessment" and "capitalizing on static analysis techniques".

The paper by Amelung, Piotrowski and Rösner (2006, p. 88) presented an "approach for supporting computer science education with software", as well as the "assessment of assignments and tests, including the automatic assessment of" these.

"The last general reason for involving peer review" and/or "peer assessment in computer science education at university is a chance for students to" obtain "more specific and accurate feedback" (Dropčová, 2016, p. 6).

Unveiling competence in the classroom, a multidimensional assessment of computer science "teachers' self-efficacy in coding education within K-12" classrooms, the study reported on by Sat and Kadirhan (2024, p. 1) presented instruments "for measuring computer science (CS) teachers' self-efficacy in" such scenarios.

In their paper, Sitthiworachart, Joy and Sutinen (2008) reviewed "the uses of e-assessment within the domain of Computer Science Education", which were factors "contributing to the success of the" e-assessment approach.

MAIN FOCUS OF THE CHAPTER

Issues, Problems

This section of the chapter will present the authors' perspectives on the issues, problems, etc., as these relate to the main theme of the book on Effective Computer Science Education in K-12 Classrooms, and arguments supporting the authors' position on Effective Information Technology Education in Grade 10-12 Classrooms, South Africa in the Further Education and Training Phase. It will also compare and contrast with what had been, or is currently being, done as it relates to the specific topic of the chapter.

"Programming education is an important educational process that enables the development of children's problem solving and algorithmic thinking skills" (Dilmen, Kert, & Uğraş, 2023, p. 10839). The *Education and Information Technologies* journal article by the latter authors therefore examined children's coding experiences in a block-based coding environment based on a usability study on code.org.

The main focus of the *ACM Transactions on Computing Education* journal article by Isayama, Ishiyama, Relator and Yamazaki (2016, p. 2) is on computer science education at the primary and lower "secondary school levels. However, because" it is said that teaching the concept of automata is a problem, most primary and secondary students are critical and see it as difficult.

The development and application of a primary puzzle-based learning program for Computer Science Education were recommended by Oh, Kim and Kim (2014, p. 11) in a *journal* article from the *Korean association of computer education* towards "understanding of the principles of" "computer science as opposed to" a fragmented, uniform programing education, and promote learners' "problem-solving abilities in computer science."

In the study reported on by Sözeri and Kert (2021, p. 49) in an international journal article on computer science education in schools, the effects and effectiveness (or rather ineffectiveness) of interactive video content developed for "usage in programming education on" the "academic achievement and self-efficacy perception of programming" students were considered.

Curriculum Development for K-12 Computer Science

A study on the connection between the computer science education curriculum of a university and that of primary and secondary schools by Kang (2006, p. 29) in the same journal as mentioned in the previous paragraph called it a problem that there was a gap, because there was nothing regarding "an educational program or system for putting" computer science education in primary and secondary schools into practice.

"The choice of a first programming language is critical for fostering problem solving skills and remains a concern in programming instruction that should be taken into account during discussions on the Computer Science curriculum" (Goosen, 2004, p. i). Criteria and guidelines for the selection and implementation of a first programming language in high (secondary) schools therefore needed to be identified.

In their paper presentation at the *7th Workshop in Primary and Secondary Computing Education (WiPCSE)*, Sentance, Dorling, McNicol and Crick (2012) discussed the 'grand' challenges for the United Kingdom (UK) related to upskilling teachers to teach computer science within the secondary curriculum.

Overcoming Challenges in K-12 Computer Science Education

The main focus of an online journal article by Kalelioğlu, Gülbahar and Kert (2020) was on teaching *computing* at secondary school level and understanding teachers' experiences and challenges in this regard.

As part of *symposium proceedings* on the challenges *of change in education*, the paper by Segal, Schuck, Brady, Deer and Segal (1999) considered innovation in primary science teacher education, as well as taking responsibility for learning through computer-mediated communication and classroom interactions.

Professional Development for K-12 Educators

Learning science in a *society* full *of computers*, the journal article by Pinto, et al. (2012, p. 28) described education using computer simulations for pre- and in-service primary school teacher training to teach science. The latter authors reported on "teachers from higher education, one from an undergraduate program and" one other, as they wanted to explore what epistemic practices (EPs) "occur between theory (T) and the observable-world (OW), in both pathways (from T to OW and from OW to T)."

Teaching Approaches and Strategies

Using *self-regulated learning* strategies to enhance the effectiveness of an online course in emergency remote teaching was the main focus of the conference paper by Kert, Erkoç, Ibrahim and Callaway (2021).

Tools and Resources for K-12 Computer Science Education

Case Studies of Successful K-12 Computer Science Programs

Amadi, Mba and Cornelius (2022, p. 493), in an *international journal* article on *Advance Research, Ideas, and Innovations in Technology*, pointed to the findings of their study showing that Computer Science Education "is a very effective tool" with regard to the availability and utilization of, as well as "for providing teaching resources for" effective computer science education and "successful technical vocational education and training for youth empowerment in Anambra state."

Moving from theory to the observable-world and vice-versa, the technology journal article by Pinto, et al. (2014, p. 86) reported on "a multi-case study with two teachers" from "a primary teacher education course." The latter authors used multimodal narratives in a description of teaching science with experimental work and computer simulations and asked what challenges were needed to promote such epistemic practices?

A *European journal* article on *social sciences studies* was aimed at "computer science teachers and primary education" teachers' perceptions on using digital games as learning tools (Kougioumtzidou, Botsoglou, & Zygouris, 2023, p. 119). ". One hundred twenty teachers participated", of which 70 from the field of computer science, in order to establish the obstacles and factors, "not to mention the barriers ... that lead to their effective use".

Inclusive Practices in Computer Science Education

Effective measures to foster girls' interest in secondary computer science education was the focus of a literature review reported on by Happe, Buhnova, Koziolek and Wagner (2021, p. 2811) in an *Education and Information Technologies* journal article. "In combination with the growing shortage of qualified computer science personnel, this" was done towards developing "effective interventions to recruit and retain girls in computer science education".

In the study reported on by Erkul and Kert (2022, p. 1) in a Yıldız journal article on educational research, a scale for monitoring "the gender-based tendencies of university students towards ubiquitous learning environments were analyzed."

Enhancing the computational thinking skills of students with disabilities was discussed by Kert, Yeni and Erkoç (2022, p. 625) in a journal article on *instructional science*. Computational thinking and computer science "are becoming more widely adopted in K-12 education. However, there is a lack of focus on CT and CS access for children with" disabilities.

Professional Development for K-12 Educators

Informal education as an effective form for the development of professional competence in the modern computer science teacher was the focus of the *Zhytomyr Ivan Franko State University journal* article on *pedagogical sciences* by Tokarska (2021, p. 40). The issue of "CS teachers in the field of informal education remained insufficiently covered and" the "competence of computer science teachers in the system of informal education" therefore needed to be explored.

Assessment and Evaluation in Computer Science Education

In terms of "the challenges associated with e-assessment, such as concerns" about assessment in computer science, Alamr, Leon-Urrutia and Carr (2023, p. 378) hoped "to provide a comprehensive understanding of the current state of research in" this regard.

SOLUTIONS AND RECOMMENDATIONS

This section of the chapter will discuss solutions and recommendations in dealing with the issues or problems presented in the preceding section.

Solutions

The journal article by Rustamov, Khomidov and Goipov (2019) not only provided "an overview of the successes, problems and shortcomings in the field of" teaching computer science in higher education, but also indicated that "the ongoing changes in the development of software" presented new solutions in this regard.

Assessment and Evaluation in Computer Science Education

The paper by Khamis and Idris (2008) in the *proceedings of the 12th WSEAS international conference on computers* detailed "the issues and possible solutions that" are related to the *assessment* of object-oriented programming skills in the core education of computer science and information technology. Due to the "decline in student enrolments in computer science," it had become important that lecturers know the impact of their education on graduates.

Professional Development for K-12 Educators

An overview and example solution with regard to school level computer science education and computer science teacher training in the United States (US) by Ray, Whitehead, Shamim, Summers and Obando (2011) presented at the *Society for Information Technology* and *Teacher Education International Conference* specified that "computer science education standards appear in the state standards for grades 9-12 across the nation. There is a 70% average adoption for level I (K-8)."

Inclusive Practices in Computer Science Education

Moving towards a game-based learning solution for female under-representation in Computer Science education and the workplace, a survey of issues and interventions by Osunde, Windall, Bacon and Mackinnon (2013) indicated that the "numbers of females studying and working in *computing* progressively decreases disproportionately from early secondary education (age 11-14) to the workforce stage."

Recommendations

Assessment and Evaluation in Computer Science Education

The Role of Parents and Community in Computer Science Education

In terms of "assessment in computer science classrooms," in a landscape study by Yadav, et al. (2015, p. v) made recommendations "that the *computer science education community* develops valid and reliable computer science *assessments*" for the *evaluation* of assessment in secondary computer science education.

FUTURE RESEARCH DIRECTIONS

This section of the chapter will discuss future and emerging trends, as well as provide insights about the future of the theme of the book on Effective Computer Science Education in K-12 Classrooms from the perspective of the chapter focus on Effective Information Technology Education in Grade 10-12 Classrooms, South Africa in the Further Education and Training Phase. The viability of a paradigm, model, implementation issues of proposed programs, etc., may be included in this section. If appropriate, this section will suggest future research directions within the domain of the topic.

Future Trends and Innovations in K-12 Computer Science Education

Tools and Resources for K-12 Computer Science Education

A chapter in the *Handbook of Research on Developments andFuture Trends* offered a reflection on teaching observation for computer science and engineering to design effective teaching resources (Gill, Thibodeau, Kaur, Naeem, & Stockman, 2023, p. 307) for *educators* at "higher education institutions, as this practice" enables them to better "teach in transnational higher education (TNE)" and/or BSc/MSc computer science programs.

Introduction to Computer Science in K-12 Education

Professional Development for K-12 Educators

"The introduction of computer science education … in schools is required to prepare … learners for future work and develop the required 21st century skills. However, for competent and confident learners, the *educators* need to be" provided with applicable *professional development* opportunities (Gouws & Lotriet, 2024, p. 187).

CONCLUSION

This section of the chapter will provide a discussion of the overall coverage of the chapter and concluding remarks.

Against the background of effective CSE in Kindergarten/Grade R-12 classrooms, the purpose of this chapter was to specifically investigate effective IT education in grade 10-12 classrooms in South Africa, where the subject IT is offered in the FET phase. As such, the chapter e.g., provided an introduction to Computer Science in R-12 education, as well as effective teaching approaches and strategies in the South African context.

REFERENCES

Alamr, S. M., Leon-Urrutia, M., & Carr, L. A. (2023, September). E-assessment in Computer Science Higher Education. *Proceedings of the 15th International Conference on Education Technology and Computers* (pp. 378-383). ACM. DOI: 10.1145/3629296.3629357

Allison, J. (2020, December). A framework for effective continuing professional development: The case of computer science teachers within further education colleges. *International Conference on Computational Science and Computational Intelligence (CSCI)* (pp. 898-903). IEEE. DOI: 10.1109/CSCI51800.2020.00168

Amadi, G. E., Mba, C. J., & Cornelius, N. U. (2022). Availability and utilization of teaching resources for effective computer science education for youth empowerment in Anambra state. *International Journal of Advance Research, Ideas, and Innovations in Technology*, 8(1), 489–493.

Amelung, M., Piotrowski, M., & Rösner, D. (2006, June). EduComponents: Experiences in e-assessment in computer science education. *Proceedings of the 11th annual SIGCSE conference on Innovation and technology in computer science education* (pp. 88-92). ACM. DOI: 10.1145/1140124.1140150

Bai, H. (2024). Introducing Computational Thinking and Coding to Teacher Education Students. In Bosch, C., Goosen, L., & Chetty, J. (Eds.), *Navigating Computer Science Education in the 21st Century* (pp. 170–186). IGI Global., DOI: 10.4018/979-8-3693-1066-3.ch009

Dilmen, K., Kert, S. B., & Uğraş, T. (2023). Children's coding experiences in a block-based coding environment: A usability study on code.org. *Education and Information Technologies*, 28(9), 10839–10864. DOI: 10.1007/s10639-023-11625-8

Dropčová, V. (2016). *Peer Review and Peer Assessment in Higher Computer Science Education.* (PhD thesis). Comenius University.

Erkul, D., & Kert, S. B. (2022). A scale for monitoring students' tendencies to ubiquitous learning environments. *Yıldız Journal of Educational Research*, 7(1), 1–11. DOI: 10.14744/yjer.2022.001

Gill, S. S., Thibodeau, D., Kaur, R., Naeem, U., & Stockman, T. (2023). Reflection on Teaching Observation for Computer Science and Engineering to Design Effective Teaching Resources in Transnational Higher Education. In *Handbook of Research on Developments and Future Trends in Transnational Higher Education* (pp. 307–325). IGI Global. DOI: 10.4018/978-1-6684-5226-4.ch016

Goodfellow, M., & Liaskos, K. (2023, June). Tips for effective blended learning for computer science education. *Proceedings of the Conference on Innovation and Technology in Computer Science Education.* 2, pp. 589-590. ACM. DOI: 10.1145/3587103.3594159

Goosen, L. (1999). *Doeltreffende onderrig van Rekenaarstudie in die sekondêre skool, met spesifieke verwysing na uitkomsgerigte onderwys (Effective teaching of Computer Studies in the secondary school, with specific reference to Outcomes-Based Education.* (MEd dissertation). Potchefstroom University for Christian Higher Education.

Goosen, L. (2004). *Criteria and Guidelines for the Selection and Implementation of a First Programming Language in High Schools.* Potchefstroom Campus: North West University., Retrieved from http://hdl.handle.net/10394/226

Goosen, L. (2020a). Effective Teaching of Information Technology for Meaningful Change in Secondary Education. In M. Motseke, M. Chitiyo, U. I. Ogbonnaya, O. C. Dada, & G. Charles-Ogan (Ed.), *Proceedings of the South Africa International Conference on Education (SAICEd)* (pp. 212-222). Pretoria: African Academic Research Forum.

Goosen, L. (2020b). A Model for Effectively Teaching Information Technology. (R. Silhavy, P. Silhavy, & Z. Prokopova, Eds.) *Advances in Intelligent Systems and Computing, 1294*, 357-371. DOI: 10.1007/978-3-030-63322-6_29

Gouws, P. M., & Lotriet, H. H. (2024). Introducing Computer Science Education Through Robotics Education in Community-Engaged Contexts: Reflecting on Good Practice. In Bosch, C., Goosen, L., & Chetty, J. (Eds.), *Navigating Computer Science Education in the 21st Century* (pp. 187–205). IGI Global., DOI: 10.4018/979-8-3693-1066-3.ch010

Happe, L., Buhnova, B., Koziolek, A., & Wagner, I. (2021). Effective measures to foster girls' interest in secondary computer science education: A Literature Review. *Education and Information Technologies*, 26(3), 2811–2829. DOI: 10.1007/s10639-020-10379-x

Ibeto, I., & Baghban Karimi, O. (2023, June). Effective Use of Open Educational Resources in Computer Science Education: A Query to Inform Open Textbook Development. *Proceedings of the Conference on Innovation and Technology in Computer Science Education. 2.* ACM. DOI: 10.1145/3587103.3594167

Ibrahim, M., Callaway, R., Kert, S. B., & Erkoç, M. F. (2021, March). Enhancing Self-Regulated Learning Strategies for College Students Through Discussion Reflections in Online Learning Environment. *Society for Information Technology & Teacher Education International Conference* (pp. 185-196). Association for the Advancement of Computing in Education (AACE).

Isayama, D., Ishiyama, M., Relator, R., & Yamazaki, K. (2016). Computer science education for primary and lower secondary school students: Teaching the concept of automata. [TOCE]. *ACM Transactions on Computing Education*, 17(1), 1–28. DOI: 10.1145/2940331

Işik Arslanoğlu, İ., Kert, S. B., & Tonbuloğlu, İ. (2023). Think together, design together, code together: The effect of augmented reality activity designed by children on the computational thinking skills. *Education and Information Technologies*, 1–30. DOI: 10.1007/s10639-023-12153-1

Kalelioğlu, F., Gülbahar, Y., & Kert, S. B. (2020). Teaching computing at secondary school level: Understanding teachers' experiences and challenges. *Ilkogretim Online*, 19(3), 1781–1796. Advance online publication. DOI: 10.17051/ilkonline.2020.735161

Kang, S.-C. (2006). A study on the connection between the computer science education curriculum of university and that of primary and secondary school. *The Journal of Korean Association of Computer Education*, 9(3), 29–45.

Kert, S. B., & Erko, Ç. (2020). The effect of robotics on six graders' academic achievement, computational thinking skills and conceptual knowledge levels. *Thinking Skills and Creativity*, 38, 100714. Advance online publication. DOI: 10.1016/j.tsc.2020.100714

Kert, S. B., Erkoç, M. F., Ibrahim, M., & Callaway, R. (2021, October). Using Self-Regulated Learning Strategies to Enhance the Effectiveness of an Online Course in Emergency Remote Teaching. *14th International Computer and Instructional Technologies Symposium (ICITS)*. Rize, Türkiye. Retrieved from https://orc.library.atu.edu/faculty_pub_lead/21/

Kert, S. B., Yeni, S., & Erkoç, M. F. (2022). Enhancing computational thinking skills of students with disabilities. *Instructional Science*, 50(4), 625–651. DOI: 10.1007/s11251-022-09585-6

Khamis, N., & Idris, S. (2008, July). Issues and solutions in assessing object-oriented programming skills in the core education of computer science and information technology. *Proceedings of the 12th WSEAS International Conference on Computers* (pp. 458-463). ACM. Retrieved from https://dl.acm.org/doi/abs/10.5555/1513605.1513687

Kougioumtzidou, E., Botsoglou, K., & Zygouris, N. (2023). Computer science and primary education teachers' perceptions, in using digital games as learning tools. Obstacles and factors that lead to their effective use. *European Journal of Social Sciences Studies*, 9(1). Advance online publication. DOI: 10.46827/ejsss.v9i1.1528

Kovač, M. M., & Eret, L. (2012, May). Correlation educational model in primary education curriculum of mathematics and computer science. *Proceedings of the 35th International Convention (MIPRO)* (pp. 1393-1397). Opatija, Croatia: IEEE.

Mensan, T., & Osman, K. (2018). Development of BIC-Science Module: An Interdisciplinary Approach of Computer Science and Primary Science Education. In Kong, S. C., Andone, D., Biswas, G., Crick, T., Hoppe, H. U., & Hsu, T. C.. .... (Ed.), *Proceedings of the International Conference on Computational Thinking Education* (pp. 93-96). The Education University of Hong Kong.

Ngugi, J. K., & Goosen, L. (2021). Innovation, Entrepreneurship, and Sustainability for ICT Students Towards the Post-COVID-19 Era. In Carvalho, L. C., Reis, L., & Silveira, C. (Eds.), *Handbook of Research on Entrepreneurship, Innovation, Sustainability, and ICTs in the Post-COVID-19 Era* (pp. 110–131). IGI Global., DOI: 10.4018/978-1-7998-6776-0.ch006

Oh, J., Kim, J., & Kim, J. (2014). Development and Application of Primary Puzzle-Based Learning Program for Computer Science Education. *The Journal of Korean association of computer education, 17*(3), 11-23.

Osunde, J., Windall, G., Bacon, E. A., & Mackinnon, L. (2013, Sep). Female under-representation in Computer Science education and workplace-A survey of issues and interventions, moving towards a game-based learning solution. *Building new cultures of learning.* University of Nottingham. Retrieved from https://oro.open.ac.uk/54981/

Özcan, M., & Kert, S. (2020). Use of mobile applications in collocation teaching. *Cypriot Journal of Educational Sciences*, 15(5), 1176–1190. Advance online publication. DOI: 10.18844/cjes.v15i5.4629

Paiva, J. C., Leal, J. P., & Figueira, Á. (2022). Automated assessment in computer science education: A state-of-the-art review. [TOCE]. *ACM Transactions on Computing Education*, 22(3), 1–40. DOI: 10.1145/3513140

Pinto, A., Barbot, A., Viegas, C., Silva, A. A., Santos, C. A., & Lopes, J. B. (2012). Teacher education using computer simulations—pre and in-service primary school teacher training to teach science. *Learning science in the society of computers, 6*, pp. 28-36. Retrieved from https://cidtff.web.ua.pt/producao/jorge_bernardino_oliveira/3_fromcblis-2012_proceedings_v6.pdf

Pinto, A., Barbot, A., Viegas, C., Silva, A. A., Santos, C. A., & Lopes, J. B. (2014). Teaching science with experimental work and computer simulations in a primary teacher education course: What challenges to promote epistemic practices? *Procedia Technology*, 13, 86–96. DOI: 10.1016/j.protcy.2014.02.012

Prickett, T., Crick, T., Harvey, M., Walters, J., & Yang, L. (2020, April 1). Exploring resilience for effective learning in computer science education. *Cambridge Computing Education Research Symposium.* University of Cambridge. Retrieved from https://nrl.northumbria.ac.uk/id/eprint/42892/1/CCERS2020_abstract_FINAL.pdf

Ray, L., Whitehead, C., Shamim, K., Summers, W., & Obando, R. (2011, March). School Level Computer Science Education and Computer Science Teacher Training in the US: An Overview and an Example Solution. *Society for Information Technology & Teacher Education International Conference* (pp. 3931-3938)). Association for the Advancement of Computing in Education (AACE). Retrieved from https://www.learntechlib.org/p/36946/

Rustamov, M. M., Khomidov, M. E., & Goipov, E. A. (2019). Teaching Computer Science in Higher Education: Problems and Solutions. *Экономика и социум, 11*(66), 105-108. Retrieved from https://elibrary.ru/item.asp?id=42200285

Sat, M., & Kadirhan, Z. (2024). Unveiling competence in the classroom: A multidimensional assessment of computer science teachers' self-efficacy in coding education. *Education and Information Technologies*, 1–29. DOI: 10.1007/s10639-024-12503-7

Segal, G., Schuck, S., Brady, L., Deer, C. E., & Segal, G. (1999). Innovation in primary science teacher education: Taking responsibility for learning through computer-mediated communication and classroom interactions. *Challenge of Change in Education Symposium Proceedings*, (pp. 318-330).

Sentance, S., Dorling, M., McNicol, A., & Crick, T. (2012). Grand challenges for the UK: upskilling teachers to teach computer science within the secondary curriculum (Paper presentation). *7th Workshop in Primary and Secondary Computing Education (WiPCSE).* Hamburg, Germany. DOI: 10.1145/2481449.2481469

Sitthiworachart, J., Joy, M., & Sutinen, E. (2008, November). Success factors for e-assessment in computer science education. *E-Learn: World Conference on E-Learning in Corporate, Government, Healthcare, and Higher Education* (pp. 2287-2293). Association for the Advancement of Computing in Education (AACE). Retrieved from https://www.learntechlib.org/p/29993/

Sözeri, M. C., & Kert, S. B. (2021). Ineffectiveness of online interactive video content developed for programming education. *International Journal of Computer Science Education in Schools*, 4(3), 49–69. DOI: 10.21585/ijcses.v4i3.99

Tokarska, O. A. (2021). Informal education as an effective form of development of professional competence of modern computer science teacher. *Zhytomyr Ivan Franko State University Journal Pedagogical Sciences*, 1(104), 40–49. DOI: 10.35433/pedagogy.1(104).2021.40-49

Yadav, A., Burkhart, D., Moix, D., Snow, E., Bandaru, P., & Clayborn, L. (2015). *Sowing the seeds: A landscape study on assessment in secondary computer science education. Comp. Sci. Teachers Assn., NY, NY.* Computer Science Teachers Association.

Chapter 4
Information Security Awareness in K12 Computer Science Education

Tuba Kaynarca İdil
https://orcid.org/0009-0000-5326-1122
Anadolu University, Turkey

ABSTRACT

Today's world is developing in many aspects like health, transport, communication. The area of technology is a kind of locomotive of the train because it affects the whole advancing arenas. Although shining development facilitates our lives and increases the life quality, it also causes some technologic threads. According to International Telecommunication Union (ITU) statistics, an estimated 5.3 billion people, or 66 per cent of the world's population, use the Internet. How nice to reach each other rapidly even though we are far away from each other, but what about hackers, malicious people? This chapter focuses on the importance of information security and cybersecurity education at K12 Level.

INFORMATION SECURITY AWARENESS IN K12 COMPUTER SCIENCE EDUCATION

Today's world is developing in many aspects like health, transport, communication. The area of technology is a kind of locomotive of the train because it affects the whole advancing arenas. Although, shining development facilitates our lives and increases the life quality, it also causes some technologic threads. According

DOI: 10.4018/979-8-3693-4542-9.ch004

to International Telecommunication Union (ITU) statistics (2022), an estimated 5.3 billion people, or 66 per cent of the world's population, use the Internet. How nice to reach each other rapidly even though we are far away from each other, but what about hackers, malicious people? Let's give thought to a concrete case. You have bought a tablet computer. If you are conscious about the unknown features the tablet and also security settings, you read the user guide or watch informative videos. The reason of that action is to use it effectively and protect your data from undesirable attainment. So, you have knowledge about your *new* technology and aware about your actions for usage and the outcomes. Another statistic of International Telecommunication Union reports *"Globally, 71 per cent of young people aged between 15 and 24 use the Internet"*. It means Internet usage is an indispensable part of youth all around the world. The question is, how youth can use Internet properly? For "proper" what is meant to be explained is using the internet and also information technology while respecting the right of other people, contributing internet resources with correct information, avoiding damaging content like violence, protecting personal rights in digital world. The question is shortened: "How?". Like being informative via reading user guide, the young people should be educated about using information technologies. In other words, the students should be aware in order to be protected against malicious cases and people.

In this chapter, the subjects below are handled:

- Definitions and distinctions of the terms of information security awareness and cyber security awareness
- How governments approach to security education for digital world
- To prevent children from developing technology and/or to work on educating and awareness
- Why the security in digital world is critical for people especially for K12 students
- Which aspects of cybersecurity awareness are prior for K12 students
- Learning process and activity suggestions in information security education

Terms From Different Views

Two terms we encounter with are: "information security awareness and cyber security awareness". Researchers defines these terms generally similar or connected. However, some of them define cybersecurity comprises information technology or vice versa. According to Von Solms & Van Niekerk (2013), cybersecurity and information security has partially different scopes. Moreover, the researchers say that information security is a part of cybersecurity; cybersecurity is interested to whole parts in cyber area whereas information security is related to safeness of information in that area. However, according to Barzilay (2013), cybersecurity is relevant with cyber risks and it is under the scope of information security.

Cybersecurity is a kind of process which protect and safeguard networks, computer systems, and data from cyber threats that attach to the confidentiality, integrity, and accessibility of information systems (Medoh & Telukdarie, 2022). Keser and Güldüren (2015) define information security as providing precautions against to unauthorized access of "information" assets, in order to prevent the use, modification, disclosure or elimination.

If there is a threat, the risks should be taken into consideration. Quayyum et al. (2021), has worked on a systematic literature review and the researchers exhibit the risks relying on the researches in the field. They present 10 main subjects:

- Online Privacy (e.g. Third party tracking, privacy on social networks)
- Online Harassment (e.g. Cyberbullying, cyberstalking)
- Stranger Danger (e.g. Cybergrooming, catfishing)
- Social Engineering (e.g. Phishing, identity theft)
- Content Related Risks (e.g. Violent, harmful, deviant content, spam, copyright)
- Sexual Solicitation (e.g. Risky sexual behavior)
- Technology Based Threats (e.g. Legacy threats, spyware, hacking, malware)
- Economic Risks (e.g. Financial scams, online gambling)
- Internet Addiction
- Password Practice and Management

All of the risks have an importance on students' education. Because some of the risks are more common, the educators are focusing on them. The governments develop policy in order to prevent kind of risks. We will seek answers in line with resources on both cyber security education and information security education.

Conspicuous Cyber Reports for Recent Years

Federal Bureau of Investigation has published Internet Crime Report of 2023 via Internet Crime Complaint Center (IC3). IC3 collects complaints from American public and provides us to identify changes in the threat landscape and publishes the report for FBI. At this title, the changes can be examined for several aspects at this report (Federal Bureau of Investigation, 2023).

From 2019 to 2023 (Page 7)
2019 – Complaints 467,361 and Loss $3.5 Billion

2023 – Complaints 880,418 and Loss $12.5 Billion

Over the last 5 years, complaints and loss has increased and the total complaints is 3.79 Million whereas total loses $37.4 Billion.

In 2023 average complaints received daily is 2,412; average complaints received per year (last 5 years) 758.000; complaints reported since inception is over 8 million (Page 16).

According to loss comparison for the top five reported crime types for the years of 2019 to 2023, the most complained crime type is Phishing (Page 8) and the least one is Botnet (Page 20).

The Federal Union Agency for Cybersecurity, ENISA, is the Union's agency dedicated to achieving a high common level of cybersecurity across Europe and the foundation was established in 2004. According to ENISA Threat Landscape 2023 report (European Union Agency for Cybersecurity, 2023), the ransomware and threats against availability ranked at the top during the reporting period.

For the future of cybersecurity, Cabaj et al. (2018) claims that, in real time conditions, wide ranging cyber threats can be realized, and it shows that the capability to detect, analyze, and defend against such threats in near real-time conditions is not easy to get rid of anymore. Therefore, developed technologies will be more active like threat intelligence, big data, and machine learning techniques. Intelligent and next-generation big-data analytical techniques can not only solve the problems but also interpret and extract data. J. Esteves who is dean of Porto Business School focuses on his article basis of IBM reports that cybersecurity will shift from being human-dependent to being human-focused because the human errors in cybersecurity is heavily on (Esteves, n.d.). To sum up, according to the researchers, for the future it will be required to deal with cyber threats via artificial intelligence, big data and machine learning. At the aspect of career at cyber area, according to the U.S. Bureau of Labor Statistics: In the 10 years between 2019 and 2029, employment of information security analysts will grow by 31%, much faster than the average for all occupations. It should be said that, as cyber threats increase, the professionals on this field increase for the future. Moreover, the report says that "Global imperative Cybercrime is predicted to cost the world $8 trillion in 2023, according to Cybersecurity Ventures" (Seppi, 2024). It is an indicator of the fact that cybersecurity will be an up-to-date field and a huge investment area all over the world.

Importance of Security Education in K12 for Digital World

If there is a problem and risk about cybersecurity, the solutions should be considered with a wide aspect. The reason of this precaution, the threat can leak because of physical weaknesses like using out of date technology, technical problems, software exploits or unconscious people. The articles about cyber solutions generally do not skip to emphasize people impact and offer solutions about awareness, training and education for permanence. Eminağaoğlu and Gökşen (2009) offer solutions in their article about information security troubles in Turkey and they focus on people factor and they assume that people perhaps the most crucial one because this factor can provide long term and successful information security. It is clear that people will be being informed about cyber threats when they educated as early as possible. Global Education Monitoring Report (UNESCO, 2023) suggests that education systems need to strengthen preventative measures and the members should be aware of presence and digital footprint in digital world. It is not only related to the students the parents and school members are also be aware of their students' privacy. The report also reveals an interesting finding: "*Analysis of 163 education technology products recommended for children during the COVID-19 pandemic found that 89% could or did collect information on children in educational settings or outside school hours.*". The whole results lead to conclusion, the stakeholders of schools should be well informed and educated about digital World with a well structured and regular education.

Ibrahim et al. (2024) study on academic research about the question: "What aspects of cybersecurity topics, competencies, skills, and behaviors are prevalent within K-12 education literature throughout the world?". In this research 14 conference papers (58%), 10 journal articles (42%), the gray literature included seven articles (39%), six websites (33%), three documents (17%), and two reports (11%) are examined. According to the results, the main terms and their percentage weight are founded as: cybersecurity in general (26%), awareness (26%), behavior (15%), Internet usage and presence (13%), ethics (9%), cyberbullying (6%) and privacy (6%). The results show that, the researchers focus on general cybersecurity terms like cyberattacks, cryptography, cyber-defense, cybersecurity training, ICT policy, digital literacy and so on; awareness terms like assessment of awareness, computer use awareness, internet security awareness, cyber-wellness awareness. Although the governments especially developed governments have a mission about the long-term politics about cybersecurity education, and the cybersecurity field are worked progressively, the researchers drew a dramatic conclusion about their research. They claimed that most aspects of cybersecurity are not being systematically taught at K-12 around the world and cybersecurity is not being implemented in international curricula.

Governments' Point of View on Security Education

Information and Communication Sciences (ICT) have not been taken into consideration sufficiently in schools' curricula up to 2000s. Over time, ICT has an important role on the other disciplines via making a productive perspective (Erümit

& Keles, 2023). When it comes to perspective of governments, cyber risks have a huge area to harm the all systems including schools. Therefore, governments have some precautions in terms of awareness, training and education level. According to National Institute of Standards and Technology (NIST) Special Report, awareness level is explained as "Awareness presentations are intended to allow individuals to recognize IT security concerns and respond accordingly.", training level is explained as "Training strives to produce relevant and needed security skills and competencies.", education level is explained as "The 'Education' level integrates all of the security skills and competencies of the various functional specialties into a common body of knowledge, adds a multidisciplinary study of concepts, issues, and principles (technological and social), and strives to produce IT security specialists and professionals capable of vision and pro-active response.". From beginner to advanced level (Figure 1), the hierarchy is like (Wilson and Hash, 2003):

Figure 1. Hierarchy of Precautions

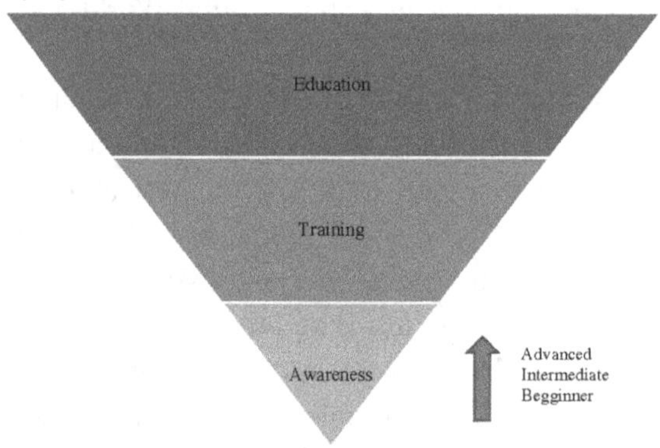

Governments have awareness, training and education level precautions with different cybersecurity policies. According to U.S. Department of Homeland Security Cybersecurity and Infrastructure Security Agency (January, 2023) report, precautions are presented and "Create a training and awareness campaign at all levels" is one of the precautions. In order to make the stakeholders of the school (staff, teacher and students) aware about cybersecurity, free trainings can be provided, curated and administrated to fill the gaps. These kinds of trainings can be provided by CISA (Cybersecurity and Infrastructure Security Agency) through the Federal Virtual Training Environment. And the report emphasizes that investment in training is just as important as investment in cybersecurity capabilities, tools, and solutions. National Institute of Standards and Technology (NIST) is conducting a conference every year about K12 Cybersecurity Education. This annual conference is supported by National Initiative for Cybersecurity Education (NICE) which was created to improve long term cybersecurity effectiveness (Catota et al., 2019). This conference brings together K12 educators and those interested in cybersecurity in K12 level and aims to discuss about not only cybersecurity awareness but also learning about cybersecurity career awareness and innovative cybersecurity educational approaches (NICE K12 Cybersecurity Education Conference, 2024). In Australia, ACSC (Australian Cyber Security Centre) part of the Australian Signals Directorate, is a centre leading the government's efforts to improve cyber security. It provides educational sources for parents' and careers' own actions. Students Wellbeing Hub has been developed by Education Services Australia for the Australian Government Department of Education. The hub provides educational resources in wide range field like health and sport and it also provides information, videos and games about cyber safety (Students Wellbeing Hub, 2024). Canada is also one of the countries follows the developing cybersecurity education for students. Cybersecurity Classroom Training Program (CCTP) is a project announced as Canada's largest cybersecurity education program for high schools launches in partnership between Cisco and STEM Fellowship in 2021. At the Project website (Cisco, 2021), the aim of the project and its budget is explained like: "*The CCTP addresses the growing need for cybersecurity awareness and education, and provides early exposure to the various tools, technologies, and career paths available in IT and digital industries. Funded by a $12 million in-kind investment from Cisco, the program aims to engage upwards of 40,000 students and 2,000 teachers across Canada by 2023 and inspire the next generation of IT leaders*". In order to increase cybersecurity talent, federal, state and private organizations promote certification, workshops, trainings and education. In addition, graduate and undergraduate degrees about information security and cybersecurity have been establishing into many universities all over the world. One of them is cooperation protocol signed between the Presidency of the Republic of Türkiye Digital Transformation Office and the Council of Higher Education on October 5, 2022 (Presidency of the Republic of Türkiye Digital Transformation Office, 2024 Updated Version). According to this protocol, cybersecurity vocational schools are activated with associate's degree under Ankara, İstanbul, Gebze Technical and Ege University. Moreover, in order to improve cybersecurity workforce government agencies, provide resources to colleges and universities. For example, Florida Center for Cybersecurity (also known as Cyber Florida), which is a state funded organization, under the roof of University of South Florida (USF) has a wide range activity about cybersecurity like trainings, podcasts, events and programs. Cyberlaunch is an example and according to the program introduction, this program aims to "*introduce high school students to the universe of cybersecurity careers through the fun of a statewide competition*" (Cyberlaunch, 2024).

Also, some Professional business foundings like Palo Alto Networks offers project namely Cyber A.C.E.S. Activities in Cybersecurity Education for Students. At the Project website, a motto meets us "Empowering Digital Safety for Our Youth". Then the lesson roadmap is explained with the age range from 5 to 15 including passwords, digital footprint, verifiable postings, interactions & bullying. The project introduces the main goal as: "*We aim to demystify cybersecurity through interactive learning, equipping kids ages 5 to 15 with an understanding of how to protect their digital future.*" (Cyber A.C.E.S., 2024).

Information security and cybersecurity is an up-to-date topic that grows and transforms according to developing technologies and new technics. Therefore, both companies and educational institutions should keep up to date articles, models, solutions and innovations. For example, Microsoft presents a threat model namely STRIDE. The threat model explained as "*the process of identifying potential security threats to the application and ensuring that proper mitigations against the threats are in place*" (Microsoft Cooperation, 2023). STRIDE model is summarized like (Table 1):

Table 1. Microsoft STRIDE Model

Threat	Security property
Spoofing	Authentication
Tampering	Integrity
Repudiation	Nonrepudiation
Information Disclosure	Confidentiality
Denial of Service	Availability
Elevation of Privilege	Authorization

Microsoft uses this model and it is still part of Microsoft Security Development Lifecycle (SDL). For each threat, Microsoft provides a solution detailed in the report.

To sum up, not only official institutions and organizations, but also private companies invest about cybersecurity education for the future.

When it comes to availability of the cybersecurity in official curricula of the countries' ministry of education, the titles and subtitles of cybersecurity can be handled below.

According to PISA 2023 rankings, when comparing performance of countries and economies in mathematics, the top 10 countries are (OECD, 2022):

1. Singapore – 575
2. Macau – 552

3. Chinese Taipei – 547
4. Hong Kong – 540
5. Japan – 536
6. Korea – 527
7. Estonia – 510
8. Switzerland – 508
9. Canada – 497
10. Netherlands – 493
39. Türkiye – 453

At this table, the cybersecurity topics in computer science course in K12 in Türkiye, China Hong Kong, Japan, Korea and Singapore will be handled (Table 3).

Türkiye

"Information and Software Technologies" course is an elective course from 1st to 4th grade whereas in 5th and 6th grade it is compulsory. When the curriculum is considered, information security related topics are available (Republic of Türkiye Ministry of National Education, 2018).

In 2nd unit for elementary grade, the theme is "Ethics and Security". The theme includes general but critical topics like human rights in technology usage, responsibilities in digital world, physical security precautions (hardware usage), privacy, data sharing and its responsibilities, how to making a strong password, ethical rules in online platforms and internet, digital footprint, malicious people in digital world and protection ways against them.

In 5th unit, "Ethics and Security" theme that we encounter with again in 5th grade and in 2nd unit is in 6th grade. 5th unit includes ethical principles, human rights in digital world, digital citizenship, digital identity, personal information security, password security and privacy. In 6th grade, the topics are expanded and the unit includes ethics on internet, cyberbullying, copyright, cybercrimes, digital footprint, digital content which is proper for cognitive and moral development, confidentiality, integrity, availability which are the main principles of cybersecurity, information protection methods, malwares, security technologies like applications.

These topics are augmented with materials. The materials are remarkable and they are developed according to instructional technology principles. Also, there are teacher guides in order to use the materials effectively.

China

Hong Kong educational system maintains 6 years of primary, 3 years of junior secondary and 3 years of senior secondary school and the compulsory education is 9 years covering primary and secondary school. When it comes to topics related to information security and cybersecurity, topics and terms are handled in the curricula like: ethics and rules in the process of exchanging and sharing information, privacy, to learn and use digital systems with a safe way in daily life, the importance of protecting digital information, the importance of private key, smart technologies, malicious people in digital world, personal data (username, password, personal citizenship card security) and security with developing technologies (Ministry of Education of the People's Republic of China, 2022). It shows that, Chinese government attaches importance on information security with wide aspect.

Japan

Japan educational system maintains 6 years of primary, 3 years of secondary and 3 years of high school and the compulsory education is 9 years covering primary and secondary school. In Japanese educational system, as it is shown in the curriculum management model of Ministry of Education, Culture, Sports, Science and Technology – Japan (Ministry of Education, Culture, Sports, Science and Technology (MEXT), 2020), information technologies are the part of the other disciplines and Japanese Education System prefers to use the information technology with an effective technology integration. The topics featured are to comprehend the term information and information technologies; information ethics, management the information, data about ourselves and others and the importance of saving the data, responsibility for the transfer and exchange of information, basic information security required in daily life, information protection methods, rules and etiquette in communication networks, individual rights to information and their importance, risks related to misuse of information technology, laws and systems related to information, scientific cybersecurity approach to protect and maintain public order in the virtual space, the impact of information and behavior spreading in the information society and effects of information media use on health. It is clear that Japan educational system attaches importance to information technologies with a broad subject area.

South Korea

South Korea educational system maintains 6 years of primary, 3 years of secondary and 3 years of high school and the compulsory education is 9 years covering primary and secondary school. Some topics about cybersecurity - which are included in national curriculum in South Korea- are digital ethics, copyright, digital crimes, digital addiction, personal data, information security, digital culture (National Curriculum Information Center, 2022).

Singapore

Singapore educational system maintains 6 years of primary, 4-5 years of secondary (Levent & Yazıcı, 2015) and 3 or 5 years of high school according to the school type and the compulsory education is 10-11 years covering primary and secondary school.

In Singapore, computer education framework comprises three dimensions:

- Computer as a science
- Computer as a tool
- Computer in society

The subtitles of three main titles are as shown at the Table 2:

Table 2. Singapore computer education framework

Titles / Subtitles	Computational Thinking	Systems Thinking	Use of Computer	Use of Applications	Safe & Responsible Use	Ethical & Legal Use	21st Century Competencies
Science	X	X					
Tool			X	X			
Society					X	X	X

When the Society title is examined, some of topics are heavily studied on: critical and inventive thinking, information and communication skills, data privacy, computer crimes, netiquette, ethics, computer security, safety, addiction, viruses and civic literacy, global awareness and cross-cultural skills (Ministry of Education Singapore, 2017). In the other syllabus security and privacy again the one of the major topics (Ministry of Education Singapore, 2024). Moreover, Cybersecurity education is delivered as part of Cyber Wellness lessons within the Character and Citizenship Education (CCE) Curriculum. Ms Mariam Jaafar, who is Ministry of Education Singapore parliament member, replies the question about cybersecurity awareness in curriculum as "*Beyond the formal curriculum, the Cyber Security Agency of Singapore (or CSA) supports MOE's efforts by providing assembly talks and other enrichment programs in schools. A cybersecurity module is also incorporated into the Code for Fun program for all Upper Primary students, where they are exposed to concepts like encryption and ways to protect oneself against cyberattacks."* (Jafaar, 2022). It can be said that, Singapore education system follows the current developments in digital World and educate the students at this aspect.

Table 3. Country and grade

Country - Region / Educational Grade	Elementary	Middle	High
	Compulsory		Non-Compulsory
Türkiye	Grade 1-4 Primary School	Grade 5-8 Secondary School	Grade 9-12 High School
South Korea	Grade 1-6 Primary School	Grade 7-9 Secondary School	Grade 9-12 High School
China (Hong Kong)	Grade 1-6 Primary School	Grade 7-9 Junior Secondary School	Grade 9-12 Senior Secondary School
Japan	Grade 1-6 Primary School	Grade 7-9 Secondary School	Grade 9-12 High School
Singapore	Grade 1-6 Primary School	Grade 7-10 Secondary School	3 to 5 years according to school type High School

To sum up, governments' point of view on security education shows that governments not only offer cybersecurity education via official institutions like ministry of education, but also develop programs, projects and fund institutions, private companies. It can be said that these kinds of projects clearly support the official education and they will continue to exist.

Prevent or Educate – Prevent and Educate

Cyber threats term includes "threat" and it would be scary for students especially younger ones. "Don't do it, never use computer it is dangerous, never click on, don't register this site" never and not doing words may prevent children to do act in some way, but are they the solution for preparing children to the digital world? At this point, research about collaboration between parents and children about cybersecurity can be given an example. Quayyum (2023) has studied on parent-children collaboration and the children age range is between 9-12. It was a game-based study and the researcher emphasize the children are safe online will be more successful when the parents have a proactive role in interacting. Moreover, students can be able to think critically, have a decision-making ability and the parents can be do as a guide for their children cognitive growth. If the collaboration is created safely, the children can share positive and negative experiences with their family, it can be a critical point, as well. As a result, the parents should be informed their students about dangers in digital world, but they educate their children with a positive way and also the rules or agreements should be applied by all members of the family.

Learning security in digital area is not a quick and easy process. It is needed to be effective structured learning environment, clear goals and objectives, activities enhancing learning. As it is said above, "threat" and "security" can be scary concepts. Moreover, not only the students, but also teachers and parents should be the people in learning process who apply in real life what they learn. Here the questions are: Which skills should be improved? What can be the objectives in cybersecurity education? How the learning process can be constructed?

Learning Process

Cybersecurity spans across a wide range of fields like management, information technologies, education, industry, therefore it uses skills that needed to developed in cybersecurity education. According to John et al. (2020), suggested primary skills in cybersecurity education are:

- Leadership skills
- Teamwork
- Interpersonal skills
- Technical skills
- Problem solving
- Critical thinking
- Life-long learning

The researchers claim that because cybersecurity is a rapid growing field, the main goal would be to develop professional people who are influential leaders being able to use such skills.

Learning process is a depth term that educational scientist, educational psychologist, educators, academicians, teachers have been working for centuries. Generally, they work on three main questions: how is learning process realized, which factors affect learning process and how the learning process can be more effective. Jean Piaget, Jerome Bruner, Robert Mills Gagne and David Ausubel, Lev Vygotsky, Erik Erikson and lots of researchers worked on learning and development. Models and theories of each researcher are handled for creating an effective and efficient learning process and shading light on the process.

Piaget's learning and cognitive development model as shown in the figure can be examined. Here, Piaget exhibit 4 stages of cognitive development, which are very crucial for understanding students' learning process. And Piaget shows learning types around the circle (Figure 2).

Figure 2. Learning Types by Piaget

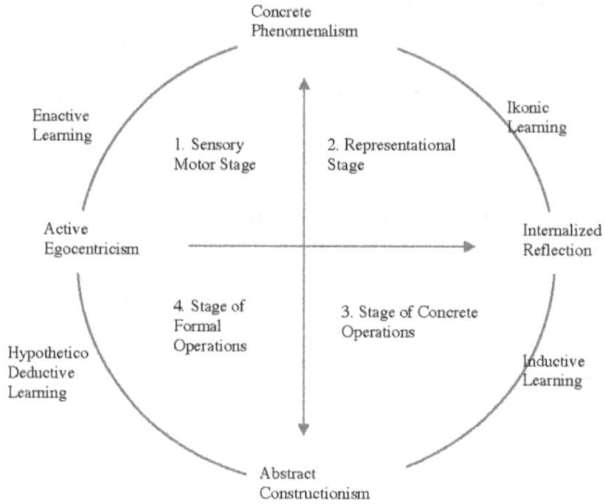

Piaget's models of learning and cognitive development (Kolb, 2014)

The figure can help the teachers in order to determine how they create teaching process for their students.

Instructional process should be planned according to pedagogical models and methods. Bloom et al. (1956) presents a hierarchical learning step that divides the learning objectives according to the aim of steps. Anderson et al. (2001) revised and redefined the taxonomy (Figure 3).

Figure 3. Objective Pyramids

For each step, objectives can be created by using the verbs that facilitate to measure the learning goals. According to a sample of 30 published lists, sample of 104 unique words are shown in the Table 4 (Stanny, 2016):

Table 4. Verbs using for objectives

Knowledge	Understand	Apply	Analyze	Evaluate	Create
Cite	Classify	Act	Analyze	Appraise	Arrange
Define	Compare	Apply	Appraise	Argue	Assemble
Describe	Convert	Calculate	Categorize	Assess	Combine
Identify	Defend	Choose	Classify	Choose	Compose
Label	Describe	Compute	Compare	Compare	Construct
List	Discuss	Construct	Contrast	Conclude	Create
Locate	Distinguish	Demonstrate	Criticize	Criticize	Design
Match	Estimate	Dramatize	Diagram	Critique	Develop
Memorize	Explain	Employ	Differentiate	Defend	Devise
Name	Express	Illustrate	Discriminate	Estimate	Formulate
Outline	Extend	Interpret	Distinguish	Evaluate	Generate
Recall	Generalize	Manipulate	Divide	Judge	Invent
Recite	Identify	Modify	Examine	Manage	Modify
Recognize	Infer	Operate	Infer	Prepare	Organize
Record	Interpret	Practice	Outline	Rearrange	Plan
Relate	Locate	Prepare	Point out	Reconcile	Prepare
Repeat	Paraphrase	Produce	Question	Set up	Produce
Reproduce	Predict	Relate	Relate	Synthesize	Rate
Select	Recognize	Schedule	Select		Revise
	Report	Show	Separate		Write
	Restate	Sketch	Subdivide		
	Review	Solve	Test		
	Rewrite	Use			
	Summarize				
	Translate				

The verbs are not limited to the table, for more, the related articles and referred article can be investigated. So, for each activity for the cybersecurity topic or course, firstly the aim of the topic should be determined. After, the objectives are cleared, the recommended verbs can be used.

Constructivism learning theory, according to Bruner (1991), is defined as active construction of new knowledge based on a learner's prior experience. Woolfolk (1993) explains the constructivism with the fact that the student actively constructs their own knowledge. In other words, the students are active while learning. 5E and 7E models are used in generally at this kind of process. Based on 5E model, 7E model is also used for cognitive development in learning process. These models provide learning cycle which is a concept of how people learn from experience. 7E learning cycle give an importance to the learner's prior knowledge. 7E model can be defined as Elicit, Engage, Explore, Explain, Elaborate, Evaluate, Extend. Whereas in explore step, students record data, design experiments, interpret results and create graphs, in explain step students explain the concept and link between new experiences and explored scientific concept and in elaborate step students apply their knowledge and transfer their learning (Adesoji & Idika, 2015).

Activities below can be used in these steps according to created lesson plans by teachers. The students are expected as an active learner and they can create their knowledge and learning way with the help of constructivist activities.

Activity Suggestions for Students

Educational games are one of the tools that are used to facilitate learning the cybersecurity. According to Francia et al. (2014), digital games can develop cognitive, spatial and motor skills and they can improve creativity. Moreover, playing well designed games allow students to fail without fear. Escape room games, serious games, puzzle games are the example used in cybersecurity education. To illustrate, in the puzzle game the gamer should solve the problem according to the given sources. In escape room games, there would be a Caesar cipher and encrypted message needed to be decrypted. Also, serious games are used at wide range of area like health, trade and industry. However, Thornton and Turley (2020) claim that without thoughtful pedagogical background and substructure, the digital games may serve as one step upward from entertainment.

Educators carefully approach the topic of how can we provide an effective guidance about teaching cyber security basics to the students. They can develop different kinds of physical or digital activities about each topic of cybers security and they can arrange the level of challenge. Here are some suggestions for activities intended to make the process more effective and joyful.

To Make the Students Being Informed About Cyber Security

It is clear that we cannot protect ourselves from something we have no knowledge about. Thus, firstly students may be informed about information security and its consequences. The teachers can prepare presentation including interactive question- answer parts, real life videos, what if cases and competitions. For sure, the presentation should be prepared grade or age level of students, pedagogical aspects of learning and cultural effects of society considered. Kaspersky, which is an international cybersecurity company in the United Kingdom, presents a joyful ABC of cybersecurity terms called cybersecurity alphabet at the website (Cybersecurity Alphabet, (2019). The other ABCs of cybersecurity is from Bitdefender, which is a company provides cybersecurity solutions, and its illustration made by haileyyamada.com (Cybersecurity ABCs, 2019).

Table 5. ABCs of cybersecurity

Letter	Kaspersky - Alphabet	Bitdefender - Alphabet
A	Authentication	Adware
B	Backup	Backup
C	Captcha	Cookie
D	Digital footprint	Denial of Service (DOS) Attack
E	Encryption	Encryption
F	Fraud	Firewall
G	Geolocation	Gateway
H	Honeypot	Https
I	IP address	IP Spoofing
J	Jailbreak	Jamming
K	Keylogger	Keylogger
L	Login	Logic Bomb
M	Malware	Malware
N	NFT	Network
O	Oversharing	Outsider Threat
P	Phishing	Phishing
Q	QR Code	Quarantine
R	Ransomware	Ransomware
S	Spam	Social Engineering
T	Trojan	Trojan Horse
U	URL	Uniform
V	VPN	Vishing
W	Wi-Fi	Worm
X	Exploit	XML Encryption
Y	Cyberbullying	Yottable
Z	ZIP File	Zombie Machines

Activity Time!

For elementary and middle school, the terms needed to learn can be included the activities. Whole terms above may result to confusion, so, some of them can be eliminated. For the rest of the words, a game may provide to learn the terms both with fun and permanency. The game can be complicated according to the level of students.

- Before the game the teacher writes each word on a small paper, gives a number for a word, folds and puts the paper in a jar.
- The teacher should make it according to the number of groups, like if there are 4 groups, the teacher writes the word 4 times and there can be 4 jars for the students.
- The teacher should make a jar for herself/himself. In total there can be 5 jars.
- Creates groups including 4-5 students.
- Wants from students to find a group name.
- Gives each jar to each group.
- Gives a time approximately 2 minutes for each word.
- Tells about the instruction: Each group opens the papers and writes their definition of the words on a A4 paper with the words' numbers.
- The crucial part students should discuss about the meaning of the word and control the time.
- At the end of the time, teacher writes the group names on the board.
- The teacher picks a paper in her/his jar and read the term.
- Each group tells their definitions orderly.
- If a group makes the definition correctly, earns 10 points.
- If a group makes the definition incorrectly, earns 0 points.
- At the end of the activity, the total scores are explained.
- The best group will be announced as cyber security librarians.

Activity Time!

For the high school students, a concept map activity may provide to learn the terms efficiently, because the students should think about each term in order to place the word on the most accurate place.

The activity consists of three parts: Researching, Planning and Mapping

At the first part, the students should make a research and increase the number of cyber security terms.

The rule is that the only two words, which are new, can be part of a branch.

The minimum number of words is 60 (If they want, they use the total of words above but they should rise the number anyway).

At second part, the students should have a plan about how the words can be a group.

Who makes the most branches, will the best concept mapping hero.

Any branch shouldn't cover the other.

At the last part, the students get the blank posters.

They make their concept maps via drawing or gluing the words.

The main title would be cyber security.

Human Rights and Ethics about Cyber Security and Cyberbullying

Some of countries like Türkiye, law about cybersecurity is generated as a consequence of the increased digital guilty. People have human rights in case of cyber guilty exposure under this kind of law umbrella. It should be said that people have human rights whereas responsibilities for others. So, the teachers make clear the rights and responsibilities for students. For example, a photograph including friends can be shared in social media but firstly the people in that photograph should give permission for sharing. Or, a child photograph shouldn't be shared in case of parent refuse. Cyberbullying is a kind of guilty and there would be some punishment according to the countries' law. Generally, students have no enough information about rights, responsibilities, punishment regarding cyber world. Thus, teaching such areas is very crucial before the subtitles handled; then the student will be well informed about their rights.

Activity Time!

In the class, groups of 5-6 students are formed. In this group there would be an information technologies expert, there would be a lawyer and 3-4 independent evaluator. The groups may choose the roles for each person in the group.

The lawyer: Defends the rights of the victim

The information technologies expert: Finds out the rights action and faults both Jane and the malicious person.

The evaluators: Analyze the whole case according to the laws and human rights. They should tell the true way that Jane should did.

All people should analyze the text and they together examine the cases, behaviors and utterances. The lawyer and IT expert are the speakers.

The activity is a disputation and the main goal of the activity is to find the fault in the letter and the activities provision in law.

10 minute is given to the groups in order to they can analyze the letter. Then they take notes like "it is a fault and the behavior would be like…" or "it is a guilty in accordance with the law in that country. For this letter Turkish Penal Code (2004) is handled as an example.

A girl at 13 age tells the story what happened a month ago. She gets a message from her friend "Hey, Jane, there is a social media account that was created via using your name, surname and photograph. You should control" and the friend sends the account connection to Jane. Jane opens it and the friend tells the truth. It was Jane's name and surname and the profile photograph belongs to her. And she tells:

"When I have noticed that the social media account was created using my personal information. Immediately I've sent a message to the account holder.

- *Hey, who are you and why use my personal information!*

  Then I have noticed that the holder blocks my account and I have lost the account. Then from my friend's social media account (she has shared her password with me), I've written another message.
- *What is your problem? It is a cyber guilty and I will complain about you to my parents. Who are you?*
- *Okay, it was just a joke. Maybe I'm your friend as you have already known.*
- *A friend? It is the worst joke.*
- *You are always arrogant like now. You always insult your friends; it is your punishment. I will show to everybody what you backbite about your classmates.*
- *Don't do it! It is a huge lie..*
- *I'm intelligent than you think about. I've recorded your voice while you're cheating.*
- *Please, don't do it..*
- *It is over.*

Jane keeps telling the story. It was an awful day for me. One day after, my classmates have not wanted to see me, talk to me. I've get lonely and I have had some health problems due to this case. Now, I want to claim my rights and file a legal complaint.

It is expected from the groups that making like items according to their analysis.

1. *"The friend sends the account connection to Jane. Jane opens it"*

   Jane should think about the link is secure or not firstly. It seems like an urgent issue and it can contain fake links.

2. *"Immediately I've sent a message to the account holder"*. It is not a guilty but it may not be preferred because the malicious people may throw off the track.
3. *"Then from my friend's social media account (she has shared her password with me)"*

    No one should share a personal account password even if the person is a close friend.
4. *" I will complain about you to my parents." This action is true, in case of cyberbullying the case should be shared with the parents.*
5. *"it was just a joke". Even if it is a joke, it doesn't chance the situation, it is a guilty..* Turkish Penal Code, Article 123
6. *You are always arrogant like now"*. Insulting is a guilty. Turkish Penal Code, Article 125
7. To open an account on behalf of others without their permission is a cyberbullying guilty. Turkish Penal Code, Article 135-136
8. *"Maybe I'm your friend as you have already known." Is a disturbing action.* Turkish Penal Code, Article 123
9. *"I will show to everybody what you backbite about your classmates.". Sharing private conversation in a digital and open platform is a guilty.* Turkish Penal Code, Article 132-134
10. *"I've recorded your voice while you're cheating." Recording the voice without any permission is a guilty.* Turkish Penal Code, Article 133
11. Jane couldn't share the case with anybody else. It was wrong, she should share firstly her parents and her responsible teacher.

After time is up, the teacher reads the letter word by word. The groups stop the teacher where they highlighted the sentence and present their claims.

Personal Data – Can Be Shared / Cannot Be Shared

When the cybersecurity term is handled, maybe the first word occurred into our minds is privacy. We have some personal data and part of them is private. Therefore, some of our data we can share with familiar people whereas we shouldn't share private ones. There are lots of social engineering and stealing the private personal data case resulting in financial and emotional damage. Although this steal story seems like a kind of chatting in normal, it can include tricks aim to catch the desired private data. When we look at the cases, the innocents use expressions like "I didn't understand, I didn't feel to say something crucial, I did trust etc". Therefore, shareable and not shareable data should be divided into our students' mind in order to the fact that they can be more aware about what they tell about.

Activity Time!

For the elementary school students, materials providing to study on can be used for sharable and not sharable personal data. For example, within the scope of Republic of Türkiye National Education Information Technology and Software course student materials, a table including sharable and non-sharable personal data is used as a material for this topic (Republic of Türkiye Ministry of National Education, 2018). The students should find who gives their private data and who don't. A sample table can be used or a unique table can be created by the teacher (Table 6).

Table 6. Activity table 1

Question/ Person	Jane	David	Adam	Rose	Amelia	William
Can you share your citizenship ID or password serial number?	My citizenship ID is: 4568672	My Passport serial number is: 34091299	My Passport serial number is: I don't know	My Passport serial number includes "7"	My citizenship ID includes "3" and "6"	My citizenship ID is: 2310984
What is your school system password?	My school system password is: 098098	I cannot say anything about my school system password	My school system password includes the number of "3" 6 times	My school system password includes the smallest counter number for 6 times	I cannot tell my password	I cannot tell my password but it contains a number that is not positive nor negative 6 times.
Where is your house?	My house is in London, England	My house is the green house at the end of the Flower Street, at this region	My house address is No:32, 554th Flower Street, Downtown, California	My house is the 3rd floor of yellow apartment in front of Shopping Mall	My house is in the Hat Village in Prague	My house is in one of the white apartment buildings

Activity Time!

For the middle school student, the teacher may distribute **a blank table** to students and wants to fill the table according to the instructions like:

Jane shares her private data for 3 times.

David shares his private data for 2 times.

Adam shares his private data for 1 time.

Rose doesn't share her private data.

Amelie shares her private data for 2 times.
William shares his private data for 2 times.
The usable data:
House address
Citizenship ID
Business address of mother
The birthdate of father
The birthdate
A system password
PS: The students can use another data different from above.

User Name and Password

As an adult, let we think for a second how much we have a username and a password in digital world. For buying a book, making market shopping, using social media platforms, transacting on a government site... As we have so much account, sometimes we forget about login data insomuch that create a new account. In other words, username and password dual will be our friends until a more innovative solution usage adopted. Hence, the right username and password creating method should be teach to students as early as possible. Especially for the passwords, generally people prefer to use so simple characters that are capable to hacked easily. The main reason is remembering the password quickly and not struggling the change password process. That is the most desired situations for a hacker because the hacker doesn't struggle to solve the password for a long time.

On this topic, there are two words being confused: cypher and password. If a teacher wants to get students' attraction, the teacher can handle the "cypher" term firstly, because the historical cases witnesses cypher cases that would change the course of fate. Students may interest the encryption and decryption terms and they want to try a kind of activity. Here is the point welcoming the students to cypher world.

When it comes to "password", the teacher may mention about estimation methods with examples like password numbers in birthday date or letters in name or surname. The other issue would be brute force attacks made by computers. For more up-to-date developments, the teacher may show the quantum computers and their working logics, moreover how it is easy as winking to break a complex password for them.

Activity Time!

For elementary and middle school, an encryption game would increase the students' interest. In regarding the grade of the class, the challenge level can be increased or decreased. The teacher first of all teaches about "caesar cipher" history and how it is used. To reinforce the knowledge, the teacher makes some encryption and decryption examples. Here, the teacher uses different encryption method. There is a key and encrypted sentence. After that, the teacher talks about the instruction of the activity.

First of all, the goal of the activity.

The goal is to find the secret object into the pirate's room in order to eliminate his dangerous plans.

There is an encrypted message which is a conundrum. The answer of the conundrum is the object in this room.

Steps:

1. The groups should solve the encrypted sentences.
2. Each group tell what they find.
3. The groups collect the decrypted sentences and make a logical order to create the puzzle.
4. The groups find the answer and the object.

Figure 4. Activity Figure 1

LETTER	A	B	C	D	E	F	G	H	I	J	K	L	M	N	O	P	Q	R	S	T	U	V	W	X	Y	Z
ENCRYPTED	T	Y	H	P	S	Q	W	X	C	V	J	U	I	O	M	L	Z	A	E	B	R	G	F	K	N	D

The main sentences (Figure 4):

WHERE ARE THE LAKES EMPTY
THE MOUNTAINS FLAT
AND THE RIVERS STILL
The encrypted sentences
FXSAS TAS BXS UTJSE SILBN

BXS IMROBTCOE QUTB
TOP BXS ACGSAE EBCUU
The puzzle: Where are the lakes empty, the mountains flat and the rivers still
The answer: Map
The encrypted sentences share among the 3 group of students.
The groups solve the cipher.
There would be the main sentences.
The groups order the sentences for a meaningful form.
The last part, the students work to find the answer: MAP
They work to find the map on this picture (Figure 5).

Figure 5. A ship room (Resource: Freepik.com / Picture with free licence)

Activity Time!

For high school students, the "caesar cipher" topic is handled. After that, the teacher gives the duty: To write a program that each letter will match a letter five before itself.
For example:
The input: F
The output: A
The input: T
The output: O

Activity Time!

For the elementary school level, the teacher may want the students to create 2 passwords with 4 characters. One of them will be easy and the other will be hard to solve. After, students present their password examples and the way of make the password easy and hard.

Activity Time!

For the middle school, password production activity can be realized. Each student grouped with a friend. Then the teacher gives instruction. The groups realize the instructions and they make a poster. After, each group changes the poster with another one and control the other group's poster. If there is a fault, they note in order to discuss about the poster owner.

The instruction may like:

Give an example,

- 3 characters – 2 passwords – Password difficulty level is the same (ex. 333 – 444)
- 5 characters – 2 passwords – Password difficulty level is not same (ex. 3As25– 00000)
- 6 characters – 3 passwords – Password difficulty will be ordered (ex. 999999– 121212 – 4aD+0.)
- 4 characters – 3 passwords – Password difficulty level is the same for two (ex. 6666 – 7777 – 43LKtp)

Activity Time!

For high school students, a basic programing can make to create passwords. The teacher gives the instruction like:

- Write a program that creates random number, it should be an integer.
- Created numbers will be 8 characters.
- Each character can start from 1, ends at 6.
- Between each character, don't forget to make a blank.

The teacher can make some challenges into the instructions. The student would write the codes like in C language:

```
#include <stdio.h>
```

```
#include <stdlib.h>
int main()
{
int i, generatedpassword; for(i = 0 ; i < 8 ; i++)
{
generatedpassword = rand() % 6 + 1;
printf("%d\t", generatedpassword);
}
return 0;
}
```

Social Engineering

Imagine a castle, with thick and high walls, little windows, armored doors, deliberately surrounded by dangerous animals and stationed with armed soldiers. If an enemy has no required and developed technology to destroy the castle and it seems approximately impossible to get rid of the precautions, what the enemy plans? Right answer, conquering "within". Some strategies never change even though the eras change. Social engineers are very adept to resemble a friend, a helpful person, a sensitive person, a polite person. If they would be opposite way, who believes, talks, trusts? They are also adept to get information into a conversation, collect o puzzle pieces and make the puzzle completed. The last part is so dangerous because they complete the aimed puzzle, it means they are ready to steal what they want. So, social engineers are known as patient people. For the students, creating role playing cases would be joyful and informative.

Activity Time!

A teacher can prefer to talk about real world cases, like poisoned child case because of eating time expired chocolate, with her/his students. The students pay attention, because they may experience bad stories like that child. In some cases, the teachers apply for an instructional method in order to make the students more aware: creative drama. Creative drama, is a kind of live presentation way similar to real world cases for educational and instructional goals (Hesapçıoğlu, 1997). Another definition is (Davis and Belm, 1978 as cited in Hendrix and Shannon, 2012) an improvisational, non-exhibitional, process-centered form of drama where drama participants are guided by a leader to imagine, enact, and reflect upon human experience. According to San (1991), students' learning process should include emotionality and experiences. The main reason is that the students' emotions, imaginations, imaginative thinking should be connected through the process for students' active participation. It is possible to use one of so many technics of creative drama. The most used types of it in the especially elementary classroom are non-fiction dramatization, improvisation and role play (Fry, 1996).

The teacher can prefer to use role play creative drama in social engineering part. Firstly, the objectives should be written and the scenario of the creative drama should be prepared. The teacher can use the topic below:

There may be 2 students who will realize role play drama. One of them is a student and the another one is stranger. Stranger follows the student's social media accounts (let's think about the student is older than 13 and can use social media legally) and the stranger collect information about the student's family. The mother likes oil paintings and she has a collection from famous paintings. The main goal is to learn the student's home address in order to steal some paintings. The stranger finds a way to learn the address. After the last lesson of the school the stranger finds the student and gets talking. The stranger says lots of information about the student.

- Hi, I'm Maya.
- Hi, sorry I don't remind who you are.
- Oh, really? I am your mother's friend from university. You are Jane right?
- Yeah, you know my name.
- Not just your name. Your mother talk to me about you when we were at university, you like dark chocolate and cake with cherry, don't you? (Jane posted a photograph on her Instagram account with the "I like dark chocolate, it is the best" and on another photograph she make a comment with "My mother does the best for me, cake witthhhh cherrrryyy".)
- Yeah, that's true.
- Jane, I need your help. I want to send a gift for my dear friend but I don't know your home address. Can you share your address with me? But please don't say to your mother, it should be surprise!
- Sure! The address is...

    The drama stops. The teacher makes some question about the case and pose the questions to all class.

- How Maya gets the Jane's trust?
- Is it a real name, Maya, what do you think?
- If you are Jane, would you share the address? Why?
- If you are the stranger, social engineer, how would you get the address without raising any suspicious?

    What is aimed in that drama is to make empathy and think about true and false behaviors against to the strangers. The critical part is to see how a social engineer thinks and approaches to victims. The drama can be expanded and improvisation can diversify the case.

Activity Time!

In different countries a game is still very popular: Wolf man. It is known as werewolf, wolvesville.. The rule of the game is simple. Approximately 6 - 10 people play the game, however it is possible to play the game 3-30 people. There is a village, everyone has a role in this game, some of them is villager, and some of them is werewolf. There would be special roles like witch, vampire, doctor, seer and angel, the roles can be diversified. Special roles have special characteristics in the game but the whole rules can be produced uniquely. The basic aim for a wolfman is to survive until the game ends. The basic aim of the villagers to catch the wolfman. For every night a villager is kidnapped by the wolfman, so the villager should find the wolfman. The critical point is wolfman is seem as a villager and the real villagers can catch the wolfman only the clues in the wolfman talks about the night. There is a moderator who gets information about the whole gamers and remind the play time. There are role cards at the beginning and each gamer selects one without seeing what he/she select and knowing the others' role. There is a kidnapped case and everybody prepares a talk about the night but one of them is lying: wolfman. The game can be played in different forms but it is really joyful and mysterious.

The reason to explain the werewolf game is that the winner is the person who displays the secret best or who catches the clues best. For sure, the game includes non-pedagogical parts like kidnapping a villager or eat a villager. Therefore, the game can be transformed as a pedagogical and instructional game. A student group is created and there would be a hacker who catches the personal data. An IT expert would be a special character like a seer. A steal case can be made by the moderator (teacher) and the group work to find the secret hacker.

Malware and Spyware

In social engineering title, a castle metaphor is handled. Let's moving on the metaphor and the new question: How does an enemy can leak to castle unseen? The answer is clear: finding a secret path or seem like the castle community – citizen. Generally, spywares use the both ways together. How they do that? To illustrate, when a person downloads a software on his/her computer from unreliable source, the program will be downloaded with extras. These extra items can be spywares that nearly unseen and stationed secretly then the mission starts. Interestingly, the welldone developed software cannot be catch by the antivirus program. One of the reasons of it, the software doesn't look like a spyware in the first sight. In other words, the spyware uses incognito like a real spy. A spyware is a malware but malware includes so many kinds of software. Some of them are Internet worms, computer viruses, trojan horses (Rieck et. al, 2008), adware, downloader, backdoor, packed, web toolbar, exploit, net tool (Kim et. al, 2020).

Activity Time!

For the middle school and high school, the activity can be applied with different level challenges and diversity. The activity is to prepare a classroom newspaper the contains incidents about malware and spywares in different countries.

- The teacher makes the groups with random selection
- There would be groups with 4-5 students.
- Let's think about 6 continents and for each group there will be one continent matched to the group.
- The students make research about news in that continent and make a classroom newspaper. The name of the newspaper should be creative.
- All groups present their work.

For the high school level, the students can find the news with cause and effect. The groups can examine the punishments (if the criminals are caught) according to law articles in that country.

Phishing

Phishing is a very popular cyber-attack and some companies send regularly an informative email to their workers about phishing attacks. The reason of why phishing is very easy way to catch the required data is that if the target person is pensive, busy, unwary or unconscious and make a quick reaction. The attack depends on a click, harmful activity can start and finish in the twinkle of an eye. Certainly, a successful phishing trick hide the real harmful link, sometimes the victims don't be aware of which transaction they do. When it comes to children, they may not sift the real or fake links even if they know how can separate them. Thus, making real life phishing activities may make them more ready for the attacks.

Activity Time!

Jigsaw is a unit within Google and its aim is to research about threats to open societies and to develop solutions (jigsaw.google.com/). The unit developed a phishing quiz (https://phishingquiz.withgoogle.com/) for testing the level of phishing awareness. It includes 8 real world e-mails and the users should make a decision about the e-mail is reliable or not. In order to make a decision, the users should control the links on the e-mail or think about the content.

Phishing Quiz Tricks:

1. Fake Google Drive link
2. Similar words usage – Efacks / Efax
   Strange end of the link like "mailru382.co"
3. Unknown shortened names like "TK"
   Link to "This Photograph" but the photograph is unclear
   Link to unknown Internet address
4. Not matching emails between historical and current inbox
   Unexpected PDFs
5. Urgent emails and steps taken with concern
   Not matching a real site address like "google.support"
   Changing the password via unknown site redirect
6. Fake mails seem like set from a governmental system

Misuse of Websites

Today's world presents us a huge information source in digital: websites. Surfing on the Internet, researching, learning, shopping and lots of activities can be realized via websites. These are kind of stations for special aims. However, for malicious people these stations can be a hunting ground. How?

HTTP - HTTPS

HTTP (Hyper Text Transfer Protocol) is a protocol that is needed by a web server in order to process the request from users. In other words, it provides communication between client and server (Jafaar et al., 2019). HTTPS is more secure version of HTTP. At banking systems, governmental websites, e-commerce websites generally https protocol is used for their secure processes.

Raffle Ads

Websites sometimes uses raffle ads for their campaigns and promotions. If a website is not reliable, the ads generally would be dangerous. These kinds of ads aim to catch clicks so they would be colorful and attractive.

Collecting Redundant Data

Websites can use a type of membership system in order to work more effective for their audience. To record the members with unique data, they can make the parts of membership form obligatory. Membership candidates can share their private data without questioning about why the data is required. The websites can use the extra data with sharing it third parties or selling them for a financial source. Actually, terms and condition letter can explain how the data will use and share with others, however it doesn't mean the occasion is secure or regular.

Cookies

Cookies provide the users with suggested items according to the users previously choices. For example, if a user is looking forward to a red dress, and the websites uses cookies, probably the user meets diverse wearing labels which have dress models. It may save the time for user instead of look the labels' websites. Moreover, cookies can provide to hold the sessions open and remind the shopping cart. However, it is hard to say that cookies are totally beneficial and aims only time saving or facilitating the process. Cookies can collect different data like location, preferences of use, language, passwords, IP address etc.

Activity Time!

For the high school students, a group activity may facilitate to learn how SSL certificate provides security. The teacher creates heterogenous groups with 4-5 student. The task Is to research about how https is more secure than http, and which conditions provides the security. After they collect data, each group should draw the process via their creativeness. They should draw the man in the middle, also. After the drawings over, each group hangs the drawings on the wall or the board. Then each group member gives point between 1-5 according to the scale items (Table 7).

Table 7. Activity table 2

Items/Points	**1**	**2**	**3**	**4**	**5**
Creativity					
Drawing					
Content					

The best drawing according to 3 criteria will be chosen.

REFERENCES

Adesoji, F. A., & Idika, M. I. (2015). Effects of 7E Learning Cycle Model and Case-Based Learning Strategy on Secondary School Students' Learning Outcomes in Chemistry. *Journal of the International Society for Teacher Education*, 19(1), 7–17.

Anderson, L. W., Krathwohl, D. R., Airasian, P. W., Cruikshank, K. A., Mayer, R. E., Pintrich, P. R., Raths, J., & Wittrock, M. C. (2001). A Taxonomy for Learning, Teaching, and Assessing: A Revision of Bloom's Taxonomy of Educational Objectives. *Reference and Research Book News: Dublin, OH, USA*, 16, 1–336.

Barzilay, M. (2013). A simple definition of cybersecurity.

Bloom, B. S., Engelhart, M. D., Furst, E. J., Hill, W. H., & Krathwohl, D. R. (1956). *Taxonomy of educational objectives: The classification of educational goals. Handbook 1: Cognitive domain*. Longman.

Bruner, J. (1990). *Acts of meaning*. Harvard University Press.

Cabaj, K., Kotulski, Z., Księżopolski, B., & Mazurczyk, W. (2018). Cybersecurity: Trends, issues, and challenges. *EURASIP Journal on Information Security*, 2018(1), 1–3. DOI: 10.1186/s13635-018-0080-0

Catota, F. E., Morgan, M. G., & Sicker, D. C. (2019). Cybersecurity education in a developing nation: *The Ecuadorian environment.Journal of Cybersecurity*, 5(1). Advance online publication. DOI: 10.1093/cybsec/tyz001

Cisco The Newsroom. (2021). [Online]. Available: https://newsroom.cisco.com/c/r/newsroom/en/us/a/y2021/m11/canada-s-largest-cybersecurity-education-program-for-high-schools-launches-in-partnership-between-cisco-and-stem-fellowship.html. Access Date: 31.08.2024

Cyber, A. C. E. S. (2024). [Online]. Available: https://start.paloaltonetworks.com/cyber-aces.html. Access Date: 29.08.2024

Cyberlaunch. (2024). [Online]. Available: https://cyberflorida.org/cyberlaunch/. Access Date: 31.08.2024

Cybersecurity ABCs. (2019). [Online]. Available: https://haileyyamada.com/cybersecurity-abcs/. Access Date: 28.06.2024

Cybersecurity Alphabet. (2024). [Online]. Available: https://www.kaspersky.com/blog/cybersecurity-alphabet/. Access Date: 28.06.2024

Davis, J. H., & Belm, T. (1978). Terminology of drama/theatre with and for children: A redefinition. *Children's Theatre Review*, 27(1), 10–11.

Eminağaoğlu, M., & Gökşen, Y. (2009). Information Security; What Is and What Is Not, Information Security Problems in Turkey and Some Related Solutions. *Dokuz Eylul University The Journal of Graduate School of Social Sciences,* 11(4), 01-15

Erümit, S. F., & Keles, E. (2023). Examining computer science education of Asia-Pacific countries successful in the PISA. *Journal of Educational Technology and Online Learning*, 6(1), 82–104. DOI: 10.31681/jetol.1154913

Esteves, J. (n.d). What Is the Future of Cybersecurity? [Online]. Available: https://www.ie.edu/insights/ideas-to-shape-the-future/idea/what-is-the-future-of-cybersecurity/. Access Date: 27.08.2024

European Union Agency For Cybersecurity. (October 2023). Enısa Threat Landscape 2023, July 2022 to June 2023. [Online]. Available: https://www.enisa.europa.eu/publications/enisa-threat-landscape-2023. Access Date: 31.08.2024

Federal Bureau of Investigation. (2023). *Internet Crime Report,* Internet Crime Complaint Centre. [Online]. Available: https://www.ic3.gov/Media/PDF/AnnualReport/2023_IC3Report.pdf. Access Date: 31.08.2024

Francia, G.III, Thornton, D., Trifas, M., & Bowden, T. (2014). *Gamification of information security awareness training. Emerging trends in ICT security*. Morgan Kaufmann.

Fry, S. M. (1996). *A handbook for using creative dramatics in elementary Ohio history* (Doctoral dissertation, University of Dayton.).

Hendrix, R., Eick, C., & Shannon, D. (2012). The Integration of Creative Drama in an Inquiry-Based Elementary Program: The Effect on Student Attitude and Conceptual Learning. *Journal of Science Teacher Education*, 23(7), 823–846. DOI: 10.1007/s10972-012-9292-1

Hesapçıoğlu, M. (1997). *Teaching Principles and Methods*. Beta Publications.

Ibrahim, A., McKee, M., Sikos, L. F., & Johnson, N. F. (2024). [Cybersecurity Education Around the World. *IEEE Access*.]. *Systematic Reviews*, •••, K-12.

International Telecommunication Union (ITU). (2022). Facts and Figures 2022. [Online]. Available: https://www.itu.int/itu-d/reports/statistics/facts-figures-2022/ Access Date: 01.08.2024

Jaafar, G. A., Abdullah, S. M., & Ismail, S. (2019). Review of recent detection methods for HTTP DDoS attack. *Journal of Computer Networks and Communications*, 2019(1), 1283472. DOI: 10.1155/2019/1283472

Jaafar, M. (Mar. 3, 2022). Introducing Cybersecurity Awareness as Part Core Curriculum Primary Schools. [Online]. Available: https://www.moe.gov.sg/news/parliamentary-replies/20220303- introducing-cybersecurity-awareness-as-part-of-the-core-curriculumin-primary-schools

John, S. N., Noma-Osaghae, E., Oajide, F., & Okokpujie, K. (2020). Cybersecurity Education: The Skills Gap, Hurdle!. *Innovations in Cybersecurity Education*, 361-376.

Keser, H., & Güldüren, C. (2015). Development Of Information Security Awareness Scale. *Kastamonu Education Journal*, 23(3), 1167–1184.

Kim, D. W., Shin, G. Y., & Han, M. M. (2020). Analysis of feature importance and interpretation for malware classification. *Computers, Materials & Continua*, 65(3), 1891–1904. DOI: 10.32604/cmc.2020.010933

Kolb, D. A. (2014). *Experiential learning: Experience as the source of learning and development.* FT press.

Levent, F., & Yazıcı, E. (2015). Examination of Factors Affecting Success of Singapore Education System. *Marmara University Atatürk Education Faculty Journal of Educational Sciences*, 39(39), 121–143.

Medoh, C., & Telukdarie, A. (2022). The future of cybersecurity: A system dynamics approach. *Procedia Computer Science*, 200, 318–326. DOI: 10.1016/j.procs.2022.01.230

Microsoft Cooperation. (2023). *Microsoft Secure Development Documentation*, [Online]. Available: https://learn.microsoft.com/pdf?url=https%3A%2F%2Flearn.microsoft.com%2Fen-us%2Fazure%2Fsecurity%2Fdevelop%2Ftoc.json. Access Date: 23.07.2024

Ministry of Education. Culture, Sports, Science and Technology (MEXT). (2020). *Developing Skills to Use Information*. Ministry of Education, Culture, Sports, Science and Technology, Elementary and Secondary Education Bureau, Information Education and Foreign Language Education Division, [Online]. Available: https://www.mext.go.jp/content/20201002-mxt_jogai01-100003163_1.pdf. Access Date: 04.08.2024

Ministry of Education of the People's Republic of China. (2022). *Compulsory Education Information Technology Curriculum Standards 2022 Edition*, [Online]. Available: http://www.moe.gov.cn/, https://www.ictr.edu.cn/download_center/ywjy .html, Access Date: 01.07.2024.

Ministry of Education Singapore. (2017). *O-Level Computing Syllabus - Upper Secondary*, [Online]. Available: https://www.moe.gov.sg/-/media/files/secondary/ syllabuses/science/2021-o-level-computing-teaching-and-learning-syllabus.pdf Access Date: 01.08.2024.

Ministry of Education Singapore. (2024). *Computing Teaching and Learning Syllabus.* [Online]. Available: https://www.moe.gov.sg/-/media/files/secondary/fsbb/syllabus/ 2024-g3-computing-teaching-and-learning-syllabus.pdf Access Date: 01.08.2024.

National Curriculum Information Center (NCIC). (2022*). Basic Curriculum, Utilization of Information and Communication, 408- 428,* [Online]. Available: https://ncic.re .kr/mobile.brd.ntc.view.do;jsessionid=3988D6B62A20BF3282FBCE62F14F7E2B ?articleNo=10000070, Access Date: 21.06.2024

NICE K12 Cybersecurity Education Conference. (2024). [Online]. Available: https://www.nist.gov/itl/applied-cybersecurity/nice/events/nice-k12-cybersecurity -education-conference, Access Date: 16.07.2024.

OECD. (2022). *OECD PISA Reports Volume 1*, [Online]. Available: https://www .oecd.org/en/publications/2023/12/pisa-2022-results-volume-i_76772a36/full-report/component-9.html#tablegrp-d1e2203-92e1015b90, Access Date: 12.07.2024.

Phishing Quiz, [Online]. Available: https://phishingquiz.withgoogle.com/ Access Date: 29.06.2024

Picture: https://www.freepik.com/free-vector/pirate-capitan-ship-cabin-wooden -room-interior_30701210.htm#fromView=search&page=2&position=2&uuid= b1e51d02-25ea-462a-91e3-b6aa708637a0

Presidency of the Republic of Türkiye Digital Transformation Office. (2024 Updated Version). Cybersecurity Vocational Schools Project. [Online]. Available: https:// cbddo.gov.tr/projeler/siber-myo/, Access Date: 29.08.2024.

Quayyum, F. (2023). Collaboration between parents and children to raise cybersecurity awareness. In Proceedings of the 2023 *European Interdisciplinary Cybersecurity Conference* (pp. 149-152). DOI: 10.1145/3590777.3590802

Quayyum, F., Cruzes, D. S., & Jaccheri, L. (2021). Cybersecurity awareness for children: A systematic literature review. *International Journal of Child-Computer Interaction*, 30, 100343. DOI: 10.1016/j.ijcci.2021.100343

Republic of Türkiye Ministry of National Education. (2018). *Information Technologies and Software Course Level 2 Activity Book*, [Online]. Available: https://tegm.meb.gov.tr/meb_iys_dosyalar/2019_04/15151914_BiliYim_Teknolojileri_ve_YazYlYm_Dersi_2._Seviye_Etkinlik_KitabY_Ylkokul_2018-2019.pdf, Access Date: 07.07.2024

Republic of Türkiye Ministry of National Education. (2018). *Information Technologies and Software Course Curriculum,* (2018). Ankara, 2018.

Rieck, K., Holz, T., Willems, C., Düssel, P., & Laskov, P. (2008, July). Learning and classification of malware behavior. In *International Conference on Detection of Intrusions and Malware, and Vulnerability Assessment* (pp. 108-125). Berlin, Heidelberg: Springer Berlin Heidelberg.

San, İ. (1990). Eğitimde Yaratıcı Drama. [JFES]. *Ankara University Journal of Faculty of Educational Sciences*, 23(2), 573–582.

Seppi, M. (2024). Cyber Security Career Roadmap: Building a Secure Future. International University of Applied Science. [Online]. Available: https://www.iu.org/blog/career-paths/cyber-security-career/#:~:text=Exploring%20the%20Cybersecurity%20career%20landscape&text=According%20to%20the%20U.S.%20Bureau,the%20average%20for%20all%20occupations. Access Date: 31.08.2024

Stanny, C. J. (2016). Reevaluating Bloom's Taxonomy: What measurable verbs can and cannot say about student learning. *Education Sciences*, 6(4), 37. DOI: 10.3390/educsci6040037

Students Wellbeing Hub. (2024). [Online]. Available: https://studentwellbeinghub.edu.au/. Access Date: 30.08.2024

Thornton, D., & Turley, F. (2020). Dynamic Difficulty Adjustment in Cybersecurity Awareness Games: Analysis of Player Behavior and the Potential of Electroencephalography. *Innovations in Cybersecurity Education*, 3-17.

Turkish Penal Code. (2004). [Online]. Available: https://www.mevzuat.gov.tr/mevzuat?MevzuatNo=5237&MevzuatTur=1&MevzuatTertip=5. Access Date: 25.08.2024

UNESCO. (2023). *Global Education Monitoring Report 2023: Technology in education– A tool on whose terms?* UNESCO.

U.S. Department of Homeland Security Cybersecurity and Infrastructure Security Agency. (2023, January) Report, [Online]. Available: https://www.cisa.gov/sites/default/files/2023-01/K-12report_FINAL_V2_508c_0.pdf, Access Date: 16.07.2024.

Von Solms, R., & Van Niekerk, J. (2013). From information security to cyber security. *Computers & Security*, 38, 97–102. DOI: 10.1016/j.cose.2013.04.004

Wilson, M., & Hash, J. (2003). Building an information technology security awareness and training program. *NIST Special publication*, 800(50), 1-39.

Woolfolk, A. E. (1993). *Educational psychology*. Allyn and Bacon.

Chapter 5
Innovations Focusing on Artificial Intelligence in Computer Science Education

Ertürk Erdağı
https://orcid.org/0000-0001-8619-8879
Republic of Türkiye Ministry of National Education, Turkey

ABSTRACT

Computer science education is a field that needs constant development due to technological developments. Especially in recent years, the widespread use of the concept of artificial intelligence in all scientific fields has affected the field of computer science education. Today, the concept of artificial intelligence is used on a very large scale in many fields other than technical fields. This has enabled the integration of the artificial intelligence universe with all fields with an interdisciplinary approach. Artificial intelligence is capable of directing the entire educational process rather than being a stand-alone educational content during computer science education. Students can use this field to solve all problems in their field of expertise during and after their education. In this section, artificial intelligence techniques and subfields used in computer science education, artificial intelligence trends, challenges related to artificial intelligence, and the interaction of the curriculum with artificial intelligence are discussed.

DOI: 10.4018/979-8-3693-4542-9.ch005

1. INTRODUCTION

Computer science education is a field that needs continuous development due to technological developments. Especially in recent years, the widespread use of artificial intelligence in all scientific fields has affected the field of computer science education. Today, the concept of artificial intelligence is used on a very large scale in many fields other than technical fields. This situation has enabled the integration of the artificial intelligence universe with all fields with an interdisciplinary approach. Artificial intelligence is capable of directing the entire education process rather than being a stand-alone educational content during computer science education. Students can use this field during and after their education in all problems in their specialization areas. In this section, artificial intelligence techniques and subfields used in computer science education, examples of their use in the educational environment, challenges related to artificial intelligence and the interaction of the curriculum with artificial intelligence are discussed.

2. MACHINE LEARNING

2.1. Technical Information for Machine Learning

Machine learning is a discipline that has revolutionized the field of computer science. Machine learning can be explained as an advanced branch of computational algorithms that aims to imitate human intelligence using data (El Naqa and Murphy 2015). Machine learning algorithms, which automate prediction and decision-making processes by learning from data, find wide application areas both in the academic world and in industry. The place and importance of machine learning in computer science education is increasing, and students gain in-depth knowledge and skills in analytical thinking, problem solving and data science.

Figure 1. Machine learning fields of study (Wahid 2017)

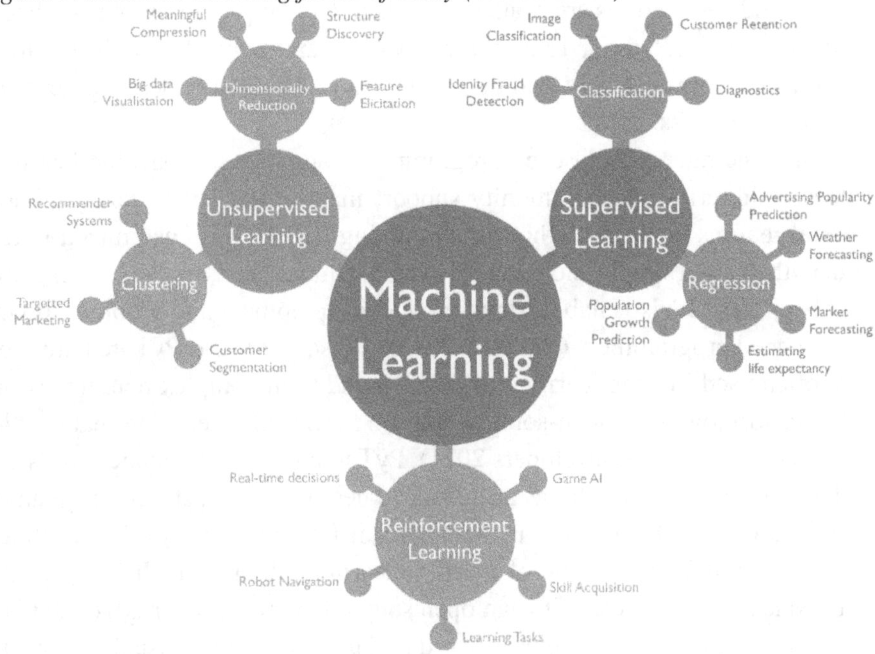

Machine learning deals with the development of algorithms and models that aim to learn from data. In Figure 1, a few of the fields of machine learning are presented visually. Only through this figure can one observe the wide range of fields of study. Machine learning is divided into three main categories: supervised learning, unsupervised learning and reinforcement learning.

In the supervised learning model, the process is managed using labeled data sets. The concept of supervision stems from the need to relate the labeled learning system to training examples (Cunningham, Cord, and Delany 2008). Regression and classification are the most common applications of supervised learning. Using these techniques, learners develop predictive models based on a given data set.

Unsupervised learning is the process of extracting knowledge from unlabeled data. Clustering and dimensionality reduction techniques are used to discover underlying structures and patterns in the data. There are some advantages over supervised learning (Dike et al. 2018).

Reinforcement learning allows agents to learn by interacting with a reward system. This technique is used especially in areas such as robotics and game theory. This learning model is based on some behaviors in human psychology (Wiering and Van Otterlo 2012).

It is possible to conduct experiments using machine learning tools and libraries. Many tools and applications are available for this. Popular programming languages and libraries include Python, TensorFlow, PyTorch and Scikit-Learn. These tools make the learning process fast and efficient with rapid product development and trial-and-error processes.

Python is the most widely used programming language for machine learning. Its extensive libraries and community support make it ideal for students. There are several reasons why the Python programming language is customized in this section. Python has a simple and readable syntax, which speeds up the learning process for beginners. It also enables rapid product development and problem solving for experienced programmers (Raschka 2015). TensorFlow and PyTorch are tools that are often used in deep learning to develop and train complex neural network models. TensorFlow is an open-source platform for machine learning that enables end-to-end development (Developers 2021). PyTorch is used for image processing as well as machine learning. It has an advanced neural network structure (Imambi, Prakash, and Kanagachidambaresan 2021). Scikit-Learn is a Python-based library that allows easy implementation of machine learning algorithms. It is frequently used for educational purposes. It is an open source library (Kramer 2016). Jupyter Notebook is an open-source, browser-based tool used to support visualizations detailing workflows, software code, data and the research process. It helps to create documentation of machine learning experiments and projects (Randles et al. 2017).

2.2. Use of Machine Learning in Education

In education, elements such as student assessment, prediction of student performance, and taking precautions for negative situations as a result of prediction are some of the important steps. In the traditional approach, these processes are carried out only by the teacher. Thanks to the developing technology, this is done with the support of various technological tools. In recent years, this technological situation has gained momentum with machine learning (Kucak, Juricic, and Dambic 2018). With machine learning, it is possible to easily predict a student's performance, take measures for a low performance, or achieve a higher level of success by rewarding. As a result of a prediction modeling for student performance with machine learning, additional lessons or study plans can be arranged for weaknesses (Anozie and Junker 2006). For example, in a study by Anand et al. the groups of students in a programming course were determined with a machine learning approach according to their performance in prerequisite courses, their performance in co-requisite courses, and their performance in current course study results (Anand et al. 2018). In the study by Erdağı and Tunalı, a machine learning-based statistical application was carried out for the assignment of teachers in the Ministry of National Education. A prediction model was created to determine the best candidate based on the data obtained from teachers and to direct them to the school in need (Erdağı and Tunalı 2022).

With machine learning, a consistent assessment and evaluation tool can be created for students. This tool can provide a consistent and effective process of assessment and evaluation (Luckin, Holmes, and Forcier 2016). Machine learning-based assessment can provide teachers and students with information about how students are learning, as well as continuous feedback about the support needed and progress toward learning goals (El-Alfy and Abdel-Aal 2008). Vaculík et al. followed a method for students to acquire and measure a learning outcome. Students were given theoretical information through presentations and animations and supported by exercises. They prepared a questionnaire to test students' knowledge. Finally, they used supervised machine learning algorithms to perform an automatic evaluation of the accuracy of the results (Vaculík et al. 2013). Creating high-quality test sets for the assessment process can be crucial and often requires experts. As a solution, expert-generated tools can be created that take into account the student's previous test solutions to create test sets with better test coverage (Tang et al. 2016).

Achieving a personalized learning goal is very important in the learning process (Alenezi and Faisal 2020). In their study, Whitehill and Seltzer suggested that online learning videos should be presented and evaluated according to students' individual characteristics in order to achieve the goal in an online learning environment supported by video resources (Whitehill and Seltzer 2017). Faisal et al. used a recommendation system to help students choose the best learning plan based on the idea that the learning activity will be different according to the characteristics of each student (Faisal, AlAmeeri, and Alsumait 2015).

3. NATURAL LANGUAGE PROCESSING

3.1. Technical Information for Natural Language Processing

Since natural language processing can be associated with the field of artificial intelligence and the social trend towards artificial intelligence has increased in recent years, it can be stated that it is an important field of study within the scope of the efficiency of computer science education and future planning.

Natural language processing includes stages such as text preprocessing, statistical data generation, tokenization, and language modeling. These stages can create differences for the problem to be solved.

Figure 2. Natural Language Processing tasks (Saleem 2022)

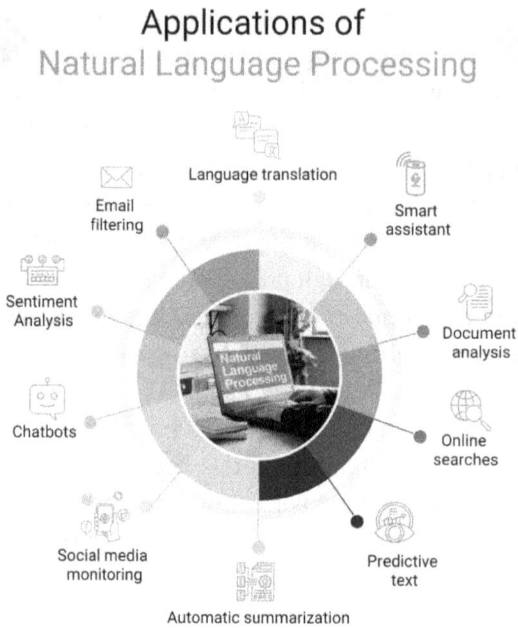

Figure 2 shows a few of the tasks that natural language processing is trying to solve. A lot of work, especially with the support of generative artificial intelligence, has become a trend today.

Although the field of natural language processing seems to work on a text-based basis, in recent years, it has actually been creating various elements by using the power of generative artificial intelligence. It no longer only generates text-based data, but also solves difficult tasks such as grammar checking of the generated text. With the concept of large language model and generative artificial intelligence, problems that were difficult to solve a few years ago can now be solved in seconds (Erdağı 2023).

Text preprocessing is a set of techniques and algorithms used to translate language content into a machine-understandable format and to perform analysis on this translated format. This preprocessing is done in order to organize the complex structure of the language and to remove unnecessary information. Unnecessary information in the text makes it easier to be understood by the machine. An example of this step is converting the letters in the text into lowercase letters. In this way, the distinction between uppercase and lowercase letters in the text will be eliminated and a healthy analysis will be performed (Başkaya and Aydin 2017). A healthier analysis can be performed by the machine by removing punctuation marks in the text. This process can also be done at some points (such as sentence separation or punctuation analysis) by first obtaining information and then performing this step. In some cases, numbers in the text can have a negative impact. Removing these numbers is an example of text preprocessing. Text preprocessing is not only used in natural language processing, but also in a similar field, text mining.

Words as textual expressions do not make sense in natural language processing. The algorithms to be used work on vector structures rather than these structures. In the text preprocessing stage, these text-based data are converted into word vectors. In some cases, threshold values are set in the text. This is used to eliminate the negative effects of a text that is too short or too long. For example, there may be structural difficulties in understanding a sentence that is too long or a sentence that is too short. The process of translating the table structure in the text into plain text is carried out at this stage (Aydoğan and Karci 2019).

The language model can be statistical or artificial intelligence based, which learns the structural situation, grammar and meaning of the language depending on the language used in the natural language processing process and can use this learned situation in subsequent situations (Bellegarda 2004). The basic element here is to understand the text, to produce or predict the text in line with the task given on the text it understands. In the process of performing these operations, language features are used. These features are conveyed in some cases by statistical methods and in some cases by using techniques such as artificial neural networks. The use of models is used in many tasks. For example, in the translation of a text, tasks such as predicting the language, completing the text, predicting the next word are realized with the use of language models.

The increase in the amount of data in research processes can reduce the quality of the research, but it can also affect it positively as it provides a rich content source. The fact that the correct determination of the point sought in a wide range of content is late makes the use of natural language processing techniques inevitable. At this point, elements such as the interpretation of the text, searching on a large-scale text, and the correct identification of the source can be evaluated in this context. The most common example of this is the search engine. Situations such as completing the words in a content written while searching and preparing the content very quickly are provided by these techniques. The use of data in libraries that can be accessed online is similar to search engines. Here, these techniques enable a person to quickly and accurately access a topic within the research in the educational process on a search engine or an online library (Yue et al. 2012).

3.2. Use of Natural Language Processing in Education

The efficiency of the learning process is based on mutual interaction. While this interaction enriches the learning environment and process, it also sheds light on the measurement and evaluation phase to be carried out at the end of the process (Karabilgin and Şahin 2006). However, it is not fully possible to differentiate this feedback situation in the learning process. This is due to the fact that it is difficult to identify all the points where feedback should be provided or that a personalized feedback situation cannot be provided (Sahranç 2013). As a precaution, natural language processing methods can be used to automate the feedback situation in the light of the data obtained. In this way, while a personalized structure is created, an easy structure can be created thanks to this situation created by rule-based or artificial intelligence methods.

Natural Language Processing models have the potential to transform teaching and learning through personalized learning, on-demand support, and other innovative approaches (Odden, Marin, and Rudolph 2021). Natural Language Processing models can be used to analyze and process large amounts of textual data such as academic articles, textbooks, and other course materials. As a result of this analysis, personalized recommendations can be provided to students based on their learning needs and preferences. Educational support and guidance services can be provided to students with Natural Language Processing models. Chatbots and virtual assistants can be used for this process (Fuchs 2023). Erdağı conducted a study using natural language processing techniques to select training for teachers and school administrators. In the study, the similarities between the training contents that can be selected and the knowledge of teachers and school administrators were analyzed with various statistical methods and a recommendation system was prepared (Erdağı 2024).

In the process of evaluating an application or an exam, natural language processing techniques can be used to evaluate spelling errors, grammatical deficiencies, and whether the content is taken from another source or not (Talan and Aktürk 2021).

Since natural language processing focuses on text-based data, it can be used in processes related to questions and answers to questions. Applications such as creating a question by scanning the content, making sense of a created question and determining the scope of the subject, scanning the answer to the question on the content can be evaluated in this context. This application can also be partially applied within the scope of automated feedback. ChatBot applications, which are frequently used not only in the educational environment but also by commercial organizations in recent years, are also created with Natural Language Processing techniques. In this part, it is part of this process that the question of the person gains meaning and the answer is found on a determined content pool and transmitted to the user. In this way, a faster and more efficient response is provided without the need for the user to scan the question. This structure can also be considered within the scope of the educational process and can be used in all processes as a question and answer application (Gupta and Gupta 2012). In addition, the use of these structures in the hybrid model can create a more efficient learning environment by increasing the interaction between the student and the system in the instructor position. For the student, this can create an active learning environment.

In the educational process, the digital resources created often provide important parts of a wide subject scope. A dense text in the material may prevent the material from being efficient. At this point, there is a need for textual summarization of an educational material to be created or a topic to be presented. Summarization studies have become increasingly popular in the field of natural language processing in recent years. Summarization can be done by extracting the context of important sentences and words in the text with statistical methods, as well as by learning the content through a modeling and expressing it in new words with abstraction-based summarization (Pandiaraja et al. 2022). Statistical methods are an easier stage in this context. This is because there is no contextual analysis of the words and vocabulary in the text and no analysis of the text in terms of meaning. With abstractive summarization, it is more difficult to apply all the rules of the language being studied and to create meaningful and contextual text with new words. These techniques can be used in the process of summarizing the resources created in computer science, in an educational material to be created and disseminated. It is possible to summarize a text given in different ways online and offline with a proportional or limited number of words (Mishra et al. 2014). Language differences are important in the formation of the summary. In Erdağı and Tunalı's study, natural language processing techniques were used to summarize news prepared in Turkish language. For the summary, Turkish major vowel harmony, minör vowel harmony and both rules were applied together. A better result was obtained than existing statistical methods (Erdağı and Tunalı 2024).

Murad et al. developed a recommendation system in a learning management system using natural language processing methods. In this recommendation system, demographic structure was used for students, and the elements that would be most useful for the student on the basis of content were presented with text analysis methods (Murad et al. 2018).

4. COMPUTER VISION

4.1. Technical Information for Computer Vision

Computer vision is an important and rapidly developing subfield of computer science. Computer vision involves the process of analyzing, processing and using digital images for various purposes. Computer vision in education enables students to understand, apply and develop this technology (Stockman and Shapiro 2001).

Today, the number of visual materials uploaded to the Internet in the form of personal, medical, scientific and social networks is increasing exponentially. Computer vision gains great importance at this point because it is used to understand the content of images, to identify what people see in one or more images, and to reconstruct features such as shape, illumination and color distributions in the image when necessary (Szeliski 2022). On the other hand, since the image element is frequently used in distance education and online classes, both the image and the video stream need to be of good quality. In this context, recent developments in computer vision and algorithms have provided significant improvements (Jin, Tan, and Jiang 2020).

Object recognition and object detection applications can be developed using computer vision techniques. Such projects play an important role especially in security systems, automated driving technologies and robotics applications. Medical image processing covers techniques for analyzing and processing medical images. Facial recognition technologies are widely used in security and user authentication systems. Computer vision techniques also find wide application in the fields of art and entertainment. Creative applications can be developed by working on projects such as photo editing, digital image creation and visual effects (Szeliski 2022).

Figure 3. How computer vision works (Turing 2024)

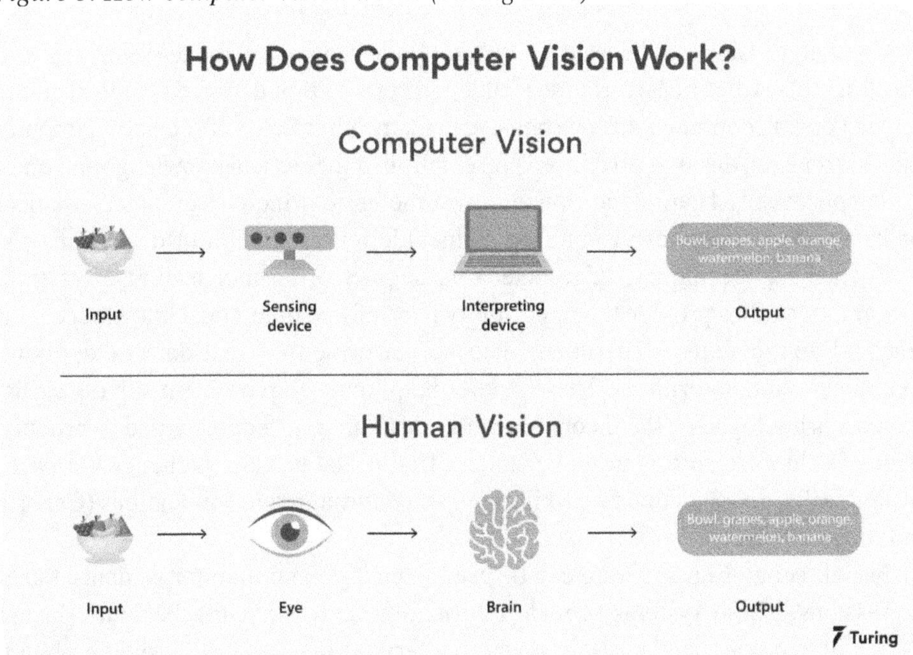

Figure 3 compares the basic working principle of computer vision algorithms with human vision. Computer vision involves the processing of digital images using various techniques and algorithms. Image representation refers to the expression of images as pixel matrices. Each pixel has a specific color and intensity value. The association of pixels creates the image. Image filtering is the techniques used for noise reduction, edge detection, and various image enhancement processes, which are unwanted elements in the image or other elements outside the image that are trying to be reached. Edge detection is used to detect important structural features in images. Its most important purpose is the detection of intensity changes (R. Sun et al. 2022). Segmentation is the process of dividing the image into meaningful parts or objects. In this way, the image is fragmented and meaningful parts are obtained. Feature extraction is the extraction and analysis of certain features from images. This analysis helps to reveal meaningful parts and wholes on an image (Nixon and Aguado 2019). Various tools and platforms used in computer vision education enable the translation of theoretical knowledge into practice. OpenCV is a popular library for image processing and computer vision. It can be used in various programming languages such as Python and C++ (Bradski and Kaehler 2008).

4.2. Use of Computer Vision in Education

Computer vision can be used not as a tool but as a goal in the teaching process. Teaching this structure as a course enables the production of various tools that can help not only in computer science but also in many other fields of science. Computer vision is realized through a balanced presentation of theoretical knowledge and practical applications. Theoretical courses cover the basic principles and mathematical background of computer vision. Topics include representation of digital images, basic filtering techniques, edge detection, segmentation and feature extraction. Laboratory studies provide the opportunity to reinforce theoretical knowledge with practical applications. Experiments can be performed on real data by applying computer vision algorithms. These studies help to develop problem solving skills. Projects bring together the theoretical and practical knowledge learned to produce original solutions. In this way, the student first needs to gain mathematical background skills, and then practical skills are gained through real applications (Cazorla and Viejo 2015).

Facial recognition software can be used to capture and monitor students' facial expressions. These systems provide information about students' behavior during the learning process and allow teachers to intervene in case of a possible problem. This can be used not only for negative situations, but also for analyzing the student's positive reactions. It can allow the investigation of the emotional state of the student (Akgun and Greenhow 2022).

Deniz et al. aimed to reduce the time spent by teachers for attendance with the face recognition system and mood analysis they developed. They also integrated an emotion recognition model so that teachers can better monitor students' emotional states in the educational environment. The negativity in a student's emotional state is analyzed instantly with image processing methods and allows the teacher to take precautions or intervene (Deniz et al. 2019).

Figure 4. Instant face detection during class with computer vision (Deniz et al. 2019)

In the visual in Figure 4, the faces of four different students were detected during the lesson, allowing the emotion detection of the students.

Zheng developed an application on human robot interaction to ensure language development in multilingual classrooms. He conducted a study on models such as computer vision and deep learning as a solution to the problem of students' lack of self-confidence in language skills lessons. In this way, students' mouth movements in speaking skills were detected instantaneously and the students' skills were improved with guiding corrections (Zheng 2023).

Although technological developments applied in online assessments are positive in terms of educational environments, negative practices such as cheating and academic plagiarism are experienced due to the lack of an adequate control system to prevent negative situations that may occur in such applications. For this reason, applications have been created in which students can analyze facial expressions and many types of objects can be identified to obtain real-time information and draw conclusions from the situation (Pezoa and Domínguez 2017).

Various applications such as face detection of the student in front of the computer and tracking eye movements can be realized. In addition to face detection, gesture detection and object detection can be used within the framework of this application. Méndez-Ortega et al. conducted a study on this problem by using research questions such as copying an online exam and transferring it directly to another student, copying online courses, and using computer vision for cheating in online assessment (Méndez-Ortega et al. 2021).

Figure 5. General view of the bibliometric map generated from Scopus data (Sophokleous et al. 2021)

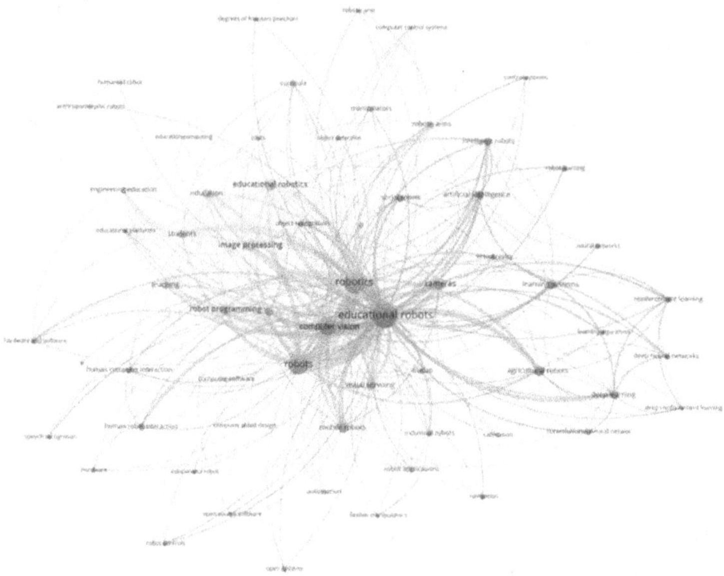

Figure 5 shows a bibliometric map based on two criteria, computer vision and educational robotics, created by Sophokleous et al. The lines between the concepts reveal their similarity. The map focuses on the concepts of computer vision, robotics and educational robotics. This map shows that computer vision can have a very wide place in the educational environment, even though it is limited to robotics (Sophokleous et al. 2021).

5. GENERATIVE ARTIFICIAL INTELLIGENCE

5.1. Technical Information for Generative Artificial Intelligence

Generative artificial intelligence is an artificial intelligence system that can create new and original content using various data sources (Goodfellow et al. 2014). Due to the high quality of the data obtained with generative artificial intelligence, it has become almost indistinguishable from man-made works. The latest advances in machine learning and deep learning, prediction models, classifications or recommendations created within the scope of traditional methods are almost ready to be replaced by realistic applications created with generative artificial intelligence.

Figure 6. Conceptual structure of generative aritificial intelligence (Banh and Strobel 2023)

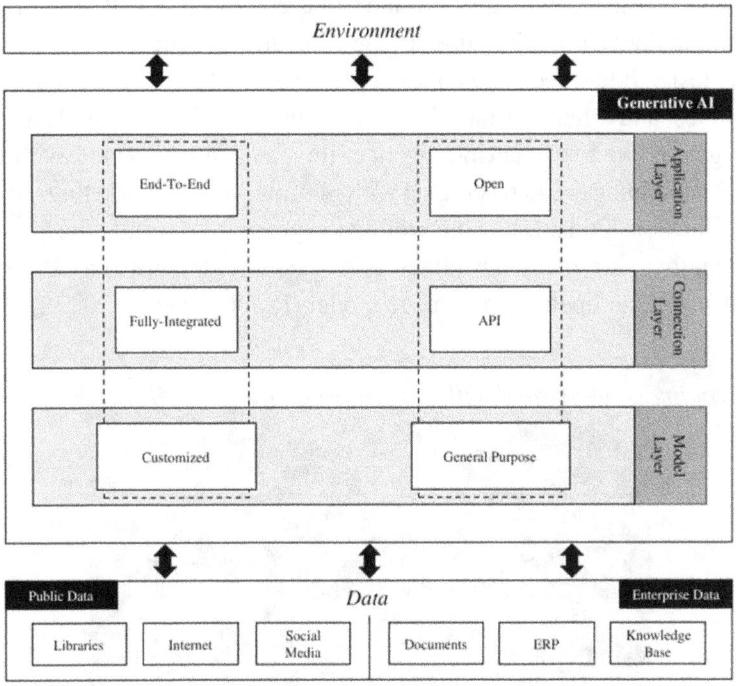

One of the biggest advantages of generative artificial intelligence models is that they enable the development of new business models and applications without the need to train them from scratch (Burström et al. 2021). The reason why it does not need to be trained from scratch is that generative artificial intelligence models are trained beforehand and the structure called fine-tuning enables performance and expectation to be increased by correcting and updating. At this point, there are opportunities for many different tasks on environments such as Hugging Face. Figure 6 presents the conceptual structure of the implementation process of generative artificial intelligence (Banh and Strobel 2023).

Textual studies with generative artificial intelligence enable text generation and natural language processing applications to be performed on the generated text. The task expected to be realized here is to create a human-like written text or to perform subtasks on a created text in a similar way to human experiences. ChatGPT, produced by OpenAI, is in the form of a chatbot that mimics textual conversations with the user and can direct the progress of the text like a human dialog (Achiam et al. 2023). ChatGPT is a large language model. It can be used for various natural language processing tasks such as text completion, text generation and language translation.

The texts produced feed many fields. The texts produced for many fields such as marketing, education, etc. show a satisfactory performance that is indistinguishable from human-made texts (Mondal, Das, and Vrana 2023). The ChatGPT infrastructure includes a transformer architecture, a type of neural network for natural language processing tasks. It has been and continues to be trained on a large text dataset from books, articles, and other text-based sources online (Baidoo-Anu and Ansah 2023).

Using generative artificial intelligence, images can be created with the clues given. Synthetic images can be created with minimal cost in marketing, advertising, design and fashion. Considering the production process, cost and time to achieve the same image, there are many advantages. For example, images can be created with Stable Diffusion, an open source image model (Rombach et al. 2022).

Figure 7. An image generated with generative artificial intelligence

The image generator in Figure 7 was created using artificial intelligence. "A serene cherry blossom park in full bloom with petals gently falling into a meandering stream." was entered as text and the image was created. The image was created with clue words and phrases entered using Copilot Designer.

The success of generative artificial intelligence in image creation has now been replaced by video. In the past few years, videos have been produced from text using generative artificial intelligence. What is interesting here is that these videos and the pictures in the video have never been put together before. Considering the time it takes to shoot a 10-second video and the subsequent production costs, a video created with just a few words and phrases can be considered revolutionary (Esser et al. 2023). The videos created can be for entertainment purposes or for sales-marketing, training and customer support. Professional videos can be created with virtual avatars and synthetic voiceovers on many platforms.

With generative artificial intelligence, difficult tasks such as code generation and code error detection can be done easily in the field of software development in recent years. Models such as CodeBERT (Feng et al. 2020) are trained to generate source code using natural language for software programming. Given hints about the desired software or module, code generation can be achieved in almost any language. This is both advantageous and disadvantageous for a software development specialist. The possible narrowing of the employment area can be seen as a disadvantage. In software development processes, the use of these tools for speed and performance enhancing processes can also be seen as an advantageous point. With GitHub Copilot, which is integrated into Visual Studio, automatically written code fragments can be created, a code fragment can be completed, unit tests can be created, and bug fixing tasks can be performed (J. Sun et al. 2022).

Sound materials can be created using generative artificial intelligence. Generated voice materials are getting closer and closer to the human voice. In particular, tasks that can be difficult in synthetic vocalization, such as stress and intonation, can now be easily performed using natural language processing techniques. Audio material production can be used to support a variety of applications such as digital assistants, customer service operations, music production, audiobook creation, and access tools (Moussawi, Koufaris, and Benbunan-Fich 2021). Considering the process and production costs for this process when the music element is used in many areas, it is conceivable that in the very near future this data can be generated entirely by generative artificial intelligence.

5.2. Use of Generative Artificial Intelligence in Education

Generative artificial intelligence can offer different education methods in line with the individual needs of students. It can dynamically produce content according to the student's interests, abilities and expectations. In this way, students can manage the learning process at their own pace (Baker, Smith, and Anissa 2019). Chen et al. showed that a conversational tool built with generative artificial intelligence can provide students with personalized mathematics lessons that can provide better learning outcomes than traditional methods. The tool was able to provide appropriate explanations that could address students' misconceptions and adapt to students' level of understanding (Chen, Chen, and Heffernan 2020).

A measurement and evaluation system can be created with generative artificial intelligence. An automated assessment system can be created provided that certain boundaries are drawn for a test instrument or an open-ended question. In the study by Kim et al. a model was trained with generative artificial intelligence on a dataset of essays evaluated by humans. This model was then applied to essays written by high school students and as a result, a high success rate of 0.86 was obtained. The model was able to identify the key features of a well-written essay and provided feedback similar to human evaluations (Kim, Park, and Lee 2019).

While language translation was a difficult task a few years ago, it is now an advanced task, especially thanks to improved language models and attention mechanisms. Johnson et al. used a dataset of bilingual sentence pairs and trained a generative artificial intelligence-based model on this dataset. The study showed that the model can understand the meaning of sentences in one language and translate them correctly into another language (Johnson et al. 2017).

Generative artificial intelligence makes it easy to create course material, exam questions and projects. Models such as GPT offer various examples and ideas on many topics. This convenience can be used in many ways such as generating data, realizing projects, and generating ideas in the educational process (Brown et al. 2020).

Generative artificial intelligence can provide students with various problem scenarios and help them find solutions. This improves the student's problem solving skills. Applications such as code completion and error correction on code are example applications for generative artificial intelligence. Students receive great support for the software development process (Becker et al. 2023).

Figure 8. Number of academic studies on generative artificial intelligence in education (Bahroun et al. 2023)

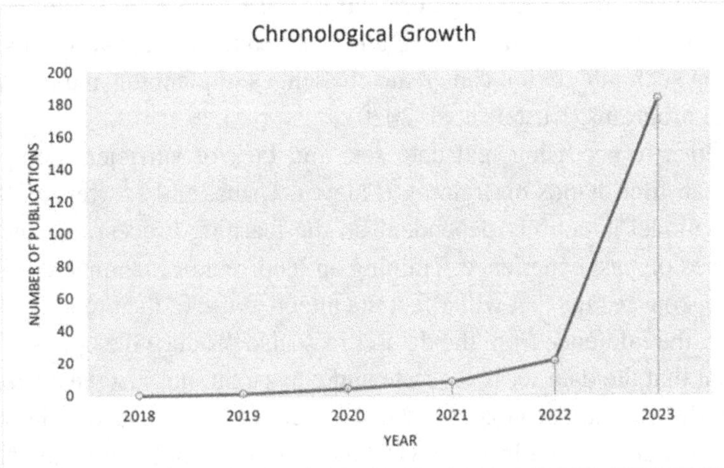

The graph in Figure 8 shows the development of academic studies on the use of generative artificial intelligence in education over the years. Especially since the end of 2022, there has been a great increase in studies thanks to the accelerated increase in technological developments (Bahroun et al. 2023). By 2024, it would be quite simple to predict that this number will be much higher.

6. CHALLENGES FOR ARTIFICIAL INTELLIGENCE

While the rapid development of artificial intelligence technologies offers great opportunities in computer science education, it also brings with it various challenges. These challenges range from teaching methods to ethical issues, from infrastructure deficiencies to faculty training.

As developers in education or future adopters of artificial intelligence technology may have a direct role in shaping society, it is important to recognize and address challenges in this area. This includes ethical design of artificial intelligence algorithms, mitigating risks in the results obtained through artificial intelligence applications, and improving data collection and other research practices (Borenstein and Howard 2021).

New techniques and tools are constantly being developed in artificial intelligence and its sub-fields, requiring continuous updating of machine learning curricula or content that uses machine learning as a tool. This represents a serious challenge for educational institutions, as it is not always easy to quickly change and approve academic curricula (Goode, Chapman, and Margolis 2012). Artificial intelligence is in the field of collaboration with various disciplines such as mathematics, statistics, computer science, and ethics. Therefore, it is necessary to adopt an interdisciplinary approach to provide effective artificial intelligence education. However, ensuring and coordinating such integration can create challenges in planning and implementing educational programs (Kusters et al. 2020).

Difficulties in accessing real data sets and lack of sufficient computational resources can limit hands-on training (Paleyes, Urma, and Lawrence 2022). The supervised model is entirely dependent on the learning process and the datasets created based on past experience. Training an incorrect or incomplete dataset may lead to erroneous results that will affect the intended use of the proposed approach. In this case, the inference from the dataset may also produce the opposite result. It is important that the data set is accurate and consistent, not just the correct choice of model (Alenezi and Faisal 2020). Various technological inadequacies may arise when data sets are created in the environment. For example, in an application to be performed with face recognition, the student's face cannot be fully captured, the distance cannot be adjusted correctly, a problematic data may occur, and the subsequent application may produce incorrect results. For this part, situations such as the student wearing glasses, coloring his/her hair, wearing a hat, etc. may cause the data not to be taken (Hwang et al. 2020).

When GPT was first published, it was revealed that the training data consisted of a wide range of sources such as books, online blog posts, etc. obtained by scrapping method, including personal data (Wu, Duan, and Ni 2024). Since these data are still in the process of education and scrapping, there is a great doubt whether they contain personal data or not. It is not clear whether permission is obtained from the people related to these data. In fact, it does not seem very possible to obtain this approval within this method. The collection and use of back-end data as input in productive artificial intelligence must be in full compliance with the laws of the country (El-Mahamdi et al. 2023).

Although artificial intelligence applications have benefits for all fields, they also have social and ethical problems. Various explanations have been made by the famous scientist Stephan Hawking about this problem. Especially in the educational environment, this situation can cause problems both in the data dimension and in the process dimension. Artificial intelligence applications may cause the prejudice and discrimination of the existing system to continue. Because the application will be fed from the existing data, it may cause a situation involving a possible bias to continue. These prejudices may include racism, the continuation of the perspective towards disadvantaged students, unfair and inequality practices (Ali et al. 2019). One of the biggest ethical issues regarding the use of artificial intelligence in K-12 education is privacy. Since artificial intelligence applications are fed by data, the storage and processing of these data in an application for current students is seen as a privacy problem. On the other hand, taking their faces in computer vision applications for students and not knowing how this data is used with third-party programs that cannot be intervened is a big problem (Akgun and Greenhow 2022). Generative artificial intelligence models are only as good as the data they are trained on, and if the training data contains bias, the model will be biased. For example, if the model is trained on a dataset consisting primarily of content written by students from a certain demographic group, it may not be able to correctly evaluate content written by students from other demographic groups (D'Mello et al. 2014).

When ChatGPT and other generative artificial intelligence-based models are not capable of providing the same level of human interaction as a real teacher or trainer, this can lead to a lack of interaction. This can be a disadvantage for students who want to not only connect with the teacher in an educational sense, but also emotionally connect with the teacher and gain an advantage in a more educational environment. In a study conducted by D'Mello et al. 2014, students who interacted with a virtual tutor with human-like emotional behavior had better learning outcomes than students who interacted with a virtual tutor without this behavior (D'Mello et al. 2014).

7. IMPACT OF ARTIFICIAL INTELLIGENCE IN COMPUTER SCIENCE EDUCATION CURRICULUM

Artificial intelligence support in computer science education requires a comprehensive and structured curriculum. This curriculum balances theoretical knowledge with practical applications to provide students with an in-depth understanding of the subject. Theoretical courses in artificial intelligence cover the basic principles, algorithms and mathematical background of artificial intelligence. These courses enable students to learn how algorithms work, which algorithms to use in which situations and how to evaluate the performance of these algorithms. Practical applications give students the opportunity to apply their theoretical knowledge to real-world problems. Students experience model development, training and evaluation processes by working on data sets. Artificial intelligence-based projects encourage students to work independently and develop creative solutions. The computer science education community has made progress in developing the necessary infrastructure for comprehensive computer science education. Several computer science curriculum standards have been published. A framework was created by bringing stakeholders together to create a document intended to guide standards and curriculum developers (K-12 Computer Science Framework Steering Committee 2016).

In the near future, as more and more artificial intelligence-based products and services will emerge, knowledge of artificial intelligence and computer science will be the basis for careers in many professions. This is especially the case when computer science education is updated in accordance with the changing trend of technology (Kandlhofer et al. 2016). Artificial intelligence technologies are increasingly being used to keep pace with innovations in this field and to provide students with the skills they need to become future technologists. In computer science education, artificial intelligence-oriented studies play an important role in updating the curriculum (Passey 2017).

Computer Science educators generally believe that hands-on experience in a computer laboratory environment is an effective way for students to gain experience. In addition to traditional methods such as textbook support and classroom environment, hands-on practice can provide students with insight into science methods, research practices, and experimental methodology (Shana and Abulibdeh 2020). There are studies showing that conducting experimental work in a laboratory environment provides positive development on students and increases motivation for effective learning (Taylor et al. 2013).

For the curriculum study on the use of artificial intelligence in the educational environment, Kandlhofer et al. presented steps such as presenting topics in a fun way to raise awareness, acquiring the theoretical knowledge underlying certain artificial intelligence topics and problem solving, obtaining data and advancing the theoretical knowledge of artificial intelligence, and finally solving high-level abstract problems with artificial intelligence. Experimental studies were conducted in each module and it was revealed that it would be efficient to present this model as a hybrid with innovative educational methods such as discovery learning, inquiry learning, collaborative learning, problem-based learning, project-based learning, storytelling, peer teaching (Kandlhofer et al. 2016).

Generative artificial intelligence is fed from various data sources and generates new elements. This field can be used to create curricula and subject coverage. Apart from the traditional curriculum structure, it can be used to create a personalized structure and determine the subject scope. Examples in the subject content can provide fast and accurate generation of elements such as text, visuals and audio. Instead of classical tools for the measurement and evaluation methods brought by the curriculum, artificial intelligence can be used for project-based or multi-domain structures. The evaluation processes of homework, projects or exams can be used as an efficient tool provided that the boundaries are determined. It will be a great advantage for the trainer to use these tools for difficulties in finding a sample or for an enriched environment. The fact that the sources that the generative artificial intelligence feeds on are dynamic will ensure that the curriculum progresses quickly and accurately (Liu et al. 2024).

Although the current structural situation for computer science education varies according to the policies of the countries, the consensus is that artificial intelligence needs to be integrated into the curriculum to a large extent. In the study by Proctor et al. on this subject, it was envisaged that the existing elective courses should be reduced in order to add courses related to artificial intelligence and its sub-fields as compulsory for the integration process, but this was also negatively received by some communities (Proctor, Bigman, and Blikstein 2019).

The concept of visualization has an important place in computer science education. Visualizing and conveying abstract concepts can be seen as an important task. For this task, integrating machine learning and generative artificial intelligence algorithms based on data into the curriculum can produce satisfactory results (Naps et al. 2002).

8. CONCLUSION

In this section, technical information on machine learning, natural language processing, computer vision and generative artificial intelligence, examples of their use in the educational environment, challenges related to the use of artificial intelligence and its sub-fields, and the impact of artificial intelligence on the curriculum of computer science education are discussed.

Since artificial intelligence and its sub-fields are still evolving, it is necessary to conduct continuous research on new trend studies in order to keep up to date technical knowledge. It is important to use this research not only for theoretical knowledge but also for practical application. Especially with generative artificial intelligence, which is the most recent and open to development in terms of using large language models, studies can be carried out using many materials. Tasks that were very difficult only a few years ago, such as audio, video, text generation, language recognition, language translation, data comparison, can now be accomplished in a very short time with high performance.

In addition to the positive aspects of artificial intelligence, there are also various challenges. Confidentiality and privacy issues in the process of obtaining data and the bias that may occur during data processing are just a few of these challenges. These challenges have been identified as issues that require measures to be taken at the level of countries and even unions with the developing technology. Failure to adapt to the developing technology, lack of allocation of sufficient resources and the possibility of lack of expert training in this field are just a few of the problems.

All models related to artificial intelligence and its sub-fields are used in educational environments today. It is used in many fields even outside computer science education. The fact that it has a wide range of uses creates an environment that will continuously feed it. It is inevitable that developments in educational environments and developments in artificial intelligence technologies affect each other. Despite the developing technology, it is necessary to make arrangements in educational environments and to update the curriculum contents. In the current structure, the fact that many countries keep the issue on the agenda with their strategic documents, opening departments in universities and encouraging academic development are seen as positive news. However, in undeveloped countries or communities where this integration is difficult, this situation is seen as a negative situation.

REFERENCES

Achiam, J., Adler, S., Agarwal, S., Ahmad, L., Akkaya, I., Aleman, F. L., Almeida, D., Altenschmidt, J., Altman, S., Anadkat, S., & Associates. (2023). 'Gpt-4 Technical Report'. *arXiv Preprint arXiv:2303.08774*.

Akgun, S., & Greenhow, C. (2022). 'Artificial Intelligence in Education: Addressing Ethical Challenges in K-12 Settings'. *AI and Ethics*, 2(3), 431–440. DOI: 10.1007/s43681-021-00096-7 PMID: 34790956

Alenezi, H. S., & Faisal, M. H. (2020). 'Utilizing Crowdsourcing and Machine Learning in Education: Literature Review'. *Education and Information Technologies*, 25(4), 2971–2986. DOI: 10.1007/s10639-020-10102-w

Ali, H., Murad, S., & Shah, Z. (2023). Spot the Fake Lungs: Generating Synthetic Medical Images Using Neural Diffusion Models. In Longo, L., & O'Reilly, R. (Eds.), *Artificial Intelligence and Cognitive Science* (pp. 32–39). Springer Nature Switzerland. DOI: 10.1007/978-3-031-26438-2_3

Ali, S., Payne, B. H., Williams, R., Park, H. W., & Breazeal, C. (2019, June). Constructionism, ethics, and creativity: Developing primary and middle school artificial intelligence education. In International workshop on education in artificial intelligence k-12 (eduai'19) (Vol. 2, pp. 1-4). mit media lab Palo Alto, California.

Anand, V. K., Abdul Rahiman, S. K., Ben George, E., & Huda, A. S. 2018. 'Recursive Clustering Technique for Students' Performance Evaluation in Programming Courses'. Pp. 1–5 in *2018 Majan International Conference (MIC)*. DOI: 10.1109/MINTC.2018.8363153

Anozie, N., & Junker, B. W. (2006, July). Predicting end-of-year accountability assessment scores from monthly student records in an online tutoring system. Educational Data Mining: Papers from the AAAI Workshop. Menlo Park, CA: AAAI Press.

Aydoğan, M., & Karcı, A. (2019). Kelime temsil yöntemleri ile kelime benzerliklerinin incelenmesi. Çukurova Üniversitesi Mühendislik-Mimarlık Fakültesi Dergisi, 34(2), 181-196.

Bahroun, Z., Anane, C., Ahmed, V., & Zacca, A. (2023). 'Transforming Education: A Comprehensive Review of Generative Artificial Intelligence in Educational Settings through Bibliometric and Content Analysis'. *Sustainability (Basel)*, 15(17), 12983. DOI: 10.3390/su151712983

Baidoo-Anu, D., & Ansah, L. O. (2023). Education in the era of generative artificial intelligence (AI): Understanding the potential benefits of ChatGPT in promoting teaching and learning. *Journal of AI*, 7(1), 52–62.

Baker, T., Smith, L., & Anissa, N. (2019). *Exploring the Future of Artificial Intelligence in Schools and Colleges*. NESTA.

Banh, L., & Strobel, G. (2023). 'Generative Artificial Intelligence'. *Electronic Markets*, 33(1), 63. DOI: 10.1007/s12525-023-00680-1

Başkaya, F., & Aydin, İ. (2017, September). Haber metinlerinin farkli metin madenciliği yöntemleriyle siniflandirilmasi. In *2017 International Artificial Intelligence and Data Processing Symposium (IDAP)* (pp. 1-5). IEEE.

Becker, B. A., Denny, P., Finnie-Ansley, J., Luxton-Reilly, A., Prather, J., & Santos, E. A. (2023, March). Programming is hard-or at least it used to be: Educational opportunities and challenges of ai code generation. In *Proceedings of the 54th ACM Technical Symposium on Computer Science Education* V. 1 (pp. 500-506).

Bellegarda, J. R. (2004). 'Statistical Language Model Adaptation: Review and Perspectives'. *Speech Communication*, 42(1), 93–108. DOI: 10.1016/j.specom.2003.08.002

Borenstein, J., & Howard, A. (2021). 'Emerging Challenges in AI and the Need for AI Ethics Education'. *AI and Ethics*, 1(1), 61–65. DOI: 10.1007/s43681-020-00002-7 PMID: 38624388

Bradski, G., & Kaehler, A. (2008). *Learning OpenCV: Computer Vision with the OpenCV Library*. O'Reilly Media, Inc.

Brown, T. B., Mann, B., Ryder, N., Subbiah, M., Kaplan, J. D., Dhariwal, P., Neelakantan, A., Shyam, P., Sastry, G., & Askell, A. (2020). Language Models Are Few-Shot Learners. *Advances in Neural Information Processing Systems*.

Burström, T., Parida, V., Lahti, T., & Wincent, J. (2021). 'AI-Enabled Business-Model Innovation and Transformation in Industrial Ecosystems: A Framework, Model and Outline for Further Research'. *Journal of Business Research*, 127, 85–95. DOI: 10.1016/j.jbusres.2021.01.016

Cazorla, M., & Viejo, D. (2015). 'JavaVis: An Integrated Computer Vision Library for Teaching Computer Vision'. *Computer Applications in Engineering Education*, 23(2), 258–267. DOI: 10.1002/cae.21594

Chen, Y., Chen, Y., & Heffernan, N. (2020). Personalized math tutoring with a conversational agent. arXiv preprint arXiv:2012.12121.

Cunningham, P., Cord, M., & Delany, S. J. (2008). Supervised Learning. In Cord, M., & Cunningham, P. (Eds.), *Machine Learning Techniques for Multimedia: Case Studies on Organization and Retrieval* (pp. 21–49). Springer. DOI: 10.1007/978-3-540-75171-7_2

D'Mello, S., Craig, S., Witherspoon, A., & Graesser, A. (2014). 'Affective and Learning-Related Dynamics during Interactions with an Intelligent Tutoring System'. *International Journal of Human-Computer Studies*, 72(6), 415–435.

Deniz, S., Lee, D., Kurian, G., Altamirano, L., Yee, D., Ferra, M., . . . Oh, P. (2019, January). Computer vision for attendance and emotion analysis in school settings. In 2019 IEEE 9th Annual Computing and Communication Workshop and Conference (CCWC) (pp. 0134-0139). IEEE.

Developers, TensorFlow. 2021. 'TensorFlow'. Zenodo. DOI: 10.5281/zenodo.4758419

Dike, H. U., Zhou, Y., Deveerasetty, K. K., & Wu, Q. 2018. 'Unsupervised Learning Based On Artificial Neural Network: A Review'. Pp. 322–27 in *2018 IEEE International Conference on Cyborg and Bionic Systems (CBS)*. Shenzhen: IEEE. DOI: 10.1109/CBS.2018.8612259

El-Alfy, E.-S. M., & Abdel-Aal, R. E. (2008). 'Construction and Analysis of Educational Tests Using Abductive Machine Learning'. *Computers & Education*, 51(1), 1–16. DOI: 10.1016/j.compedu.2007.03.003

El-Mahamdi, E., S. Farhadkhani, R. Guerraoui, and others. 2023. 'On the Impossible Safety of Large Language Models'.

El Naqa, I., & Murphy, M. J. (2015). What Is Machine Learning? In El Naqa, I., Li, R., & Murphy, M. J. (Eds.), *Machine Learning in Radiation Oncology: Theory and Applications* (pp. 3–11). Springer International Publishing. DOI: 10.1007/978-3-319-18305-3_1

Erdağı, E. 2023. 'Bilgisayar Bilimi Eğitiminde Doğal Dil İşleme'. Pp. 205–18 in *Teoriden Uygulamaya Bilgisayar Bilimi Eğitimi*. Ankara: Nobel Akademik Yayıncılık.

Erdağı, E. (2024). 'A Model for Automating Course Selection for Teachers and Managers with Natural Language Processing Methods'. 9(2).

Erdağı, E., & Tunalı, V. (2022). 'Assignment of Part-Time Teachers in the Ministry of National Education with Artificial Learning Techniques'.

Erdağı, E., & Tunalı, V. (2024) 'Comparison of Feature-Based Sentence Ranking Methods for Extractive Summarization of Turkish News Texts'. *Sigma Journal of Engineering and Natural Sciences – Sigma Mühendislik ve Fen Bilimleri Dergisi* 321–34. .DOI: 10.14744/sigma.2023.00076

Esser, P., Chiu, J., Atighehchian, P., Granskog, J., & Germanidis, A. (2023). Structure and content-guided video synthesis with diffusion models. In *Proceedings of the IEEE/CVF International Conference on Computer Vision* (pp. 7346-7356).

Faisal, M. H., AlAmeeri, A. W., & Alsumait, A. A. (2015, December). An adaptive e-learning framework: crowdsourcing approach. In *Proceedings of the 17th International Conference on Information Integration and Web-based Applications & Services* (pp. 1-5).

Feng, Z., Guo, D., Tang, D., Duan, N., Feng, X., Gong, M., . . . Zhou, M. (2020). Codebert: A pre-trained model for programming and natural languages. arXiv preprint arXiv:2002.08155.

Fuchs, K. (2023). Exploring the Opportunities and Challenges of NLP Models in Higher Education: Is Chat GPT a Blessing or a Curse? *Frontiers in Education*, 8, 1166682. DOI: 10.3389/feduc.2023.1166682

Goode, J., Chapman, G., & Margolis, J. (2012). 'Beyond Curriculum: The Exploring Computer Science Program'. *ACM Inroads*, 3(2), 47–53. DOI: 10.1145/2189835.2189851

Goodfellow, I., Pouget-Abadie, J., Mirza, M., Xu, B., Warde-Farley, D., Ozair, S., & Bengio, Y. (2014). Generative adversarial nets. *Advances in Neural Information Processing Systems*, •••, 27.

Gupta, P., & Gupta, V. (2012). 'A Survey of Text Question Answering Techniques'. *International Journal of Computer Applications*, 53(4), 1–8. DOI: 10.5120/8406-2030

Hwang, G.-J., Xie, H., Wah, B. W., & Gašević, D. (2020). 'Vision, Challenges, Roles and Research Issues of Artificial Intelligence in Education'. *Computers and Education: Artificial Intelligence*, 1, 100001. DOI: 10.1016/j.caeai.2020.100001

Imambi, S., Prakash, K. B., & Kanagachidambaresan, G. R. (2021). PyTorch. In Prakash, K. B., & Kanagachidambaresan, G. R. (Eds.), *Programming with TensorFlow: Solution for Edge Computing Applications* (pp. 87–104). Springer International Publishing. DOI: 10.1007/978-3-030-57077-4_10

Jin, L., Tan, F., & Jiang, S. (2020). 'Generative Adversarial Network Technologies and Applications in Computer Vision'. *Computational Intelligence and Neuroscience*, 1459107(1), 1–17. DOI: 10.1155/2020/1459107 PMID: 32802024

Johnson, M., Schuster, M., Le, Q. V., Krikun, M., Wu, Y., Chen, Z., Thorat, N., Viégas, F., Wattenberg, M., Corrado, G., Hughes, M., & Dean, J. (2017). 'Google's Multilingual Neural Machine Translation System: Enabling Zero-Shot Translation'. *Transactions of the Association for Computational Linguistics*, 5, 339–351. DOI: 10.1162/tacl_a_00065

K-12 Computer Science Framework Steering Committee. (2016). *K-12 Computer Science Framework. Technical Report*. Association for Computing Machinery.

Kandlhofer, M., Steinbauer, G., Hirschmugl-Gaisch, S., & Huber, P. (2016, October). Artificial intelligence and computer science in education: From kindergarten to university. In 2016 IEEE frontiers in education conference (FIE) (pp. 1-9). IEEE.

Karabilgin, Ö. S., & Şahin, H. (2006). 'Eğitim Etkinliğini Değerlendirmede Öğrenci Geri Bildiriminin Kullanımı'. *Tıp Eğitimi Dünyası*, 21(21), 27–33.

Kim, S., Park, J., & Lee, H. (2019). 'Automated Essay Scoring Using a Deep Learning Model'. *Journal of Educational Technology Development and Exchange*, 2(1), 1–17.

Kramer, O. (2016). Scikit-Learn. In Kramer, O. (Ed.), *Machine Learning for Evolution Strategies* (pp. 45–53). Springer International Publishing.

Kucak, D., Juricic, V., & Dambic, G. 2018. 'Machine Learning in Education - a Survey of Current Research Trends'. Pp. 0406–10 in *DAAAM Proceedings*. Vol. 1, edited by B. Katalinic. DAAAM International Vienna. DOI: 10.2507/29th.daaam.proceedings.059

Kusters, R., Misevic, D., Berry, H., Cully, A., Le Cunff, Y., Dandoy, L., Díaz-Rodríguez, N., Ficher, M., Grizou, J., Othmani, A., Palpanas, T., Komorowski, M., Loiseau, P., Frier, C. M., Nanini, S., Quercia, D., Sebag, M., Fogelman, F. S., Taleb, S., & Wehbi, F. (2020). 'Interdisciplinary Research in Artificial Intelligence: Challenges and Opportunities'. *Frontiers in Big Data*, 3, 577974. Advance online publication. DOI: 10.3389/fdata.2020.577974 PMID: 33693418

Liu, R., Zenke, C., Liu, C., Holmes, A., Thornton, P., & Malan, D. J. (2024, March). Teaching CS50 with AI: leveraging generative artificial intelligence in computer science education. In *Proceedings of the 55th ACM Technical Symposium on Computer Science Education* V. 1 (pp. 750-756).

Luckin, R., & Holmes, W. (2016). Intelligence unleashed: An argument for AI in education.

Méndez-Ortega, M. G., Herrera-Granda, E. P., Prado Malte, A. E., & Heredia Enríquez, R. B. (2021). 'Supervision and Control of Students during Online Assessments Applying Computer Vision Techniques: A Systematic Literature Review'. *Universal Journal of Educational Research*, 9(5), 1000–1013. DOI: 10.13189/ujer.2021.090513

Mishra, R., Bian, J., Fiszman, M., Weir, C. R., Jonnalagadda, S., Mostafa, J., & Del Fiol, G. (2014). 'Text Summarization in the Biomedical Domain: A Systematic Review of Recent Research'. *Journal of Biomedical Informatics*, 52, 457–467. DOI: 10.1016/j.jbi.2014.06.009 PMID: 25016293

Mondal, S., Das, S., & Vrana, V. G. (2023). 'How to Bell the Cat? A Theoretical Review of Generative Artificial Intelligence towards Digital Disruption in All Walks of Life'. *Technologies*, 11(2), 44. Advance online publication. DOI: 10.3390/technologies11020044

Moussawi, S., Koufaris, M., & Benbunan-Fich, R. (2021). 'How Perceptions of Intelligence and Anthropomorphism Affect Adoption of Personal Intelligent Agents'. *Electronic Markets*, 31(2), 343–364. DOI: 10.1007/s12525-020-00411-w

Murad, D. F., Heryadi, Y., Wijanarko, B. D., Isa, S. M., & Budiharto, W. (2018, September). Recommendation system for smart LMS using machine learning: a literature review. In 2018 international conference on computing, engineering, and design (ICCED) (pp. 113-118). IEEE.

Naps, T. L., Rößling, G., Almstrum, V., Dann, W., Fleischer, R., Hundhausen, C., . . . Velázquez-Iturbide, J. Á. (2002). Exploring the role of visualization and engagement in computer science education. In Working group reports from ITiCSE on Innovation and technology in computer science education (pp. 131-152).

Nixon, M., & Aguado, A. (2019). *Feature Extraction and Image Processing for Computer Vision*. Academic Press.

Odden, T. O. B., Marin, A., & Rudolph, J. L. (2021). How has Science Education changed over the last 100 years? An analysis using natural language processing. *Science Education*, 105(4), 653–680.

Oppenlaender, J. (2022, November). The creativity of text-to-image generation. In *Proceedings of the 25th international academic mindtrek conference* (pp. 192-202).

Paleyes, A., Urma, R. G., & Lawrence, N. D. (2022). Challenges in deploying machine learning: A survey of case studies. *ACM Computing Surveys*, 55(6), 1–29.

Pandiaraja, P., Boopesh, K. B., Deepthi, T., Laksmi Priya, M., & Noodhana, R. (2022). An Analysis of Document Summarization for Educational Data Classification Using NLP with Machine Learning Techniques. In Iyer, B., Crick, T., & Peng, S.-L. (Eds.), *Applied Computational Technologies, Smart Innovation, Systems and Technologies* (pp. 127–143). Springer Nature. DOI: 10.1007/978-981-19-2719-5_12

Passey, D. (2017). Computer science (CS) in the compulsory education curriculum: Implications for future research. *Education and Information Technologies*, 22, 421–443.

Pezoa, W. G., & Domínguez, M. J. (2017, October). Combined approach using artificial vision and neural networks for facial recognition. In *2017 CHILEAN Conference on Electrical, Electronics Engineering, Information and Communication Technologies (CHILECON)* (pp. 1-5). IEEE.

Proctor, C., Bigman, M., & Blikstein, P. (2019, February). Defining and designing computer science education in a k12 public school district. In *Proceedings of the 50th ACM technical symposium on computer science education* (pp. 314-320).

Randles, B. M., Pasquetto, I. V., Golshan, M. S., & Borgman, C. L. (2017, June). Using the Jupyter notebook as a tool for open science: An empirical study. In *2017 ACM/IEEE Joint Conference on Digital Libraries (JCDL)* (pp. 1-2). IEEE.

Raschka, S. (2015). *Python Machine Learning*. Packt Publishing Ltd.

Rombach, R., Blattmann, A., Lorenz, D., Esser, P., & Ommer, B. (2022). High-resolution image synthesis with latent diffusion models. In *Proceedings of the IEEE/CVF conference on computer vision and pattern recognition* (pp. 10684-10695).

Sahranç, Ü. (2013). 'Bir Durumluk Akış Modeli: Stres Kontrolü, Genel Özyeterlik, Durumluk Kaygı, Yaşam Doyumu Ve Akış İlişkileri'. *Sakarya Üniversitesi Eğitim Fakültesi Dergisi*, (16), 122–144.

Saleem, A. (2022). 'Applications of Natural Language Processing | Data Science Dojo'. Retrieved 23 May 2024 (https://datasciencedojo.com/blog/natural-language-processing-applications/)

Shana, Z., & Abulibdeh, E. S. (2020). 'Science Practical Work and Its Impact on High Students' Academic Achievement'. *JOTSE*, 10(2), 199–215. DOI: 10.3926/jotse.888

Sophokleous, A., Christodoulou, P., Doitsidis, L., & Chatzichristofis, S. A. (2021). 'Computer Vision Meets Educational Robotics'. *Electronics (Basel)*, 10(6), 730. DOI: 10.3390/electronics10060730

Stockman, G., & Shapiro, L. G. (2001). *Computer Vision* (1st ed.). Prentice Hall PTR.

Sun, J., Liao, Q. V., Muller, M., Agarwal, M., Houde, S., Talamadupula, K., & Weisz, J. D. (2022, March). Investigating explainability of generative AI for code through scenario-based design. In *Proceedings of the 27th International Conference on Intelligent User Interfaces* (pp. 212-228).

Sun, R., Lei, T., Chen, Q., Wang, Z., Du, X., Zhao, W., & Nandi, A. K. (2022). 'Survey of Image Edge Detection'. *Frontiers in Signal Processing*, 2, 826967. Advance online publication. DOI: 10.3389/frsip.2022.826967

Szeliski, R. (2022). *Computer Vision: Algorithms and Applications*. Springer Nature. DOI: 10.1007/978-3-030-34372-9

Talan, T., & Aktürk, C. (2021). *Bilgisayar Bilimlerinde Teorik Ve Uygulamalı Araştırmalar*. Efe Akademi Yayınları.

Tang, T., Smith, R., Rixner, S., & Warren, J. (2016, July). Data-driven test case generation for automated programming assessment. In *Proceedings of the 2016 ACM Conference on Innovation and Technology in Computer Science Education* (pp. 260-265).

Taylor, E., Breed, M., Hauman, I., & Homann, A. (2013). *Choosing Learning Methods Suitable for Teaching and Learning in Computer Science*. International Association for Development of the Information Society.

Turing. 2024. 'All You Need to Know about Computer Vision and How It Works'. Retrieved 23 May 2024 (https://www.turing.com/kb/all-you-need-to-know-about-computer-vision)

Vaculík, K., Popelínský, L., Mráková, E., & Jurco, J. (2013, October). Tutoring and automatic evaluation of logic proofs. In European Conference on e-Learning (p. 495). Academic Conferences International Limited.

Wahid, A. (2017) 'Big Data and Machine Learning for Businesses'. *SlideShare*. Retrieved 23 May 2024 (https://www.slideshare.net/slideshow/big-data-and-machine-learning-for-businesses/75413684)

Whitehill, J., & Seltzer, M. 2017. 'A Crowdsourcing Approach to Collecting Tutorial Videos -- Toward Personalized Learning-at-Scale'. Pp. 157–60 in *Proceedings of the Fourth (2017) ACM Conference on Learning @ Scale, L@S '17*. New York, NY, USA: Association for Computing Machinery.

Wiering, M. A., & Van Otterlo, M. (2012). 'Reinforcement Learning'. *Adaptation, Learning, and Optimization*, 12(3), 729.

Wu, X., Duan, R., & Ni, J. (2024). 'Unveiling Security, Privacy, and Ethical Concerns of ChatGPT'. *Journal of Information and Intelligence*, 2(2), 102–115. DOI: 10.1016/j.jiixd.2023.10.007

Yue, X., Di, G., Yu, Y., Wang, W., & Shi, H. (2012). 'Analysis of the Combination of Natural Language Processing and Search Engine Technology'. *Procedia Engineering*, 29, 1636–1639. DOI: 10.1016/j.proeng.2012.01.186

Zheng, X. (2023). Robot translation based on computer vision for cultural psychology of english culture education. International journal of humanoid robotics, 20(02n03), 2250006.

Chapter 6
Low-Code Programming for K-12 Education

İbrahim Halil Özdemir
https://orcid.org/0000-0001-9291-7112
Ege University, Turkey

Fırat Sarsar
https://orcid.org/0000-0002-3611-8137
Ege University, Turkey

Brendan Calandra
Georgia State University, USA

ABSTRACT

Computer science is crucial in the information age, driving an international movement towards digital literacy. The rapid development of digital technologies, especially data science and AI, necessitates a deeper understanding of human-machine interactions. CS literacy is essential for individual and societal success, leading to increased research on programming instruction from an early age. Programming is now integral to K-12 curricula worldwide. To enhance computer programming education, strategies must address both cognitive and affective aspects. Low-code programming, which enables application creation with minimal manual coding, is a promising approach. This book chapter introduces low-code programming as a valuable toolset for K-12 Computer Science Education.

DOI: 10.4018/979-8-3693-4542-9.ch006

Introduction

In this chapter, the authors will present low-code programming as a viable pathway to K12 students' acquisition of coding knowledge, skills and self-efficacy. With this chapter, we hope to introduce the toolset and provide some guidance for teachers, learning experience designers, and instructional designers on how and why to successfully integrate a low-code programming approach into curricula and instructional strategies for K12 learning environments.

Programming and computational thinking have been widely regarded as a skill set and even basic literacy that is fundamental for individuals to be able to participate and succeed in the information age (Danhieux, 2022; Lindberg, Laine, & Haaranen, 2018; Sun, Hu & Zhou, 2021; Theodoropoulos & Lepouras, 2020; Wong, Cheung, Ching, & Huen, 2015). In fact, at least a basic set of skills within these domains are increasingly required in many areas of work and study within and beyond the bounds of computer science. (Lindberg, Laine, & Haaranen, 2018). This phenomenon has created a large and comprehensive movement in Computer Science Education (CSEd) (Aivaloglou & Hermans, 2019; Antanenko & Abramowitz, 2023; Blikstein & Moghadam, 2018; Lee, Francom & Nuatomue, 2022; Zhu & Wang, 2024). Indeed, there has been a surge in the interest in programming education, i.e., focusing on understanding how programs are created (Sun, Guo, & Zhou, 2022). This movement has more recently begun to focus on CSEd starting at the early stages of an individuals' educational journey (Aivaloglou & Hermans, 2019; He, Guo, Lu, Xu & Gong, 2020) leading to an increased focus on CSEd in K-12 (Sim & Lau, 2022), childhood is widely acknowledged as a pivotal period that significantly impacts individuals' cognitive and intellectual development. (Grover & Pea, 2013). Therefore, the inclusion of programming teaching in the curriculum with this period is an important achievement. While teaching programming and computer science to achieve this outcome has been a long-standing practice, the teaching of current and modern programming techniques (e.g. block-based programming and unplugged programming) has emerged more recently (Blikstein & Moghadam, 2018; Lee, Francom, & Nuatomue, 2022; Tank et al., 2024). According to data from the World Bank, computer science and programming courses are mandatory in nearly half of the world's high-income countries (Coşkunserçe, 2023). Additionally, research by Balanskat and Engelhard (2015) indicates that many countries have successfully integrated programming and computer science into their curricula. The ongoing integration of programming education in many countries aims to enhance K-12 students' learning experiences and advance their understanding of programming processes (Sáez-López, Román-González, & Vázquez-Cano, 2016). Besides the learning experience and understanding of programming, teaching programming can also help to develop computational thinking skills, which play a critical role for 21st century learners (Tikva & Tambouris, 2021). This is because programming, by its very nature, provides a necessary infrastructure for the acquisition of computational thinking (Basogain, Olabe, Olabe, & Rico, 2018). In addition, the programming skill gained through programming education at the K-12 level can be explained as a feature that emerges from the dimensions of "metacognition, cognition, processing and communication", which includes 17 sub-skills in its own context (Sun, Guo, & Zhou, 2022). With the contribution of those working in this field, efforts to expand programming education at the K-12 level continue to accelerate (Sim & Lau, 2022).

While the teaching of modern programming in many countries now starts in primary school and even preschool (Aivaloglou & Hermans, 2019; Tank, et al. 2024), this comes with its own set of challenges. One common challenge or barrier to CSEd, especially for beginners, has to do with the complex and comprehensive structure of text-based programming languages (Garneli, Giannakos, & Chorianopoulos, 2015). For example, younger or less experienced students can encounter problems with making sense of traditional programming flows and programming terminology (Garneli, Giannakos, & Chorianopoulos, 2015). In addition, text-based programming languages make it difficult for individuals who are in the concrete processing period or who have recently transitioned to the abstract processing period to construct meaning (Sun & Zhou, 2023; Ye, Liang, Ng & Chai, 2023).

This problem can be divided into two main categories: issues related to selecting a programming language and challenges associated with translating solutions into practice (Sim & Lau, 2022). First, to better understand the problem of selecting a programming language, it's helpful to examine the classification of existing languages. (Haigh & Ceruzzi, 2021; Lachaux, Roziere, Chaussot & Lample, 2020; Özdemir, Kışla & Tito, 2023; Sim & Lau, 2022). See Figure 1.

Figure 1. Generational classification of programming languages (Sim & Lau, 2022).

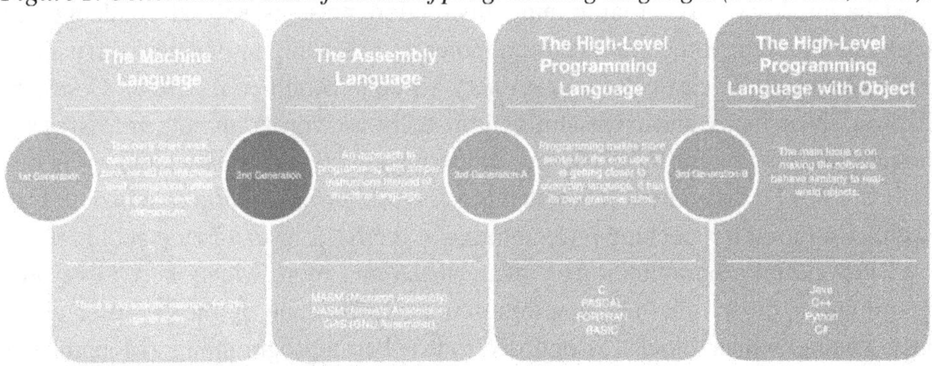

As shown in Figure 1, in the categorization of programming languages until the current period, each generation of programming language has aimed to be simpler and more understandable than the previous generation. The focus is on the most comfortable perception and understanding of languages by the end user (Sim & Lau, 2022) which can also be considered as a means to overcome the linguistic difficulties encountered in teaching programming (Joque, 2016).

Another challenge in teaching programming is translating the problem-solving context, fundamental to programming, into practical exercises (Altadmri & Brown, 2015). The key to developing an effective programming solution is a clear, precise, and accurate definition of the problem to be solved. The most significant difficulty faced by K-12 students in programming instruction is their inability to abstract the given problem (Sim & Lau, 2022). This difficulty can impact the development of their computational thinking skills.

Visual-based languages have recently been presented an alternative to text-based languages in part to address the aforementioned challenges and help facilitate the learning process (Erümit, 2020; Garneli, Giannakos, & Chorianopoulos, 2015; Mladenović, Boljat & Žanko, 2018). This is largely because the visual programming approach enables students to create programs through readily available visual components rather than long and complex lines of code (Mladenović, Žanko & Aglić Čuvić, 2021). Block-based programming is one example of visual programming that can be found across K12 CS curricula (Coşkunserçe, 2023; Sim & Lau, 2022; Sun, Guo, & Zhou, 2022; Xu, Wang & Wang, 2023).

Block based programming in K12 CSEd

Simple block-based programming environments such as Scratch and Blokly have appeared across research and practice in CSEd, especially at the K-12 level. Text-based, high-level programming instruction presents several challenges in terms of structure and comprehension, potentially leading to practical difficulties in K-12 education, particularly in primary schools (Smith et al., 2020). Concepts like variables, loops, and expressions within text-based programming processes are notably challenging for K-12 learners, hindering effective problem-solving (Grover & Basu, 2017). To address this issue, block-based programming stands out as an optimal solution for teaching programming at the K-12 level. (Tsung et al., 2022).

Block-based programming is a more visual and more widely accessible programming approach that allows programming to be done by the end-user using visual and graphical blocks, as opposed to text-based programming (Mohamad et al., 2011). Block-based programming can be thought of as a puzzle. The basic logic is to drag and drop the ready-made visual blocks in the correct algorithm. Therefore, programming with block-based tools is dragging and dropping ready-made programming instructions in a meaningful way (Weintrop, 2019). Figure 2 shows the structure of an example block-based program. This program was created using Scratch, which was developed by MIT.

Figure 2. Example Block Based Programming

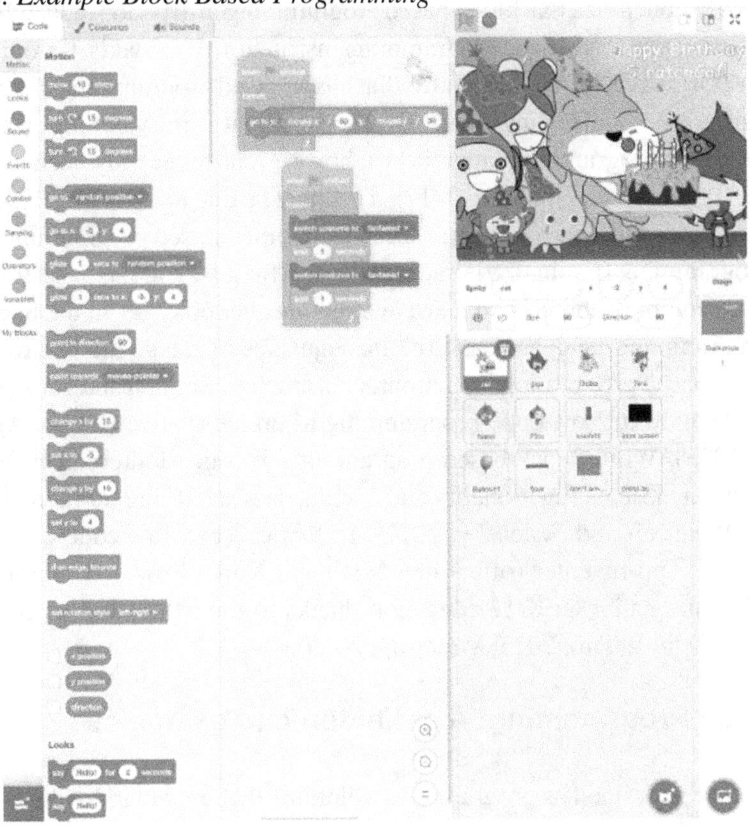

The first tools that come to mind when it comes to block-based programming tools are undoubtedly Scratch, Alice, and Blockly (Das, Marghitu, Mandala, & Howard, 2021). Today, these and similar block-based programming environments and tools enable learners to be productive, put their ideas to work to test them, interact with computers (human-computer interaction), explore new topics, and experience innovative programming learning (Xu, Ritzhaupt, Tian, & Umapathy, 2019).

For young K-12 learners, the block-based learning approach can have a significant impact as it enables them to construct algorithms instead of creating syntax (Mladenović, Boljat & Žanko, 2018). In addition, block-based programming enables young learners to engage in problem solving skills (Sun, Guo & Zhou, 2022). What's more, early K-12 learners can achieve a more effective learning experience with the visual interface provided by the block-based approach (Noone & Mooney, 2018).

In their study, Weintrop and Wilensky (2017) found that K-12 learners achieved more targeted outcomes and showed more interest in the given CS course during the learning process with block-based programming. Similarly, Mladenović, Boljat & Žanko (2018) concluded that block-based programming instruction reduced learners' misconceptions and facilitated programming instruction. Papadakis, Kalogiannakis, Zaranis, & Orfanakis (2016) concluded that block-based programming increased the interest in the process of coding for K-12 learners without a programming background.

Block-based programming approaches, however, have recently been called into question. (Weintrop & Wilensky, 2017). This may be due to difficulty encountered by more advanced learners in the transition from block-based programming to text-based programming (Espinal, Vieira, & Guerrero-Bequis, 2023; Noone & Mooney, 2018). The complex and comprehensive structure that emerges in the use of text-based programming languages and the inadequacies of the solutions provided by basic block-based programming environments (such as Scratch and Blokly) justify the consideration of Low-code programming as an alternative (Pinho, Aguiar, & Amaral, 2023). While block-based programming is a good alternative for young learners, it may lose its functionality and become less satisfying for more advanced learners (Weintrop and Wilensky, 2017). In this context, low-code development tools such as App Inventor (offered by MIT) and Kuika Low-code platform may be a viable alternative in K-12 education thanks to their drag-and-drop structure (Özdemir, Kışla, & Tito, 2023; Weintrop, 2019).

Low-code Programming: A definition and examples

Low-code is defined as programming solutions that enable individuals with no programming background to carry out a fast and easy application development processes through visual interfaces and drag-and-drop technologies (Sahay, Indamutsa, Ruscio, Pierantonio, 2020). The "What You See Is What You Get" architecture of low-code programming, unlike text-based programming and block-based programming, visually shows the output to the learners instantly, and can output various types of applications that cannot be done with block-based programming (Özdemir, Kışla ve Tito, 2023; Pinho, Aguiar, & Amaral, 2023). Low-code development, which has increased in popularity in recent years and its integration into the processes of different disciplines in daily life, enables fast application development that requires minimal or no coding.

The graphical user interface and drag-and-drop features of a low-code platform automate the development process in various aspects by eliminating dependencies on traditional software development approaches and block-based programming platforms (Bock & Frank, 2021). In addition, one of the most important features of Low-code programming is that individuals with no programming background can develop different types of applications on a single platform or interface through a visual interface (Martinez and Pfister, 2023). For example, using a Low-Code tool, web, mobile, IoT, and artificial intelligence applications can be created without writing text-based programs.

As mentioned above, through Low-code development, end-users can output various types of applications. These can be categorized as Web applications, Mobile Applications (specific to different operating systems), process automation, IoT applications, and artificial intelligence applications (Sufi, 2023). Although these application types may seem difficult to develop, they can be easily produced thanks to the visual interface and minimal coding requirement of Low-code development platforms (Pinho, Aguiar, & Amaral, 2023). A further advantage of the visual interface is that users who carry out Low-code programming process can also see the final output while preparing the applications they develop by taking advantage of the WYSIWYG (What You See Is What You Get) structure.

The details of these application types mentioned above are presented below.

> Web Applications: Low-code platforms enable the development and publishing of unique web applications through a visual interface and a set of pre-prepared components that require minimal technical knowledge and ease of use by the end user. Many low-code development tools allow these web applications to be responsive (Luo, Liang, Wang, Shahin, & Zhan, 2021). Figure 3 shows a screenshot from a sample web application programmed with Low-code.

Figure 3. A sample web application developed with Low-code

Figure 3 shows a sample responsive web application programmed through Kuika Low-code platform.

Mobile Applications: Mobile applications are expected to be designed to appeal to different operating systems and to respond to the features of mobile devices. Such an expectation brings along a very complex process in a typical programming scenario. Low-code programming, on the other hand, simplifies mobile application programming and publishing to meet the requirements of different operating systems and mobile devices with drag-and-drop technologies thanks to the visual and graphical interface it provides (Martinez & Pfister, 2023). Figure 4 shows a screenshot from a sample native mobile application programmed with Low-code.

Figure 4. A sample mobile application developed with low-code

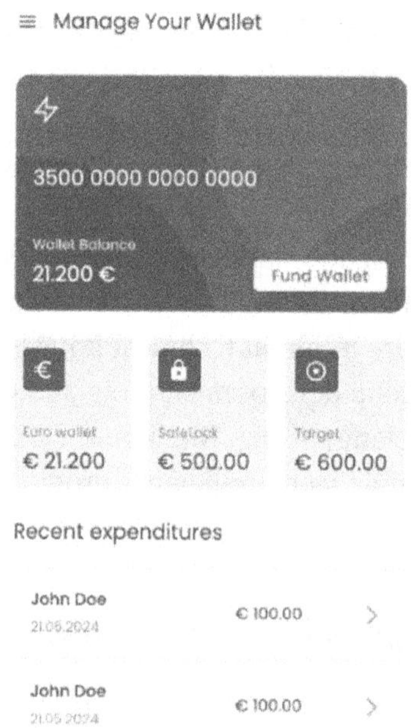

Figure 4 shows an example of the wallet management screen of a mobile application programmed in Low-code.

Process Automation: The digitization and automation of processes in an organization can be achieved through Low-code programming. Through low-code development, a workflow process can be realized with drag-and-drop diagram tools (Ciucan-Rusu et al., 2023).

IoT Applications: Internet of Things (IoT) applications involve a complex development process due to its concept. The basis of the concept is based on the communication between hardware and software. Therefore, there are many variables when developing IoT applications. However, Low-code development simplifies the complexity of these components for the end user. Ready-made integration tools, ready-made and reusable Wi-Fi and Bluetooth components combined with a visual interface make the development process easier and faster (Ihirwe, Ruscio, Mazzini, Pierini, & Pierantonio, 2020).

Figure 5 shows a screenshot from a sample IoT application programmed with Low-code.

Figure 5. A sample IoT application developed with low-code

Figure 5 shows an example of a dashboard screen of a mobile application programmed in Low-code and communicating with a Bluetooth scale.

Artificial Intelligence Applications: Artificial intelligence applications are undoubtedly the most discussed topic of the current era. Despite its growing popularity, developing AI applications in traditional software development processes is far from being simple. Through low-code programming, you can create your own AI application in a drag-and-drop structure through pre-prepared components or integrate with tools such as Open AI. One does not need to know any programming language while performing these processes

(Rao, Tsay, Kate, Hellendoorn, & Hirzel, 2024; Sahay, Indamutsa, Ruscio, & Pierantonio, 2020; Sufi, 2023; Viilegas, García-Ortiz, & Sánchez-Viteri, 2021).

Figure 6 shows a screenshot from a sample artificial intelligence application programmed with Low-code.

Figure 6. A sample AI application developed with low-code

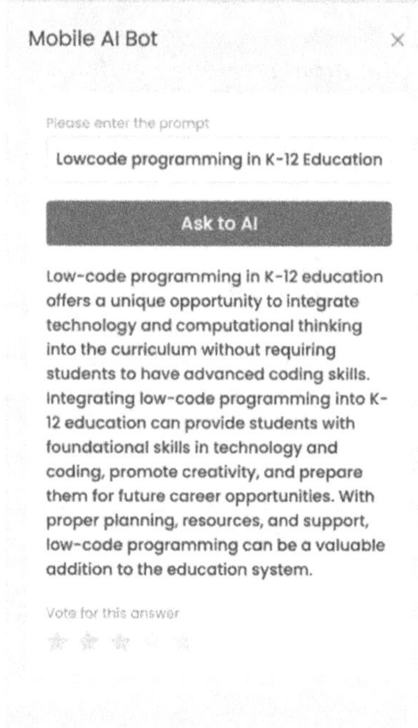

Figure 6 shows a screenshot of an artificial intelligence application developed in Kuika with low-code programming. As can be seen in the screenshot, there is an input structure that allows the end user to enter a prompt, a response generated by the AI and a voting structure that allows the end user to vote on the response.

In the process of programming/developing the types of applications presented above, several advantages are achieved through Low-code programming.

These advantages can be listed as time saving, economic/cost saving, simplification of processes, not requiring much technical know-how, facilitating organization, minimizing effort and improving quality (Ciucan-Rusu et al., 2023; Ihirwe, Ruscio, Mazzini, Pierini, & Pierantonio, 2020; Rao, Tsay, Kate, Hellendoorn, & Hirzel, 2024; Sufi, 2023; Viilegas, García-Ortiz, & Sánchez-Viteri, 2021).

Block-based Programming versus Low-code Programming

The features and structure of block-based programming provide learners with ready-made logic blocks and limit the learners with the functional framework of the blocks (Weintrop & Wilensky, 2017). In addition, the focus in block-based programming is to provide the student with abstract programming logic and flow, as opposed to creating an output for the end user (Espinal, Vieira, & Guerrero-Bequis, 2023). Due to this structure, block-based programming is an alternative and innovative approach for the beginning or first step. Still, in light of the needs of the current period, it can be quite limited in terms of enabling students to gain more in-depth programming skills and participate in more complex projects (Weng, Ng, Cui & Leung, 2023). For example, block-based programming, which has a very important role in teaching basic topics such as loops, conditions, and variables in the early stages of programming education, is not able to bring learners to a level that can meet the requisite competence of the current period in the process of integrating the programming knowledge base into real life scenarios (Wörister & Knobelsdorf, 2023). Especially in this are, which we call the data age, the block-based programming approach used in programming teaching may not provide the desired answer. Due to the nature of block-based programming, the basic workflow and algorithm are prioritized before data (Begosso, Begosso & Christ, 2020). In addition, as mentioned in the introduction part, one of the biggest challenges experienced in programming teaching is the transition process from block-based programming to text-based programming. Block-based programming currently enables learners to perceive programming as a simple structure consisting of "blocks" while overlooking the terminology and complex infrastructure of programming (Espinal, Vieira, & Guerrero-Bequis, 2023; Noone & Mooney, 2018). In addition, block-based programming provides a perspective that is far from focusing on the visual user interface with the blocks it offers. The product quality of the outputs obtained may not align with the requirements of the current period. In contrast to block-based programming, Low-code programming, a new approach to teaching and programming, is the product of the integration of visual programming and minimal text-based programming due to its reusable and ready-to-use component-based structure (Pinho, Aguiar, & Amaral, 2023). Due to the nature of low-code programming, learners can implement real-world examples, unlike block-based programming. Although Low-code programming is similar to block-based programming due to its drag-and-drop development method, the "What You See Is What You Get" architecture of Low-code programming allows learners to concretise abstract concepts in the programming process while simultaneously obtaining the user interface (Cai et al., 2023; Özdemir, Kışla & Tito, 2023). This feature establishes Low-code programming ahead of block-based programming and other alternative programming approaches (Elshan, Ebeli Söllner & Leimeister,

2023). Low-code programming allows working with data in the data age in addition to the possibilities provided by block-based programming in teaching programming and allows business logic organizations at a more advanced level than block-based programming (Hirzel, 2023; Özdemir, Kışla & Tito, 2023). Low-code programming, which enables the development and management of current business organizations such as mobile applications, prepares learners for the needs of the current era (Matook, Maggie Wang, Koeppel & Guerin, 2024). The primary distinction between low-code programming and block-based programming is that the output which is not an animation or a game with a rule set (such as Scratch, Blockly and Code.org), but applications that can operate in the environments of the current era (iOS, Android and Web, and sometimes desktop applications) (Alamin et al., 2023; Begosso, Begosso & Christ, 2020; Weng, Ng, Cui & Leung, 2023).

Low code programming for K12

Low-code programming has its place in K-12 CSEd (Mladenovic, Granic, Zaharija, & Krpan, 2023). Environments with visual interfaces that enable low-code programming allow K-12 learners to minimize potential errors that can arise when writing long lines of code from scratch. In addition, they allow for a learning experience based on diagnosis and identification rather than a rote learning experience. In addition, low code environments also provide an easy way to learn programming due to its learning structure that minimizes the cognitive load of learners (Gresse von Wangenheim, Hauck, Pachecco, & Bertonceli Bueno, 2021; Sońta & Przegalinska, 2024). Especially in this respect, the Low-code programming approach is in line with the teaching goals and current needs for teaching computational thinking skills in K-12 education to prepare students for future career opportunities.

The low-code programming approach allows students to develop their programming skills while at the same time strengthening their computational thinking abilities. It also allows students to gain essential skills such as problem-solving, logical thinking, and creativity (Wang & Wu, 2020). In addition to these skills, robotics and maker skills, the important technologies and skills of the current era, have become more accessible through Low-code programming (Brouzos, Panayiotou, Tsardoulias, & Symeonidis, 2023; Sufi, 2023).

Although the low-code programming approach is still a new concept for teachers, it provides a great advantage for them as well. Regardless of their level of programming knowledge, teachers can more effectively and easily integrate programming instruction into their lesson plans using Low-code development platforms.

In addition, they can develop applications in various fields (web, mobile, and artificial intelligence) and present them in a fiction that will increase interaction and motivation with learners in the learning process. In their study, McHugh, Carrol, and Connoly (2023) reported that K-12 teachers' values, confidence, attitudes, self-efficacy, and perceived use levels for professional development improved as they became familiar with Low-code programming and gained Low-code programming skills. In addition, it is stated that K-12 teachers can have a product-oriented, accessible, creative, and critical-thinking structure with Low-code programming. In the next section, we will provide a roadmap for designing and implementing curricula for low-code programming.

Low-code programming for K12: A roadmap

The integration of low-code programming in K-12 education offers a transformative approach that can significantly enhance both teaching and learning experiences. By systematically integrating low-code programming, students and teachers can achieve success in programming, making it essential to create a clear and detailed roadmap for its implementation in K-12 education.

Analysis

In programming education at the K-12 level, the target audience to which Low-code programming will be applied should be analyzed in detail. In addition, how to solve existing problem situations should also be analyzed. An important point is to analyze the knowledge sets that teachers have and need. Finally, an analysis of the current technological possibilities of K-12 curricula and the Low-code environments available in the market should be carried out. After the results of the analysis, it is necessary to start working on designing and developing curricula in the light of potential technologies.

Curriculum Development

At the K-12 level, a suitable curriculum should be prepared for the learners by taking into account the existing computer science curricula and achievements of the grade levels where Low-code programming will be carried out, in a way to support the cognitive development of the learners, taking into account the needs of the learners. Basic concepts, algorithm design and development, and problem-solving skills, which are very important for K-12 level programming education, should be supported with Low-code programming. In parallel with the curriculum development process, it is crucial for institutions to set a clear vision and strategy for Low-code programming.

Teacher Training

Comprehensive training programs should be organized for teachers who will be the implementers of the developed curricula to use Low-code programming tools and pedagogical approaches effectively. Through teacher training, teachers should be provided with practical information, various applications, best practices, and best practices on how to use Low-code programming in programming instruction. The teacher training should be planned within the framework of lifelong learning and continuous learning models that will support the professional development of teachers and should be organized according to the needs of teachers. Through these trainings, K-12 teachers' knowledge and skill levels will be improved, and their beliefs and attitudes will improve in parallel (Ertmer, Ottenbreit-Leftwich, Sadık, Şendurur, & Şendururur, 2012).

Technological Infrastructure

In programming education, K-12 institutions where Low-code programming will be used are expected to be capable of providing the necessary infrastructure for the institution, teachers, and learners. In this process, Low-code environments should be provided and institutionally disseminated, and technology integration models should be applied.

Preparing Support Structures for Teachers

It is crucial to provide support systems for teachers to facilitate using Low-code approaches in programming education at the K-12 level. These support systems, additional training, video tutorials, and resources, frequently asked questions for potential questions, and a helpdesk for teachers will increase the success of the process. A successful setup can be achieved if the support processes are customized in the context of the questions teachers have. In addition, establishing a professional network for teachers and even identifying leaders in this network will increase the efficiency of the process.

Preparing Support Structures for Learners

One of the most critical points in the integration of Low-code programming at the K-12 level is the design and preparation of structures that can support learners. In this context, it is crucial for the success of the process to provide learning platforms and interactive learning tools to support the learning environment in which the curriculum will be implemented, to create a community with learners and to provide tasks within this community, and to provide learners with additional resources and materials that will enrich the learning experience of the learners.

One of the most important processes that should be carried out in parallel with all these topics is the institutional adoption process.

Institutional Adoption

Institutional adoption is a key factor in the successful integration of low-code programming into K-12 education. Institutional adoption is possible when the institution establishes decision-making mechanisms for adoption in a shared democracy, with the participation of all its constituents. In this process, it is important to identify leaders for the relevant decision mechanisms and to ensure the dynamism of the organization. In this context, the following steps can facilitate institutional adoption:

Vision and Leadership: Establish a clear vision for the role of low-code programming in the school's educational strategy. School leaders should communicate the benefits and goals of integrating low-code tools to all stakeholders, ensuring alignment with the institution's broader educational objectives.

Policy Development: Develop and implement policies that support the use of low-code programming. This includes creating guidelines for its use in the classroom, ensuring student data privacy, and setting standards for digital citizenship.

Resource Allocation: Secure funding and allocate resources for the necessary technological infrastructure, professional development for teachers, and curricular materials. This might involve applying for grants, reallocating existing funds, or seeking partnerships with technology providers.

Community Engagement: Engage with parents, local businesses, and community organizations to build support for low-code programming initiatives. Demonstrating the potential for enhancing students' future career opportunities can help garner broader community backing.

Evaluation and Feedback: Establish mechanisms for ongoing evaluation and feedback. Regularly assess the effectiveness of low-code programming initiatives through student performance data, teacher feedback, and technological usability studies. Use this data to make informed adjustments to the program.

Scalability and Sustainability: Plan for scalability and sustainability from the outset. Develop a phased implementation plan that allows for gradual integration across different grade levels and schools. Ensure that there are plans in place to sustain the program long-term, including regular updates to technology and continuous professional development for teachers.

One of the most important points in the context of these topics is to recognize the tools in the Low-code ecosystem and to include these tools in the roadmap during the integration process.

Table 1 below presents a comparison of Low-code platforms available for teachers and organizations. The features provided by the Low-code platforms mentioned in Table 1 can be considered in the context of the roadmap presented and can be used alone or in combination with each other to bring advantages for K-12 programming education.

Table 1. Comparison of Platforms that can be used in K-12 Programming Education

Features - Platform	Responsive Web Applications	Mobile Apps	Process Automation	IoT Applications	Artificial Intelligence Applications	Own Learning Systems	Education Support(Free)
App Inventor		Android only		✓		✓	✓
Kuika	✓	Native Android and iOS	✓	✓	✓	✓	✓
Mendix	✓	Native Android and iOS	✓	✓	✓	✓	N/A
Outsystems	✓	Native Android and iOS	✓	✓		✓	N/A
Microsoft Power App	✓	Native Android and iOS	✓	With additional service(Azure)	✓	✓	N/A

CONCLUSION

Low-code programming has the potential to play an important role for K-12 learners who are new to programming and learning programming. K-12 education is a critical period when students acquire basic knowledge and skills. Teaching students the basics of computer science during this period is vital to prepare them for the technological world of the present and future. Especially in programming education, the complex context of text-based programming as well as the features and outputs that block-based programming does not offer at some points, further emphasize the importance of low-code programming in computer science education.

Low-code platforms provide an accessible entry point into the world of programming by minimizing the syntactical complexities that often deter beginners. They allow students to focus on core programming concepts and logical problem-solving without the initial barrier of mastering syntax. This is crucial in building confidence and fostering an early interest in computer science. Furthermore, low-code programming can serve as a bridge between block-based programming environments, which are typically used in elementary education, and more advanced text-based programming languages encountered in higher education and professional environments.

As part of the process of integrating low-code programming as a bridge to K-12 education, learners are expected to be introduced to and embrace the fundamental concepts of block-based programming in computer science courses in the early years of the learning process. In the initial years of primary education (first 4-6 years), it is important for students to be introduced to drag-and-drop methodologies and to experience basic programming concepts, including algorithms, variables, and loops. This process facilitates students' to have and understanding of computing and prepares them for more advanced programming skills.

In the later years of K-12 education, it is important for students to be introduced to low-code programming tools in a manner that incorporates their existing skills in order to raise individuals who are suited to the needs of this era. In particular, the integration of low-code tools into computer science courses at the high school level becomes inevitable. The ease of use, user-friendliness, and drag-and-drop functionality of low-code programming tools are highly effective in advancing the programming skills of high school students.

As stated in the literature (Espinal, Vieira, & Guerrero-Bequis, 2023; Kışla, Özdemir & Tito, 2023; Noone & Mooney, 2018), block-based programming remains simple after a certain point and may be insufficient to meet daily needs and real-life problems. Since text-based programming requires an abstract and complex approach, the importance of low-code programming, which is an up-to-date and innovative programming approach, is increasing in K-12 education (especially after the first 6 years). Low-code tools facilitate students to work on more complex tasks, create solutions to real-world problems, and develop their programming skills hands-on.

At this point, it is important to further examine the examples presented in this chapter and the integration roadmap in detail, to create an effective learning experience. Practical implementation of low-code programming in the classroom requires careful curriculum design that aligns with educational standards and learning outcomes. Teachers must be provided with adequate professional development and resources to effectively facilitate low-code programming lessons. Additionally, integrating project-based learning approaches can enhance the applicability of low-code programming, allowing students to engage in real-world problem-solving and innovation.

It is also critical to plan for the adoption of low-code programming at the K-12 level. This includes considering the technical infrastructure required, such as access to computers and reliable internet connections, as well as ensuring that the software used is age-appropriate and pedagogically sound. Collaboration with educational stakeholders, including policymakers, educators, and industry partners, can help in creating a supportive ecosystem for the successful integration of low-code programming.

However, in the existing literature, the number of theoretical and practical resources on how to use and integrate low-code programming in teaching processes is limited. More empirical research is needed to evaluate the long-term impacts of low-code programming on students' computational thinking skills, creativity, and overall engagement in computer science. Furthermore, case studies and best practice guides can provide valuable insights into effective teaching strategies and curriculum design.

Looking forward, the potential of low-code programming extends far beyond initial education. As students' progress, the skills acquired through low-code platforms can form a solid foundation for advanced studies in computer science and related fields. The ability to quickly prototype and develop applications can be a significant advantage in higher education and the workforce, where rapid development cycles and innovation are highly valued. Moreover, as the technology behind low-code platforms continues to evolve, the gap between low-code and traditional programming will likely narrow, making low-code solutions even more powerful and versatile.

Therefore, it is hoped that this chapter can provide a starting point for those interested in the integration of low-code programming at the K-12 level. By leveraging the potential of low-code platforms, educators can demystify programming for young learners, equipping them with the essential skills needed for the digital age. This chapter aims to inspire further exploration and implementation of low-code programming in K-12 education, contributing to the development of a future-ready generation. As we look ahead, the integration of low-code programming into the education system holds the promise of nurturing a generation of innovators and problem-solvers, ready to meet the challenges of an increasingly digital and automated world.

REFERENCES

Aivaloglou, E., & Hermans, F. (2019, February). Early programming education and career orientation: the effects of gender, self-efficacy, motivation and stereotypes. In *Proceedings of the 50th ACM technical symposium on computer science education* (pp. 679-685). DOI: 10.1145/3287324.3287358

Alamin, M. A. A., Uddin, G., Malakar, S., Afroz, S., Haider, T., & Iqbal, A. (2023). Developer discussion topics on the adoption and barriers of low code software development platforms. *Empirical Software Engineering*, 28(1), 4. DOI: 10.1007/s10664-022-10244-0 PMID: 36407813

Altadmri, A., & Brown, N. C. (2015, February). 37 million compilations: Investigating novice programming mistakes in large-scale student data. In *Proceedings of the 46th ACM technical symposium on computer science education* (pp. 522-527). DOI: 10.1145/2676723.2677258

Antonenko, P., & Abramowitz, B. (2023). In-service teachers'(mis) conceptions of artificial intelligence in K-12 science education. *Journal of Research on Technology in Education*, 55(1), 64–78. DOI: 10.1080/15391523.2022.2119450

Balanskat, A., & Engelhardt, K. (2014). *Computing our future: Computer programming and coding-Priorities, school curricula and initiatives across Europe*. European Schoolnet.

Basogain, X., Olabe, M. Á., Olabe, J. C., & Rico, M. J. (2018). Computational thinking in pre-university blended learning classrooms. *Computers in Human Behavior*, 80, 412–419. DOI: 10.1016/j.chb.2017.04.058

Begosso, L. C., Begosso, L. R., & Christ, N. A. (2020, October). An analysis of block-based programming environments for CS1. In *2020 IEEE Frontiers in Education Conference (FIE)* (pp. 1-5). IEEE.

Blikstein, P., & Moghadam, S. H. (2018). *Pre-college computer science education: A survey of the field*. Google LLC.

Bock, A. C., & Frank, U. (2021). Low-code platform. *Business & Information Systems Engineering*, 63(6), 733–740. DOI: 10.1007/s12599-021-00726-8

Brouzos, R., Panayiotou, K., Tsardoulias, E., & Symeonidis, A. (2023). A Low-Code Approach for Connected Robots. *Journal of Intelligent & Robotic Systems*, 108(2), 28. DOI: 10.1007/s10846-023-01861-y

Cai, Y., Mao, S., Wu, W., Wang, Z., Liang, Y., Ge, T., . . . Duan, N. (2023). Low-code llm: Visual programming over llms. *arXiv preprint arXiv:2304.08103*, 2.

Ciucan-Rusu, L., Timus, M., Stefan, D., Comes, C. A., Bunduchi, E., & Poptamas, M. A. (2023, September). Low-code solutions integration for digital process automation-application in management. In *2023 22nd RoEduNet Conference: Networking in Education and Research (RoEduNet)* (pp. 1-5). IEEE. DOI: 10.1109/RoEduNet60162.2023.10274938

Coşkunserçe, O. (2023). Comparing the use of block-based and robot programming in introductory programming education: Effects on perceptions of programming self-efficacy. *Computer Applications in Engineering Education*, 31(5), 1234–1255. DOI: 10.1002/cae.22637

Danhieux, P. (2022, September 12). Navigating the developer shortage crisis: A time to define the developer of the future. Forbes. Retrieved May 15, 2024, from https://www.forbes.com/sites/forbestechcouncil/2022/09/12/navigating-the-developer-shortage-crisis-a-time-to-define-the-developer-of-the-future/?sh=75d222da2a5c

Das, M., Marghitu, D., Mandala, M., & Howard, A. (2021, July). Accessible block-based programming for k-12 students who are blind or low vision. In *International Conference on Human-Computer Interaction* (pp. 52-61). Cham: Springer International Publishing. DOI: 10.1007/978-3-030-78095-1_5

Elshan, E., Ebel, P., Söllner, M., & Leimeister, J. M. (2023). Leveraging low code development of smart personal assistants: An integrated design approach with the SPADE method. *Journal of Management Information Systems*, 40(1), 96–129. DOI: 10.1080/07421222.2023.2172776

Ertmer, P. A., Ottenbreit-Leftwich, A. T., Sadik, O., Sendurur, E., & Sendurur, P. (2012). Teacher beliefs and technology integration practices: A critical relationship. *Computers & Education*, 59(2), 423–435. DOI: 10.1016/j.compedu.2012.02.001

Erümit, A. K. (2020). Effects of different teaching approaches on programming skills. *Education and Information Technologies*, 25(2), 1013–1037. DOI: 10.1007/s10639-019-10010-8

Espinal, A., Vieira, C., & Guerrero-Bequis, V. (2023). Student ability and difficulties with transfer from a block-based programming language into other programming languages: A case study in Colombia. *Computer Science Education*, 33(4), 567–599. DOI: 10.1080/08993408.2022.2079867

Garneli, V., Giannakos, M. N., & Chorianopoulos, K. (2015, March). Computing education in K-12 schools: A review of the literature. In *2015 IEEE Global Engineering Education Conference (EDUCON)* (pp. 543-551). IEEE. DOI: 10.1109/EDUCON.2015.7096023

Gresse von Wangenheim, C., Hauck, J. C., Pacheco, F. S., & Bertonceli Bueno, M. F. (2021). Visual tools for teaching machine learning in K-12: A ten-year systematic mapping. *Education and Information Technologies*, 26(5), 5733–5778. DOI: 10.1007/s10639-021-10570-8 PMID: 33967587

Grover, S., & Basu, S. (2017, March). Measuring student learning in introductory block-based programming: Examining misconceptions of loops, variables, and boolean logic. In *Proceedings of the 2017 ACM SIGCSE technical symposium on computer science education* (pp. 267-272). DOI: 10.1145/3017680.3017723

Grover, S., & Pea, R. (2013). Computational thinking in K-12: A review of the state of the field. *Educational Researcher*, 42(1), 38–43. DOI: 10.3102/0013189X12463051

Haigh, T., & Ceruzzi, P. E. (2021). *A new history of modern computing*. MIT Press. DOI: 10.7551/mitpress/11436.001.0001

He, Y. T., Guo, B. J., Lu, J., Xu, Y. P., & Gong, M. (2020, December). Research of scratch programming recommendation system based on med and knowledge graph. In 2020 5th International Conference on Mechanical, Control and Computer Engineering (ICMCCE) (pp. 2158-2163). IEEE. DOI: 10.1109/ICMCCE51767.2020.00469

Hirzel, M. (2023). Low-code programming models. *Communications of the ACM*, 66(10), 76–85. DOI: 10.1145/3587691

Ihirwe, F., Di Ruscio, D., Mazzini, S., Pierini, P., & Pierantonio, A. (2020, October). Low-code engineering for internet of things: a state of research. In *Proceedings of the 23rd ACM/IEEE international conference on model driven engineering languages and systems: companion proceedings* (pp. 1-8). DOI: 10.1145/3417990.3420208

Joque, J. (2016). The invention of the object: Object orientation and the philosophical development of programming languages. *Philosophy & Technology*, 29(4), 335–356. DOI: 10.1007/s13347-016-0223-5

Lachaux, M. A., Roziere, B., Chanussot, L., & Lample, G. (2020). Unsupervised translation of programming languages. *arXiv preprint arXiv*:2006.03511.

Lee, S. J., Francom, G. M., & Nuatomue, J. (2022). Computer science education and K-12 students' computational thinking: A systematic review. *International Journal of Educational Research*, 114, 102008. DOI: 10.1016/j.ijer.2022.102008

Lindberg, R. S., Laine, T. H., & Haaranen, L. (2019). Gamifying programming education in K-12: A review of programming curricula in seven countries and programming games. *British Journal of Educational Technology*, 50(4), 1979–1995. DOI: 10.1111/bjet.12685

Luo, Y., Liang, P., Wang, C., Shahin, M., & Zhan, J. (2021, October). Characteristics and challenges of low-code development: the practitioners' perspective. In *Proceedings of the 15th ACM/IEEE international symposium on empirical software engineering and measurement (ESEM)* (pp. 1-11). DOI: 10.1145/3475716.3475782

Martinez, E., & Pfister, L. (2023). Benefits and limitations of using low-code development to support digitalization in the construction industry. *Automation in Construction*, 152, 104909. DOI: 10.1016/j.autcon.2023.104909

Matook, S., Maggie Wang, Y., Koeppel, N., & Guerin, S. (2024). Metacognitive skills in low-code app development: Work-integrated learning in information systems development. *Journal of Information Technology*, 39(1), 41–70. DOI: 10.1177/02683962231170238

Mladenović, M., Boljat, I., & Žanko, Ž. (2018). Comparing loops misconceptions in block-based and text-based programming languages at the K-12 level. *Education and Information Technologies*, 23(4), 1483–1500. DOI: 10.1007/s10639-017-9673-3

Mladenović, M., Žanko, Ž., & Aglić Čuvić, M. (2021). The impact of using program visualization techniques on learning basic programming concepts at the K-12 level. *Computer Applications in Engineering Education*, 29(1), 145–159. DOI: 10.1002/cae.22315

Mladenovic, S., Granic, A., Zaharija, G., & Krpan, D. (2023). LOW-CODE AND NO-CODE APPROACH TO TEACHING ARTIFICIAL INTELLIGENCE. In *17th International Technology,Education and Development Conference*.

Mohamad, S. N. H., Patel, A., Latih, R., Qassim, Q., Na, L., & Tew, Y. (2011, July). Block-based programming approach: challenges and benefits. In *Proceedings of the 2011 international conference on electrical engineering and informatics* (pp. 1-5). IEEE.

Noone, M., & Mooney, A. (2018). Visual and textual programming languages: A systematic review of the literature. *Journal of Computers in Education*, 5(2), 149–174. DOI: 10.1007/s40692-018-0101-5

Özdemır, İ. H., Kişla, T., & Tito, S. S. (2023, June). Mobile Programming with Kuika: A Course Design. In 2023 32nd Annual Conference of the European Association for Education in Electrical and Information Engineering (EAEEIE) (pp. 1-6). IEEE.

Papadakis, S., Kalogiannakis, M., Zaranis, N., & Orfanakis, V. (2016). Using Scratch and App Inventor for teaching introductory programming in secondary education. A case study. *International Journal of Technology Enhanced Learning*, 8(3-4), 217–233. DOI: 10.1504/IJTEL.2016.082317

Pinho, D., Aguiar, A., & Amaral, V. (2023). What about the usability in low-code platforms? A systematic literature review. *Journal of Computer Languages*, 74, 101185. DOI: 10.1016/j.cola.2022.101185

Rao, N., Tsay, J., Kate, K., Hellendoorn, V., & Hirzel, M. (2024, March). Low-Code for AI. In *Proceedings of the 29th International Conference on Intelligent User Interfaces* (pp. 837-852).

Sáez-López, J. M., Román-González, M., & Vázquez-Cano, E. (2016). Visual programming languages integrated across the curriculum in elementary school: A two year case study using "Scratch" in five schools. *Computers & Education*, 97, 129–141. DOI: 10.1016/j.compedu.2016.03.003

Sim, T. Y., & Lau, S. L. (2022, November). Review on challenges and solutions in novice programming education. In *2022 IEEE International Conference on Computing (ICOCO)* (pp. 55-61). IEEE. DOI: 10.1109/ICOCO56118.2022.10031657

Smith, A., Mott, B., Taylor, S., Hubbard-Cheuoua, A., Minogue, J., Oliver, K., & Ringstaff, C. (2020). Toward a block-based programming approach to interactive storytelling for upper elementary students. In *Interactive Storytelling: 13th International Conference on Interactive Digital Storytelling, ICIDS 2020, Bournemouth, UK, November 3-6, 2020* [Springer International Publishing.]. *Proceedings*, 13, 111–119.

Sońta, M., & Przegalinska, A. (2024). Say 'yes' to 'no-code'solutions: how to teach low-code and no-code competencies to non-IT students. In *Handbook of Social Computing* (pp. 330–342). Edward Elgar Publishing. DOI: 10.4337/9781803921259.00030

Sufi, F. (2023). Algorithms in low-code-no-code for research applications: A practical review. *Algorithms*, 16(2), 108. DOI: 10.3390/a16020108

Sun, L., Guo, Z., & Zhou, D. (2022). Developing K-12 students' programming ability: A systematic literature review. *Education and Information Technologies*, 27(5), 7059–7097. DOI: 10.1007/s10639-022-10891-2

Sun, L., & Zhou, L. (2023). Does text-based programming improve K-12 students' CT skills? Evidence from a meta-analysis and synthesis of qualitative data in educational contexts. *Thinking Skills and Creativity*, 49, 101340. DOI: 10.1016/j.tsc.2023.101340

Tank, K. M., Ottenbreit-Leftwich, A., Moore, T. J., Yang, S., Wafula, Z., Kim, J., ... & Chu, L. (2024). Investigating Sequencing as a Means to Computational Thinking in Young Learners.

Theodoropoulos, A., & Lepouras, G. (2020). Digital game-based learning and computational thinking in P-12 education: a systematic literature review on playing games for learning programming. Handbook of research on tools for teaching computational thinking in p-12 education, 159-183.

Tikva, C., & Tambouris, E. (2021). Mapping computational thinking through programming in K-12 education: A conceptual model based on a systematic literature review. *Computers & Education*, 162, 104083. DOI: 10.1016/j.compedu.2020.104083

Tsung, S., Wei, H., Li, H., Wang, Y., Xia, M., & Qu, H. (2022, June). Blocklens: visual analytics of student coding behaviors in block-based programming environments. In *Proceedings of the Ninth ACM Conference on Learning@ Scale* (pp. 299-303). DOI: 10.1145/3491140.3528298

Villegas-Ch, W., García-Ortiz, J., & Sánchez-Viteri, S. (2021). Identification of the factors that influence university learning with low-code/no-code artificial intelligence techniques. *Electronics (Basel)*, 10(10), 1192. DOI: 10.3390/electronics10101192

Wang, C. H., & Wu, K. C. (2022, December). A preliminary study on interdisciplinary programming learning based on cloud computing low-code development platform. In *2022 International Conference on Computer and Applications (ICCA)* (pp. 1-5). IEEE. DOI: 10.1109/ICCA56443.2022.10039663

Weintrop, D. (2019). Block-based programming in computer science education. *Communications of the ACM*, 62(8), 22–25. DOI: 10.1145/3341221

Weintrop, D., & Wilensky, U. (2017). Comparing block-based and text-based programming in high school computer science classrooms. [TOCE]. *ACM Transactions on Computing Education*, 18(1), 1–25. DOI: 10.1145/3089799

Weng, X., Ng, O. L., Cui, Z., & Leung, S. (2023). Creativity development with problem-based digital making and block-based programming for science, technology, engineering, arts, and mathematics learning in middle school contexts. *Journal of Educational Computing Research*, 61(2), 304–328. DOI: 10.1177/07356331221115661

Wong, G. K., Cheung, H. Y., Ching, E. C., & Huen, J. M. (2015, December). School perceptions of coding education in K-12: A large scale quantitative study to inform innovative practices. In *2015 IEEE international conference on teaching, Assessment, and learning for engineering (TALE)* (pp. 5-10). IEEE. DOI: 10.1109/TALE.2015.7386007

Wörister, F., & Knobelsdorf, M. (2023, November). A Block-Based Programming Environment for Teaching Low-Level Computing (Discussion Paper). In *Proceedings of the 23rd Koli Calling International Conference on Computing Education Research* (pp. 1-7).

Xu, E., Wang, W., & Wang, Q. (2023). A meta-analysis of the effectiveness of programming teaching in promoting K-12 students' computational thinking. *Education and Information Technologies*, 28(6), 6619–6644. DOI: 10.1007/s10639-022-11445-2

Xu, Z., Ritzhaupt, A. D., Tian, F., & Umapathy, K. (2019). Block-based versus text-based programming environments on novice student learning outcomes: A meta-analysis study. *Computer Science Education*, 29(2-3), 177–204. DOI: 10.1080/08993408.2019.1565233

Ye, H., Liang, B., Ng, O. L., & Chai, C. S. (2023). Integration of computational thinking in K-12 mathematics education: A systematic review on CT-based mathematics instruction and student learning. *International Journal of STEM Education*, 10(1), 3. DOI: 10.1186/s40594-023-00396-w

Zhu, M., & Wang, C. (2024). K-12 computer science teaching strategies, challenges, and teachers' professional development opportunities and needs. *Computers in the Schools*, 41(1), 1–22. DOI: 10.1080/07380569.2023.2178868

Chapter 7
Mapping the Anatomy of Novice-Generated Mistakes in Learning Programming

Fatih Erdoğdu
https://orcid.org/0000-0003-1022-8570
Zonguldak Bülent Ecevit University, Turkey

Seyfullah Gökoğlu
https://orcid.org/0000-0003-0074-7692
Bartın University, Turkey

ABSTRACT

Programming has become very important in modern education. Research shows that exposing students to coding at a young age positively contributes to their academic, cognitive and professional development. However, students may make some mistakes during the programming process, which are considered a natural part of programming. In this context, the aim of this study is to classify various mistakes encountered by novice programmers while learning programming. For this purpose, a literature review was conducted, and it was found that there are basically two types of mistakes: strategic mistakes and knowledge-based mistakes. It was found that these mistakes are divided into groups within themselves. This book chapter recommends that researchers and practitioners conduct practical studies of the mistakes uncovered and conduct qualitative research in which the mistakes can be examined in greater depth.

DOI: 10.4018/979-8-3693-4542-9.ch007

INTRODUCTION

Programming, telling computers what to do, is one of the most important parts of technology. For K-12 students, learning to code means preparing for the world of the future. However, some common mistakes can be made when beginning this process. Knowing these mistakes and learning to learn from them can make programming more fun and efficient. Beginning programmers often make the following mistakes: copying and pasting code without fully understanding it, ignoring or not understanding error messages, choosing the wrong programming language to start with, and ignoring basic concepts. These mistakes not only make learning more difficult but can also reduce student motivation. Although copying and pasting the code without understanding how it works may seem like a solution in the short term, in the long term it makes it difficult to understand programming. This method can prevent students from developing the ability to write their own code (DEV Community, 2023). Ignoring or not understanding error messages makes it impossible to solve problems and improve code (LearnPython.com, 2023). These mistakes usually arise from a lack of patience and carelessness. Choosing the wrong programming language is also a big problem (freeCodeCamp, 2023). Some languages are easier and more fun, especially for beginners. For example, the Python language with its simple and understandable structure is very suitable for beginners (Mladenovi et al., 2018). Starting with more difficult languages can discourage students from learning. Ignoring basic concepts, especially without understanding important topics like algorithms and data structures, makes writing code and solving problems difficult (EnjoyAlgorithms, 2023). Therefore, it is important to understand programming mistakes by classifying them.

With the rapid advancement of technology, programming knowledge is no longer a luxury but a necessity. Therefore, computer education should be accessible and become a priority area of learning in the 21st century. In this educational process, programming knowledge teaches students important skills such as critical thinking, problem solving, and creative thinking. Since many schools put a lot of effort into teaching programming (Lye & Koh, 2014), various difficulties in learning and executing programming for beginners have been identified. Ashraf and Ashraf (2024) claimed that mistakes are inevitable for students while learning programming. Since programming courses require demanding tasks and logical thinking (Durak et al., 2019), there are usually high dropout and failure rates, especially in the first year of computer science courses (Ayalew et al., 2018; Navarro-Cota et al., 2024). There is a very close connection between programming and problem-solving skills (Wong, 2024). Programming is the translation of the problem-solving process into computer language. The steps to be followed to solve a problem are expressed as code in the programming process. The goal of programming education is to acquire skills such as understanding and analyzing the problem, developing algorithms, logical thinking, debugging, creativity, and innovation (Romero et al., 2017). During this process, it is a natural process to encounter mistakes while writing code and trying to solve them. Katai and Toth (2010) found that complex processes such as programming make learning difficult. In addition to the complex structure, the abstract structure is also a factor that makes learning difficult. Teaching programming, while inherently difficult, involves future skills that must be taught appropriately in K-12 classrooms. Therefore, it is considered important to uncover the anatomy of programming mistakes that beginners encounter while learning programming in K-12 classrooms. This study discusses the mistakes made while learning programming and the causes of these mistakes. Understanding what causes mistakes and how to fix them is the key to learning programming successfully. In this way, students can make greater progress in the programming world and overcome the difficulties they encounter more easily. This can have a positive impact on students' 21st century skills and academic success. Therefore, classifying programming mistakes can be the first step in programming lessons. Based on the classifications in this part of the book, teachers can implement activities as part of programming lessons that focus on these mistakes and make learning programming easier. Thanks to these classifications, teachers can also find the sources and causes of their students' programming mistakes.

MAIN FOCUS OF THE CHAPTER

The Importance of Programming at the K-12 Level

Research show that exposing students to coding at a young age positively contributes to their academic, cognitive and professional development (Bers, 2020). Hu (2024) suggests that by integrating programming into the curriculum, students can develop other essential 21st century skills such as critical thinking, creativity, communication, collaboration, problem solving, as well as computational thinking. It can be said that one of the most important contributions is the development of computational thinking skills. Computational thinking: This is a skill that is in many ways consistent with 21st century skills such as creativity, critical thinking, and problem solving (Binkley et al., 2012). Lye and Koh (2014) emphasize the role of computational thinking in promoting problem-solving skills and logical thinking and state that students should be exposed to programming concepts from a young age so that they acquire basic digital skills necessary for navigating the Digital World Age is very important and can be developed.

There is a lot of research in the literature showing that programming can improve students' computational thinking skills at the K-12 level. For example, Sun et al. (2021) examined the effect of programming on computational thinking using the meta-analysis method, using 114 effect sizes from 86 experimental studies. The research showed that programming generally improved K-12 students' numeracy skills. Zhang et al. (2024) found that the development of students' computational thinking skills has received great attention in the era of artificial intelligence and used experimental research to investigate the effects of robot programming approaches on computational thinking skills. In the experiment, a total of 118 students aged five to six were divided into two groups and experienced two different approaches to robot programming. As a result of the research, it was observed that the computational thinking skills of both groups in which robot programming was used significantly improved. Sun et al. (2024) emphasized that the development of computational thinking skills has recently become widespread worldwide and examined the effects of computer-assisted and non-computer-assisted programming activities on computational thinking skills. Using the quasi-experimental research method, researchers conducted programming activities with 124 elementary school students for 10 weeks. The results show that non-computer programming activities are more effective than computer-based programming activities at younger age groups and that programming activities generally improve computational thinking skills. Stressing that computational thinking is a new literacy skill of the future, Sun and Liu (2024) examined the effects of visual and text-based programming approaches on the computational thinking skills of 6th grade students. According to the results of the research, conducted using a semi-experimental method with 98 students, it was found that both programming approaches made a positive contribution to the development of computational thinking skills and that the gamified Python programming approach was more useful in developing computational thinking skills than thinking the block-based visual programming approach. In another study comparing the effects of block-based and text-based programming methods on computational thinking skills, D. Sun et al. (2024) evaluated the impact of these two approaches on the transition process to professional programming learning. Using the quasi-experimental research method, 64 secondary school students were divided into two groups and used different programming methods for five weeks. Both groups then switched to professional text-based programming for the following eight weeks. The results showed that students who progressed from the introductory level to professional text-based programming achieved significantly better computational thinking skills, exhibited more coding and debugging behavior and less apathetic behavior, and interacted more with the teacher. Yurdakök and Kalelioğlu (2024) compared the effect of a physical programming tool and a text-based programming lesson on the computational thinking skills of secondary school students. In the mixed-method research, 85 secondary school students used the physical programming tool called Micro:bit to learn Python programming for 6 weeks. According to the findings of the pre- and post-tests, a significant and positive difference was found in students' computational thinking skills and perceptions of self-efficacy in computational thinking skills. Su et al. (2024) investigated whether the pair programming method helps students develop computational thinking skills. In the study, a total of 32 fifth graders worked on scratch tasks in 16 pairs. Group discourses on learning topics consisting of nine projects were analyzed using the epistemic network analysis method. The results showed that the pair programming method could play a supporting role in learning computational thinking skills and concepts related to computational thinking.

The research findings listed above and numerous studies in the literature show that programming education positively contributes to the computational thinking skills of students at the K-12 level. However, when examining the research, it is apparent that there are many different approaches to programming education. The most important of these approaches may be listed as text-based programming, block-based programming, visual programming, robotic programming, pair programming and unplugged programming. Which approach to take when teaching programming can vary depending on factors such as the student's level, school facilities, curriculum, and teacher characteristics. What is the ideal and effective teaching approach to improve students' programming skills is one of the valid and current research questions (Tareq & Raja Yusof, 2024). This question shows us that we continue to encounter various difficulties and limitations when learning programming. Cheah (2020) conducted a literature review on factors that contribute to difficulties in learning and teaching programming. As a result of the analysis, it was found that there are many factors that contribute to the difficulties of programming in teaching and learning. However, these factors can generally be classified into four main factors: (1) programming phases, (2) problem-solving skills, (3) ineffective pedagogy, and (4) personal traits and attitude.

Dale and Weems (2014) divide the programming process into two phases and state that each phase requires different types of knowledge and skills. These phases are the problem-solving phase and the implementation phase. In order for students to successfully master a programming language, they must complete these phases one after the other. It is emphasized that it is very important for students to acquire the knowledge and skills of each level in order to avoid later mistakes. In the problem-solving phase, the student must learn programming and data structure concepts to analyze a problem. To understand the problem, analysis and specification steps must be performed. In this phase, the type, location and number of variables should be determined. A general solution called an algorithm is then created using the identified variables. Algorithms are English-language expressions that describe how and what a computer program should do to process data. Algorithms include step-by-step instructions for operations to be performed by the computer and other functions such as computation, data processing, and automatic decision making. Algorithms are generally expressed as command-like verbal expressions, pseudocodes, or flowcharts. After an algorithm is created, the program is created to verify the developed solution. The verification process includes ensuring that the program's flow logic is in the correct order, that the correct types of decision options are used, that appropriate and effective programming cycles are used, and that each function executed produces the correct output. The steps taken during the problem-solving phase determine the program results. Therefore, in this phase, cognitive skills such as reasoning and logical thinking are important to develop an effective and robust algorithm.

After the problem-solving phase is completed, the implementation phase begins. This phase is where the actual programming code is created, and programmers improve the code based on the information gathered in the problem-solving phase. Once the program is developed, extensive testing is carried out to verify the effectiveness of the program. The tests are carefully carried out using different types of input data and repetitive processes to ensure that the system is stable. This process is intended to ensure that the program works properly with its goal of solving a specific task without mistakes. Dale and Weems (2024) claimed that if the test result does not meet the intended goal, it is recommended to repeat the problem-solving phase to verify the actions taken and correct the resulting mistakes.

During the programming process, students encounter various difficulties. Although many programming tools and teaching approaches have been developed to facilitate learning and teaching programming, several problems still exist today. Learning programming concepts and creating semantic structures by merging these structures can be difficult for students at first. For this reason, students may find programming difficult, tedious, and even frustrating (Aparicio et al., 2018). Garner (2003) found that students understand programming concepts well when teachers explain programming, but they have difficulty developing solutions to problems when programming individually. Sentance and Csizmadia (2017) based the reasons for the difficulties encountered in the programming process on three categories: teacher, student, resources. Teacher challenges; as such, subject knowledge, differentiation, lack of time, approaches to teaching, dry (difficult to teach) topics, assessment and lack of support are listed. Challenges relating to students; these are listed as students' lack of understanding, problem-solving skills, students' resilience, math skills, literacy skills, remembering, and students not practicing. Difficulties related to resources are listed as technical problems, lack of resources, and finding quality resources. Cheah (2020) asserted that due to such problems, high failure rates and high dropout rates occur even in the first phase of introductory programming courses.

One of the difficulties that students often encounter when programming is programming mistakes. Programming mistakes, which are particularly committed by novice programmers, manifest themselves in different ways. Ranjeeth and Naidoo (2011) assessed students' programming mistakes into three groups: arbitrary, executive, and structural. Arbitrary errors are mistakes that occur when students act arbitrarily without taking certain programming restrictions into account. Execution errors are mistakes that arise due to the student's inability to perform manipulations even though he/she has understood the principles of programming. Structural errors are mistakes that arise from not understanding the context of the problem being programmed or not understanding a basic principle for the solution. Prokofyeva et al. (2017) listed the mistakes students commonly make while programming as follows: (1) Logical errors in creating algorithms, (2) Misunderstanding and misuse of programming language features, (3) Using incorrect data types, (4) Using Loops and Conditional Expressions. not used correctly, (5) missing or incorrect steps in solving programming problems, (6) using incorrect syntax, (7) making mistakes in memory management, and (8) defining or using functions incorrectly. Palominos et al. (2018) states that the mistakes students encounter in the programming process are generally mistakes caused by syntax. Sklirou (2017), programming mistakes made by students; he explained that they include incorrect use of variables, incorrect use of operators, use of reserved words in the wrong places, missing or misspelled commands, failure to create algorithmic structures correctly, and syntax or logic errors.

Vasilopoulos and Van Schaik (2019), student programming mistakes; it is emphasized that there are mistakes related to (1) the creation of variables, (2) the use of commands, (3) the correctness of the program syntax, (4) the correctness of the command sequence, (5) the executability of the program and (6) the correct execution of the program. Bishop-Clark (1998) discussed students' programming mistakes from a logical perspective and defined them as major logical mistakes and minor logical mistakes. Major logic errors are students' misrecognition of basic structures (e.g., choice or loop structures) or a combination of three or more minor logic mistakes. Minor logic mistakes include errors such as placing an expression in the wrong place, swapping two lines of code, not initializing a variable, or not defining a less important variable. Rodrigo et al. (2013) examined the mistakes students encountered while programming according to low, medium, and high levels of success and found that student success had no influence on the errors made and that students generally made similar types of mistakes. Researchers identify student programming errors; syntax mistakes include the mixing of the assignment operator with the equality comparator, the misuse of different variants of print expressions, the misuse or non-use of parameters, the misuse of object-oriented design principles such as information hiding and encapsulation, and the inability to find different reasons why they occurred mistake. Özdener (2008) explained that the reasons for the errors that students encounter in the programming process are perceptual and that the misconceptions that lead students to make errors are (1) believing that a shorter program is more efficient, and (2) thinking that the program uses the fewer variables is more efficient. According to Kwon (2017), students make the following mistakes when programming: (1) misusing variables or not using them, (2) not understanding the purpose and use of variables, and (3) not using variable names. Veerasamy et al. (2016), student programming mistakes generally occur in the form of knowledge mistakes and inability to complete programming tasks. Students often make knowledge mistakes when they have wrong concepts and cannot solve programming problems. Additionally, relatively few students make rule- and skill-based mistakes. Wang et al. (2011) states that students' programming mistakes generally include syntax errors, structural mistakes, logical mistakes, and untested scenarios. Syntax mistakes are errors that occur because expressions do not follow the rules of the programming language or are used incorrectly. Structural mistakes are errors such as flaws in the structure of the program, unused variables or assignments, and unnecessary pieces of code. Logical mistakes are errors that affect the correctness of the program, such as: logical mistakes, incorrect algorithms or incorrect evaluation of conditions. Untested scenarios are mistakes that occur because students do not adequately test their programs.

As detailed above, many mistakes are made in the programming process, which are expressed by researchers in different ways. In addition, the mistakes encountered may differ depending on the programming language or method used. In addition to identifying mistakes in the programming process, researchers have also investigated the causes of these mistakes. For example, Kwon (2017) examined the mental models of novice programmers. The researcher concluded that incorrect use of variables, redundancy of codes and poor problem-solving strategies were the major challenges in this process. In another study, the deficits of novice programmers were revealed and categorized by analyzing students' answers to the final exam (Veerasamy et al., 2016). When conducting a summative assessment, lack of programming knowledge and inability to remember correct instructions while programming were identified as major problems. Implementing summative assessments in programming instructions can result in students becoming unable to observe, format, and interpret. Therefore, when learning programming, it is a bit difficult to deal with logical notations and all kinds of mistakes. From a cognitive perspective, Ranjeeth and Naidoo (2011) analyzed students' answers in a programming exam and examined the relationship between cognitive maturity and mistakes types in a programming course. The results showed that students with lower cognitive maturity engaged in superficial learning of programming concepts. In addition, Özdener (2008) analyzed students' programming process and reported that students had misconceptions about algorithms in terms of runtime efficiency. Butler and Morgan (2007) claimed that it is difficult for novice programmers to learn algorithms and methods, understand the difference between syntax and semantics, and the lifetime of variables.

When reviewing previous studies, it appears that the anatomy of mistakes encountered in the programming process cannot be clearly revealed and uncertainties exist. It is believed that capturing the anatomy of the mistakes encountered will be helpful for students to program effectively and for teachers to carry out the programming teaching process efficiently. It is expected that the resulting conceptual map will serve as a guide for instructors in the process of teaching programming. This chapter presents the anatomy of mistakes novice programmers make when learning to code. Examining the current literature, it is found that the most common mistakes made by novice programmers can be divided into two categories: (1) strategic mistakes and (2) knowledge-based mistakes.

The Anatomy of Mistakes

In this book chapter, the mistakes that beginners make when learning programming are divided into strategic mistakes and knowledge-based mistakes. As a result of the literature review, it was seen that strategic mistakes and knowledge-based mistakes emerged. Because it has been revealed in this literature review that students make mistakes due to either their lack of knowledge about programming or their deficiencies in how a program works (Tirronen et al., 2015; Gupta et al., 2017; Brennan, 2021). Strategic mistakes are discussed as planning mistakes, semantic mistakes, parallelism and egocentricity. Knowledge mistakes are classified and explained as syntax mistakes, mistakes related to programming structure, and mistakes related to computer operation logic. This framework explains the reasons for such mistakes and how they arise. The classification and categorization of these mistakes is shown in Figure 1.

Figure 1. Programming Mistakes

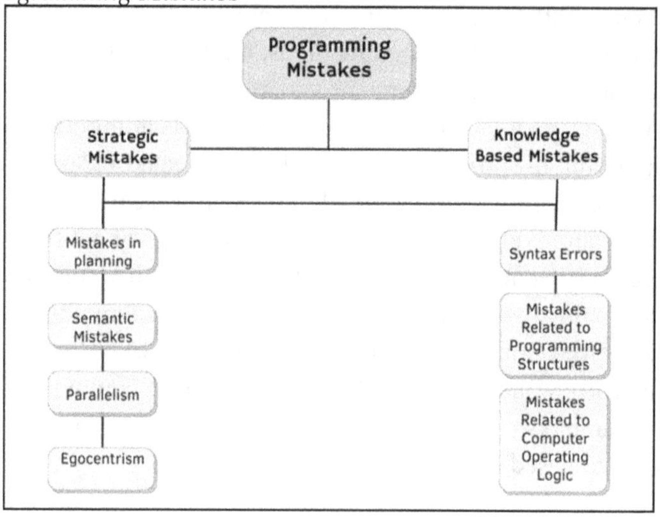

Strategic Mistakes

Strategic mistakes are usually caused by the programmer's inexperience or lack of attention to detail and can cause compilation or build problems (Gupta et al., 2017). These mistakes, especially made by inexperienced programmers, cause programmers to struggle with syntax mistakes, hinder programming progress, and can result in significant time loss (Brown & Altadmri, 2017; Denny et al., 2012). Brown and Altadmri (2017) claimed that these mistakes can be detrimental to the learning process as they prevent the program from running correctly and disrupt the learning process.

Strategic mistakes usually arise from incorrect decisions during the programming process. Therefore, they can be divided into conceptual mistakes. Conceptual mistakes occur during the programming process, usually due to a lack of technical knowledge or misunderstanding. These mistakes can directly affect the functionality, reliability and performance of the program. Conceptual mistakes in programming are fundamental mistakes that arise from a misunderstanding of basic programming concepts rather than mere (core) syntactic or logical errors in the code. These mistakes can lead to persistent problems and unexpected behavior during software development. Research has emphasized the importance of addressing misunderstandings at a deeper level by distinguishing between conceptual mistakes and coding mistakes (Cortinovis et al., 2023). Tirronen et al. (2015) stated that three categories of conceptual mistakes occur in novice programmers: parallelism, intentionality, and egocentrism mistakes. These errors indicate a fundamental lack of understanding of programming principles, which can hinder learning and problem-solving skills. In this study, we classified conceptual mistakes as planning mistakes, semantic mistakes, parallelism mistakes, and egocentrism mistakes.

Mistakes in Planning

Planning mistakes can significantly affect the success of programming. Beginning programmers often have difficulty drawing up programming plans to create functional solutions. It is emphasized that difficulties in creating plans are the cause of most mistakes made by novice programmers (Castro & Fisler, 2020). Difficulties in drawing up plans can affect the overall quality of the software by leading to mistakes in the design and implementation of the program.

Understanding the structure and flow of a program is critical to effective planning and execution. Planning errors can lead to inefficiency, longer development times and poor software quality. To reduce planning errors, it is important for programmers to reflect on failed plans, identify mistakes, and develop strategies to resolve them (Baek et al., 2019). By learning from mistakes and failures in the planning phase, programmers can improve their problem-solving skills and improve the quality of their programs. It is of great importance to plan before writing code, so the purpose and problem must be clearly determined first. Problem statements accompanied by step-by-step solutions have been shown to be particularly beneficial for novices in programming education (Muldner, Jennings & Chiarelli 2022). At this point, teachers can show step-by-step solutions to the problem through similar examples.

Semantic Mistakes

Semantic mistakes in programming refer to errors that occur at a deeper level than syntax problems and involve a misunderstanding of the meaning or logic behind the code. These mistakes can result in programs being written that do not function completely correctly (Patrick et al., 2014). Beginning programmers often struggle with semantic mistakes that, although minor, have a significant impact on the functionality of the software (Ahadi et al., 2018). These errors are different from syntactic errors because they involve problems with the logic or meaning of the code rather than its structure (Avci et al., 2016). Dealing with semantic errors requires a thorough understanding of programming concepts and the ability to identify and correct misunderstandings that can lead to such mistakes (Cortinovis et al., 2023). It is very important for programmers to think about failed plans, identify semantic errors and develop strategies to fix them. To reduce semantic mistakes, first the mistakes should be identified and strategies to solve them should be determined

(Baek et al., 2019). For this purpose, teachers can prepare guidelines to reduce these mistakes of students.

Parallelism

Parallelism mistakes in programming occur particularly when transitioning from sequential code to parallel code. Beginning programmers often have difficulty identifying and implementing parallelization options in the code they write. Various types of errors can occur in parallel programming, including those specific to parallel programming, such as data races and deadlocks (Brođanac et al., 2022). To resolve concurrency errors, it is important that programmers understand the nuances of parallel programming and be able to identify and resolve common mistakes. Tools like Semantic Mutation Testing (SMT) are designed to identify and fix semantic mistakes in parallel programs. Furthermore, Alghamdi et. al (2020) asserted that the use of parallelizing compilers and advanced testing techniques can help effectively detect and resolve concurrency mistakes

Egocentrism

Egocentric mistakes in programming refer to a cognitive bias in which programmers focus too much on their own perspectives or assumptions, leading to mistakes in problem solving and code development (Kwon, 2017). Kwon (2017) highlights the importance of addressing egocentric mistakes to improve the computational thinking skills of novice programmers. To overcome egocentrism in programming, students must distinguish between the programmer's intent and actual instructions that are explicitly encoded, which promotes a more objective and effective approach to programming (Kwon & Cheon, 2019). Egocentric mistakes in the programming process can hinder problem-solving and decision-making processes. By raising awareness of egocentric biases, encouraging diverse perspectives, and providing training that incorporates multiple perspectives, programmers may improve their computational thinking skills and improve the quality of their code.

Egocentric mistakes in programming often occur when a developer fails to get out of his own perspective and ignores the needs or perspectives of users. These errors can be examined based on two subfactors: discrepancy and intent. Inconsistency is when the code written by the developer does not meet the expected results. This is often because user needs are not fully understood or taken into account. For example, if a developer designs an interface based on their own usage habits, that interface may not be suitable for the general user base. Intent refers to the situation where the developer writes code that aims for a specific behavior or result, but that intent does not match the user experience. For example, adding a feature may ignore how that feature will be reflected or perceived by the user. In both cases, egocentrism results from the developer's inability to step outside of their own perspective and negatively impacts the overall usability of the software due to a lack of user-centered thinking. Therefore, to develop effective and user-friendly software, it is crucial that developers avoid errors of egocentricity and consider the user perspective.

Knowledge-based Mistakes

Students' previous experiences and knowledge can affect the mistakes they make in the programming processes. In situations such as learning incorrect information or lack of programming experience, inexperienced programmers can often make mistakes due to lack of knowledge. In this section, we will particularly focus on syntax errors, mistakes related to the programming structure and operating logic of the computer.

Syntax Errors

Syntactic knowledge is a concept that refers to the correct application of grammar and sentence structures that must be followed when writing a program, and a programmer cannot become a good programmer if he only has syntactic knowledge (Qian & Lehman, 2017). Mistakes such as mismatched parentheses, parentheses, quotes, variable definition errors, incorrect use of operators, use of lowercase/uppercase letters, and variable type errors are the most common syntax errors. Syntax errors are one of the first problems students encounter, especially when starting new programming. Since the spelling rules of each programming language can be different, this causes confusion for inexperienced programmers. Syntax errors are considered a hurdle in learning programming for students who are new to programming (Stefik and Siebert, 2013). It is also observed that students conduct randomized controlled trials when writing code to overcome this hurdle (Stefik and Siebert, 2013). To avoid this situation, it may be advisable to include appropriate syntax notes in all programming languages. This allows students to write the right codes directly instead of trying to write the right code. Ding, Shi & Li (2024) state that although different types of error classifications are made, the basis of all errors is syntax errors. Syntax errors and spelling errors can be confused with each other, in short, when an inexperienced programmer writes code. While accidentally deleting the character is defined as a typographical error, it can also occur as a syntax error (Ding, Shi, & Li, 2024). Finally, syntax errors seem to be the cause of all programming errors and are often made, especially by inexperienced programmers. Therefore, it is necessary to teach programming syntax effectively and efficiently as part of programming education at the K-12 level. To reduce the number of syntax errors, it is important to take precautions such as: writing careful code, using modern code editors, checking the code regularly, not writing too many lines at once, and practicing. It may be useful at this point to provide students with working with exercises to solve similar problems (Renkl, 2014). Moreover, the teacher should relate both theory and practice after the theoretical lecture. Syntax errors in programming at the K-12 level play a crucial role in student learning. These mistakes provide important benefits such as learning the rules of the language, improving error detection and solving skills, understanding programming logic, learning caution, and achieving a sense of achievement. Therefore, syntax errors are an indispensable part of programming education and help students improve their programming skills.

Mistakes Related to Programming Structures

Programming is the writing of code that instructs computers to perform specific tasks and solve problems. The structure of this process is organized within the framework of programming language-specific rules and concepts. Understanding the structure of programming is the foundation for writing effective and error-free code. The basic structure of programming consists of syntax, variables, data types, control structures, functions, procedures, error management, input and output operations. Therefore, to write correct code, it is necessary to learn this programming structure properly. Knowing the programming structure also helps you decide what strategy you want to pursue before writing code (Brennan, 2021). Before any code is written, the structure of the program must first be revealed (Steve, 2004). This is possible if you know the structure of programming well. For example, errors can be made in the structure of basic operations such as loops and conditional statements (Robins et al., 2003).

Mistakes Related to Computer Operating Logic

The operating logic of a computer mainly involves the interaction between hardware and software (De Michell and Gupta, 1997). Hardware consists of the physical parts of the computer: processor, memory, storage units, input/output devices, etc. This hardware processes information through electrical signals. Programming is used to determine how this hardware works. Programming languages contain instructions written in a format that humans can understand. These instructions allow the computer to perform certain functions. For example, opening a web browser, printing a document, or playing a game. A programming language contains instructions written in a language that the computer can understand. These instructions are used in the computer's hardware to generate or interpret certain electrical signals. Therefore, the programming language is the basic building block of the software.

That is, the programming language is a tool that controls the operating logic of the computer. A program defines how computer hardware is used to perform a specific task. It controls the operation of the computer through the programming language and provides instructions to achieve the desired results. Therefore, the relationship between the operating logic and programming of the computer describes how the computer's hardware is controlled and controlled by the software. In summary, knowing the working logic of the computer can make it easier for you to develop programming skills. Because the individual understands how the code he writes works in the background of the computer, how the code is compiled, and through which stages it reaches the user.

FUTURE RESEARCH DIRECTIONS

Many future research directions can be identified within this section. First, an experimental study can be conducted by examining the encodings developed as part of programming education at the K-12 level. Thus, programming mistakes that occur in an experimental study can be classified and categorized. In addition, programming training can be organized at the K-12 level to eliminate the causes and effects of programming mistakes. This way we get to the bottom of the problem and take precautions before the problem occurs. In addition, methods should be developed that can specifically reduce the number of syntax errors. For example, editors can be developed and offered to users that automatically indicate syntax errors. However, detailed research can be carried out by conducting extensive applied studies on all mistakes presented within the scope of this book section, or the classification can be expanded by adding various mistakes. Finally, since English concepts are incorporated into the programming process, knowledge of the English language is considered important. However, it may be difficult for a programmer with poor English skills to write code and this is one of the sources of errors. Therefore, it is important to develop coding platforms and put them into practice in the native language.

CONCLUSION

The purpose of this book chapter is to classify the mistakes in the programming process at the K-12 level and examine their causes. During the literature search carried out on this subject, two different programming mistakes came to light. These are divided into strategic mistakes and knowledge-based mistakes. Strategic mistakes are divided into four different types. These are planning mistakes, semantic mistakes, egocentrism and parallelism. Knowledge-based mistakes are divided into three groups. These are syntax errors, mistakes related to the programming structure, and mistakes related to the operating logic of the computer. These mistakes are usually caused by students not understanding the logic of programming, not writing detailed code, and making strategic mistakes.

Teachers have the most important role in reducing the classified programming mistakes. Therefore, for programming to be easy to learn, teachers should have the right strategy in addition to their knowledge. For this reason, teachers should provide students with plenty of similar examples in programming education, make them practice after each theoretical lecture, show problem solving step by step through similar examples and motivate students. For this purpose, various games can be used. By using these teaching methods, teachers can minimize the types of mistakes classified.

REFERENCES

Ahadi, A., Lister, R., & Mathieson, L. (2018). Syntax error based quantification of the learning progress of the novice programmer (world). 10–14. DOI: 10.1145/3197091.3197121

Alghamdi, A. M., & Eassa, F. E. (2019). OpenACC Errors Classification and Static Detection Techniques. *IEEE Access : Practical Innovations, Open Solutions*, 7, 113235–113253. DOI: 10.1109/ACCESS.2019.2935498

Alghamdi, A. S. A., Alghamdi, A. M., Eassa, F. E., & Khemakhem, M. A. (2020). ACC_TEST: Hybrid Testing Techniques for MPI-Based Programs. *IEEE Access : Practical Innovations, Open Solutions*, 8, 91488–91500. DOI: 10.1109/ACCESS.2020.2994172

Aparicio, J. T., Aparicio, M., & Costa, C. J. (2018). A Virtual Robot to support Programming Learning. ISR 2018; *50th International Symposium on Robotics*, 1–4. https://ieeexplore.ieee.org/document/8470585

Ashraf, T. A., & Ashraf, T. A. (2024). The Impact of Inter-language Related Errors among Non-English Majors at Tertiary Level Students in Bangladesh. *Language in India, 24*(1). http://languageinindia.com/jan2024/v24i1jan2024.pdf#page=12

Avci, G., Mehuljic, M., & Schüller, P. (2016). Giving hints for logic programming examples without revealing solutions. *2016 24th Signal Processing and Communication Application Conference (SIU)*, 513–516. DOI: 10.1109/SIU.2016.7495790

Ayalew, Y., Tshukudu, E., & Lefoanea, M. (2018). Factors affecting programming performance of first year students at a University in Botswana. African Journal of Research in Mathematics, *Science and Technology Education, 22*(3), 363-373. https://hdl.handle.net/10520/EJC-12a2c586fa

Baek, Y., Wang, S., Yang, D., Ching, Y.-H., Swanson, S., & Chittoori, B. (2019). Revisiting Second Graders' Robotics with an Understand/Use-Modify-Create (U2MC) Strategy. *European Journal of STEM Education, 4*(1), 07. https://doi.org/ DOI: 10.20897/ejsteme/5772

Bers, M. U. (2020). *Coding as a playground: Programming and computational thinking in the early childhood classroom*. Routledge. DOI: 10.4324/9781003022602

Binkley, M., Erstad, O., Herman, J., Raizen, S., Ripley, M., Miller-Ricci, M., & Rumble, M. (2012). Defining Twenty-First Century Skills. In Griffin, P., McGaw, B., & Care, E. (Eds.), *Assessment and Teaching of 21st Century Skills (pp* (pp. 17–66). Springer Netherlands., DOI: 10.1007/978-94-007-2324-5_2

Bishop-Clark, C. (1998). Comparing Understanding of Programming Design Concepts Using Visual Basic and Traditional Basic. *Journal of Educational Computing Research*, 18(1), 37–47. DOI: 10.2190/0FG3-BVDK-2XB9-P1F6

Brennan, K. (2021). How kids manage self-directed programming projects: Strategies and structures. *Journal of the Learning Sciences*, 30(4-5), 576–610. DOI: 10.1080/10508406.2021.1936531

Brođanac, P., Novak, J., & Boljat, I. (2022). Has the time come to teach parallel programming to secondary school students? *Heliyon*, 8(1), e08662. Advance online publication. DOI: 10.1016/j.heliyon.2021.e08662 PMID: 35028449

Brown, N. C. C., & Altadmri, A. (2017). Novice Java Programming Mistakes: Large-Scale Data vs. Educator Beliefs. *ACM Transactions on Computing Education, 17*(2), 7:1-7:21. DOI: 10.1145/2994154

Butler, M., & Morgan, M. (2007). Learning challenges faced by novice programming students studying high level and low feedback concepts. *Proceedings ascilite Singapore*, 1(99-107). https://www.ascilite.org/conferences/singapore07/procs/butler.pdf

Castro, F. E. V., & Fisler, K. (2020, February). Qualitative Analyses of Movements Between Task-level and Code-level Thinking of Novice Programmers (world). *51st ACM Technical Symposium on Computer Science Education.* DOI: 10.1145/3328778.3366847

Cheah, C. S. (2020). Factors Contributing to the Difficulties in Teaching and Learning of Computer Programming: A Literature Review. *Contemporary Educational Technology*, 12(2), ep272. DOI: 10.30935/cedtech/8247

Community, D. E. V. (2023). What are some common mistakes that beginners make when learning to code, and how can you avoid them? *DEV Community*. Retrieved from https://dev.to

Cortinovis, R., Bolton, P. F., & Caceffo, R. (2023). An Open List of Computer Programming Student's Common Problems and its Leverage in Teaching Practice. *Simpósio Brasileiro de Educação Em Computação (EDUCOMP),* 108–118. DOI: 10.5753/educomp.2023.228328

Dale, N. B., & Weems, C. (2014). *Programming and Problem Solving with C.* Jones & Bartlett Publishers.

De Michell, G., & Gupta, R. K. (1997). Hardware/software co-design. *Proceedings of the IEEE*, 85(3), 349–365. DOI: 10.1109/5.558708

Denny, P., Luxton-Reilly, A., & Tempero, E. (2012). All syntax errors are not equal. *Proceedings of the 17th ACM Annual Conference on Innovation and Technology in Computer Science Education*, 75–80. https://doi.org/DOI: 10.1145/2325296.2325318

Ding, G., Shi, X., & Li, S. (2024). Integrating programming errors into knowledge graphs for automated assignment of programming tasks. *Education and Information Technologies*, 29(5), 5947–5980. DOI: 10.1007/s10639-023-12026-7

Durak, H. Y., Yilmaz, F. G. K., & Yilmaz, R. (2019). Computational Thinking, Programming Self-Efficacy, Problem Solving and Experiences in the Programming Process Conducted with Robotic Activities. *Contemporary Educational Technology*, 10(2), 173–197. DOI: 10.30935/cet.554493

Enjoy Algorithms. (2023). Guide to master DSA and crack the coding interview. Retrieved from https://www.enjoyalgorithms.com/blog/guide-to-master-dsa-and-crack-the-coding-interview

freeCodeCamp. (2023). Mistakes every programmer makes when learning to code – and how to fix them. f*reeCodeCamp*. Retrieved from https://freecodecamp.org

Garner, S. (2003, June). Learning resources and tools to aid novices learn programming. In *Informing science & information technology education joint conference* (pp. 213–222). INSITE., https://proceedings.informingscience.org/IS2003Proceedings/docs/036Garne.pdf DOI: 10.28945/2613

Gupta, R., Pal, S., Kanade, A., & Shevade, S. (2017). DeepFix: Fixing Common C Language Errors by Deep Learning. *Proceedings of the AAAI Conference on Artificial Intelligence*, 31(1), 1. Advance online publication. DOI: 10.1609/aaai.v31i1.10742

Hu, L. (2024). Programming and 21st century skill development in K-12 schools: A multidimensional meta-analysis. *Journal of Computer Assisted Learning*, 40(2), 610–636. DOI: 10.1111/jcal.12904

Katai, Z., & Toth, L. (2010). Technologically and artistically enhanced multi-sensory computer-programming education. *Teaching and Teacher Education*, 26(2), 244–251. DOI: 10.1016/j.tate.2009.04.012

Kwon, K. (2017). Novice programmer's misconception of programming reflected on problem-solving plans. *International Journal of Computer Science Education in Schools*, 1(4), 14–24. DOI: 10.21585/ijcses.v1i4.19

Kwon, K., & Cheon, J. (2019). Exploring problem decomposition and program development through block-based programs. *International Journal of Computer Science Education in Schools*, 3(1), 1. Advance online publication. DOI: 10.21585/ijcses.v3i1.54

LearnPython.com. (2023). 8 most common programming errors made by beginners. *LearnPython.com*. Retrieved from https://learnpython.com

Lye, S. Y., & Koh, J. H. L. (2014). Review on teaching and learning of computational thinking through programming: What is next for K-12? *Computers in Human Behavior*, 41, 51–61. DOI: 10.1016/j.chb.2014.09.012

Muldner, K., Jennings, J., & Chiarelli, V. (2022). A review of worked examples in programming activities. *ACM Transactions on Computing Education*, 23(1), 1–35. DOI: 10.1145/3560266

Navarro-Cota, C., Molina, A. I., Redondo, M. A., & Lacave, C. (2024). Individual differences in computer programming: A systematic review. *Behaviour & Information Technology*, •••, 1–19. DOI: 10.1080/0144929X.2024.2317377

Özdener, N. (2008). A comparison of the misconceptions about the time-efficiency of algorithms by various profiles of computer-programming students. *Computers & Education*, 51(3), 1094–1102. DOI: 10.1016/j.compedu.2007.10.008

Palominos, F. E., Palominos, S. K., Durán, C. A., Córdova, F. M., & Díaz, H. (2018). Challenges in the use of a support tool with automated review in student learning of programming courses. *Procedia Computer Science*, 139, 424–431. DOI: 10.1016/j.procs.2018.10.260

Patrick, M., Alexander, R., Oriol, M., & Clark, J. A. (2014). Probability-Based Semantic Interpretation of Mutants. *2014 IEEE Seventh International Conference on Software Testing, Verification and Validation Workshops,* 186–195. DOI: 10.1109/ICSTW.2014.18

Prokofyeva, N., Uhanova, M., Katalnikova, S., Synytsya, K., & Jurenoks, A. (2017). Introductory Programming Training of First Year Students. *Procedia Computer Science*, 104, 286–293. DOI: 10.1016/j.procs.2017.01.137

Qian, Y., & Lehman, J. (2017). Students' misconceptions and other difficulties in introductory programming: A literature review. *ACM Transactions on Computing Education*, 18(1), 1–24. DOI: 10.1145/3077618

Ranjeeth, S., & Naidoo, R. (2011). An Investigation into the Relationship between the Level of Cognitive Maturity and the Types of Errors Made by Students in a Computer Programming Course. *The International College Teaching Methods & Styles Journal*, 3(2), 31–40. DOI: 10.19030/ctms.v3i2.5279

Renkl, A. (2014). Toward an instructionally oriented theory of example-based learning. *Cognitive Science*, 38(1), 1–37. DOI: 10.1111/cogs.12086 PMID: 24070563

Robins, A., Rountree, J., & Rountree, N. (2003). Learning and teaching programming: A review and discussion. *Computer Science Education*, 13(2), 137–172. DOI: 10.1076/csed.13.2.137.14200

Rodrigo, M., Andallaza, T. C. S., Castro, F. E. V. G., Armenta, M. L. V., Dy, T. T., & Jadud, M. C. (2013). An Analysis of Java Programming Behaviors, Affect, Perceptions, and Syntax Errors among Low-Achieving, Average, and High-Achieving Novice Programmers. *Journal of Educational Computing Research*, 49(3), 293–325. DOI: 10.2190/EC.49.3.b

Romero, M., Lepage, A., & Lille, B. (2017). Computational thinking development through creative programming in higher education. *International Journal of Educational Technology in Higher Education*, 14(1), 1–15. DOI: 10.1186/s41239-017-0080-z

Sentance, S., & Csizmadia, A. (2017). Computing in the curriculum: Challenges and strategies from a teacher's perspective. *Education and Information Technologies*, 22(2), 469–495. DOI: 10.1007/s10639-016-9482-0

Sklirou, T. S. (2017). Programming in secondary education: Applications, new trends and challenges. *2017 IEEE Global Engineering Education Conference (EDUCON)*, 580–585. DOI: 10.1109/EDUCON.2017.7942904

Stefik, A., & Siebert, S. (2013). An empirical investigation into programming language syntax. [TOCE]. *ACM Transactions on Computing Education*, 13(4), 1–40. DOI: 10.1145/2534973

Steve, M. (2004). *Code complete: a practical handbook of software construction*. Microsoft Press.

Su, Y.-S., Wang, S., & Liu, X. (2024). Using Epistemic Network Analysis to Explore Primary School Students' Computational Thinking in Pair Programming Learning. *Journal of Educational Computing Research*, 62(2), 559–593. DOI: 10.1177/07356331231210560

Sun, D., Zhu, C., Xu, F., Li, Y., Ouyang, F., & Cheng, M. (2024). Transitioning From Introductory to Professional Programming in Secondary Education: Comparing Learners' Computational Thinking Skills, Behaviors, and Attitudes. *Journal of Educational Computing Research*, 62(3), 647–674. DOI: 10.1177/07356331231204653

Sun, L., Hu, L., & Zhou, D. (2021). Which way of design programming activities is more effective to promote K-12 students' computational thinking skills? A meta-analysis. *Journal of Computer Assisted Learning*, 37(4), 1048–1062. DOI: 10.1111/jcal.12545

Sun, L., & Liu, J. (2024). Effects of Gamified Python Programming on Primary School Students' Computational Thinking Skills: A Differential Analysis of Gender. *Journal of Educational Computing Research*, 62(3), 846–874. DOI: 10.1177/07356331231225269

Sun, L., Liu, J., & Liu, Y. (2024). Comparative experiment of the effects of unplugged and plugged-in programming on computational thinking in primary school students: A perspective of multiple influential factors. *Thinking Skills and Creativity*, 52, 101542. DOI: 10.1016/j.tsc.2024.101542

Tareq, Z.-A., & Raja Yusof, R. J. (2024). Modeling a Problem-Solving Approach Through Computational Thinking for Teaching Programming. *IEEE Transactions on Education*, 67(2), 282–291. DOI: 10.1109/TE.2024.3354425

Tirronen, V., Uusi-Mäkelä, S., & Isomöttönen, V. (2015). Understanding beginners' mistakes with Haskell. *Journal of Functional Programming*, 25, e11. DOI: 10.1017/S0956796815000179

Vasilopoulos, I. V., & Van Schaik, P. (2019). Koios: Design, Development, and Evaluation of an Educational Visual Tool for Greek Novice Programmers. *Journal of Educational Computing Research*, 57(5), 1227–1259. DOI: 10.1177/0735633118781776

Veerasamy, A. K., D'Souza, D., & Laakso, M.-J. (2016). Identifying Novice Student Programming Misconceptions and Errors From Summative Assessments. *Journal of Educational Technology Systems*, 45(1), 50–73. DOI: 10.1177/0047239515627263

Wang, T., Su, X., Ma, P., Wang, Y., & Wang, K. (2011). Ability-training-oriented automated assessment in introductory programming course. *Computers & Education*, 56(1), 220–226. DOI: 10.1016/j.compedu.2010.08.003

Wong, G. K. (2024). Amplifying children's computational problem-solving skills: A hybrid-based design for programming education. *Education and Information Technologies*, 29(2), 1761–1793. DOI: 10.1007/s10639-023-11880-9

Yurdakök, E. A., & Kalelioğlu, F. (2024). The Effect of Teaching Physical Programming on Computational Thinking Skills and Self-Efficacy Perceptions Towards Computational Thinking. *Journal of Educational Computing Research*, 62(3), 785–815. DOI: 10.1177/07356331231220313

Zhang, X., Chen, Y., Hu, L., Bao, Y., Tu, Y.-F., & Hwang, G.-J. (2024). A metaphor-based robot programming approach to facilitating young children's computational thinking and positive learning behaviors. *Computers & Education*, 215, 105039. DOI: 10.1016/j.compedu.2024.105039

Chapter 8
Methods for Accessible Computer Science and Computer Programming Education for Visually Impaired and Blind Students

Habibe Güneş
https://orcid.org/0000-0002-3479-2195
Firat University, Turkey

ABSTRACT

Just like our fingerprints, we are born different from each other with many characteristics. What is expected from education is to respect these differences, to highlight individuals' unique and special characteristics, and to create experiences that will enable them to maximize their talents. However, when structuring education for individuals with special needs, it should be tailored to their individual needs and provide accessibility that allows them to develop skills relevant to the current technological age. In this book chapter, suggestions are presented for developing the basic skills of visually impaired individuals in computer science and coding education.

DOI: 10.4018/979-8-3693-4542-9.ch008

INTRODUCTION

The Universal Declaration of Human Rights, the Convention on the Rights of the Child, the International Covenant on Economic, Social and Cultural Rights, the United Nations Convention on the Rights of the Child, and the Salamanca Statement on Special Needs Education all emphasize that education is a fundamental right and freedom accessible to everyone (Ciftci, 2021). Accordingly, education should be organized in a way that is supported by the state, equally accessible to all, and provides an environment where individuals can develop their vocational and technical skills. However, the emphasis on the need for education to be specifically tailored to individuals with special needs is highlighted only in the Salamanca Statement, created in 1994. Additionally, reviewing the United Nations' (UN) 2030 Agenda reveals that it includes 17 Sustainable Development Goals (SDGs) aimed at achieving a better and more sustainable world for everyone. The fourth Sustainable Development Goal encompasses "ensuring inclusive and equitable quality education and promoting lifelong learning opportunities for all." To speak about educational equity, it is essential to provide maximum opportunities and necessary supports for children to participate in computer science courses and extracurricular activities, regardless of gender, race, ethnicity, disability, and other factors (Milne & Ladner, 2019). Despite international efforts to achieve such a goal, many visually impaired students seeking degrees in computer science face significant challenges and must overcome social and technical barriers. One of the challenges is learning programming as a fundamental skill for obtaining a degree in computer science (Alotaibi et al., 2020). In addition to education, there is a disadvantage for visually impaired individuals in the workforce due to the lack of education tailored to their individual differences. Disabled individuals (DIs) are often excluded from the growing IT job market, with a general inequality in employment and recruitment opportunities between disabled and non-disabled individuals. In 2022, it was observed that 21.3% of disabled individuals in the US were employed, while 65.4% of non-disabled individuals were employed. Specifically, blind and visually impaired (BLV) professionals have lower employment rates compared to their visually impaired peers. As the software industry rapidly expands, the employment rate of BLV professionals is even lower; a 2022 survey revealed that only 1.7% of software professionals were BLV individuals. However, a general trend of increasing numbers of BLV software employees has been observed (Bureau of Labor Statistics, 2023; Stack Overflow, 2022).

To overcome these challenges, it is crucial to structure education for individuals with special needs, considering the rights and freedoms outlined in these declarations. This is important for enabling disabled individuals to smoothly continue their social lives, adapt to society, and comfortably sustain their lives. Since each individual possesses distinct characteristics, it is not possible to evaluate everyone under the same conditions, and standard educational conditions will be insufficient for individuals who require special education. Therefore, individuals with special educational needs must have the right to education under equal conditions in accordance with the principle of equality, and education must be planned and provided based on the individual characteristics of each disabled student. According to the World Health Organization, among the 285 million individuals with special needs, visually impaired individuals can navigate their lives more easily by receiving education through the enhancement and utilization of their other senses, as they cannot perceive the external world through their sense of sight. In this process, the use of assistive technologies is also widely applied in the education of visually impaired students.

In contemporary times, assistive technologies are widely used by educators to individualize and differentiate the teaching process for at-risk students, those with exceptional talents, and other students. Students with visual impairments are mentally similar to other students, but they require auditory or tactile tools in their learning experiences and communications (Safak, 2017). To access information, they often rely on their senses of touch, hearing, taste, and smell (Demir & Sen, 2009). Additionally, the Special Education Services Regulation in Turkey (2018) stipulates that support for visual content, such as descriptions or tactile representations, should be available. In this context, it is crucial to organize teaching according to students' needs and subjects, and to identify and use appropriate methods, techniques, and tools (Okcu et al., 2016; Yazici et al., 2021). Studies have examined the effectiveness of material usage in supporting and facilitating the education of students with visual impairments in various ways (Karakoc, 2016; Kizilaslan & Sozbilir, 2017; Sahin & Yorek, 2009). However, when examining the contents of education provided to individuals with special needs, it is evident that the supportive tools used in the lessons, assessment processes, and programs are not sufficiently suited to the individuals' specific requirements (Zorluoglu & Sozbilir, 2017). Similarly, among the challenges faced by disabled students in academic settings are issues such as access to mostly printed study materials, the need for additional time and resources to convert these materials into electronic formats, difficulties in accessing information, and slides that are not sufficiently explained by teachers (Guttman, 2011). Accessibility is, however, a crucial issue for visually impaired individuals.

Despite programs like AccessComputing, which aim to assist disabled students in reaching higher education and career goals in computer science by offering mentoring, internships, and other opportunities, such programs have not yet permeated daily classroom environments (Burgstahler & Ladner, 2006). Therefore, to expand diversity efforts in supporting computer science professionals, it is crucial to understand the challenges they must overcome (Baker et al., 2019). Internationally recognized education standards or reports, such as those from ISTE, often highlight computer science (CS) and computer programming (CP) activities as expected competencies for future students, yet these remain insufficiently accessible for students with visual impairments or blindness (Kert et al., 2022). Although recent emphasis has been placed on the importance of integrating accessibility into computer science curricula to develop effective individuals in the field, there are still very few tools and resources available to support educators in higher education (Baker et al., 2020; Baker et al., 2022). Therefore, accessibility is a critical topic that needs to be incorporated into computer science curricula (Elglaly et al., 2024).

Disabled students are known to be less inclined towards STEM fields and are more likely to leave STEM programs compared to their non-disabled peers (Burgstahler & Ladner, 2006). This is because, despite the use of assistive technologies to increase accessibility for visually impaired individuals in mathematics, science, and language courses, resources related to computer science education and coding remain limited. To address this limitation, the DO-IT (Disabilities, Opportunities, Internetworking, and Technology) Center was established with the aim of empowering individuals with disabilities through technology and education. The center aims to maximize the potential of disabled individuals by promoting awareness and accessibility in classroom and workplace environments, making communities more vibrant, diverse, and inclusive. The DO-IT Center supports the success of disabled individuals in challenging academic programs and careers and promotes the application of universal design in physical spaces, information technology, education, and services. It also provides online content, publications, and videos for presentations, exhibitions, and classroom use. Resources are available for disabled students, K-12 educators, higher education faculty and administrators, librarians, employers, parents, and mentors.

However, challenges remain, particularly in computer programming and coding activities, which involve teaching abstract concepts and pose numerous accessibility issues for individuals with low vision or complete blindness. Identifying context, code structure, and syntax errors can be particularly challenging when using screen readers (Baker et al., 2015; Mealin, 2012). It has been assumed that many visually impaired software engineers do not use many tools integrated into development environments (IDEs), and this lack of exposure in schools contributes to this issue (Mealin & Murphy-Hill, 2012). Recently, advances such as voice-command programming tools, eye-tracking systems, and systems tracking head movements have made programming more accessible. Examples of touch-based programming also exist (Huff Jr et al., 2021). Stefik and colleagues (2011) developed a training infrastructure with an accessible programming environment called Sodbeans, a programming language named Hop, and a multisensory (auditory and tactile) curriculum. Their summer workshop for visually impaired students showed a significant increase in students' programming self-efficacy. Nevertheless, it is recognized that many studies remain superficial, and there is a need for increased efforts in implementing accessible lesson materials and tools, supporting faculty training on accessibility, and prioritizing social integration of visually impaired students (Baker et al., 2019; Cujdikova & Stankovicova, 2022). Ensuring the use of high-quality accessible materials and tools requires collaboration between faculty, curriculum developers, educational technology researchers, companies, university IT departments, and offices serving disabled students. Faculty members should be involved to provide subject matter expertise, and university staff responsible for adaptations should provide more specialized expertise regarding specific problems faced by students and the creation of alternative materials. Additionally, when curriculum developers and educational technology researchers consider the needs of disabled students from the outset, the need for adaptations will decrease. More research is needed to improve the process of creating accessible materials. Currently, fundamental challenges include the time, expertise, and specialized equipment required to provide accessible alternatives. This not only burdens students but also requires faculty to prepare materials well in advance. The production of alternative materials falls on a few specialists, which delays accessibility for visually impaired students and faculty until accessible materials are returned. Some initiatives, such as using the Tactile Graphics Assistant to improve the process of creating tactile formats for images in textbooks, have begun. However, this is only a partial solution, and further improvements are needed to accelerate and make the production of alternative materials feasible by non-specialists. This situation can support everyone involved in providing adaptations, allowing students and faculty to play a more active role. It has been observed that faculty members need more support in educating visually impaired individuals, as they often rely solely on the visually impaired students themselves for information. Therefore, it is crucial to equip faculty with Universal Design Techniques to enable students with disabilities to participate in classes with a few adaptations, similar to programs like AccessComputing. Faculty members and disability service experts can join application communities to help determine steps to make classes and programs more accessible and inclusive, and to attract more disabled students. Finally, visually impaired students should be consciously integrated socially. Adaptations made to complete assignments functionally are seen as a tool to access education for disabled students. However, it has been found that these arrangements are often inadequate, and alternative assignments that require a participant to work alone with a partner or set up a completely different system can increase isolation. First, visually impaired students should have access to areas, machines, and activities organized by departments. Recruitment activities aimed at increasing diversity should explicitly include disability as an underrepresented group. Lastly, adapted curricula should minimize social isolation and replace assignments considered visually overly complex for visually impaired students with more inclusive alternatives for the entire class (Baker et al., 2019). Further research on developing more accessible technologies could enhance the participation of visually impaired students in group work and other assignments. As technologies become more accessible, the burden on students to find suitable adaptations will decrease. All these developments are examples of initiatives to increase accessibility in programming education. Thus, this book chapter aims to present examples of assistive technologies used in computer science education for minority groups, such as visually impaired or blind individuals, where resources are still insufficient but development efforts are ongoing. It will also provide suggestions for activities that can be used in programming education and examples from Turkey and around the world.

By the end of this chapter, readers will:

- Be able to understand the importance of accessibility for individuals with visual impairments and describe current practices by viewing the world from different perspectives.
- Gain knowledge about existing practices in computer science and computer programming education.
- Recognize current practices used in Turkey and worldwide and understand their purposes.

Accessibility in Computer Science Education

In terms of terminology, "assistive technologies" refer to the services and equipment necessary to compensate for disabilities and enhance performance. "Access technologies," on the other hand, encompass hardware and software applications used to enable individuals with visual impairments to access computers, the internet, and other resources. Known access technologies include screen readers, electronic and screen magnifiers, text recognition applications, Braille equipment, and books in DAISY format (Pădure, 2010).

Assistive technologies typically involve the use of screen reader programs and accessible text editors. For effective computer science and programming education, it is crucial that instructional materials and development tools are provided in an accessible manner. Educational materials should be compatible with screen readers and readable without any loss of information. Learning keyboard shortcuts for frequently used functions in development environments provides significant convenience for visually impaired users. Software used in education must adhere to accessibility standards and be continuously updated in accordance with these standards (Vartic & Oprisan, 2019).

Screen Readers

Screen readers are software programs designed to convert text content on computers and mobile devices into spoken words or Braille output, providing accessibility for individuals with visual impairments. These tools play a crucial role in ensuring that websites, documents, emails, and text within applications are accessible. By facilitating equal access to information, screen readers also ease the use of software and applications for visually impaired users (Milne & Ladner, 2019). For example, ethnographic studies in foreign language instruction have demonstrated how learners utilized screen reader technologies such as JAWS and NVDA to access various resources. This indicates that visually impaired students can effectively learn language and technology skills needed in daily life, such as using Office programs, through assistive technologies (Mulyati et al., 2023; Susanto & Nanda, 2018).

JAWS (Job Access With Speech)

JAWS (Job Access With Speech) is a screen reader that converts on-screen information into audible speech, enabling visually impaired individuals to interact with computers. This technology allows users to perform tasks that would otherwise require sight, such as word processing. The task analysis model, which breaks tasks into smaller components, is particularly helpful for teaching visually impaired individuals. The loss of vision necessitates reliance on other functional senses. Therefore, visually impaired students require detailed, step-by-step instructional models to learn features or systems on a computer or laptop. Teachers and trainers must develop instructional materials in the form of task analysis models tailored to the characteristics and needs of visually impaired students. Field studies have shown that the task analysis instructional materials, especially those related to Microsoft Office Word, are still too basic and lack sufficient detail. Consequently, there is a need for development to enhance the ability of visually impaired individuals to use JAWS effectively (Mulyati et al., 2023). JAWS is one of the most widely used screen readers. Developed by Freedom Scientific in 1989, this software integrates with the Windows operating system. In addition to its ability to read text aloud, JAWS enables users to process commands quickly. Users can navigate through menus, select, and edit text using keyboard shortcuts. JAWS is also a fundamental tool for visually impaired users in software development. When coding, the screen reader reads the syntax, variable names, and functions, helping users gain understanding of coding (Mulyati et al., 2023). With its own user interface, JAWS allows users to manage their accessibility settings and customize their personal preferences.

NVDA (NonVisual Desktop Access)

NVDA is an open-source screen reader. Developed as an alternative to JAWS, NVDA is completely free and is preferred by many users around the world. NVDA works seamlessly with web browsers, office software, and many other applications. One of NVDA's key features is its ability to automatically receive updates, which is crucial for keeping the software up-to-date with the latest technology and accessibility standards. NVDA users can also read text aloud while coding and use developer tools without issues. However, despite being powerful tools, screen readers have certain limitations. For example, complex and poorly structured HTML documents may not be effectively read by some screen readers. This often results from developers lacking sufficient knowledge of web accessibility, leading to poorly structured content. Therefore, it is crucial for developers to adhere to accessibility standards and create screen reader-friendly designs.

Accessible Text Editors and IDEs

Accessible text editors and Integrated Development Environments (IDEs) are designed to facilitate coding, editing, and debugging processes for programmers. The effective use of these tools by visually impaired individuals can make a significant difference in overall programming education.

Visual Studio Code (VSCode)

Visual Studio Code, developed by Microsoft, is a popular text editor that supports a wide range of programming languages. It features an accessible interface for screen reader users, with most key functionalities accessible via keyboard shortcuts. VSCode allows users to benefit from features such as auto-completion, debugging, and integrations through its extensions. Additionally, it offers a variety of settings that users can customize to enhance accessibility. As an open-source platform, VSCode is continuously updated and improved by the community.

Integrated Development Environments (IDEs) play a crucial role in learning a programming language by providing programmers with extensive development capabilities. They understand the syntax of programming languages and offer features such as code compilation, error checking, testing, and debugging, which streamline and simplify the coding process. IDEs help students efficiently engage in programming, testing, and debugging processes, allowing them to develop better coding habits and facilitate the learning process of new languages. Therefore, educators have started to incorporate IDEs into beginner-level Python courses, significantly improving students' coding experiences. However, not all IDEs are suitable for beginner-level Python courses. Selecting a satisfactory IDE can be challenging for educators. For beginner-level Python courses, there is a pressing need for an IDE that offers both sufficient educational features and is widely used among professional software engineers. Four criteria can be considered for choosing an appropriate IDE:

1. **Cross-Platform Support**: The IDE should support multiple platforms, allowing students to install and use it on various operating systems and hardware.
2. **Ease of Use**: The IDE should be user-friendly, enabling students to write code effectively with a simple and intuitive interface.
3. **Functionality**: The IDE should offer extensive functionalities such as code compilation, project organization, and multi-language support.
4. **Industry Adoption**: The IDE should be widely used among professional software engineers, bridging the gap between beginner-level courses and future career needs.

Microsoft Visual Studio Code (VS Code) is considered an ideal IDE that meets these four criteria (Tan et al., 2023). Python has become the most taught programming language in universities and is particularly favored in beginner-level computer science courses. There are three main reasons for this: Python has a beginner-friendly, simplified syntax and emphasizes natural language, making it easier to learn and apply compared to other programming languages with complex rules. Python is also a powerful tool used in various fields such as machine learning, big data, scientific computing, and data analysis. Students from diverse backgrounds use Python for purposes ranging from financial analysis to simulating protein structures in biology. Students enrolled in computer science or related fields are likely to continue using Python throughout their careers. According to the PYPL index and the Stack Overflow Developer Survey 2021, Python stands out as the most popular and fastest-growing programming language as of June 2022. At this juncture, IDEs play a significant role. IDEs integrate the processes of writing code, testing, and debugging, greatly enhancing the software development process. Using an IDE in Python courses helps students write more accurate code and develop good coding practices. Therefore, choosing an appropriate IDE for Python courses is critical for supporting students' academic and professional success (Tan et al., 2023).

Eclipse

Eclipse is an IDE used for various programming languages, including Java. Its adherence to accessibility standards ensures that visually impaired users can effectively write code on this platform. The Eclipse interface is designed with accessibility principles in mind to ensure screen readers function correctly. Eclipse features a comprehensive plugin ecosystem, allowing users to find the tools that best meet their needs. Additionally, it provides access to extensive documentation and resources that guide users through various software development processes (Baker et al., 2015). To enable students with visual impairments or vision disabilities to receive computer science education, various assistive technologies are employed. Screen readers and accessible text editors/IDEs play a crucial role in this regard. Tools like JAWS and NVDA provide students with access to written content and programming languages, while accessible development environments such as VSCode and Eclipse make coding processes more user-friendly. The importance of accessible educational tools lies in their potential to increase the presence of visually impaired individuals in the technology field in the future.

Examples of Web Accessibility

To enhance accessibility for visually impaired individuals on web pages accessed via mobile or browsers, several key considerations should be observed:

- **Minimize Image Use:** Use as few images as possible.
- **Provide Meaningful Alt Text:** Offer meaningful and understandable alternative descriptions for images and multimedia objects.
- **Avoid Relying on Color Alone:** Colors should not be used solely to emphasize or highlight text.
- **Use High Contrast Colors:** Employ contrasting colors for background and text.
- **Select Readable Fonts:** Choose fonts that are clearly legible and widely used.
- **Limit Clicks for Access:** Ensure that accessing frequently used information requires no more than three clicks.
- **Design Accessible Forms and Tables:** Ensure forms and tables are designed to be accessible.
- **Utilize CSS for Layout:** Use CSS to format the webpage layout.
- **Provide Text Alternatives for Media:** Offer written counterparts for audio and video files.
- **Offer HTML Alternatives for Plugins:** Ensure that all information presented through plugins has HTML alternatives.
- **Test Accessibility:** Test web pages using applications that enhance accessibility (Yucel & Acarturk, 2006; W3C, 2024).

The internet is a crucial source of information for visually impaired individuals; however, access can be limited due to compatibility issues between web browsers and assistive technologies (Edwards, 2008; Guttman, 2011). Therefore, the above principles should be considered when designing web pages. Additionally, platforms like WordPress offer plugins to improve accessibility, such as WP Accessibility, which provides tools for color contrast, text size adjustments, and screen reader support (WP Accessibility, 2024). To assess and enhance web page accessibility, browser extensions like DesignChecker can be used (Huh & Pavel, 2024).

Artificial Intelligence (AI) for Enhancing Accessibility

Artificial Intelligence (AI) can significantly ease the lives of individuals with visual impairments and improve accessibility in various ways. From voice control systems to visual content descriptions, AI helps to empower these individuals and reduce barriers in their daily lives. With the advancement of AI, significant strides are being made toward creating a more inclusive technology world and providing equal opportunities for everyone.

AI enables the development of applications and devices that operate through voice commands. These systems assist visually impaired individuals in controlling smartphones, computers, and other devices through spoken instructions. For example, Google Assistant helps users interact with their smartphones, home devices, and various apps by sending messages, making calls, and playing music through voice commands. Similarly, Amazon's Alexa controls smart home devices, provides information, facilitates shopping, and handles daily tasks via voice commands. Apple's Siri offers voice-controlled access to applications, sends messages, makes phone calls, and searches for information on iPhones and other Apple devices. Microsoft's Cortana, operating on Windows, assists users in controlling various features of their computer through voice commands.

For spatial awareness, applications like Be My Eyes, similar to Turkey's From Your Eyes, provide volunteer assistance to visually impaired users. Through video calls via the app, users can get help from volunteers to identify objects around them or navigate their surroundings. Microsoft's Seeing AI recognizes texts, objects, and faces, providing vocal descriptions. Another application, Aira, offers real-time audio guidance by connecting users with live helpers through video calls. Google's Lookout also helps by identifying texts, objects, and labels in the environment and providing vocal notifications. AI enables the development of systems that analyze and recognize visual content. For instance, AI-based applications can describe the objects, human faces, and other critical information in an image or video, helping visually impaired individuals gain more information about their surroundings and better understand their environment.

AI-based systems that convert visual content to text provide significant convenience for visually impaired individuals. Optical Character Recognition (OCR) technology allows the reading of written documents, books, or labels aloud or converting them to Braille. This enhances access to information and supports independence. For example, applications like Google Keep and Microsoft OneNote can recognize text from photos or scanned documents and convert them into editable digital text. Tools like Adobe Acrobat Reader also use OCR technology to make texts searchable and editable.

Text-to-speech applications facilitate access to information by reading texts aloud. Applications like Voice Dream Reader and Natural Reader can read PDFs, e-books, and other text-based files aloud, allowing users to listen and gain information. Additionally, educational software like Kurzweil 3000 supports the learning process by providing text-to-speech functionality along with text highlighting and note-taking features.

AI can also personalize access to educational content and materials. AI-based educational tools can tailor instructional materials and methods to the learning styles of visually impaired individuals, offering a more effective learning experience. Furthermore, AI enables the development of autonomous navigation systems. These systems assist visually impaired individuals in navigating public spaces or unfamiliar environments more safely. For example, AI-based applications can provide voice instructions and feedback to guide users, helping them avoid obstacles. Additionally, AI can enhance social interactions. Chatbots and virtual assistants can help visually impaired individuals establish more social connections and receive emotional support, reducing feelings of loneliness and improving overall quality of life.

Supportive Environments for Teaching Programming to Visually Impaired Students

Programming concepts can be highly abstract, posing several challenges when creating a supportive learning environment for visually impaired students. Firstly, programming tools need to be accessible to the student and compatible with assistive technologies such as screen readers, screen magnifiers, or refreshable Braille displays. Secondly, programming tasks should provide engaging and motivating feedback. Many common programming exercises used to attract young programmers, such as GUI programming or creating graphic games, may not be accessible to visually impaired students. Therefore, finding engaging and accessible alternative programming activities can encourage more visually impaired students to learn programming (Kane & Bigham, 2014).

There are various projects and initiatives worldwide aimed at increasing accessibility in computing and coding. These projects aim to enable disabled individuals to use information technology more effectively and develop their coding skills. Various organizations offer different alternatives in this regard:

1. **Microsoft's Accessibility Tools:** Microsoft has developed a range of tools to enhance accessibility. The Windows operating system provides features like screen readers, magnifiers, and voice commands. Additionally, Microsoft's "AI for Accessibility" program encourages the development of accessibility solutions using artificial intelligence.
2. **Google's Accessibility Initiatives:** Google runs several projects to improve accessibility. For example, it offers screen readers like "TalkBack" and instant text transcription tools like "Live Transcribe." Google's "Accessibility Scanner" app helps identify accessibility issues in applications.
3. **Apple's Accessibility Features:** Apple offers many accessibility features on iOS and macOS devices, including VoiceOver (screen reader), Magnifier (magnifier), and Switch Control (switch control). Apple also guides developers in implementing accessibility standards through its "Accessibility APIs."
4. **Web Accessibility Initiatives:** Web content accessibility is promoted through standards like WCAG (Web Content Accessibility Guidelines). WCAG provides guidance to ensure web pages are accessible to visually impaired, hearing-impaired, and other disabled individuals.
5. **Accessible Coding Education Programs:** Accessible coding education programs help individuals with disabilities develop coding skills. For example, "Coding with a Disability" programs and online courses support people with various disabilities in learning coding.
6. **OpenAI's Accessibility Research:** OpenAI conducts research on how artificial intelligence can be used in the field of accessibility. These studies aim to develop AI-based solutions to improve technology access for disabled individuals.
7. **Kodable and Similar Educational Tools:** Tools that promote coding education provide accessible coding training for children. For instance, Kodable allows children to learn the basics of coding in an engaging and accessible way.
8. **GitHub's Accessibility Efforts:** GitHub offers various features and tools to make its software development platform more accessible. It also provides resources to inform and train developers on accessibility issues.

These projects and initiatives aim to enhance accessibility in the computing and coding world, providing broader access to technology. However, it's essential to ensure that the assistive technologies used in coding are compatible with widely accepted programming languages and integrate seamlessly. It is known that traditional programming concepts can be integrated with assistive technologies to remove barriers for visually impaired students (Kane & Bigham, 2014). Traditional programming tools and integrated development environments (IDEs) often rely on visual information for structure and assistance, which can be problematic for visually impaired users. To address this issue, researchers have developed various techniques. For example, APL is a voice programming language designed by visually impaired programmers, and Quorum (formerly Hop) is a language designed for both visually impaired and sighted novice programmers (Sánchez & Aguayo, 2006). However, these specialized programming languages may come with limitations, as knowledge gained from them might not transfer well to general programming tasks and may be restricted by certain functionalities, libraries, or development tools (Stefik et al., 2011). Other projects have produced accessible variations of existing programming tools. For example, accessible versions of tools like Visual Basic and LEGO Mindstorms have been developed. Additionally, research has been conducted to enhance the accessibility of mainstream programming languages and IDEs. Emacspeak is a screen reader for the Emacs text editor that supports various text editing tasks, including programming. Smith and colleagues developed a plugin for the Eclipse IDE that allows visually impaired programmers to navigate code hierarchies with auditory feedback. The PLUMB EXTRA3 educational tool offers visually impaired programming students the opportunity to explore data structures spatially using a talking graphical exploration tool. Ludi & Reichlmayr (2011) used entry-level robotics kits like Mindstorms to teach computer science concepts to visually impaired and low-vision students in grades 7-12.

Due to the difficulties visually impaired students face in understanding the overall structure of code, block-based, language-based, and auditory programming languages are generally more suitable tools for teaching programming. However, popular applications may not be widely accessible for students with motor impairments or visual disabilities (Milne & Ladner, 2019). Additionally, these environments still have some limitations. The primary challenge with block-based programming tools is the technical difficulties involved in making libraries like Blockly accessible. These challenges include ensuring compatibility with screen readers and defining keyboard shortcuts. The irregular shapes of blocks and the difficulties screen readers have in understanding these blocks make these challenges even more complex. Moreover, making the spatial structure of block-based programs understandable to screen readers and enabling block manipulation in a way that is compatible with screen readers is a significant struggle. Various strategies have been developed to address these challenges and improve the accessibility of existing web-based environments. Enhancing the accessibility of block-based programming environments (BBPEs) can be an effective option for overcoming the programming difficulties faced by visually impaired individuals. Specifically, Blocks4All, an accessible BBPE, has been developed and implemented for iPads. This environment is compatible with the VoiceOver screen reader, which is familiar to visually impaired children, and sends commands to a Dash robot. The goal of this work is to replace the inaccessible drag-and-drop method with a more accessible way to create and edit programs (Milne & Ladner, 2019). On another front, physical-based applications, such as robots and microcontrollers, can support the programming learning process (Psycharis et al., 2022). Additionally, the increasing accessibility of digital production technologies, such as 3D printers, offers opportunities to create accessible physical and tactile objects for programming education for visually impaired and low-vision students (Kane & Bigham, 2014).

Code Jumper

One of the most well-known tools for teaching programming through tactile means is the Code Jumper application (Code Jumper, 2024). As shown in Figure 1, Code Jumper is a robotic educational tool specifically designed for visually impaired children. Developed by Microsoft, this tool aims to make coding and computer science topics accessible and enjoyable for visually impaired individuals. Code Jumper consists of a set of colorful and tactilely distinct pieces. These pieces help children understand basic coding concepts. By assembling these pieces, students physically express coding commands, thereby gaining a hands-on understanding of computer science. Coding operations are performed using auditory feedback and tactile cues, which allows visually impaired users to benefit from this technology.

Figure 1. Code Jumper

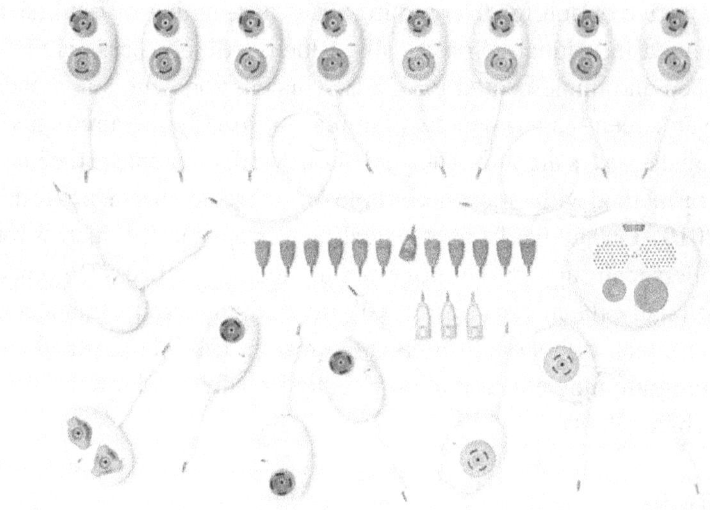

Code Jumper teaches children skills such as algorithm creation, problem-solving, and creative thinking while providing a fun and interactive experience. In a study involving lower secondary blind students, three different assistive technologies were used: an auditory text-based programming language, Code Jumper (a physical programming language), and Coshi. Coshi is a text-based programming environment that allows controlling a virtual robot with voice commands. It provides students with the ability to control a virtual robot using voice commands and offers the opportunity to create new micro-worlds. The programming language includes simple directional commands and allows the modification of sound patterns, enabling the creation of various motivational difficulty levels. By using these three tools together, various educational scenarios were created, and lessons were taught to students using these scenarios. It was observed that students used all three environments positively, adopted all functionalities, and progressively moved on to more complex programming concepts. These tools, with features similar to block-based programming languages, help students focus on algorithms while avoiding syntax errors. Additionally, the environments and tools support students' constructivist learning (Jašková, 2022).

Cubetto

Cubetto is a hands-on coding activity designed for children aged 3 and up, specifically aimed at pre-school education. It allows young children to engage in screen-free coding while learning fundamental programming concepts (Cubetto, 2024). The programming game includes a wooden robot, a physical programming console (board) with 16 uniquely shaped colored coding blocks, a beautifully designed map, and an activity book. To program the robot, different coding blocks must be placed in their positions on the board to create an algorithm. Each block is coded for different commands such as forward, right, left, and loops. After pressing GO, the robot moves according to the programmed sequence on the game map. The shapes of the blocks indicate which code segments to use in the flowchart, making it suitable for visually impaired students as well. Cubetto can be used both individually and in group settings, allowing for team-based learning. It can also be adapted with Braille labels or embossed surfaces created with a 3D printer.

Figure 2. Cubetto

Cubetto, Figure 2 shows that it features large, uniquely tactile pieces that eliminate the need for a mouse or touchscreen to select a block, making it easier to work with visually impaired students. Light and sound cues for each action link coding to all steps of the journey, reducing memory load and strengthening the connection between instructions and actions. Additionally, the 10x10 square game mat can be customized with different tasks and stories. Besides with Cubetto we can also;

- Add daily schedule elements for Cubetto to preview a student or the class' school journey
- Using him as a game piece for giant size group games

- Put numbers or phonemes, or words on the cubetto map to create literacy (e.g. word building, sentence building) or numeracy activities (e.g. addition, shape building)
- Attaching a marker or pen to Cubetto to make a drawing tool for a giant picture
- Adding percussion musical instruments – xylophone, cymbals, chimes to his route to create a song.
- Adding blocks, people or other 3D elements to map for an adventure.

Cubetto can be a break through device for students in an integrated or a designated special needs classroom setting. As Cubetto finds its way to more and more classrooms, we're looking forward to teachers sharing more ways the friendly wooden robot with the unique coding interface engages students with special needs with the essentials of programming and coding (Cubetto Robot Kit, 2024).

EarSketch

Earsketch is an educational platform specifically developed to combine music production and computer programming. Developed by the Georgia Institute of Technology, Earsketch provides users with the opportunity to develop their programming skills while learning the process of creating music. It allows users to create music by writing code in Python and JavaScript. On the platform, users can compose their own music using the available sound loops, effects, and instruments. This approach aims to bridge the gap between music production and coding, providing a fun and creative learning environment, particularly for young people and students. As shown in Figure 3, Earsketch is commonly used by educators to integrate programming and music education in the classroom, offering students the chance to enhance both their creative and analytical thinking skills (EarSketch, 2024).

Figure 3. EarSketch Interface

In British Columbia, the Applied Design, Skills, and Technologies curriculum emphasizes the importance of "designing, acquiring skills, and applying technologies" in today's world, acknowledging that these abilities play a crucial role in the education of future citizens. In the context of promoting digital literacy throughout the K-12 education process, teaching coding empowers students to control technology and develop mastery in skills such as logic, problem-solving, critical thinking, and sequencing. In a workforce environment where digital skills are increasingly important, teaching coding skills to visually impaired students can spark interest and potentially lead to exciting career paths in this field.

In this regard, the PRCVI (Provincial Resource Centre for the Visually Impaired) team, in collaboration with SET-BC (Special Education Technology – British Columbia), works to create or make accessible resource materials and kits to support the development of coding skills for visually impaired students at various grade levels. They recommend the Code and Go Robot Mouse Kit, adapted for primary school students. This kit is an important tool for early age coding skill development and has been adapted for visually impaired students. It requires students to create routes of varying difficulty levels and then guide a robot mouse along a pre-planned path to its destination, a piece of cheese. The adapted Code and Go kit is equipped with tactile and high-contrast markers, braille labels, and simplified tactile graphics. Additionally, an activity guide with tactile guides for interacting with the robot mouse and related components is provided. This kit allows visually impaired students to participate in coding activities alongside their classmates, offering opportunities to develop collaboration, problem-solving, and communication skills. It is also used as a tool to support mobility specialists in working with students on planning and implementing simple routes. For primary school students, the Code and Go Robot Mouse Kit provides a low-tech, practical approach. It is complemented by tools like Swift Playgrounds, which offer more complex digital product creation opportunities for older students using coding languages. Apple has made Swift Playgrounds accessible with VoiceOver technology. Notably, the development of Swift Playgrounds Tactile Puzzle Worlds graphics, in collaboration with the San Francisco Lighthouse, represents a significant advancement (PRCVI, 2024). The use of such innovative tools for coding education for visually impaired students contributes to their full participation in the digital world.

Quorum (Former Hop)

Quorum is a programming language designed with accessibility in mind, specifically for individuals with visual impairments and students with special educational needs. It aims to make the software development process more accessible by providing a simple and user-friendly syntax and is primarily used for educational purposes (Stefik et al., 2024). However, it also functions as a general-purpose programming language and can be used in various software projects. Quorum was developed to facilitate coding for visually impaired individuals. The design of the programming language is compatible with assistive technologies like screen readers, allowing the language to be used without the need for visual access. The syntax of Quorum is simple and understandable, making it easier for beginners and especially for students with special educational needs to learn the language. Programming terms and structures are expressed in a clear and natural language, making coding more intuitive.

Quorum provides a wide range of educational materials to support teaching and learning. These resources are developed to help teachers and students learn and use the language effectively. Additionally, online communities and resources offer support for users during the learning process. Quorum can be used in various application areas such as game development, simulations, and educational software. It offers simple tools and libraries for game development, allowing students to create their own games and develop their programming skills in the process (Stefik et al., 2024). The language's flexibility, as shown in Figure 4, enables coding across different platforms and environments. It is also designed to be inherently accessible and text-based. Its syntax and semantics have undergone rigorous testing for ease of learning through randomized controlled trials. Consequently, the syntax is much simpler compared to many other programming languages, making it less daunting for beginners (Milne & Ladner, 2019).

Figure 4. Quorum Studio

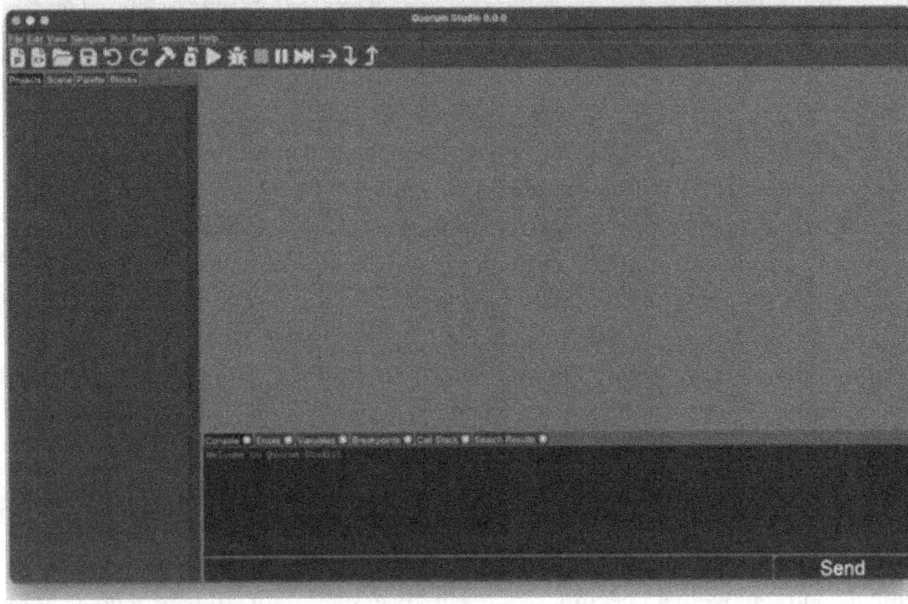

The platform, supported by a strong community, has been developed by accessibility experts and educators. Quorum comes with resources such as forums, documentation, and example projects to help users solve problems. It includes its own integrated development environment (IDE) called "Quorum Studio." This IDE provides the tools needed to write, run, and debug Quorum code. Quorum Studio can be easily installed after download. Code is written using a simple syntax and can be executed within the Quorum IDE. When the program runs, the IDE displays the output of the code to the user. The program can also be used to develop more complex applications, such as games, mathematical simulations, or data processing applications. The application is compatible with both Windows and Mac, and it can also work with programming applications in LEGO's robotics kits (Quorum, 2024).

Initiatives to Enhance Accessibility in Turkey

In Turkey, various initiatives are underway in the fields of artificial intelligence and coding to help visually impaired students keep up with current technology. For example, the SenseCode-AI project at Yıldız Technical University aims to equip visually impaired students with skills in artificial intelligence and to create a specialized teaching design for them (Kert et al., 2021). Another initiative, the "From Your Eyes" project developed by founder Zülal Tannur, enables visually impaired users to receive a description from artificial intelligence within seven seconds after uploading an image to the app. If users believe the descriptions need improvement, they can send them to a pool of volunteers (describers) through the app. The describers review the images and text again to make necessary improvements before returning the updated description to the user (From Your Eyes, 2024).

National projects like TUBITAK 4008 aim to provide support for all students with special educational needs. This project support covers individuals with diagnoses of intellectual disabilities, hearing impairments, visual impairments, physical disabilities, autism spectrum disorders, multiple disabilities, language and speech disorders, learning difficulties, and emotional/behavioral disorders. Researchers use this project type to provide assistance to students by developing interventions and providing material support for educational challenges faced by visually impaired individuals in daily life (TÜBİTAK 4008, 2024). In addition, the Ministry of National Education (MoNE) has teaching programs and technological supports for the education of visually impaired students. For example, applications such as software that translates texts into Braille and audiobooks are used to facilitate the learning process for students (MoNE, 2015; MoNE, 2020). However, as is the case globally, there are still not enough initiatives in Turkey for coding education. As a national coding movement becomes increasingly essential for students who want to learn coding in the age of artificial intelligence, there is a need to increase efforts in this area to ensure equal educational opportunities for everyone.

Result

In the age of artificial intelligence, computers and other technologies are integral to personal life, professional work, and university education. These technologies play a critical role for visually impaired students as well. Visual impairment affects how students access information, and digital technologies facilitate overcoming these barriers and making information more accessible. Therefore, it is crucial for visually impaired students to learn how to use digital technologies from an early age. Effective use of digital technologies helps promote independence in their learning and increases their chances of success in the job market.

In this context, computer science education and coding emerge as critical areas for enabling visually impaired individuals to fully benefit from technological opportunities. Special software, hardware, and methods developed for their education not only provide technical skills but also have the potential to enhance their independence and promote more active participation in societal life. Specifically, education programs that start from an early age will strengthen the confidence and problem-solving skills of individuals with disabilities.

For future efforts, making teaching materials more accessible, increasing teacher training, and spreading innovative technologies in this field are of great importance. Additionally, developing new educational tools tailored to the needs of visually impaired individuals and considering their feedback in this process will contribute to building an inclusive education system. Every step taken in this area is believed to make a significant difference in enabling individuals with disabilities to fully participate in the information world and realize their potential. An inclusive computer science education that reaches every segment of society will contribute significantly not only to individual development but also to societal progress. In this regard, increasing awareness at both individual and societal levels, ensuring technological equality, and guaranteeing equal access to opportunities for everyone are crucial.

REFERENCES

W3C (2024). https://www.w3.org/WAI/fundamentals/accessibility-intro/

Accessibility, W. P. (2024). https://wordpress.org/plugins/wp-accessibility/

Alotaibi, H., Al-Khalifa, H. S., & AlSaeed, D. (2020). Teaching Programming to Students with Vision Impairment: Impact of Tactile Teaching Strategies on Student's Achievements and Perceptions. *Sustainability*, 12(13), 5320. DOI: 10.3390/su12135320

Baker, C. M., Bennett, C. L., & Ladner, R. E. (2019). Educational experiences of blind programmers. In *Proceedings of the 50th ACM Technical Symposium on Computer Science Education* (pp. 759-765). DOI: 10.1145/3287324.3287410

Baker, C. M., El-Glaly, Y. N., & Shinohara, K. (2020). A systematic analysis of accessibility in computing education research. In *Proceedings of the 51st ACM Technical Symposium on Computer Science Education* (pp. 107-113). DOI: 10.1145/3328778.3366843

Baker, C. M., Elglaly, Y. N., Ross, A. S., & Shinohara, K. (2022). Including accessibility in computer science education. In *Proceedings of the 24th International ACM SIGACCESS Conference on Computers and Accessibility* (pp. 1-5).

Baker, C. M., Milne, L. R., & Ladner, R. E. (2015). Structjumper: A tool to help blind programmers navigate and understand the structure of code. In *Proceedings of the 33rd Annual ACM Conference on Human Factors in Computing Systems* (pp. 3043-3052). DOI: 10.1145/2702123.2702589

Bureau of Labor Statistics U.S. Department of Labor. 2023. Persons with a Disability: Labor Force Characteristics – 2022. https://www.bls.gov/news.release/pdf/disabl.pdf

Burgstahler, S., & Ladner, R. (2006). An alliance to increase the participation of individuals with disabilities in computing careers. *ACM SIGACCESS Accessibility and Computing*, (85), 3–9. DOI: 10.1145/1166118.1166119

Çiftçi, E. (2021). *Görme engelli öğrencilere ortaokul matematiği öğreten matematik öğretmenlerinin öğretim uygulamaları ve karşılaştıkları zorluklar* (Master's thesis, Eğitim Bilimleri Enstitüsü).

Cubetto. (2024). Cubetto: Teaching Children How to Code without Screens https://www.perkins.org/resource/cubetto-teaching-children-how-code-without-screens/

Cubetto Robot Kit. (2024). Cubetto Robot Kit Brings Coding to Students with Special Needs. https://www.bridges-canada.com/blogs/bridges-news/cubetto-coding-robot-ideal-for-students-with-special-needs

Cujdikova, M., & Stankovicova, M. (2022). The summer computer school for students with visual impairment in preparation for university. In *ICERI2022 Proceedings* (pp. 7789-7797). IATED. DOI: 10.21125/iceri.2022.2003

Demir, T., & Şen, Ü. (2009). Görme engelli öğrencilerin çeşitli değişkenler açısından öğrenme stilleri üzerine bir araştırma. *Journal of International Social Research,* 2(8), 154–161.

Edwards, A. D. (2008). Assistive Technologies. In Harper, S., & Yesilada, Y. (Eds.), *Web Accessibility. Human-Computer Interaction Series.* Springer., DOI: 10.1007/978-1-84800-050-6_10

Elglaly, Y. N., Baker, C. M., Ross, A. S., & Shinohara, K. (2024, March). Beyond HCI: The Need for Accessibility Across the CS Curriculum. In *Proceedings of the 55th ACM Technical Symposium on Computer Science Education* V. 1 (pp. 324-330). DOI: 10.1145/3626252.3630788

From Your Eyes. (2024). https://www.farkyaratanlar.org/tr-tr/haberler-duyurular/fark-yaratan-roportaj-from-your-eyes--zulal-tannur

Guttman, F. (2011). Accesibilitatea studen ilor cu deficien e de vedere în Universită ile clujene, în: Calitatea vie ii, XXII, nr. 2, 2011, p. 201-214, on-line: https://www.revistacalitateavietii.ro/2011/CV-2-2011/05.pdf

Huff, E. W.Jr, Boateng, K., Moster, M., Rodeghero, P., & Brinkley, J. (2021). Exploring the perspectives of teachers of the visually impaired regarding accessible k12 computing education. In *Proceedings of the 52nd acm technical symposium on computer science education* (pp. 156-162). DOI: 10.1145/3408877.3432418

Huh, M., & Pavel, A. (2024). DesignChecker: Visual Design Support for Blind and Low Vision Web Developers. *arXiv preprint arXiv:2407.17681.* DOI: 10.1145/3654777.3676369

Jašková, Ľ. (2022). Three programming environments friendly to blind students in lower secondary education. In *EDULEARN22 Proceedings* (pp. 8099-8108). IATED. https://doi.org/DOI: 10.21125/edulearn.2022.1917

Jumper, C. (2024). About Code Jumper. https://codejumper.com/

Kane, S. K., & Bigham, J. P. (2014). Tracking@ stemxcomet: teaching programming to blind students via 3D printing, crisis management, and twitter. In *Proceedings of the 45th ACM technical symposium on Computer science education* (pp. 247-252). DOI: 10.1145/2538862.2538975

Karakoç, T. (2016). *Görme yetersizliği olan öğrencilerin araştırmaya dayalı öğrenme yaklaşımı modellerinden rehberli keşfetme modelinin deneysel işlemleri kazanmalarına, akademik başarılarına ve fen bilgisine ait tutumlarına etkisi.* Yayımlanmamış Doktora Tezi. Gazi Üniversitesi, Eğitim Bilimleri Enstitüsü.

Kert, S. B., Read, J., Uğraş, T., Erkoç, M. F., Özçakır, F. C., Berksoy, İ., . . . Zubair, M. S. (2021). Design Ideas For A Learning Material To Teach Coding To Children With Visual Impairment. In *ICERI2021 Proceedings* (pp. 5864-5871). IATED. DOI: 10.21125/iceri.2021.1318

Kert, S. B., Yeni, S., & Fatih Erkoç, M. (2022). Enhancing computational thinking skills of students with disabilities. *Instructional Science*, 50(4), 625–651. DOI: 10.1007/s11251-022-09585-6

Kızılaslan, A., & Sözbilir, M. (2017). *Herkes İçin bilim: görme engelli öğrenciler için örnek uygulamalar*. Çizgi Kitabevi.

Ludi, S., & Reichlmayr, T. (2011). The use of robotics to promote computing to pre-college students with visual impairments. *ACM Transactions on Computing Education*, 11(3), 1–20. DOI: 10.1145/2037276.2037284

Mealin, S., & Murphy-Hill, E. (2012). An exploratory study of blind software developers. *2012 IEEE Symposium on Visual Languages and Human-Centric Computing (VL/HCC)*, 71–74. https://doi.org/DOI: 10.1109/VLHCC.2012.6344485

Milne, L. R., & Ladner, R. E. (2019). Position: Accessible block-based programming: Why and how. In *2019 IEEE Blocks and Beyond Workshop (B&B)* (pp. 19-22). IEEE.

MoNE. (2015). MEB'ten görme engelli öğrencilere teknolojik destek. https://www.aa.com.tr/tr/bilim-teknoloji/mebten-gorme-engelli-ogrencilere-teknolojik-destek/73990

MoNE. (2020). Görme engelli öğrencilerimiz için metinleri braılle alfabesine çeviren program ücretsiz olarak kullanımda. https://www.meb.gov.tr/gorme-engelli-ogrencilerimiz-icin-metinleri-braille-alfabesine-ceviren-program-ucretsiz-olarak-kullanimda/haber/20630/tr

Mulyati, E. N., Sabatini, R., Nuraeni, I., & Fitriani, N. (2023). Development of Ict Learning Task Analysis about Microsoft Office Word on Jaws (Job Access with Speech) Application for Visually Impaired Students Class X At Slbn Pajajaran Bandung City. *resmilitaris, 13*(2), 2030-2039.

Okcu, B., Yazıcı, F., & Sozbilir, M. (2016). Ortaokul düzeyindeki görme engelli öğrencilerin okuldaki öğrenim sürecine dair görüşleri. *Amasya Üniversitesi Eğitim Fakültesi Dergisi*, 5(1), 51–83.

Overflow, S. (2022). Stack Overflow Developer Survey 2022. https://survey.stackoverflow.co/2022/?utm_source=socialshare&utm_medium=social&utm_campaign=dev-survey-2022

Özel, E. H. Y. (2018).. . *T.C. Resmi Gazete*, (30471), 22–77.

PRCVI. (2024). Inclusive Coding for Students with Visual Impairments. https://www.prcvi.org/outreach/school-based-services/inclusive-coding-for-students-with-visual-impairments/

Psycharis, S., Theodorou, P., Spanidis, Y., & Kydonakis, P. (2022). Teaching Programming Skills to Blind and Visually Impaired Learners. In Guralnick, D., Auer, M. E., & Poce, A. (Eds.), *Innovations in Learning and Technology for the Workplace and Higher Education. TLIC 2021. Lecture Notes in Networks and Systems* (Vol. 349). Springer., DOI: 10.1007/978-3-030-90677-1_26

Safak, P. (2017). Braille yazı sistemi, tarihçesi ve dünyada Braille. P. Şafak (Ed.), *Görenler için braille (kabartma) yazı rehberi içinde* (1. Baskı., ss. 2–23). Ankara: Pegem Akademi Yayınları

Sahin, M., & Yorek, N. (2009). Teaching Science to Visually Impaired Students: A Small-Scale Qualitative Study. *Online Submission*, 6(4), 19–26.

Sánchez, J., & Aguayo, F. 2006. APL: Audio programming language for blind learners. Computers Helping People with Special Needs, Springer, 1334–1341.

Stefik, A., Allee, W., Contreras, G., Kluthe, T., Hoffman, A., Blaser, B., & Ladner, R. (2024, March). Accessible to whom? Bringing accessibility to blocks. In *Proceedings of the 55th ACM Technical Symposium on Computer Science Education* V. 1 (pp. 1286-1292). DOI: 10.1145/3626252.3630770

Stefik, A. M., Hundhausen, C., & Smith, D. (2011). On the design of an educational infrastructure for the blind and visually impaired in computer science. In *Proceedings of the 42nd ACM technical symposium on Computer science education* (pp. 571-576). DOI: 10.1145/1953163.1953323

Susanto, S., & Nanda, D. S. (2018). Teaching and learning English for visually impaired students: An ethnographic case study. English Review. *Journal of English Education*, 7(1), 83–92.

TUBITAK 4008. (2024). Özel Gereksinimli Bireylere Yönelik Kapsayıcı Toplum Uygulamaları Destekleme Programı. https://tubitak.gov.tr/tr/destekler/bilim-toplum/ulusal-destek-programlari/4008-ozel-gereksinimli-bireylere-yonelik-kapsayici-toplum-uygulamalari-destekleme-programi

Vartic, V., & Oprisan, E. (2019). Use of Assistive Technologies in Accessibility of Information for Students with Visual Impairments. *eLearning & Software for Education, 2*.

WHO. (2024). Assistive technology. https://www.who.int/news-room/fact-sheets/detail/assistive-technology

Yazici, F., Gul, S., Sozbilir, M., Cakmak, S., & Aslan, C. (2021). Altıncı sınıfa devam eden görme engelli öğrencilerin Fen Bilimleri dersine yönelik öğrenme ihtiyaçlarının belirlenmesi. *Millî Eğitim Özel Eğitim ve Rehberlik Dergisi*, 1(1), 26–64.

Yücel, C., & Acartürk, C. (2006). *Görme engelliler için web sayfalarına erişebilirliğin sağlanması*. Pamukkale Üniversitesi Akademik Bilişim Konferansı.

Zorluoglu, S. L., & Sozbilir, M. (2017). Teaching the concept of density through insoluble liquids to visually impaired students. *Journal of Theory and Practice in Education*, 13(2), 211–231.

KEY TERMS AND DEFINITIONS

Assistive technology: A general term encompassing assistive technology, assistive products, and associated systems and services. Assistive products are technologies that help individuals maintain or improve their functions related to cognition, communication, hearing, mobility, self-care, and vision, thereby supporting their health, well-being, participation, and social integration (WHO, 2024).

Coding: The process of writing instructions for computers to perform specific tasks or solve problems, typically using programming languages. It involves creating software, applications, or systems that can automate tasks or provide solutions.

Accessibility: Ensuring that all individuals have equal opportunities by making technology beneficial and usable for everyone. It involves designing products, services, and environments that accommodate a diverse range of abilities and needs.

Visual impairment: A condition where an individual has reduced or completely lost vision due to a disorder or disease affecting the eye or brain. This can range from partial loss of vision to complete blindness.

Visual disorder: A broad term referring to any condition affecting visual acuity or function. This includes both eye disorders and conditions affecting the brain's ability to process visual information, resulting in impaired vision.

Chapter 9
Online Assessment in K12 Computer Science Education

Betül Tonbuloğlu
https://orcid.org/0000-0003-1542-2380
Distance Education Application and Research Center, Yildiz Technical University, Turkey

ABSTRACT

The use of online assessment methods in K12 computer science education, which allow students to be assessed via networked computers, increases efficiency and accuracy by facilitating data collection, analysis and reporting, and enables large-scale tests to be implemented easily and at low costs. Online assessment, which can be applied in different types such as diagnostic, formative and summative performance-based, criterion-referenced, self-assessment and peer assessment, can also be applied for different purposes such as online skills assessment, online aptitude assessment, online coding assessment, psychometric assessment. Traditional assessment tools such as online exams and standardized tests can be used for online assessment of K12 computer science education, while alternative assessment methods such as e-portfolios, digital rubrics, self-assessment and peer assessment can be preferred. Online exams, which are considered traditional assessment tools, stand out with different advantages such as the use of many question types in their structure, so that CS subjects with different content can be measured with question types suitable for their own dynamics, and the automatic evaluation and reporting of measurement results. In addition, online exams can be assigned as tasks to classes created in a virtual environment, their completion can be tracked, collective feedback can be provided and students' progress can be monitored. Standardized tests, which are generally used to assess cognitive skills, stand out with their features such as taking

DOI: 10.4018/979-8-3693-4542-9.ch009

into account basic competence areas and being valid and reliable tools. Automated Assessment Tools, one of the alternative online assessment methods, are widely used for purposes such as the assessment of programming skills and code analysis, and provide many advantages such as making the quality of the assessment independent from the teacher and providing more qualified feedback to students, as well as saving educators from a significant workload. E-portfolios are more than just a space for students to accumulate their individual work, they can also be used for accreditation, application, graduate employability, evidence of professional competence, material repository, and many other purposes. Peer assessment makes important contributions to process assessment in CS education by using different types of assessment such as written assessment, evaluation of coding projects, debugging and algorithm analysis. Digital rubrics, on the other hand, are one of the alternative assessment tools frequently used in computer science education in order to understand at what level of expertise a learning outcome is acquired by students for which subheadings. Many different online assessment applications such as Rubric-Maker, Project Quantum, Computational Thinking Test, Bebras, LeetCode, Codetester, Mahara, etc. can be used in the assessment of K12 Computer Science education, which includes basic topics such as information technologies and information processing systems, computer networks, media creation and editing, data and analysis, algorithms and programming, ethics and cyber security. In this way, assessment designs can be created effectively and easily, ease of access can be provided, time and cost savings can be made, participation can be increased, and fast and advanced feedback can be provided. However, extra security measures such as authentication, plagiarism control, and proctored exams are needed to ensure the reliability of online assessment practices. Different types of proctored online exams such as live proctoring, recorded proctoring, and automated proctoring can be implemented; in addition, measures such as limiting the exam time, randomizing questions, locking internet browsers, voice recognition, face recognition, monitoring keyboard dynamics, and tracking typing style also positively affect the reliability of online exams. Online assessment methods have the potential to provide significant gains in terms of making a comprehensive assessment of students' knowledge, skills and competencies when applied in a contextually appropriate manner with strategies and tools appropriate to the outcomes in the K12 CS education content

INTRODUCTION

Computer science education at the K-12 level is an increasingly recognized discipline that prepares students for the digital age by equipping them with digital literacy skills and developing their critical thinking abilities. Computer science education emphasizes computational thinking to develop problem-solving skills and facilitate the understanding of complex concepts, encourages systems thinking, and supports the development of students' analytical abilities. In this sense, it can be said to play a vital role in preparing students for the demands of the modern workforce and fostering innovation. Evaluating the effectiveness of computer science education helps to identify areas for improvement, such as teacher preparation and curriculum effectiveness (Passey, 2016). In addition, it can lead to the development of teaching methods and resources, benefit students from diverse backgrounds, and improve overall educational outcomes (Prickett et al., 2020). Furthermore, assessment of computer science education at the K-12 level enables policymakers and educators to make informed decisions to improve curricula and better meet the demands of a rapidly evolving technological environment (Passey, 2016). Thus, assessment practices in computer science education play a critical role in promoting digital literacy and technology innovation.

The assessment process is one of the most critical elements in education as it serves to determine students' knowledge, skills and understanding and promotes learning while achieving educational goals. Assessments contribute to improving the overall quality of education and validating educational standards in various institutions. They also influence students' learning strategies and attitudes towards learning environments (Thomson & Falchikov, 1998). Therefore, the assessment process, which plays a multifaceted role in education, shapes student learning experiences and contributes to educational excellence.

The use of technology in the evaluation process is very important because it facilitates data collection, analysis and reporting, increasing efficiency and accuracy. It can be said that the use of technology in assessment processes began in the 1920s when Sidney L. Presses designed a machine for automatic testing (Skinner, 1958). As schools started to use automated scoring systems and standardized assessment, technology facilitated the implementation of large-scale tests at low costs (Alruwais et al., 2018). The use of information and communication technologies (ICT) in the assessment process, from designing assignments to storing results, is referred to as e-assessment (Joint Information Systems Committee, 2007; Jordan, 2013). Online assessment is defined as exams that allow students to take tests on networked computers from anywhere (Lewis, 2020).

Online assessment is the process of using technology to improve learning outcomes and covers a wide range of applications from formative assessments to summative exams. As one of the innovative assessment methods, online assessment can facilitate personalized feedback and real-time monitoring to improve the overall assessment experience and outcomes. As with traditional assessment, online assessment processes are generally carried out to evaluate learning outcomes, provide feedback, and award grades or certificates (Bukhari et al., 2022). However, the use of digital tools or platforms comes to the fore in these processes. Online assessment offers many advantages such as providing feedback and shaping instructional plans based on assessment results (Pu & Xu, 2021), guiding practitioners and developers to select or create appropriate systems for measurement and assessment purposes (Topuz et al., 2022), and supporting students' participation in online learning (Veugen et al., 2022). In addition, Sitthisak et al. (2008) argued that assessments using computers with web-based assessment tools can guide students to develop questions for themselves, thus supporting self-assessment. Nevertheless, online assessment processes also have different problems in many aspects such as fairness, equity, validity and reliability. There are many studies that emphasize various challenges such as cheating, cheating, plagiarism and fake identity that can negatively affect the quality and quality of online assessment practices (Flavin, 2021; Mellar et al., 2018; Peytcheva-Forsyth et al., 2018). Therefore, the evolving landscape of online assessment requires continuous research to optimize assessment practices and ensure their effectiveness in various educational settings.

It is seen that online assessment practices can be applied in many different ways. Examples include digitization of paper-based assessment systems, online administration of multiple-choice tests, and online tests that assess problem-solving skills (Ridgway et al., 2004). Traditional assessment tools such as online exams and standardized tests/questionnaires, as well as alternative assessment methods such as e-portfolios, digital rubrics, self-assessment and peer assessment can be preferred for online assessment of computer science education offered at K12 level. For example, there are Web 2.0 tools such as Socrative, Kahoot, Mentimeter, Quiziz that can be used in online assessment for purposes such as selecting, classifying, modifying, sorting, summarizing, organizing and explaining appropriate codes in the evaluation of programming instruction offered within the scope of computer science education. In addition, applications such as CodeRunner, MindReader, Quick Rubric, Mahara can be utilized for online assessment of computer science course contents (Gündüz & Tosik, 2023).

The importance of online assessment in computer science education has been emphasized in many studies. Hsueh et al. (2023) designed an online assessment platform to help assess software engineering students' abilities in an online Python programming course, aiming to understand the relationship between learning behavior and final learning outcomes and to improve students' learning achievement. Bastian and Mühling (2019) developed an online assessment system suitable for the K12 level to track code snippets, which reduced misunderstandings compared to typical pen-and-paper assessments and allowed for a more detailed examination of cognitive processes. Unlike traditional assessments that only consider the completed program submitted by the student, Robinson and Carroll (2016) proposed an online assessment system that can track student tasks during the programming task, automatically evaluate the code generation process and the final product, and provide adaptive feedback. Similarly, Koh et al. (2014) developed an assessment system that provides real-time formative assessment of in-class programming tasks, allowing students to see which higher-order concepts they have mastered and which ones they struggle with while writing code in real time. Shanley et al. (2022) noted the importance of design, facilitation, and assessment strategies used by teachers in computer science education to optimize the learning experience. All these examples point to the current importance and urgency of using and improving online assessment methods in computer science education.

In this book chapter, firstly, the purpose and importance of online assessment in Computer Science education will be discussed, and the scope and types of online assessment will be explained. Then, practical tools and examples of applications that can be used in online assessment of K12 computer science education will be presented. The opportunities and challenges presented by online assessment in computer science education will be discussed, and how to increase the effectiveness of online assessment in various educational settings will be discussed.

Assessment, E-assessment and Online Assessment

Assessment processes, which serve to measure and monitor students' learning outcomes, constitute one of the most fundamental components of education. Assessment is a comprehensive construct that not only refers to the process of monitoring the progress of learning (Spivey & McMillan, 2014), but also includes making judgments about the quality and institutionalization levels of courses and programs (Osabutey et al., 2022). Vonderwell et al. (2007) define assessment as all activities carried out by teachers and students to obtain information to change the teaching and learning process. Through assessment processes, feedback can be provided on student progress and achievement of learning goals. The evaluation of student performances according to the set learning objectives and standards shows educators the level of effectiveness of teaching practices and educational programs. This allows educators to identify strong and weak areas in the teaching process. For example, Barros (2022) focused on the options and alternatives to be considered when selecting assessment criteria for computer programming courses, thus providing a short guide for undecided teachers. Ruiz et al. (2022), in a study involving young women and students from low socio-economic backgrounds, proposed formative assessment tools to promote participation in computing and design equitable computing learning environments at the K12 level. In addition, assessment processes play a major role in ensuring quality assurance of education programs and increasing the accountability of institutions. Quality assessment results have an important place in terms of making innovations and improvements in the education system and educational institutions (Aziz et al., 2018). Archer (2017) stated that assessment is carried out for basic purposes such as supporting learning, accountability and certification, thus supporting quality education, tracking progress and facilitating transfer. Assessment processes are of great importance for stakeholders, policy makers and accreditation bodies to make the right decisions on resource allocation, program improvement and educational policy development (Aziz et al., 2018). In this context, there are studies that aim to develop an assessment and accreditation framework for computing courses and discuss how to manage the components of academic programs (Bayyapu, 2022; Mohiudddin et al., 2019).

The changing and evolving nature of education over time has led to changes in assessment processes. The electronic process in which information and communication technologies (ICT) are used in all assessment stages and activities is called e-assessment (Appiah & Tonder, 2018; Joint Information Systems Committee, 2007; Jordan, 2013). In e-assessment processes, information technologies are used in many different evaluation stages such as exam preparation, scoring and grading of results, and statistical analysis, inferences and reporting (Osuji, 2017). The rapid development of computer-assisted instruction, intelligent tutoring systems, online learning and learning analytics have played a major role in the development of e-assessment (Csapó & Molnár, 2019).

In computer science education, e-assessment processes can be used for many different purposes. Amelung et al. (2008) suggested the use of e-assessment in computer science education to test and evaluate assignments instantly and to provide students with immediate feedback to enable further learning opportunities. Alamr et al. (2023) stated that e-assessment offers many advantages such as efficient grading and automatic feedback, but it has different challenges such as academic integrity and providing personalized feedback. They also noted that e-assessment is a topic of interest in the field of computer science in higher education and pointed out different types of e-assessment such as coding exercises and peer assessments. Sierra et al. (2014) conducted a study on the e-assessment tool applied in the programming course offered in engineering education and stated that with this tool, students can verify whether the programs are working correctly and the results can be displayed on the server side.

Whitelock et al. (2006), in their framework on how the e-assessment process works, identified motivation as the main factor that drives the process and constitutes the first step of the cycle. The next steps of e-assessment are designing, creating, testing, delivering outputs, processing data, receiving feedback, evaluating outputs and reviewing feedback. After the feedback review phase, the design and creation phases are returned to the design and creation phases, so that necessary adjustments and improvements can be made depending on the results and feedback (Figure 1) (Alruwais et al., 2018). Conducting the e-assessment process in a repetitive cycle is critical for improving the process according to the deficiencies in the assessment process.

Figure 1. **Cycle of e-assessment (Whitelock vd., 2006).**

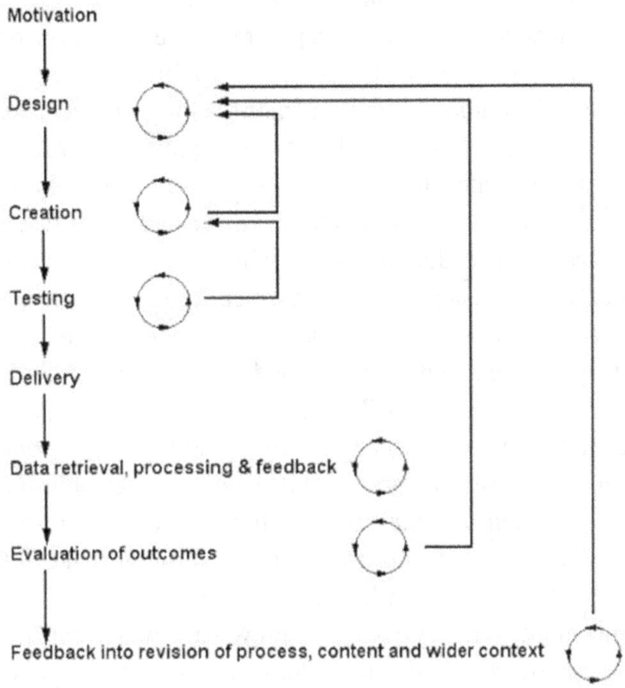

Online assessment, which is a subset of e-assessment, is defined as assessment processes that involve the use of computers to manage and analyze processes and are conducted over networked computers (Astini, 2020; Lewis, 2020). Online assessments provide significant time savings compared to traditional assessment methods and allow instructors to provide immediate feedback to large groups of students (Marden et al., 2013). Students who receive instant feedback can make the necessary improvements in their learning processes by correcting their mistakes faster, thus improving their learning experience. Statistical reports of the exams can be created more easily and the scores can be learned instantly when the exam is completed (Sharma & Holbah, 2022). In addition, students' motivation to study can be kept high thanks to the flexibility given to students and instructors regarding the time and place of the assessment, links to learning resources during and after the assessment, and opportunities for review (Velan et al., 2008). Nguyen et al. (2017), in their study investigating the design of online assessment and its impact on student engagement, stated that educators' use of different strategies can have a positive impact on student engagement. Other advantages offered by the use of online assessment are: adaptive assessment by adjusting the difficulty level of the test to the students' ability level, providing personalized tests according to the actual needs of the student, time flexibility, automatic scoring, data processing and statistical analysis, and scaling (Csapó & Molnár, 2019).

Online assessment can be used in computer science education in many different contexts. Lu et al. (2023) stated that the use of online assessment techniques in computer science education facilitates instant tracking of students' progress, provides immediate feedback to students, helps prepare students for 21st century digital skills, and computer educators have a positive disposition towards online assessment techniques. Munisamy et al. (2024) similarly emphasized the effectiveness of online assessment in measuring student proficiency in programming education. Ljubic et al. (2023) stated that by using online assessment tools, they were able to present computer science education in a more qualified way, prevent delayed feedback and biased evaluations, make a fairer grading, and provide a consistent evaluation process by eliminating possible biases. They emphasized that through the Online Judge system they used in their study, teachers were able to create various problems in both programming and database areas, while students received instant feedback on the accuracy and efficiency of their code, helping students identify their mistakes, optimize their solutions, and improve their programming and SQL proficiency. Moosvi et al. (2023), on the other hand, stated the advantages of the open-source online assessment platform they used to improve student learning in undergraduate Computer Science courses, especially its support for multiple question types in algorithmically generated questions and its use in other coding languages. These and other examples show that online assessment can be used actively and efficiently in computer science education in many ways.

In addition to the advantages of online assessment, there are also some challenges. The main ones are the lack of supervision and the potential for cheating due to the easy access to online resources. Gonsalves (2023) also emphasized this limitation by stating that students' wide access to materials on the internet allows them to solve questions through internet searches. Therefore, the importance of implementing various strategies to accurately assess student progress and prevent cheating in online assessments is emphasized (Alharbi et al., 2021). Examples of measures that can be taken to prevent plagiarism and cheating include electronic surveillance systems, browser locks, authentication methods, face recognition, voice recognition, keyboard dynamics, writing style and plagiarism tools (Koçdar et al., 2022). Apart from the negative impact of cheating and plagiarism on the reliability of online assessment, there are other factors that limit online assessment. Sharma and Holbah (2022) list the challenges of online assessment as quality expectations, assessment security, time limitation, ethical aspects, digital literacy and expertise, and learning outcomes. Inequality in access to appropriate technologies, internet accessibility, technological failures, and home environment are also seen as limitations of online assessment (Iftikhar & Cheema, 2022; Mate & Weidenhofer, 2021; Sharma & Holbah, 2022).

Online assessment, with all its strengths and limitations, is one of the most preferred types of assessment in today's world where online learning environments are becoming increasingly widespread. This is due to the opportunities it provides in different aspects such as facilitating access to hard-to-reach populations, user-friendliness, efficiency and cost-effectiveness of data collection mechanisms, time-saving, ease of recording assessments and objectivity in grading (Al Roomy, 2022; Bailey et al., 2013). Online assessment is a valuable tool for increasing accessibility, immediate feedback, flexibility and efficiency, improving learning outcomes and ensuring the effectiveness and fairness of assessment processes. However, it is important for educators and institutions to consider the opportunities and challenges that this type of assessment presents in the design and implementation of online assessment strategies.

Types of Online Assessment

Online assessment has a broad structure that covers different processes such as assessing student readiness to learn, providing feedback by evaluating learning progress, and determining the level of understanding achieved by students. Diagnostic assessment is carried out at the beginning of the learning process to learn about students' prior knowledge, strengths and weaknesses in order to tailor the learning process to individual student needs and to provide a basis for future assessment. Diagnostic assessments are very important to understand what level of knowledge students have at the beginning of a lesson or unit. Csapó and Molnár (2019) stated that one of the biggest problems teachers face in teaching heterogeneous classes is the difficulty in adapting instruction to the individual needs of each student, and defined diagnostic assessment as a type of assessment that is used to understand students' readiness for a learning task and therefore can also measure prerequisite knowledge. Brendefur et al. (2018) stated that this type of assessment is often followed by various supportive activities such as remedial instruction to remove barriers and facilitate data-based decision-making. Online diagnostic assessments also provide insight for teachers to decide which content, experiments, teaching methods, or assessments they can structure in their courses and how (Slavin, 2002).

Formative assessment involves ongoing assessment and continuous feedback throughout the learning process to support learning. Formative assessment, which can take different forms such as exams, assignments or discussions, aims to monitor progress, identify areas for improvement and adjust teaching strategies accordingly, thereby increasing student understanding and performance. Through this type of assessment, it is possible to learn students' learning needs immediately, facilitate learning and provide immediate feedback to students (Good, 2011). Sweeney et al. (2017) emphasized the advantages of formative assessment by stating that online exams help sustain course engagement when administered regularly and with low risk. Online formative assessments can take place within the framework of the teacher's instructions in the online teaching process and in the context of classroom interaction, as well as through the evaluation of student work and products (project, performance, presentation, e-portfolio, article review, worksheet, etc.) (Csapó & Molnár, 2019). Beerepoot (2023) also stated that online formative assessment can take place in large online classrooms or outside of classrooms through practice tests.

Summative assessment is a type of assessment that takes place at the end of the learning period or program to evaluate the overall achievement of students, which is considered important to measure the degree of achievement of learning objectives and to determine whether students are ready to move to the next level. There are different online assessment methods such as open book exams, online quizzes or peer assessments (Amer et al., 2022). Although summative assessment enables to determine the learning goals achieved and to make inferences about the quality of teaching, it has some disadvantages such as the fact that teaching becomes exam-oriented, assessment results cannot be used to personalize teaching due to the time difference between exam and feedback time, it has a negative impact on school climate and increases teacher stress (Koretz, 2018; Saeki et al., 2018). Diagnostic, formative and summative assessment types are summarized in Figure 2.

Figure 2. **Diagnstic, Formative and Summative assessment types**

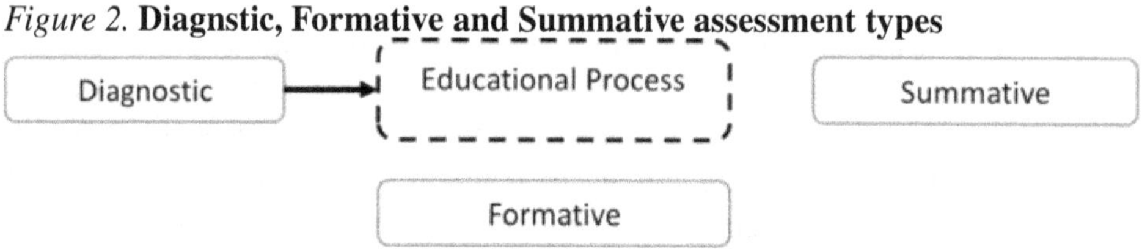

Apart from diagnostic, formative and summative assessments, there are different types of online assessments such as performance-based, criterion-referenced, self-assessment and peer assessment (Reddy, 2023). Through performance-based assessments, students can demonstrate how they can use their knowledge and skills in real situations through activities such as demonstrations and presentations. Criterion-referenced tests, which rate students' performance according to specific criteria, allow for more objective assessment. Self-evaluation through tools such as self-evaluation checklists or reflection journals allows students to measure their own progress. Peer assessment can be done through tools such as online discussion groups and feedback forums.

Online assessments can be conducted in different types as well as for different purposes. Some of these can be listed as online skill assessment, online aptitude assessment, online coding assessment, psychometric assessment, video based online assessment (Xobin, 2024, Figure 3). In this way, online assessment can be utilized for skill, aptitude, coding, psychometric assessment and video-based assessment.

Figure 3. **Types of online assessment tests (Xobin, 2024)**

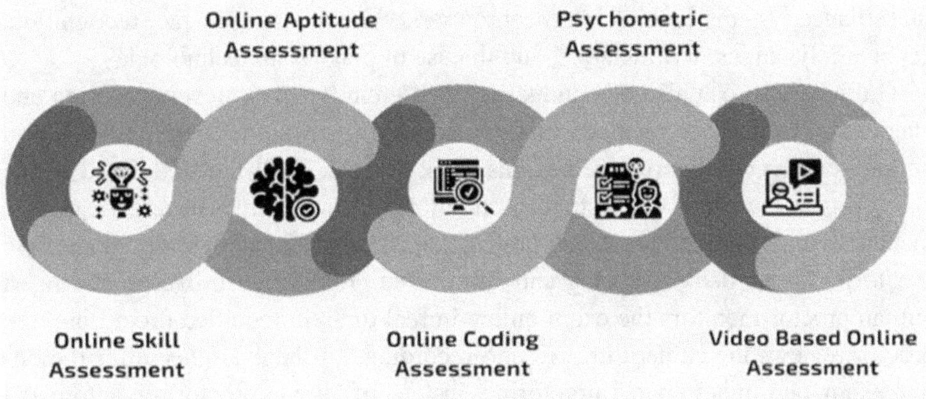

Online assessment, when applied in different types depending on different educational processes and needs, provides educational stakeholders with advantages such as increased objectivity, personalized assessment, rapid feedback, cost-effectiveness and time efficiency. However, in all types of online assessment, special attention needs to be paid to issues such as the quality of questions, alignment with the intended learning outcomes, and the quality of feedback provided to students.

Reliability in Online Assessment and Online Proctoring Tools

As with traditional assessment methods, it is important that online assessment is conducted in accordance with certain principles. Arifuddin et al. (2021) list these principles as validity and reliability, objectivity, fairness, integration, openness, comprehensiveness, continuity, systematicity, criteria-based, and accountability. One of the most emphasized principles for online assessment is the principle of reliability due to the ease of access to online resources and lack of supervision during assessment.

There are some strategies that can be used to ensure the reliability of online exams and to prevent academic dishonesty. Boitshwarelo et al. (2017) stated some of these methods as increasing the number of questions in the test pool in online exams and randomizing the order of questions for each exam. Measures such as limiting the test duration, randomizing both the question pool and the questions in the pool can also be shown among the measures that can be taken (Amer et al., 2022). Koçdar et al. (2021) stated that many security measures can be taken for online exams, such as verifying the identity of the student with fingerprint-like tools, using electronic surveillance systems, locking internet browsers, voice recognition, face recognition, keyboard dynamics, writing style, and the use of plagiarism technologies.

Online exams can also be conducted in different types to prevent cheating and plagiarism. One of the methods that can be used to ensure academic integrity in online exams is online proctored exams. Hussein et al. (2020), who defined online proctoring as the use of virtual tools to monitor student activities during the assessment activity, examined proctored online exams under 3 headings. These are Live proctoring, Recorded proctoring and Automated proctoring. In live proctoring, a human proctor monitors the exam online in real time, in recorded proctoring, the proctor reviews the camera images and recordings of the examinee after the online exam, and in automated proctoring, instead of human proctoring, automated systems identify possible fraud and cheating and warn the human proctor about these people (Hussein et al., 2020). Each of these types of proctoring has different advantages and limitations. In live proctoring, the proctor must be competent in the use of technology and the exam time must be adjusted according to the proctor. In addition, live proctoring is not considered very suitable for essays and long-term studies, and is especially recommended for oral exams (Sietses, 2016). Linden and González (2021) stated that the use of online platforms such as Zoom, which are not specifically designed for test proctoring, can be a cost-effective and valid method for test proctoring. While the flexibility of the exam time is an advantage in recorded proctoring, reviewing each recording is a factor that increases the workload. Automated proctoring, on the other hand, is considered more scalable and cost-effective as artificial intelligence algorithms replace humans (Jose, 2016). However, the establishment and dissemination of these systems requires a certain cost and business awareness. There are also comments that students may develop different strategies against AI algorithms or that AI may misinterpret and report events (Sietses, 2016).

Sietses (2016) stated that there are 3 levels of online proctoring and explained these levels as follows: 1st level: screen capture and single camera; 2nd level: screen capture and two cameras; 3rd level: full logging, screen capture, two cameras and only live proctoring or recording. Sietses (2016) presented the types of questions for which online proctoring is more appropriate and their importance and risk levels as shown in Figure 4.

Figure 4. **Importance and risk ratings of tests with online proctoring (Sietses, 2016)**

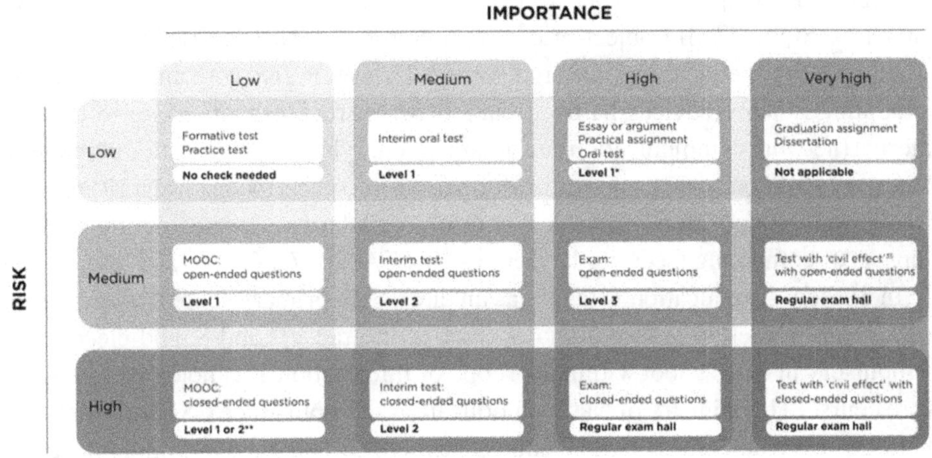

It is stated that the unproctored nature of online assessment negatively affects the validity and reliability of assessment (Dermo, 2009). However, Sietses (2016) states that despite all the measures taken, the security options offered by online proctoring are not yet sufficient and that well-equipped computer laboratories and paper-based exams can be good alternatives. Technologies that will increase online exam security continue to develop rapidly.

Scope of K12 Computer Science Education

Computer Science (CS) education is a scientific discipline that covers a wide range of topics and approaches that can be acquired directly and indirectly. CS education aims to equip students with the necessary knowledge and skills in algorithms, programming languages, data structures, software development and other related areas to understand and navigate the digital society (Romeike, 2019). Bocconi et al. (2022) state that more and more countries are adopting and incorporating CS curricula into their curricula, thereby supporting the development of thinking skills.

The scope of CS education is constantly updated and dynamic due to the rapid development of technology. Since examining the scope of CS education will facilitate the discussion of online assessment tools suitable for this scope, this section will briefly explain how the scope of CS education at K12 level is handled in different countries.

The basic stage of UK CS education consists of 4 levels. These levels generally cover topics such as computer systems and networks, media creation (animation, video production, audio production, web page, photo editing, 3D modeling), programming, data and information (databases and spreadsheets), digital media, mobile application development, cyber security, computer networks, network security, databases, SQL, HTML, object-oriented programming (NCCE, 2023b).

In the US, CS education is offered at the K12 level in five core units. These are computing systems (devices, hardware and software, troubleshooting), networks and internet (network communication and organization, cybersecurity), data and analysis (storage, collection, visualization, transformation, inference, models), algorithms and programming (algorithms, variables, control, modularity, program development), impacts of computing (security law, ethics) (CSTA, 2017a; CSTA, 2017b).

In Turkey, CS education is taught as an elective in primary school, compulsory for 2 hours a week in grades 5 and 6, elective in grades 7 and 8, and elective or compulsory in high school within the scope of Information Technologies and Software course. The Ministry of National Education's 5th-6th grade CS course content includes units on Information Technologies, ethics and safety, communication, research and collaboration, product creation, problem solving and programming. These units cover the importance of information technologies, computer systems, file management, ethical values, digital citizenship, privacy and security, computer networks, research, visual processing - word processing - spreadsheet - audio and video processing and presentation programs, problem solving approaches and programming (TTKB, 2018). The secondary education curriculum includes basic modules on introduction to programming and algorithms, robotic coding, mobile application development, programming languages (Java, C++, C#, DART, PHP, Javascript, Python), and artificial intelligence applications (TTKB, 2023).

CS is a very comprehensive and dynamic discipline, as can be seen in examples from different countries. Currently, the scope of CS education at the K12 level can be said to consist of core topics such as information technologies and computing systems, computer networks, media creation and editing, data and analysis, algorithms and programming, ethics and cybersecurity. In this context, this course aims to support the development of students' technological literacy levels and thinking skills by focusing on basic practices such as promoting an inclusive computing culture, communication, collaboration, abstraction, creating, testing and improving computational artifacts, and solving computational problems (CSTA, 2017b).

Online Assessment in K12 Computer Science Education

Students' success in a particular discipline depends on acquiring functional knowledge as well as declarative knowledge specific to that discipline, and learning the study and communication skills required by that discipline (Entwistle & Tait, 1995). Therefore, student assessments, typical assessment tasks and grading practices also differ across disciplinary settings (Neumann et al., 2002). The extent to which assessment criteria reflect quality also varies across disciplines. Dunn et al. (2003) noted that not only the assessment tasks but also the concerns about assessment vary across disciplines; for example, the concern about the assessment of creativity skills is not the same in science and history courses.

One of the most important advantages of online assessment in CS education is its formative feedback capacity. As it is a discipline with a predominance of applied subjects, formative online assessments are extremely important for students to monitor and improve their own learning. Formative online assessment tasks can be annotated, teacher and peer assessments can be accessed instantly, students can receive immediate feedback, and thus personalized and adaptive learning and assessment environments can be created. The feedback provided to students is not limited to the learning content. Keuning et al. (2018) stated that there are constructive feedback types in online assessment that provide information about tasks, concepts, errors, information about how to proceed, and metacognition (such as why the answer is correct). In CS education, especially in the assessment of applied subjects, it is very important for the student to receive feedback not only about the mistakes made by the student, but also about the use of the system, the explanations of the tasks given, and the ways to progress, so that the student can improve his/her learning by drawing meaningful conclusions from the assessment process.

CS education is a discipline that focuses on technical knowledge, high-level cognitive and intellectual skills (problem solving, abstraction, creative thinking, critical thinking, etc.) and aims to acquire them (Gündüz & Tosik, 2023). Therefore, the assessment of CS education needs to cover both content knowledge and thinking skills that allow for the effective presentation of this knowledge (Kallia, 2017). As discussed in the previous section, CS education at the K12 level has a broad content that covers core topics such as information technologies, computing systems, computer networks, media creation and editing, data analysis, algorithms and programming, ethics and cybersecurity. Online assessment methods need to be selected and adapted to the specific characteristics and learning objectives of these subjects.

Many different online evaluation methods can be utilized in the evaluation of K12 CS education contents. Some examples of these could be as follows: Information technology and information processing systems topics cover applications such as devices, hardware and software, troubleshooting, the importance of information technologies, file management. For online assessment of these topics, scenario-based questions and simulations of practical situations can be used to help students analyze and propose solutions to real-world information processing challenges. These scenarios can also contribute to the development of students' concretization and problem solving skills. Online assessment tasks in the context of computer networks can consist of network simulation exercises in which students are responsible for configuring network components, troubleshooting connectivity issues and optimizing network performance. Students can make use of virtual network environments to practice network protocols, topologies and security measures. Media creation and editing skills can be assessed through e-portfolios or project work where students showcase multimedia projects such as videos, graphics, audio and image files, computational files, 3D designs, web pages or interactive presentations. Online peer assessments and self-assessment tools can be used to evaluate the media created in this process. In this way, students can be provided with feedback on their creativity skills and technical competencies from multiple perspectives. Online quizzes or assignments that require students to analyze and visualize data sets, interpret results, and model meaningful conclusions can be given to assess the outcomes related to data analysis. By including data visualization tools and statistical software in the online assessment platform, students can be supported to demonstrate their data analysis skills in a practical and interactive way. In addition, screen recordings of student applications in these tools can be evaluated and the student's progress in the process can be monitored. Ethics and cybersecurity assessments can include case studies and ethical dilemmas presented through online scenarios, videos and simulations. Students may be asked to analyze ethical issues related to information integrity, information security, privacy, and intellectual property presented online, discuss these issues with their peers in online forums, develop solutions and recommendations related to ethical standards and cybersecurity, and share them in interactive environments. Algorithm development and programming instruction is one of the most important topics in CS education. The evaluation of the algorithms and codes created can be achieved through programming assignments to be carried out through online coding platforms. Through these assessments, students' algorithmic thinking and problem solving skills, programming competencies and debugging skills can be tested practically.

Utilizing online assessment methods that are appropriate for the comprehensive and dynamic K12 CS education content provides a comprehensive assessment of students' knowledge, skills, and competencies. Different strategies such as scenario-based questions, simulations, portfolio submissions, data analysis tasks, coding tasks, and ethical case studies facilitate the effective assessment of basic knowledge, skills, and practices in CS subjects and lead to more effective learning experiences. These assessment tools can be utilized in face-to-face as well as distance learning environments. McMillan and Hearn (2008) stated that the use of these assessment tools during in-class instruction enables students to provide quick feedback, understand their mistakes immediately, and actively try to correct these mistakes.

Traditional Online Assessment Methods and Application Examples for K12 Computer Science Education

Online Exams

Online exams provide many advantages such as flexibility in time and space, affordability compared to traditional exams, ease of creating, managing and grading exams (Attia, 2014; Schmidt et al., 2009) and are preferred by students more than traditional exams (Butler- Henderson & Crawford, 2020). Online exams are one of the online assessment methods that can be widely applied for many outcomes in CS education at the K12 level. Wójcik and Rataj (2022), in their research on CS students' online exams, applied online exams in six different CS courses: Practical Algorithms, Discrete Mathematics, Software Engineering, Programming, Team Projects, and Artificial Intelligence.

Among the advantages of this assessment method is that many question types such as multiple choice, true/false, matching, gap filling, multiple response, short and long answer open-ended questions, essay, scale, ranking, file uploading can be used in online exams. In this way, it is possible to measure CS subjects with different scopes with question types suitable for their own dynamics and to automatically evaluate and report the measurement results. The National Center for Computing Education (NCCE, 2023b) includes many examples of questions that can be used in formative and summative assessment of CS courses in its Computing Curriculum. To give examples of these question types among the contents defined in 4 levels, examples of summative multiple-choice questions published for the unit titled "Using media - Gaining support for a cause" for Key Stage 1- Age 7 students and for Key stage 4- Age 14-16- Impacts of technology unit are shown in Figure 5. In addition to these types of multiple-choice questions, different types of questions can be included in online exams.

Figure 5. **Examples of multiple choice questions that can be used in summative assessment of CS course (NCCE, 2023b)**

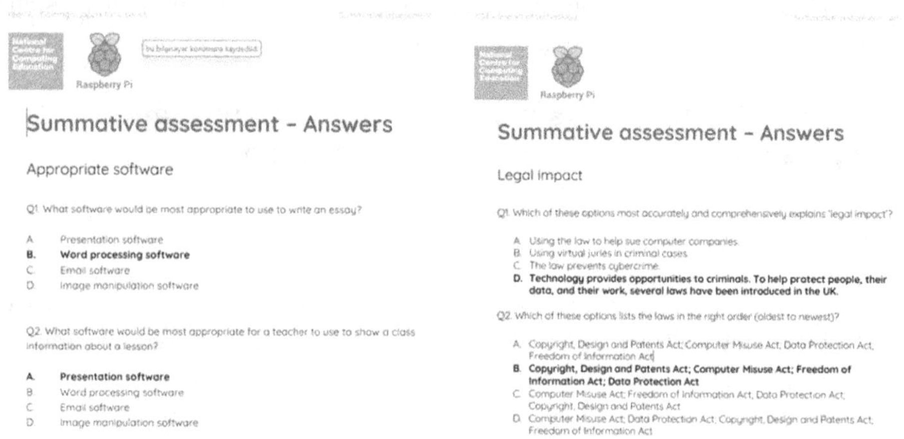
Raspberry Pi

Summative assessment - Answers

Appropriate software

Q1. What software would be most appropriate to use to write an essay?

A. Presentation software
B. Word processing software
C. Email software
D. Image manipulation software

Q2. What software would be most appropriate for a teacher to use to show a class information about a lesson?

A. Presentation software
B. Word processing software
C. Email software
D. Image manipulation software

Raspberry Pi

Summative assessment - Answers

Legal impact

Q1. Which of these options most accurately and comprehensively explains 'legal impact'?

A. Using the law to help sue computer companies.
B. Using virtual juries in criminal cases.
C. The law prevents cybercrime.
D. Technology provides opportunities to criminals. To help protect people, their data, and their work, several laws have been introduced in the UK.

Q2. Which of these options lists the laws in the right order (oldest to newest)?

A. Copyright, Design and Patents Act; Computer Misuse Act; Data Protection Act; Freedom of Information Act
B. Copyright, Design and Patents Act; Computer Misuse Act; Freedom of Information Act; Data Protection Act
C. Computer Misuse Act; Freedom of Information Act; Data Protection Act; Copyright, Design and Patents Act
D. Computer Misuse Act; Data Protection Act; Copyright, Design and Patents Act; Freedom of Information Act

Programming and algorithm building skills can also be measured in different ways with online exams. Schulte et al. (2010) stated that different types of questions such as selecting the correct code, finding the code that completes the skeleton code, finding the code that changes the algorithm logic, completing the code in an alternative way, writing the desired code sequence in any language, classifying and reorganizing the code by writing the purpose of the code can be used to measure programming skills in online exams. In addition, thanks to the multimedia opportunities offered by the online environment, many different question types such as Word Cloud, Guess the Number, 100 points, Grid, Quick Form, Pin on Image can be used as in the Mentimeter application (Figure 6). Different exam strategies such as competing for points in a multiple-choice exam and earning points by guessing the correct answer, as in the Kahoot application, can also be applied in online exams.

Figure 6. **Question types in the Mentimeter app**

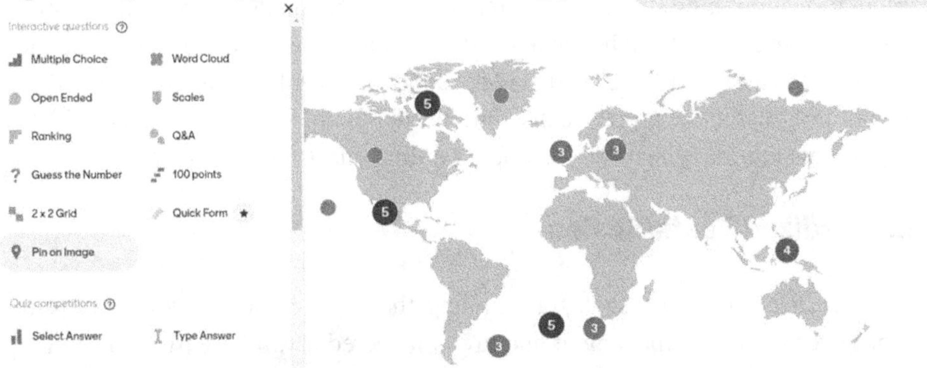

In CS teaching with the question types shown in Figure 6, students can be evaluated online in the process with different activities such as marking computer hardware on the picture, predicting the number that a piece of code will produce, showing the measures that can be taken regarding information security with a word cloud.

Project Quantum (Diagnosticquestions, 2024) is an example of online exam applications in the field of CS. In this platform, which includes question banks of high quality multiple-choice questions for the assessment of computer science education in schools, the questions are grouped under Computer Science-Foundations, Information Technology-Applications and Digital Literacy- Implications (Figure 7).

Figure 7. Online Exam Creation Platform- Diagnosticquestions. (https://diagnosticquestions.com/Quantum)

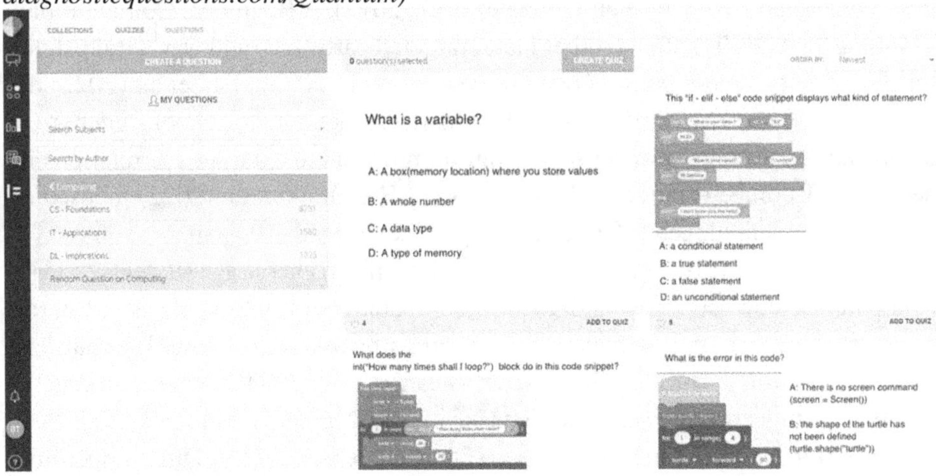

In this platform, which includes CS questions on many different topics such as computational thinking, logic, prediction, explanation, boolean operators, abstractions, state, etc., classes can be created, students can be assigned to classes, created quizzes can be assigned as tasks to classes, collective feedback can be provided and students' progress in the process can be monitored. In this respect, it can be said that this platform has many features beyond an online question repository.

Standardized Tests/Scales

Standardized tests and scales are among the most commonly used measures of computer science achievement and are considered a valid measure of learning outcomes (Randolph, 2008). These measurement tools, which are generally used in the assessment of cognitive skills and focus on remembering and understanding levels according to Bloom's taxonomy (Román-González et al., 2019), stand out with their advantages such as taking into account the basic competence areas and being valid and reliable tools.

There are many examples of standardized tests and scales for CS. There are some standardized tests developed specifically to measure computational thinking skills (El-Hamamsy et al., 2022; Román-González et al., 2017; Tsai et al., 2022; Zapata-Cáceres et al., 2020). Although these tests differ in some aspects, such as the age groups they address or the skills they focus on, they generally focus on the valid and reliable measurement of computational thinking. For example, the Computational Thinking Test, which is administered online and consists of 28 multiple-choice questions, is a diagnostic assessment tool that aims to measure computational thinking skills such as sequencing, completing, or debugging algorithms and is administered to students aged 10-16 (Román-González et al., 2017). A Beginners Computational Thinking Test (BCTt), on the other hand, targeted early ages and was administered for the primary school period (Zapata-Cáceres et al., 2020). Tsai et al. (2022) developed the Computational Thinking Test to assess elementary school students' CT competencies in subjects other than programming and to examine the relationship between CT competencies and dispositions. El-Hamamsy et al. (2022) focused on developing an unplugged CT test targeting students aged 7-9 years.

Another example of a standardized test that aims to encourage students to learn Computer Science concepts and acquire computational thinking skills is Bebras, an international attempt. Created in 2003 in Lithuania, the Bebras International Competition aims to stimulate interest in education among K-12 students around the world, and students are given specific tasks in CS (Dagiene & Futschek, 2008). An example of these tasks can be given as in Figure 8 (Bebras, 2024). This competition, which is carried out in schools using computers or mobile devices, aims to develop problem solving skills, including decomposing complex tasks into simpler components, algorithm design, pattern recognition, pattern generalization, and abstraction, as well as introducing computing concepts (Bebras, 2024).

Figure 8. **Example of a Bebras task (Bebras, 2024)**

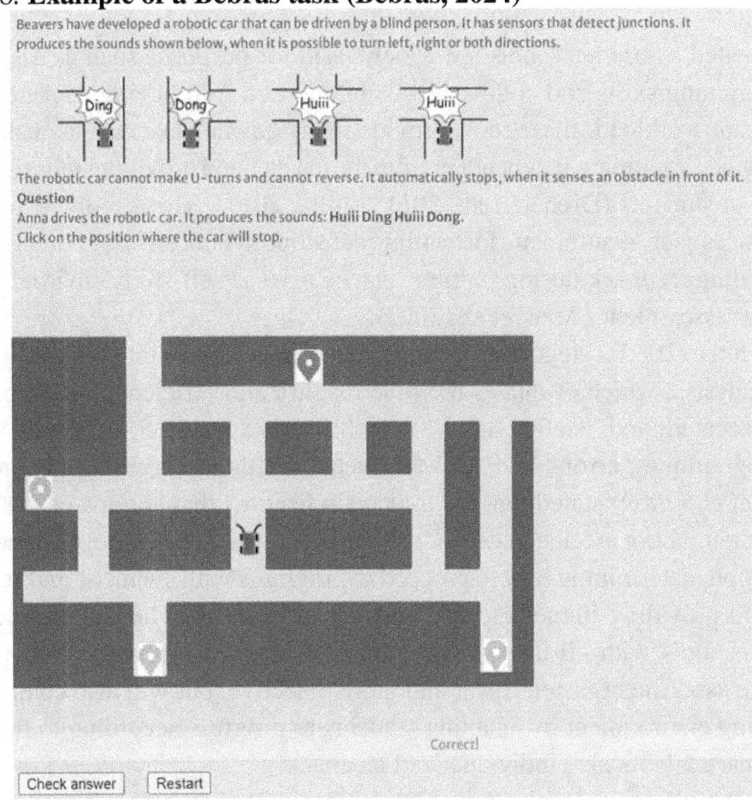

Regardless of the purpose, scope, audience and context in which they are used, such standardized tests have an important role to play in achieving more valid and reliable results in CS. Implementing such tools online will enable faster learning and reporting of the characteristics of larger audiences, and thus faster action in planning and improving the training offered.

Alternative Online Assessment Methods for K12 Computer Science Education

Automated Assessment Tools

Automated assessment tools are widely used for purposes such as assessment of programming skills and code analysis. In addition to relieving educators from a significant workload, these tools provide many advantages such as making the quality of the assessment independent from the teacher and providing more qualified feedback to students (Dreher et al., 2011; Kallia, 2017). These tools, which offer conveniences such as automatic formatting, detecting syntax errors, giving warnings and providing feedback during runtime, can be used as self-study environments as well as for assessment (Amer et al., 2022).

Ala-Mutka (2005) categorized automated evaluation tools into two groups: “dynamic analysis”, which evaluates the functionality and efficiency of the program as it is executed, and “static checks”, which provide feedback on issues such as style, programming errors, and software metrics without executing the program. Tiantian et al. (2009) stated that the four main features that automated evaluation systems should have are adequate testing, checking whether the program meets the specification, determining how to proceed in programs with syntactic and semantic errors, and providing immediate and corrective feedback. The use of automated assessment tools with all these features in computer science education will not only make assessment faster, easier and more objective, but will also contribute to the learning environment by enabling students to progress according to their own learning pace and receive individualized feedback.

One example of an application for automated evaluation tools is LeetCode. Leetcode is an online platform that allows people interested in software development to practice topics such as algorithms and data structures, includes learning resources, discussion forums and additional tools, and supports many programming languages. In this platform, which can be used by creating an account, predefined questions according to certain difficulty levels are presented with a description, input and output formats and a sample input/output, and it is expected to produce the output by writing an algorithm. The Description section contains explanations, examples, clues, similar questions and a discussion area. Editorial section includes video solutions, solution articles, different solution approaches and user comments on these approaches. Solutions section provides access to other users' solutions. In the Submissions section, the user's previously written codes and errors can be viewed (Figure 9).

Figure 9. **LeetCode interface**

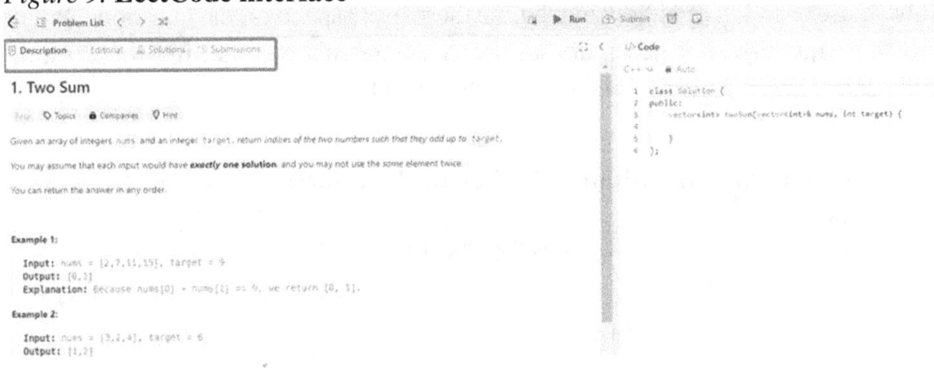

When the user completes the code solution, the generated code can be tested and the correctness of the solution can be displayed (Figure 10). In addition, the user can also practice by creating their own questions. Questions similar to the interview questions used in recruitment processes can be submitted through the discussion forum and shared on these topics.

Figure 10. **Online code evaluation in the LeetCode tool**

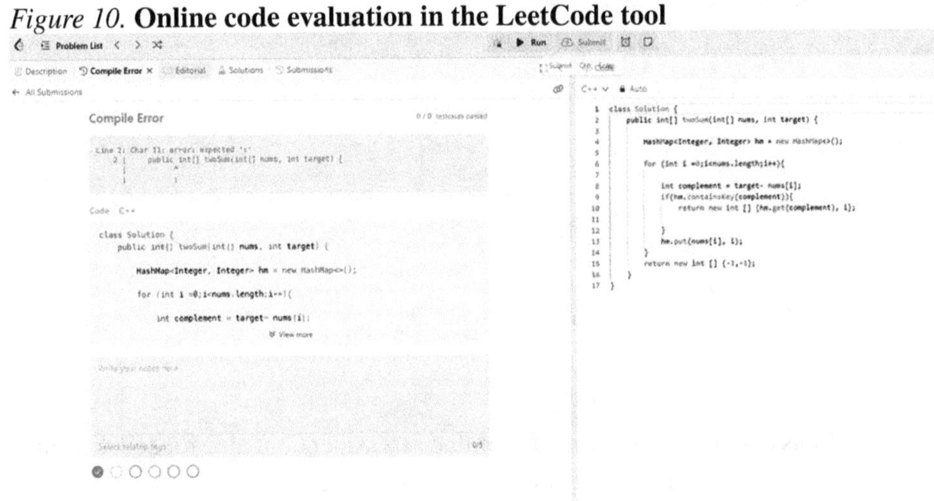

Another example of an automated assessment tool is Codetester. This evaluation tool, which supports Java, Javascript, Python and Ruby languages, can be used free of charge upon registration. The user interface is quite simple. It has the advantage that it can create custom code evaluations, is fully automated and can review code submissions. With this tool, it is possible to create assessments with multiple questions, and it is possible to access information about how many users are trying to solve these questions and how much time these users spend on the questions. When creating a question, it is necessary to specify the instructions, starting code, testing code and solution code for the question (Figure 11).

Figure 11. **Question definition interface in the Codetester automated assessment tool**

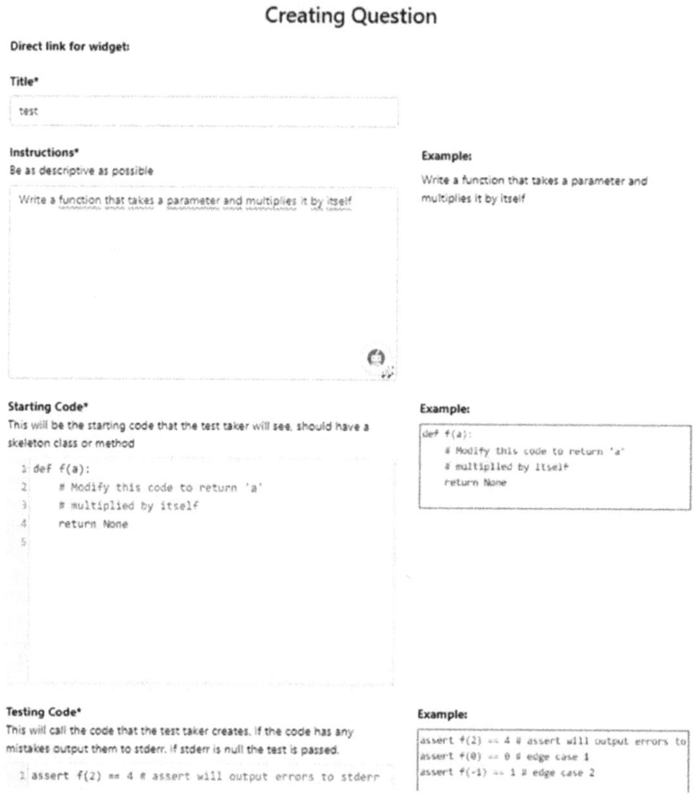

These tools can be used not only for online assessment but also for self-learning and peer learning. When the assessment questions are completed, a sharing link is generated so that the assessment can be shared with others. Assessment questions can also be sent directly to e-mail addresses via Codetester. There is also a free widget that you can embed on your site to allow users to test their code by typing it into a web page.

E-portfolio

Portfolios, which can be used effectively in the assessment of computer science education, aim to collect and evaluate student products through a purposeful and systematic process (McMillan, 2014). It is seen as a student-centered approach that encourages students' thinking skills and supports learner autonomy (Little, 2009). E-portfolios enable individual progress and academic preparation to be created, shared and published more easily in a web-based environment (Lorenzo & Ittelson, 2005). E-portfolios enable students to manage and evaluate their own learning and increase students' participation in the assessment process (Sharifi et al., 2017).

E-portfolios are more than just a space for students to accumulate their individual work. Downer and Slade (2019) note that e-portfolios can also be used for many different purposes, such as accreditation, admissions, graduate employability and evidence of professional competence. Sharing e-portfolios that contain many materials can also encourage peer learning by creating a repository of materials.

Mahara, one of the e-portfolio applications, is a digital assessment platform that enables the creation of digital diaries, uploading files, embedding third-party resources from the web, and collaborating with other users in groups (Mahara, 2024). In this application, portfolios can be created as collections or pages, license rights of each uploaded file are specified, and the portfolio can be searched by file name, description and tags (Figure 12).

Figure 12. **Mahara E-portfolio tool** (*https://mahara.org/*)

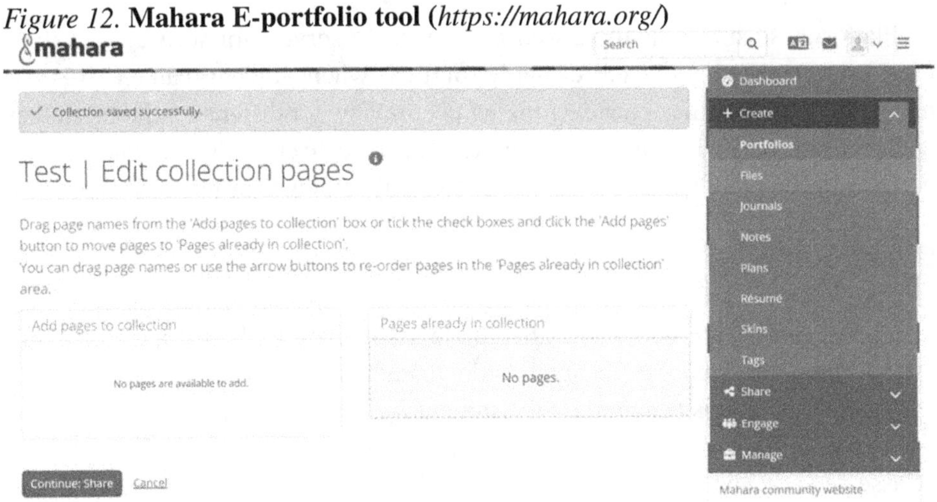

In addition to creating an e-portfolio on this platform, the student's friends list and groups can also be accessed. Students can interact with their friends by posting on their own wall.

Peer Review

Peer assessment makes significant contributions to process evaluation in CS education by using different types of assessment such as written assessment, evaluation of coding projects, debugging and algorithm analysis. Peer assessment, which is seen as an effective technique in developing students' high-level cognitive skills (Gündüz & Tosik, 2023), also contributes significantly to the collaborative working environment and social interaction. Peer code review tasks, which are considered within the scope of peer assessment, are one of the most effective methods in the development of code writing and editing skills. Peers' efforts to identify errors by examining the code leads to a deeper understanding of the sources of errors. Smith et al. (2012) listed the objectives of peer review for teaching software testing as follows:

1. Identify testing as a fun and competitive activity
2. Facilitating students to learn from each other
3. Demonstrate the importance of testing by uncovering hidden bugs in students' code
4. Create a mechanism for assessing test skills

Platforms such as GitHub, a web-based storage service for software development projects, can be given as examples of areas where students can receive peer reviews on the code they create. Utilizing peer review for different CS topics other than programming will contribute to students' capacity to critically evaluate existing projects and their ability to develop their projects according to different perspectives.

Digital Rubrics

Digital rubrics are one of the alternative assessment tools that are frequently used in computer science education in order to understand at what level of expertise a learning outcome is acquired by the student for which sub-headings. In rubrics, which enable more detailed assessments than other assessment tools, what should be assessed and how it should be assessed is determined by the instructor from the beginning. Figure 13 shows an example of an assessment rubric that can be used in a CS course (NCCE, 2023b).

Figure 13. **An example of an evaluation rubric that can be used in CS course (NCCE, 2023b)**

Year 7 - Gaining support for a cause | Assessment rubric

National Centre for Computing Education | Raspberry Pi

Assessment rubric

Year 7 - Gaining support for a cause

Learner:		Teacher:		Date:	

	Emerging [1]	Expected [2]	Exceeding [3]	Score
Audience	• Some evidence of thought for the audience	• Has appropriately identified the audience and there is some evidence that content is tailored for the audience	• Has identified the audience and it is clear that the content is fully appropriate for the audience	
Sources	• Has used at least one source to support argument, but it is not fully or appropriately referenced and there is no indication of credibility	• Has used two or more sources of information, which are referenced appropriately, and it can be proven that some information came from credible sources	• Has used a range of sources to support their argument, and all sources are fit for purpose and referenced appropriately, and their credibility has been justified	

The creation of these rubrics in a digital environment facilitates the process and feedback, allowing for more functional and sustainable assessments (Gündüz and Tosik, 2023). Jubaedah et al. (2020) also stated that the integration of information technologies into the assessment process will facilitate the creation and summarization of student assessment reports, so the creation and use of electronic rubrics will provide significant advantages.

Rubric-maker, one of the digital rubric creation tools, enables easy and fast digital rubric creation with its features such as selecting levels (primary, elementary, secondary, post secondary), determining topics, sub-topics and descriptions and assigning points to each of them (Figure 14).

Figure 14. **Rubric-Maker - Digital Rubric Creation Tool** (*https://rubric-maker.com/*)

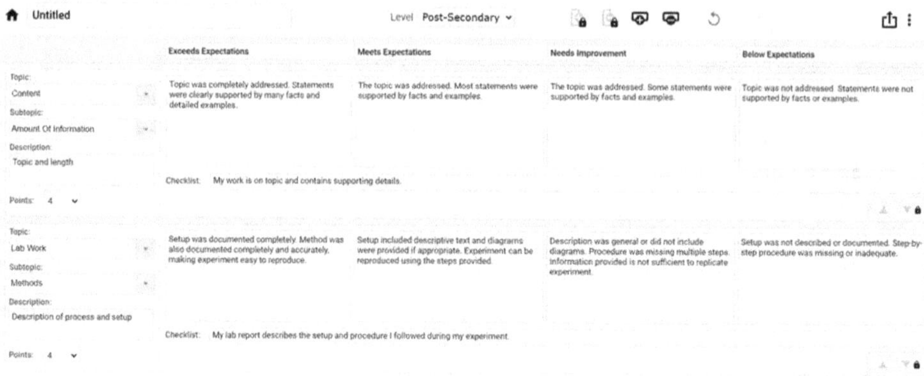

Digitally created rubrics can be printed out as PDFs or checklists. There are also other online rubric creation applications such as Quick Rubric.

CONCLUSION

Online assessment methods and tools have significant potential in K12 computer science education. Especially in this discipline, which has a comprehensive and dynamic content, there is a need for assessment methods that can be dynamically created and updated, that allow for process evaluation, and that provide immediate feedback to improve learning. Online assessment provides many advantages such as easy publishing of instructions and tests, automatic grading of exams, easier and faster access to peer assessment through online discussion forums, collective or individualized feedback to the whole class, and easier inclusion of remote students in assessment. The use of online exams, standardized tests, automated assessment tools, e-portfolios, digital rubrics, peer assessments and other assessment tools created in the digital environment is seen as effective in monitoring the development of thinking skills as well as providing diagnostic, formative and summative assessment of discipline-specific subjects. While online exams can be used to evaluate students' skills such as coding, sequencing, and debugging, different methods such as e-portfolios, digital rubrics, projects, self- and peer-assessment can be used to evaluate their efforts and higher-order thinking skills. Rubric-Maker, Project Quantum, Computational Thinking Test, Computational Thinking Test, Bebras, LeetCode, Codetester, Mahara are some examples of practical applications that can be used for online assessment. These applications enable effective and easy creation of assessment designs, increase participation and collaboration by reaching large communities, provide fast and advanced feedback, enable context-specific assessments, and offer time and cost advantages. In addition to all these opportunities and conveniences, there may be situations where the IT infrastructure is not robust or comprehensive enough to provide reliable and equally good service to all students, or where education stakeholders do not have sufficient digital literacy skills. It is important to take extra measures for academic integrity, such as verifying whether submitted work belongs to students, checking for plagiarism, authentication of students taking online exams, measures to prevent cheating, and proctored exams. In the assessment of computer science education, all the opportunities and challenges offered by online assessment should be handled in a balanced way, and assessment methods and tools that are appropriate to the context and outcomes should be included in the education process.

REFERENCES

Al Roomy, M. A. (2022). Exploring Teacher's Perspectives about Online Assessment during the COVID-19 Pandemic in a Saudi Context. *Arab World English Journal (AWEJ). Special Issue on CALL*, (8), 3–16. DOI: 10.24093/awej/call8.1

Alamr, S. M., Leon-Urrutia, M., & Carr, L. A. (2023, September). E-assessment in Computer Science Higher Education. In *Proceedings of the 15th International Conference on Education Technology and Computers* (pp. 378-383). https://doi.org/ DOI: 10.1145/3629296.3629357

Alharbi, A. S., Alhebshi, A. A., & Meccawy, Z. (2021). Efl students' and teachers' perceptions of google forms as a digital formative assessment tool in saudi secondary schools. *Arab World English Journal*, 7(1), 140–154. DOI: 10.24093/awej/call7.10

Alruwais, N., Wills, G., & Wald, M. (2018). Advantages and challenges of using e-assessment. *International Journal of Information and Education Technology (IJIET)*, 8(1), 34–37. DOI: 10.18178/ijiet.2018.8.1.1008

Amelung, M., Forbrig, P., & Rösner, D. (2008, June). Towards generic and flexible web services for e-assessment. In *Proceedings of the 13th annual conference on Innovation and technology in computer science education* (pp. 219-224). https://doi.org/DOI: 10.1145/1384271.1384330

Amer, A., Sidhu, G., Bo, Z., & Srinivasan, S. (2022). A Short Review of Online Learning Assessment Strategies. *International Journal of Pedagogy and Teacher Education*, 6(2), 89–103. https://jurnal.uns.ac.id/ijpte/article/view/66579. DOI: 10.20961/ijpte.v6i2.66579

Appiah, M., & Tonder, F. (2018). E-Assessment in higher education: A review. *International journal of business and economic research, 9*(6), 1454-1460. https://www.researchgate.net/profile/Martin-Appiah/publication/329775612_E-Assessment_in_Higher_Education_A_Review/links/5c1a2f61458515a4c7e90a08/E-Assessment-in-Higher-Education-A-Review.pdf

Archer, E. (2017). The assessment purpose triangle: Balancing the purposes of educational assessment. *Frontiers in Education*, 2, 41. Advance online publication. DOI: 10.3389/feduc.2017.00041

Arifuddin, A., Turmudi, T., & Rokhmah, U. N. (2021). Alternative assessments in online learning during covid-19 pandemic: The strenghths and weaknesses. *International Journal of Elementary Education*, 5(2), 240. DOI: 10.23887/ijee.v5i2.33532

Astini, N. K. S. (2020). Pemanfaatan Teknologi Informasi dalam Pembelajaran Tingkat Sekolah Dasar pada Masa Pandemi Covid-19. *Lampuhyang*, 11(2), 13–25. DOI: 10.47730/jurnallampuhyang.v11i2.194

Attia, M. A. (2014). Postgraduate students' perceptions toward online assessment: The case of the faculty ofeducation, Umm Al- Qura university. *In Education for a Knowledge Society in Arabian Gulf Countries* (pp.151–173). https://doi.org/DOI: 10.1108/S1479-367920140000024015

Aziz, S., Mahmood, M., & Rehman, Z. (2018). Implementation of cipp model for quality evaluation at school level: A case study. *Journal of Education and Educational Development*, 5(1), 189. DOI: 10.22555/joeed.v5i1.1553

Bailey, J., Pavlou, M., Copas, A., McCarthy, O., Carswell, K., Rait, G., Hart, G., Nazareth, I., Free, C., French, R., & Murray, E. (2013). The sexunzipped trial: Optimizing the design of online randomized controlled trials. *Journal of Medical Internet Research*, 15(12), e278. DOI: 10.2196/jmir.2668 PMID: 24334216

Barros, J. P. (2022). Assessment for Computer Programming Courses: A Short Guide for the Undecided Teacher. In *CSEDU (2)* (pp. 549-554). https://www.scitepress .org/Link.aspx?doi=10.5220/0011095800003182

Bastian, M., & Mühling, A. (2019, November). Let's Look a Layer Deeper: Design and First Results of a New Test System in the Context of Program Tracing. In *Proceedings of the 19th Koli Calling International Conference on Computing Education Research* (pp. 1-2). https://doi.org/DOI: 10.1145/3364510.3366155

Bayyapu, N. (2022, December). PDC Course Development and Assessment Process for the betterment of Teaching-Learning Process. In *2022 IEEE 29th International Conference on High Performance Computing,Data and Analytics Workshop (HiPCW)* (pp. 12-19). IEEE. https://doi.org/DOI: 10.1109/HiPCW57629.2022.00007

Bebras. (2024). https://www.bebras.org/

Beerepoot, M. T. P. (2023). Formative and summative automated assessment with multiple-choice question banks. *Journal of Chemical Education*, 100(8), 2947–2955. DOI: 10.1021/acs.jchemed.3c00120

Bocconi, S., Chioccariello, A., & Kampylis, P. (2022). Reviewing computational thinking in compulsory education: state of play and practices from computing education, (Ed. A.Inamorato dos Santos; Y. Punie; R. Cachia; N. Giannoutsou). European Commission, Joint Research Centre, Publications Office of the European Union. http://doi.org/DOI: 10.2760/126955

Boitshwarelo, B., Reedy, A. K., & Billany, T. (2017). Envisioning the use of online tests in assessing twentyfirst century learning: A literature review. *Research and Practice in Technology Enhanced Learning*, 12(1), 16. DOI: 10.1186/s41039-017-0055-7 PMID: 30595721

Brendefur, J. L., Johnson, E. S., Thiede, K. W., Strother, S., & Severson, H. H. (2018). Developing a multi-dimensional early elementary mathematics screener and diagnostic tool: The primary mathematics assessment. *Early Childhood Education Journal*, 46(2), 153–157. DOI: 10.1007/s10643-017-0854-x PMID: 29576730

Bukhari, G., Saleem, J., Bukhari, S., Ishaq, M., & Butt, M. (2022). Challenges in conducting online assessments in undergraduate medical and dental education: A scoping review. *Biomedica*, 38(3), 123–128. DOI: 10.51441/BioMedica/5-764

Butler-Henderson, K., & Crawford, J. (2020). A systematic review of online examinations: A pedagogical innova-tion for scalable authentication and integrity. *Computers & Education*, 159, 104024. DOI: 10.1016/j.compedu.2020.104024 PMID: 32982023

Csapó, B., & Molnár, G. (2019). Online diagnostic assessment in support of personalized teaching and learning: The eDia system. *Frontiers in Psychology*, 10, 443648. DOI: 10.3389/fpsyg.2019.01522 PMID: 31333546

CSTA. (2017a). K12 Computer Science Standards. https://members.csteachers.org/documents/en-us/46916364-83ab-4f51-85fb-06b3b25b417c/1/

CSTA. (2017b). View the CSTA K-12 Standards. https://csteachers.org/k12standards/interactive

Dagiene, V., & Futschek, G. (2008). Bebras international contest on informatics and computer literacy:Criteria for good tasks. *In International Conference on Informatics in Secondary Schools- Evolution and Perspectives* (pp. 19–30). Berlin, Germany: Springer. DOI: 10.1007/978-3-540-69924-8_2

Dermo, J. (2009). E-assessment and the student learning experience: A survey of student percep tions of e-assessment. *British Journal of Educational Technology*, 40(2), 203–214. DOI: 10.1111/j.1467-8535.2008.00915.x

Diagnosticquestions. (2024). https://diagnosticquestions.com/Quantum

Downer, T., & Slade, C. (2019). Starting early: Using ePortfolios to prepare first year midwifery students for professional practice. In Trimmer, K., Newman, T., & Padró, F. (Eds.), *Ensuring quality in professional education* (Vol. I, pp. 73–98). Palgrave Macmillan., https://link.springer.com/chapter/10.1007/978-3-030-01096-6_4 DOI: 10.1007/978-3-030-01096-6_4

Dreher, C., Reiners, T., & Dreher, H. (2011). Investigating factors affecting the uptake of automated assessment technology. *Journal of Information Technology Education*, 10, 161–181. DOI: 10.28945/1492

Dunn, L., Morgan, C., O'Reilly, M., & Parry, S. (2003). *The student assessment handbook: New directions in traditional and online assessment*. Routledge., DOI: 10.4324/9780203416518

El-Hamamsy, L., Zapata-Cáceres, M., Barroso, E. M., Mondada, F., Zufferey, J. D., & Bruno, B. (2022). The competent computational thinking test: Development and validation of an unplugged computational thinking test for upper primary school. *Journal of Educational Computing Research*, 60(7), 1818–1866. DOI: 10.1177/07356331221081753

Entwistle, N., & Tait, H. (1995). *Approaches to studying. New Directions for Teaching and Learning, 64, Winter* (Hativa, N., & Marincovic, M., Eds.). JosseyBass.

Flavin, M. (2021). A Disruptive Innovation perspective on students' opinions of online assessment. *Research in Learning Technology*, 29, •••. https://journal.alt.ac.uk/index.php/rlt/article/view/2611/2887. DOI: 10.25304/rlt.v29.2611

Gonsalves, C. (2023). On chatgpt: What promise remains for multiple choice assessment? *Journal of Learning Development in Higher Education*, (27). Advance online publication. DOI: 10.47408/jldhe.vi27.1009

Good, R. (2011). Formative use of assessment information: It's a process, so let's say what we mean. *Practical Assessment, Research & Evaluation*, 16, 1–6.

Gündüz, M., & Tosik, E. G. (2023). Bilgisayar Bilimi Eğitiminde Çevrimiçi Değerlendirme Uygulamaları [Online Assessment Applications in Computer Science Education]. *Teoriden Uygulamaya Bilgisayar Bilimi Eğitimi* [Computer Science Education from Theory to Practice]. (Ed. S. B. Kert), Nobel Publishing.

Hsueh, N., Lai, L., & Tseng, W. (2023). Design of an online programming platform and a study on learners' testing ability. *Electronics (Basel)*, 12(22), 4596. DOI: 10.3390/electronics12224596

Hussein, M., Yusuf, J., Deb, A., Fong, L., & Naidu, S. (2020). An Evaluation of Online Proctoring Tools. *Open Praxis.*, 12(4), 509–525. DOI: 10.5944/openpraxis.12.4.1113

Iftikhar, S., & Cheema, K. (2022). Medical students' perception of online assessment at a private medical college. *Health Professions Educator Journal*, 5(2), 15–18. DOI: 10.53708/hpej.v5i2.1258

Joint Information Systems Committee (JISC). 2007. Effective practice with e-assessment: An overview of technologies, policies and practice in further and higher education. http://www.jisc.ac.uk/media/documents/themes/elearning/effpraceassess.pdf

Jordan, S. (2013). E-assessment: Past, present and future. *New Directions in the Teaching of Physical Sciences*, 9(1), 87–106. DOI: 10.11120/ndir.2013.00009

Jose, S. (2016, December 15). Online proctoring is trending: Here is all you must know. Talview. Retrieved from https://blog.talview.com/a-complete-guide-to-online-remote-proctoring

Jubaedah, Y., Yulia, C., Muktiarni, M., & Maosul, A. (2020). Usability testing electronic rubric of performance assessment. In *Journal of Physics: Conference Series, 1456(1)*. IOP Publishing., DOI: 10.1088/1742-6596/1456/1/012016

Kallia, M. (2017). Assessment in computer science courses: A literature review. *Royal Society*, 1-60. https://royalsociety.org/-/media/policy/projects/computing-education/assessment-literature-review.pdf

Keuning, H., Jeuring, J., & Heeren, B. (2018). A systematic literature review of automated feedback generation for programming exercises. [TOCE]. *ACM Transactions on Computing Education*, 19(1), 1–43. DOI: 10.1145/3231711

Koçdar, S., Karadeniz, A., & Göksel, N. (2022). Çevrim İçi Ölçme ve Değerlendirmede Kimlik Tanıma ve Doğrulama Sistemlerinin Kullanımı: Üniversite Öğrencilerinin Deneyimleri [Authentication and Authorship Systems in Online Assessment: Experiences of University Students]. *Adam Academy Journal of Social Sciences*, 12(1), 1–32. DOI: 10.31679/adamakademi.1038184

Koh, K. H., Basawapatna, A., Nickerson, H., & Repenning, A. (2014, July). Real time assessment of computational thinking. In *2014 IEEE Symposium on visual languages and human-centric computing (VL/HCC)* (pp. 49-52). IEEE. https://www.webofscience.com/wos/woscc/full-record/WOS:000361019600012

Koretz, D. (2018). Moving beyond the Failure of Test-Based Accountability. *American Educator*, 41(4), 22–26. https://eric.ed.gov/?id=EJ1164385

Lewis, S. E. (2020). Chemistry assessments through the sudden implementation of online instruction. *Journal of Chemical Education*, 97(9), 3418–3422. DOI: 10.1021/acs.jchemed.0c00697

Linden, K., & González, P. (2021). Zoom invigilated exams: A protocol for rapid adoption to remote examinations. *British Journal of Educational Technology*, 52(4), 1323–1337. DOI: 10.1111/bjet.13109

Little, D. (2009). Language learner autonomy and the European language portfolio: Two L2 English examples. *Language Teaching*, 42(2), 222–233. DOI: 10.1017/S0261444808005636

Ljubic, S., Skoki, A., Hržić, F., & Salkanovic, A. (2023). Empowering Computer Engineering Education: Leveraging Cloud-Based Programming Platforms and Online Assessment Tools. *BOOKOF*, 43. https://www.researchgate.net/profile/Francesca-Finestrone/publication/378268879_HELMeTO_2023_Book-of-abstracts/links/65d08fd601325d4652114308/HELMeTO-2023-Book-of-abstracts.pdf

Lorenzo, G., & Ittelson, J. (2005). An overview of e-portfolios. EDUCAUSE Learning Initiative. ELI Paper, 1-28. Retrieved May 8, 2014, from https://net.educause.edu/ir/library/pdf/ELI3001.pdf

Lu, S., Eloanyi, C. B., & Olelewe, C. J. (2023). Computer educators' perception of the utilization of online assessment in the Covid-19 era. *Computer Applications in Engineering Education*, 31(4), 983–1000. DOI: 10.1002/cae.22618

Mahara. (2024). https://demo.mahara.org/

Marden, N. Y., Ulman, L. G., Wilson, F., & Velan, G. M. (2013). Online feedback assessments in physiology: Effects on students' learning experiences and outcomes. *Advances in Physiology Education*, 37(2), 192–200. DOI: 10.1152/advan.00092.2012 PMID: 23728137

Mate, K. E., & Weidenhofer, J. (2021). Considerations and strategies for effective online assessment with a focus on the biomedical sciences. *FASEB bioAdvances*, 4(1), 9–21. DOI: 10.1096/fba.2021-00075 PMID: 35024569

McMillan, J. H., & Hearn, J. (2008). Student Self-Assessment: The Key to Stronger Student Motivation and Higher Achievement. *Educational Horizons*, 87(1), 40–49.

McMillan, J. H., & Hellsten, L. (2010). *Classroom assessment: Principles and practice for effective standards-based instruction*. Pearson Education. https://researchportal.murdoch.edu.au/esploro/outputs/book/Classroom-Assessment-Principles-and-Practice-for/991005631470107891

Mellar, H., Peytcheva-Forsyth, R., Kocdar, S., Karadeniz, A., & Yovkova, B. (2018). Addressing cheating in e-assessment using student authentication and authorship checking systems: Teachers' perspectives. *International Journal for Educational Integrity*, 14(1), 1–21. DOI: 10.1007/s40979-018-0025-x

Mohiudddin, K., Islam, A., Mohd, S., & Shariff, M. (2019). Evaluation of an academic program: The case of computing accreditation commission framework in higher education. *International Journal of Emerging Technologies in Learning*, 14(11), 70. DOI: 10.3991/ijet.v14i11.10178

Moosvi, F., Eddelbuettel, D., Zilles, C., Wolfman, S. A., Fund, F., Alford, L. K., & Schroeder, J. (2023, March). Creating Algorithmically Generated Questions Using a Modern, Open-sourced, Online Platform: PrairieLearn. In *Proceedings of the 54th ACM Technical Symposium on Computer Science Education* V. 2 (pp. 1177-1177). https://doi.org/DOI: 10.1145/3545947.3569634

Munisamy, M., Osman, S. Z. M., & Sanmugam, M. (2024). Code, Click, Learn: A Systematic Review Of Online Assessment Tools In 21st Century Programming Education. *International Journal of Medical Education*, 6(20), 358–377. DOI: 10.35631/IJMOE.620027

NCCE. (2023b). National Centre of Computing Education. https://teachcomputing.org/curriculum

Neumann, R., Parry, S., & Becher, T. (2002). Teaching and learning in their disciplinary contexts: A conceptual analysis. *Studies in Higher Education*, 27(4), 405–417. DOI: 10.1080/0307507022000011525

Nguyen, Q., Rienties, B., Toetenel, L., Ferguson, R., & Whitelock, D. (2017). Examining the designs of computer-based assessment and its impact on student engagement, satisfaction, and pass rates. *Computers in Human Behavior*, 76, 703–714. DOI: 10.1016/j.chb.2017.03.028

Osabutey, E. L., Senyo, P. K., & Bempong, B. F. (2022). Evaluating the potential impact of online assessment on students' academic performance. *Information Technology &Amp. Information Technology & People*, 37(1), 152–170. DOI: 10.1108/ITP-05-2021-0377

Osuji, S. (2017). The use of e-assessment in the Nigerian higher systems. *Turkish Online Journal of Distance Education*, 13(4), 140–152.

Passey, D. (2016). Computer science (cs) in the compulsory education curriculum: Implications for future research. *Education and Information Technologies*, 22(2), 421–443. DOI: 10.1007/s10639-016-9475-z

Peytcheva-Forsyth, R., Aleksieva, L., & Yovkova, B. (2018). The impact of prior experience of e-learning and e-assessment on students' and teachers' approaches to the use of a student authentication and authorship checking system. *EDULEARN18 Proceedings*, 2311-2321. https://bit.ly/3OCGK80

Prickett, T., Walters, J., Yang, L., Harvey, M., & Crick, T. (2020). Resilience and effective learning in first-year undergraduate computer science. *Proceedings of the 2020 ACM Conference on Innovation and Technology in Computer Science Education*. https://doi.org/DOI: 10.1145/3341525.3387372

Pu, S., & Xu, H. (2021). Examining changing assessment practices in online teaching: A multiple-case study of efl school teachers in china. *The Asia-Pacific Education Researcher*, 30(6), 553–561. DOI: 10.1007/s40299-021-00605-6

Randolph, J. (2008). A methodological review of the program evaluations in k-12 computer science education. *Informatics in Education*, 7(2), 237–258. DOI: 10.15388/infedu.2008.15

Reddy, S. (2023). Best Assessment Software for Schools- E-tutor. https://etutor.co/blog/assessment-software/

Ridgway, J., McCusker, S., & Pead, D. (2004). Literature review of e-assessment. https://telearn.hal.science/hal-00190440

Robinson, P. E., & Carroll, J. (2016). An online system for monitoring and assessing the programming process. *Bulletin of the IEEE Technical Committee on Learning Technology*, 18(2/3), 2. https://www.webofscience.com/wos/woscc/full-record/WOS:000398346100002

Román-González, M., Moreno-León, J., & Robles, G. (2019). Combining assessment tools for a comprehensive evaluation of computational thinking interventions. *Computational thinking education*, 79-98. https://library.oapen.org/bitstream/handle/20.500.12657/23182/1006971.pdf?sequenc#page=85

Román-González, M., Pérez-González, J. C., & Jiménez-Fernández, C. (2017). Which cognitive abilities underlie computational thinking? Criterion validity of the Computational Thinking Test. *Computers in Human Behavior*, 72, 678–691. DOI: 10.1016/j.chb.2016.08.047

Romeike, R. (2019). The role of computer science education for understanding and shaping the digital society. In Sustainable ICT, Education and Learning: IFIP WG 3.4 International Conference, SUZA 2019, Zanzibar, Tanzania, April 25–27, 2019, Revised Selected Papers 1 (pp. 167-176). Springer International Publishing. https://link.springer.com/chapter/10.1007/978-3-030-28764-1_19

Ruiz, P., Nestor, E., Mills, K., Coenraad, M., & Burke, Q. (2022, March). Designing Equity-Centered Formative Assessment Artifacts for Computing. In *Proceedings of the 53rd ACM Technical Symposium on Computer Science Education V. 2* (pp. 1121-1121). https://www.webofscience.com/wos/woscc/full-record/WOS:000947124200075

Saeki, E., Segool, N., Pendergast, L., & von der Embse, N. (2018). The influence of test-based accountability policies on early elementary teachers: School climate, environmental stress, and teacher stress. *Psychology in the Schools*, 55(4), 391–403. DOI: 10.1002/pits.22112

Schmidt, S. M. P., Ralph, D. L., & Buskirk, B. (2009). Utilizing online exams: A case study. *Journal of College Teaching and Learning*, 6(8), 1. DOI: 10.19030/tlc.v6i8.1108

Schulte, C., Clear, T., Taherkhani, A., Busjahn, T., & Paterson, J. H. (2010). An introduction to program comprehension for computer science educators. *Proceedings of the 2010 ITiCSE working group reports*, 65-86. https://doi.org/DOI: 10.1145/1971681.1971687

Shanley, N., Martin, F., Hite, N., Pérez-Quiñones, M. A., Ahlgrim-Delzell, L., Pugalee, D., & Hart, E. (2022). Teaching programming online: Design, facilitation and assessment strategies and recommendations for high school teachers. *TechTrends*, 66(3), 483–494. DOI: 10.1007/s11528-022-00724-x PMID: 35434728

Sharifi, M., Soleimani, H., & Jafarigohar, M. (2017). E-portfolio evaluation and vocabulary learning: Moving from pedagogy to andragogy. *British Journal of Educational Technology*, 48(6), 1441–1450. DOI: 10.1111/bjet.12479

Sharma, V. K., & Holbah, W. A. (2022). Online Language Assessment the Exception, Not the Rule: For Inclusive Language Learning. *Arab World English Journal (AWEJ). Special Issue on CALL*, (8), 299–313. DOI: 10.24093/awej/call8.20

Sierra, A. J., Ariza, T., Fernández-Jiménez, F. J., Bellido, S., & Martínez-Gotor, A. (2014). E-assessment tool within PBL in programming subjects at engineering. In *EDULEARN14 Proceedings* (pp. 7074–7080). IATED., https://library.iated.org/view/SIERRA2014EAS

Sietses, L. (2016). White Paper Online Proctoring. Questions and answers about remote proctoring. *SURFnet*. Retrieved from https://www.surf.nl/files/2019-04/whitepaper-online-proctoring_en.pdf

Sitthisak, O., Gilbert, L., & Davis, H. C. (2008). An evaluation of pedagogically informed parameterised questions for self-assessment. *Learning, Media and Technology*, 33(3), 235–248. https://www.tandfonline.com/doi/abs/10.1080/17439880802324210. DOI: 10.1080/17439880802324210

Skinner, B. F. (1958). Teaching machines. *Science*, 128(3330), 969–977. https://app.nova.edu/toolbox/instructionalproducts/edd8124/fall11/1958-Skinner-TeachingMachines.pdf. DOI: 10.1126/science.128.3330.969 PMID: 13592277

Slavin, R. E. (2002). Evidence-based education policies: Transforming educational practice and research. *Educational Researcher*, 31(7), 15–21. DOI: 10.3102/0013189X031007015

Smith, J., Tessler, J., Kramer, E., & Lin, C. (2012, September). Using peer review to teach software testing. In *Proceedings of the ninth annual international conference on International computing education research* (pp. 93-98). https://doi.org/DOI: 10.1145/2361276.2361295

Spivey, M. F., & McMillan, J. J. (2014). Classroom versus online assessment. *Journal of Education for Business*, 89(8), 450–456. DOI: 10.1080/08832323.2014.937676

Sweeney, T., West, D., Groessler, A., Haynie, A., Higgs, B., Macaulay, J., Mercer-Mapstone, L., & Yeo, M. (2017). Where's the Transformation? Unlocking the Potential of Technology Enhanced Assessment. *Teaching & Learning Inquiry*, 5(1), 1–13. DOI: 10.20343/5.1.5

Thomson, K., & Falchikov, N. (1998). 'Full on until the sun comes out': The effects of assessment on student approaches to studying. *Assessment & Evaluation in Higher Education*, 23(4), 379–390. DOI: 10.1080/0260293980230405

Tiantian, W., Xiaohong, S., Peijun, M., Yuying, W., & Kuanquan, W. (2009) Autolep: An automated learning and examination system for programming and its application in programming course. *InFirst International Workshop on Education Technology and Computer Science,* 43-46. IEEE. DOI: 10.1109/ETCS.2009.18

Topuz, A. C., Saka, E., Fatsa, Ö. F., & Kurşun, E. (2022). Emerging trends of online assessment systems in the emergency remote teaching period. *Smart Learning Environments*, 9(1), 17. Advance online publication. DOI: 10.1186/s40561-022-00199-6

Tsai, M. J., Chien, F. P., Wen-Yu Lee, S., Hsu, C. Y., & Liang, J. C. (2022). Development and validation of the computational thinking test for elementary school students (CTT-ES): Correlate CT competency with CT disposition. *Journal of Educational Computing Research*, 60(5), 1110–1129. DOI: 10.1177/07356331211051043

TTKB. (2018). Bilişim Teknolojileri ve Yazılım Öğretim Programı [Information Technologies and Software Curriculum]. https://mufredat.meb.gov.tr/ProgramDetay.aspx?PID=1383

TTKB. (2023). Ortaöğretim Bilişim Teknolojileri ve Yazılım Dersi Öğretim Programı. [Secondary Education Information Technologies and Software Course Curriculum]. https://mufredat.meb.gov.tr/ProgramDetay.aspx?PID=1353

Velan, G. M., Jones, P., McNeil, H. P., & Kumar, R. K. (2008). Integrated online formative assessments in the biomedical sciences for medical students: Benefits for learning. *BMC Medical Education*, 8(1), 52. Advance online publication. DOI: 10.1186/1472-6920-8-52 PMID: 19032738

Veugen, M. J., Gulikers, J., & Brok, P. (2022). Secondary school teachers' use of online formative assessment during covid-19 lockdown: Experiences and lessons learned. *Journal of Computer Assisted Learning*, 38(5), 1465–1481. DOI: 10.1111/jcal.12699 PMID: 35942306

Vonderwell, S., Liang, X., & Alderman, K. (2007). Asynchronous discussions and assessment in online learning. *Journal of Research on Technology in Education*, 39(3), 309–328. DOI: 10.1080/15391523.2007.10782485

Whitelock, D., Reudel, C., & Mackenzie, D. (2006). *E-assessment : Case studies of effective and innovative practice a JISC*. Jt. Inf. Syst. Comm.

Wójcik, J., & Rataj, M. (2022). The impact of covid-19 on online final exam scores among computer science students. *European Conference on Knowledge Management, 23(*2), 955-964. https://doi.org/DOI: 10.34190/eckm.23.2.644

Xobin. (2024). What is an Online Assessment? Everything You Need to Know. https://xobin.com/blog/guide-to-online-assessment/

Zapata-Cáceres, M., Martín-Barroso, E., & Román-González, M. (2020, April). Computational thinking test for beginners: Design and content validation. In *2020 IEEE Global Engineering Education Conference (EDUCON)*. pp. 1905-1914. IEEE. https://doi.org/DOI: 10.1109/EDUCON45650.2020.9125368

Chapter 10
Professional Development for K-12 Educators

Veysel Bilal Arslankara
https://orcid.org/0000-0002-9062-9210
T.C. Millî Eğitim Bakanlığı, Turkey

Elif Arslankara
T.C. Millî Eğitim Bakanlığı, Turkey

İlyas Asan
MONE, Turkey

Mehmet Külekçi
MONE, Turkey

Süleyman Sadi Seferoğlu
Hacettepe University, Turkey

ABSTRACT

This chapter covers professional development and literacy in K-12 education, focusing on technology integration and leadership. It emphasizes the need for continuous education and support for teachers, highlighting personalized, collaborative, and sustained development. Key areas include: Data and information literacy: critical evaluation and use of information through inquiry-based and project-based learning. Digital literacy: integrating technology, teaching responsible use of digital tools, and digital citizenship. Research-oriented teaching: fostering curiosity and critical thinking, enhancing students' research skills. Leadership: teacher leaders creating

DOI: 10.4018/979-8-3693-4542-9.ch010

positive environments through vision, collaboration, and resilience. Overall, the chapter presents a holistic approach to prepare students for the 21st century.

Professional development is a process and a set of activities designed to enhance educators' professional knowledge, skills, and attitudes (Guskey, 2000). This process and these activities include directed instruction and learning experiences organized to help teachers acquire professional knowledge, skills, and tendencies, as well as to support the application of this knowledge (NPDCI, 2008). Thus, it aims to improve teachers' effectiveness to enhance students' learning performance (Sparks & Loucks-Harsley, 1989). Day (1999) defines professional development as all natural learning experiences and purposeful planned activities that directly or indirectly benefit individuals, groups, or schools and contribute to the quality of classroom education.

In recent years, data-driven professional development has been considered the most effective approach to adequately prepare educators and enhance their educational and intervention practices after entering the profession (Buysse et al., 2009). Policymakers increasingly focus on professional development to ensure that educators working in K-12 have the necessary foundational knowledge and skills for effective practices, preparing them for teaching and intervention practices or assisting them in improving existing practices (NPDCI, 2008).

Participation in professional development activities has been shown to have a positive impact on teachers' beliefs and practices, as well as positive effects on the implementation of education reforms in their classrooms (Villegas-Reimers, 2003). In a study conducted by Youngs (2001), four different professional development models (teacher networks, coaching and mutual visitation, student assessment, and school improvement) were examined, and each model was found to strengthen teachers' knowledge, skills, and tendencies. Borko and Putnam (1995) also stated that professional development activities for teachers have a significant impact on teachers' pedagogical content knowledge and pedagogical content beliefs, enabling teachers to change their teaching techniques and thus improve students' learning processes. Additionally, the importance of professional development for early childhood educators is emphasized to provide high-quality services to children and families and to improve schools (Borko, 2004; Buysse et al., 2009).

As one of the most important professions nurturing societal development, teaching, especially in K-12, emphasizes the significance of teacher qualifications and professional development (Bümen et al., 2012). Debates over the quality, intensity, standards, and implementation forms of professional development programs particularly affect the professional development of K-12 teachers and specialists (Bümen et al., 2012; Gür and Çelik, 2009).

Professional development for K-12 educators is highly crucial, and its prominence stems from several important reasons. Constantly evolving educational and instructional methods, the emergence of new technologies, and changes in student profiles necessitate educators to be equipped with up-to-date knowledge and skills (Guskey, 2002). This is because educators need to continually improve themselves to enhance student success, which is expected by individuals and society alike. Professional development enhances teaching quality by improving educators' knowledge and skills (Shulman, 1987), allowing for more effective lesson planning, catering to different learning styles, and boosting students' academic achievement (Hattie, 2009). Moreover, research has shown that educators who participate in professional development have students with higher academic achievement (Good et al., 2001), attributing this to educators being equipped with current knowledge and skills and employing more effective teaching methods.

Professional development strengthens educators' pedagogical approaches and instructional techniques, thereby progressing towards providing more effective teaching. Professional development programs provide educators with opportunities to explore new ideas and approaches and implement them in their own classrooms (Fullan, 2007), fostering innovation in education (Cuban, 1984). Furthermore, professional development contributes to elevating instructional quality. Well-prepared and equipped teachers deliver more effective lessons and provide opportunities to enhance students' learning experiences.

Successful implementation of educational reforms is also a significant reason for the importance of professional development. Educators must be knowledgeable about evolving curricula, instructional methods, or assessment techniques. K-12 educators will continuously need professional development to develop and implement instructional strategies suitable for different student groups. This facilitates coping with student diversity and enables making correct and effective plans. Professional development programs allow educators to come together to share knowledge and experiences (Little, 1990), enhancing professional solidarity and collaboration, thereby facilitating continuous improvement of the education system.

With changing living conditions, many changes have occurred in individuals and societies, such as social and economic opportunities, the education system, professions, and definitions of roles and duties in professions. Parallel to these changes in the education system, changes are also occurring in traditional teaching roles and behaviors. As emphasized in William Arthur Wood's quote, "The ordinary teacher tells, the good teacher explains, the superior teacher demonstrates, and the great teacher inspires," the roles of teachers in the education system are no longer limited to being mere lecturers. Teachers are expected to serve as inspirational leaders.

With digital technologies becoming more widespread and accessible, people from all walks of life have begun to use these technologies more extensively. However, this does not imply that everyone who uses digital technology knows how to use these tools appropriately and correctly. Furthermore, the fact that today's children are immersed in technology and digital tools from birth does not necessarily mean that they know how to use these tools effectively. Teachers should be able to use these skills in their own lives and transfer these skills to students. Having certain skills in the digital world we live in plays an important role in integrating technology more effectively into our lives and living with technology correctly.

Professional development is critically important for educators to improve and keep their knowledge and skills current. Opportunities in this regard range from one-time workshops to academic courses offered by a variety of providers (Buysse et al., 2009). Different programs can vary greatly in terms of the philosophy, content, and format of learning experiences. The term "professional development" generally brings to mind formal processes such as conferences, seminars, workshops, collaborative team efforts, or university courses. However, this concept also encompasses informal learning forms that occur in contexts such as discussions with colleagues, individual reading and research, peer observation, and peer learning (Mizell, 2010). In addition, informal activities such as following professional journals, attending professional meetings, and even watching TV programs related to relevant disciplines can be considered as part of professional development (Ganser, 2000).

As stated in this book chapter, we will try to discuss what professional development means for K-12 educators and why it is important; What are the professional development opportunities and in which areas the impact of professional development is observed; Strategies that support professional development and where professional development will develop in the future will be examined. In addition, concepts such as data and information literacy teaching, digital literacy teaching, curious and constantly researching teaching, and pioneering teaching, which are among the new concepts of our age, will be explained.

1. PROFESSIONAL DEVELOPMENT FOR EDUCATORS

In the rapidly evolving field of education, continuous professional development (PD) for K-12 educators is paramount. As technology advances and pedagogical approaches evolve, educators must stay abreast of new methodologies, tools, and practices to effectively meet the diverse needs of their students. Professional development is not only about enhancing teachers' knowledge and skills but also about fostering a culture of continuous improvement and lifelong learning within the educational community.

Professional development (PD) for educators is a systematic approach aimed at enhancing the teaching practices, knowledge, and skills of teachers. It involves a range of activities such as workshops, seminars, online courses, and collaborative learning communities, all designed to support educators in their continuous professional growth. PD is vital because it helps teachers stay updated with the latest educational research, technological advancements, and innovative pedagogical strategies. In an era where educational demands are rapidly changing, ongoing professional learning ensures that educators are equipped to meet the diverse needs of their students and adapt to new educational challenges (Dogan, Pringle, & Mesa, 2016).

The significance of professional development goes beyond individual teacher improvement; it is crucial for the overall effectiveness of the educational system. Research has consistently demonstrated that high-quality PD is linked to improved teaching practices and better student outcomes. For instance, a study by Wallace (2009) found that professional development has a moderate impact on teacher practices and a smaller but significant effect on student achievement when mediated by teacher practices (Wallace, 2009). Furthermore, professional development that focuses on specific content areas and instructional strategies has been shown to be particularly effective in enhancing teachers' ability to engage students and improve their learning outcomes (Supovitz & Turner, 2000). Investing in professional development not only empowers teachers but also drives the success of students and the broader educational community.

Professional development is critical for several reasons. Firstly, it ensures that teachers remain current with the latest educational research and best practices. This is essential for maintaining high standards of teaching and learning. For instance, Guskey (2002) emphasizes that effective PD leads to improved teaching practices and student outcomes. One study demonstrated that professional development has a moderate effect on teacher practice and a smaller but significant effect on student achievement when mediated by teacher practice (Wallace, 2009). Furthermore, professional development helps teachers to integrate new technologies into their classrooms, which is increasingly important in the 21st century. Research by Lawless and Pellegrino (2007) indicates that PD focused on technology integration significantly enhances teachers' ability to use digital tools to support student learning.

Additionally, effective PD contributes to the development of inquiry-based teaching practices and fosters an investigative classroom culture, which are crucial for enhancing student engagement and achievement in subjects such as science (Supovitz & Turner, 2000). The integration of professional learning communities (PLCs) into PD initiatives has also been shown to help teachers increase their pedagogical content knowledge (PCK) and improve instructional practices, which subsequently boosts student learning outcomes (Dogan, Pringle, & Mesa, 2016).

Various models of professional development exist, each with its strengths and challenges. Traditional models, such as workshops and seminars, provide opportunities for teachers to learn from experts and gain new insights. However, these models often suffer from a lack of follow-up and sustained support (Desimone, 2009).

More contemporary models emphasize continuous, collaborative learning. Professional Learning Communities (PLCs) and coaching/mentoring programs are examples of these models. PLCs refer to groups of educators who work together regularly to share experiences, discuss challenges, and develop solutions. Research by Vescio, Ross, and Adams (2008) shows that PLCs can lead to significant improvements in instructional practices and student outcomes. Similarly, mentoring and coaching programs provide personalized, context-specific support to teachers, helping them implement new strategies effectively (Kraft, Blazar, & Hogan, 2018).

1.1. Effective Professional Development Practices

For professional development to be effective, it must be well-designed and thoughtfully implemented. Key characteristics of effective PD include relevance, active learning, collaboration, and sustained duration (Darling-Hammond et al., 2017).

Effective professional development (PD) is crucial for fostering meaningful and lasting improvements in teaching practices and student outcomes. One of the most significant factors that contribute to the effectiveness of PD is its alignment with evidence-based practices. Research indicates that PD programs grounded in the latest educational research are more likely to result in positive changes in the classroom. For instance, programs that focus on content-specific training and the development of pedagogical content knowledge have been shown to enhance teachers' instructional capabilities and improve student learning outcomes (Lynch, Hill, Gonzalez, & Pollard, 2019). By integrating research-driven strategies into PD, educators can be confident that the methods they are learning are not only theoretically sound but also practically effective.

Another key aspect of effective PD is the incorporation of reflective practice. Teachers who are encouraged to reflect on their teaching methods and student outcomes as part of their PD experience tend to develop a deeper understanding of their own practice and are better equipped to make informed adjustments. Reflective practice allows educators to critically analyze their successes and challenges, fostering a culture of continuous improvement. Studies have shown that PD programs that include opportunities for reflection, such as peer observations and feedback sessions, are more successful in promoting lasting changes in teaching practices (Supovitz & Turner, 2000).

Moreover, the role of school leadership in supporting effective PD cannot be overstated. School leaders play a critical role in creating an environment that values professional learning and encourages teachers to engage fully in PD opportunities. When school administrators actively support PD initiatives, provide resources, and participate in learning activities alongside teachers, it reinforces the importance of continuous professional growth. Research has shown that schools with strong leadership support for PD are more likely to see improvements in teaching practices and student outcomes (Wetherill, Burton, Calhoun, & Thomas, 2001).

Another essential component of effective PD is the focus on building teacher autonomy and agency. Teachers who feel empowered to take ownership of their professional learning are more likely to implement new strategies and sustain changes in their practice. PD programs that provide teachers with choices in their learning paths, encourage experimentation, and support risk-taking can lead to more innovative and responsive teaching. Research suggests that when teachers have a sense of control over their professional development, they are more engaged and motivated, leading to better outcomes for both teachers and students (Andrews & Richmond, 2019).

Effective PD practices emphasize the importance of cultural responsiveness. As classrooms become increasingly diverse, it is essential that PD programs equip teachers with the skills and knowledge to address the cultural and linguistic needs of their students. Culturally responsive PD helps teachers to understand and value the diverse backgrounds of their students, leading to more inclusive and equitable teaching practices. Studies have shown that PD programs focusing on cultural competence and responsiveness can significantly improve student engagement and achievement, particularly for students from marginalized communities (Hudley & Mallinson, 2017).

An exemplary PD program focused on enhancing teachers' inquiry-based instructional practices in science education. This program provided intensive training on subject-matter knowledge and offered comprehensive support for transforming instructional practices. The approach helped teachers foster an inquiry-driven classroom culture, which subsequently led to significant improvements in student achievement (Supovitz & Turner, 2000).

Hybrid-based learning environments that integrate the best practices of traditional classroom instruction with online learning have proven effective in PD. These environments enable teachers to apply newly acquired knowledge and skills directly in their classrooms, thereby enhancing instructional practices. This model supports the seamless transition of professional learning into classroom implementation, contributing to improved educational outcomes (Larrimore, 2013).

Another successful model involves personalized PD that is tailored to the specific needs of educators, implemented within a collaborative community of practice. This model fosters a supportive environment where teachers can engage in meaningful professional growth, thereby enhancing their self-efficacy and instructional effectiveness. The collaborative nature of this approach encourages the sharing of best practices and continuous improvement (Cua, 2020).

A PD program that supported teachers in integrating technology into inquiry-based science instruction demonstrated substantial improvements in classroom practices. This approach, grounded in constructivist learning theories, enabled teachers to effectively incorporate technology into their teaching, thereby enhancing students' inquiry-based learning experiences and overall academic performance in science subjects (Gerard, Varma, Corliss & Linn, 2011).

A notable example of effective PD involved integrating action research (AR) into the professional growth of computer science teachers. In this program, teachers conducted small-scale research projects within their own classrooms, focusing on authentic instructional challenges. The iterative process of inquiry and reflection within a social learning context significantly improved teaching practices and contributed to the professional development of participating educators (Brandes & Armoni, 2019).

1.2. Challenges in Professional Development

Despite its importance, it can be said that professional development faces various difficulties. One of the biggest challenges is lack of time and resources. Many teachers struggle to find time for PD in the midst of their demanding schedules. Additionally, funding availability may limit access to quality PD opportunities.

Another challenge concerns the quality and relevance of PD programs. Not all PDs are good. Poorly designed programs may fail to meet teachers' needs or lead to meaningful changes in practice. It is crucial that PD programs are evaluated and evaluated regularly to ensure they are effective and aligned with educational goals (Garet et al., 2001).

In addition to time and resource constraints, another significant challenge in professional development (PD) is the lack of alignment between PD programs and the specific needs of teachers. Research indicates that many PD programs fail to consider the diverse contexts in which teachers operate, resulting in a one-size-fits-all approach that is often ineffective. For instance, culturally and linguistically diverse classrooms require tailored PD that addresses the unique challenges these environments present. When PD programs do not align with the specific needs of teachers, they are less likely to be implemented effectively, leading to minimal impact on student outcomes (Hudley & Mallinson, 2017).

Another challenge is the difficulty in maintaining the relevance and effectiveness of PD over time. As educational policies, curricula, and student needs evolve, PD programs must adapt to remain effective. However, many PD initiatives are static, failing to evolve alongside these changes, which can lead to outdated practices being perpetuated in the classroom. This issue is particularly pronounced in subject areas like STEM, where rapid advancements in technology and pedagogy require continuous updating of PD content. Without ongoing revisions and adaptations, PD can quickly become irrelevant, reducing its overall efficacy (Fairman, Smith, Pullen & Lebel, 2020).

Furthermore, there is often a gap in support systems for teachers after they have participated in PD programs. Teachers may struggle to apply new strategies in their classrooms without sufficient follow-up support or opportunities to reflect and refine their practices. Research has shown that when district-level administrators fail to provide ongoing support and resources, the impact of PD is significantly diminished. Continuous engagement and support are crucial for helping teachers integrate new knowledge into their daily teaching practices, ensuring that PD leads to meaningful and sustained improvements in student learning (Puhala, 2018).

One of the primary challenges for computer science (CS) educators in professional development (PD) is the rapid pace of technological advancements. CS educators often struggle to stay current with the latest developments in programming languages, software tools, and educational technologies. For instance, a study highlighted that many newly assigned CS teachers felt inadequately prepared to teach the rapidly evolving curriculum due to the PD programs focusing more on general concepts rather than on practical, up-to-date skills needed in the classroom. This disconnect between PD content and the actual technological demands of the classroom can result in educators being ill-equipped to deliver effective instruction (Northrup, Borowczak & Slater, 2022).

Another significant challenge is the lack of specific pedagogical training tailored to the unique needs of CS education. Many PD programs for CS educators focus on the technical content but neglect the pedagogical strategies necessary for effective teaching. This gap often leaves educators without the tools to engage students in complex CS concepts or to differentiate instruction based on varying levels of student proficiency. For example, research has shown that without adequate pedagogical support, teachers may struggle to implement student-centered learning approaches, which are crucial for fostering critical thinking and problem-solving skills in CS education (Puhala, 2018).

Additionally, CS educators often face challenges related to the integration of interdisciplinary approaches within the CS curriculum. PD programs frequently overlook the importance of blending CS with other STEM fields, leaving teachers unprepared to create interdisciplinary connections that enhance students' learning experiences. This issue is particularly pressing given the increasing emphasis on integrating CS with subjects like mathematics, science, and engineering to develop comprehensive STEM education. Without sufficient interdisciplinary PD, CS educators may find it challenging to design curricula that reflect the interconnected nature of these disciplines, potentially limiting students' holistic understanding of CS and its applications (Fairman et al., 2020).

1.3. The Role of Technology in Professional Development

Technology plays a significant role in modern professional development. Online PD programs, webinars, and virtual coaching have expanded access to high-quality PD, allowing teachers to learn at their own pace and convenience. Studies have shown that online PD can be as effective as traditional face-to-face PD, particularly when it includes interactive elements and opportunities for collaboration (Fishman et al., 2013). Moreover, technology facilitates the creation of online communities of practice where educators can connect, share resources, and support each other. These virtual communities extend the benefits of PD beyond the boundaries of a single school or district, encouraging a broader professional network.

Technology plays a pivotal role in the professional development (PD) of computer science (CS) educators, offering numerous tools and platforms that enhance both the delivery and effectiveness of PD programs. One of the primary ways technology can be leveraged is through online learning platforms, which provide flexible and accessible opportunities for CS educators to engage in continuous learning. These platforms offer courses on the latest programming languages, software development tools, and emerging technologies, allowing educators to stay current with industry trends. For example, online learning platforms like Coursera and edX have been utilized by CS educators to deepen their understanding of advanced topics such as machine learning and cybersecurity, which can then be integrated into their teaching practices (Scher & O'Reilly, 2009).

Moreover, technology facilitates collaborative learning among CS educators through online communities and professional networks. Virtual communities such as GitHub, Stack Overflow, and various educator forums enable teachers to share resources, discuss challenges, and collaborate on projects regardless of geographic location. This peer-to-peer interaction is crucial for solving immediate classroom issues and fostering a sense of community among educators. For instance, collaboration on open-source projects or co-creation of lesson plans in these platforms enhances instructional practices by incorporating diverse perspectives and experiences (Hudley & Mallinson, 2017).

Technology also allows for the use of real-time data analytics in PD, enabling CS educators to track their progress and adapt their learning paths according to their specific needs. Learning management systems (LMS) with integrated analytics tools provide educators with insights into their learning patterns, strengths, and areas needing improvement. For example, platforms like Moodle and Canvas offer dashboards that monitor engagement and performance, allowing educators to focus on areas requiring further development. This data-driven approach to PD ensures that the learning experience is personalized and responsive to the unique needs of each educator, leading to more effective outcomes (Puhala, 2018).

Furthermore, the integration of virtual reality (VR) and augmented reality (AR) into PD offers CS educators immersive learning experiences that enhance their understanding of complex concepts. VR environments can simulate advanced coding scenarios or software development processes, providing a risk-free setting for practice and experimentation. AR can overlay instructional content onto physical objects, offering a hands-on learning experience that bridges theoretical knowledge and practical application. These technologies make PD more engaging and help educators develop skills directly transferable to their classroom teaching, ensuring that their instructional practices are aligned with contemporary educational demands (Northrup et al., 2022).

Finally, technology supports the implementation of microlearning in PD, which is particularly beneficial for CS educators who have limited time for extensive professional development. Microlearning involves delivering content in small, manageable chunks accessible on-demand, often via mobile devices. This approach allows educators to learn at their own pace and revisit content as needed. Platforms like LinkedIn Learning and YouTube offer short, focused tutorials on specific topics such as coding techniques or software tools, which educators can integrate into their daily routines. Microlearning thus provides a flexible and efficient way for CS educators to continuously upgrade their skills without requiring extensive time commitments (Scher & O'Reilly, 2009).

In conclusion, professional development is a critical component of effective K-12 education. By staying current with new research, methodologies, and technologies, teachers can continuously improve their practice and better support their students' learning. Effective PD is characterized by relevance, active learning, collaboration, and sustained duration. While there are challenges to overcome, particularly regarding time and resources, the integration of technology offers promising solutions to enhance access and engagement in professional development.

2. PROFESSIONAL DEVELOPMENT PROCESS

Professional development (PD) opportunities for K-12 educators are essential for maintaining the dynamism and effectiveness of the education system. These opportunities provide teachers with the skills, knowledge, and strategies needed to adapt to changing educational landscapes, incorporate new technologies, and address the diverse needs of their students. The impact of effective professional development on teaching practices and student outcomes is well-documented, making it a critical investment for educational institutions.

There are numerous professional development opportunities available to educators, ranging from formal programs to informal learning experiences. These opportunities can be categorized into several key types:

Workshops and seminars. Traditional PD opportunities often take the form of workshops and seminars, where educators gather to learn about specific topics or strategies from experts. These sessions can vary in length from a few hours to several days and can cover a wide range of subjects, such as classroom management, curriculum design, and technology integration. Despite their popularity, workshops and seminars must be well-designed and interactive to ensure meaningful learning experiences (Desimone, 2009).

Online courses and webinars. With the rise of digital technology, online courses and webinars have become increasingly popular. These formats offer flexibility, allowing teachers to learn at their own pace and on their own schedule. Research by Fishman et al. (2013) shows that online PD can be as effective as face-to-face PD when it includes interactive elements and opportunities for engagement.

Professional learning communities (PLCs). PLCs are collaborative groups of educators who meet regularly to discuss their practice, share resources, and solve common problems. These communities foster a culture of continuous improvement and support, helping teachers to implement new strategies and reflect on their practice. Vescio, Ross, and Adams (2008) found that PLCs can lead to significant improvements in both teaching practices and student outcomes.

Mentoring and coaching. Mentoring and coaching provide personalized support to teachers, helping them to develop their skills and apply new strategies in their classrooms. Mentors and coaches offer guidance, feedback, and encouragement, which can be especially beneficial for novice teachers. Kraft, Blazar, and Hogan (2018) found that coaching programs have a positive impact on both instructional practices and student achievement.

Conferences and networking events. Attending conferences and networking events allows educators to connect with peers, learn from leading experts, and stay updated on the latest trends and research in education. These events provide valuable opportunities for professional growth and collaboration.

The impact of professional development on educators and their students is profound and multifaceted. Effective PD leads to improved teaching practices, enhanced student learning, and overall school improvement.

One of the primary goals of professional development is to enhance teachers' instructional practices. PD programs that are well-designed and aligned with teachers' needs can lead to significant changes in the classroom. For instance, Garet et al. (2001) found that PD focused on active learning and content knowledge significantly improves teaching practices. When teachers are equipped with new strategies and tools, they will be able to create more engaging and effective learning experiences for their students.

The ultimate measure of PD's effectiveness is its impact on student learning. Research consistently shows that high-quality PD leads to better student outcomes. For example, a study by Yoon et al. (2007) found that sustained, intensive PD is associated with increases in student achievement. By improving teachers' content knowledge and instructional skills, PD helps to create a more supportive and effective learning environment for students.

Participation in PD can also boost teachers' confidence and morale. When teachers feel supported and capable of implementing new strategies, they are more likely to feel satisfied with their work and committed to their profession. This positive attitude can, in turn, enhance their interactions with students and colleagues, contributing to a positive school climate.

PD contributes to overall school improvement by fostering a culture of continuous learning and collaboration. Schools that prioritize PD are better equipped to adapt to changes, address challenges, and implement innovative practices. According to Darling-Hammond et al. (2017), schools with strong PD programs tend to have higher levels of teacher collaboration and student achievement.

3. STRATEGIES AND FUTURE ORIENTATIONS

Professional development (PD) is an essential component in the educational landscape, aimed at enhancing the skills and knowledge of K-12 educators. Effective PD strategies are critical for ensuring that teachers can adapt to new educational demands, integrate technology into their classrooms, and meet the diverse needs of their students. As we look towards the future, it is crucial to explore innovative approaches and future directions in professional development that can sustain and further enhance educational practices.

Implementing effective PD strategies requires a multifaceted approach that meets the diverse needs of educators. Some basic strategies that support the professional development process should be expressed.

A personalized PD tailors learning experiences to teachers' individual needs, interests and goals. This approach recognizes that teachers are at different stages in their careers and have unique professional development needs. Borko's (2004) research highlights the importance of differentiated professional learning that addresses specific teacher contexts and experiences. Personalized PD can include one-on-one coaching, self-paced online courses, and personalized action plans.

However, collaborative learning communities such as Professional Learning Communities (PLCs) foster a culture of shared learning and collective inquiry. PLCs encourage teachers to work together to solve problems, share best practices, and support each other's professional development. Vescio, Ross, and Adams (2008) say that PLCs can lead to significant improvements in teaching practices and student outcomes by promoting sustainable collaborative learning.

Another strategy is job-embedded professional development. Integrates professional learning into teachers' daily work. This approach involves real-time, practical application of new strategies in the classroom, often supported by instructional coaches or mentors. According to Croft et al. (2010), work-embedded PD is highly effective because it relates directly to teachers' work and provides immediate opportunities for practice and feedback.

Technology, on the other hand, provides innovative solutions for PD, making it more accessible and flexible. Online platforms, webinars, and virtual learning communities enable teachers to engage in PD at their own pace and connect with peers across the globe. A study by Dede et al. (2009) found that technology-enhanced PD can significantly improve teachers' content knowledge and instructional practices. Additionally, using digital tools for PD allows for the creation of multimedia resources, interactive modules, and virtual simulations that enhance learning experiences.

Another strategy to recommend is reflective practice. Encouraging this is a very important strategy in PD. Reflective practice involves teachers critically analyzing their teaching methods, assessing their effectiveness, and making adjustments based on their reflections. Research by Schön (1983) underscores the importance of reflection in professional growth. Tools such as reflective journals, peer observations, and video analysis can support teachers in this process.

As we look to the future of professional development, it is possible to mention several emerging trends and directions that promise to reshape the PD landscape. These are blended learning approaches, data-based professional development, social emotional learning, equality and participation in professional development, and sustainable professional development.

Blended learning offers a flexible and comprehensive approach to professional learning by combining online and face-to-face PD experiences. This model helps teachers leverage the strengths of both digital and face-to-face interactions. According to Graham (2006), blended learning environments are an element that increases the effectiveness of PD by providing a variety of learning opportunities and promoting a sense of community among participants.

Using data analytics to inform PD is an emerging trend. Data-driven PD analyzes student performance data, teacher evaluations, and other metrics to identify areas of need and adapt PD accordingly. A study by Marsh, Pane, and Hamilton (2006) states that data-based decision-making can provide a more targeted and effective PD process, thus improving learning.

PD programs increasingly incorporate social-emotional learning (SEL) components to address the holistic development of students. SEL-focused PD helps teachers develop skills that support students' emotional and social well-being, which is crucial to creating a positive learning environment. A study by Jennings and Greenberg (2009) found that teachers who received SEL training were better equipped to manage classroom dynamics and support student participation.

Sustainability in PD ensures that professional learning is ongoing and adaptable to future changes in education. This involves creating a culture of continuous improvement, where PD is not seen as a one-time event but as a fundamental aspect of teaching. Systems for ongoing support, such as mentoring programs and professional networks, are critical for sustaining PD efforts.

In conclusion, effective strategies for supporting the professional development process and innovative future directions are essential for enhancing K-12 education. Personalized and collaborative learning, job-embedded experiences, technology integration, and reflective practice are key strategies that contribute to effective PD. Looking ahead, blended learning, data-driven approaches, SEL, equity and inclusion, and sustainability will play pivotal roles in shaping the future of professional development. By embracing these strategies and future directions, we can ensure that educators are well-equipped to meet the evolving demands of the 21st-century classroom and provide high-quality education for all students.

3.1. Data and Information Literacy Teaching

In today's digital age, data and information literacy have become essential skills for students. The ability to critically evaluate, interpret, and use information is crucial for success in both academic and real-world contexts. As educators, it is imperative to integrate data and information literacy teaching into the K-12 curriculum to prepare students for the challenges of the 21st century. This chapter explores the importance of data and information literacy, effective teaching strategies, and the role of technology in enhancing these skills.

Data and information literacy encompass a range of skills that enable individuals to effectively locate, evaluate, and use information. These skills are foundational for academic success, informed citizenship, and lifelong learning. According to the

American Library Association (ALA), information literacy is abilities requiring individuals to "recognize when information is needed and have the ability to locate, evaluate, and use effectively the needed information" (ALA, 2000). In the context of data literacy, this situation involves the ability to read, interpret, and analyze data, which is increasingly important in a data-driven world. Data literacy enables students to make evidence-based decisions, understand and create visualizations, and critically assess the reliability and validity of data sources (Wolff, Gooch, Cavero Montaner, Rashid, & Kortuem, 2016).

Data and information literacy are not only essential for students but are also crucial for computer science educators in their professional development. As educators are expected to integrate data-driven insights into their teaching practices, it is imperative that they themselves possess strong data and information literacy skills. For instance, computer science educators can utilize data analytics tools to assess student performance, identify learning gaps, and tailor instruction to meet the specific needs of their students. By analyzing data on student outcomes, educators can make informed decisions about which instructional strategies are most effective, thereby improving the overall quality of education they provide. This process of data-driven decision-making is a direct application of data literacy in an educational context, and it underscores the importance of these skills in modern teaching practices (Gummer & Mandinach, 2015).

Furthermore, the ability to effectively interpret and utilize data can empower computer science educators to contribute to educational research and curriculum development. By leveraging data literacy skills, educators can conduct action research within their classrooms, gathering and analyzing data to explore the impact of new teaching methods or technologies on student learning. This research can then be shared with the broader educational community, contributing to the ongoing development of evidence-based teaching practices. Additionally, information literacy allows educators to critically evaluate existing research and data sources, ensuring that they are incorporating the most reliable and valid information into their teaching. This not only enhances their professional growth but also ensures that students are receiving an education that is informed by the latest and most accurate knowledge available in the field (Koltay, 2017).

Effective teaching strategies are essential for developing students' data and information literacy skills. For instance, inquiry-based learning involves students actively engaging in the process of inquiry by asking questions, conducting research, and drawing conclusions. This method encourages critical thinking and allows students to practice information literacy skills in a meaningful context. For instance, Kuhlthau, Maniotes, and Caspari (2015) advocate for the Guided Inquiry Design framework, which provides a structured approach to inquiry-based learning and supports the development of information literacy. Project-based learning is one of them. It is a dynamic classroom approach in which students actively explore real-world problems and challenges. PBL encourages students to take ownership of their learning, engage in deep research, and apply their findings to create projects. This method not only enhances information literacy but also fosters collaboration and communication skills (Bell, 2010).

As stated above, integrating data analysis activities into the curriculum helps students develop data literacy skills. These activities can include analyzing datasets, creating data visualizations, and interpreting statistical results. According to Means, Chen, DeBarger, and Padilla (2011), engaging students in hands-on data analysis promotes a deeper understanding of mathematical concepts and improves their ability to use data effectively.

Teaching students how to critically evaluate information sources is a crucial aspect of information literacy. Exercises that involve comparing multiple sources, assessing the credibility of information, and identifying biases help students develop the skills needed to navigate the vast amounts of information available online. Metzger and Flanagin (2013) emphasize the importance of teaching students to critically evaluate digital information to foster informed and responsible internet use.

Technology plays a vital role in teaching data and information literacy. Digital tools and platforms can facilitate access to a wide range of information sources, support collaborative research, and provide opportunities for creating and sharing knowledge. Tools such as Google Scholar, data visualization software, and educational databases can enhance students' learning experiences and support the development of literacy skills (Hicks, 2018).

Technology has transformed the way we access, analyze and communicate information. Therefore, technology is a powerful tool to improve data and information literacy teaching. Therefore, it is considered important to explore some ways that technology can support this process. At this point, the Internet, arguably the most perfect invention, comes into the mix. The internet provides students with access to an unprecedented amount of information. Online databases, digital libraries, and open-access journals offer a wealth of resources that can support research and learning. Educators guides students in using these resources effectively and ethically.

Taking their access and knowledge one step further, students learn to visualize data with data visualization tools such as Tableau, Google Data Studio, and Microsoft Excel. These tools help students to understand complex data sets, identify patterns, and communicate findings clearly. Visualization is a key component of data literacy, making it easier for students to interpret and analyze data (Roth, Bowen, & McGinn, 1996).

When using these tools, they can use collaborative platforms. Collaborative platforms such as Google Docs, Microsoft Teams, and Slack enable students to work together on research projects, share resources, and provide feedback. These platforms support the development of information literacy skills by fostering communication, collaboration, and critical thinking. At the same time, interactive learning environments that include online courses, simulations, and educational games provide students with engaging and immersive experiences. These environments can strengthen information literacy skills through interactive exercises and real-time feedback (Clark and Mayer, 2016).

The use of all these tools and environments brings with it an important concept. Digital citizenship education teaches students how to use technology responsibly and ethically. This includes understanding digital footprints, protecting personal information, and recognizing the impact of their online actions. Integrating digital citizenship into the curriculum supports the development of information literacy by promoting responsible and ethical use of information (Ribble, 2015).

Data and information literacy are critical skills for students in the digital age. By integrating effective teaching strategies such as inquiry-based learning, project-based learning, data analysis activities, and critical evaluation exercises, educators can help students develop these essential skills. The role of technology in enhancing data and information literacy cannot be overstated; it provides access to information, supports data visualization, facilitates collaboration, and creates interactive learning environments. As we continue to navigate the complexities of the information age, it is imperative that we equip students with the skills they need to critically evaluate, interpret, and use information effectively.

3.2. Digital Literacy Teaching

In the contemporary educational landscape, digital literacy is a cornerstone of effective learning and teaching. As digital technologies permeate every aspect of daily life, it is crucial for K-12 educators to equip students with the skills necessary to navigate and leverage these technologies effectively. Digital literacy encompasses a range of competencies, including the ability to use digital tools, evaluate online information, and engage in safe and ethical online behaviors. This chapter explores the importance of digital literacy, effective teaching strategies, and the role of educators in fostering these essential skills.

Digital literacy is defined as the ability to use information and communication technologies to find, evaluate, create, and communicate information, requiring both cognitive and technical skills. The American Library Association (ALA) emphasizes that digital literacy involves the ability to use technology, communications tools, and networks to access, manage, integrate, evaluate, and create information (ALA, 2013).

The importance of digital literacy in K-12 education cannot be overstated. Digital literacy prepares students for the demands of the modern workforce, where digital skills are increasingly vital. Moreover, digital literacy supports lifelong learning, enabling individuals to adapt to new technologies and continuously update their skills. Hobbs' (2010) research argues for the conclusion that digital literacy is necessary for full participation in the digital society, including effective communication, critical thinking, and informed citizenship.

Effective teaching strategies are essential for developing students' digital literacy skills. In this context, the first thing we encounter is technology integration into the curriculum. Integrating digital tools and resources into various subject areas helps students see the relevance of digital literacy in different contexts. This approach ensures that digital literacy is not taught in isolation but is embedded in everyday learning activities. For example, using online research tools in social studies projects or creating digital presentations in science classes can enhance students' digital skills while reinforcing subject knowledge (Harris, Mishra, & Koehler, 2009).

Another strategy is considered project-based learning. Project-based learning encourages students to engage in meaningful, real-world projects that require the use of digital tools. PBL provides opportunities for students to develop digital literacy by researching online, collaborating with peers using digital platforms, and creating digital artifacts such as videos, websites, and presentations. According to Bell (2010), PBL fosters critical thinking and problem-solving skills, which are integral components of digital literacy.

An important component of digital literacy is teaching students how to critically evaluate online information. Teaching students how to critically evaluate online information is a key component of digital literacy. This teaches them to assess the credibility of sources, recognize biases, and distinguish between reliable and unreliable information. Metzger and Flanagin (2013) emphasize the importance of critical evaluation skills in helping students navigate the vast amount of information available online and make informed decisions.

Educators play a pivotal role in fostering digital literacy. Their attitudes, knowledge, and skills significantly influence how effectively they can teach digital literacy to their students. It is possible to express some ways that educators can support digital literacy development under the following headings.

Professional development. Continuous professional development is essential for educators to stay current with the latest digital tools and pedagogical strategies. Professional development programs should focus on enhancing teachers' digital skills and providing them with practical strategies for integrating technology into their teaching (Darling-Hammond, Hyler, & Gardner, 2017). Training sessions, workshops, and online courses can equip teachers with the knowledge and confidence needed to effectively teach digital literacy.

Modeling digital literacy. Educators should model digital literacy in their own practices. By demonstrating how to use digital tools effectively, critically evaluate online information, and engage in ethical online behaviors, teachers can set a positive example for their students. This modeling can be particularly effective in showing students the real-world applications of digital literacy skills (Bandura, 1977).

Creating a supportive learning environment. A supportive learning environment encourages students to explore and experiment with digital tools. This includes providing access to technology, fostering a culture of collaboration and innovation, and offering guidance and feedback. According to Ertmer and Ottenbreit-Leftwich (2010), a positive learning environment is crucial for promoting students' confidence and competence in using digital technologies.

Incorporating digital literacy standards. Incorporating digital literacy standards into the curriculum ensures that digital literacy is systematically and comprehensively addressed. Standards such as the International Society for Technology in Education (ISTE) Standards for Students provide a framework for integrating digital literacy into teaching and learning (ISTE, 2016). These standards outline the essential skills and knowledge that students need to thrive in a digital world.

Encouraging lifelong learning. Educators should encourage students to view digital literacy as a lifelong learning process. Lifelong learning is essential for staying relevant in a rapidly changing digital landscape (Dweck, 2006).

In conclusion, digital literacy is a critical skill for students in the digital age. By integrating effective teaching strategies such as technology integration, project-based learning, critical evaluation, digital citizenship education, and collaborative learning, educators can help students develop the necessary digital literacy skills. The role of educators is pivotal in fostering these skills through professional development, modeling, creating supportive environments, incorporating standards, and encouraging lifelong learning. As we move forward, it is essential to prioritize digital literacy teaching to prepare students for the demands and opportunities of the 21st century.

4. LEADERSHIP IN TEACHING

Leadership in teaching is a critical component of effective education. It involves the ability to inspire, guide, and support both students and colleagues towards achieving educational goals. Effective teacher leadership can enhance classroom practices, improve student outcomes, and contribute to the overall success of the school community. This chapter explores the importance of leadership in teaching, key characteristics of effective teacher leaders, and strategies for developing leadership skills among educators.

Leadership in teaching is essential for several reasons. First, it contributes to the creation of a positive and productive learning environment. Teacher leaders play a pivotal role in establishing high expectations, fostering a culture of collaboration, and promoting continuous improvement (Danielson, 2006). They influence not only their students but also their peers, helping to create a shared vision of educational excellence.

Second, teacher leadership is crucial for implementing and sustaining educational reforms. Research by Fullan (2007) indicates that successful school reforms are often driven by strong teacher leaders who are committed to innovation and improvement. These leaders act as change agents, helping to translate policy into practice and ensuring that new initiatives are effectively integrated into the school culture.

Third, leadership in teaching enhances professional development. Teacher leaders often serve as mentors and coaches, providing guidance and support to their colleagues. This collaborative approach to professional development promotes shared learning and helps to build a community of practice within the school (Hargreaves & Fullan, 2012).

4.1. Key Characteristics of Effective Teacher Leaders

Effective teacher leaders possess a range of characteristics that enable them to inspire and influence others. Effective teacher leaders have a clear vision of what they want to achieve and the steps needed to get there. They are able to articulate this vision to others and inspire them to work towards common goals. According to Kouzes and Posner (2012), visionary leaders are able to create a sense of purpose and direction that motivates and energizes their followers.

Collaboration is a cornerstone of effective teacher leadership. Teacher leaders work closely with their colleagues, sharing ideas, resources, and best practices. This collaborative approach fosters a sense of community and collective responsibility for student success (Waldron & McLeskey, 2010).

Strong communication skills are essential for teacher leaders. They must be able to listen actively, provide constructive feedback, and convey information clearly and persuasively. Effective communication helps to build trust and rapport with students, colleagues, and other stakeholders (Danielson, 2006).

Empathy allows teacher leaders to understand and respond to the needs and concerns of others. By demonstrating empathy, teacher leaders can build strong relationships and create a supportive and inclusive school environment (Goleman, 1998).

Teacher leaders must be resilient in the face of challenges and setbacks. They are able to persevere through difficulties, maintain a positive attitude, and find solutions to problems. Resilience is essential for sustaining long-term improvement and achieving success (Patterson, Collins, & Abbott, 2004).

4.2. Strategies for Developing Leadership Skills Among Educators

Developing leadership skills among educators is crucial for fostering a culture of continuous improvement and excellence. Schools and districts should provide professional development programs focused on leadership skills. These programs can include workshops, seminars, and courses on topics such as effective communication, conflict resolution, and change management. Research by Darling-Hammond, Hyler, and Gardner (2017) highlights the importance of high-quality professional development in building leadership capacity among teachers.

Mentoring and coaching programs can provide educators with the guidance and support needed to develop their leadership skills. Experienced teacher leaders can serve as mentors, offering advice, feedback, and encouragement to their colleagues. This one-on-one support helps to build confidence and competence in emerging leaders (Kraft, Blazar, & Hogan, 2018).

Providing opportunities for teachers to take on leadership roles within the school can help them develop their skills and experience. This can include roles such as department heads, curriculum coordinators, and professional learning community leaders. By taking on these roles, teachers can gain practical experience in leadership and contribute to school improvement efforts (York-Barr & Duke, 2004).

Engaging teachers in collaborative leadership projects can help them develop their skills and build a sense of collective responsibility. These projects can involve working together to address specific school challenges, develop new programs, or implement instructional improvements. Collaborative projects provide opportunities for teachers to practice leadership in a supportive and cooperative environment (Harris & Lambert, 2003).

Leadership in teaching is a vital element of effective education. Teacher leaders play a critical role in creating positive learning environments, implementing educational reforms, and enhancing professional development. By developing key characteristics such as vision, collaboration, communication, empathy, and resilience, teacher leaders can inspire and influence their students and colleagues. Strategies such as professional development programs, mentoring and coaching, opportunities for leadership roles, collaborative leadership projects, and reflective practice are essential for developing leadership skills among educators.

CONCLUSION

The exploration of professional development for K-12 educators, the integration of data and information literacy, the emphasis on digital literacy and the critical role of leadership in teaching collectively highlight the multifaceted nature of modern education. Each of these elements is integral to cultivating a learning environment that prepares students for the complexities of the 21st century.

Professional development is fundamental to maintaining high standards in teaching and learning. It ensures educators are equipped with the latest methodologies, technologies, and strategies to address diverse student needs. By focusing on personalized, collaborative, and sustained professional development, educators can continuously improve their practice and significantly impact student outcomes (Guskey, 2002; Desimone, 2009).

Teaching data and information literacy is essential in an era where information is abundant and readily accessible. Educators must guide students in navigating this vast landscape, helping them develop the skills to critically evaluate, interpret, and use information effectively. Strategies such as inquiry-based learning and project-based learning are crucial in fostering these skills, ensuring students are well-prepared for academic and professional challenges (Kuhlthau, Maniotes, & Caspari, 2015; Bell, 2010).

Digital literacy encompasses a range of competencies necessary for students to thrive in a digital world. Effective teaching strategies include integrating technology across the curriculum, promoting digital citizenship, and encouraging collaborative learning. These approaches help students develop the ability to use digital tools responsibly and creatively, essential for lifelong learning and informed citizenship (Hobbs, 2010; Ribble, 2015).

Leadership in teaching is crucial for creating a positive and effective educational environment. Teacher leaders inspire and guide their colleagues and students, fostering a culture of collaboration and continuous improvement. Developing leadership skills among educators through professional development, mentoring, and opportunities for leadership roles ensures the sustainability and success of educational initiatives (Fullan, 2007; Darling-Hammond, Hyler, & Gardner, 2017).

The synthesis of these elements underscores the importance of a holistic approach to education that prioritizes continuous professional development, the integration of digital and information literacy, fostering inquisitive and research-oriented mindsets, and developing strong leadership within teaching. Future directions should focus on interdisciplinary research, authentic assessment, global collaboration, and sustainable practices to further enhance educational outcomes.

By embracing these strategies, educators can create dynamic and inclusive learning environments that empower students to succeed in an ever-evolving digital and information-rich world. This comprehensive approach to education not only addresses current challenges but also prepares students to be adaptable, critical thinkers capable of making informed decisions in their personal and professional lives.

REFERENCES

American Library Association (ALA). (2000). *Information literacy competency standards for higher education*. ALA.

American Library Association (ALA). (2013). *Digital literacy, libraries, and public policy*.

Andrews, D., & Richmond, G. (2019). Professional development for equity: What constitutes powerful professional learning? *Journal of Teacher Education*, 70(5), 408–409. DOI: 10.1177/0022487119875098

Bell, S. (2010). Project-based learning for the 21st century: Skills for the future. *The Clearing House: A Journal of Educational Strategies, Issues and Ideas*, 83(2), 39–43. DOI: 10.1080/00098650903505415

Borko, H. (2004). Professional development and teacher learning: Mapping the terrain. *Educational Researcher*, 33(8), 3–15. DOI: 10.3102/0013189X033008003

Borko, H., & Putnam, R. T. (1995). Expanding a teacher's knowledge base: A cognitive psychological perspective on professional development. In Guskey, T. R., & Huberman, M. (Eds.), *Professional development in education: New Paradigms and Practices* (pp. 35–65). Teachers College Press.

Brandes, O., & Armoni, M. (2019). The Effects of a Professional Development Workshop Focusing on Action Research on the Practice of High-School Computer Science Teachers. *Proceedings of the 14th Workshop in Primary and Secondary Computing Education*.https://doi.org/DOI: 10.1145/3361721.3361725

Bümen, N. T., Ateş, A., Çakar, E., Ural, G., & Acar, V. (2012). Professional development of teachers in the Turkish context: Issues and suggestions. *Journal of National Education. Education and Social Sciences*, 41(194), 31–50.

Buysse, V., Winton, P. J., & Rous, B. (2009). Reaching consensus on a definition of professional development for the early childhood field. *Topics in Early Childhood Special Education*, 28(4), 235–243. DOI: 10.1177/0271121408328173

Clark, R. C., & Mayer, R. E. (2016). *E-learning and the science of instruction: Proven guidelines for consumers and designers of multimedia learning*. John Wiley & Sons. DOI: 10.1002/9781119239086

Croft, A., Coggshall, J. G., Dolan, M., Powers, E., & Killion, J. (2010). *Job-embedded professional development: What it is, who is responsible, and how to get it done well*. National Comprehensive Center for Teacher Quality.

Cua, K. (2020). A personalized approach to professional development through a community of practice. Doctoral Dissertation, University of Kentucky, https://doi.org/DOI: 10.13023/ETD.2020.068

Cuban, L. (1984). *How teachers taught: Constancy and change in American classrooms*. Longman.

Danielson, C. (2006). *Teacher Leadership That Strengthens Professional Practice*. ASCD.

Darling-Hammond, L., Hyler, M. E., & Gardner, M. (2017). *Effective Teacher Professional Development*. Learning Policy Institute. DOI: 10.54300/122.311

Day, C. (1999). *Developing teachers: The challenges of lifelong learning*. Falmer Press.

Dede, C., Ketelhut, D. J., Whitehouse, P., Breit, L., & McCloskey, E. M. (2009). A research agenda for online teacher professional development. *Journal of Teacher Education*, 60(1), 8–19. DOI: 10.1177/0022487108327554

Desimone, L. M. (2009). Improving impact studies of teachers' professional development: Toward better conceptualizations and measures. *Educational Researcher*, 38(3), 181–199. DOI: 10.3102/0013189X08331140

Dillenbourg, P. (1999). *Collaborative learning: Cognitive and computational approaches*. Elsevier.

Dogan, S., Pringle, R., & Mesa, J. (2015). The impacts of professional learning communities on science teachers' knowledge, practice and student learning: A review. *Professional Development in Education*, 42(4), 569–588. DOI: 10.1080/19415257.2015.1065899

Dweck, C. S. (2006). *Mindset: The New Psychology of Success*. Random House.

Ertmer, P. A., & Ottenbreit-Leftwich, A. T. (2010). Teacher technology change: How knowledge, confidence, beliefs, and culture intersect. *Journal of Research on Technology in Education*, 42(3), 255–284. DOI: 10.1080/15391523.2010.10782551

Fairman, J., Smith, D., Pullen, P., & Lebel, S. (2020). The challenge of keeping teacher professional development relevant. *Professional Development in Education*, 49(2), 197–209. DOI: 10.1080/19415257.2020.1827010

Fishman, B. J., Konstantopoulos, S., Kubitskey, B. W., Vath, R. J., Park, G., Johnson, H., & Edelson, D. C. (2013). Comparing the impact of online and face-to-face professional development in the context of curriculum implementation. *Journal of Teacher Education*, 64(5), 426–438. DOI: 10.1177/0022487113494413

Fullan, M. (2007). *The New Meaning of Educational Change* (4th ed.). Teachers College Press.

Ganser, T. (2000). An Ambitions Vision of Professional Development for Teachers. *NASSP Bulletin*, 84(618), 6–12. DOI: 10.1177/019263650008461802

Garet, M. S., Porter, A. C., Desimone, L., Birman, B. F., & Yoon, K. S. (2001). What makes professional development effective? Results from a national sample of teachers. *American Educational Research Journal*, 38(4), 915–945. DOI: 10.3102/00028312038004915

Gerard, L., Varma, K., Corliss, S., & Linn, M. (2011). Professional Development for Technology-Enhanced Inquiry Science. *Review of Educational Research*, 81(3), 408–448. DOI: 10.3102/0034654311415121

Goleman, D. (1998). *Working with Emotional Intelligence*. Bantam Books.

Good, J., Miller, V., & Cathy, G. (2004). *Reforming Professional Development at the School Site: New Standards and New Practices*. University of Arkansas.

Graham, C. R. (2006). Blended learning systems: Definition, current trends, and future directions. In *Handbook of blended learning: Global perspectives, local designs* (pp. 3–21). Pfeiffer Publishing.

Gür, B. S., & Çelik, Z. (2009). National education system in Turkey: Structural problems and suggestions. *Politics. Economics and Social Research Foundation*, 1, 29–32.

Guskey, T. R. (2000). *Evaluating professional development*. Corwin Press.

Guskey, T. R. (2002). Professional development and teacher change. *Teachers and Teaching*, 8(3), 381–391. DOI: 10.1080/135406002100000512

Hargreaves, A., & Fullan, M. (2012). *Professional Capital: Transforming Teaching in Every School*. Teachers College Press.

Harris, A., & Lambert, L. (2003). *Building Leadership Capacity for School Improvement*. Open University Press.

Harris, J., Mishra, P., & Koehler, M. (2009). Teachers' technological pedagogical content knowledge and learning activity types: Curriculum-based technology integration reframed. *Journal of Research on Technology in Education*, 41(4), 393–416. DOI: 10.1080/15391523.2009.10782536

Hattie, J. (2009). *Visible learning: A synthesis of over 800 meta-analyses relating to achievement*. Routledge.

Hicks, A. (2018). Technology and professional identity of librarians: The making of the cybrarian. *Journal of Academic Librarianship*, 44(4), 534–541.

Hobbs, R. (2010). *Digital and Media Literacy: A Plan of Action*. Aspen Institute.

Hudley, A., & Mallinson, C. (2017). "It's worth our time": A model of culturally and linguistically supportive professional development for K-12 STEM educators. *Cultural Studies of Science Education*, 12(3), 637–660. DOI: 10.1007/s11422-016-9743-7

ISTE. (2016). *ISTE Standards for Students*. International Society for Technology in Education.

Jennings, P. A., & Greenberg, M. T. (2009). The prosocial classroom: Teacher social and emotional competence in relation to student and classroom outcomes. *Review of Educational Research*, 79(1), 491–525. DOI: 10.3102/0034654308325693

Koltay, T. (2017). Data literacy for researchers and data librarians. *Journal of Librarianship and Information Science*, 49(1), 14–33. DOI: 10.1177/0961000615616450

Kouzes, J. M., & Posner, B. Z. (2012). *The Leadership Challenge: How to Make Extraordinary Things Happen in Organizations* (5th ed.). Jossey-Bass.

Kraft, M. A., Blazar, D., & Hogan, D. (2018). The effect of teacher coaching on instruction and achievement: A meta-analysis of the causal evidence. *Review of Educational Research*, 88(4), 547–588. DOI: 10.3102/0034654318759268

Larrimore, D. (2013). Examining the effectiveness of K-12 professional development delivered through a hybrid-based learning environment, Doctoral Dissertation, Towson University, https://doi.org/DOI: 10.13016/M29H8N

Lawless, K. A., & Pellegrino, J. W. (2007). Professional development in integrating technology into teaching and learning: Knowns, unknowns, and ways to pursue better questions and answers. *Review of Educational Research*, 77(4), 575–614. DOI: 10.3102/0034654307309921

Little, J. W. (1990). The Persistence of Privacy: Autonomy and Initiative in Teachers' Professional Relations. *Teachers College Record*, 91(4), 509–536. DOI: 10.1177/016146819009100403

Lynch, K., Hill, H., Gonzalez, K., & Pollard, C. (2019). Strengthening the research base that informs stem instructional improvement efforts: A meta-analysis. *Educational Evaluation and Policy Analysis*, 41(3), 260–293. DOI: 10.3102/0162373719849044

Marsh, J. A., Pane, J. F., & Hamilton, L. S. (2006). *Making sense of data-driven decision making in education*. RAND Corporation.

Means, B., Chen, E., DeBarger, A., & Padilla, C. (2011). *Teachers' ability to use data to inform instruction: Challenges and supports*. US Department of Education.

Metzger, M. J., & Flanagin, A. J. (2013). Credibility and trust of information in online environments: The use of cognitive heuristics. *Journal of Pragmatics*, 59, 210–220. DOI: 10.1016/j.pragma.2013.07.012

Mizell, H. (2010). *Why professional development matters*. Learning Forward.

National Professional Development Center on Inclusion. (2008). *What do we mean by Professional development in the early childhood field?* The University of North Carolina, FPG Child Development Institute, Author.

Northrup, A., Borowczak, A., & Slater, T. (2022). K-12 teachers' perceptions and experiences in starting to teach computer science. *Education Sciences*, 12(11), 742. Advance online publication. DOI: 10.3390/educsci12110742

Patterson, J., Collins, L., & Abbott, G. (2004). Effective Leadership in the Eye of the Storm. *NASSP Bulletin*, 88(638), 2–14.

Puhala, J. (2018). Changing Classroom practice: Elementary teacher experiences of a professional development program. *Technology. Knowledge and Learning*, 25(1), 129–147. DOI: 10.1007/s10758-018-9370-3

Ribble, M. (2015). *Digital citizenship in schools: Nine elements all students should know*. International Society for Technology in Education.

Roth, W.-M., Bowen, G. M., & McGinn, M. K. (1996). Interpretive scientific research methods. *Journal of Research in Science Teaching*, 33(3), 157–173.

Scher, L., & O'Reilly, F. (2009). Professional development for k–12 math and science teachers: What do we really know? *Journal of Research on Educational Effectiveness*, 2(3), 209–249. DOI: 10.1080/19345740802641527

Schön, D. A. (1983). *The reflective practitioner: How professionals think in action*. Basic Books.

Shulman, L. S. (1987). Knowledge and Teaching: Foundations of the New Reform. *Harvard Educational Review*, 57(1), 1–22. DOI: 10.17763/haer.57.1.j463w79r56455411

Sparks, D., & Loucks-Horsley, S. (1989). Development for Teachers. *Journal of Staff Development*, 10(4), 40–57.

Supovitz, J., & Turner, H. (2000). The effects of professional development on science teaching practices and classroom culture. *Journal of Research in Science Teaching*, 37(9), 963–980. DOI: 10.1002/1098-2736(200011)37:9<963::AID-TEA6>3.0.CO;2-0

Thomas, J. W. (2000). *A review of research on project-based learning*. Autodesk Foundation.

Vescio, V., Ross, D., & Adams, A. (2008). A review of research on the impact of professional learning communities on teaching practice and student learning. *Teaching and Teacher Education*, 24(1), 80–91. DOI: 10.1016/j.tate.2007.01.004

Villegas-Reimers, E. (2003). *Teacher professional development: an international review of the literature*. International Institute for Educational Planning.

Waldron, N. L., & McLeskey, J. (2010). Establishing a collaborative school culture through comprehensive school reform. *Journal of Educational & Psychological Consultation*, 20(1), 58–74. DOI: 10.1080/10474410903535364

Wallace, M. (2009). Making sense of the links: Professional development, teacher practices, and student achievement. teachers college record. *Teachers College Record*, 111(2), 573–596. DOI: 10.1177/016146810911100205

Wetherill, K., Burton, G., Calhoun, D., & Thomas, C. (2001). Redefining professional career development in the twenty-first century: A systemic approach. *High School Journal*, 85(2), 54–66. DOI: 10.1353/hsj.2001.0026

Wolff, A., Gooch, D., Cavero Montaner, J. J., Rashid, U., & Kortuem, G. (2016). Creating an understanding of data literacy for a data-driven society. *The Journal of Community Informatics*, 12(3). Advance online publication. DOI: 10.15353/joci.v12i3.3275

Yoon, K. S., Duncan, T., Lee, S. W. Y., Scarloss, B., & Shapley, K. L. (2007). Reviewing the evidence on how teacher professional development affects student achievement. *Issues & Answers*. REL 2007-No. 033.

York-Barr, J., & Duke, K. (2004). What do we know about teacher leadership? Findings from two decades of scholarship. *Review of Educational Research*, 74(3), 255–316. DOI: 10.3102/00346543074003255

Youngs, P. (2001). District and state policy influences on professional development and school capacity. *Educational Policy*, 15(2), 278–301. DOI: 10.1177/0895904801015002003

Chapter 11
Teaching Machine Learning Through Educational Robotics

Gamze Mercan
https://orcid.org/0000-0001-5515-999X
Hacettepe University, Turkey

Zümrüt Varol Selçuk
Ordu University, Turkey

ABSTRACT

This study explores the pivotal role of educational robotics (ER) in enriching K–12 curriculums with machine learning (ML) and artificial intelligence (AI) concepts, highlighting the necessity of demystifying these advanced technologies for the younger generation. With the integration of AI into everyday devices, the urgency to familiarize students with AI and ML has escalated, making it essential for educational systems to adapt. Our research delves into the impact of ER as a practical tool for imparting complex AI and ML principles, fostering not only a deeper understanding but also stimulating interest in STEM fields. This investigation is grounded in the exploration of current ER applications and their potential to transform traditional learning environments into hubs of innovation and critical thinking. By analyzing various ER platforms and their effectiveness in teaching ML concepts, this study aims to offer insights into developing a comprehensive framework that can be utilized by educators to integrate AI and ML into the classroom dynamically and interactively.

DOI: 10.4018/979-8-3693-4542-9.ch011

INTRODUCTION

Technological advancements have profoundly reshaped numerous facets of modern life, embedding themsleves into daily activities and enhancing engagement within the digital realm. This integration facilitates tasks, making them more efficient and practical. These technological transformations are also reflected in the educational sector, where innovative learning methodoligies supported by technological advancments are emerging. These methods, grounded in practical applications, aim to improve teaching and learning techniques, offering adaptable and sustainable systems that support educational growth.

In education, the focus on intellectual development and effective learning approaches through technological progress has become central to modern educational systems. These systems seek solutions that prioritize the learning process, ensuring that technological advancements serve to augment human learning rather than replace it. The advent of tabletop technologies has particularly transformed perspectives of learning and knowledge acquisition, with machine learning (ML) methods undergoing significant examination and improvement. This evolution necessitates a dedicated effort to understand and implement these methods efficiently.

In the educational domain, the emergence of novel learning methodologies enhanced by technological innovations has commenced. These methods are not speculative but grounded in practical applications within the educational field. They aim to improve teaching and learning methods, offering sustainable and adaptable systems that support educational growth. The emphasis on intellectual evolution and effective learning approaches through technological progress has become central to modern educational systems, which seek solutions that are both eloquent and durable.

The challenge, however, lies in creating solutions that not only embrace technological progress but also prioritize the learning process. The definitive aim is for mechanisms to learn from humans, rather than the reverse. The advent of tabletop technologies has particularly shifted perspectives of learning and insight procurement. The evolution of machine learning (ML) methods, involving the procurement and application of insight, is under considerable examination and improvement. This evolution necessitates time and dedication to fully grasp and implement efficiently.

The application of technological progress in education serves numerous purposes, facilitating learning methods and fostering the procurement of new, pertinent skills. These skills are vital across diverse sectors, including automotive, aerospace, medical offerings, legal, economic offerings, and the creative fields. Appropriate use of technological progress in education enables the assimilation of new insight and skills, fostering competencies necessary for modern life.

Moreover, technological progress plays a pivotal role in the analysis and analysis of extensive data. The ability to manage large volumes of information and extract meaningful insights is increasingly crucial. Education that integrates technological progress supports this analytical capability, preparing individuals to efficiently manage and leverage vast datasets.

In recent years, artificial intelligence (AI) has become an integral part of daily devices such as smartphones, influencing individuals who are not necessarily experts in the field (De la Higuera, 2019). The significant increase in computing power over the last twenty years has enabled applications to achieve results that were previously out of reach. Machine learning (ML), a crucial subset of AI, involves techniques that enable computers to learn from data (Alpaydin, 2020). ML methods are utilized in a variety of commonly used devices and services, including facial recognition in social media photo tagging and speech recognition in voice-activated personal assistants. Additionally, ML techniques are employed in targeted advertising on social networks. Heys (2018) suggests that advancements in ML techniques and applications are poised to transform various aspects of life, such as work, education, entertainment, and human relationships. As ML services become more widespread, it becomes essential for the general public to comprehend the underlying methodologies. Despite the extensive use of ML, there remains a lack of public understanding, which leads to baseless fears about AI and automation overshadowing their potential positive societal impacts. This viewpoint is reinforced by the Royal Society Technical Report (2017), which highlights the necessity for people of all ages, particularly children, to grasp the basics of ML methods. The growing demand for fresh talent in AI startups underlines the importance of initiatives by governments and organizations to aid individuals, especially digital natives, in developing a foundational understanding of AI technologies (Muro, Whiton, & Maxim, 2019; Bessen, 2018; Touretzky, Gardner-McCune, Martin, & Seehorn, 2019).

The Fourth Industrial Revolution necessitates new skills from the global workforce (Marr, 2016; Marr, 2018; Chatzopoulos, Papoutsidakis, Kalogiannakis, & Psycharis, 2020). P21's Frameworks for 21st Century Learning outline the essential skills and knowledge that students need to thrive in their future careers and lives, including creativity, innovation, critical thinking, problem-solving, communication, and collaboration (Battelle for Kids, 2019). These educational objectives are furthered by the STEM (Science, Technology, Engineering, Math) initiative (Alimisis & Moro, 2016; Barker, Nugent, Grandgenett, & Adamchuk, 2012; Benitti, 2012) and are complemented by STEAM (Science, Technology, Engineering, Arts, Math), which incorporates art education (Kim & Park, 2012). STEM education, which integrates curriculum information and assessment to enhance science education by seamlessly combining these disciplines (Breiner, Harkness, Johnson, & Koehler, 2012), is becoming more prevalent than traditional learning methods. Constructivist learning, often employed in STEM education, is recognized as more comprehensible and skill-enriching for students (Takacs, Eigner, Kovacs, Rudas, & Haidegger, 2016) and is crucial for the sustainable development of a country's economy by nurturing critical thinkers and the next generation of innovators (Xie, Fang, & Shauman, 2015).

Educational robotics (ER) has attracted significant interest from educators and researchers as a supportive tool for formal education, particularly in STEM and STEAM curricula (Tselegkaridis & Sapounidis, 2022; Alimisis, 2013). The primary motivation for incorporating ER tools into classrooms is rooted in Seymour Papert's constructivist theories (Papert, 1980). ER represents tangible learning artifacts that can enhance student interest in STEM fields (Alimisis & Moro, 2016; Atmatzidou & Demetriadis, 2016; Mataric, Koenig, & Feil-Seifer, 2007) and foster technical competencies such as programming (Alimisis & Kynigos, 2009; Atmatzidou, Markelis, & Demetriadis, 2008). ER creates a dynamic and engaging learning environment where students are actively involved in learning through a constructivist approach, emphasizing the learning process rather than solely the outcomes (Eguchi, 2017). Working with robots allows students to grasp concepts that are typically considered challenging. Research has shown that ER helps students develop essential cross-disciplinary skills such as critical thinking, problem-solving, decision-making, communication, and teamwork (Benitti, 2012; Blanchard, Freiman, & Lirrete-Pitre, 2010; Atmatzidou & Demetriadis, 2012). Additionally, robotics enhances computational thinking skills (Repenning, Webb, & Ioannidou, 2010; Lee et al., 2011) and positively impacts students' motivation, self-confidence, and creativity (Miller, Nourbakhsh, & Siegwart, 2008; Khanlari, 2013), contributing to a more enjoyable learning experience. Robots have become integral in STEM courses as they embody the interdisciplinary approach of STEM education (Takacs et al., 2016; Atmatzidou & Demetriadis, 2016; Naya et al., 2017).

Given the success of educational robots in various settings, there exists an opportunity to introduce ML through ER. This study will first present the current state of ML instruction in K–12 education, followed by an introduction to a range of commercial robots suitable for teaching ML concepts. Finally, we propose a new approach utilizing manipulatives as the preferred ER platform for introducing ML concepts.

THE AIM AND IMPORTANCE OF THE STUDY

The aim of this study is to investigate the role of educational robotics (ER) as a conduit for imparting machine learning (ML) and artificial intelligence (AI) concepts within the K–12 educational curriculum. Given the pervasive impact of AI in contemporary society and its seamless incorporation into everyday gadgets, there exists a critical need to demystify these technologies and make them accessible to all layers of the population, especially the youth who will inevitably become both the consumers and developers of future AI systems (De la Higuera, 2019; Heys, 2018).

This research addresses the considerable gap in AI literacy by developing a framework that educators can adopt to introduce the fundamentals of ML and AI in an engaging and interactive manner through the use of ER. The importance of this study is underscored by the rapid evolution of the global job market, as the Fourth Industrial Revolution demands a workforce skilled in areas such as problem-solving, critical thinking, and digital literacy (Marr, 2016; Marr, 2018). ER offers an immersive learning experience that can foster these skills, aligning with the aims of STEM and STEAM education initiatives (Alimisis & Moro, 2016; Kim & Park, 2012).

Furthermore, the research is pivotal in examining how ER can be a powerful educational tool that promotes interest in STEM fields, enhances computational thinking, and supports the evolution of vital 21st-century skills (Benitti, 2012; Repenning, Webb, & Ioannidou, 2010). The incorporation of ER into classrooms is not merely a pedagogical enhancement but a necessity for preparing students to navigate and contribute to a future where AI and ML are integral to all aspects of life.

The proposed study will contribute to the field by providing insights into current practices of teaching ML in K–12 education, evaluating commercial robots for educational purposes, and proposing novel approaches for using robotics to teach ML concepts. Through this research, we aspire to lay the groundwork for educational systems that will empower the next generation to harness the potential of AI and robotics, thereby ensuring societal progress and economic sustainability.

BACKGROUND

The emphasis of this part of the chapter is the literature review concerning the interplay between educational robotics (ER), machine learning (ML), and their implementation within the K–12 educational sphere. This literature review is pivotal in mapping the current state of insight and practice, identifying gaps, and understanding the trajectory of future educational approaches.

Artificial Intelligence and Machine Learning as a Subfield of Learning

Machine learning, one of the leading fields within artificial intelligence, has made remarkable progress in recent years. Today, energy resources in our world are rapidly diminishing, and all sectors are in a race against time to save energy and minimize wasted effort in any task. One of the important steps of saving is to ensure that the learning of any information is accomplishd in the shortest time and with the least amount of error (Sakulkueakulsuk et al., 2018). There are diverse obstacles to learning during the time allocated for educational activities; for example, contexts such as laboratories, where students can conduct practical experiments, are limited. Therefore, the role of technological progress platforms, which are used to save time, effort, and expense during the learning process, is becoming increasingly prominent. These platforms offer dynamic systems that are constantly being updated and improved and are able to follow and integrate the latest evolutions in artificial intelligence into the learning process (Kış, 2019).

Machine learning in the field of education has started to be taught within the scope of artificial intelligence. The demand for information that can be processed faster and remembered for longer has led to a rise in interest in machine learning in educational settings (Marshall, 2015). ML, which operates based on the principle of increasing the efficiency of learning by using data efficiently, also brings the ability to solve complex problems that humans have difficulty understanding (Cevyak & Kayakuş, 2020). ML also provides a considerable benefit in diagnosing and remedying learning difficulties encountered in education (Özkan, 2015). In situations where it is necessary to emphasis on individual learning needs, ML can play an important role by enabling personalized education tailored to each student's needs.

ML generally takes place in small group work contexts where problem-solving activities are carried out together. Education is conducted by programming in small groups and integrating the curriculum with the learning aims of the ML field. By addressing the educational needs of students and offering problem-solving tasks, students are provided with the opportunity to tackle real-world issues in the classroom (Marques, Gresse von Wangenheim, & Hauck, 2020). The spread of ML in educational programs offers different scientific and intellectual possibilities for students to develop their computational thinking, creativity, and problem-solving skills (Zimmermann-Niefield, Turner, Murchy, Kane & Shapiro, 2019). ML provides opportunities for authentic applications in education that are connected with daily life, enabling the evolution of self-efficacy and innovative skills (Shapiro, Feinberg & Nemorin, 2018). The incorporation of ML in education also allows for the introduction of diverse software and programs, boosting the educational process and providing a system that can think and act like a human.

ML also involves certain risks. The security of the information used in ML must be ensured, and privacy must be protected. In particular, attention should be paid to the use of personal data and information. Students must be able to grasp not only the benefits but also the potential harms and risks of ML. They should be informed about how the algorithms work and how they can protect their personal data (Gülçiçek, 2006).

ML is divided into three types: supervised learning, unsupervised learning, and semi-supervised (or reinforcement) learning. In supervised learning, the system learns from the data provided, and its performance is measured by the classification or prediction outcomes (Kırıkçı & Oğuzlar, 2018). In unsupervised learning, the system tries to make sense of the input data without pre-existing labels or outcomes (Aydogan & Karci, 2018). Lastly, reinforcement learning differentiates itself by not having predefined labels or outcomes for the data it methods (Peters, 2019).

Types of Machine Learning

Machine learning is employed in diverse areas within education. It is instrumental in assessment and evaluation, predicting success, developing course materials, and improving learning systems—vital components of intelligent educational systems. However, the research in Turkey on the application of machine learning in education is limited. For this reason, only a handful of studies have been reviewed and are presented in the table below. The areas where machine learning is used in education are given in Table 1

Table 1. Uses of machine learning in education and examples

Authors and Year	Type	Target Audience	Machine Learning Software Used	Machine Learning Algorithm	Method	Purpose	Result
Filiz (2019)	Doctoral Thesis	8th Grade Students	Logistic Regression, Support Vector Machines	Experimental	To understand the impact of students' mathematical achievement and their success in other classes	In the final exams, the machine learning algorithms, particularly LDA and SVM-POLY, were successful.	
Selvi (2020)	Master's Thesis	6th, 7th, and 8th Grade Students	KNIME Analytics Platform	-	Experimental	To identify the factors that affect students' success in schools	The performance of students was most effectively predicted by Random Forest method among machine learning models.
Jiménez Chaves and Torres (2019)	Article	Students	-	Data mining, K-means clustering algorithm	Experimental	To identify the different profiles of the students	The decrease in the number of failures has been observed with the application of the model.

continued on following page

Table 1. Continued

Authors and Year	Type	Target Audience	Machine Learning Software Used	Machine Learning Algorithm	Method	Purpose	Result
Villalobos-Roman-Cañizares and Palacios-Pacheco (2020)	Article	University Students	MapReduce	-	-	To contribute to the learning process by using machine learning technologies and other artificial intelligence learning systems	Significant improvements have been observed in the learning process with the use of artificial intelligence and machine learning.
Kotsiantis, Pierrakeas, and Pintelas (2004)	Article	University Students	-	Naive Bayes	Experimental	To predict student performance by analyzing it with machine learning	The application of machine learning techniques has resulted in a low performance prediction error.
Sobnath, Kaduk, Rehman, and Issa (2020)	Article	Students with Disabilities	-	Decision Trees, Logistic Regression	Not Experimental	To increase the job placement probability by identifying specific features	The model has been successful in identifying job placement probabilities.
Verma, Adhikari, Khanduri, Tandon, Rawat, and Singh (2020)	Article	University Students	-	Support Vector, Logistic Regression Algorithms	System Development	To predict students' performance in learning systems	The logistic regression model showed a prediction accuracy of 86.84%, while the SVM model showed an accuracy of 67% for dropout predictions.
Hasan and Khan (2020)	Article	Computer Science Students at the University	-	Hybrid Machine Learning	System Development	To predict the dropout rates and improve student performance	The hybrid machine learning system provided better results than other algorithms.
Ahmad, Hussain, Ahmad, and Din (2020)	Article	Physics Department Students in Higher Education and Lecturers	-	-	Quantitative	To predict the students' academic performance using demographic and academic factors	The model has provided significant predictions about the students' academic performance.
Sharma, Joshi, Agarwal, and Kulkarni (2020)	Article	Undergraduate Students	MS Azure	KNN	-	To compare learning achievements based on the teaching methods used	Students performed better in the courses that utilized machine learning.
Küchenmann, Klein, Beckers, Kumari, and Kuhn (2020)	Article	High School Students	-	Support Vector, Random Forest, Multiple Kernel Learning	Quantitative	To apply machine learning techniques to solve spatial-temporal problems	SVM and Machine LearningP showed the best performance among the models.

continued on following page

Table 1. Continued

Authors and Year	Type	Target Audience	Machine Learning Software Used	Machine Learning Algorithm	Method	Purpose	Result
Abdulameer and Abdullah (2019)	Article	Higher Education Students	Python	Full Range Algorithms	Quantitative	To determine the efficiency of video-based learning systems	The video learning system, when implemented with the Decision Tree and k-NN algorithms, provided better results than other algorithms.
Park, Ahn, Jang, Yu, Kim, Bae, and Yoo (2020)	Article	Elementary School Students	-	-	Quantitative	To develop a machine learning-based education system for teaching programming	The implementation of machine learning platforms has led to improved learning outcomes.
Zhu (2019)	Master's Thesis	High School and University Students	MIT App Inventor, TensorFlow.js	-	Not Experimental	To improve learning efficiency by integrating Artificial Intelligence into mobile applications	The integration of Artificial Intelligence into educational apps has facilitated learning.
Lin, Van Brummelen, Lukin, Williams, and Breazeal (2020)	Article	Elementary and Middle School Students	-	System Development (Zhorai)	-	To assist in understanding machine learning concepts	The conversational platform has helped children to understand the concepts of machine learning.
Peters (2019)	Master's Thesis	High School Students	Python	Support Vector	-	To teach students programming languages using machine learning	The use of machine learning in robotic platforms has resulted in an increase in student motivation.
Khan, Cheng, and Bee (2018)	Article	Elementary School Students	Python	KNN	System Development	To identify learning styles in tablet-based education systems	The education platform based on machine learning showed a risk of 32% in dropout predictions.
Roy, Roy, and Sinha (2018)	Article	Children under 18 years old	-	Support Vector, Bayes, k-Nearest Neighbors (FRNN)	System Development	To determine the internet usage patterns through a machine learning-based approach	The keyboard usage patterns were predicted with an accuracy of 92%.

Authors and Year	Type	Target Audience	Machine Learning Software Used	Machine Learning Algorithm	Method	Purpose	Result
Duzhin and Gustafsson (2018)	Article	University Students and Teachers	-	Random Forest, k-Nearest Neighbors Algorithms	Not Experimental	To help teachers identify the most influential factors in group learning	The study found that group learning in some cases leads to better results than individual learning.
Hamilton and Plattner (2013)	Article	K-12 Students	MATLAB	SVM, Naive Bayes	Experimental	To forecast the potential career interests of K-12 students	The study has provided insights into the potential career interests of K-12 students.

Machine learning is used in education for a range of purposes, from voice recognition to identifying at-risk students (Shapiro, 2019). Identifying students who are at risk of dropping out is particularly important in placing interventions in a timely manner at schools (Mduma, Kalegele & Machuve, 2019). It is evident from the table that there have been limited comprehensive studies on this topic. The scope of thesis work is inherently limited. The machine learning software predominantly chosen for these studies are Python and MATLAB. Moreover, the majority of these studies are experimental in nature. Looking at the results of these studies, it is clear that the aims were generally accomplishd, and overall positive outcomes were obtained. Table 1 aggregates a compendium of research examining the intersection of machine learning (Machine Learning) applications within educational paradigms, varying from foundational school years to advanced tertiary education. The investigations span a spectrum of methodologies, aims, and outcomes, unified by their employment of Machine Learning to enhance educational methods and outcomes. Research types cataloged in the table include doctoral theses, master's theses, and peer-reviewed articles, reflecting the academic rigor and depth of exploration into this progressive subject. The breadth of the target audience, detailed in the table, underscores the versatility of Machine Learning applications across educational levels, targeting specific student groups such as 8th graders, university students, and even learners with disabilities. The software and algorithms utilized, such as Logistic Regression, Support Vector Machines, and decision-tree based methods like Random Forest, denote the technological underpinnings that drive these studies. These tools are applied in both experimental and system evolution methodologies to fulfill purposes ranging from predicting academic performance to identifying learning styles and key factors affecting educational success. Significantly, the results column encapsulates the effectiveness of Machine Learning in educational settings. For example, the usage of Logistic Regression and SVM has been noted to predict student dropout rates with considerable accuracy. Meanwhile, a study employing Random Forest techniques was particularly adept at forecasting student performance. Moreover, the application of machine learning has not been limited to conventional academic outcomes alone. Certain studies have emphasised on boosting practical understanding, as seen in the implementation of Machine Learning in programming education for elementary students, and in creating conversational platforms to elucidate Machine Learning concepts to younger learners.

Table 1 conveys a narrative of successful incorporation of Machine Learning in education, evidencing notable enhancements in both teaching methodologies and student learning experiences. It underscores the promise of machine learning as a considerable enabler in the evolution of educational practices, reflecting a pivotal shift towards data-driven, personalized learning.

MACHINE LEARNING (ML) TEACHING APPLICATIONS IN K-12

In light of the aforementioned considerations, we present an overview of educational robotics platforms equipped with intrinsic artificial intelligence (Artificial Intelligence) capabilities, thereby obviating the need for reliance on external platforms for acquiring Artificial Intelligence skills. Our emphasis lies on robotics platforms programmable in languages accessible to students, supplemented with illustrative examples and instructional materials within their documentation. Furthermore, the selected robotics platforms are compact in size, rendering them suitable for incorporation into typical K-12 classroom contexts. Notably, our selection criteria did not impose restrictions based on the machine learning (Machine Learning) capabilities of the robots. These capabilities encompass a spectrum of Machine Learning models, spanning from elementary color recognition to sophisticated models capable of facial recognition, emotion analysis, sound classification, and pose detection.

Additionally, we offer an examination of existing tools tailored for teaching Machine Learning concepts within the K-12 domain and pertinent scholarly literature, aiming to underscore the contrasting readiness levels between conventional (virtual) teaching tools and educational robotics.

Existing Tools for Teaching Machine Learning

The incorporation of Machine Learning (ML) fundamentals into higher education institutions (HEIs) has become a staple of university curricula, exposing students to critical concepts and techniques that drive modern AI developments. However, this exposure is often lacking among younger students who interact with smart devices, such as Amazon's Alexa, on a daily basis without understanding the underlying technologies. Introducing ML concepts at an early educational stage and equipping educators with the appropriate teaching tools presents a significant challenge (Sulmont et al., 2019).

To address this, several tools have been developed to introduce ML concepts to K–12 students. One such tool is the "Artificial Intelligence for Oceans" program, which is designed for students from grade three upwards. This program teaches essential ML concepts, including training data and ML bias, while aligning with the United States' Computer Science Teachers Association (CSTA) Computer Science Standards (Code.org, n.d.). Moreover, a variety of online tools and resources enhanced with AI and ML have been created to make learning engaging and accessible for children (Scratch Lab, n.d.; Machine Learning for Kids, n.d.).

Despite these efforts, many initiatives are primarily aimed at experienced educators and tailored for specific teaching environments, often involving small class sizes. This specificity can make it difficult to adapt these tools to standard classroom settings. A notable example is Teachable Machine, which uses ML classification models that do not require extensive prior knowledge, thus making it accessible for a wider audience (Carney et al., 2020). Additionally, platforms like LearningMachine Learning enable students to create their own ML applications, while tools such as Zhorai help children explore ML concepts and knowledge representation in an interactive manner (Rodríguez-García et al., 2021; Lin et al., 2022). Other curricula, such as PopBots and IRobot, have been designed to introduce AI into secondary education, though their implementation remains largely experimental (Williams et al., 2019; Burgsteiner et al., 2016).

A significant barrier to incorporating AI in K–12 education is the lack of comprehensive AI curricula integrated into core subjects. This is a notable challenge, as highlighted by Van Brummelen and Lin (2020). Interestingly, China stands out as the only country that has systematically introduced AI education in some of its schools (Jing, 2018).

Despite these challenges, various initiatives aimed at introducing ML concepts to younger students have gained traction in recent years. For instance, Hitron et al. (2018) and Vartiainen & Tedre (2020) have noted several emerging efforts. A systematic study by Marques et al. (2020) mapped the state-of-the-art in teaching ML at elementary and high school levels, revealing a rapid increase in instructional units (IUs) developed in recent years. These IUs range from short, one-hour workshops to semester-long courses and are mostly extracurricular rather than part of the standard curriculum. Tedre et al. (2021) explored emerging trends in educational technology theory and practice related to teaching ML in K–12 education, concluding that teaching ML poses greater challenges than integrating computational thinking into school curricula. Despite these difficulties, Hintz et al. (2018) emphasize the clear necessity for early understanding of how ML-based and data-driven systems can address real-world problems.

Advanced Educational Robotics for Machine Learning

This section delves into advanced educational robotic tools that meet the criteria outlined in earlier sections. These selected robots are equipped with pre-installed modules that enable them to recognize faces (facial recognition), individuals (face detection), emotions, sounds, objects, colors, and hand gestures. Notably, Arduino robotic kits or BBC micro are excluded from this list as they do not inherently possess ML capabilities. To gain such capabilities, these kits would require additional platforms or programming in languages that may be challenging for younger learners. Here, we focus on six standalone AI-powered educational robots: Zumi, RoboMaster S1, ClicBot, Cozmo, MINDSTORMS Robot Inventor, and Cogbots (Zumi, n.d.; RoboMaster, n.d.; Clicbot, n.d.; Cozmo, n.d.; Mindstorms, n.d.; Cogbots, n.d.).

Zumi is a compact, constructible kit designed to build a self-driving vehicle. It educates young individuals on how autonomous vehicles use sensors and cameras for navigation and environmental understanding through AI. Built around a Raspberry Pi0, Zumi includes six infrared sensors, a gyroscope, an accelerometer, a Pi-specific camera, and a 128x64 pixel OLED display. It supports programming in Blockly and Python, enabling tasks such as color recognition and facial recognition through ML algorithms. Educational resources are provided for users aged six and older (Zumi, n.d.).

RoboMaster S1 is an educational robotics platform that blends AI with practical applications in math and physics through programming instruction. It supports Scratch and Python, featuring high-definition, low-latency video transmission, AI computation, and simultaneous programming capabilities. The S1 moves using four Mecanum wheels, each with 12 rollers, allowing omnidirectional movement. Its AI capabilities include gesture recognition, sound recognition, road and traffic light recognition, and identification of up to 44 vision markers. It targets users aged 10 to 16 with a variety of online resources available (RoboMaster S1, n.d.).

ClicBot is a modular robotics kit that offers both educational and entertainment functionalities through AI. Its design allows for easy assembly and disassembly, promoting creativity in robot construction. The central control and power unit includes a 2.1-inch rotational touchscreen that serves as the robot's eye, equipped with AI for facial recognition, gesture sensors, and a camera. Additional modules feature touch sensors and connection ports. ClicBot supports Blockly-based and Python programming, suitable for ages 6 to 16+ (ClicBot, n.d.).

Cozmo provides an interactive AI learning experience, equipped with proximity sensors, a gyroscope, a cliff detector, and a camera for face and emotion recognition. Cozmo displays emotions through a screen and speaker and includes three LED cubes for interactive games. Cozmo's programming options include Code Lab and

Python, with resources for advanced developers through SDKs, targeting ages 6 to 16+ (Cozmo, n.d.).

LEGO® MINDSTORMS® Robot Inventor introduces ML through a programming app that is compatible with the kit, supporting both Scratch and Python. It includes a variety of sensors and motors, with the potential to add a force sensor. The platform offers extensive programming possibilities for object and voice command recognition, suitable for ages 8 to 16+ (MINDSTORMS Robot Inventor, n.d.).

CogBots are open-source robotics kits available in CogBot and CogMini versions, created in collaboration with Google and UNESCO. They feature a 3D-printed skeleton, an Arduino ESP32 board controller, and use a smartphone's sensors. They support programming with Scratch and integrate Google's Teachable Machines for learning AI concepts, aimed at ages 8 to 16+ (CogBots, n.d.).

The exploration of these advanced educational robotic tools underscores their significant potential in teaching ML within STEM disciplines, providing hands-on learning experiences. However, several challenges are noted, such as space requirements, proprietary software limitations, and the necessity for wireless connectivity. As an alternative, educational robotic arms are suggested due to their static nature and USB connectivity, offering advantages for classroom management and effective programming tasks in ML (Some Conceptual Guidelines for Teaching Machine Learning with STEM-Based Robotics, n.d.).

Teaching Machine Learning with STEM-Based Robotics: Conceptual Guidelines and Strategies

In the evolving landscape of education, the incorporation of STEM (Science, Technology, Engineering, and Mathematics) principles through educational robots presents a forward-thinking method for teaching machine learning (Machine Learning) concepts. While the innovation behind such educational tools as Zumi, RoboMaster S1, ClicBot, Cozmo, LEGO® MINDSTORMS® Robot Inventor, and CogBots marks a considerable advancement in learning methodologies, their deployment within the classroom setting brings to light a set of challenges that need addressing to maximize their educational potential.

The mobility of these robots, although a key feature of their design, necessitates considerable space, making them less suitable for the constrained contexts of most classrooms, especially for the larger models like RoboMaster S1 ("RoboMaster S1," n.d.). Furthermore, the proprietary nature of the software limits the customizability of lesson plans, thereby restricting the educational scope. The necessity for a wireless internet connection for operation and the lack of customizable machine learning models further limit hands-on learning experiences and experimentation opportunities for students. An exception to some of these constraints is the LEGO®

MINDSTORMS® Robot Inventor kit, which offers greater flexibility in terms of customization and connectivity (MINDSTORMS Robot Inventor, n.d.).

To address these limitations, the adoption of educational robotic arms has been proposed. These robotic arms, unlike their cellular counterpcreative fields, are stationary and necessitate considerablely less space, making them a practical option for classroom settings. Their operation does not depend on wireless connectivity, as they can be directly connected to a computer or student workstation via USB, boosting reliability and ease of use. Furthermore, the static nature of these arms simplifies classroom management for teachers and emphasises on programming tasks directly related to machine learning, making the learning experience more pertinent and impactful.

The guidelines for implementing these technologies efficiently in teaching scenarios include:

Utilization of low-cost and recycled materials. Encouraging the use of affordable and recycled materials for building and programming robots, such as the approach taken by Cogbots, promotes sustainability and accessibility (CogBots, n.d.).

Workspace optimization. By designing robots that necessitate minimal operational space, educators can more easily integrate these tools into the classroom environment. This strategy also implies that robots do not need advanced controllers if they can efficiently connect to a computer.

Preference for direct connections. To circumvent the issues associated with wireless connectivity, the use of USB cables for connecting robots to computers is recommended, ensuring a stable and straightforward setup.

Development of concise teaching scenarios. Creating short and emphasised teaching scenarios that fit within the constraints of typical class durations can considerablely enhance learning outcomes. Incorporating tasks that allow the robot to act as an assistant to the student not only facilitates learning but also fosters a personal connection with the technological progress.

Encouragement of experimentation. Allowing students to adjust critical parameters, such as the number of hidden layers in neural networks through tools like TensorFlow Playground, enables a hands-on learning experience and a deeper understanding of machine learning concepts (TensorFlow Playground, n.d.).

By adopting these approaches, educators can overcome the challenges associated with using educational robots in the classroom and unlock the full potential of these innovative tools in teaching machine learning concepts. The emphasis on practical, accessible, and engaging teaching methodologies aligns with the goals of STEM education, preparing students for the technological progress of the future.

CONCLUSION AND RECOMMENDATIONS

In the rapidly evolving landscape of contemporary education, the imperative to integrate artificial intelligence (Artificial Intelligence), particularly machine learning (Machine Learning), into the curriculum is undeniable. As we navigate through the 21st century, the necessity to equip students with a deep understanding of these technologies becomes increasingly urgent, given their considerable impact across all sectors of society. STEM education, with a particular emphasis on robotics, emerges as a pivotal tool in making the abstract concepts of Artificial Intelligence and Machine Learning more tangible and comprehensible to students. This approach aligns with the broader educational goal of preparing students not only to navigate but also to innovate within the digital world that surrounds them.

To assess the effectiveness of this innovative approach to teaching Artificial Intelligence and Machine Learning, we plan to conduct pre- and post-assessment tests. These assessments will not only gauge students' understanding and retention of the material but also provide valuable data on the impact of hands-on learning with robotics on students' comprehension of Artificial Intelligence and Machine Learning. The outcomes of these assessments will be compared against the results from the previous year's courses, which introduced Machine Learning concepts without the use of robotic aids.

FUTURE RESEARCH DIRECTIONS

The incorporation of robotics into the educational framework, particularly for the facilitation of artificial intelligence (Artificial Intelligence) and machine learning (Machine Learning) concepts, stands at the frontier of contemporary pedagogical methodologies. As this field burgeons, it unfurls a plethora of research trajectories that promise to recalibrate our approach to STEM education, catering to the demands of an increasingly digitalized society. Herein, we delineate several pivotal future research directions that will contribute considerablely to the academic discourse surrounding the use of robotics in educational settings.

In conclusion, these future research directions underscore the multifaceted nature of educational robotics as a domain that intersects technological innovation, pedagogical theory, and ethical considerations. Through rigorous investigation and interdisciplinary collaboration, the incorporation of robotics into education holds the promise of not only boosting STEM education but also preparing students to navigate and contribute to a technologically intricate world with informed ethical sensibilities and innovative capabilities.

REFERENCES

Abdulameer, M. M. H., & Abdullah, M. Z. (2019). Toward Generating a New Video Education Lectures Dataset and Performance Comparison with Various Machine Learning Algorithms. *Annals of Tropical Medicine and Health*, 22(12), 279–298. DOI: 10.36295/ASRO.2019.221230

Ahmad, S. A., Hussain, I., Ahmad, R., & Din, M. N. U. (2020). Performance Based Prediction of the Students in the Physics Subject using Traditional and Machine Learning Approach at Higher Education Level. [IJITL]. *International Journal of Innovation in Teaching and Learning*, 6(1), 174–190. DOI: 10.35993/ijitl.v6i1.997

Aki Tamashiro, M., Van Mechelen, M., Schaper, M.-M., & Sejer Iversen, O. (2021). Introducing Teenagers to Machine Learning through Design Fiction: An Exploratory Case Study. Interact. Des. Child., 471–475.

Alimisis, D. (2013). Educational robotics: Open questions and new challenges. *Themes in Science and Technology Education*, 6(1), 1.

Alimisis, D., & Kynigos, C. (2009). Constructionism and robotics in education. In Alimisis, D. (Ed.), *Teacher Education on Robotic-Enhanced Constructivist Pedagogical Methods* (pp. 11–26). ASPETE.

Alimisis, D., & Moro, M. (2016). Special issue on educational robotics. *Robotics and Autonomous Systems*, 77, 74–75. DOI: 10.1016/j.robot.2015.12.006

Alpaydin, E. (2020). *Introduction to Machine Learning* (4th ed.). MIT Press.

Atmatzidou, S., & Demetriadis, S. (2016). Advancing students' computational thinking skills through educational robotics: A study on age and gender pertinent differences. *Robotics and Autonomous Systems*, 75, 661–670. DOI: 10.1016/j.robot.2015.10.008

Atmatzidou, S., & Demetriadis, S. N. (2012). Evaluating the Role of Collaboration Scripts as Group Guiding Tools in Activities of Educational Robotics: Conclusions from Three Case Studies. In *Proceedings of the 2012 IEEE 12th International Conference on Advanced Learning Technologies* (pp. 298–302). IEEE. DOI: 10.1109/ICALT.2012.111

Atmatzidou, S., & Markelis, I. (2008). The use of LEGO Mindstorms in elementary and secondary education: Game as a way of triggering learning. In *Proceedings of the International Conference of Simulation, Modeling and Programming for Autonomous Robots (SIMPAR)* (pp. 22–30). Venice, Italy.

Barker, B. S., Nugent, G., Grandgenett, N., & Adamchuk, V. I. (2012). *Robots in K-12 Education: A New Technology for Learning*. IGI Global. DOI: 10.4018/978-1-4666-0182-6

Battelle for Kids. (2019). *Framework for 21st Century Learning. Partnership for 21st Century Learning*. Retrieved from.

Benitti, F. B. V. (2012). Exploring the educational potential of robotics in schools: A systematic review. *Computers & Education*, 58(3), 978–988. DOI: 10.1016/j.compedu.2011.10.006

Bessen, J. (2018). Artificial Intelligence and Jobs: The Role of Demand (Working Paper No. 24235). National Bureau of Economic Research.

Blanchard, S., Freiman, V., & Lirrete-Pitre, N. (2010). Strategies used by elementary schoolchildren solving robotics-based complex tasks: Innovative potential of technological progress. *Procedia: Social and Behavioral Sciences*, 2(2), 2851–2857. DOI: 10.1016/j.sbspro.2010.03.427

Breiner, J. M., Harkness, S. S., Johnson, C. C., & Koehler, C. M. (2012). What Is STEM? A Discussion About Conceptions of STEM in Education and Partnerships. *School Science and Mathematics*, 112(1), 3–11. DOI: 10.1111/j.1949-8594.2011.00109.x

Burgsteiner, H., Kandlhofer, M., & Steinbauer, G. (2016). IRobot: Teaching the Basics of Artificial Intelligence in High Schools. In *Proceedings of the AAArtificial Intelligence Conference on Artificial Intelligence*, Phoenix, AZ, USA, 12–17 February 2016, 30, 1. DOI: 10.1609/aaai.v30i1.9864

Calypso. (n.d.). Retrieved from

Carney, M., Webster, B., Alvarado, I., Phillips, K., Howell, N., Griffith, J., Jongejan, J., Pitaru, A., & Chen, A. (2020). Teachable Machine: Approachable Web-Based Tool for Exploring Machine Learning Classification. In *Proceedings of the CHI 2020*, Honolulu, HI, USA, 25–30 April 2020. DOI: 10.1145/3334480.3382839

Chatzopoulos, A., Papoutsidakis, M., Kalogiannakis, M., & Psycharis, S. (2020). Innovative Robot for Educational Robotics and STEM. In Kumar, V., & Troussas, C. (Eds.), *Intelligent Tutoring Systems* (pp. 95–104). Springer International Publishing. DOI: 10.1007/978-3-030-49663-0_13

Clicbot. (n.d.). Retrieved from

Code.org. (n.d.). *Artificial Intelligence for Oceans*. Retrieved from.

CogBots. (n.d.). Retrieved from

Cognimates Team. (2020). *Cognimates*. Retrieved from.

Computer Science Teachers Association. (2020). *CSTA Standards for Computer Science Teachers*. Retrieved from.

Cozmo. (n.d.). Retrieved from

De la Higuera, C. (2019). A Report about Education, Training Teachers and Learning Artificial Intelligence: Overview of Key Issues. Working Paper Prepared for the Knowledge Societies Division, Communication and Information Sector of the UNESCO. Retrieved from

Eguchi, A. (2017). Bringing robotics in classrooms. In Khine, M. S. (Ed.), *Robotics in STEM Education* (pp. 3–31). Springer. DOI: 10.1007/978-3-319-57786-9_1

Eguchi, A. (2022). Understanding Machine Learning Through Artificial Intelligence-powered Educational Robotics—Pilot Study with Undergraduate Students. In Lepuschitz, W., Merdan, M., Koppensteiner, G., Balogh, R., & Obdržálek, D. (Eds.), *Robotics in Education* (pp. 52–62). Springer. DOI: 10.1007/978-3-031-12848-6_5

Eguchi, A. (2023). Machine Learning Application with Artificial Intelligence-Robotics Tool—What We Learned from Pilot Studies. In Cascalho, J. M., Tokhi, M. O., Silva, M. F., Mendes, A., Goher, K., & Funk, M. (Eds.), *Robotics in Natural Settings* (pp. 383–394). Springer. DOI: 10.1007/978-3-031-15226-9_36

Evangelista, I., Blesio, G., & Benatti, E. (2018). Why Are We Not Teaching Machine Learning at High School? A Proposal. In Proceedings of the 2018 World Engineering Education Forum—Global Engineering Deans Council (WEEF-GEDC) (pp. 1–6).

Filiz, A. (2019). *Dergi Adı, Cilt(Sayı)*. Sayfa Aralığı. [Çalışmanın Başlığı]

Filiz, E. (2019). An Application of Machine Learning Methods on Trend Data: International Study of Trends in Mathematics and Science 2015, Turkey Case. (Unpublished doctoral dissertation). Yıldız Technical University, Institute of Science, Istanbul.

Google Teachable Machine. (n.d.). Retrieved from

Hasan, M., & Khan, B. (2020). Variability in the Effectiveness of Psychological Interventions based on Machine Learning in STEM Education. *GSE Journal*, 233, 1–16.

Heys, J. (2018). Machine Learning as a Tool to Identify Critical Assignments. *Chemical Engineering Education*, 52(4).

Ho, J. W., Scadding, M., Kong, S. C., Andone, D., Biswas, G., Hoppe, H. U., & Hsu, T. C. (2019). Classroom activities for teaching artificial intelligence to primary school students. In *Proceedings of the International Conference on Computational Thinking Education* (pp. 157–159).

Inventor Mindstorms, APP. (n.d.). Retrieved from

Jiménez Chaves, V. E., & Torres, M. G. (2019). Analysis of Pre-school Education from Paraguay through Machine Learning Techniques. *Revista de la Sociedad Científica del Paraguay*, 24(2), 293–304. DOI: 10.32480/rscp.2019-24-2.293-304

Jing, M. (2018). China Looks to School Kids to Win the Global Artificial Intelligence Race. South China Morning Post. Retrieved from

Khan, R. U., Cheng, J. L. A., & Bee, O. Y. (2018). Machine Learning and Dyslexia: Diagnostic and Classification System (DCS) for Kids with Learning Disabilities. International Journal of Engineering & Technology, 7(3.18), 97-100.

Khanlari, A. (2013). Effects of robotics on 21st-century skills. *European Scientific Journal*, 9(13), 26–36.

Kotsiantis, S., Pierrakeas, C., & Pintelas, P. (2004). Predicting Students' Performance in Distance Learning Using Machine Learning Techniques. *Applied Artificial Intelligence*, 18(5), 411–426. DOI: 10.1080/08839510490442058

Küchenmann, S., Klein, P., Beckers, S., Kumari, N., & Kuhn, J. (2020). Classification of Students' Conceptual Understanding in STEM Education using their Visual Attention Distributions: A Comparison of Three Machine-Learning Approaches. In *Proceedings of the CSEDU 2020*, Prague, 36-46.

Lee, I., Martin, F., Denner, J., Coulter, B., Allan, W., Erickson, J., Malyn-Smith, J., & Werner, L. (2011). Computational thinking for youth in practice. *ACM Inroads*, 2(1), 32–37. DOI: 10.1145/1929887.1929902

Levy, R. B.-B., & Ben-Ari, M. M. (2015). Robotics Activities–Is the Investment Worthwhile? In Brodnik, A., & Vahrenhold, J. (Eds.), *Informatics in Schools. Curricula, Competences, and Competitions* (pp. 22–31). Springer. DOI: 10.1007/978-3-319-25396-1_3

Lin, P., Brummelen, J. V., Lukin, G., Williams, R., & Breazeal, C. (2020). Zhorai: Designing a Conversational Agent for Children to Explore Machine Learning Concepts. In *Proceedings of the AAArtificial Intelligence Conference on Artificial Intelligence*, New York, NY, USA, 7–12 February 2020, 34. DOI: 10.1609/aaai.v34i09.7061

Lin, P., Van Brummelen, J., Lukin, G., Williams, R., & Breazeal, C. (2020, April). Zhorai: Designing a Conversational Agent for Children to Explore Machine Learning Concepts. In *Proceedings of the AAArtificial Intelligence Conference on Artificial Intelligence* (Vol. 34, No. 09, pp. 13381-13388). DOI: 10.1609/aaai.v34i09.7061

Machine Learning for Kids. (n.d.). Retrieved April 01, 2024, from

Marques, L. S., Gresse Von Wangenheim, C., & Hauck, J. C. R. (2020). Teaching Machine Learning in School: A Systematic Mapping of the State of the Art. *Inform. Educ.*, 19, 283–321. DOI: 10.15388/infedu.2020.14

Marr, B. (2018). What Is Industry 4.0? Here's a Super Easy Explanation for Anyone. [Retrieved from]. *Forbes*, •••, 4–7.

Mataric, M. J., Koenig, N., & Feil-Seifer, D. (2007). Materials for enabling hands-on robotics and STEM education. In Proceedings of the AAArtificial Intelligence Spring Symposium: Semantic Scientific Knowledge Integration (pp. 99–102). Stanford University.

Melchior, A., Cohen, F., Cutter, T., & Leavitt, T. (2005). *More than Robots: An Evaluation of the FIRST Robotics Competition Participant and Institutional Impacts*. Heller School for Social Policy and Management, Brandeis University.

Mindstorms Inventor Kit. (n.d.). Retrieved from

Muro, M., Whiton, J., & Maxim, R. (2019). *What Jobs Are Affected by Artificial Intelligence?* Better-Paid, Better-Educated Workers Face the Most Exposure. Brookings Institution.

Narahara, T., & Kobayashi, Y. (2018). Personalizing homemade bots with plug & play Artificial Intelligence for STEAM education. In *SIGGRAPH Asia 2018 Technical Briefs* (pp. 1–4). ACM. DOI: 10.1145/3283254.3283270

Naya, M., Varela, G., Llamas, L., Bautista, M., Becerra, J. C., Bellas, F., Prieto, A., Deibe, A., & Duro, R. J. (2017). A versatile robotic platform for educational engagement. In Proceedings of the 2017 9th IEEE International Conference on Intelligent Data Acquisition and Advanced Computing Systems: Technology and Applications (IDAACS) (Vol. 1, pp. 138–144).

Nourbakhsh, I. R., Crowley, K., Bhave, A., Hamner, E., Hsiu, T., Perez-Bergquist, A., Richards, S., & Wilkinson, K. (2005). The Robotic Autonomy Mobile Robotics Course: Robot Design, Curriculum Design and Educational Assessment. *Autonomous Robots*, 18(1), 103–127. DOI: 10.1023/B:AURO.0000047303.20624.02

Papert, S. (1980). *Mindstorms: Children, Computers, and Powerful Ideas* (Vol. 1). Basic Books.

Park, D., Ahn, J., Jang, J., Yu, W., Kim, W., Bae, Y., & Yoo, I. (2020). The Development of Software Teaching-Learning Model based on Machine Learning Platform. *Journal of The Korean Association of Information Education*, 24(1), 49–57. DOI: 10.14352/jkaie.2020.24.1.49

Peters, L. (2019). An Educational Programming Environment for Teaching the Principles of Machine Learning using Lego Mindstorms (Unpublished doctoral dissertation). University of Applied Sciences Leipzig.

Petre, M., & Price, B. (2004). Using Robotics to Motivate 'Back Door' Learning. *Education and Information Technologies*, 9(2), 147–158. DOI: 10.1023/B:EAIT.0000027927.78380.60

Repenning, A., Webb, D., & Ioannidou, A. (2010). Scalable game design and the evolution of a checklist for getting computational thinking into public schools. In *Proceedings of the 41st ACM Technical Symposium on Computer Science Education* (pp. 265–269). ACM. DOI: 10.1145/1734263.1734357

Robomaster S1. (n.d.). Retrieved from

Rodríguez-García, J. D., Moreno-León, J., Román-González, M., & Robles, G. (2021). Introducing Artificial Intelligence Fundamentals with LearningMachine Learning: Artificial Intelligence made easy. In *Proceedings of the Eighth International Conference on Technological Ecosystems for Enhancing Multiculturality*, Barcelona, Spain, 26–29 October 2021, 18–20.

Rousseau, V. (2022). Lego Mindstorms: One-Legged Robot Learning How to Crawl with q-Learning [Video]. YouTube. Retrieved from

Royal Society. (2017). *Machine Learning: The Power and Promise of Computer That Learn by Example* [Technical Report]. The Royal Society.

Scratch Extensions. (n.d.). Retrieved from

Scratch Lab's Face Sensing. (n.d.). Retrieved from

Selvi, A. (2020). Prediction of Student Success in Transition from Primary to Secondary Education Exams in Bilecik Province Using Machine Learning Methods. (Unpublished Master's thesis). Bilecik Şeyh Edebali University, Institute of Natural Sciences, Bilecik.

Sharma, R., Joshi, S., Agarwal, A., & Kulkarni, V. (2020). UniAssist-Implementation of Machine Learning Based Higher Education University Recommendation System. [IJREAM]. *International Journal for Research in Engineering Application & Management*, 6(1), 262–266.

Sobnath, D., Kaduk, T., Rehman, I. U., & Issa, R. (2020). Feature Selection for UK Disabled Students Engagement Post Higher Education: A Machine Learning Approach for a Predictive Employment Model. *IEEE Access : Practical Innovations, Open Solutions*, 8, 159530–159541. DOI: 10.1109/ACCESS.2020.3018663

Steinbach, P., Seibold, H., & Guhr, O. (2021). Teaching Machine Learning in 2020. In *Proceedings of the First Teaching Machine Learning and Artificial Intelligence Workshop* (pp. 1–6). [Accessed online:(41/steinbach21a.html)]

Sulmont, E., Patitsas, E., & Cooperstock, J. R. (2019). What Is Hard about Teaching Machine Learning to Non-Majors? Insights from Classifying Instructors' Learning Goals. ACM Transactions on Computing Education, 19, 33:1–33:16.

Takacs, A., Eigner, G., Kovacs, L., Rudas, I. J., & Haidegger, T. (2016). Teacher's Kit: Development, Usability, and Communities of Modular Robotic Kits for Classroom Education. *IEEE Robotics & Automation Magazine*, 23(4), 30–39. DOI: 10.1109/MRA.2016.2548754

Tedre, M., Toivonen, T., Kahila, J., Vartiainen, H., Valtonen, T., Jormanainen, I., & Pears, A. (2021). Teaching Machine Learning in K-12 Computing Education: Potential and Pitfalls. arXiv, arXiv:2106.11034.

TensorFlow Playground. (n.d.). Retrieved from

Tim, T. (2022). Reinforcement Learning with Lego Mindstorms—Crawling Robot [Video]. YouTube. Retrieved from

Touretzky, D. S., Gardner-McCune, C., Martin, F., & Seehorn, D. (2019). K-12 Guidelines for Artificial Intelligence: What Students Should Know. In *Proceedings of the ISTE Conference*, 23–26 June 2019, Philadelphia, PA, USA.

Tselegkaridis, S., & Sapounidis, T. (2022). Exploring the Features of Educational Robotics and STEM Research in Primary Education: A Systematic Literature Review. *Education Sciences*, 12(2), 305. DOI: 10.3390/educsci12050305

Van Brummelen, J., & Lin, P. (2020). Engaging Teachers to Co-Design Integrated Artificial Intelligence Curriculum for K-12 Classrooms. arXiv, arXiv:2009.11100.

Vartiainen, H., Tedre, M., & Valtonen, T. (2020). Learning machine learning with very young children: Who is teaching whom? *International Journal of Child-Computer Interaction*, 25, 100182. DOI: 10.1016/j.ijcci.2020.100182

Verma, G., Adhikari, S., Khanduri, V., Tandon, S., Rawat, S., & Singh, P. (2020). Machine Learning Model for Prediction of Stress Levels in Students of Technical Education. Artificial IntelligenceJR Proceedings, 45-52. DOI: 10.21467/proceedings.100.5

Villalobos-Roman-Cañizares, M., & Palacios-Pacheco, X. (2020). Improvement of an Online Education Model with the Integration of Machine Learning and Data Analysis in an LMS. *Applied Sciences (Basel, Switzerland)*, 10(15), 5371. DOI: 10.3390/app10155371

Vollstedt, A. M., Robinson, M., & Wang, E. (2007). Using robotics to enhance science, technological progress, engineering, and mathematics curricula. In *Proceedings of the American Society for Engineering Education Pacific Southwest Annual Conference* (pp. 1–9). University of Nevada.

Williams, R., Park, H. W., & Breazeal, C. (2019). A is for Artificial Intelligence: The Impact of Artificial Intelligence Activities on Young Children's Perceptions of Robots. In *Proceedings of the 2019 CHI Conference on Human Factors in Computing Systems*, Glasgow, UK, 4–9 May 2019, 1–11. DOI: 10.1145/3290605.3300677

Williams, R., Park, H. W., Oh, L., & Breazeal, C. (2019). PopBots: Designing an Artificial Intelligence Curriculum for Early Childhood Education. In *Proceedings of the AAArtificial Intelligence Conference on Artificial Intelligence*, Honolulu, HI, USA, 27 January–1 February 2019, 33, 1. DOI: 10.1609/aaai.v33i01.33019729

Xie, Y., Fang, M., & Shauman, K. (2015). STEM Education. *Annual Review of Sociology*, 41(1), 331–357. DOI: 10.1146/annurev-soc-071312-145659 PMID: 26778893

Yang, W. (2022). Artificial Intelligence education for young children: Why, what, and how in curriculum design and implementation. *Computer Education and Artificial Intelligence*, 3, 100061. DOI: 10.1016/j.caeai.2022.100061

Yu, W. J., Jang, J. H., Ahn, J. M., Park, D. R., Yoo, I. H., Bae, Y. K., & Kim, W. Y. (2019). Design of Artificial Intelligence Education Program based on Design-based Research. *Int. J. Adv. Smart Converg.*, 8, 113–120.

Zhu, K. (2019). An Educational Approach to Machine Learning with Mobile Applications. (Unpublished doctoral dissertation). Massachusetts Institute of Technology.

Zumi. (n.d.). Retrieved from

ADDITIONAL READING

Hamilton, D., & Plattner, K. (2013). *Exploring Potential for Machine Learning on Dataset about K-12 Teacher Professional Development. CS 229 Machine Learning Final Projects*. Stanford University.

Marques, L. S., Gresse von Wangenheim, C., & Hauck, J. C. (2020). Teaching Machine Learning in School: A Systematic Mapping of the State of the Art. *Informatics in Education*, 19(2), 283–321. DOI: 10.15388/infedu.2020.14

Murphy, R. F. (2019). Artificial Intelligence Applications to Support K-12 Teachers and Teaching. RAND Corporation, Santa Monica, CA, USA. *Tech. Rep.*, PE135, 2019. DOI: 10.7249/PE315

Roy, S., Roy, U., & Sinha, D. (2018). Protection of Kids from Internet Threats: A Machine Learning Approach for Classification of Age-group based on Typing Pattern. In *Proceedings of the International MultiConference of Engineers and Computer Scientists*, Vol. 1.

Sakulkueakulsuk, B., Vitoon, S., Ngarmkajornwiwat, P., Pataranutaporn, P., Surareungchai, W., & Pataranutaporn, P. (2018). Kids making Artificial Intelligence: Integrating Machine Learning, Gamification, and Social Context in STEM Education. In *2018 IEEE International Conference on Teaching, Assessment, and Learning for Engineering (TALE)*, 1005-1010. DOI: 10.1109/TALE.2018.8615249

Zhu, K. (2019). An educational approach to machine learning with cellular applications. (Unpublished doctoral dissertation). Massachusetts Institute of Technology, USA

Zimmermann-Niefield, A., Turner, M., Murphy, B., Kane, S. K., & Shapiro, R. B. (2019, June). Youth Learning Machine Learning through Building Models of Athletic Moves. In *Proceedings of the 18th ACM International Conference on Interaction Design and Children* (pp. 121-132). DOI: 10.1145/3311927.3323139

KEY TERMS AND DEFINITIONS

Artificial Intelligence (AI): The simulation of human intelligence methods by mechanisms, especially computer systems, encompassing learning, reasoning, and self-correction.

Cognitive Development: The process of growth and change in intellectual capabilities, affecting how individuals perceive, think, and understand their world through engagements, experiences, and genetic potential.

Curriculum Integration: The process of teaching and assessing numerous subjects or areas of insight together, emphasizing the interconnections between concepts across different disciplines.

Educational Robotics (ER): A pedagogical approach that utilizes robotic kits or platforms as tools for boosting learning, particularly in STEM subjects, by providing hands-on experiences and fostering active engagement.

K–12 Education: A comprehensive education system encompassing primary and secondary education, which includes Kindergarten through to the 12th grade, before higher education.

Machine Learning (Machine Learning): A subset of artificial intelligence emphasising on the evolution of algorithms and statistical models that enable computers to perform tasks without explicit instructions, through pattern recognition and inference.

STEM Education: An interdisciplinary approach to learning that combines the study of Science, Technology, Engineering, and Mathematics to foster critical thinking, problem-solving, and innovation.

Chapter 12
Teaching Programming Through Metaphors

Erkan Geçitli
http://orcid.org/0000-0001-7700-8690
Ministry of National Education, Turkey

Bünyamin Yurdakul
https://orcid.org/0000-0001-8401-7202
Ege University, Turkey

ABSTRACT

This chapter aims to provide computer science stakeholders with a perspective on teaching programming through metaphors. The chapter emphasises that the difficulties encountered in learning programming stem from the structure of programming as a learning task, individual traits, and many factors, including curriculum and teaching approaches as interactional setting variables. First, the need for pedagogical approach to teaching programming is emphasized, briefly introducing the teaching approaches used in programming. Teaching programming through metaphor is introduced as an alternative approach to teaching programming concepts. It explains metaphor as a concept, conceptual metaphor theory, and the use of metaphor in teaching programming concepts. Then, the need to reveal the pattern of the teaching process through in-depth qualitative studies is highlighted as a future research direction. Finally, it is argued that using metaphor is not limited to teaching of concepts, but can also improve thinking skills, differentiate teaching and support teachers' professional development.

DOI: 10.4018/979-8-3693-4542-9.ch012

INTRODUCTION

To educate digital citizens ready for today's societal transformation, countries are either designing Computer Science (CS) as a separate curriculum or integrating CS knowledge, skills and attitudes into their curricula. CS is an academic discipline that encompasses computing pedagogy (Passey, 2017) and forms the foundation of the computing (Webb et al., 2017). First introduced at the University of Cambridge in 1953 and opened as a department at Purdue University in 1962, CS is still discussed in the field of curriculum studies with its updated technologies and dynamic content (Forsström & Kaufmann, 2018; Fluck et al., 2016; Webb et al., 2017). Although programming has been equated with CS and has hindered curricular studies of the discipline (Denning et al., 1989), it as part of the CS curricula is an important on-going pedagogical debate in CS education due to widespread problems in learning it (Chao, 2016; Cheah, 2020).

Erümit and Berigel (2018) define programming as the design of strategies to solve a problem. Nouri et al. (2020) see programming as a way of creating, solving problems and implementing ideas in the digital world. Forsström and Kaufmann (2018) report that programming skills are becoming increasingly important for 21st century skills, and many countries are integrating programming into their curricula to provide students with skills such as problem solving and logical thinking. The literature shows that starting to teach programming at an early age is crucial for the development of programming skills and that early teaching of programming can prevent learning difficulties that may occur in later years (Fagerlund et al., 2021; Webb et al., 2017; Zurnacı & Turan, 2022). Teaching programming is mostly carried out with unplugged activities in preschool and with physical, block or text-based programming tools in middle and high school, but what and how pedagogical approaches should be is often lacking. As stated by Li et al. (2023), the search for effective teaching strategies for programming is needed to improve higher order thinking skills such as computational thinking, problem solving, creative thinking and critical thinking. In this context, learning programming concepts using metaphors as scaffolding can be seen as one of the effective ways to improve teaching programming. In fact, Pérez-Marín et al. (2018) also discuss teaching programming through metaphor as an alternative approach. The rationale for this can be found in Lakoff and Johnson's (1980) statement that "...human thought processes are largely metaphorical..." (p. 6). In addition, Dewi and Sørensen (2023) state that metaphors are related to higher order thinking skills and that by focusing teachers and students on the cognitive potential of metaphors, both higher order thinking skills and student learning can be improved.

BACKGROUND

There may be many factors that prevent students from learning programming. In the literature, the abstract concepts and processes of programming (Funcke, 2014; Luxton-Reilly, 2016; Robins, 2019) and programming language syntax (Santos et al., 2020), students' higher-order thinking skills (Çakır, 2019; Li et al, 2023); teachers' competencies in teaching programming (Pérez-Marín et al., 2020; Qian & Lehman, 2017; Sarpong et al., 2013); and attempts to teach complex programming languages with traditional teaching methods (Cheah, 2020; Gaspar & Langevin, 2007) influence programming learning. Given this evidence, it is thought that *learning task*, *individual traits*, and *interactional setting variables* should be focused on for effective programming instruction.

Programming, one of the *learning task* variables, is a skill that involves abstract concepts. A concept is used to define a concrete entity or model an abstract object (Wang, 2010), and learning it requires recognising categories and new examples of these categories (Sammut, 2010), categorising stimuli into specific categories, and creating information in the mind (Ülgen, 2004). Therefore, learning programming concepts requires cognitive activities such as recognising the features of the relevant concept, distinguishing it from similar ones, and grouping them with appropriate criteria and logical thinking. For students who are new to programming, learning programming concepts and concept sets simultaneously requires intensive cognitive processes (Funcke, 2014; Shuhidan, 2012). Students' difficulty in learning programming concepts prevents them from creating programs that can effectively solve real-life problems (Rudder et al., 2007). The findings in the literature that students have difficulty in understanding the difficult and abstract concepts of programming (Cheah, 2020) and the syntax of programming languages (Bosse & Gerosa, 2017; Leinonen et al., 2019) show that the conditions related to concept learning should be considered in teaching programming.

Difficulties in learning programming stemming from *individual traits* can be related to cognitive and affective domains. For example, inadequacy of students' self-efficacy skills (Tsai, 2019), and their negative attitudes (Cheah, 2020; Robins, 2019) to learning programming can be accepted as affective difficulties. Students who have problems learning the basic concepts of programming and solving given programming problems may develop negative attitudes towards programming over time. Especially at the beginning of CS courses, students begin to show negative attitudes towards programming, which could lead to a decrease in success (Luxton-Reilly, 2016). During programming, students encounter many frustrating events ranging from syntax errors to misunderstood features of the programming language (Drosos et al., 2017), which hinders their intrinsic motivation to continue learning (Qian & Lehman, 2017; Robins, 2019). For cognitive difficulties, misconceptions can be given as an example. According to Qian & Lehman (2017), misconceptions about syntactic, conceptual and strategic knowledge can occur in the process of learning programming. In addition, students' lack of high-level thinking skills makes it difficult for them to solve complex programming problems (Chetty & Barlow-Jones, 2014). Problem solving, whether defined as a component of computational thinking or metacognitive thinking, is closely related to programming. Furthermore, trying to realise learning about programming concepts and processes without identifying students' prior knowledge (Bosse & Gerosa, 2017; Cheah, 2020) learning deficits or focusing on their existing misconceptions about the concepts or processes to be learned can be seen as another difficulty related to the cognitive domain. Therefore, it can be argued that students should be empowered in terms of the affective and cognitive domains in learning programming processes.

The most important variable in the *interactional setting* is undoubtedly the teacher factor. In order to estimate the interactional setting in the most effective way, teachers are expected to plan their teaching process effectively (Humble, 2019). The planning can take into account the prior knowledge about programming concepts that students bring to the learning situation about the new learning task (Shrestha et al., 2020). In the learning situations, positive learning experiences can be provided with more student-centred, active learning approaches (Cheah, 2020; Papadakis & Orfanakis, 2017) and effective feedback strategies (Drosos et al., 2017; Koulouri et al., 2014). For example, according to Mohorovicic & Strcic (2011), it is important to choose appropriate teaching strategies that enable students to develop positive attitudes towards programming. In this way, positive and sufficient conditions can be created in the learning of programming.

To overcome the difficulties arising from the *learning task*, *individual traits* and *interactional setting* variables in teaching programming, it may be useful to examine the teaching approaches used in the interactional setting. Kert (2018) introduces the approaches used in teaching programming as learner-oriented and tool-oriented approaches. Learner-oriented approaches are based on students' programming skills, while tool-oriented approaches focus on teaching the tool or programming language used in the teaching process. In addition, the use of artificial intelligence tools in teaching programming has increased in recent years. Examples of learner-centred approaches used in teaching programming include gamification, digital storytelling, interdisciplinary approach, pair programming, differentiated instruction, project and inquiry-based instruction and blended learning; while block, text, physical, and unplugged approaches are examples of tool-oriented approaches.In this section, the authors argue that teaching programming through metaphors can be used in combination with both learner-oriented and tool-oriented approaches, and that regardless of the approach employed, the use of metaphors can contribute to the learning task, individual traits, and interactional setting variables in teaching programming.

As a learner-centred approach, gamification increases extrinsic and intrinsic motivation and engages the learners in learning situations (Manzano-León et al., 2021; Rodrigues et al., 2021). However, despite the popularity and increasing interest in gamification (Pfeiffer et al., 2020; Zhan et al., 2022), the expected results have not yet been achieved in teaching programming (Lindberg et al., 2019; Shahid et al., 2019). Digital storytelling encourages the development of digital literacy and language skills, as well as reflective thinking, emotional intelligence (de Jager et al., 2017), and creative thinking and writing skills (Yıldız Durak, 2018), thus ensuring active participation. Similarly, project-based teaching allows students to actively and directly participate in the teaching process (Çelik et al., 2018) and can bridge the gap between learning abstract knowledge and applying that knowledge to authentic programming tasks (Peng et al., 2017). In fact, when used in combination with peer assessment, it can be a solution to the problem of failure among students who are new to programming (Sobral, 2021). An interdisciplinary approach can offer much more than teaching a concept, principle, or teaching programming in practice (Hubálovský, 2012). In the inquiry-based environment, when students are guided in self-directed research on a topic (Lazonder et al., 2016), their discovery and learning processes are supported (Vanicek, 2015). Pair programming is known to be effective in increasing attitudes, success and programming self-efficacy when learning programming (Campe et al., 2020; Dongo et al., 2016; Wei et al., 2021) and is preferred over individual programming approaches (Celepkolu & Boyer, 2018). In flipped learning, students take responsibility for learning by controlling their own learning process (Lin & Hwang, 2019) and develop skills such as critical thinking, creativity, communication and collaboration (Chis et al., 2018; Wang et al., 2017). Blended learning combines different aspects of strategies used to teach programming, providing flexibility for students and contributing to teacher performance (Dangwal, 2017; Djenic & Mitic, 2017; Smith & Hill, 2019; Alammary, 2019; Lazarinis et al., 2019). Finally, differences in students' prior knowledge or programming skills make learning challenging (Gil Fonseca et al., 2018). Although the use of differentiated instruction in teaching programming is quite limited in the literature (e.g. Geçitli & Bümen, 2020; Gibbs & Beamish, 2020), it can be said that many teaching techniques used in differentiated instruction (e.g. station, graded activity, story-based learning) can be a solution to programming learning difficulties.

One of the tool-oriented approaches is block-based programming, which is particularly popular with beginners (Lin & Weintrop, 2021), supporting the view that programming can be learned by anyone (Bau et al., 2017). Block-based programming is based on the metaphor of puzzles that provide users with visual clues about how and where commands can be used, likening writing programs to dragging and dropping instructions (Weintrop & Wilensky, 2017; Weintrop, 2019). The aim is to allow students and teachers to focus on algorithms rather than struggling with syntax, thus enabling students to learn faster by eliminating syntax problems (Mladenović et al., 2018). Unlike the block-based approach to programming, text-based programming supports learning the syntax of the programming language. While learning text-based programming, students can use the prior knowledge learned in the block-based approach and develop programs like those of professional programmers (Sentance & Waite, 2017; Weintrop & Wilensky, 2017). Mladenović et al. (2018) also mention that text-based mini-languages, despite their simplicity, may not be suitable for K-12 level students. Beginners' interest in programming has shifted from block-based programming to physical programming with the development of physical technologies (Morrison et al., 2019). Robots, smart objects, do-it-yourself kits, virtual robot programming environments, and robot programming languages are widely used in physical programming education (Numanoğlu & Keser, 2017). Programming concepts are taught by providing students with educational content in a game format through programming robots (Shim et al., 2016). Concrete objects such as robots attract attention as they make the programming course practical and less abstract (Serrano Pérez & Juárez López, 2019). Teaching programming with robots used for educational purposes is based on constructivist theory and is used in STEM applications with an interdisciplinary approach (Merkouris et al., 2017). Unplugged programming, as a pedagogical approach to introduce students to CS without having to involve computers (Bell & Vahrenhold 2018), provides the use of many innovative applications for different age groups and learning through discovery (Kalelioğlu, 2020). It is reported to have positive effects especially for beginners in CS education at primary and secondary school levels (del Olmo-Muñoz et al., 2020). Games, presented as magic tricks and puzzles, provide opportunities to practice the kind of thinking that computer scientists deal with (Munasinghe et al., 2023). Finally, according to Denny et al. (2024), AI teaching assistants can be helpful in providing comprehensive and high-quality feedback in programming education. Zhu and Van Brummelen (2021) found that conversational AI tools contribute to students' learning of programming, and they have knowledge about how artificial intelligence works. In this context, considering the variety of artificial intelligence tools that can be used in programming education and the need to determine the pedagogically effective and efficient ones among these tools, it can be said that teachers should act meticulously and carefully.

Although there is interest in how to teach programming, it is also suggested that a complete consensus should not be expected considering the variables of individual traits, learning task and interactional setting. Research on teaching programming tends to focus on instructional tools, and pedagogical research remains limited, as some authors (Erümit et al., 2019; Popat & Starkey 2019) have pointed out. However, pedagogical research can help CS teachers make difficult programming concepts more understandable and contribute to the development of students' higher-order thinking skills. As part of the emerging pedagogical research to overcome the difficulties in learning programming (Cao et al., 2016; Harper et al., 2024; Moape et al., 2018), it can be said that the use of metaphors in learning programming can be an effective pedagogical approach.

USING METAPHOR AS A TEACHING APPROACH

The literature on the use of metaphor as an effective pedagogical approach in teaching programming provides stakeholders with a limited perspective on how to conduct a metaphor-based teaching process. In this section, after introducing the concept of metaphor and the conceptual metaphor theory, some implications for the use of metaphor in an educational situation, especially in teaching programming concepts, are presented with reference to the existing literature.

The Concept of Metaphor

Metaphor comes from the Greek word metapherein ("meta" to change, "pherein" to carry) (Levine, 2005). Metaphors give form to an abstract concept by allowing us to understand it in concrete and familiar terms (Morgan, 2006). They carry explanatory structures from one familiar domain of experience to another that needs to be understood or reconstructed, and they structure our perceptions and understanding of reality (Kövecses, 2005, 2010; Lakoff & Johnson, 1999). Metaphors require seeing similarities between domains, carrying the meaning far beyond any structural similarity (Krippendorff, 1993). They connect abstract and difficult-to-understand expressions with recognisable ones. According to Lakoff and Johnson (1980), it is not only related to language, but is also quite common in thought and action.

In analysing the concept of metaphor, it may also be helpful to review the concepts of analogy, metonymy, synecdoche and personification. According to Gentner et al. (1987) "…an analogy is a mapping of knowledge from one domain (the base) into another (the target) which conveys that a system of relations that holds among the base objects also holds among the target objects." Two situations share a common pattern of relationship model, even if they are different, the relationship between these two situations can be generally said analogous (Gray & Holyoak, 2021). While metaphors involve more cultural and personal experience, analogies involve less personal experience. For example, when a group is asked to create a metaphor about the concept of peace, if they mostly say 'white dove', this may be an example of analogy formation (Özelmacı & Çakır, 2019). In addition, "both metaphors and analogies serve as devices to express comparison, facilitating understanding through relational thinking" (Harper et al. 2024, p. 464). Metonymy is "a cognitive process in which one conceptual entity, the vehicle, provides mental access to another conceptual entity, the target, within the same idealized cognitive model." (Radden & Kövecses, 1999, p. 21). Lakoff and Johnson (1980) explain, "Like metaphors, metonymic concepts structure not just our language but our thoughts, attitudes and actions" (p. 40). In synecdoche, the category is taken into account when defining the relations, whereas in metonymy, the transfer of the entity is in question (Seto, 1999). Kövecses (2002) claims that one of the best source domains is the human being itself. Hence, personification as an ontological metaphor allows us to understand the diversity of experiences with nonhuman entities for human motivations, characteristics, and activities (Lakoff & Johnson, 1980). A number of theories have been developed in order to define the relationship between metaphor and concepts such as analogy, metonymy, synecdoche and personification. Among these theories, the conceptual metaphor theory of Lakoff and Johnson (1980) is one of the most well known ones in the literature.

The Conceptual Metaphor Theory

According to Parsons (2018), until the conceptual metaphor theory was defined by Lakoff and Johnson, the common view of metaphor was that it was a linguistic tool and had no fundamental importance for cognition. George Lakoff and Mark Johnson put forward the conceptual metaphor theory in their work *Metaphors We Live by* published in 1980 and defined metaphor as a fundamental aspect of thought and the basis of abstract thinking. They argued that understanding metaphor as a rhetorical tool is a matter of cognition, not language (Ruiz de Mendoza Ibáñez, & Pérez Hernández, 2011; Parsons, 2018). The impact of metaphor on language and cognition has led to the emergence of classical and contemporary metaphorical approaches, with classical metaphorical theory being accepted as a poetic expression in which one or more words are used to express a similar concept outside their traditional meaning, as if it had been forgotten for years that it was a theory (Lakoff, 1993). Lakoff and Johnson's (1980) work on cognitive metaphor, known as conceptual metaphor theory, was renamed contemporary metaphor theory in the following decade (Ruiz de Mendoza Ibáñez, & Pérez Hernández, 2011). According to Lakoff and Johnson (1980), the generalisations that govern metaphors in language are in thought, and in the contemporary understanding of metaphor, the word metaphor means a match between domains in the conceptual system. Lakoff and Johnson (1980) summarise their view of metaphor as follows:

Metaphor is for most people a device of the poetic imagination and the rhetorical flourish... Metaphor is typically viewed as characteristic of language alone, a matter of words rather than thought or action. ... Metaphor is pervasive in everyday life, not just in language but in thought and action. Our ordinary conceptual system, in terms of which we both think and act, is fundamentaly metaphorical in nature. (p. 4)

Lakoff and Johnson (1980) consider the division of metaphors into orientational, ontological and structural as artificial; they argue that all metaphors are structural in that all map structures to structures, ontological in that all create target domain entities, and most of them are orientational in that they map orientational image schemas.

Structural metaphors are metaphors in which a concept is expressed according to a different structure (Ruiz de Mendoza Ibáñez, & Pérez Hernández, 2011) and generally involve the use of a concept from one domain by an intellectual concept from another domain (Lakoff & Johnson, 1980). Structural metaphors provide a rich knowledge structure from the source domain to the target domain, allowing target B to be understood through the structure of source A (Kövecses, 2010). For example, war is an abstract concept that is often paired with target domains such as argument and love, and when we talk about war, we also talk about argument and love (Lakoff & Johnson, 1980). It is known that war is a very complex process involving planning, attacking, defending, counterattacking, fighting, winning, losing, ceasefire, etc., and unknown abstract concepts can be defined by talking about war (Li, 2010). Lakoff and Johnson (2015) note a culture in which arguments are not viewed in terms of war as "... Try to imagine a culture where arguments are not viewed in terms of war, where no one wins or loses, where there is no sense of attacking or defending, gaining or losing ground." (pp. 5-6).

Orientational metaphors organise a concept according to a whole conceptual system and most of them are related to spatial orientation (Lakoff & Johnson, 1980). While structural metaphors provide a richer structure about conceptual structures, orientational metaphors can provide more accessible data than conceptual metaphors because they are more restricted (Langston, 2002). For example, Lakoff and Johnson (1980) give the following example of orientational metaphors about the physical basis for personal well-being:

VIRTUE IS UP; DEPRAVITY IS DOWN

He is *high*-minded. She has *high* standards. She is *upright*. She is an *upstanding* citizen.

That was a *low* trick. Don't be *underhanded*. I wouldn't *stoop* to that. That would be *beneath* me. He *fell* into the *abyss* of depravity. That was a *low-down* thing to do (pp. 16-17)

Ontological metaphors help to describe experiences related to the environment and provide an additional basis that goes beyond the limited domain of orienting metaphors, beyond mere orientation, by allowing us to talk about, categorise and group physical objects or the actual matter that makes up the universe (Lakoff & Johnson, 1980). For example, statements such as "time is an entity", "I don't have enough time", or "Thank you for giving me time" are observable and allow time to be understood and its properties to be quantified (Barr et al., 2002). Lakoff and Johnson (1980) explain ontological metaphors with the following two examples:

THE MIND IS A MACHINE

We're still trying to *grind out* the solution to this equation. My mind just isn't *operating* today.

Boy, the *wheels* are *turning* now!

I'm a *little rusty* today.

We've been working on this problem all day and now we' re *running out of steam* (p. 27).

THE MIND IS A BRITTLE OBJECT

Her ego is very *fragile*.

You have to *handle him with care* since his wife' s death. He *broke* under cross-examination.

She is *easily crushed*.

The experience *shattered* him.

I'm going to *pieces*.

His mind *snapped* (p. 28).

Following the contemporary metaphor theory, metaphors, which have been shown to be related not only to language but also to thought and action, have begun to be also used in the teaching of difficult-to-learn and abstract concepts in literature, science, social science and education. In education, for example, they are utilised to find an attractive and memorable label for difficult concepts, to understand abstract and complex concepts, and to extend existing thinking about the concept (Ahlgren et al., 2021; Low, 2008).

Metaphor can help students by examining the characteristics of a concept that is difficult to conceptualise in terms of another, more accessible and familiar concept in their prior knowledge. Shuell (1990) explains the power of metaphor in teaching concepts by saying: "If a picture is worth 1000 words, a metaphor is worth 1000 pictures! For a picture provides only a static image while a metaphor provides a conceptual framework for thinking about something." (p. 102). Therefore, the use of metaphor in teaching can be an effective scaffolding for cognitive processes. As Harper et al. (2024) suggested, "Rooted deeply within our cognitive structures, conceptual metaphors serve as scaffolds, guiding our comprehension of one domain by mapping it onto another." (p. 464). Thus, metaphor is not only a matter of language, but can also improve students' learning and their cognitive skills (Dewi & Sørensen, 2023; Low, 2008; Pérez-Marín et al., 2020). As a result, metaphor has been increasingly used as a cognitive tool in teaching programming in recent years.

Using Metaphor in Programming Instruction

With regard to the interactional setting variable, one of the most important factors that makes learning programming difficult is undoubtedly the teaching of programming. The use of metaphor in teaching can contribute to the search for solutions to problems related to learning programming, which are also discussed in the literature (Cao et al., 2016; Moape et al., 2018; Pérez-Marín et al., 2020; Pérez-Marín et al., 2018; Zhang et al., 2024). For example, Zhang et al. (2024) showed that a metaphor-based robot programming approach can facilitate childrens's superior learning performance and more positive learning behaviours to help them achieve their learning objectives.

When teaching programming concepts, teachers can use metaphors by drawing on their experience. For example, the concept of *function* can be structurally related to the concept of function in mathematics. The concept of a function, in terms of being able to be called from anywhere in a program, processing the values it contains and producing results, can be linked to the concept of a *factory*, which is assumed to exist in students' prior knowledge, and can be treated as *Functions are factories*. In fact, the factory metaphor is one of the first metaphorical examples that teachers think of and it is a stereotypical metaphor. In terms of this function, it can be explained by analogy under the umbrella of metaphor. The metaphors that can be used to teach the concept of function are not limited to the factory. Assuming that metaphor is defined by relations between source and target domains, various metaphors can be produced from unlimited source domains in everyday life for the concept of function in the target domain of programming. Payphones, which have been widely used in the past, contain many features of the function concept of programming, such as the tokens they contain, the talk time they produce according to the size of the token, and the ability to make direct calls without requiring a token for emergencies when necessary. With these features, the metaphor *Functions are payphones* can be developed by making the abstract concept of function easier to understand. As in the example given, in concept teaching, the source domain should cover all the features of the target domain. Otherwise, the limitations of the source domain may lead to limited learning of the concept or misconceptions.

Inappropriate selection of the source and target domain of the metaphor or failure to properly emphasise the relationship between them can lead to misconceptions. Funcke (2014) mentions that metaphors used inappropriately in teaching can damage the model constructed in the mind. Therefore, misconceptions should be considered when using metaphors in programming education. For example, Hermans et al. (2018) state that the commonly used box metaphor for the concept of *variable* is effective in teaching, but can lead to misconceptions. The concept of variable in programming can be explained by the fact that it can take different values in different parts of the program. The *box* metaphor is explained by the fact that the things you put in it will be taken out over time and replaced by something else. The misconception of this metaphor may be due to several reasons. Variables in a program can take the same or different types of data. If the teacher uses the box metaphor in the lesson, the objects placed in the box may find different responses in the minds of the students. This situation may lead to the schema covering the properties of the variable concept being formed differently than expected. Therefore, when using metaphors, teachers should carefully consider the properties of the concept in the target domain and define metaphors appropriately to prevent limited or mislearning that may occur later. In addition, to avoid misconceptions, it may be useful to support the metaphors planned to be used with experiences related to the target domain. For example, after introducing the metaphor of a box to students, they can be asked to write a program to find out how many boxes of different sizes, are needed to transport someone, so that the same or different types of items can be transported together. Students can be expected to make connections between the box metaphor and the program they have prepared. In this way, supporting the comprehensive features of the target concept with activities can contribute to the formation of a deeper network of meaning and concept development. In these processes, the fact that metaphors can carry different meanings together should be taken into account, the metaphors to be used in teaching should be carefully selected and the selected metaphors should be determined based on a certain theory.

Conceptual metaphor theory requires that the relationships between the source and target domains should be revealed in the metaphors developed. In Figure 1, the structural features of the concept of *loop* are associated with the *bear's hibernation* by considering the target and source domains defined in the theory. The first day the bear *fell asleep* was associated with the concept of *initialization*, *each day* the bear slept was associated with the concept of *increment*, *having enough energy or not* was associated with the concept of *condition*, and the *awakening* of the bear from hibernation was associated with the concept of *exit* from the loop.

Figure 1. Source and target domain relationship of loop concepts in programming with bear hibernation

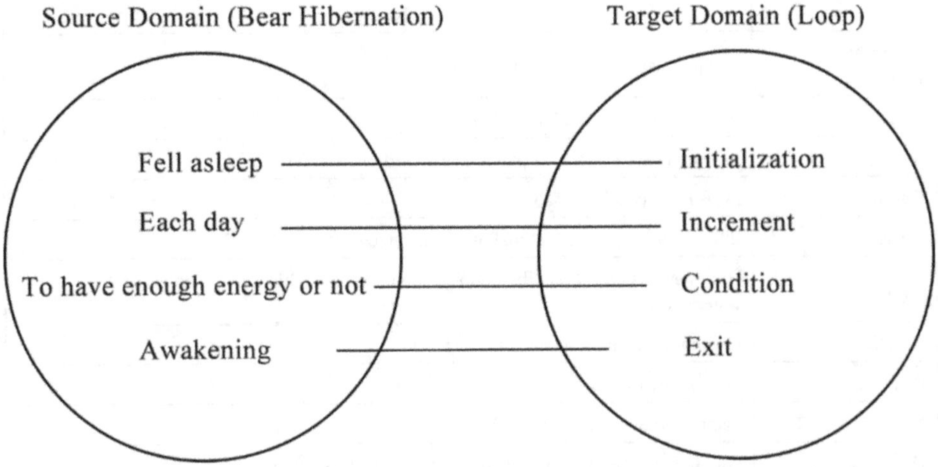

At the K-12 level, teachers can also collaborate with teachers of other courses to identify the source domain. They can discuss the characteristics of concepts or meanings of words in different subject-matter content. For example, the scientific characteristics of the *term mouth* of the digestive system in science courses can be analysed with science teachers, and the use of the *word mouth* in language and culture in language courses can be analysed with language teachers. In the science course, the mouth is seen as an organ of the digestive system and as the beginning of digestion, while in Turkish, the mouth can sometimes mean a place to *exit* or *enter* as a compound word with the word *doorway* (in Turkish word *kapı ağzı*). Therefore, the metaphor of *input is the doorway* can be developed to teach the concepts of *input* and *output* from programming concepts. Interdisciplinary work of teachers in this way can contribute to analysing the concepts that can be selected from the source domain of different disciplines, establishing interdisciplinary connections through language, increasing the interaction of teachers and thus supporting their professional development. Furthermore, making linguistic connections of concepts from different disciplines can facilitate the transfer of knowledge for students. In terms of curriculum studies, it can also support horizontal articulation.

Metaphors can be predetermined in order to avoid misconceptions, enable students to think deeply about concepts and metaphors, and plan activities. To give readers an idea, examples of metaphors that can be used when teaching programming concepts in the literature (Hermans et al., 2018; Pérez-Marín et al., 2018, 2020) and the authors' experiences are given in Table 1. However, the examples of metaphors to be used in teaching programming concepts given in the table are not limited to them.

Table 1. Some Examples of Metaphors that can be used in Teaching Programming Concepts

Concept	Metaphor
Algorithm, flowchart	Recipe, map, game rules, installation guide
Variable	Box, ice cream bowl, labelled jars
Input	Ingredients (*e.g.*, cake or pastry), keyboard, mouth, form filling
Output	PC screen, cake or pastry
Decision	Intelligent fridge, student making decision, crossroads
Loop	Hibernation (*e.g.*, Bear hibernation), you laying the table for X people, hand mixer, water cycle
Function	Payphones, factory, ice cream machine
Parameter	Token, raw material
Memory	Pantry, storage, warehouse, library
File processing	Population registry book, classroom files, library systems

These metaphor examples can be used by reviewing them in terms of the characteristics of the target concept. Teachers can avoid misconceptions by considering the scope and nature of the concept to be taught. CS teachers can identify the characteristics of the metaphors in this domain, having identified the source domain for teaching programming concepts during their preparation for teaching through metaphors. In this way, they can avoid possible misconceptions by considering the scope and nature of the concept to be learned. In addition, they can prepare teaching materials that show the relationships between the source domain and the target domain. In their teaching processes, they can ask their students to prepare concept maps related to the source domain and help them to discover their prior knowledge. They can support the materials they prepare with scenarios by taking into account the grade level and the different levels of the students. In this way, they can reveal their students' experience of the source domain. They can enrich their explanations with positive and negative examples by carrying out their teaching processes through concept development processes. In addition, teachers can support their teaching skills with gestures (Hostetter & Alibali, 2008; Larsson and Stolpe, 2023, 2024; Manches, et al., 2020) related to the concepts of the target domain.

In the Figure 2, based on conceptual metaphor theory, some suggestions for CS teachers who will teach programming concepts are shown in relation to the variables of *learning task*, *individual traits* and *interactional settings*.

Figure 2. Some suggestions for using metaphor in teaching programming for CS teachers

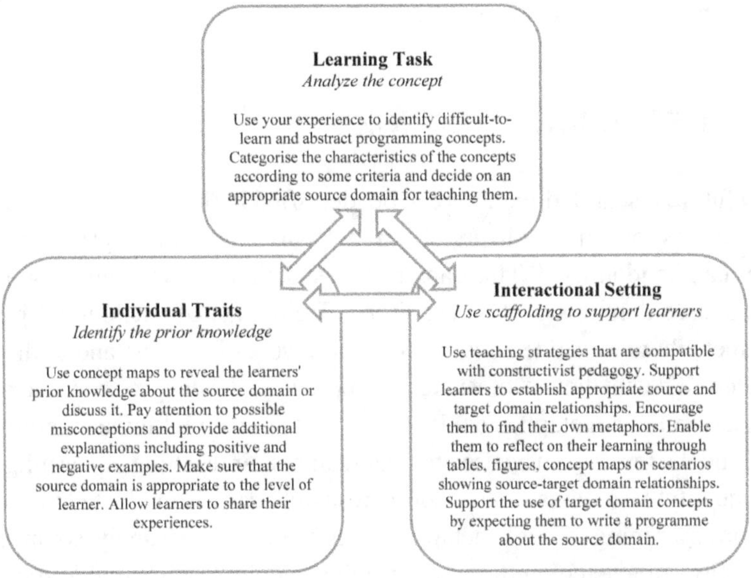

When teaching programming concepts and processes, CS teachers should be careful that the metaphors they pre-determine or create in the classroom facilitate learning of the programming concepts, are appropriate for the purpose, and do not create misconceptions in students. Metaphors that create misconceptions in students may cause difficulties in developing products that require students to use higher order thinking skills, leading to negative attitudes towards the course and early withdrawal from the course. It is important for teachers to decide which metaphors to use when planning programming activities, and to think broadly about the concept that corresponds to the programming field. When deciding on metaphors, it is possible to use those whose effects have been previously analysed in the literature. However, determining metaphors by taking into account the differences of students in each class can facilitate students' understanding of concepts. Since students' experiences with the source domain may be different, the teacher should think about the possible effects of the metaphors to be used in class and carefully examine how the concepts are perceived.

When preparing metaphor-based lesson plans, it is important to make use of source domains from daily life to establish appropriate source-target domain relationships. These domains for metaphor are not limited to the metaphor set by the teacher, and supporting students to develop their own metaphors can make it easier for them to see source-target domain relationships. Due to the positive contribution of metaphor-based teaching to students' concept acquisition and students' digital product development processes, it can raise students' expectations of teaching environments to a higher level, and these expectations can be taken into account in the development of CS course teaching plans.

FUTURE RESEARCH DIRECTIONS

Many future research directions can be identified in this section. The metaphors used by teachers and students in programming courses or found in printed and digital resources can be identified. This can provide stakeholders with an insight into the potential source domains of the metaphors. The impact of teaching programming through metaphors on students with different levels of interest and ability can be investigated. The influence of stakeholders' cultural backgrounds and personal experiences on their metaphorical language and conceptual understanding can be analysed and the results can be used to understand their teaching or learning actions. In-depth qualitative studies such as action research, can be conducted to reveal how learning programming through metaphor takes place. Content analysis can reveal the pattern or flow of a teaching through metaphor. Findings can provide stakeholders with a perspective on how the CS curriculum is planned, implemented and evaluated.

CONCLUSION

The aim of this chapter is to provide CS stakeholders, and in particular CS teachers, with a perspective on teaching programming through metaphors. The chapter highlights that the difficulties in learning programming arise from the nature of programming as a *learning task*, *individual trait* variables such as attitudes, self-efficacy, self-regulation, prior knowledge, and many factors such as curriculum, teaching approaches, and teacher competence as *interactional setting* variables. Considering these variables in teaching programming concepts may support Qian et al. (2018) in that an effective CS teacher should have both subject-matter content knowledge and pedagogical content knowledge. That is, in relation to the *learning task* variable, teachers' analysis of programming concepts may help them to monitor their subject-matter content knowledge. In relation to the *individual* variable, teachers' identification of students' prior knowledge and their efforts to establish a relationship between source and target domains by choosing appropriate metaphors can help them to get to know their students. With regard to the *interactional setting variable*, the use of metaphors as cognitive scaffolds can raise awareness of the need to develop their teaching methods to CS teachers. Thus, it can contribute to both the subject-matter content knowledge and the pedagogical competence of CS teachers.

Consequently, the use of metaphors that are derived from a particular theoretical framework and aligned with the intended objective can be accepted as an effective cognitive tool to facilitate the teaching of complicated and abstract concepts pertaining to programming. Metaphors can encourage students to use programming concepts in problem solving by making programming more fun and easy, and can prevent students from developing negative attitudes towards programming courses and dropping out of the course early. Furthermore, the use of metaphors in teaching programming can help to improve of students' programming skills and higher order cognitive skills such as computational thinking, algorithmic thinking and problem solving, which are closely related to programming.

NOTE

This chapter is derived from the first author's Ph.D. dissertation, entitled "Effects of Using Metaphors in Text-Based Programming Instruction: A Mixed Method Study", supervised by the second author.

REFERENCES

Ahlgren, K., Golden, A., & Magnusson, U. (2021). Metaphor in education: A multilingual and Scandinavian perspective. *Metaphor and the Social World*, 11(2), 196–211. DOI: 10.1075/msw.00015.ahl

Alammary, A. (2019). Blended learning models for introductory programming courses: A systematic review. *PLoS One*, 14(9), 1–26. DOI: 10.1371/journal.pone.0221765 PMID: 31487316

Barr, P., Biddle, R., & Noble, J. (2002). A taxonomy of user-interface metaphors. In Jones, S., & Masoodian, M. (Eds.), *Proceedings of the SIGCHI-NZ Symposium on Computer-Human Interaction* (pp.25-30). Association for Computing Machinery. DOI: 10.1145/2181216.2181221

Bau, D., Gray, J., Kelleher, C., Sheldon, J., & Turbak, F. (2017). Learnable programming: Blocks and beyond. *Communications of the ACM*, 60(6), 72–80. DOI: 10.1145/3015455

Bell, T., & Vahrenhold, J. (2018). CS Unplugged-How is it used, and does it work? In Böckenhauer, H. J., Komm, D., & Unger, W. (Eds.), Lecture Notes in Computer Science: Vol. 11011. *Adventures Between Lower Bounds and Higher Altitudes*. Springer., DOI: 10.1007/978-3-319-98355-4_29

Bosse, Y., & Gerosa, M. A. (2017). Difficulties of programming learning from the point of view of students and instructors. *IEEE Latin America Transactions*, 15(11), 2191–2199. DOI: 10.1109/TLA.2017.8070426

Çakır, R. (2019). Programlama öğretimi ve düşünme becerileri. In Korkmaz, Ö. (Ed.), *Programlama öğretimi yaklaşımları* (pp. 15–36). Nobel Akademik.

Campe, S., Denner, J., Green, E., & Torres, D. (2020). Pair programming in middle school: Variations in interactions and behaviors. *Computer Science Education*, 30(1), 22–46. DOI: 10.1080/08993408.2019.1648119

Cao, Y., Porter, L., & Zingaro, D. (2016). Examining the value of analogies in introductory computing. In *Proceedings of the 2016 ACM Conference on International Computing Education Research* (pp. 231-239). ACM. DOI: 10.1145/2960310.2960313

Celepkolu, M., & Boyer, K. E. (2018). Thematic analysis of students' reflections on pair programming in cs1. In *49th ACM Technical Symposium on Computer Science Education* (pp.771-776). Association for Computing Machinery. DOI: 10.1145/3159450.3159516

Çelik, H. C., Ertas, H., & İlhan, A. (2018). The impact of project-based learning on achievement and student views: The case of AutoCAD programming course. *Journal of Education and Learning*, 7(6), 67–80. DOI: 10.5539/jel.v7n6p67

Chao, P. Y. (2016). Exploring students' computational practice, design and performance of problem-solving through a visual programming environment. *Computers & Education*, 95, 202–215. DOI: 10.1016/j.compedu.2016.01.010

Cheah, C. S. (2020). Factors Contributing to the Difficulties in Teaching and Learning of Computer Programming: A Literature Review. *Contemporary Educational Technology*, 12(2), 1–14. DOI: 10.30935/cedtech/8247

Chetty, J., & Barlow-Jones, G. (2014). Novice students and computer programming: Toward constructivist pedagogy. *Mediterranean Journal of Social Sciences*, 5(14), 240–251. DOI: 10.5901/mjss.2014.v5n14p240

Chis, A. E., Moldovan, A. N., Murphy, L., Pathak, P., & Muntean, C. H. (2018). Investigating flipped classroom and problem-based learning in a programming module for computing conversion course. *Journal of Educational Technology & Society*, 21(4), 232–247.

Dangwal, K. L. (2017). Blended learning: An innovative approach. *Universal Journal of Educational Research*, 5(1), 129–136. DOI: 10.13189/ujer.2017.050116

de Jager, A., Fogarty, A., Tewson, A., Lenette, C., & Boydell, K. M. (2017). Digital Storytelling in Research: A Systematic Review. *The Qualitative Report*, 22(10), 2548–2582. DOI: 10.46743/2160-3715/2017.2970

del Olmo-Muñoz, J., Cózar-Gutiérrez, R., & González-Calero, J. A. (2020). Computational thinking through unplugged activities in early years of primary education. *Computers & Education*, 150, 103832. DOI: 10.1016/j.compedu.2020.103832

Denning, P. J., Comer, D. E., Gries, D., Mulder, M. C., Tucker, A., Turner, A. J., & Young, P. R. (1989). Computing as a discipline. *Computer*, 22(2), 63–70. DOI: 10.1109/2.19833

Denny, P., MacNeil, S., Savelka, J., Porter, L., & Luxton-Reilly, A. (2024). Desirable characteristics for AI teaching assistants in programming education. In *Proceedings of the 2024 on Innovation and Technology in Computer Science Education (ITiCSE),* Vol. 1 (pp. 408–414). Association for Computing Machinery. DOI: 10.1145/3649217.3653574

Dewi, A. N., & Sørensen, B. (2023). Higher-order thinking skills and metaphor. *Southern Semiotic Review*, 18(ii), 1–35. DOI: 10.33234/SSR.18.1

Djenic, S., & Mitic, J. (2017). Teaching Strategies and Methods in Modern Environments for Learning of Programming. International Association for Development of the Information Society. Retrieved June 23, 2024 from https://files.eric.ed.gov/fulltext/ED579455.pdf

Dongo, T., Reed, A. H., & O'Hara, M. (2016). Exploring pair programming benefits for MIS majors. *Journal of Information Technology Education: Innovations in Practice*, 15, 223–239. DOI: 10.28945/3625

Drosos, I., Guo, P. J., & Parnin, C. (2017). HappyFace: Identifying and predicting frustrating obstacles for learning programming at scale. In *2017 IEEE Symposium on Visual Languages and Human-Centric Computing (VL/HCC)* (pp. 171-179). IEEE. DOI: 10.1109/VLHCC.2017.8103465

Erümit, A., & Berigel, M. (2018). Programlama dillerinin tarihi ve programlama öğretimi. In Gülbahar, Y., & Karal, H. (Eds.), *Kuramdan Uygulamaya Programlama Öğretimi* (pp. 1–36). Pegem Akademi.

Erümit, K. A., Karal, H., Şahin, G., Aksoy, D. A., Aksoy, A., & Benzer, A. İ. (2019). A model suggested for programming teaching: Programming in seven steps. *Education in Science*, 44(197), 155–183. DOI: 10.15390/EB.2018.7678

Fagerlund, J., Häkkinen, P., Vesisenaho, M., & Viiri, J. (2021). Computational thinking in programming with Scratch in primary schools: A systematic review. *Computer Applications in Engineering Education*, 29(1), 12–28. DOI: 10.1002/cae.22255

Fluck, A., Webb, M., Cox, M., Angeli, C., Malyn-Smith, J., Voogt, J., & Zagami, J. (2016). Arguing for computer science in the school curriculum. *Journal of Educational Technology & Society*, 19(3), 38–46.

Forsström, S., & Kaufmann, O. (2018). A literature review exploring the use of programming in mathematics education. *International Journal of Learning. Teaching and Educational Research.*, 17(12), 18–32. DOI: 10.26803/ijlter.17.12.2

Funcke, M. (2014). *Developing high-fidelity mental models of programming concepts using manipulatives and interactive metaphors.* [Doctoral dissertation, Rhodes University], Repository http://hdl.handle.net/10962/d1017929

Gaspar, A., & Langevin, S. (2007). Restoring coding with intention in introductory programming courses. In B. Sweeney & D. Feinstein (Eds.), *The 8th ACM SIGITE conference on information technology education*, (pp. 91-98). ASCM. DOI: 10.1145/1324302.1324323

Geçitli, E., & Bümen, N. (2020). Kademelendirilmiş etkinlik yoluyla metin tabanlı programlama öğretimi: İşbirlikli bir eylem araştırması. *Asya Öğretim Dergisi*, 8(2), 64–85. DOI: 10.47215/aji.791967

Gentner, D., Faikenhain, B., & Skorstad, J. (1987). Metaphor: The Good, The Bad and the Ugly. In *Proceedings of the 1987 workshop on Theoretical issues in natural language processing (TINLAP'87).* (pp. 176–180). Association for Computational Linguistics. DOI: 10.3115/980304.980345

Gibbs, K., & Beamish, W. (2020). Differentiated instruction: A programming tool for inclusion. In van Rensburg, H., & O'Neill, S. (Eds.), *Inclusive Theory and Practice in Special Education* (pp. 174–191). IGI Global., DOI: 10.4018/978-1-7998-2901-0.ch009

Gil Fonseca, N., Macedo, L., & Mendes, A. J. (2018). Supporting differentiated instruction in programming courses through permanent progress monitoring. In *Proceedings of the 49th ACM Technical Symposium on Computer Science Education* (pp. 209-214). ACM. DOI: 10.1145/3159450.3159578

Gray, M. E., & Holyoak, K. J. (2021). Teaching by analogy: From theory to practice. *Mind, Brain and Education : the Official Journal of the International Mind, Brain, and Education Society*, 15(3), 250–263. DOI: 10.1111/mbe.12288

Harper, C., Tran, K., & Cooper, S. (2024). Conceptual metaphor theory in action: Insights into student understanding of computing concepts. In *Proceedings of the 55th ACM Technical Symposium on Computer Science Education* (SIGCSE 2024) V. 1. (pp. 463–469). Association for Computing Machinery. DOI: 10.1145/3626252.3630812

Hermans, F., Swidan, A., Aivaloglou, E., & Smit, M. (2018). Thinking out of the box: comparing metaphors for variables in programming education. In A. Mühling ve Q. Cutts (Eds.), *Proceedings of the 13th workshop in primary and secondary computing* education (pp.1-8). ACM. DOI: 10.1145/3265757.3265765

Hostetter, A. B., & Alibali, M. W. (2008). Visible embodiment: Gestures as simulated action. *Psychonomic Bulletin & Review*, 15(3), 495–514. DOI: 10.3758/PBR.15.3.495 PMID: 18567247

Hubálovský, S. (2012). Research of methods of a multidisciplinary approach in the teaching of algorithm development and programming. In Cápay, M., Mesárošová, M., & Palmárová, V. (Eds.) *9th International Scientific Conference on Distance Learning in Applied Informatics-DIVAI* (pp. 147-156).

Humble, N., Mozelius, P., & Sällvin, L. (2019). Teacher chalenges and choice of programming tools for teaching k-12 technology and mathematics. In *International Conference on Education and New Developments (END 2019)*, (pp. 431-435). inScience Press. DOI: 10.36315/2019v1end099

Kalelioğlu, F. (2020). Bilgisayarsız bilgisayar bilimi öğretimi. In Gülbahar, Y. (Ed.), *Bilgi İşlemsel Düşünmeden Programlamaya* (pp. 183–206). Pegem Akademi.

Kert, B. S. (2018). Programlama öğretimi için pedagojik yaklaşımlar. In Gülbahar, Y., & Karal, H. (Eds.), *Kuramdan Uygulamaya Programlama Öğretimi* (pp. 37–65). Pegem Akademi.

Koulouri, T., Lauria, S., & Macredie, R. D. (2014). Teaching introductory programming: A quantitative evaluation of different approaches. [TOCE]. *ACM Transactions on Computing Education*, 14(4), 1–28. DOI: 10.1145/2662412

Kövecses, Z. (2002). Cognitive-linguistic comments on metaphor identification. *Language and Literature*, 11(1), 74–78. DOI: 10.1177/096394700201100107

Kövecses, Z. (2005). *Metaphor in culture: Universality and variation*. Oxford University Press. DOI: 10.1017/CBO9780511614408

Kövecses, Z. (2010). *Metaphor-A Practical Introduction*. Oxford University Press.

Krippendorff, K. (1993). Major metaphors of communication and some constructivist reflections on their use. *Cybernetics & Human Knowing*, 2(1), 3–25. Retrieved June 9, 2024, from https://repository.upenn.edu/server/api/core/bitstreams/defeb3a5-5162-4b0b-8026-a3bb09981e50/content

Lakoff, G. (1993). The contemporary theory of metaphor. In Ortony, A. (Ed.), *Metaphor and Thought* (pp. 202–251). Cambridge University Press. DOI: 10.1017/CBO9781139173865.013

Lakoff, G., & Johnson, M. (1980). *Metaphors we live by*. Chicago University Press.

Lakoff, G., & Johnson, M. (1999). *Philosophy in the flesh: The embodied mind and its chalenge to western thought*. Basic Books.

Langston, W. (2002). Violating orientational metaphors slows reading. *Discourse Processes*, 34(3), 281–310. DOI: 10.1207/S15326950DP3403_3

Larsson, A., & Stolpe, K. (2023). Hands on programming: Teachers' use of metaphors in gesture and speech make abstract concepts tangible. *International Journal of Technology and Design Education*, 32(3), 1–19. DOI: 10.1007/s10798-022-09755-0

Larsson, A., & Stolpe, K. (2024). Exploring the metaphoric nature of programming teachers' reflections on action-a case study with teaching in mind. *International Journal of Technology and Design Education*, 32(5), 1–18. DOI: 10.1007/s10798-023-09826-w

Lazarinis, F., Karachristos, C. V., Stavropoulos, E. C., & Verykios, V. S. (2019). A blended learning course for playfully teaching programming concepts to school teachers. *Education and Information Technologies*, 24(2), 1237–1249. DOI: 10.1007/s10639-018-9823-2

Lazonder, A. W., & Harmsen, R. (2016). Meta-analysis of inquiry-based learning: Effects of guidance. *Review of Educational Research*, 86(3), 681–718. DOI: 10.3102/0034654315627366

Leinonen, A., Nygren, H., Pirttinen, N., Hellas, A., & Leinonen, J. (2019). Exploring the applicability of simple syntax writing practice for learning programming. In *Proceedings of the 50th ACM Technical Symposium on Computer Science Education* (pp. 84-90). ACM. DOI: 10.1145/3287324.3287378

Levine, P. M. (2005). Metaphors and images of classrooms. *Kappa Delta Pi Record*, 41(4), 172–175. DOI: 10.1080/00228958.2005.10532066

Li, W., Huang, J. Y., Liu, C. Y., Tseng, J. C., & Wang, S. P. (2023). A study on the relationship between student' learning engagements and higher-order thinking skills in programming learning. *Thinking Skills and Creativity*, 49, 101369. DOI: 10.1016/j.tsc.2023.101369

Li, X. (2010). Conceptual metaphor theory and the teaching of English and Chinese idioms. *Journal of Language Teaching and Research*, 1(3), 206–210. https://doi.org/10.4304/jltr.1.3.206-210

Lin, , H. CHwang, , G. J. (2019). Research trends of flipped classroom studies for medical courses: A review of journal publications from 2008 to 2017 based on the technology-enhanced learning model. *Interactive Learning Environments*, 27(8), 1011–1027. DOI: 10.1080/10494820.2018.1467462

Lin, Y., & Weintrop, D. (2021). The landscape of Block-based programming: Characteristics of block-based environments and how they support the transition to text-based programming. *Journal of Computer Languages*, 67, 101075. DOI: 10.1016/j.cola.2021.101075

Lindberg, S. (2019). Gamification for self-directed learning in higher education. In *EDULEARN19 Proceedings* (pp. 1764-1773). IATED. DOI: 10.21125/edulearn.2019.0507

Low, G. (2008). Metaphor and education. In Gibbs, R. W. (Ed.), *The Cambridge handbook of metaphor and thought* (pp. 212–231). DOI: 10.1017/CBO9780511816802.014

Luxton-Reilly, A. (2016). Learning to program is easy. In *Proceedings of the 2016 ACM Conference on Innovation and Technology in Computer Science Education (ITiCSE '16)*. Association for Computing Machinery, USA, 284–289. DOI: 10.1145/2899415.2899432

Manches, A., McKenna, P. E., Rajendran, G., & Robertson, J. (2020). Identifying embodied metaphors for computing education. *Computers in Human Behavior*, 105(10585), 1–11. DOI: 10.1016/j.chb.2018.12.037

Manzano-León, A., Camacho-Lazarraga, P., Guerrero, M. A., Guerrero-Puerta, L., Aguilar-Parra, J. M., Trigueros, R., & Alias, A. (2021). Between level up and game over: A systematic literature review of gamification in education. *Sustainability (Basel)*, 13(4), 2247. DOI: 10.3390/su13042247

Merkouris, A., Chorianopoulos, K., & Kameas, A. (2017). Teaching programming in secondary education through embodied computing platforms: Robotics and wearables. [TOCE]. *ACM Transactions on Computing Education*, 17(2), 1–22. DOI: 10.1145/3025013

Mladenović, M., Boljat, I., & Žanko, Ž. (2018). Comparing loops misconceptions in block-based and text-based programming languages at the K-12 level. *Education and Information Technologies*, 23(4), 1483–1500. DOI: 10.1007/s10639-017-9673-3

Moape, T., Ojo, S., & Van Wyk, E. (2018). A metaphor-driven interactive multimedia simulation for teaching and learning of programming concepts. In P. Cunningham & M. Cunningham (Eds.), *2018 IST-Africa Week Conference* (p. 1-25). IEEE.

Mohorovicic, S., & Strcic, V. (2011). An overview of computer programming teaching methods. In *Proceedings of the 22nd Central European Conference on Information and Intelligent Systems* (pp. 47-52.). Faculty of Organization and Informatics Varazdin. Retrieved May 12, 2024, from https://www.proquest.com/conference-papers-proceedings/overview-computer-programming-teaching-methods/docview/1322999502/se-2?accountid=10699

Morgan, G. (2006). Images of Organization. *Sage (Atlanta, Ga.).*

Morrison, C., Villar, N., Hadwen-Bennett, A., Regan, T., Cletheroe, D., Thieme, A., & Sentance, S. (2019). Physical programming for blind and low vision children at scale. *Human-Computer Interaction*, 36(5-6), 535–569. DOI: 10.1080/07370024.2019.1621175

Munasinghe, B., Bell, T., & Robins, A. (2023). Unplugged activities as a catalyst when teaching introductory programming. *Journal of Pedagogical Research*, 7(2), 56–71. DOI: 10.33902/JPR.202318546

Nouri, J., Zhang, L., Mannila, L., & Norén, E. (2020). Development of computational thinking, digital competence and 21st century skills when learning programming in K-9. *Education Inquiry*, 11(1), 1–17. DOI: 10.1080/20004508.2019.1627844

Numanoğlu, M., & Keser, H. (2017). Programlama öğretiminde robot kullanımı-Mbot örneği. *Bartın Üniversitesi Eğitim Fakültesi Dergisi*, 6(2), 497–515. DOI: 10.14686/buefad.306198

Özelmacı, Ş., & Çakır, U. (2017). Metaforlar ve benzerlileri ile ilgili söylenenler. In Kılcan, B. (Ed.), *Metafor ve Eğitimde Metaforik Çalışmalar İçin Bir Uygulama Rehberi* (pp. 1–14). Pegem Akademi. DOI: 10.14527/9786052410806.02

Papadakis, S., & Orfanakis, V. (2017). The combined use of Lego Mindstorms NXT and App Inventor for teaching novice programmers. In Alimisis, D., Moro, M., & Menegatti, E. (Eds.), *Educational Robotics in the Makers Era. Edurobotics 2016 2016. Advances in Intelligent Systems and Computing* (Vol. 560). Springer., DOI: 10.1007/978-3-319-55553-9_15

Parsons, P. C. (2018). Conceptual metaphor theory as a foundation for communicative visualization design. In *IEEE VIS Workshop on Visualization for Communication* (VisComm 2018). Retrieved June 15, 2024, from https://www.dvclab.net/wp-content/uploads/2019/02/Parsons-Conceptual-Metaphor-Theory-as-a-Foundation-for-Com.pdf

Passey, D. (2017). Computer science (CS) in the compulsory education curriculum: Implications for future research. *Education and Information Technologies*, 22(2), 421–443. DOI: 10.1007/s10639-016-9475-z

Peng, J., Wang, M., & Sampson, D. (2017). Scaffolding project-based learning of computer programming in an online learning environment. In *2017 IEEE 17th International Conference on Advanced Learning Technologies (ICALT)* (pp. 315-319). IEEE. DOI: 10.1109/ICALT.2017.17

Pérez-Marín, D., Hijon-Neira, R., Bacelo, A., & Pizarro, C. (2020). Can computational thinking be improved by using a methodology based on metaphors and scratch to teach computer programming to children? *Computers in Human Behavior*, 105849, 1–10. DOI: 10.1016/j.chb.2018.12.027

Pérez-Marín, D., Hijón-Neira, R., & Martín-Lope, M. (2018). A methodology proposal based on metaphors to teach programming to children. *IEEE Revista Iberoamericana de Technologias del Aprendizaje*, 13(1), 46–53. DOI: 10.1109/RITA.2018.2809944

Pfeiffer, A., Bezzina, S., Koenig, N., & Kriglstein, S. (2020). Beyond classical gamification: In-and Around-Game gamification for education. In *Proceedings of the 19th European Conference on e-Learning ECEL 2020* (pp. 415-420). https://doi.org/DOI: 10.34190/EEL.20.007

Popat, S., & Starkey, L. (2019). Learning to code or coding to learn? A systematic review. *Computers & Education*, 128, 365–376. DOI: 10.1016/j.compedu.2018.10.005

Qian, Y., Hambrusch, S., Yadav, A., & Gretter, S. (2018). Who needs what: Recommendations for designing effective online professional development for computer science teachers. *Journal of Research on Technology in Education*, 50(2), 164–181. DOI: 10.1080/15391523.2018.1433565

Qian, Y., & Lehman, J. (2017). Students' misconceptions and other difficulties in introductory programming: A literature review. [TOCE]. *ACM Transactions on Computing Education*, 18(1), 1–24. DOI: 10.1145/3077618

Radden, G., & Kövecses, Z. (1999). Towards a theory of metonymy. In Panther, K.-U., & Radden, G. (Eds.), *Metonymy in Language and Thought* (pp. 17–59). John Benjamins., DOI: 10.1075/hcp.4.03rad

Robins, A. (2019). Novice programmers and introductory programming. *The Cambridge Handbook of Computing Education Research, Cambridge Handbooks in Psychology*, 327-376. Retrieved June 4, 2024, from https://www.otago.ac.nz/computer-science/otago706761.pdf

Rodrigues, L., Toda, A. M., Oliveira, W., Palomino, P. T., Avila-Santos, A. P., & Isotani, S. (2021, March). Gamification works, but how and to whom? an experimental study in the context of programming lessons. In *Proceedings of the 52nd ACM technical symposium on computer science education* (pp. 184-190). ACM. DOI: 10.1145/3408877.3432419

Rudder, A., Bernard, M., & Mohammed, S. (2007). Teaching programming using visualization. In *Proceedings of the Sixth IASTED International Conference on Web-Based Education* (pp. 487-492). ACTA Press. Retrieved June 16, 2024, from https://uwispace.sta.uwi.edu/server/api/core/bitstreams/cf1424a5-dc26-4204-a864-72c7bd3161ac/content

Ruiz de Mendoza Ibáñez, F. J., & Pérez Hernández, L. (2011). The Contemporary Theory of Metaphor: Myths, Developments and Challenges. *Metaphor and Symbol*, 26(3), 161–185. DOI: 10.1080/10926488.2011.583189

Sammut, C. (2010). Concept Learning. In Sammut, C., & Webb, G. I. (Eds.), *Encyclopedia of Machine Learning* (pp. 205–208). Springer. DOI: 10.1007/978-0-387-30164-8

Santos, S., Tedesco, P., Borba, M., & Brito, M. (2020). Innovative approaches in teaching programming: A systematic literature review. *InProceedings of the 12th International Conference on Computer Supported Education (CSEDU 2020).* Vol. 1, (pp. 205-214). Science and Technology Publications. DOI: 10.5220/0009190502050214

Sarpong, K. A. M., Arthur, J. K., & Amoako, P. Y. O. (2013). Causes of failure of students in computer programming courses: The teacher-learner perspective. *International Journal of Computer Applications*, 77(12), 27–32. DOI: 10.5120/13448-1311

Sentance, S., & Waite, J. (2017). PRIMM: Exploring pedagogical approaches for teaching text-based programming in school. Barendsen, E., & Hubwieser, P. (Eds.), In *Proceedings of the 12th Workshop on Primary and Secondary Computing* Education (pp.113-114), Association for Computing Machinery. DOI: 10.1145/3137065.3137084

Serrano Pérez, E., & Juárez López, F. (2019). An ultra-low cost line follower robot as educational tool for teaching programming and circuit's foundations. *Computer Applications in Engineering Education*, 27(2), 288–302. DOI: 10.1002/cae.22074

Seto, K. (1999). Distinguishing metonymy from synecdoche. In K. U. Panther ve G. Radden, (Eds.), *Metonymy in language and thought* (pp. 91-120). John Benjamins Publishing. DOI: 10.1075/hcp.4.06set

Shahid, M., Wajid, A., Haq, K. U., Saleem, I., & Shujja, A. H. (2019). A review of gamification for learning programming fundamental. In *2019 International Conference on Innovative Computing (ICIC)* (pp. 1-8). IEEE. DOI: 10.1109/ICIC48496.2019.8966685

Shim, J., Kwon, D., & Lee, W. (2016). The effects of a robot game environment on computer programming education for elementary school students. *IEEE Transactions on Education*, 60(2), 164–172. DOI: 10.1109/TE.2016.2622227

Shrestha, N., Botta, C., Barik, T., & Parnin, C. (2020). Here we go again: Why is it difficult for developers to learn another programming language? In *Proceedings of the ACM/IEEE 42nd International Conference on Software Engineering* (pp. 691-701). IEEE. DOI: 10.1145/3377811.3380352

Shuell, T. J. (1990). Teaching and learning as problem solving. *Theory into Practice*, 29(2), 102–108. DOI: 10.1080/00405849009543439

Shuhidan, S. M. (2012). *Probing the minds of novice programmers through guided learning* (Publication No. 9921861240001341) [Doctoral dissertation, RMIT University]. RMIT Research Repository. https://researchrepository.rmit.edu.au/esploro/outputs/doctoral/Probing-the-minds-of-novice-programmers/9921861240001341

Smith, K., & Hill, J. (2018). Defining the nature of blended learning through its depiction in current research. *Higher Education Research & Development*, 38(2), 383–397. DOI: 10.1080/07294360.2018.1517732

Sobral, S. R. (2021). Project based learning with peer assessment in an introductory programming course. *International Journal of Information and Education Technology (IJIET)*, 11(7), 337–341. DOI: 10.18178/ijiet.2021.11.7.1532

Tsai, C. Y. (2019). Improving students' understanding of basic programming concepts through visual programming language: The role of self-efficacy. *Computers in Human Behavior*, 95, 224–232. DOI: 10.1016/j.chb.2018.11.038

Ülgen, G. (2004). *Kavram Geliştirme: Kuramlar ve Uygulamalar* (3rd ed.). Pegema yayıncılık.

Vanicek, J. (2015). Programming in Scratch using inquiry-based approach. Brodnik, A., & Vahrenhold, J. (Eds.), In *International Conference on Informatics in Schools: Situation, Evolution, and Perspectives* (pp. 82-93). Springer. DOI: 10.1007/978-3-319-25396-1_8

Wang, X. M., Hwang, G. J., Liang, Z. Y., & Wang, H. Y. (2017). Enhancing students' computer programming performances, critical thinking awareness and attitudes towards programming: An online peer-assessment attempt. *Journal of Educational Technology & Society*, 20(4), 58–68.

Wang, Y. (2010). On concept algebra for computing with words (CWW). *International Journal of Semantic Computing*, 4(03), 331–356. DOI: 10.1142/S1793351X10001061

Webb, M., Davis, N., Bell, T., Katz, Y. J., Reynolds, N., Chambers, D. P., & Sysło, M. M. (2017). Computer science in K-12 school curricula of the 2lst century: Why, what and when? *Education and Information Technologies*, 22(2), 445–468. DOI: 10.1007/s10639-016-9493-x

Wei, X., Lin, L., Meng, N., Tan, W., Kong, S.-C., & Kinshuk, . (2021). The effectiveness of partial pair programming on elementary school students' computational thinking skills and self-efficacy. *Computers & Education*, 160, 104023. Advance online publication. DOI: 10.1016/j.compedu.2020.104023

Weintrop, D. (2019). Block-based programming in computer science education. *Communications of the ACM*, 62(8), 22–25. DOI: 10.1145/3341221

Weintrop, D., & Wilensky, U. (2017). Comparing block-based and text-based programming in high school computer science classrooms. [TOCE]. *ACM Transactions on Computing Education*, 18(1), 1–25. DOI: 10.1145/3089799

Yıldız Durak, H. (2018). Digital story design activities used for teaching programming effect on learning of programming concepts, programming self-efficacy, and participation and analysis of student experiences. *Journal of Computer Assisted Learning*, 34(6), 740–752. DOI: 10.1111/jcal.12281

Zhan, Z., Tong, Y., Lan, X., & Zhong, B. (2022). A systematic literature review of game-based learning in Artificial Intelligence education. *Interactive Learning Environments*, 32(3), 1137–1158. DOI: 10.1080/10494820.2022.2115077

Zhang, X., Chen, Y., & Hu, , LBao, , YTu, , Y-FHwang, , G. (2024). A metaphor-based robot programming approach to facilitating young children's computational thinking and positive learning behaviors. *Computers & Education*, (105039), 1–16. DOI: 10.1016/j.compedu.2024.105039

Zhu, J., & Van Brummelen, J. (2021). Teaching students about conversational ai using convo, a conversational programming agent. In *2021 IEEE Symposium on Visual Languages and Human-Centric Computing* (pp. 1-5). IEEE. DOI: 10.1109/VL/HCC51201.2021.9576290

Zurnacı, B., & Turan, Z. (2022). Türkiye'de okul öncesinde kodlama eğitimine ilişkin yapılan çalışmaların incelenmesi. *Kocaeli Üniversitesi Eğitim Dergisi*, 5(1), 258–286. DOI: 10.33400/kuje.1062803

Chapter 13
Tools and Resources for K-12 Computer Science Education

İsmail Tonbuloğlu
https://orcid.org/0000-0001-7059-9125
Marmara University, Turkey

ABSTRACT

K-12 computer science education utilizes a variety of tools and resources that make significant contributions. Tools such as unplugged computer science tools, block-based computer science tools, text-based computer science tools, physical computer science tools, robotic kits, artificial intelligence, etc. have an important place in K-12 computer science education. It is crucial to incorporate computer science instruction into the basic courses of K-12 students, as well as to incorporate these tools into the curriculum. Worldwide resources have a significant impact on the enrichment and dissemination of K-12 computer science education. The content and resources created by platforms like Computer Science Teachers Association (CSTA), International Society for Technology in Education (ISTE), National Centre for Computing Education (NCCE), etc. contribute significantly to K-12 computer science education. Websites such as K-12 Computer Science, CS for ALL, Teach Computing, Code.org, Scratch, etc. are also important platforms that have become learning communities in computer science education.

DOI: 10.4018/979-8-3693-4542-9.ch013

1. INTRODUCTION

Tools and resources make important contributions to the analysis, design, development, implementation and evaluation processes while designing computer science education. Within the scope of the chapter, tools and resources that can be utilized in K-12 computer science education will be evaluated. The chapter aims to focus on the tools and resources necessary to develop students' computational thinking skills in K-12 computer science education.

In K-12 computer science education, various resources and tools play an important role in introducing computer science concepts and computational thinking. Computational thinking encompasses a range of specific thinking skills for problem solving including abstraction, decomposition, pattern recognition, logic and algorithm design, evaluation (Grover & Pea, 2018). Unplugged computer science tools, block-based computer science tools, text-based computer science tools, physical computer science tools, robotics kits, artificial intelligence tools have an important place in K-12 computer science education. It's critical to integrate these tools into the curriculum and to incorporate computer science education entering the basic courses of primary and high school students (Ballard & Haroldson, 2021). Studies conducted in the field show how crucial it is to introduce students to computer science education at a young age, and there is a growing movement in K–12 education to start computer science education early(Chittora & Baynes, 2020). Furthermore, among the resources now used in K–12 computer science teaching include augmented reality, virtual reality, artificial intelligence, and data science. According to Ersözlü and Clark (2019), the educational technology tools now employed in computer science education are essential for helping students build computational thinking abilities and serve as a basis for more complex ideas. In addition to being essential elements of contemporary K–12 computer science education, augmented reality (AR), virtual reality (VR), and artificial intelligence (AI) also provide immersive and dynamic learning environments. Another approach suggests that workshops focused on data science examples can help students understand algorithms and make inferences from data, and demonstrate practical applications of AI in education (Chittora & Baynes, 2020). By visualizing difficult concepts and offering hands-on experiences, augmented reality and virtual reality technologies have been demonstrated to increase student engagement and improve learning outcomes. Moreover, AI applications in K-12 computer science education offer personalized learning experiences and adaptive feedback mechanisms. Abdulrhman et al. (2023) emphasize that artificial intelligence (AI) systems are constantly evolving to operate efficiently and mimic human thought processes, highlighting the potential of AI to enhance educational practices.

The resources created within the scope of the world have a significant impact on the dissemination of K-12 computer science education. The contribution of resources like Computer Science Teachers Association (CSTA, 2017), National Center for Computing Education (NCCE, 2023), International Society for Technology in Education (ISTE, 2024a), etc. to K-12 computer science education will be assessed in this section. Initiatives to integrate and enhance computer science education into the curriculum are instrumental in advancing Computer science instruction in grades K–12. Furthermore, organizations such as ISTE, CSTA, NCCE, etc. play a significant part in shaping the scope of computer science education by providing professional development opportunities, curriculum resources and networking platforms for educators to raise the standard of instruction in computer science in K-12 settings. Moreover, in line with developments in countries such as the US and the UK, the focus of Computer science education in grades K–12 is shifting from a focus on information and communication technology (ICT) to more elaborately structured computer science concepts (Dagienė & Stupurienė, 2016; Hubwieser et al., 2014). In order to provide teachers with the skills they need to successfully teach computer science topics in K–12 classrooms, K–12 computer science education places a strong emphasis on the integration of both content and computer science concepts into curriculum (Yadav et al., 2017). Together with developments in teacher preparation and curriculum development, the cooperative efforts of groups like CSTA, ISTE, and NCCE are enhancing K–12 computer science education globally and helping to guarantee that students have the computational thinking abilities required for the future.

By synthesizing different perspectives and examples, the chapter will contribute to ongoing efforts to improve K-12 computer science education by providing educators with practical tools and resources to enhance students' computational thinking skills.

2. K-12 COMPUTER SCIENCE EDUCATION TOOLS

Unplugged computer science tools, block-based computer science tools, text-based computer science tools, physical computer science tools, robotics kits, artificial intelligence tools find an important place in K-12 computer science education.

2.1 Unplugged Computer Science Tools

Computer Science Unplugged Tools include a variety of activities that aim to teach basic computer science concepts and computational thinking skills without using programming or digital tools (Battal et al., 2021; Nishida et al., 2009). Computer science education for young children supports developmental processes such as problem solving, imagination, cognitive challenges, social interactions, motor skill development, emotional exploration and making different choices (Bers, 2020). For example, the Computer Science Unplugged project offers free learning actions to engage pupils with computer science concepts in an interesting and fun way (Nuhu, 2018). Computer science unplugged tools are valuable in that they enable educators to teach computer science regardless of access to hardware or the internet and are inclusive of all students (Ballard & Haroldson, 2021; Washbrooke, 2024). Studies have highlighted the effectiveness of unplugged programs in simplifying programming concepts and developing programming skills among students (Mukhirez et al., 2022). It has also shown that unplugged activities can increase students' collaboration, creativity, problem-solving skills, and motivation (Tonbuloğlu & Tonbuloğlu, 2019; Yildiz & Karal, 2021). For example, Huang et al. (2023) created an environment that improves the coding and computational thinking skills of primary school students with the Combined with Scratch block-based game called “Coding Ocean”. In the game where augmented reality technology is included, learners make positive contributions in the areas of abstraction, problem decomposition, pattern recognition, computational thinking and programming skills throughout the treasure hunt game fiction. Overall, Unplugged Computer Science Tools provide a unique and engaging way to introduce students to basic computer science concepts, develop computational thinking skills, and spark interest in the field without the need for computers or digital tools.

2.2 Block-based Computer Science Tools

Block-based programming tools have become prominent in educational settings, especially in computer science education. These tools provide a visual and intuitive way for students to grasp programming concepts without the complexity of traditional text-based languages. Examples of block-based computer science tools include Scratch, MIT App Inventor, and Pencil Code (Hu et al., 2020; Wangenheim et al., 2021; Bau et al., 2015). Block-based computer science tools are considered essential for introductory programming in K-12 settings. They are a fundamental element for novice students before moving on to text-based programming (Seralidou & Douligeris, 2022). To support programming learning at different educational levels, various interfaces have been designed to provide teachers and students with tools to facilitate programming instruction (Wang, 2021).

Scratch, a widely used block-based programming language, provides a user-friendly environment for creating interactive stories, games and animations. It uses colorful blocks that come together to create scenarios and is accessible to novice programmers of all ages (Hu et al., 2020; Sáez-López et al., 2020).

App Inventor is another example of a block-based tool that enables users to create mobile applications for Android devices. It simplifies the app development process by using visual blocks to represent code logic, allowing users to focus on app functionality rather than syntax (Wangenheim et al., 2021).

Pencil Code is a block-based coding tool made to facilitate the use of text-based web programming languages by novices. It provides students with a smooth transition by serving as a link between text-based and block-based programming (Bau et al., 2015).

Deng et al. (2019) conducted an eight-week study with ninety-nine K-10 students in Visual Basic (text-based) and Pencil Code (block-based) programming environments. At the end of the instruction, it was found that students who learned in the text-based and block-based programming environment not only significantly improved their computational thinking, but also became more confident and enjoyed learning programming. In addition, students showed more communication and interaction behaviors while learning block-based (Pencil Code) programming. Block-based computer science tools not only make understanding programming fundamentals easier, but also encourage computational thinking, problem-solving skills, and creativity among students. By providing a hands-on and engaging way to learn coding, block-based computer science tools play an important role in fostering interest and proficiency in programming from an early age (Hu et al., 2020; Wangenheim et al., 2021; Bau et al., 2015).

2.3 Text-based Computer Science Tools

Languages like Python, Java and C are actively used in educational settings to teach programming concepts and skills (Kim & Lee, 2020). **Python** is a popular text-based programming language used in educational settings to teach students the fundamentals and skills of programming (Doss et al., 2016). **Java** is another popular text-based programming language used in educational settings to teach programming fundamentals (Alomari et al., 2020). Jython is a text-based programming language used in educational settings to introduce computer science concepts (Rubinstein & Chor, 2014). The **C programming language** is often used to teach programming and computational thinking (Kandemir et al., 2020). Another example is **Dolittle**, a text-based educational programming language that supports students in the transition from block-based languages to text-based languages (Engelberger et al., 2021). Another way to think about a programming learning environment that facilitates the switch from block-based to text-based programming is **TABLET.** (Santo et al., 2022). There are also tools such as **Hybrid Java** that combine the benefits of visual and text-based programming languages for a comprehensive learning experience (Peel et al., 2022). Pedagogical strategies used in classrooms to effectively integrate text-based computer science tools into learning environments include teaching an introduction to programming with an emphasis on computational thinking concepts and practices. The programming pedagogy framework consists of four main components: programming paradigm, implementation strategy, teaching methods and teaching techniques (Kandemir et al., 2020). Text-based computer science tools can be selected according to learner goals, age group and learning process.

2.4 Physical Computer Science Tools

Physical Computer Science Education Tools encompass a variety of resources that integrate physical components with computer science concepts to enhance learning experiences. "Physical Computing" which blends hardware and software to construct interactive physical systems that sense and react to the real world, is one of the key tools in this subject. (Hodges et al., 2020). This approach is increasingly recognized as an important element in modern computer science education, offering hands-on experiences that bridge the gap between the digital and physical domains. An example of Physical Computing is the use of **Arduino**, a microcontroller platform that allows users to create interactive projects by connecting sensors and other hardware components to build physical computing systems (Sarı et al. 2022; Roumen & Fernaeus, 2021). Learners can use Arduino to create projects such as a weather station that collects data from sensors and displays it in real time. Another example is the **"Raspberry Pi",** a small, affordable computer that can be used for various physical computer science projects. Learners can program the Raspberry Pi to control lights, motors, and other physical devices to create interactive systems such as a smart home automation system or a robot (Sentance, 2023). Another example in this field is the **"Micro:bit",** a pocket-sized microcontroller board designed for education that allows students to create various projects by connecting sensors, LEDs and other components (Kalelioglu & Sentance, 2020).

Tools for "Physical Computing" like Arduino, Raspberry Pi, Micro:bit, etc. provide hands-on learning experiences that bridge the digital and physical worlds, allowing students to apply computational concepts to real-world scenarios. By interacting with these tools, students can develop their problem solving skills and creativity. They can gain a better knowledge of how to interact with and create the physical world using computer science principles. With the use of "Physical Computing" resources, students can investigate how computer science and the physical world interact. Physical Computing also fosters creativity and innovation in learning computer science through concrete, hands-on projects.

2.5 Robotic Kits

Computer science tools play an important role in introducing students to computer science concepts, developing their computational thinking skills and preparing them for further studies and careers in computer science. Many robotic kits are used in computer science education. One of the prominent robotic kits is LEGO kits. From past to present, LEGO Mindstorms NXT (2006), LEGO Education WeDo (2009), LEGO Mindstorms EV3 (2013), LEGO Boost (2017), and LEGO Spike Prime (2019) kits are the robotic education sets utilized in computer science education processes. LEGO robotics education sets generally consist of intelligent brick, various sensors and motors. The sets, which appeal to various age groups at the K-12 level, aim to introduce students to robotics and programming in a fun and engaging way. These LEGO robotics educational kits have been effective in teaching students robotics, programming and engineering concepts in an interactive and hands-on way (Fanchamps et al., 2021). Furthermore, research underscores the importance of LEGO robotics kits in enhancing STEM education, promoting creativity, problem-solving skills, and interdisciplinary learning among students. LEGO robotics kits are reported to be valuable tools in engaging students and promoting hands-on learning experiences in robotics and programming (AlQarzaie, et al., 2022; Çetin & Demircan, 2020; Zhong & Xia, 2020).

Another robotic kit is the **"Makey Makey",** which allows learners to transform everyday objects into touchpads and connect them to a computer, encouraging creativity and exploration in physical computing projects (Olympiou & Zacharia, 2011). The use of Makey Makey in teaching introductory programming concepts to primary school children is being investigated. Makey Makey allows users to connect everyday objects such as fruit or play dough to create a tangible user interface that can manipulate software on a computer, receiving input similar to a mouse or keyboard. The research demonstrates the practical applications of Makey Makey in educational settings, emphasizing its importance in hands-on learning experiences and encouraging creativity in physical computing projects (Hijón-Neira et al., 2020).

Another kit, **"BBC micro:bit"** is a pocket-sized microcontroller designed for educational purposes, offering students a simple introduction to physical computing and coding. The BBC micro:bit is a pocket-sized microcontroller designed for educational purposes, offering students a simple introduction to physical computing and coding. The device is widely used in educational settings to enhance students' understanding of programming concepts and encourage creativity in hands-on learning experiences (Stanojević et al., 2021).

The **"LittleBits"** kit is ideal for introducing electronic and physical computing concepts, as the electronic building blocks are held together with magnets, allowing users to create circuits and prototypes without soldering. It emphasizes that

LittleBits are used as electronic building blocks for hands-on learning of science concepts and serve as a STEM solution for children's educational experiences (Kewalramani et al., 2020). Research highlights the practical application of LittleBits in STEM education and emphasizes its role in introducing students to electronic and physical computing concepts in an engaging and interactive way. A noteworthy kit for Science, Technology, Engineering, and Mathematics (STEM) education is the STORMLab, an inexpensive modular robotic kit (Susilo et al., 2016). This kit offers versatile activities that can be seamlessly integrated into core STEM subjects and enhance students' interdisciplinary learning experiences.

The pedagogical emphasis in computer science education with Robotic Kits should always be on challenging students and helping them to understand in depth, rather than on using robotic devices and programming language. When structuring the pedagogical process, the questions 1) "What happened?", 2) "What was supposed to happen?", 3) "Did it work in the first step?", 4) "Did it work in the second step?", 5) "Where did it go wrong?" can be used as an encouraging key (Glezou, 2020). Robotic kits provide students with hands-on experiences in computer science education, allowing them to explore the intersection of hardware and software in building interactive systems. These educational kits play a crucial role in engaging students, stimulating creativity and supporting hands-on learning experiences in computer science education.

2.6 Artificial Intelligence Tools

In computer science education, especially in programming education processes, artificial intelligence tools that offer features such as code completion, code editing, code interpretation, code interpretation, debugging/editing, etc. allow personalization of the learning environment. Safurai, Phind, GitFluence, Codeium, and Replit are a few examples of artificial intelligence tools that can be used in computer science teaching that provide the aforementioned capabilities. (Kayalı et al., 2023). Among the subfields of computer science education, data analysis is one area where artificial intelligence technologies are particularly notable. In computer science education, artificial intelligence tools are used for discovering, analyzing, visualizing, sharing, interpreting, etc. data quickly and effectively. Artificial intelligence tools such as Swot Analysis, Graphy HQ, RTutor, Comment Analyzer, Pandachat etc. stand out in data analysis (Kayalı et al., 2023). According to a study that use a metaphorical approach to analyze the literature on the subject, using artificial intelligence tools in computer science instruction improves student motivation, performance, and attitude. However, it was stated that there are limitations in terms of application to the teaching processes of instructors and ethical aspects (García-Martínez, et al., 2023). ISTE's Elementary Educator AI Guide, Secondary Educator AI Guide and Computer Science Educator AI Guide documents can be utilized in integrating artificial intelligence tools in computer science education of K-12 educators (ISTE, 2024b).

3. K-12 COMPUTER SCIENCE EDUCATION RESOURCES

The global creation of resources has greatly influenced the spread of computer science education in grades K–12. Resources for K–12 computer science education include a broad variety of instruments, approaches, and structures designed to foster students' comprehension of computational thinking and computer science ideas from an early age. Resources like Computer Science Teachers Association (CSTA, 2017), Association for Computing Machinery (ACM, 2024), International Society for Technology in Education (ISTE, 2024a), National Center for Computing Education (NCCE, 2023), etc. have significantly improved the teaching of computer science in K–12. Computational thinking (CT) in K–12 education is supported by a wealth of resources offered by organizations involved in computer science education, including workshops, teacher tools, and academic events (So et al., 2019). By offering advice and assistance to educators, these organizations have a significant impact on the landscape of computer science education. Let's take a look at some of the prominent resources in the field that contribute to computer science education through their activities and the services they create and offer.

3.1 Association for Computing Machinery (ACM)

The Association for Computing Machinery (ACM) is an international professional association in the field of computer science. Since 1947, ACM has been organizing professional and academic scientific research, publications, competitions, and conferences in the discipline of computing and providing resources for computer science educators and students (ACM, 2024). ACM has approximately eighty thousand members today. For many years, ACM has also made contributions to the discipline by developing and upgrading the undergraduate degree curricula in subjects including computer science, software engineering, information systems, computer engineering, and information technology. Although ACM has spent many years learning about the various subfields of computer science, it has continued to contribute to computer science education by deepening in computer science education with a specialized organization through the ***Computer Science Teachers Association (CSTA)*** since 2004.

3.2 Computer Science Teachers Association (CSTA)

An significant source of digital tools and information for computer science teaching is the Computer Science Teachers Association (CSTA). The essential support that CSTA offers to instructors and students has a significant impact on the landscape of computer science education. Academic references highlight the importance of CSTA's initiatives and the impact of digital resources in computer science education. In elementary, middle, and high schools as well as in higher education and business, CSTA has been advocating and supporting computer science education since 2004 (CSTA, 2024).

Scaico & Costa's (2014) study highlights the role of organizations such as CSTA in contributing to curriculum models and guidelines for establishing computer science teaching in schools. In order to give teachers organized frameworks and resources to successfully incorporate computer science concepts into their curricula, CSTA's digital resources are essential. So et al. (2019) has conducted additional research that emphasizes the computational thinking resources offered by CSTA and the International Society for Technology in Education (ISTE) for K–12 education. These resources include teacher support, workshops and academic activities and emphasize the importance of integrating computational thinking into educational practices. Furthermore, Garet et al.'s (2001) research highlights the effectiveness of professional development programs that focus on specific content areas, such as mathematics and science, in improving teachers' instructional practices and students' conceptual understanding. CSTA provides digital resources to educators with the goal of improving their pedagogical approaches to computer science education. In collaboration with organizations such as ISTE, CSTA plays an important role in supporting computer science education by providing resources, workshops, and scholarly events that enhance computational thinking and teaching practices in K-12 settings.

3.3 International Society for Technology in Education (ISTE)

Leading the way in technology integration and the advancement of digital literacy in education is the International Society for Technology in Education (ISTE). ISTE provides digital content and resources in various fields to develop educators' technological competencies and promote effective teaching practicesArtificial intelligence, computational thinking, digital citizenship, edtech choices, international cooperation, STEAM in education, and teacher preparation are its main areas of emphasis. In addition, educational technology standards for students, teachers, education leaders and coaches are published. It offers supportive guides on “Essential Conditions” and “Adopting the Standards” for the process of published educational technology standards. It offers content as Books, blog posts, topic guides, podcasts, podcasts, and journals (ISTE, 2024a). It provides educators with a virtual learning environment for certification, school collaboration, professional development, and career advancement. It also contributes to computer science education through conferences, workshops and exchange programs.

Academic research reflects ISTE's impact on various fields of activity and on education. Basilotta-Gómez-Pablos et al. (2022) highlight ISTE's "Standards for Educational Technology for Teachers" (NETS-T) as a framework for developing teachers' digital competencies in higher education. They also underline that ISTE focuses on promoting digital skills among educators to improve teaching practices. Gomez et al. (2021) address in a different study how ISTE creates new standards for educators to use and integrate technology in order to improve student learning and promote instructors' technological and pedagogical competencies. The study emphasizes how important it is for ISTE to establish guidelines for teachers to follow while utilizing technology in the classroom. Ebersole (2019) explores the impact of the ISTE Standards for Educators on pre-service teacher education programs and emphasizes the importance of integrating these standards into courses and field experiences. She shows how ISTE's standards influence teacher preparation and technology integration in education programs. The research collectively demonstrates ISTE's significant contributions to promoting digital literacy, technology integration, and professional development among educators and highlights the organization's multifaceted involvement in advancing the use of technology in education.

3.4 National Centre for Computing Education (NCCE)

The National Centre for Computing Education (NCCE) is an organization focused on advancing computer science education and promoting digital literacy. NCCE runs a range of activities to support educators and students to develop their computer science skills and technological competencies. The UK Department for Education and its auxiliary partners provide funding for NCCE. It has become a significant investment in improving computer science education in the UK. It is run by STEM Learning. NCCE consists of the Teach Computing, Isaac Computer Science and Computing Quality Framework programs. NCCE is a structure that provides support in many areas such as curriculum, content, certification, support, best practices, good practices, careers, etc. for the computer science education processes of primary, middle and high school students (NCCE, 2024).

3.5 Australian Computer Society (ACS)

ACS is the professional representative of the computer science industry in AustraliaSince its founding in 1966, this premier professional society for computer science has represented Australia's technology community in industry, government, and education with over 47,000 members. ACS promotes computer science education, research and industrial development. It enhances computer science education by offering assistance in areas including professional development, publications, employer solutions, ethics and conduct, education and grievances, events, startup and scale-up, and publications (ACS, 2024).

3.6 British Computer Society (BCS)

BCS is an organization committed to ensuring that everyone's experience with technology is a positive one. It has been working since 1957. It has more than seventy thousand members in 150 different countries, including educators, policymakers, business leaders, practitioners, etc. The organization is structured on four main areas. Membership, Inspiration, Progression and Influence are the four main areas. It supports members to gain the skills, expertise and connections they need to develop their careers, shape the digital future and professionalize. Creates a talent network for its members that enables more careers in digital business processes. It supports its members and people to advance in their careers and provides learning and development opportunities. It organizes various events to increase the impact of computer science. Learned publishing, academy of computing, certifications, digital apprenticeships, jobs board, digital skills, books are the prominent areas of activity (BCS, 2024).

3.7 Information Technologies Educators Association

Information Technologies Educators Association (ITE) carries out activities for computer science education in Turkey with more than five thousand volunteer educators. ITE organizes publications, trainings, summits, and national teacher summits together with teachers, academics, education faculty students, and computer science professionals (ITE, 2024).

(CACS), Japan Society for Software Science and Technology (JSSST), New Zealand Association for Computing, Digital, and Information Technology Education (NZACDITE), Computer Science Teachers' Association of Nigeria (CSTAN), etc. work to promote computer science education in their own countries and around the world. They do this by developing, producing educational content, and providing resources. We have also briefly mentioned some of these organizations' resources in this section.

4. COMPUTER SCIENCE EDUCATION WEB SITES

Massively open online access platforms such as Coursera, edX, Khan Academy, etc. make significant contributions to computer science education. In addition to mass open online platforms, there are websites focused and specialized in computer science. We can summarize the prominent websites that contribute to computer science education as follows.

4.1 K–12 Computer Science - k12cs.org

A framework for computer science education has been developed by the Association for Computing Machinery, Code.org, Computer Science Teachers Association, National Math and Science Initiative, and K-12 Computer Science Cyber Innovation Center. One important tool for computer science education is the K–12 Computer Science Framework, which is built on the five different core concepts and seven different core practices listed in Figure 1 (K-12 Computer Science, 2024). A detailed curriculum is available on the K-12 Computer Science (K12CS) website. It also offers resources supporting the curriculum, practice guides, assessment methods, glossary, teaching methods and techniques, teacher development, books, etc.

Figure 1. The K–12 Computer Science Framework's Principles and Methods (https://k12cs.org/wp-content/uploads/2018/07/concepts_practices.png)

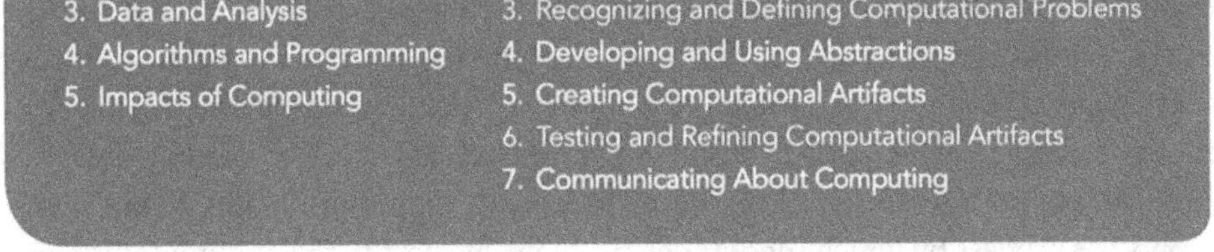

4.2 CSforALL - csforall.org

CSforALL is a central resource for K-12 computer science (CS) educators and organizations. It establishes a network to give every child in the US access to high-quality computer science education. The Association of Computing Machinery (ACM), the College Board, the National Center for Women & Information Technology (NCWIT), and the Computer Science Teachers Association (CSTA) have taken joint leadership of it since September 2016. Supporting curriculum work supports school, instructor, and student collaborations. It shares examples of activities, content and projects in accordance with the K-12 Computer Science Framework with all students and instructors (CSforALL, 2024).

4.3 Teach Computing - teachcomputing.org

The British Department for Education founded the National Centre for Computing Education (NCCE). Several organizations, including the UK Department of Education, provide funding and support for NCCE. It bases its work on three different programs. The first area is the "Teach Computing" curriculum, which provides training, resources and guidance for teaching computing at 4 different levels free of charge. Figure 2 shows the levels, age ranges, number of units and number of lessons. The contents of all levels can be accessed free of charge on the website.

Figure 2. Teach Computing Curriculum Key Stage Details (https://teachcomputing.org/curriculum)

Key Stage 1	Key Stage 2	Key Stage 3	Key Stage 4
Year 1-2, Age 5-7	**Year 3-6**, Age 7-11	**Year 7-9**, Age 11-14	**Year 10-11**, Age 14-16
Units: 13 Lessons: 72	Units: 24 Lessons: 144	Units: 19 Lessons: 115	Units: 22 Lessons: 178

The second area, "Isaac Computer Science", provides an online learning environment for computer science teachers and students. For teachers, the section offers access to lesson plans of different teachers, lesson plan preparation, access to colleagues' resources, assessment resources, etc. For students, it offers self-paced quality learning content and environment, online workshops, free trainings, project and career opportunities, etc. As the third area, the "Computing Quality Framework" supports a process by which schools can evaluate and certify their computer science education processes.

4.4 Computing at School - www.computingatschool.org.uk

Established in 2008, Computing at School (CAS) was a pioneer in computer science teaching in the United Kingdom and has now expanded globally. CAS has supported more than 44000 teachers with communities of practice, resources, discussion forums, computer science events. In all its activities it focuses on three aims: "TeachTogether", "TechTeach" and "Teachspiration". It carries out core activities such as communities of practice, national conference, student events, collaborations, etc. for K-12 level. CAS is supported by the British Computing Society (BCS) and The Chartered Institute for IT. The website has a large library of resources covering all aspects of the current UK curriculum and all key stages. The library includes worksheets, activities, lesson plans, schemes of work, content, etc., filterable by resource type.

4.5 Mr Fraser Computing Resources - www.mrfraser.org

Mr. Fraser is a computer science tutor and IT manager at a secondary school. The website provides free notes, presentations, links, code samples and links for IGCSE, GCSE, A-Level and IB Computing. In addition, there are 40 videos prepared for computer science education. The coding section includes a brief explanation of the structure of computer language and links to coding tutorials and resources to help you improve your skills, whether you are a beginner or an expert. The programming section is quite comprehensive. Python, Java, C# programming, Linux, web design and development, cybersecurity, Visual Basic programming, game development, and general programming resources such as IDEs and compilers are shared in a rich selection.

4.6 For Inspiration and Recognition of Science and Technology (FIRST) - www.firstinspires.org

An organization called For Inspiration and Recognition of Science and Technology (FIRST) is designed to provide robotics programs in PreK–12 classrooms and organized after-school activities for students aged 4–18. It has been contributing to computer science education since 1989 with its platform structure. International competitions are held for FIRST® LEGO® League (Grades PreK–8; Ages 4–16), FIRST® Tech Challenge (Grades 7–12; Ages 12–18), and FIRST® Robotics Competition teams (Grades 9–12; Ages 14–18). FIRST competitions are competitions that include processes such as designing, building, programming, problem solving, and use LEGO, Android, etc. structures. The FIRST platform is a platform that offers resources, trainings, participation in communities, and opportunities to obtain materials.

4.7 DENEYAP Türkiye - www.deneyap.org

The curricula of DENEYAP Technology Workshops, which are implemented within the Turkish Technology Team Foundation, are available free of charge on the digital platform. The Scientific and Technological Research Council of Turkey (TÜBİTAK) created the content. For middle and high school computer science instruction, different workshop contents are presented. Design and Production, Robotics and Coding, Cyber Security, Software Technologies, Mobile Applications, Artificial Intelligence, Online Software Technologies, Aerospace, Electronic Programming and Internet of Things (EPIT), and Advanced Robotics are among the topics covered in the middle school workshop curriculum. Design and Production, Robotics and Coding, Information Technology, Cyber Security, Online Software Technologies, Energy Technologies, Mobile Applications, Artificial Intelligence, Advanced Robotics, Aerospace, Electronic Programming and Internet of Things (EPIT) are among the topics covered in the high school workshop curriculum. Turkish Technology Team Foundation also organizes "The Aerospace And Technology Festıval (TEKNOFEST) organization since 2018. Turkish Technology Team Foundation makes significant contributions to computer science education through the competitions, publications, entrepreneurship summits and content it organizes and supports.

4.8 Other Resources

Codecademy (codecademy.com), FreeCodeCamp (freecodecamp.org), Raspberry Pi Foundaiton (raspberrypi.org and projects.raspberrypi.org/en/codeclub), Raspberry Pi (raspberrypi.com), Sololearn (sololearn.com), European Schoolnet (eun.org), Programmr (programmr.com), Codewars (codewars.com), Home and Learn (homeandlearn.co. uk), Project Euler (projecteuler.net), Sentinus (sentinus.co.uk), Raspberry Pi Computing Education Research Centre (computingeducation-research.org), AccessCSforAll (washington.edu/accesscomputing and washington.edu/accesscomputing/accesscsforall), Creative Technology Research Lab (ctrl.education.ufl.edu) etc. Some of the platforms are interactive platforms for learning programming languages. They offer courses in web development, data science, artificial intelligence and many other areas. Learners can get feedback and work on projects while writing code. Some of the platforms offer free training and practice in computer science areas such as web development, data science, etc. They provide resources for both beginners and experienced developers.

Code.org's Professional Learning Programs (https://code.org/professional-learning), Google for Education's CS First (https://csfirst.withgoogle.com/s/en/home & https://edu.google.com/intl/ALL_kr/for-educators/product-guides/csfirst/) and Microsoft Learn Educator Center (https://learn.microsoft.com/en-us/training/educator-center/) are qualified and free platforms that support the professional development of computer science educators and students.

In addition to these resources, there are websites focused on specific areas of computer science education. Most of these websites have turned into a learning community rather than just a website. Code.org, Scratch, CS Unplugged, Bootstrap, codehs.com are some examples of online platforms. These and similar platforms offer useful tools, curricula, and activities to help K–12 children understand computer science ideas, coding techniques, and the fundamentals of computational thinking in an engaging and hands-on manner.

5. CONCLUSION

In computer science education, it is seen that robotic kits, block-based computer science tools, and computer science tools without computers become more prominent in kindergarten and primary school. Later on, text-based computer science tools, physical computer science tools, robotic kits and artificial intelligence computer science tools are utilized. In Zhu and Wang's (2023) study, it was suggested to start with a visual and block-based visual programming language and then move on to textual languages like Python, Java, and C++ in computer science education structured to develop computational thinking, problem solving, and basic mathematics skills at the K–12 level through computer science tools. In addition, computer science education can be integrated into different curricular areas to promote mathematics, science, engineering and the arts through project-based approaches (Bers, 2020). In addition to all of these procedures, Zhu and Wang (2023) assert that it is essential for K–12 computer science educators to engage in and gain from a learning community that offers ongoing professional development and assistance. Organizations such as ACM,NCCE, ISTE, CSTA, etc. make important contributions to the need for continuous professional development for computer science educators. In addition, websites and digital resources for computer science education; computer science education, which has a dynamic structure, stands out as an important element.

REFERENCES

Abdulrhman, S. H., Abttan, R. A., Mijwil, M. M., & Alkhazraji, A. (2023). Artificial intelligence applications in english language teaching: A short survey. *Asian Journal of Applied Sciences*, 10(6). Advance online publication. DOI: 10.24203/ajas.v10i6.7111

ACM. (2024). Association for Computing Machinery (ACM). https://www.acm.org/about-acm/about-the-acm-organization

ACS. (2024). Australian Computer Society (ACS). https://www.acs.org.au/

Alomari, H. W., Ramasamy, V., Kiper, J. D., & Potvin, G. (2020). A user interface (ui) and user experience (ux) evaluation framework for cyberlearning environments in computer science and software engineering education. *Heliyon*, 6(5), e03917. DOI: 10.1016/j.heliyon.2020.e03917 PMID: 32426541

AlQarzaie, K. N., & AlEnezi, S. A. (2022). Using lego mindstorms in primary schools: Perspective of educational sector. [iJOE]. *International Journal of Online and Biomedical Engineering*, 18(01), 139–147. DOI: 10.3991/ijoe.v18i01.27579

Ballard, E. D., & Haroldson, R. (2021). Analysis of computational thinking in children's literature for k-6 students: Literature as a non-programming unplugged resource. *Journal of Educational Computing Research*, 59(8), 1487–1516. DOI: 10.1177/07356331211004048

Basilotta-Gómez-Pablos, V., Matarranz, M., Casado-Aranda, L., & Otto, A. (2022). Teachers' digital competencies in higher education: A systematic literature review. *International Journal of Educational Technology in Higher Education*, 19(1), 8. Advance online publication. DOI: 10.1186/s41239-021-00312-8

Battal, A., Afacan Adanır, G., & Gülbahar, Y. (2021). Computer science unplugged: A systematic literature review. *Journal of Educational Technology Systems*, 50(1), 24–47. DOI: 10.1177/00472395211018801

Bau, D., Dawson, M., & Pickens, C. S. (2015). *Pencil code. Proceedings of the 14th International Conference on Interaction Design and Children*. https://doi.org/DOI: 10.1145/2771839.2771875

BCS. (2024). British Computer Society. https://www.bcs.org/about-us/

Bers, M. U. (2020). *Coding as a playground: Programming and computational thinking in the early childhood classroom*. Routledge. DOI: 10.4324/9781003022602

Çetin, M., & Demircan, H. Ö. (2020). Empowering technology and engineering for STEM education through programming robots: A systematic literature review. *Early Child Development and Care*, 190(9), 1323–1335. DOI: 10.1080/03004430.2018.1534844

Chittora, S., & Baynes, A. (2020). Interactive visualizations to introduce data science for high school students. *Proceedings of the 21st Annual Conference on Information Technology Education*. https://doi.org/DOI: 10.1145/3368308.3415360

CSforALL. (2024). About CSforALL. https://www.csforall.org/

CSTA. (2017). K-12 Computer Science Standards. https://members.csteachers.org/documents/en-us/46916364-83ab-4f51-85fb-06b3b25b417c/1/

CSTA. (2024). Computer Science Teachers Association (CSTA). https://csteachers.org/about-csta/

Dagienė, V., & Stupurienė, G. (2016). Informatics concepts and computational thinking in k-12 education: A lithuanian perspective. *Journal of Information Processing*, 24(4), 732–739. DOI: 10.2197/ipsjjip.24.732

Deng, W., Pi, Z., Lei, W., Zhou, Q., & Zhang, W. (2019). Pencil code improves learners' computational thinking and computer learning attitude. *Computer Applications in Engineering Education*, 28(1), 90–104. DOI: 10.1002/cae.22177

Doss, B. D., Cicila, L. N., Georgia, E. J., Roddy, M. K., Nowlan, K. M., Benson, L. A., & Christensen, A. (2016). A randomized controlled trial of the web-based ourrelationship program: Effects on relationship and individual functioning. *Journal of Consulting and Clinical Psychology*, 84(4), 285–296. DOI: 10.1037/ccp0000063 PMID: 26999504

Ebersole, E. (2019). Preservice teacher experience with technology integration: How the preservice teacher's efficacy in technology integration is impacted by the context of the preservice teacher education program. *International Dialogues on Education Journal*, 6(2). Advance online publication. DOI: 10.53308/ide.v6i2.64

Engelberger, F., Galaz-Davison, P., Bravo, G., Rivera, M., & Ramírez-Sarmiento, C. A. (2021). Developing and implementing cloud-based tutorials that combine bioinformatics software, interactive coding, and visualization exercises for distance learning on structural bioinformatics. *Journal of Chemical Education*, 98(5), 1801–1807. DOI: 10.1021/acs.jchemed.1c00022

Ersözlü, A., & Clark, A. C. (2019). Augmented reality research in education: A bibliometric study. *Eurasia Journal of Mathematics, Science and Technology Education*, 15(10). Advance online publication. DOI: 10.29333/ejmste/103904

Fanchamps, N. L., Slangen, L., Hennissen, P., & Specht, M. (2021). The influence of SRA programming on algorithmic thinking and self-efficacy using Lego robotics in two types of instruction. *International Journal of Technology and Design Education*, 31(2), 203–222. DOI: 10.1007/s10798-019-09559-9

García-Martínez, I., Batanero, J. M. F., Fernández-Cerero, J., & León, S. P. (2023). Analysing the impact of artificial intelligence and computational sciences on student performance: Systematic review and meta-analysis. *Journal of New Approaches in Educational Research*, 12(1), 171–197. DOI: 10.7821/naer.2023.1.1240

Garet, M. S., Porter, A. C., Desimone, L. M., Birman, B. F., & Yoon, K. S. (2001). What makes professional development effective? results from a national sample of teachers. *American Educational Research Journal*, 38(4), 915–945. DOI: 10.3102/00028312038004915

Glezou, K. V. (2020). Robotics as a Powerful Vehicle Toward Learning and Computational Thinking in Secondary Education of 21st Century. Papadakis, S., & Kalogiannakis, M. (Eds.). *Handbook of research on using educational robotics to facilitate student learning* (p. 1-40). IGI Global.

Gomez, F. C.Jr, Trespalacios, J., Hsu, Y., & Yang, D. (2021). Exploring teachers' technology integration self-efficacy through the 2017 iste standards. *TechTrends*, 66(2), 159–171. DOI: 10.1007/s11528-021-00639-z PMID: 34378007

Grover, S., & Pea, R. (2018). Computational thinking: A competency whose time has come. *Computer science education: Perspectives on teaching and learning in school, 19*(1), 19-38.

Hijón-Neira, R., Perez-Marin, D., Pizarro, C., & Connolly, C. (2020). The effects of a visual execution environment and makey makey on primary school children learning introductory programming concepts. *IEEE Access : Practical Innovations, Open Solutions*, 8, 217800–217815. DOI: 10.1109/ACCESS.2020.3041686

Hodges, S., Sentance, S., Finney, J., & Ball, T. (2020). Physical computing: A key element of modern computer science education. *Computer*, 53(4), 20–30. DOI: 10.1109/MC.2019.2935058

Hu, Y., Chen, C., & Su, C. (2020). Exploring the effectiveness and moderators of block-based visual programming on student learning: A meta-analysis. *Journal of Educational Computing Research*, 58(8), 1467–1493. DOI: 10.1177/0735633120945935

Huang, S., Tarng, W., & Ou, K. (2023). Effectiveness of ar board game on computational thinking and programming skills for elementary school students. *Systems*, 11(1), 25. DOI: 10.3390/systems11010025

Hubwieser, P., Armoni, M., Giannakos, M. N., & Mittermeir, R. T. (2014). Perspectives and visions of computer science education in primary and secondary (k-12) schools. *ACM Transactions on Computing Education*, 14(2), 1–9. DOI: 10.1145/2602482

ISTE. (2023). International Society for Technology in Education Standarts https://iste.org/standards

ISTE. (2024a). International Society for Technology in Education (ISTE). https://iste.org/about

ISTE. (2024b). Artificial Intelligence in Education. https://iste.org/ai

ITE. (2024). Information Technologies Educators Association. https://bte.org.tr/bizkimiz/

K-12 Computer Science. (2024). K–12 Computer Science Framework. https://k12cs.org/

Kalelioglu, F., & Sentance, S. (2020). Teaching with physical computing in school: the case of the micro: bit. *Education and Information Technologies*, 25(4), 2577–2603. DOI: 10.1007/s10639-019-10080-8

Kandemir, C. M., Kalelioğlu, F., & Gülbahar, Y. (2020). Pedagogy of teaching introductory text-based programming in terms of computational thinking concepts and practices. *Computer Applications in Engineering Education*, 29(1), 29–45. DOI: 10.1002/cae.22374

Kayalı, B., Balat, Ş., & Yavuz, M. (2023). *Yapay Zeka Tabanlı Araçlar ve Uygulamaların Bilgisayar Bilimi Eğitiminde Kullanımı. Kert, S. B. (Editör), Teoriden Uygulamaya Bilgisayar Bilimi Eğitimi.* Nobel Yayın Dağıtım.

Kewalramani, S., Palaiologou, I., & Dardanou, M. (2020). Children's engineering design thinking processes: The magic of the robots and the power of blocks (electronics*). Eurasia Journal of Mathematics, Science and Technology Education*, 16(3). Advance online publication. DOI: 10.29333/ejmste/113247

Kim, S., & Lee, Y. (2020). An analysis of pre-service teachers' learning process in programming learning. *International Journal on Advanced Science, Engineering and Information Technology*, 10(1), 58–69. DOI: 10.18517/ijaseit.10.1.5723

Mukhirez, E. J., Asqule, M., & Hasan, M. S. (2022). Effectiveness of CS Unplugged Program in Developing Programming Skills for Eighth Grade Female Students. *IUG Journal of Educational & Psychological Studies,* 30(4).

NCCE. (2023). National Centre for Computing Education. https://teachcomputing.org/curriculum

NCCE. (2024). National Centre for Computing Education (NCCE). https://computingeducation.org.uk/

Nishida, T., Kanemune, S., Idosaka, Y., Namiki, M., Bell, T., & Kuno, Y. (2009). A CS unplugged design pattern. *SIGCSE Bulletin*, 41(1), 231–235. DOI: 10.1145/1539024.1508951

Nuhu, K. M., Adedokun-Shittu, N. A., & Shittu, A. J. K. (2018). Assessment of Students' Comprehension of Binary Concept Using Computer-Science-Unplugged-Method in a Selected Secondary School in Ilorin, Kwara State. *Fountain Journal of National Ad Applied Sciences*, 7(2). Advance online publication. DOI: 10.53704/fujnas.v7i2.232

Peel, A., Sadler, T. D., & Friedrichsen, P. (2022). Algorithmic explanations: An unplugged instructional approach to integrate science and computational thinking. *Journal of Science Education and Technology*, 31(4), 428–441. DOI: 10.1007/s10956-022-09965-0 PMID: 35535350

Roumen, G. J., & Fernaeus, Y. (2021). Envisioning Arduino Action: A collaborative tool for physical computing in educational settings. *International Journal of Child-Computer Interaction*, 29, 100277. DOI: 10.1016/j.ijcci.2021.100277

Rubinstein, A., & Chor, B. (2014). Computational thinking in life science education. *PLoS Computational Biology*, 10(11), e1003897. DOI: 10.1371/journal.pcbi.1003897 PMID: 25411839

Sáez-López, J., Otero, R. B., & García-Cervigón, S. D. L. (2020). Introducing robotics and block programming in elementary education. *RIED.Revista Iberoamericana De Educación a Distancia*, 24(1), 95. DOI: 10.5944/ried.24.1.27649

Santo, A. D., Farah, J. C., Martínez, M. L., Moro, A., Bergram, K., Purohit, A. K., Gelber, P., Gillet, D., & Holzer, A. (2022). Promoting computational thinking skills in non-computer-science students: Gamifying computational notebooks to increase student engagement. *IEEE Transactions on Learning Technologies*, 15(3), 392–405. DOI: 10.1109/TLT.2022.3180588

Sarı, U., Pektaş, H. M., Şen, Ö. F., & Çelik, H. (2022). Algorithmic thinking development through physical computing activities with Arduino in STEM education. *Education and Information Technologies*, 27(5), 6669–6689. DOI: 10.1007/s10639-022-10893-0

Scaico, P. D., & Costa, T. K. L. (2014). Supervised internships and their lessons: Challenges and experiences with teaching degree in computer science in brazilian scenario. *CLEI Electronic Journal*, 17(3). Advance online publication. DOI: 10.19153/cleiej.17.3.11

Sentance, S., Barendsen, E., Howard, N. R., & Schulte, C. (2023). *Computer science education: Perspectives on teaching and learning in school*. Bloomsbury Publishing. DOI: 10.5040/9781350296947

Seralidou, E. & Douligeris, C. (2022). Investigating the transition from block-based to text-based programming techniques in secondary education in greece. *European Journal of Engineering and Technology Research*, 21-27. https://doi.org/DOI: 10.24018/ejeng.2021.0.CIE.2753

So, H. J., Jong, M. S., & Liu, C. (2019). Computational thinking education in the asian pacific region. *The Asia-Pacific Education Researcher*, 29(1), 1–8. DOI: 10.1007/s40299-019-00494-w

Stanojević, D., Rosić, A., Ranđelović, B., & Stanković, Ž. (2021). Micro: Bit as a tool for improvement of education. *The International Journal of Management Science and Business Administration*, 7(2), 14–19. DOI: 10.18775/ijmsba.1849-5664-5419.2014.72.1002

Susilo, E., Liu, J., Rayo, Y. A., Peck, A. M., Montenegro, J., Gonyea, M., & Valdastri, P. (2016). Stormlab for stem education: An affordable modular robotic kit for integrated science, technology, engineering, and math education. *IEEE Robotics &Amp. IEEE Robotics & Automation Magazine*, 23(2), 47–55. DOI: 10.1109/MRA.2016.2546703

Tonbuloğlu, B., & Tonbuloğlu, I. (2019). The effect of unplugged coding activities on computational thinking skills of middle school students. *Informatics in Education*, 18(2), 403–426. DOI: 10.15388/infedu.2019.19

Wang, J. (2021). Use hopscotch to develop positive attitudes toward programming for elementary school students. *International Journal of Computer Science Education in Schools*, 5(1), 48–58. DOI: 10.21585/ijcses.v5i1.122

Wangenheim, C. G., Hauck, J. C. R., Pacheco, F. S., & Bueno, M. F. B. (2021). Visual tools for teaching machine learning in k-12: A ten-year systematic mapping. *Education and Information Technologies*, 26(5), 5733–5778. DOI: 10.1007/s10639-021-10570-8 PMID: 33967587

Washbrooke, S., & Giacaman, N. (2024). Play, Code, Learn: Fostering Computational Thinking in Primary Aged Learners Through Interactive Play. In Papadakis, S. (Ed.), *IoT, AI, and ICT for Educational Applications. EAI/Springer Innovations in Communication and Computing*. Springer., DOI: 10.1007/978-3-031-50139-5_7

Yadav, A., Stephenson, C., & Hai, H. (2017). Computational thinking for teacher education. *Communications of the ACM*, 60(4), 55–62. DOI: 10.1145/2994591

Yildiz, M., & Karal, H. (2021). A Computer Science Unplugged Activity: CityMap. *International Journal of Computer Science Education in Schools*, 5(2), 14–27. DOI: 10.21585/ijcses.v5i2.110

Zhong, B., & Xia, L. (2020). A systematic review on exploring the potential of educational robotics in mathematics education. *International Journal of Science and Mathematics Education*, 18(1), 79–101. DOI: 10.1007/s10763-018-09939-y

Zhu, M., & Wang, C. (2024). K-12 computer science teaching strategies, challenges, and teachers' professional development opportunities and needs. *Computers in the Schools*, 41(1), 1–22. DOI: 10.1080/07380569.2023.2178868

KEY TERMS AND DEFINITIONS

Coding: The process of writing instructions to agents so they can carry out a certain task.

Computational Thinking: Computational thinking is a set of techniques, approaches, and abilities for solving issues that entail comprehending issues and their resolutions in ways that could be carried out by a computer.

Computer Science: The investigation of procedures, techniques, and apparatuses that work with data to modify, store, and transmit digital information.

Programming Language: An algorithm can be implemented and communication with a computer facilitated by using a formal language, which is composed of a collection of instructions that generate different types of output.

Programming: The procedure for creating an executable program in a programming language to carry out a certain computational task.

Robotics: The procedure for creating an executable program in a programming language to carry out a certain computational task.

Compilation of References

Abdulameer, M. M. H., & Abdullah, M. Z. (2019). Toward Generating a New Video Education Lectures Dataset and Performance Comparison with Various Machine Learning Algorithms. *Annals of Tropical Medicine and Health*, 22(12), 279–298. DOI: 10.36295/ASRO.2019.221230

Abdulrhman, S. H., Abttan, R. A., Mijwil, M. M., & Alkhazraji, A. (2023). Artificial intelligence applications in english language teaching: A short survey. *Asian Journal of Applied Sciences*, 10(6). Advance online publication. DOI: 10.24203/ajas.v10i6.7111

Accessibility, W. P. (2024). https://wordpress.org/plugins/wp-accessibility/

Achiam, J., Adler, S., Agarwal, S., Ahmad, L., Akkaya, I., Aleman, F. L., Almeida, D., Altenschmidt, J., Altman, S., Anadkat, S., & Associates. (2023). 'Gpt-4 Technical Report'. *arXiv Preprint arXiv:2303.08774.*

Ackermann, E. (2001). Piaget's constructivism, Papert's constructionism: What's the difference. *Future of Learning Group Publication*, 5(3), 438.

ACM. (2024). Association for Computing Machinery (ACM). https://www.acm.org/about-acm/about-the-acm-organization

ACS. (2024). Australian Computer Society (ACS). https://www.acs.org.au/

Adesoji, F. A., & Idika, M. I. (2015). Effects of 7E Learning Cycle Model and Case-Based Learning Strategy on Secondary School Students' Learning Outcomes in Chemistry. *Journal of the International Society for Teacher Education*, 19(1), 7–17.

Ahadi, A., Lister, R., & Mathieson, L. (2018). Syntax error based quantification of the learning progress of the novice programmer (world). 10–14. DOI: 10.1145/3197091.3197121

Ahlgren, K., Golden, A., & Magnusson, U. (2021). Metaphor in education: A multilingual and Scandinavian perspective. *Metaphor and the Social World*, 11(2), 196–211. DOI: 10.1075/msw.00015.ahl

Ahmad, S. A., Hussain, I., Ahmad, R., & Din, M. N. U. (2020). Performance Based Prediction of the Students in the Physics Subject using Traditional and Machine Learning Approach at Higher Education Level. [IJITL]. *International Journal of Innovation in Teaching and Learning*, 6(1), 174–190. DOI: 10.35993/ijitl.v6i1.997

Aivaloglou, E., & Hermans, F. (2019, February). Early programming education and career orientation: the effects of gender, self-efficacy, motivation and stereotypes. In *Proceedings of the 50th ACM technical symposium on computer science education* (pp. 679-685). DOI: 10.1145/3287324.3287358

Akçay, A. O., Karahan, E., & Türk, S. (2019). Bilgi işlemsel düşünme becerileri odaklı okul sonrası kodlama sürecinde ilkokul öğrencilerinin deneyimlerinin incelenmesi. *Eskişehir Osmangazi Üniversitesi Türk Dünyası Uygulama ve Araştırma Merkezi Eğitim Dergisi*, 4(2), 38–50.

Akgun, S., & Greenhow, C. (2022). 'Artificial Intelligence in Education: Addressing Ethical Challenges in K-12 Settings'. *AI and Ethics*, 2(3), 431–440. DOI: 10.1007/s43681-021-00096-7 PMID: 34790956

Aki Tamashiro, M., Van Mechelen, M., Schaper, M.-M., & Sejer Iversen, O. (2021). Introducing Teenagers to Machine Learning through Design Fiction: An Exploratory Case Study. Interact. Des. Child., 471–475.

Al Roomy, M. A. (2022). Exploring Teacher's Perspectives about Online Assessment during the COVID-19 Pandemic in a Saudi Context. *Arab World English Journal (AWEJ). Special Issue on CALL*, (8), 3–16. DOI: 10.24093/awej/call8.1

Alamin, M. A. A., Uddin, G., Malakar, S., Afroz, S., Haider, T., & Iqbal, A. (2023). Developer discussion topics on the adoption and barriers of low code software development platforms. *Empirical Software Engineering*, 28(1), 4. DOI: 10.1007/s10664-022-10244-0 PMID: 36407813

Alammary, A. (2019). Blended learning models for introductory programming courses: A systematic review. *PLoS One*, 14(9), 1–26. DOI: 10.1371/journal.pone.0221765 PMID: 31487316

Alamr, S. M., Leon-Urrutia, M., & Carr, L. A. (2023, September). E-assessment in Computer Science Higher Education. *Proceedings of the 15th International Conference on Education Technology and Computers* (pp. 378-383). ACM. DOI: 10.1145/3629296.3629357

Alenezi, H. S., & Faisal, M. H. (2020). 'Utilizing Crowdsourcing and Machine Learning in Education: Literature Review'. *Education and Information Technologies*, 25(4), 2971–2986. DOI: 10.1007/s10639-020-10102-w

Alghamdi, A. M., & Eassa, F. E. (2019). OpenACC Errors Classification and Static Detection Techniques. *IEEE Access : Practical Innovations, Open Solutions*, 7, 113235–113253. DOI: 10.1109/ACCESS.2019.2935498

Alghamdi, A. S. A., Alghamdi, A. M., Eassa, F. E., & Khemakhem, M. A. (2020). ACC_TEST: Hybrid Testing Techniques for MPI-Based Programs. *IEEE Access : Practical Innovations, Open Solutions*, 8, 91488–91500. DOI: 10.1109/ACCESS.2020.2994172

Alharbi, A. S., Alhebshi, A. A., & Meccawy, Z. (2021). Efl students' and teachers' perceptions of google forms as a digital formative assessment tool in saudi secondary schools. *Arab World English Journal*, 7(1), 140–154. DOI: 10.24093/awej/call7.10

Ali, S., Payne, B. H., Williams, R., Park, H. W., & Breazeal, C. (2019, June). Constructionism, ethics, and creativity: Developing primary and middle school artificial intelligence education. In International workshop on education in artificial intelligence k-12 (eduai'19) (Vol. 2, pp. 1-4). mit media lab Palo Alto, California.

Ali, H., Murad, S., & Shah, Z. (2023). Spot the Fake Lungs: Generating Synthetic Medical Images Using Neural Diffusion Models. In Longo, L., & O'Reilly, R. (Eds.), *Artificial Intelligence and Cognitive Science* (pp. 32–39). Springer Nature Switzerland. DOI: 10.1007/978-3-031-26438-2_3

Alimisis, D. (2013). Educational robotics: Open questions and new challenges. *Themes in Science and Technology Education*, 6(1), 1.

Alimisis, D., & Kynigos, C. (2009). Constructionism and robotics in education. In Alimisis, D. (Ed.), *Teacher Education on Robotic-Enhanced Constructivist Pedagogical Methods* (pp. 11–26). ASPETE.

Alimisis, D., & Moro, M. (2016). Special issue on educational robotics. *Robotics and Autonomous Systems*, 77, 74–75. DOI: 10.1016/j.robot.2015.12.006

Allison, J. (2020, December). A framework for effective continuing professional development: The case of computer science teachers within further education colleges. *International Conference on Computational Science and Computational Intelligence (CSCI)* (pp. 898-903). IEEE. DOI: 10.1109/CSCI51800.2020.00168

Alomari, H. W., Ramasamy, V., Kiper, J. D., & Potvin, G. (2020). A user interface (ui) and user experience (ux) evaluation framework for cyberlearning environments in computer science and software engineering education. *Heliyon*, 6(5), e03917. DOI: 10.1016/j.heliyon.2020.e03917 PMID: 32426541

Alonso-García, S., Rodríguez Fuentes, A.-V., Ramos Navas-Parejo, M., & Victoria-Maldonado, J.-J. (2024). Enhancing computational thinking in early childhood education with educational robotics: A meta-analysis. *Heliyon*, 10(13), e33249. DOI: 10.1016/j.heliyon.2024.e33249 PMID: 39035481

Alotaibi, H., Al-Khalifa, H. S., & AlSaeed, D. (2020). Teaching Programming to Students with Vision Impairment: Impact of Tactile Teaching Strategies on Student's Achievements and Perceptions. *Sustainability*, 12(13), 5320. DOI: 10.3390/su12135320

Alpaydin, E. (2020). *Introduction to Machine Learning* (4th ed.). MIT Press.

AlQarzaie, K. N., & AlEnezi, S. A. (2022). Using lego mindstorms in primary schools: Perspective of educational sector. [iJOE]. *International Journal of Online and Biomedical Engineering*, 18(01), 139–147. DOI: 10.3991/ijoe.v18i01.27579

Alruwais, N., Wills, G., & Wald, M. (2018). Advantages and challenges of using e-assessment. *International Journal of Information and Education Technology (IJIET)*, 8(1), 34–37. DOI: 10.18178/ijiet.2018.8.1.1008

Altadmri, A., & Brown, N. C. (2015, February). 37 million compilations: Investigating novice programming mistakes in large-scale student data. In *Proceedings of the 46th ACM technical symposium on computer science education* (pp. 522-527). DOI: 10.1145/2676723.2677258

Amadi, G. E., Mba, C. J., & Cornelius, N. U. (2022). Availability and utilization of teaching resources for effective computer science education for youth empowerment in Anambra state. *International Journal of Advance Research, Ideas, and Innovations in Technology*, 8(1), 489–493.

Amelung, M., Forbrig, P., & Rösner, D. (2008, June). Towards generic and flexible web services for e-assessment. In *Proceedings of the 13th annual conference on Innovation and technology in computer science education* (pp. 219-224). https://doi.org/DOI: 10.1145/1384271.1384330

Amelung, M., Piotrowski, M., & Rösner, D. (2006, June). EduComponents: Experiences in e-assessment in computer science education. *Proceedings of the 11th annual SIGCSE conference on Innovation and technology in computer science education* (pp. 88-92). ACM. DOI: 10.1145/1140124.1140150

Amer, A., Sidhu, G., Bo, Z., & Srinivasan, S. (2022). A Short Review of Online Learning Assessment Strategies. *International Journal of Pedagogy and Teacher Education*, 6(2), 89–103. https://jurnal.uns.ac.id/ijpte/article/view/66579. DOI: 10.20961/ijpte.v6i2.66579

American Library Association (ALA). (2000). *Information literacy competency standards for higher education*. ALA.

American Library Association (ALA). (2013). *Digital literacy, libraries, and public policy*.

Amri, S., Budiyanto, C. W., Fenyvesi, K., Yuana, R. A., & Widiastuti, I. (2022). Educational robotics: Evaluating the role of computational thinking in attaining 21st-century skills. *Open Education Studies*, 4(1), 322–338. DOI: 10.1515/edu-2022-0174

Anand, V. K., Abdul Rahiman, S. K., Ben George, E., & Huda, A. S. 2018. 'Recursive Clustering Technique for Students' Performance Evaluation in Programming Courses'. Pp. 1–5 in *2018 Majan International Conference (MIC)*. DOI: 10.1109/MINTC.2018.8363153

Anderson, L. W., Krathwohl, D. R., Airasian, P. W., Cruikshank, K. A., Mayer, R. E., Pintrich, P. R., Raths, J., & Wittrock, M. C. (2001). A Taxonomy for Learning, Teaching, and Assessing: A Revision of Bloom's Taxonomy of Educational Objectives. *Reference and Research Book News: Dublin, OH, USA*, 16, 1–336.

Andrews, D., & Richmond, G. (2019). Professional development for equity: What constitutes powerful professional learning? *Journal of Teacher Education*, 70(5), 408–409. DOI: 10.1177/0022487119875098

Angeli, C., & Valanides, N. (2009). Epistemological and methodological issues for the conceptualization, development, and assessment of ICT-TPCK: Advances in technological pedagogical content knowledge (TPCK). *Computers & Education*, 52(1), 154–168. DOI: 10.1016/j.compedu.2008.07.006

Angeli, C., Voogt, J., Fluck, A., Webb, M., Cox, M., Malyn-Smith, J., & Zagami, J. (2016). A K-6 computational thinking curriculum framework: Implications for teacher knowledge. *Journal of Educational Technology & Society*, 19(3), 47–57.

Anozie, N., & Junker, B. W. (2006, July). Predicting end-of-year accountability assessment scores from monthly student records in an online tutoring system. Educational Data Mining: Papers from the AAAI Workshop. Menlo Park, CA: AAAI Press.

Antonenko, P., & Abramowitz, B. (2023). In-service teachers' (mis) conceptions of artificial intelligence in K-12 science education. *Journal of Research on Technology in Education*, 55(1), 64–78. DOI: 10.1080/15391523.2022.2119450

Aparicio, J. T., Aparicio, M., & Costa, C. J. (2018). A Virtual Robot to support Programming Learning. ISR 2018; *50th International Symposium on Robotics*, 1–4. https://ieeexplore.ieee.org/document/8470585

Appiah, M., & Tonder, F. (2018). E-Assessment in higher education: A review. *International journal of business and economic research, 9*(6), 1454-1460. https://www.researchgate.net/profile/Martin-Appiah/publication/329775612_E-Assessment_in_Higher_Education_A_Review/links/5c1a2f614585l5a4c7e90a08/E-Assessment-in-Higher-Education-A-Review.pdf

Archer, E. (2017). The assessment purpose triangle: Balancing the purposes of educational assessment. *Frontiers in Education*, 2, 41. Advance online publication. DOI: 10.3389/feduc.2017.00041

Arifuddin, A., Turmudi, T., & Rokhmah, U. N. (2021). Alternative assessments in online learning during covid-19 pandemic: The strenghths and weaknesses. *International Journal of Elementary Education*, 5(2), 240. DOI: 10.23887/ijee.v5i2.33532

Arslan, K., & Akçelik, M. (2019). Programlama eğitiminde Scratch'in kullanılması: Öğretmen adaylarının tutum ve algıları. *Ulusal Eğitim Akademisi Dergisi*, 3(1), 41–61. DOI: 10.32960/uead.455502

Ashraf, T. A., & Ashraf, T. A. (2024). The Impact of Inter-language Related Errors among Non-English Majors at Tertiary Level Students in Bangladesh. *Language in India, 24*(1). http://languageinindia.com/jan2024/v24i1jan2024.pdf#page=12

Astini, N. K. S. (2020). Pemanfaatan Teknologi Informasi dalam Pembelajaran Tingkat Sekolah Dasar pada Masa Pandemi Covid-19. *Lampuhyang*, 11(2), 13–25. DOI: 10.47730/jurnallampuhyang.v11i2.194

Atmatzidou, S., & Demetriadis, S. (2016). Advancing students' computational thinking skills through educational robotics: A study on age and gender pertinent differences. *Robotics and Autonomous Systems*, 75, 661–670. DOI: 10.1016/j.robot.2015.10.008

Atmatzidou, S., & Demetriadis, S. N. (2012). Evaluating the Role of Collaboration Scripts as Group Guiding Tools in Activities of Educational Robotics: Conclusions from Three Case Studies. In *Proceedings of the 2012 IEEE 12th International Conference on Advanced Learning Technologies* (pp. 298–302). IEEE. DOI: 10.1109/ICALT.2012.111

Atmatzidou, S., & Markelis, I. (2008). The use of LEGO Mindstorms in elementary and secondary education: Game as a way of triggering learning. In *Proceedings of the International Conference of Simulation, Modeling and Programming for Autonomous Robots (SIMPAR)* (pp. 22–30). Venice, Italy.

Attia, M. A. (2014). Postgraduate students' perceptions toward online assessment: The case of the faculty ofeducation, Umm Al- Qura university. *In Education for a Knowledge Society in Arabian Gulf Countries* (pp.151–173). https://doi.org/DOI: 10.1108/S1479-367920140000024015

Avci, G., Mehuljic, M., & Schüller, P. (2016). Giving hints for logic programming examples without revealing solutions. *2016 24th Signal Processing and Communication Application Conference (SIU)*, 513–516. DOI: 10.1109/SIU.2016.7495790

Ayalew, Y., Tshukudu, E., & Lefoanea, M. (2018). Factors affecting programming performance of first year students at a University in Botswana. African Journal of Research in Mathematics, *Science and Technology Education, 22*(3), 363-373. https://hdl.handle.net/10520/EJC-12a2c586fa

Aydoğan, M., & Karcı, A. (2019). Kelime temsil yöntemleri ile kelime benzerliklerinin incelenmesi. Çukurova Üniversitesi Mühendislik-Mimarlık Fakültesi Dergisi, 34(2), 181-196.

Aziz, S., Mahmood, M., & Rehman, Z. (2018). Implementation of cipp model for quality evaluation at school level: A case study. *Journal of Education and Educational Development*, 5(1), 189. DOI: 10.22555/joeed.v5i1.1553

Baek, Y., Wang, S., Yang, D., Ching, Y.-H., Swanson, S., & Chittoori, B. (2019). Revisiting Second Graders' Robotics with an Understand/Use-Modify-Create (U2MC) Strategy. *European Journal of STEM Education, 4*(1), 07. https://doi.org/ DOI: 10.20897/ejsteme/5772

Bahroun, Z., Anane, C., Ahmed, V., & Zacca, A. (2023). 'Transforming Education: A Comprehensive Review of Generative Artificial Intelligence in Educational Settings through Bibliometric and Content Analysis'. *Sustainability (Basel)*, 15(17), 12983. DOI: 10.3390/su151712983

Baidoo-Anu, D., & Ansah, L. O. (2023). Education in the era of generative artificial intelligence (AI): Understanding the potential benefits of ChatGPT in promoting teaching and learning. *Journal of AI*, 7(1), 52–62.

Bai, H. (2024). Introducing Computational Thinking and Coding to Teacher Education Students. In Bosch, C., Goosen, L., & Chetty, J. (Eds.), *Navigating Computer Science Education in the 21st Century* (pp. 170–186). IGI Global., DOI: 10.4018/979-8-3693-1066-3.ch009

Bailey, J., Pavlou, M., Copas, A., McCarthy, O., Carswell, K., Rait, G., Hart, G., Nazareth, I., Free, C., French, R., & Murray, E. (2013). The sexunzipped trial: Optimizing the design of online randomized controlled trials. *Journal of Medical Internet Research*, 15(12), e278. DOI: 10.2196/jmir.2668 PMID: 24334216

Baker, C. M., Bennett, C. L., & Ladner, R. E. (2019). Educational experiences of blind programmers. In *Proceedings of the 50th ACM Technical Symposium on Computer Science Education* (pp. 759-765). DOI: 10.1145/3287324.3287410

Baker, C. M., Elglaly, Y. N., Ross, A. S., & Shinohara, K. (2022). Including accessibility in computer science education. In *Proceedings of the 24th International ACM SIGACCESS Conference on Computers and Accessibility* (pp. 1-5).

Baker, C. M., El-Glaly, Y. N., & Shinohara, K. (2020). A systematic analysis of accessibility in computing education research. In *Proceedings of the 51st ACM Technical Symposium on Computer Science Education* (pp. 107-113). DOI: 10.1145/3328778.3366843

Baker, C. M., Milne, L. R., & Ladner, R. E. (2015). Structjumper: A tool to help blind programmers navigate and understand the structure of code. In *Proceedings of the 33rd Annual ACM Conference on Human Factors in Computing Systems* (pp. 3043-3052). DOI: 10.1145/2702123.2702589

Baker, T., Smith, L., & Anissa, N. (2019). *Exploring the Future of Artificial Intelligence in Schools and Colleges*. NESTA.

Balanskat, A., & Engelhardt, K. (2014). *Computing our future: Computer programming and coding-Priorities, school curricula and initiatives across Europe*. European Schoolnet.

Ballard, E. D., & Haroldson, R. (2021). Analysis of computational thinking in children's literature for k-6 students: Literature as a non-programming unplugged resource. *Journal of Educational Computing Research*, 59(8), 1487–1516. DOI: 10.1177/07356331211004048

Banh, L., & Strobel, G. (2023). 'Generative Artificial Intelligence'. *Electronic Markets*, 33(1), 63. DOI: 10.1007/s12525-023-00680-1

Barker, B. S., Nugent, G., Grandgenett, N., & Adamchuk, V. I. (2012). *Robots in K-12 Education: A New Technology for Learning*. IGI Global. DOI: 10.4018/978-1-4666-0182-6

Barragán-Sánchez, R., Romero-Tena, R., & García-López, M. (2023). Educational Robotics to Address Behavioral Problems in Early Childhood. *Education Sciences*, 13(1), 22. Advance online publication. DOI: 10.3390/educsci13010022

Barr, D., Harrison, J., & Conery, L. (2011). Computational Thinking: A Digital Age Skill for Everyone. *Learning and Leading with Technology*, 38(6), 20–23.

Barros, J. P. (2022). Assessment for Computer Programming Courses: A Short Guide for the Undecided Teacher. In *CSEDU (2)* (pp. 549-554). https://www.scitepress.org/Link.aspx?doi=10.5220/0011095800003182

Barr, P., Biddle, R., & Noble, J. (2002). A taxonomy of user-interface metaphors. In Jones, S., & Masoodian, M. (Eds.), *Proceedings of the SIGCHI-NZ Symposium on Computer-Human Interaction* (pp.25-30). Association for Computing Machinery. DOI: 10.1145/2181216.2181221

Barr, V., & Stephenson, C. (2011). Bringing computational thinking to K-12: What is involved and what is the role of the computer science education community? *ACM Inroads*, 2(1), 48–54. DOI: 10.1145/1929887.1929905

Barzilay, M. (2013). A simple definition of cybersecurity.

Basilotta-Gómez-Pablos, V., Matarranz, M., Casado-Aranda, L., & Otto, A. (2022). Teachers' digital competencies in higher education: A systematic literature review. *International Journal of Educational Technology in Higher Education*, 19(1), 8. Advance online publication. DOI: 10.1186/s41239-021-00312-8

Başkaya, F., & Aydin, İ. (2017, September). Haber metinlerinin farkli metin madenciliği yöntemleriyle siniflandirilmasi. In *2017 International Artificial Intelligence and Data Processing Symposium (IDAP)* (pp. 1-5). IEEE.

Basogain, X., Olabe, M. Á., Olabe, J. C., & Rico, M. J. (2018). Computational thinking in pre-university blended learning classrooms. *Computers in Human Behavior*, 80, 412–419. DOI: 10.1016/j.chb.2017.04.058

Bastian, M., & Mühling, A. (2019, November). Let's Look a Layer Deeper: Design and First Results of a New Test System in the Context of Program Tracing. In *Proceedings of the 19th Koli Calling International Conference on Computing Education Research* (pp. 1-2). https://doi.org/DOI: 10.1145/3364510.3366155

Bati, K. (2022). A systematic literature review regarding computational thinking and programming in early childhood education. *Education and Information Technologies*, 27(2), 2059–2082. Advance online publication. DOI: 10.1007/s10639-021-10700-2

Battal, A., Afacan Adanr, G., & Gülbahar, Y. (2021). Computer science unplugged: A systematic literature review. *Journal of Educational Technology Systems*, 50(1), 24–47. DOI: 10.1177/00472395211018801

Battelle for Kids. (2019). *Framework for 21st Century Learning. Partnership for 21st Century Learning*. Retrieved from.

Bau, D., Dawson, M., & Pickens, C. S. (2015). *Pencil code. Proceedings of the 14th International Conference on Interaction Design and Children*. https://doi.org/DOI: 10.1145/2771839.2771875

Bau, D., Gray, J., Kelleher, C., Sheldon, J., & Turbak, F. (2017). Learnable programming: Blocks and beyond. *Communications of the ACM*, 60(6), 72–80. DOI: 10.1145/3015455

Bayyapu, N. (2022, December). PDC Course Development and Assessment Process for the betterment of Teaching-Learning Process. In *2022 IEEE 29th International Conference on High Performance Computing,Data and Analytics Workshop (HiPCW)* (pp. 12-19). IEEE. https://doi.org/DOI: 10.1109/HiPCW57629.2022.00007

BCS. (2024). British Computer Society. https://www.bcs.org/about-us/

Bebras. (2024). https://www.bebras.org/

Becker, B. A., Denny, P., Finnie-Ansley, J., Luxton-Reilly, A., Prather, J., & Santos, E. A. (2023, March). Programming is hard-or at least it used to be: Educational opportunities and challenges of ai code generation. In *Proceedings of the 54th ACM Technical Symposium on Computer Science Education* V. 1 (pp. 500-506).

Beerepoot, M. T. P. (2023). Formative and summative automated assessment with multiple-choice question banks. *Journal of Chemical Education*, 100(8), 2947–2955. DOI: 10.1021/acs.jchemed.3c00120

Begosso, L. C., Begosso, L. R., & Christ, N. A. (2020, October). An analysis of block-based programming environments for CS1. In *2020 IEEE Frontiers in Education Conference (FIE)* (pp. 1-5). IEEE.

Bell, T., & Vahrenhold, J. (2018). CS Unplugged How Is It Used, and Does It Work? In *Adventures Between Lower Bounds and Higher Altitudes* (pp. 497–521). Springer. DOI: 10.1007/978-3-319-98355-4_29

Bellegarda, J. R. (2004). 'Statistical Language Model Adaptation: Review and Perspectives'. *Speech Communication*, 42(1), 93–108. DOI: 10.1016/j.specom.2003.08.002

Bell, S. (2010). Project-based learning for the 21st century: Skills for the future. *The Clearing House: A Journal of Educational Strategies, Issues and Ideas*, 83(2), 39–43. DOI: 10.1080/00098650903505415

Benetti, E., & Mazzini, G. (2020). Coding Training Proposal for Kindergarten. *2020 International Conference on Software, Telecommunications and Computer Networks (SoftCOM)*, 1–5. DOI: 10.23919/SoftCOM50211.2020.9238207

Benitti, F. B. V. (2012). Exploring the educational potential of robotics in schools: A systematic review. *Computers & Education*, 58(3), 978–988. DOI: 10.1016/j.compedu.2011.10.006

Bers, M. U., Govind, M., & Relkin, E. (2022). Coding as Another Language: Computational Thinking, Robotics and Literacy in First and Second Grade. In *Computational Thinking in PreK-5: Empirical Evidence for Integration and Future Directions* (p. 30-38). Association for Computing Machinery. DOI: 10.1145/3507951.3519285

Bers, M. U., Strawhacker, A., & Sullivan, A. (2022). *The state of the field of computational thinking in early childhood education.*

Bers, M. U. (2010). The TangibleK Robotics Program: Applied Computational Thinking for Young Children. *Early Childhood Research & Practice*, 12(2), 2.

Bers, M. U. (2018). Coding and computational thinking in early childhood: The impact of ScratchJr in Europe. *European Journal of STEM Education*, 3(3), 8. DOI: 10.20897/ejsteme/3868

Bers, M. U. (2019). Coding as another language: A pedagogical approach for teaching computer science in early childhood. *Journal of Computers in Education*, 6(4), 499–528. DOI: 10.1007/s40692-019-00147-3

Bers, M. U. (2020). *Coding as a playground: Programming and computational thinking in the early childhood classroom*. Routledge. DOI: 10.4324/9781003022602

Bers, M. U., Flannery, L., Kazakoff, E. R., & Sullivan, A. (2014). Computational thinking and tinkering: Exploration of an early childhood robotics curriculum. *Computers & Education*, 72, 145–157. DOI: 10.1016/j.compedu.2013.10.020

Bessen, J. (2018). Artificial Intelligence and Jobs: The Role of Demand (Working Paper No. 24235). National Bureau of Economic Research.

Bhakti, C., Farozin, M., & Suwarjo, S. (2022, July). A Design of Blended Learning Core Curriculum based on Personalized Learning for Career Readiness. In *Proceedings of the 1st International Conference on Social, Science, and Technology, ICSST 2021,* 25 November 2021, Tangerang, Indonesia. DOI: 10.4108/eai.25-11-2021.2318804

Binkley, M., Erstad, O., Herman, J., Raizen, S., Ripley, M., Miller-Ricci, M., & Rumble, M. (2012). Defining Twenty-First Century Skills. In Griffin, P., McGaw, B., & Care, E. (Eds.), *Assessment and Teaching of 21st Century Skills (pp* (pp. 17–66). Springer Netherlands., DOI: 10.1007/978-94-007-2324-5_2

Bishop-Clark, C. (1998). Comparing Understanding of Programming Design Concepts Using Visual Basic and Traditional Basic. *Journal of Educational Computing Research*, 18(1), 37–47. DOI: 10.2190/0FG3-BVDK-2XB9-P1F6

Black, P., & Wiliam, D. (1998). Assessment and classroom learning. *Assessment in Education: Principles, Policy & Practice*, 5(1), 7–74. DOI: 10.1080/0969595980050102

Blanchard, S., Freiman, V., & Lirrete-Pitre, N. (2010). Strategies used by elementary schoolchildren solving robotics-based complex tasks: Innovative potential of technological progress. *Procedia: Social and Behavioral Sciences*, 2(2), 2851–2857. DOI: 10.1016/j.sbspro.2010.03.427

Blikstein, P. (2013). Digital fabrication and 'making'in education: The democratization of invention. In Walter-Herrmann, J., & Büching, C. (Eds.), *FabLabs: Of machines, makers and inventors* (pp. 203–222). Transcript Publishers. DOI: 10.14361/transcript.9783839423820.203

Blikstein, P., & Moghadam, S. H. (2018). *Pre-college computer science education: A survey of the field.* Google LLC.

Bloom, B. S., Engelhart, M. D., Furst, E. J., Hill, W. H., & Krathwohl, D. R. (1956). *Taxonomy of educational objectives: The classification of educational goals. Handbook 1: Cognitive domain.* Longman.

Blumenfeld, P. C., Soloway, E., Marx, R. W., Krajcik, J. S., Guzdial, M., & Palincsar, A. (1991). Motivating project-based learning: Sustaining the doing, supporting the learning. *Educational Psychologist*, 26(3-4), 369–398. DOI: 10.1080/00461520.1991.9653139

Bocconi, S., Chioccariello, A., & Earp, J. (2018). The Nordic Approach To Introducing Computational Thinking And Programming In Compulsary Education. *Report Prepared for the Nordic@BETT2018 Steering Group.*

Bocconi, S., Chioccariello, A., & Kampylis, P. (2022). Reviewing computational thinking in compulsory education: state of play and practices from computing education, (Ed. A.Inamorato dos Santos; Y. Punie; R. Cachia; N. Giannoutsou). European Commission, Joint Research Centre, Publications Office of the European Union. http://doi.org/DOI: 10.2760/126955

Bock, A. C., & Frank, U. (2021). Low-code platform. *Business & Information Systems Engineering*, 63(6), 733–740. DOI: 10.1007/s12599-021-00726-8

Boitshwarelo, B., Reedy, A. K., & Billany, T. (2017). Envisioning the use of online tests in assessing twentyfirst century learning: A literature review. *Research and Practice in Technology Enhanced Learning*, 12(1), 16. DOI: 10.1186/s41039-017-0055-7 PMID: 30595721

Borenstein, J., & Howard, A. (2021). 'Emerging Challenges in AI and the Need for AI Ethics Education'. *AI and Ethics*, 1(1), 61–65. DOI: 10.1007/s43681-020-00002-7 PMID: 38624388

Borko, H. (2004). Professional development and teacher learning: Mapping the terrain. *Educational Researcher*, 33(8), 3–15. DOI: 10.3102/0013189X033008003

Borko, H., & Putnam, R. T. (1995). Expanding a teacher's knowledge base: A cognitive psychological perspective on professional development. In Guskey, T. R., & Huberman, M. (Eds.), *Professional development in education: New Paradigms and Practices* (pp. 35–65). Teachers College Press.

Bosse, Y., & Gerosa, M. A. (2017). Difficulties of programming learning from the point of view of students and instructors. *IEEE Latin America Transactions*, 15(11), 2191–2199. DOI: 10.1109/TLA.2017.8070426

Bradski, G., & Kaehler, A. (2008). *Learning OpenCV: Computer Vision with the OpenCV Library*. O'Reilly Media, Inc.

Brainin, E., Shamir, A., & Eden, S. (2022). Promoting Spatial Language and Ability Among SLD Children: Can Robot Programming Make a Difference? *Journal of Educational Computing Research*, 60(7), 1742–1762. DOI: 10.1177/07356331221083224

Brandes, O., & Armoni, M. (2019). The Effects of a Professional Development Workshop Focusing on Action Research on the Practice of High-School Computer Science Teachers. *Proceedings of the 14th Workshop in Primary and Secondary Computing Education*. https://doi.org/DOI: 10.1145/3361721.3361725

Bratitsis, T., Tsapara, M., Melliou, K., Busuttil, L., Vassallo, D., Callus, J., Meireles, G., Koliakou, I., Kojok, T., & Sousa, S. (2023). Cultivating Computational Thinking in Early Years Through Board Games. The Cthink.it Approach. *IMCL2023 – 15th International Conference on Interactive Mobile Communication, Technologies and Learning*, 158–161.

Breiner, J. M., Harkness, S. S., Johnson, C. C., & Koehler, C. M. (2012). What Is STEM? A Discussion About Conceptions of STEM in Education and Partnerships. *School Science and Mathematics*, 112(1), 3–11. DOI: 10.1111/j.1949-8594.2011.00109.x

Brendefur, J. L., Johnson, E. S., Thiede, K. W., Strother, S., & Severson, H. H. (2018). Developing a multi-dimensional early elementary mathematics screener and diagnostic tool: The primary mathematics assessment. *Early Childhood Education Journal*, 46(2), 153–157. DOI: 10.1007/s10643-017-0854-x PMID: 29576730

Brennan, K. (2021). How kids manage self-directed programming projects: Strategies and structures. *Journal of the Learning Sciences*, 30(4-5), 576–610. DOI: 10.1080/10508406.2021.1936531

Brennan, K., & Resnick, M. (2012, April). New frameworks for studying and assessing the development of computational thinking. In *Proceedings of the 2012 annual meeting of the American Educational Research Association*, Vancouver, Canada (*1*, p. 25)

Brođanac, P., Novak, J., & Boljat, I. (2022). Has the time come to teach parallel programming to secondary school students? *Heliyon*, 8(1), e08662. Advance online publication. DOI: 10.1016/j.heliyon.2021.e08662 PMID: 35028449

Brouzos, R., Panayiotou, K., Tsardoulias, E., & Symeonidis, A. (2023). A Low-Code Approach for Connected Robots. *Journal of Intelligent & Robotic Systems*, 108(2), 28. DOI: 10.1007/s10846-023-01861-y

Brown, N. C. C., & Altadmri, A. (2017). Novice Java Programming Mistakes: Large-Scale Data vs. Educator Beliefs. *ACM Transactions on Computing Education, 17*(2), 7:1-7:21. DOI: 10.1145/2994154

Brown, T. B., Mann, B., Ryder, N., Subbiah, M., Kaplan, J. D., Dhariwal, P., Neelakantan, A., Shyam, P., Sastry, G., & Askell, A. (2020). Language Models Are Few-Shot Learners. *Advances in Neural Information Processing Systems*.

Bruner, J. (1990). *Acts of meaning*. Harvard University Press.

Bruner, J. S. (1966). *Toward a Theory of Instruction*. Belkapp Press.

Bui, T.-L., Tran, T.-T., Dang, U. P., Nguyen, T.-H., Nguyen, T.-L., Vu, C.-T., Nguyen, M.-T., Tran, V.-N., & Hoang, A.-D. (2024). Research on STEM in Early Childhood Education from 1992 to 2022: A Bibliometric Analysis from the Web of Science Database. *European Journal of Educational Research*, 13(3), 1057–1075. DOI: 10.12973/eu-jer.13.3.1057

Bukhari, G., Saleem, J., Bukhari, S., Ishaq, M., & Butt, M. (2022). Challenges in conducting online assessments in undergraduate medical and dental education: A scoping review. *Biomedica*, 38(3), 123–128. DOI: 10.51441/BioMedica/5-764

Bümen, N. T., Ateş, A., Çakar, E., Ural, G., & Acar, V. (2012). Professional development of teachers in the Turkish context: Issues and suggestions. *Journal of National Education. Education and Social Sciences*, 41(194), 31–50.

Bureau of Labor Statistics U.S. Department of Labor. 2023. Persons with a Disability: Labor Force Characteristics – 2022. https://www.bls.gov/news.release/pdf/disabl.pdf

Burgstahler, S., & Ladner, R. (2006). An alliance to increase the participation of individuals with disabilities in computing careers. *ACM SIGACCESS Accessibility and Computing*, (85), 3–9. DOI: 10.1145/1166118.1166119

Burgsteiner, H., Kandlhofer, M., & Steinbauer, G. (2016). IRobot: Teaching the Basics of Artificial Intelligence in High Schools. In *Proceedings of the AAArtificial Intelligence Conference on Artificial Intelligence*, Phoenix, AZ, USA, 12–17 February 2016, 30, 1. DOI: 10.1609/aaai.v30i1.9864

Burleson, W. S., Harlow, D. B., Nilsen, K. J., Perlin, K., Freed, N., Jensen, C. N., Lahey, B., Lu, P., & Muldner, K. (2018). Active Learning Environments with Robotic Tangibles: Children's Physical and Virtual Spatial Programming Experiences. *IEEE Transactions on Learning Technologies*, 11(1), 96–106. DOI: 10.1109/TLT.2017.2724031

Burström, T., Parida, V., Lahti, T., & Wincent, J. (2021). 'AI-Enabled Business-Model Innovation and Transformation in Industrial Ecosystems: A Framework, Model and Outline for Further Research'. *Journal of Business Research*, 127, 85–95. DOI: 10.1016/j.jbusres.2021.01.016

Busuttil, L., Vassallo, D., Callus, J., Bratitsis, T., Tsapara, M., Melliou, K., Meireles, G., Tarraf Kojok, N., Koliakou, I., & Sousa, S. (2023). Promoting Computational Thinking in Early Childhood: A Novel Board Game Design. *ICERI Proceedings*.

Busuttil, L., & Formosa, M. (2020). Teaching Computing without Computers: Unplugged Computing as a Pedagogical Strategy. *Informatics in Education*, 19(4), 569–587. DOI: 10.15388/infedu.2020.25

Butler, M., & Morgan, M. (2007). Learning challenges faced by novice programming students studying high level and low feedback concepts. *Proceedings ascilite Singapore*, 1(99-107). https://www.ascilite.org/conferences/singapore07/procs/butler.pdf

Butler-Henderson, K., & Crawford, J. (2020). A systematic review of online examinations: A pedagogical innova-tion for scalable authentication and integrity. *Computers & Education*, 159, 104024. DOI: 10.1016/j.compedu.2020.104024 PMID: 32982023

Buysse, V., Winton, P. J., & Rous, B. (2009). Reaching consensus on a definition of professional development for the early childhood field. *Topics in Early Childhood Special Education*, 28(4), 235–243. DOI: 10.1177/0271121408328173

Cabaj, K., Kotulski, Z., Księżopolski, B., & Mazurczyk, W. (2018). Cybersecurity: Trends, issues, and challenges. *EURASIP Journal on Information Security*, 2018(1), 1–3. DOI: 10.1186/s13635-018-0080-0

Cai, Y., Mao, S., Wu, W., Wang, Z., Liang, Y., Ge, T., . . . Duan, N. (2023). Low-code llm: Visual programming over llms. *arXiv preprint arXiv:2304.08103*, 2.

Çakır, R. (2019). Programlama öğretimi ve düşünme becerileri. In Korkmaz, Ö. (Ed.), *Programlama öğretimi yaklaşımları* (pp. 15–36). Nobel Akademik.

Calypso. (n.d.). Retrieved from

Campbell, C., & Walsh, C. (2017). Introducing the new digital literacy of coding in the early years. *Practical Literacy*, 22(3), 10–12.

Campe, S., Denner, J., Green, E., & Torres, D. (2020). Pair programming in middle school: Variations in interactions and behaviors. *Computer Science Education*, 30(1), 22–46. DOI: 10.1080/08993408.2019.1648119

Canbeldek, M. (2020). *Erken çocukluk eğitiminde üreten çocuklar kodlama ve robotik eğitim programının etkilerinin incelenmesi* [Yayınlanmamış Doktora Tezi]. Pamukkale Üniversitesi.

Canbeldek, M., & Isikoglu, N. (2023). Exploring the effects of "productive children: Coding and robotics education program" in early childhood education. *Education and Information Technologies*, 28(3), 3359–3379. DOI: 10.1007/s10639-022-11315-x

Cao, Y., Porter, L., & Zingaro, D. (2016). Examining the value of analogies in introductory computing. In *Proceedings of the 2016 ACM Conference on International Computing Education Research* (pp. 231-239). ACM. DOI: 10.1145/2960310.2960313

Carney, M., Webster, B., Alvarado, I., Phillips, K., Howell, N., Griffith, J., Jongejan, J., Pitaru, A., & Chen, A. (2020). Teachable Machine: Approachable Web-Based Tool for Exploring Machine Learning Classification. In *Proceedings of the CHI 2020*, Honolulu, HI, USA, 25–30 April 2020. DOI: 10.1145/3334480.3382839

Castro, F. E. V., & Fisler, K. (2020, February). Qualitative Analyses of Movements Between Task-level and Code-level Thinking of Novice Programmers (world). *51st ACM Technical Symposium on Computer Science Education.* DOI: 10.1145/3328778.3366847

Catota, F. E., Morgan, M. G., & Sicker, D. C. (2019). Cybersecurity education in a developing nation: *The Ecuadorian environment.Journal of Cybersecurity*, 5(1). Advance online publication. DOI: 10.1093/cybsec/tyz001

Cazorla, M., & Viejo, D. (2015). 'JavaVis: An Integrated Computer Vision Library for Teaching Computer Vision'. *Computer Applications in Engineering Education*, 23(2), 258–267. DOI: 10.1002/cae.21594

Celepkolu, M., & Boyer, K. E. (2018). Thematic analysis of students' reflections on pair programming in cs1. In *49th ACM Technical Symposium on Computer Science Education* (pp.771-776). Association for Computing Machinery. DOI: 10.1145/3159450.3159516

Çelik, H. C., Ertas, H., & İlhan, A. (2018). The impact of project-based learning on achievement and student views: The case of AutoCAD programming course. *Journal of Education and Learning*, 7(6), 67–80. DOI: 10.5539/jel.v7n6p67

Çetin, M., & Demircan, H. Ö. (2020). Empowering technology and engineering for STEM education through programming robots: A systematic literature review. *Early Child Development and Care*, 190(9), 1323–1335. DOI: 10.1080/03004430.2018.1534844

Ceylan, V. K., & Kesici, A. E. (2017). Effect of blended learning to academic achievement. *International Journal of Human Sciences*, 14(1), 308–320. DOI: 10.14687/jhs.v14i1.4141

Chao, P. Y. (2016). Exploring students' computational practice, design and performance of problem-solving through a visual programming environment. *Computers & Education*, 95, 202–215. DOI: 10.1016/j.compedu.2016.01.010

Chatzopoulos, A., Papoutsidakis, M., Kalogiannakis, M., & Psycharis, S. (2020). Innovative Robot for Educational Robotics and STEM. In Kumar, V., & Troussas, C. (Eds.), *Intelligent Tutoring Systems* (pp. 95–104). Springer International Publishing. DOI: 10.1007/978-3-030-49663-0_13

Cheah, C. S. (2020). Factors Contributing to the Difficulties in Teaching and Learning of Computer Programming: A Literature Review. *Contemporary Educational Technology*, 12(2), ep272. DOI: 10.30935/cedtech/8247

Chen, Y., Chen, Y., & Heffernan, N. (2020). Personalized math tutoring with a conversational agent. arXiv preprint arXiv:2012.12121.

Chen, L., Xiao, S., Chen, Y., Song, Y., Wu, R., & Sun, L. (2024). ChatScratch: An AI-Augmented System Toward Autonomous Visual Programming Learning for Children Aged 6-12. *Conference on Human Factors in Computing Systems - Proceedings*. DOI: 10.1145/3613904.3642229

Chetty, J., & Barlow-Jones, G. (2014). Novice students and computer programming: Toward constructivist pedagogy. *Mediterranean Journal of Social Sciences*, 5(14), 240–251. DOI: 10.5901/mjss.2014.v5n14p240

Chis, A. E., Moldovan, A. N., Murphy, L., Pathak, P., & Muntean, C. H. (2018). Investigating flipped classroom and problem-based learning in a programming module for computing conversion course. *Journal of Educational Technology & Society*, 21(4), 232–247.

Chittora, S., & Baynes, A. (2020). Interactive visualizations to introduce data science for high school students. *Proceedings of the 21st Annual Conference on Information Technology Education*. https://doi.org/DOI: 10.1145/3368308.3415360

Chou, P. N. (2020). Using ScratchJr to foster young children's computational thinking competence: A case study in a third-grade computer class. *Journal of Educational Computing Research*, 58(3), 570–595. DOI: 10.1177/0735633119872908

Christidi, Z., & Christopoulou, E. (2022). Environmental Awareness in Preschool Education via Educational Robotics and STEAM Education. *2022 7th South-East Europe Design Automation, Computer Engineering,Computer Networks and Social Media Conference (SEEDA-CECNSM)*, 1–8. DOI: 10.1109/SEEDA-CECNSM57760.2022.9932911

Çiftçi, E. (2021). *Görme engelli öğrencilere ortaokul matematiği öğreten matematik öğretmenlerinin öğretim uygulamaları ve karşılaştıkları zorluklar* (Master's thesis, Eğitim Bilimleri Enstitüsü).

Cisco The Newsroom. (2021). [Online]. Available: https://newsroom.cisco.com/c/r/newsroom/en/us/a/y2021/m11/canada-s-largest-cybersecurity-education-program-for-high-schools-launches-in-partnership-between-cisco-and-stem-fellowship.html. Access Date: 31.08.2024

Ciucan-Rusu, L., Timus, M., Stefan, D., Comes, C. A., Bunduchi, E., & Poptamas, M. A. (2023, September). Low-code solutions integration for digital process automation-application in management. In *2023 22nd RoEduNet Conference: Networking in Education and Research (RoEduNet)* (pp. 1-5). IEEE. DOI: 10.1109/RoEduNet60162.2023.10274938

Clark, R. C., & Mayer, R. E. (2016). *E-learning and the science of instruction: Proven guidelines for consumers and designers of multimedia learning*. John Wiley & Sons. DOI: 10.1002/9781119239086

Clements, D. H., & Sarama, J. (2003). Young children and technology: What does the research say? *Young Children*, 58(6), 34–40.

Clicbot. (n.d.). Retrieved from

Code.org. (n.d.). *Artificial Intelligence for Oceans*. Retrieved from.

CogBots. (n.d.). Retrieved from

Cognimates Team. (2020). *Cognimates*. Retrieved from.

CollegeBoard. (2017). *AP computer science A: Course and exam description*. AP Central.

Community, D. E. V. (2023). What are some common mistakes that beginners make when learning to code, and how can you avoid them? *DEV Community*. Retrieved from https://dev.to

Computer Science Teachers Association. (2020). *CSTA Standards for Computer Science Teachers*. Retrieved from.

Cortinovis, R., Bolton, P. F., & Caceffo, R. (2023). An Open List of Computer Programming Student's Common Problems and its Leverage in Teaching Practice. *Simpósio Brasileiro de Educação Em Computação (EDUCOMP),* 108–118. DOI: 10.5753/educomp.2023.228328

Coşkunserçe, O. (2023). Comparing the use of block-based and robot programming in introductory programming education: Effects on perceptions of programming self-efficacy. *Computer Applications in Engineering Education*, 31(5), 1234–1255. DOI: 10.1002/cae.22637

Cozmo. (n.d.). Retrieved from

Critten, V., Hagon, H., & Messer, D. (2022). Can pre-school children learn programming and coding through guided play activities? A case study in computational thinking. *Early Childhood Education Journal*, 50(6), 969–981. DOI: 10.1007/s10643-021-01236-8

Croft, A., Coggshall, J. G., Dolan, M., Powers, E., & Killion, J. (2010). *Job-embedded professional development: What it is, who is responsible, and how to get it done well*. National Comprehensive Center for Teacher Quality.

Csapó, B., & Molnár, G. (2019). Online diagnostic assessment in support of personalized teaching and learning: The eDia system. *Frontiers in Psychology*, 10, 443648. DOI: 10.3389/fpsyg.2019.01522 PMID: 31333546

CSforALL. (2024). About CSforALL. https://www.csforall.org/

CSTA. (2017). K-12 Computer Science Standards. https://members.csteachers.org/documents/en-us/46916364-83ab-4f51-85fb-06b3b25b417c/1/

CSTA. (2017a). K12 Computer Science Standards. https://members.csteachers.org/documents/en-us/46916364-83ab-4f51-85fb-06b3b25b417c/1/

CSTA. (2017b). View the CSTA K-12 Standards. https://csteachers.org/k12standards/interactive

CSTA. (2024). Computer Science Teachers Association (CSTA). https://csteachers.org/about-csta/

Cua, K. (2020). A personalized approach to professional development through a community of practice. Doctoral Dissertation, University of Kentucky, https://doi.org/DOI: 10.13023/ETD.2020.068

Cuban, L. (1984). *How teachers taught: Constancy and change in American classrooms*. Longman.

Cubetto Robot Kit. (2024). Cubetto Robot Kit Brings Coding to Students with Special Needs. https://www.bridges-canada.com/blogs/bridges-news/cubetto-coding-robot-ideal-for-students-with-special-needs

Cubetto. (2024). Cubetto: Teaching Children How to Code without Screens https://www.perkins.org/resource/cubetto-teaching-children-how-code-without-screens/

Cujdikova, M., & Stankovicova, M. (2022). The summer computer school for students with visual impairment in preparation for university. In *ICERI2022 Proceedings* (pp. 7789-7797). IATED. DOI: 10.21125/iceri.2022.2003

Cunningham, P., Cord, M., & Delany, S. J. (2008). Supervised Learning. In Cord, M., & Cunningham, P. (Eds.), *Machine Learning Techniques for Multimedia: Case Studies on Organization and Retrieval* (pp. 21–49). Springer. DOI: 10.1007/978-3-540-75171-7_2

Cuny, J., Snyder, L., & Wing, J. M. (2010, November 17). (Manuscript submitted for publication). Demystifying computational thinking for noncomputer scientists. *Work (Reading, Mass.)*.

Cyber, A. C. E. S. (2024). [Online]. Available: https://start.paloaltonetworks.com/cyber-aces.html. Access Date: 29.08.2024

Cyberlaunch. (2024). [Online]. Available: https://cyberflorida.org/cyberlaunch/. Access Date: 31.08.2024

Cybersecurity ABCs. (2019). [Online]. Available: https://haileyyamada.com/cybersecurity-abcs/. Access Date: 28.06.2024

Cybersecurity Alphabet. (2024). [Online]. Available: https://www.kaspersky.com/blog/cybersecurity-alphabet/. Access Date: 28.06.2024

D'Mello, S., Craig, S., Witherspoon, A., & Graesser, A. (2014). 'Affective and Learning-Related Dynamics during Interactions with an Intelligent Tutoring System'. *International Journal of Human-Computer Studies*, 72(6), 415–435.

Dagiene, V., & Futschek, G. (2008). Bebras international contest on informatics and computer literacy:Criteria for good tasks. *In International Conference on Informatics in Secondary Schools- Evolution and Perspectives* (pp. 19–30). Berlin, Germany: Springer. DOI: 10.1007/978-3-540-69924-8_2

Dagienė, V., & Stupurienė, G. (2016). Informatics concepts and computational thinking in k-12 education: A lithuanian perspective. *Journal of Information Processing*, 24(4), 732–739. DOI: 10.2197/ipsjjip.24.732

Dale, N. B., & Weems, C. (2014). *Programming and Problem Solving with C*. Jones & Bartlett Publishers.

Dangwal, K. L. (2017). Blended learning: An innovative approach. *Universal Journal of Educational Research*, 5(1), 129–136. DOI: 10.13189/ujer.2017.050116

Danhieux, P. (2022, September 12). Navigating the developer shortage crisis: A time to define the developer of the future. Forbes. Retrieved May 15, 2024, from https://www.forbes.com/sites/forbestechcouncil/2022/09/12/navigating-the-developer-shortage-crisis-a-time-to-define-the-developer-of-the-future/?sh=75d222da2a5c

Danielson, C. (2006). *Teacher Leadership That Strengthens Professional Practice*. ASCD.

Darling-Hammond, L., Hyler, M. E., & Gardner, M. (2017). *Effective Teacher Professional Development*. Learning Policy Institute. DOI: 10.54300/122.311

Das, M., Marghitu, D., Mandala, M., & Howard, A. (2021, July). Accessible block-based programming for k-12 students who are blind or low vision. In *International Conference on Human-Computer Interaction* (pp. 52-61). Cham: Springer International Publishing. DOI: 10.1007/978-3-030-78095-1_5

Davis, J. H., & Belm, T. (1978). Terminology of drama/theatre with and for children: A redefinition. *Children's Theatre Review*, 27(1), 10–11.

Day, C. (1999). *Developing teachers: The challenges of lifelong learning*. Falmer Press.

de Jager, A., Fogarty, A., Tewson, A., Lenette, C., & Boydell, K. M. (2017). Digital Storytelling in Research: A Systematic Review. *The Qualitative Report*, 22(10), 2548–2582. DOI: 10.46743/2160-3715/2017.2970

De la Higuera, C. (2019). A Report about Education, Training Teachers and Learning Artificial Intelligence: Overview of Key Issues. Working Paper Prepared for the Knowledge Societies Division, Communication and Information Sector of the UNESCO. Retrieved from

De Michell, G., & Gupta, R. K. (1997). Hardware/software co-design. *Proceedings of the IEEE*, 85(3), 349–365. DOI: 10.1109/5.558708

Dede, C., Ketelhut, D. J., Whitehouse, P., Breit, L., & McCloskey, E. M. (2009). A research agenda for online teacher professional development. *Journal of Teacher Education*, 60(1), 8–19. DOI: 10.1177/0022487108327554

del Olmo-Muñoz, J., Cózar-Gutiérrez, R., & González-Calero, J. A. (2020). Computational thinking through unplugged activities in early years of primary education. *Computers & Education*, 150, 103832. DOI: 10.1016/j.compedu.2020.103832

Demir, T., & Şen, Ü. (2009). Görme engelli öğrencilerin çeşitli değişkenler açısından öğrenme stilleri üzerine bir araştırma. *Journal of International Social Research*, 2(8), 154–161.

Deng, W., Pi, Z., Lei, W., Zhou, Q., & Zhang, W. (2019). Pencil code improves learners' computational thinking and computer learning attitude. *Computer Applications in Engineering Education*, 28(1), 90–104. DOI: 10.1002/cae.22177

Deniz, S., Lee, D., Kurian, G., Altamirano, L., Yee, D., Ferra, M., . . . Oh, P. (2019, January). Computer vision for attendance and emotion analysis in school settings. In 2019 IEEE 9th Annual Computing and Communication Workshop and Conference (CCWC) (pp. 0134-0139). IEEE.

Denning, P. J. (2009). The profession of IT Beyond computational thinking. *Communications of the ACM*, 52(6), 28–30. DOI: 10.1145/1516046.1516054

Denning, P. J., Comer, D. E., Gries, D., Mulder, M. C., Tucker, A., Turner, A. J., & Young, P. R. (1989). Computing as a discipline. *Computer*, 22(2), 63–70. DOI: 10.1109/2.19833

Denny, P., Luxton-Reilly, A., & Tempero, E. (2012). All syntax errors are not equal. *Proceedings of the 17th ACM Annual Conference on Innovation and Technology in Computer Science Education*, 75–80. https://doi.org/DOI: 10.1145/2325296.2325318

Denny, P., MacNeil, S., Savelka, J., Porter, L., & Luxton-Reilly, A. (2024). Desirable characteristics for AI teaching assistants in programming education. In *Proceedings of the 2024 on Innovation and Technology in Computer Science Education (ITiCSE),* Vol. 1 (pp. 408–414). Association for Computing Machinery. DOI: 10.1145/3649217.3653574

Dermo, J. (2009). E-assessment and the student learning experience: A survey of student percep tions of e-assessment. *British Journal of Educational Technology*, 40(2), 203–214. DOI: 10.1111/j.1467-8535.2008.00915.x

Desimone, L. M. (2009). Improving impact studies of teachers' professional development: Toward better conceptualizations and measures. *Educational Researcher*, 38(3), 181–199. DOI: 10.3102/0013189X08331140

Developers, TensorFlow. 2021. 'TensorFlow'. Zenodo. DOI: 10.5281/zenodo.4758419

Dewi, A. N., & Sørensen, B. (2023). Higher-order thinking skills and metaphor. *Southern Semiotic Review*, 18(ii), 1–35. DOI: 10.33234/SSR.18.1

Diagnosticquestions. (2024). https://diagnosticquestions.com/Quantum

Dick, W., & Carey, L. (1996). *The systematic design of instruction* (4th ed.). HarperCollins College Publishers.

Dike, H. U., Zhou, Y., Deveerasetty, K. K., & Wu, Q. 2018. 'Unsupervised Learning Based On Artificial Neural Network: A Review'. Pp. 322–27 in *2018 IEEE International Conference on Cyborg and Bionic Systems (CBS)*. Shenzhen: IEEE. DOI: 10.1109/CBS.2018.8612259

Dillenbourg, P. (1999). *Collaborative learning: Cognitive and computational approaches*. Elsevier.

Dilmen, K., Kert, S. B., & Uğraş, T. (2023). Children's coding experiences in a block-based coding environment: A usability study on code.org. *Education and Information Technologies*, 28(9), 10839–10864. DOI: 10.1007/s10639-023-11625-8

Ding, G., Shi, X., & Li, S. (2024). Integrating programming errors into knowledge graphs for automated assignment of programming tasks. *Education and Information Technologies*, 29(5), 5947–5980. DOI: 10.1007/s10639-023-12026-7

Djenic, S., & Mitic, J. (2017). Teaching Strategies and Methods in Modern Environments for Learning of Programming. International Association for Development of the Information Society. Retrieved June 23, 2024 from https://files.eric.ed.gov/fulltext/ED579455.pdf

Dogan, S., Pringle, R., & Mesa, J. (2015). The impacts of professional learning communities on science teachers' knowledge, practice and student learning: A review. *Professional Development in Education*, 42(4), 569–588. DOI: 10.1080/19415257.2015.1065899

Dongo, T., Reed, A. H., & O'Hara, M. (2016). Exploring pair programming benefits for MIS majors. *Journal of Information Technology Education: Innovations in Practice*, 15, 223–239. DOI: 10.28945/3625

Doss, B. D., Cicila, L. N., Georgia, E. J., Roddy, M. K., Nowlan, K. M., Benson, L. A., & Christensen, A. (2016). A randomized controlled trial of the web-based ourrelationship program: Effects on relationship and individual functioning. *Journal of Consulting and Clinical Psychology*, 84(4), 285–296. DOI: 10.1037/ccp0000063 PMID: 26999504

Downer, T., & Slade, C. (2019). Starting early: Using ePortfolios to prepare first year midwifery students for professional practice. In Trimmer, K., Newman, T., & Padró, F. (Eds.), *Ensuring quality in professional education* (Vol. I, pp. 73–98). Palgrave Macmillan., https://link.springer.com/chapter/10.1007/978-3-030-01096-6_4 DOI: 10.1007/978-3-030-01096-6_4

Dreher, C., Reiners, T., & Dreher, H. (2011). Investigating factors affecting the uptake of automated assessment technology. *Journal of Information Technology Education*, 10, 161–181. DOI: 10.28945/1492

Dropčová, V. (2016). *Peer Review and Peer Assessment in Higher Computer Science Education.* (PhD thesis). Comenius University.

Drosos, I., Guo, P. J., & Parnin, C. (2017). HappyFace: Identifying and predicting frustrating obstacles for learning programming at scale. In *2017 IEEE Symposium on Visual Languages and Human-Centric Computing (VL/HCC)* (pp. 171-179). IEEE. DOI: 10.1109/VLHCC.2017.8103465

Dunn, L., Morgan, C., O'Reilly, M., & Parry, S. (2003). *The student assessment handbook: New directions in traditional and online assessment*. Routledge., DOI: 10.4324/9780203416518

Durak, H. Y., Yilmaz, F. G. K., & Yilmaz, R. (2019). Computational Thinking, Programming Self-Efficacy, Problem Solving and Experiences in the Programming Process Conducted with Robotic Activities. *Contemporary Educational Technology*, 10(2), 173–197. DOI: 10.30935/cet.554493

Dweck, C. S. (2006). *Mindset: The New Psychology of Success*. Random House.

Ebersole, E. (2019). Preservice teacher experience with technology integration: How the preservice teacher's efficacy in technology integration is impacted by the context of the preservice teacher education program. *International Dialogues on Education Journal*, 6(2). Advance online publication. DOI: 10.53308/ide.v6i2.64

Edwards, A. D. (2008). Assistive Technologies. In Harper, S., & Yesilada, Y. (Eds.), *Web Accessibility. Human-Computer Interaction Series*. Springer., DOI: 10.1007/978-1-84800-050-6_10

Eguchi, A. (2017). Bringing robotics in classrooms. In Khine, M. S. (Ed.), *Robotics in STEM Education* (pp. 3–31). Springer. DOI: 10.1007/978-3-319-57786-9_1

Eguchi, A. (2022). Understanding Machine Learning Through Artificial Intelligence-powered Educational Robotics—Pilot Study with Undergraduate Students. In Lepuschitz, W., Merdan, M., Koppensteiner, G., Balogh, R., & Obdržálek, D. (Eds.), *Robotics in Education* (pp. 52–62). Springer. DOI: 10.1007/978-3-031-12848-6_5

Eguchi, A. (2023). Machine Learning Application with Artificial Intelligence-Robotics Tool—What We Learned from Pilot Studies. In Cascalho, J. M., Tokhi, M. O., Silva, M. F., Mendes, A., Goher, K., & Funk, M. (Eds.), *Robotics in Natural Settings* (pp. 383–394). Springer. DOI: 10.1007/978-3-031-15226-9_36

El Naqa, I., & Murphy, M. J. (2015). What Is Machine Learning? In El Naqa, I., Li, R., & Murphy, M. J. (Eds.), *Machine Learning in Radiation Oncology: Theory and Applications* (pp. 3–11). Springer International Publishing. DOI: 10.1007/978-3-319-18305-3_1

El-Alfy, E.-S. M., & Abdel-Aal, R. E. (2008). 'Construction and Analysis of Educational Tests Using Abductive Machine Learning'. *Computers & Education*, 51(1), 1–16. DOI: 10.1016/j.compedu.2007.03.003

Elglaly, Y. N., Baker, C. M., Ross, A. S., & Shinohara, K. (2024, March). Beyond HCI: The Need for Accessibility Across the CS Curriculum. In *Proceedings of the 55th ACM Technical Symposium on Computer Science Education* V. 1 (pp. 324-330). DOI: 10.1145/3626252.3630788

El-Hamamsy, L., Zapata-Cáceres, M., Barroso, E. M., Mondada, F., Zufferey, J. D., & Bruno, B. (2022). The competent computational thinking test: Development and validation of an unplugged computational thinking test for upper primary school. *Journal of Educational Computing Research*, 60(7), 1818–1866. DOI: 10.1177/07356331221081753

El-Mahamdi, E., S. Farhadkhani, R. Guerraoui, and others. 2023. 'On the Impossible Safety of Large Language Models'.

Elshan, E., Ebel, P., Söllner, M., & Leimeister, J. M. (2023). Leveraging low code development of smart personal assistants: An integrated design approach with the SPADE method. *Journal of Management Information Systems*, 40(1), 96–129. DOI: 10.1080/07421222.2023.2172776

Eminağaoğlu, M., & Gökşen, Y. (2009). Information Security; What Is and What Is Not, Information Security Problems in Turkey and Some Related Solutions. *Dokuz Eylul University The Journal of Graduate School of Social Sciences,* 11(4), 01-15

Engelberger, F., Galaz-Davison, P., Bravo, G., Rivera, M., & Ramírez-Sarmiento, C. A. (2021). Developing and implementing cloud-based tutorials that combine bioinformatics software, interactive coding, and visualization exercises for distance learning on structural bioinformatics. *Journal of Chemical Education*, 98(5), 1801–1807. DOI: 10.1021/acs.jchemed.1c00022

Enjoy Algorithms. (2023). Guide to master DSA and crack the coding interview. Retrieved from https://www.enjoyalgorithms.com/blog/guide-to-master-dsa-and-crack-the-coding-interview

Entwistle, N., & Tait, H. (1995). *Approaches to studying. New Directions for Teaching and Learning, 64, Winter* (Hativa, N., & Marincovic, M., Eds.). JosseyBass.

Erdağı, E. (2024). 'A Model for Automating Course Selection for Teachers and Managers with Natural Language Processing Methods'. 9(2).

Erdağı, E. 2023. 'Bilgisayar Bilimi Eğitiminde Doğal Dil İşleme'. Pp. 205–18 in *Teoriden Uygulamaya Bilgisayar Bilimi Eğitimi*. Ankara: Nobel Akademik Yayıncılık.

Erdağı, E., & Tunalı, V. (2022). 'Assignment of Part-Time Teachers in the Ministry of National Education with Artificial Learning Techniques'.

Erdağı, E., & Tunalı, V. (2024) 'Comparison of Feature-Based Sentence Ranking Methods for Extractive Summarization of Turkish News Texts'. *Sigma Journal of Engineering and Natural Sciences – Sigma Mühendislik ve Fen Bilimleri Dergisi* 321–34. .DOI: 10.14744/sigma.2023.00076

Erkul, D., & Kert, S. B. (2022). A scale for monitoring students' tendencies to ubiquitous learning environments. *Yıldız Journal of Educational Research*, 7(1), 1–11. DOI: 10.14744/yjer.2022.001

Ersözlü, A., & Clark, A. C. (2019). Augmented reality research in education: A bibliometric study. *Eurasia Journal of Mathematics, Science and Technology Education*, 15(10). Advance online publication. DOI: 10.29333/ejmste/103904

Ertmer, P. A., & Ottenbreit-Leftwich, A. T. (2010). Teacher technology change: How knowledge, confidence, beliefs, and culture intersect. *Journal of Research on Technology in Education*, 42(3), 255–284. DOI: 10.1080/15391523.2010.10782551

Ertmer, P. A., Ottenbreit-Leftwich, A. T., Sadik, O., Sendurur, E., & Sendurur, P. (2012). Teacher beliefs and technology integration practices: A critical relationship. *Computers & Education*, 59(2), 423–435. DOI: 10.1016/j.compedu.2012.02.001

Erümit, A. K. (2020). Effects of different teaching approaches on programming skills. *Education and Information Technologies*, 25(2), 1013–1037. DOI: 10.1007/s10639-019-10010-8

Erümit, A., & Berigel, M. (2018). Programlama dillerinin tarihi ve programlama öğretimi. In Gülbahar, Y., & Karal, H. (Eds.), *Kuramdan Uygulamaya Programlama Öğretimi* (pp. 1–36). Pegem Akademi.

Erümit, K. A., Karal, H., Şahin, G., Aksoy, D. A., Aksoy, A., & Benzer, A. İ. (2019). A model suggested for programming teaching: Programming in seven steps. *Education in Science*, 44(197), 155–183. DOI: 10.15390/EB.2018.7678

Erümit, S. F., & Keles, E. (2023). Examining computer science education of Asia-Pacific countries successful in the PISA. *Journal of Educational Technology and Online Learning*, 6(1), 82–104. DOI: 10.31681/jetol.1154913

Espinal, A., Vieira, C., & Guerrero-Bequis, V. (2023). Student ability and difficulties with transfer from a block-based programming language into other programming languages: A case study in Colombia. *Computer Science Education*, 33(4), 567–599. DOI: 10.1080/08993408.2022.2079867

Esser, P., Chiu, J., Atighehchian, P., Granskog, J., & Germanidis, A. (2023). Structure and content-guided video synthesis with diffusion models. In *Proceedings of the IEEE/CVF International Conference on Computer Vision* (pp. 7346-7356).

Esteves, J. (n.d). What Is the Future of Cybersecurity? [Online]. Available: https://www.ie.edu/insights/ideas-to-shape-the-future/idea/what-is-the-future-of-cybersecurity/. Access Date: 27.08.2024

European Union Agency For Cybersecurity. (October 2023). Enısa Threat Landscape 2023, July 2022 to June 2023. [Online]. Available: https://www.enisa.europa.eu/publications/enisa-threat-landscape-2023. Access Date: 31.08.2024

Evangelista, I., Blesio, G., & Benatti, E. (2018). Why Are We Not Teaching Machine Learning at High School? A Proposal. In Proceedings of the 2018 World Engineering Education Forum—Global Engineering Deans Council (WEEF-GEDC) (pp. 1–6).

Fagerlund, J., Häkkinen, P., Vesisenaho, M., & Viiri, J. (2021). Computational thinking in programming with Scratch in primary schools: A systematic review. *Computer Applications in Engineering Education*, 29(1), 12–28. DOI: 10.1002/cae.22255

Fairman, J., Smith, D., Pullen, P., & Lebel, S. (2020). The challenge of keeping teacher professional development relevant. *Professional Development in Education*, 49(2), 197–209. DOI: 10.1080/19415257.2020.1827010

Faisal, M. H., AlAmeeri, A. W., & Alsumait, A. A. (2015, December). An adaptive e-learning framework: crowdsourcing approach. In *Proceedings of the 17th International Conference on Information Integration and Web-based Applications & Services* (pp. 1-5).

Falloon, G. (2024). Advancing young students' computational thinking: An investigation of structured curriculum in early years primary schooling. *Computers and Education, 216.0.* DOI: 10.1016/j.compedu.2024.105045

Fanchamps, N. L., Slangen, L., Hennissen, P., & Specht, M. (2021). The influence of SRA programming on algorithmic thinking and self-efficacy using Lego robotics in two types of instruction. *International Journal of Technology and Design Education*, 31(2), 203–222. DOI: 10.1007/s10798-019-09559-9

Federal Bureau of Investigation. (2023). *Internet Crime Report,* Internet Crime Complaint Centre. [Online]. Available: https://www.ic3.gov/Media/PDF/AnnualReport/2023_IC3Report.pdf. Access Date: 31.08.2024

Felder, R. M., & Silverman, L. K. (1988). Learning and teaching styles in engineering education. *Engineering Education*, 78(7), 674–681.

Feng, Z., Guo, D., Tang, D., Duan, N., Feng, X., Gong, M., . . . Zhou, M. (2020). Codebert: A pre-trained model for programming and natural languages. arXiv preprint arXiv:2002.08155.

Filiz, E. (2019). An Application of Machine Learning Methods on Trend Data: International Study of Trends in Mathematics and Science 2015, Turkey Case. (Unpublished doctoral dissertation). Yıldız Technical University, Institute of Science, Istanbul.

Filiz, A. (2019). *Dergi Adı, Cilt(Sayı)*. Sayfa Aralığı. [Çalışmanın Başlığı]

Fishman, B. J., Konstantopoulos, S., Kubitskey, B. W., Vath, R. J., Park, G., Johnson, H., & Edelson, D. C. (2013). Comparing the impact of online and face-to-face professional development in the context of curriculum implementation. *Journal of Teacher Education*, 64(5), 426–438. DOI: 10.1177/0022487113494413

Flannery, L. P., Silverman, B., Kazakoff, E. R., Bers, M. U., Bontá, P., & Resnick, M. (2013). Designing ScratchJr: support for early childhood learning through computer programming. *Proceedings of the 12th International Conference on Interaction Design and Children*, 1–10. DOI: 10.1145/2485760.2485785

Flavin, M. (2021). A Disruptive Innovation perspective on students' opinions of online assessment. *Research in Learning Technology*, 29, •••. https://journal.alt.ac.uk/index.php/rlt/article/view/2611/2887. DOI: 10.25304/rlt.v29.2611

Flood, V. J., Wang, X. C., & Sheridan, M. (2022). Embodied responsive teaching for supporting computational thinking in early childhood. *Proceedings of International Conference of the Learning Sciences, ICLS*, 855 - 862. https://www.scopus.com/inward/record.uri?eid=2-s2.0-85145770444&partnerID=40&md5=60994482aacf819ed93b47195152cee6

Fluck, A., Webb, M., Cox, M., Angeli, C., Malyn-Smith, J., Voogt, J., & Zagami, J. (2016). Arguing for computer science in the school curriculum. *Journal of Educational Technology & Society*, 19(3), 38–46.

Forsström, S., & Kaufmann, O. (2018). A literature review exploring the use of programming in mathematics education. *International Journal of Learning. Teaching and Educational Research.*, 17(12), 18–32. DOI: 10.26803/ijlter.17.12.2

Fowler, B., & Vegas, E. (2021). *How England Implemented Its Computer Science Education Program*. Center for Universal Education at The Brookings Institution.

Francia, G.III, Thornton, D., Trifas, M., & Bowden, T. (2014). *Gamification of information security awareness training. Emerging trends in ICT security*. Morgan Kaufmann.

freeCodeCamp. (2023). Mistakes every programmer makes when learning to code – and how to fix them. *freeCodeCamp*. Retrieved from https://freecodecamp.org

Fridberg, M., & Redfors, A. (2024). Teachers' and children's use of words during early childhood STEM teaching supported by robotics. *International Journal of Early Years Education*, 32(2), 405–419. DOI: 10.1080/09669760.2021.1892599

From Your Eyes. (2024). https://www.farkyaratanlar.org/tr-tr/haberler-duyurular/fark-yaratan-roportaj-from-your-eyes--zulal-tannur

Fry, S. M. (1996). *A handbook for using creative dramatics in elementary Ohio history* (Doctoral dissertation, University of Dayton.).

Fuchs, K. (2023). Exploring the Opportunities and Challenges of NLP Models in Higher Education: Is Chat GPT a Blessing or a Curse? *Frontiers in Education*, 8, 1166682. DOI: 10.3389/feduc.2023.1166682

Fullan, M. (2007). *The New Meaning of Educational Change* (4th ed.). Teachers College Press.

Funcke, M. (2014). *Developing high-fidelity mental models of programming concepts using manipulatives and interactive metaphors.* [Doctoral dissertation, Rhodes University], Repository http://hdl.handle.net/10962/d1017929

Gagné, R. M. (1985). *The conditions of learning* (4th ed.). Holt, Rinehart & Winston.

Gagne, R. M., Wager, W. W., Golas, K. C., Keller, J. M., & Russell, J. D. (2005). Principles of instructional design. *Performance Improvement*, 44(2), 44–46. DOI: 10.1002/pfi.4140440211

Ganser, T. (2000). An Ambitions Vision of Professional Development for Teachers. *NASSP Bulletin*, 84(618), 6–12. DOI: 10.1177/019263650008461802

García-Martínez, I., Batanero, J. M. F., Fernández-Cerero, J., & León, S. P. (2023). Analysing the impact of artificial intelligence and computational sciences on student performance: Systematic review and meta-analysis. *Journal of New Approaches in Educational Research*, 12(1), 171–197. DOI: 10.7821/naer.2023.1.1240

Garet, M. S., Porter, A. C., Desimone, L., Birman, B. F., & Yoon, K. S. (2001). What makes professional development effective? Results from a national sample of teachers. *American Educational Research Journal*, 38(4), 915–945. DOI: 10.3102/00028312038004915

Garneli, V., Giannakos, M. N., & Chorianopoulos, K. (2015, March). Computing education in K-12 schools: A review of the literature. In *2015 IEEE Global Engineering Education Conference (EDUCON)* (pp. 543-551). IEEE. DOI: 10.1109/EDUCON.2015.7096023

Garner, S. (2003, June). Learning resources and tools to aid novices learn programming. In *Informing science & information technology education joint conference* (pp. 213–222). INSITE., https://proceedings.informingscience.org/IS2003Proceedings/docs/036Garne.pdf DOI: 10.28945/2613

Garrison, C., & Ehringhaus, M. (2007). *Formative and summative assessments in the classroom.* Retrieved from https://www.nwea.org/blog/2017/formative-vs-summative-assessments-whats-difference/

Gärtig-Daugs, A., Weitz, K., Wolking, M., & Schmid, U. (2016, October). Computer science experimenters kit for use in preschool and primary school. *Proceedings of the 11th Workshop in Primary and Secondary Computing Education.* DOI: 10.1145/2978249.2978258

Gaspar, A., & Langevin, S. (2007). Restoring coding with intention in introductory programming courses. In B. Sweeney & D. Feinstein (Eds.), *The 8th ACM SIGITE conference on information technology education*, (pp. 91-98). ASCM. DOI: 10.1145/1324302.1324323

Geçitli, E., & Bümen, N. (2020). Kademelendirilmiş etkinlik yoluyla metin tabanlı programlama öğretimi: İşbirlikli bir eylem araştırması. *Asya Öğretim Dergisi*, 8(2), 64–85. DOI: 10.47215/aji.791967

Gee, J. P. (2003). What video games have to teach us about learning and literacy. [CIE]. *Computers in Entertainment*, 1(1), 20–20. DOI: 10.1145/950566.950595

Gentner, D., Faikenhain, B., & Skorstad, J. (1987). Metaphor: The Good, The Bad and the Ugly. In *Proceedings of the 1987 workshop on Theoretical issues in natural language processing (TINLAP'87).* (pp. 176–180). Association for Computational Linguistics. DOI: 10.3115/980304.980345

Gerard, L., Varma, K., Corliss, S., & Linn, M. (2011). Professional Development for Technology-Enhanced Inquiry Science. *Review of Educational Research*, 81(3), 408–448. DOI: 10.3102/0034654311415121

Gibbs, K., & Beamish, W. (2020). Differentiated instruction: A programming tool for inclusion. In van Rensburg, H., & O'Neill, S. (Eds.), *Inclusive Theory and Practice in Special Education* (pp. 174–191). IGI Global., DOI: 10.4018/978-1-7998-2901-0.ch009

Gil Fonseca, N., Macedo, L., & Mendes, A. J. (2018). Supporting differentiated instruction in programming courses through permanent progress monitoring. In *Proceedings of the 49th ACM Technical Symposium on Computer Science Education* (pp. 209-214). ACM. DOI: 10.1145/3159450.3159578

Gill, S. S., Thibodeau, D., Kaur, R., Naeem, U., & Stockman, T. (2023). Reflection on Teaching Observation for Computer Science and Engineering to Design Effective Teaching Resources in Transnational Higher Education. In *Handbook of Research on Developments and Future Trends in Transnational Higher Education* (pp. 307–325). IGI Global. DOI: 10.4018/978-1-6684-5226-4.ch016

Glezou, K. V. (2020). Robotics as a Powerful Vehicle Toward Learning and Computational Thinking in Secondary Education of 21st Century. Papadakis, S., & Kalogiannakis, M. (Eds.). *Handbook of research on using educational robotics to facilitate student learning* (p. 1-40). IGI Global.

Goldenberg, E. P., & Carter, C. J. (2021). Programming as a language for young children to express and explore mathematics in school. *British Journal of Educational Technology*, 52(3), 969–985. DOI: 10.1111/bjet.13080

Goleman, D. (1998). *Working with Emotional Intelligence*. Bantam Books.

Gomez, F. C.Jr, Trespalacios, J., Hsu, Y., & Yang, D. (2021). Exploring teachers' technology integration self-efficacy through the 2017 iste standards. *TechTrends*, 66(2), 159–171. DOI: 10.1007/s11528-021-00639-z PMID: 34378007

Gonsalves, C. (2023). On chatgpt: What promise remains for multiple choice assessment? *Journal of Learning Development in Higher Education*, (27). Advance online publication. DOI: 10.47408/jldhe.vi27.1009

González, Y. A. C., & Muñoz-Repiso, A. G.-V. (2017). Educational robotics for the formation of programming skills and computational thinking in childish. *2017 International Symposium on Computers in Education (SIIE)*, 1–5. DOI: 10.1109/SIIE.2017.8259652

González, Y. A. C., & Muñoz-Repiso, A. G.-V. (2018, October). A robotics-based approach to foster programming skills and computational thinking. *Proceedings of the Sixth International Conference on Technological Ecosystems for Enhancing Multiculturality*. DOI: 10.1145/3284179.3284188

Goode, J., Chapman, G., & Margolis, J. (2012). 'Beyond Curriculum: The Exploring Computer Science Program'. *ACM Inroads*, 3(2), 47–53. DOI: 10.1145/2189835.2189851

Goodfellow, I., Pouget-Abadie, J., Mirza, M., Xu, B., Warde-Farley, D., Ozair, S., & Bengio, Y. (2014). Generative adversarial nets. *Advances in Neural Information Processing Systems*, •••, 27.

Goodfellow, M., & Liaskos, K. (2023, June). Tips for effective blended learning for computer science education. *Proceedings of the Conference on Innovation and Technology in Computer Science Education.* 2, pp. 589-590. ACM. DOI: 10.1145/3587103.3594159

Good, J., Miller, V., & Cathy, G. (2004). *Reforming Professional Development at the School Site: New Standards and New Practices.* University of Arkansas.

Good, R. (2011). Formative use of assessment information: It's a process, so let's say what we mean. *Practical Assessment, Research & Evaluation*, 16, 1–6.

Google Teachable Machine. (n.d.). Retrieved from

Goosen, L. (1999). *Doeltreffende onderrig van Rekenaarstudie in die sekondêre skool, met spesifieke verwysing na uitkomsgerigte onderwys (Effective teaching of Computer Studies in the secondary school, with specific reference to Outcomes-Based Education.* (MEd dissertation). Potchefstroom University for Christian Higher Education.

Goosen, L. (2020a). Effective Teaching of Information Technology for Meaningful Change in Secondary Education. In M. Motseke, M. Chitiyo, U. I. Ogbonnaya, O. C. Dada, & G. Charles-Ogan (Ed.), *Proceedings of the South Africa International Conference on Education (SAICEd)* (pp. 212-222). Pretoria: African Academic Research Forum.

Goosen, L. (2020b). A Model for Effectively Teaching Information Technology. (R. Silhavy, P. Silhavy, & Z. Prokopova, Eds.) *Advances in Intelligent Systems and Computing, 1294*, 357-371. DOI: 10.1007/978-3-030-63322-6_29

Goosen, L. (2004). *Criteria and Guidelines for the Selection and Implementation of a First Programming Language in High Schools.* Potchefstroom Campus: North West University., Retrieved from http://hdl.handle.net/10394/226

Gordon, M., Rivera, E., Ackermann, E., & Breazeal, C. (2015). Designing a relational social robot toolkit for preschool children to explore computational concepts. *Proceedings of IDC 2015: The 14th International Conference on Interaction Design and Children*, 355–358. DOI: 10.1145/2771839.2771915

Graham, C. R. (2006). Blended learning systems: Definition, current trends, and future directions. In *Handbook of blended learning: Global perspectives, local designs* (pp. 3–21). Pfeiffer Publishing.

Graham, C. R., Henrie, C. R., & Gibbons, A. S. (2014). Developing models and theory for blended learning research. In Spector, J. M., Merrill, M. D., Elen, J., & Bishop, M. J. (Eds.), *Handbook of Research on Educational Communications and Technology* (4th ed., pp. 485–495). Springer., DOI: 10.1007/978-1-4614-3185-5_38

Gray, M. E., & Holyoak, K. J. (2021). Teaching by analogy: From theory to practice. *Mind, Brain and Education : the Official Journal of the International Mind, Brain, and Education Society*, 15(3), 250–263. DOI: 10.1111/mbe.12288

Gresse von Wangenheim, C., Hauck, J. C., Pacheco, F. S., & Bertonceli Bueno, M. F. (2021). Visual tools for teaching machine learning in K-12: A ten-year systematic mapping. *Education and Information Technologies*, 26(5), 5733–5778. DOI: 10.1007/s10639-021-10570-8 PMID: 33967587

Grover, S., & Pea, R. (2018). Computational thinking: A competency whose time has come. *Computer science education: Perspectives on teaching and learning in school, 19*(1), 19-38.

Grover, S., & Basu, S. (2017, March). Measuring student learning in introductory block-based programming: Examining misconceptions of loops, variables, and boolean logic. In *Proceedings of the 2017 ACM SIGCSE technical symposium on computer science education* (pp. 267-272). DOI: 10.1145/3017680.3017723

Grover, S., & Pea, R. (2013). Computational Thinking in K-12: A Review of the State of the Field. *Educational Researcher*, 42(1), 38–43. Advance online publication. DOI: 10.3102/0013189X12463051

Gündüz, M., & Tosik, E. G. (2023). Bilgisayar Bilimi Eğitiminde Çevrimiçi Değerlendirme Uygulamaları [Online Assessment Applications in Computer Science Education]. *Teoriden Uygulamaya Bilgisayar Bilimi Eğitimi* [Computer Science Education from Theory to Practice]. (Ed. S. B. Kert), Nobel Publishing.

Gupta, P., & Gupta, V. (2012). 'A Survey of Text Question Answering Techniques'. *International Journal of Computer Applications*, 53(4), 1–8. DOI: 10.5120/8406-2030

Gupta, R., Pal, S., Kanade, A., & Shevade, S. (2017). DeepFix: Fixing Common C Language Errors by Deep Learning. *Proceedings of the AAAI Conference on Artificial Intelligence*, 31(1), 1. Advance online publication. DOI: 10.1609/aaai.v31i1.10742

Gür, B. S., & Çelik, Z. (2009). National education system in Turkey: Structural problems and suggestions. *Politics. Economics and Social Research Foundation*, 1, 29–32.

Guskey, T. R. (2000). *Evaluating professional development*. Corwin Press.

Guskey, T. R. (2002). Professional development and teacher change. *Teachers and Teaching*, 8(3), 381–391. DOI: 10.1080/135406002100000512

Guttman, F. (2011). Accesibilitatea studen ilor cu deficien e de vedere în Universită ile clujene, în: Calitatea vie ii, XXII, nr. 2, 2011, p. 201-214, on-line: https://www.revistacalitateavietii.ro/2011/CV-2-2011/05.pdf

Haigh, T., & Ceruzzi, P. E. (2021). *A new history of modern computing*. MIT Press. DOI: 10.7551/mitpress/11436.001.0001

Hall, J. A., & McCormick, K. I. (2022). My Cars don't Drive Themselves: Preschoolers' Guided Play Experiences with Button-Operated Robots. *TechTrends*, 66(3), 510–526. DOI: 10.1007/s11528-022-00727-8

Happe, L., Buhnova, B., Koziolek, A., & Wagner, I. (2021). Effective measures to foster girls' interest in secondary computer science education: A Literature Review. *Education and Information Technologies*, 26(3), 2811–2829. DOI: 10.1007/s10639-020-10379-x

Hargreaves, A., & Fullan, M. (2012). *Professional Capital: Transforming Teaching in Every School*. Teachers College Press.

Harper, C., Tran, K., & Cooper, S. (2024). Conceptual metaphor theory in action: Insights into student understanding of computing concepts. In *Proceedings of the 55th ACM Technical Symposium on Computer Science Education* (SIGCSE 2024) V. 1. (pp. 463–469). Association for Computing Machinery. DOI: 10.1145/3626252.3630812

Harris, A., & Lambert, L. (2003). *Building Leadership Capacity for School Improvement*. Open University Press.

Harris, J., Mishra, P., & Koehler, M. (2009). Teachers' technological pedagogical content knowledge and learning activity types: Curriculum-based technology integration reframed. *Journal of Research on Technology in Education*, 41(4), 393–416. DOI: 10.1080/15391523.2009.10782536

Hasan, M., & Khan, B. (2020). Variability in the Effectiveness of Psychological Interventions based on Machine Learning in STEM Education. *GSE Journal*, 233, 1–16.

Haseski, H., Ilic, U., & Tugtekin, U. (2018). Defining a New 21st Century Skill-Computational Thinking: Concepts and Trends. *International Education Studies*, 11(4), 29–42. DOI: 10.5539/ies.v11n4p29

Hassenfeld, Z. R., & Bers, M. U. (2020). Debugging the writing process: Lessons from a comparison of students' coding and writing practices. *The Reading Teacher*, 73(6), 735–746. DOI: 10.1002/trtr.1885

Hattie, J. (2009). *Visible learning: A synthesis of over 800 meta-analyses relating to achievement*. Routledge.

Havighurst, R. J. (1952). Social and psychological needs of the aging. *The Annals of the American Academy of Political and Social Science*, 279(1), 11–17. DOI: 10.1177/000271625227900102

He, Y. T., Guo, B. J., Lu, J., Xu, Y. P., & Gong, M. (2020, December). Research of scratch programming recommendation system based on med and knowledge graph. In 2020 5th International Conference on Mechanical, Control and Computer Engineering (ICMCCE) (pp. 2158-2163). IEEE. DOI: 10.1109/ICMCCE51767.2020.00469

Hendrix, R., Eick, C., & Shannon, D. (2012). The Integration of Creative Drama in an Inquiry-Based Elementary Program: The Effect on Student Attitude and Conceptual Learning. *Journal of Science Teacher Education*, 23(7), 823–846. DOI: 10.1007/s10972-012-9292-1

Hermans, F., Swidan, A., Aivaloglou, E., & Smit, M. (2018). Thinking out of the box: comparing metaphors for variables in programming education. In A. Mühling ve Q. Cutts (Eds.), *Proceedings of the 13th workshop in primary and secondary computing* education (pp.1-8). ACM. DOI: 10.1145/3265757.3265765

Hesapçıoğlu, M. (1997). *Teaching Principles and Methods*. Beta Publications.

Heys, J. (2018). Machine Learning as a Tool to Identify Critical Assignments. *Chemical Engineering Education*, 52(4).

Hicks, A. (2018). Technology and professional identity of librarians: The making of the cybrarian. *Journal of Academic Librarianship*, 44(4), 534–541.

Hijón-Neira, R., Perez-Marin, D., Pizarro, C., & Connolly, C. (2020). The effects of a visual execution environment and makey makey on primary school children learning introductory programming concepts. *IEEE Access : Practical Innovations, Open Solutions*, 8, 217800–217815. DOI: 10.1109/ACCESS.2020.3041686

Hirzel, M. (2023). Low-code programming models. *Communications of the ACM*, 66(10), 76–85. DOI: 10.1145/3587691

Hobbs, R. (2010). *Digital and Media Literacy: A Plan of Action*. Aspen Institute.

Hodges, S., Sentance, S., Finney, J., & Ball, T. (2020). Physical computing: A key element of modern computer science education. *Computer*, 53(4), 20–30. DOI: 10.1109/MC.2019.2935058

Ho, J. W., Scadding, M., Kong, S. C., Andone, D., Biswas, G., Hoppe, H. U., & Hsu, T. C. (2019). Classroom activities for teaching artificial intelligence to primary school students. In *Proceedings of the International Conference on Computational Thinking Education* (pp. 157–159).

Horn, M. B., & Staker, H. (2011). The rise of K-12 blended learning. *Innosight institute, 5*(1), 1-17.

Hostetter, A. B., & Alibali, M. W. (2008). Visible embodiment: Gestures as simulated action. *Psychonomic Bulletin & Review*, 15(3), 495–514. DOI: 10.3758/PBR.15.3.495 PMID: 18567247

Hsueh, N., Lai, L., & Tseng, W. (2023). Design of an online programming platform and a study on learners' testing ability. *Electronics (Basel)*, 12(22), 4596. DOI: 10.3390/electronics12224596

Huang, S., Tarng, W., & Ou, K. (2023). Effectiveness of ar board game on computational thinking and programming skills for elementary school students. *Systems*, 11(1), 25. DOI: 10.3390/systems11010025

Hubálovský, S. (2012). Research of methods of a multidisciplinary approach in the teaching of algorithm development and programming. In Cápay, M., Mesárošová, M., & Palmárová, V. (Eds.) *9th International Scientific Conference on Distance Learning in Applied Informatics-DIVAI* (pp. 147-156).

Hubwieser, P., Armoni, M., Giannakos, M. N., & Mittermeir, R. T. (2014). Perspectives and visions of computer science education in primary and secondary (k-12) schools. *ACM Transactions on Computing Education*, 14(2), 1–9. DOI: 10.1145/2602482

Hudley, A., & Mallinson, C. (2017). "It's worth our time": A model of culturally and linguistically supportive professional development for K-12 STEM educators. *Cultural Studies of Science Education*, 12(3), 637–660. DOI: 10.1007/s11422-016-9743-7

Hufad, A., Faturrohman, M., & Rusdiyani, I. (2021). Unplugged coding activities for early childhood problem-solving skills. *Jurnal Pendidikan Usia Dini*, 15(1), 121–140. DOI: 10.21009/JPUD.151.07

Huff, E. W.Jr, Boateng, K., Moster, M., Rodeghero, P., & Brinkley, J. (2021). Exploring the perspectives of teachers of the visually impaired regarding accessible k12 computing education. In *Proceedings of the 52nd acm technical symposium on computer science education* (pp. 156-162). DOI: 10.1145/3408877.3432418

Hughes, J., Thomas, R., & Scharber, C. (2006). Assessing technology integration: The RAT - Replacement, Amplification, and Transformation framework. *Technology and Teacher Education Annual*, 1616-1620.

Huh, M., & Pavel, A. (2024). DesignChecker: Visual Design Support for Blind and Low Vision Web Developers. *arXiv preprint arXiv:2407.17681*. DOI: 10.1145/3654777.3676369

Hu, L. (2024). Programming and 21st century skill development in K-12 schools: A multidimensional meta-analysis. *Journal of Computer Assisted Learning*, 40(2), 610–636. DOI: 10.1111/jcal.12904

Humble, N., Mozelius, P., & Sällvin, L. (2019). Teacher chalenges and choice of programming tools for teaching k-12 technology and mathematics. In *International Conference on Education and New Developments (END 2019)*, (pp. 431-435). inScience Press. DOI: 10.36315/2019v1end099

Hussein, M., Yusuf, J., Deb, A., Fong, L., & Naidu, S. (2020). An Evaluation of Online Proctoring Tools. *Open Praxis.*, 12(4), 509–525. DOI: 10.5944/openpraxis.12.4.1113

Hu, W., Huang, R., & Li, Y. (2024). Young children's experience in unplugged activities about computational thinking: From an embodied cognition perspective. *Early Childhood Education Journal*, 52(4), 769–782. DOI: 10.1007/s10643-023-01475-x

Hu, Y., Chen, C., & Su, C. (2020). Exploring the effectiveness and moderators of block-based visual programming on student learning: A meta-analysis. *Journal of Educational Computing Research*, 58(8), 1467–1493. DOI: 10.1177/0735633120945935

Hwang, G.-J., Xie, H., Wah, B. W., & Gašević, D. (2020). 'Vision, Challenges, Roles and Research Issues of Artificial Intelligence in Education'. *Computers and Education: Artificial Intelligence*, 1, 100001. DOI: 10.1016/j.caeai.2020.100001

Ibeto, I., & Baghban Karimi, O. (2023, June). Effective Use of Open Educational Resources in Computer Science Education: A Query to Inform Open Textbook Development. *Proceedings of the Conference on Innovation and Technology in Computer Science Education. 2.* ACM. DOI: 10.1145/3587103.3594167

Ibrahim, M., Callaway, R., Kert, S. B., & Erkoç, M. F. (2021, March). Enhancing Self-Regulated Learning Strategies for College Students Through Discussion Reflections in Online Learning Environment. *Society for Information Technology & Teacher Education International Conference* (pp. 185-196). Association for the Advancement of Computing in Education (AACE).

Ibrahim, A., McKee, M., Sikos, L. F., & Johnson, N. F. (2024). [Cybersecurity Education Around the World. *IEEE Access.*]. *Systematic Reviews*, •••, K-12.

Iftikhar, S., & Cheema, K. (2022). Medical students' perception of online assessment at a private medical college. *Health Professions Educator Journal*, 5(2), 15–18. DOI: 10.53708/hpej.v5i2.1258

Ihirwe, F., Di Ruscio, D., Mazzini, S., Pierini, P., & Pierantonio, A. (2020, October). Low-code engineering for internet of things: a state of research. In *Proceedings of the 23rd ACM/IEEE international conference on model driven engineering languages and systems: companion proceedings* (pp. 1-8). DOI: 10.1145/3417990.3420208

Imambi, S., Prakash, K. B., & Kanagachidambaresan, G. R. (2021). PyTorch. In Prakash, K. B., & Kanagachidambaresan, G. R. (Eds.), *Programming with TensorFlow: Solution for Edge Computing Applications* (pp. 87–104). Springer International Publishing. DOI: 10.1007/978-3-030-57077-4_10

Inhelder, B., & Piaget, J. (1958). *The growth of logical thinking from childhood to adolescence: An essay on the construction of formal operational structures*. Psychology Press. DOI: 10.1037/10034-000

International Telecommunication Union (ITU). (2022). Facts and Figures 2022. [Online]. Available: https://www.itu.int/itu-d/reports/statistics/facts-figures-2022/ Access Date: 01.08.2024

Inventor Mindstorms, APP. (n.d.). Retrieved from

Ioannou, M., & Bratitsis, T. (2017). Teaching the Notion of Speed in Kindergarten Using the Sphero SPRK Robot. *2017 IEEE 17th International Conference on Advanced Learning Technologies (ICALT)*, 311–312. DOI: 10.1109/ICALT.2017.70

Isayama, D., Ishiyama, M., Relator, R., & Yamazaki, K. (2016). Computer science education for primary and lower secondary school students: Teaching the concept of automata. [TOCE]. *ACM Transactions on Computing Education*, 17(1), 1–28. DOI: 10.1145/2940331

Işik Arslanoğlu, İ., Kert, S. B., & Tonbuloğlu, İ. (2023). Think together, design together, code together: The effect of augmented reality activity designed by children on the computational thinking skills. *Education and Information Technologies*, 1–30. DOI: 10.1007/s10639-023-12153-1

ISTE. (2016). *ISTE Standards for Students*. International Society for Technology in Education.

ISTE. (2023). International Society for Technology in Education Standarts https://iste.org/standards

ISTE. (2024a). International Society for Technology in Education (ISTE). https://iste.org/about

ISTE. (2024b). Artificial Intelligence in Education. https://iste.org/ai

ITE. (2024). Information Technologies Educators Association. https://bte.org.tr/bizkimiz/

Jaafar, M. (Mar. 3, 2022). Introducing Cybersecurity Awareness as Part Core Curriculum Primary Schools. [Online]. Available: https://www.moe.gov.sg/news/parliamentary-replies/20220303- introducing-cybersecurity-awareness-as-part-of-the-core-curriculumin-primary-schools

Jaafar, G. A., Abdullah, S. M., & Ismail, S. (2019). Review of recent detection methods for HTTP DDoS attack. *Journal of Computer Networks and Communications*, 2019(1), 1283472. DOI: 10.1155/2019/1283472

Jašková, Ľ. (2022). Three programming environments friendly to blind students in lower secondary education. In *EDULEARN22 Proceedings* (pp. 8099-8108). IATED. https://doi.org/DOI: 10.21125/edulearn.2022.1917

Jennings, P. A., & Greenberg, M. T. (2009). The prosocial classroom: Teacher social and emotional competence in relation to student and classroom outcomes. *Review of Educational Research*, 79(1), 491–525. DOI: 10.3102/0034654308325693

Jiménez Chaves, V. E., & Torres, M. G. (2019). Analysis of Pre-school Education from Paraguay through Machine Learning Techniques. *Revista de la Sociedad Científica del Paraguay*, 24(2), 293–304. DOI: 10.32480/rscp.2019-24-2.293-304

Jing, M. (2018). China Looks to School Kids to Win the Global Artificial Intelligence Race. South China Morning Post. Retrieved from

Jin, L., Tan, F., & Jiang, S. (2020). 'Generative Adversarial Network Technologies and Applications in Computer Vision'. *Computational Intelligence and Neuroscience*, 1459107(1), 1–17. DOI: 10.1155/2020/1459107 PMID: 32802024

John, S. N., Noma-Osaghae, E., Oajide, F., & Okokpujie, K. (2020). Cybersecurity Education: The Skills Gap, Hurdle!. *Innovations in Cybersecurity Education*, 361-376.

Johnson, D. W., & Johnson, R. J. (1999). Making cooperative learning work. *Theory into Practice*, 38(2), 67–73. DOI: 10.1080/00405849909543834

Johnson, M., Schuster, M., Le, Q. V., Krikun, M., Wu, Y., Chen, Z., Thorat, N., Viégas, F., Wattenberg, M., Corrado, G., Hughes, M., & Dean, J. (2017). 'Google's Multilingual Neural Machine Translation System: Enabling Zero-Shot Translation'. *Transactions of the Association for Computational Linguistics*, 5, 339–351. DOI: 10.1162/tacl_a_00065

Joint Information Systems Committee (JISC). 2007. Effective practice with e-assessment: An overview of technologies, policies and practice in further and higher education. http://www.jisc.ac.uk/media/documents/themes/elearning/effpraceassess.pdf

Joque, J. (2016). The invention of the object: Object orientation and the philosophical development of programming languages. *Philosophy & Technology*, 29(4), 335–356. DOI: 10.1007/s13347-016-0223-5

Jordan, S. (2013). E-assessment: Past, present and future. *New Directions in the Teaching of Physical Sciences*, 9(1), 87–106. DOI: 10.11120/ndir.2013.00009

Jose, S. (2016, December 15). Online proctoring is trending: Here is all you must know. Talview. Retrieved from https://blog.talview.com/a-complete-guide-to-online-remote-proctoring

Jubaedah, Y., Yulia, C., Muktiarni, M., & Maosul, A. (2020). Usability testing electronic rubric of performance assessment. In *Journal of Physics: Conference Series, 1456(1)*. IOP Publishing., DOI: 10.1088/1742-6596/1456/1/012016

Jumper, C. (2024). About Code Jumper. https://codejumper.com/

K-12 Computer Science Framework Steering Committee. (2016). *K-12 Computer Science Framework. Technical Report.* Association for Computing Machinery.

K-12 Computer Science. (2024). K–12 Computer Science Framework. https://k12cs.org/

Kalelioglu, F., Gulbahar, Y., & Kukul, V. (2016). *A framework for computational thinking based on a systematic research review.*

Kalelioğlu, F. (2015). A new way of teaching programming skills to K-12 students: Code. org. *Computers in Human Behavior*, 52, 200–210. DOI: 10.1016/j.chb.2015.05.047

Kalelioğlu, F. (2020). Bilgisayarsız bilgisayar bilimi öğretimi. In Gülbahar, Y. (Ed.), *Bilgi İşlemsel Düşünmeden Programlamaya* (pp. 183–206). Pegem Akademi.

Kalelioğlu, F., Gülbahar, Y., & Kert, S. B. (2020). Teaching computing at secondary school level: Understanding teachers' experiences and challenges. *Ilkogretim Online*, 19(3), 1781–1796. Advance online publication. DOI: 10.17051/ilkonline.2020.735161

Kalelioglu, F., & Sentance, S. (2020). Teaching with physical computing in school: the case of the micro: bit. *Education and Information Technologies*, 25(4), 2577–2603. DOI: 10.1007/s10639-019-10080-8

Kallia, M. (2017). Assessment in computer science courses: A literature review. *Royal Society*, 1-60. https://royalsociety.org/-/media/policy/projects/computing-education/assessment-literature-review.pdf

Kandemir, C. M., Kalelioğlu, F., & Gülbahar, Y. (2020). Pedagogy of teaching introductory text-based programming in terms of computational thinking concepts and practices. *Computer Applications in Engineering Education*, 29(1), 29–45. DOI: 10.1002/cae.22374

Kandlhofer, M., Steinbauer, G., Hirschmugl-Gaisch, S., & Huber, P. (2016). Artificial intelligence and computer science in education: From kindergarten to university. *2016 IEEE Frontiers in Education Conference (FIE)*, 1–9. DOI: 10.1109/FIE.2016.7757570

Kandlhofer, M., Steinbauer, G., Hirschmugl-Gaisch, S., & Huber, P. (2016, October). Artificial intelligence and computer science in education: From kindergarten to university. In 2016 IEEE frontiers in education conference (FIE) (pp. 1-9). IEEE.

Kane, S. K., & Bigham, J. P. (2014). Tracking@ stemxcomet: teaching programming to blind students via 3D printing, crisis management, and twitter. In *Proceedings of the 45th ACM technical symposium on Computer science education* (pp. 247-252). DOI: 10.1145/2538862.2538975

Kang, S.-C. (2006). A study on the connection between the computer science education curriculum of university and that of primary and secondary school. *The Journal of Korean Association of Computer Education*, 9(3), 29–45.

Kaplancalı, U. T., & Demirkol, Z. (2017). Teaching coding to children: A methodology for kids 5+. *International Journal of Elementary Education*, 6(4), 32–37. DOI: 10.11648/j.ijeedu.20170604.11

Karabilgin, Ö. S., & Şahin, H. (2006). 'Eğitim Etkinliğini Değerlendirmede Öğrenci Geri Bildiriminin Kullanımı'. *Tıp Eğitimi Dünyası*, 21(21), 27–33.

Karakoç, T. (2016). *Görme yetersizliği olan öğrencilerin araştırmaya dayalı öğrenme yaklaşımı modellerinden rehberli keşfetme modelinin deneysel işlemleri kazanmalarına, akademik başarılarına ve fen bilgisine ait tutumlarına etkisi*. Yayımlanmamış Doktora Tezi. Gazi Üniversitesi, Eğitim Bilimleri Enstitüsü.

Katai, Z., & Toth, L. (2010). Technologically and artistically enhanced multi-sensory computer-programming education. *Teaching and Teacher Education*, 26(2), 244–251. DOI: 10.1016/j.tate.2009.04.012

Kayalı, B., Balat, Ş., & Yavuz, M. (2023). *Yapay Zeka Tabanlı Araçlar ve Uygulamaların Bilgisayar Bilimi Eğitiminde Kullanımı. Kert, S. B. (Editör), Teoriden Uygulamaya Bilgisayar Bilimi Eğitimi*. Nobel Yayın Dağıtım.

Kert, S. B., Erkoç, M. F., Ibrahim, M., & Callaway, R. (2021, October). Using Self-Regulated Learning Strategies to Enhance the Effectiveness of an Online Course in Emergency Remote Teaching. *14th International Computer and Instructional Technologies Symposium (ICITS)*. Rize, Türkiye. Retrieved from https://orc.library.atu.edu/faculty_pub_lead/21/

Kert, S. B., Read, J., Uğraş, T., Erkoç, M. F., Özçakır, F. C., Berksoy, İ., . . . Zubair, M. S. (2021). Design Ideas For A Learning Material To Teach Coding To Children With Visual Impairment. In *ICERI2021 Proceedings* (pp. 5864-5871). IATED. DOI: 10.21125/iceri.2021.1318

Kert, S. B., & Erko, Ç. (2020). The effect of robotics on six graders' academic achievement, computational thinking skills and conceptual knowledge levels. *Thinking Skills and Creativity*, 38, 100714. Advance online publication. DOI: 10.1016/j.tsc.2020.100714

Kert, S. B., & Uğraş, T. (2009, May). Programlama eğitiminde sadelik ve eğlence: Scratch örneği. *InThe First International Congress of Educational Research*, Çanakkale, Turkey.

Kert, S. B., Yeni, S., & Erkoç, M. F. (2022). Enhancing computational thinking skills of students with disabilities. *Instructional Science*, 50(4), 625–651. DOI: 10.1007/s11251-022-09585-6

Keser, H., & Güldüren, C. (2015). Development Of Information Security Awareness Scale. *Kastamonu Education Journal*, 23(3), 1167–1184.

Keuning, H., Jeuring, J., & Heeren, B. (2018). A systematic literature review of automated feedback generation for programming exercises. [TOCE]. *ACM Transactions on Computing Education*, 19(1), 1–43. DOI: 10.1145/3231711

Kewalramani, S., Palaiologou, I., & Dardanou, M. (2020). Children's engineering design thinking processes: The magic of the robots and the power of blocks (electronics). *Eurasia Journal of Mathematics, Science and Technology Education*, 16(3). Advance online publication. DOI: 10.29333/ejmste/113247

Khamis, N., & Idris, S. (2008, July). Issues and solutions in assessing object-oriented programming skills in the core education of computer science and information technology. *Proceedings of the 12th WSEAS International Conference on Computers* (pp. 458-463). ACM. Retrieved from https://dl.acm.org/doi/abs/10.5555/1513605.1513687

Khan, R. U., Cheng, J. L. A., & Bee, O. Y. (2018). Machine Learning and Dyslexia: Diagnostic and Classification System (DCS) for Kids with Learning Disabilities. International Journal of Engineering & Technology, 7(3.18), 97-100.

Khanlari, A. (2013). Effects of robotics on 21st-century skills. *European Scientific Journal*, 9(13), 26–36.

Kim, D. W., Shin, G. Y., & Han, M. M. (2020). Analysis of feature importance and interpretation for malware classification. *Computers, Materials & Continua*, 65(3), 1891–1904. DOI: 10.32604/cmc.2020.010933

Kim, S. U. (2020). A Comparative Study on the Effects of Hands-on Robot and EPL Programming Activities on Creative Problem-Solving Ability in Children. *ACM International Conference Proceeding Series*, 49–53. DOI: 10.1145/3401861.3401866

Kim, S., & Lee, Y. (2020). An analysis of pre-service teachers' learning process in programming learning. *International Journal on Advanced Science, Engineering and Information Technology*, 10(1), 58–69. DOI: 10.18517/ijaseit.10.1.5723

Kim, S., Park, J., & Lee, H. (2019). 'Automated Essay Scoring Using a Deep Learning Model'. *Journal of Educational Technology Development and Exchange*, 2(1), 1–17.

Kızılaslan, A., & Sözbilir, M. (2017). *Herkes İçin bilim: görme engelli öğrenciler için örnek uygulamalar*. Çizgi Kitabevi.

Koçdar, S., Karadeniz, A., & Göksel, N. (2022). Çevrim İçi Ölçme ve Değerlendirmede Kimlik Tanıma ve Doğrulama Sistemlerinin Kullanımı: Üniversite Öğrencilerinin Deneyimleri [Authentication and Authorship Systems in Online Assessment: Experiences of University Students]. *Adam Academy Journal of Social Sciences*, 12(1), 1–32. DOI: 10.31679/adamakademi.1038184

Koehler, M., & Mishra, P. (2009). What is technological pedagogical content knowledge (TPACK)? *Contemporary Issues in Technology & Teacher Education*, 9(1), 60–70.

Koh, K. H., Basawapatna, A., Nickerson, H., & Repenning, A. (2014, July). Real time assessment of computational thinking. In *2014 IEEE Symposium on visual languages and human-centric computing (VL/HCC)* (pp. 49-52). IEEE. https://www.webofscience.com/wos/woscc/full-record/WOS:000361019600012

Kolb, D. A. (2014). *Experiential learning: Experience as the source of learning and development.* FT press.

Koltay, T. (2017). Data literacy for researchers and data librarians. *Journal of Librarianship and Information Science*, 49(1), 14–33. DOI: 10.1177/0961000615616450

Kong, R., & Wong, G. K. (2017). Teachers' perception of professional development in coding education. *In 2017 IEEE 6th International Conference on Teaching, Assessment, and Learning for Engineering (TALE)*, 377-380.

Koretz, D. (2018). Moving beyond the Failure of Test-Based Accountability. *American Educator*, 41(4), 22–26. https://eric.ed.gov/?id=EJ1164385

Kotsiantis, S., Pierrakeas, C., & Pintelas, P. (2004). Predicting Students' Performance in Distance Learning Using Machine Learning Techniques. *Applied Artificial Intelligence*, 18(5), 411–426. DOI: 10.1080/08839510490442058

Kougioumtzidou, E., Botsoglou, K., & Zygouris, N. (2023). Computer science and primary education teachers' perceptions, in using digital games as learning tools. Obstacles and factors that lead to their effective use. *European Journal of Social Sciences Studies*, 9(1). Advance online publication. DOI: 10.46827/ejsss.v9i1.1528

Koulouri, T., Lauria, S., & Macredie, R. D. (2014). Teaching introductory programming: A quantitative evaluation of different approaches. [TOCE]. *ACM Transactions on Computing Education*, 14(4), 1–28. DOI: 10.1145/2662412

Kouzes, J. M., & Posner, B. Z. (2012). *The Leadership Challenge: How to Make Extraordinary Things Happen in Organizations* (5th ed.). Jossey-Bass.

Kovač, M. M., & Eret, L. (2012, May). Correlation educational model in primary education curriculum of mathematics and computer science. *Proceedings of the 35th International Convention (MIPRO)* (pp. 1393-1397). Opatija, Croatia: IEEE.

Kövecses, Z. (2002). Cognitive-linguistic comments on metaphor identification. *Language and Literature*, 11(1), 74–78. DOI: 10.1177/096394700201100107

Kövecses, Z. (2005). *Metaphor in culture: Universality and variation.* Oxford University Press. DOI: 10.1017/CBO9780511614408

Kövecses, Z. (2010). *Metaphor-A Practical Introduction.* Oxford University Press.

Kozulin, A. (2003). *Vygotsky's educational theory in cultural context.* Cambridge University Press. DOI: 10.1017/CBO9780511840975

Kraft, M. A., Blazar, D., & Hogan, D. (2018). The effect of teacher coaching on instruction and achievement: A meta-analysis of the causal evidence. *Review of Educational Research*, 88(4), 547–588. DOI: 10.3102/0034654318759268

Kramer, O. (2016). Scikit-Learn. In Kramer, O. (Ed.), *Machine Learning for Evolution Strategies* (pp. 45–53). Springer International Publishing.

Krippendorff, K. (1993). Major metaphors of communication and some constructivist reflections on their use. *Cybernetics & Human Knowing*, 2(1), 3–25. Retrieved June 9, 2024, from https://repository.upenn.edu/server/api/core/bitstreams/defeb3a5-5162-4b0b-8026-a3bb09981e50/content

Kucak, D., Juricic, V., & Dambic, G. 2018. 'Machine Learning in Education - a Survey of Current Research Trends'. Pp. 0406–10 in *DAAAM Proceedings*. Vol. 1, edited by B. Katalinic. DAAAM International Vienna. DOI: 10.2507/29th.daaam.proceedings.059

Küchenmann, S., Klein, P., Beckers, S., Kumari, N., & Kuhn, J. (2020). Classification of Students' Conceptual Understanding in STEM Education using their Visual Attention Distributions: A Comparison of Three Machine-Learning Approaches. In *Proceedings of the CSEDU 2020*, Prague, 36-46.

Kusters, R., Misevic, D., Berry, H., Cully, A., Le Cunff, Y., Dandoy, L., Díaz-Rodríguez, N., Ficher, M., Grizou, J., Othmani, A., Palpanas, T., Komorowski, M., Loiseau, P., Frier, C. M., Nanini, S., Quercia, D., Sebag, M., Fogelman, F. S., Taleb, S., & Wehbi, F. (2020). 'Interdisciplinary Research in Artificial Intelligence: Challenges and Opportunities'. *Frontiers in Big Data*, 3, 577974. Advance online publication. DOI: 10.3389/fdata.2020.577974 PMID: 33693418

Kwon, K. (2017). Novice programmer's misconception of programming reflected on problem-solving plans. *International Journal of Computer Science Education in Schools*, 1(4), 14–24. DOI: 10.21585/ijcses.v1i4.19

Kwon, K., & Cheon, J. (2019). Exploring problem decomposition and program development through block-based programs. *International Journal of Computer Science Education in Schools*, 3(1), 1. Advance online publication. DOI: 10.21585/ijcses.v3i1.54

Kyza, E. A., Georgiou, Y., Agesilaou, A., & Souropetsis, M. (2022). A Cross-Sectional Study Investigating Primary School Children's Coding Practices and Computational Thinking Using ScratchJr. *Journal of Educational Computing Research*, 60(1), 220–257. DOI: 10.1177/07356331211027387

Lachaux, M. A., Roziere, B., Chanussot, L., & Lample, G. (2020). Unsupervised translation of programming languages. *arXiv preprint arXiv*:2006.03511.

Lakoff, G. (1993). The contemporary theory of metaphor. In Ortony, A. (Ed.), *Metaphor and Thought* (pp. 202–251). Cambridge University Press. DOI: 10.1017/CBO9781139173865.013

Lakoff, G., & Johnson, M. (1980). *Metaphors we live by*. Chicago University Press.

Lakoff, G., & Johnson, M. (1999). *Philosophy in the flesh: The embodied mind and its chalenge to western thought*. Basic Books.

Langston, W. (2002). Violating orientational metaphors slows reading. *Discourse Processes*, 34(3), 281–310. DOI: 10.1207/S15326950DP3403_3

Larrimore, D. (2013). Examining the effectiveness of K-12 professional development delivered through a hybrid-based learning environment, Doctoral Dissertation, Towson University, https://doi.org/DOI: 10.13016/M29H8N

Larsson, A., & Stolpe, K. (2023). Hands on programming: Teachers' use of metaphors in gesture and speech make abstract concepts tangible. *International Journal of Technology and Design Education*, 32(3), 1–19. DOI: 10.1007/s10798-022-09755-0

Larsson, A., & Stolpe, K. (2024). Exploring the metaphoric nature of programming teachers' reflections on action-a case study with teaching in mind. *International Journal of Technology and Design Education*, 32(5), 1–18. DOI: 10.1007/s10798-023-09826-w

Lawless, K. A., & Pellegrino, J. W. (2007). Professional development in integrating technology into teaching and learning: Knowns, unknowns, and ways to pursue better questions and answers. *Review of Educational Research*, 77(4), 575–614. DOI: 10.3102/0034654307309921

Lazarinis, F., Karachristos, C. V., Stavropoulos, E. C., & Verykios, V. S. (2019). A blended learning course for playfully teaching programming concepts to school teachers. *Education and Information Technologies*, 24(2), 1237–1249. DOI: 10.1007/s10639-018-9823-2

Lazonder, A. W., & Harmsen, R. (2016). Meta-analysis of inquiry-based learning: Effects of guidance. *Review of Educational Research*, 86(3), 681–718. DOI: 10.3102/0034654315627366

LearnPython.com. (2023). 8 most common programming errors made by beginners. *LearnPython.com*. Retrieved from https://learnpython.com

Lee, I., Martin, F., Denner, J., Coulter, B., Allan, W., Erickson, J., Malyn-Smith, J., & Werner, L. (2011). Computational thinking for youth in practice. *ACM Inroads*, 2(1), 32–37. DOI: 10.1145/1929887.1929902

Lee, J. (2020). Coding in early childhood. *Contemporary Issues in Early Childhood*, 21(3), 266–269. DOI: 10.1177/1463949119846541

Lee, J., & Junoh, J. (2019). Implementing unplugged coding activities in early childhood classrooms. *Early Childhood Education Journal*, 47(6), 709–716. DOI: 10.1007/s10643-019-00967-z

Lee, S. J., Francom, G. M., & Nuatomue, J. (2022). Computer science education and K-12 students' computational thinking: A systematic review. *International Journal of Educational Research*, 114, 102008. DOI: 10.1016/j.ijer.2022.102008

Lee, V. R., Poole, F., Clarke-Midura, J., Recker, M., & Rasmussen, M. (2020). Introducing Coding through Tabletop Board Games and Their Digital Instantiations across Elementary Classrooms and School Libraries. *Proceedings of the 51st ACM Technical Symposium on Computer Science Education*, 787–793. DOI: 10.1145/3328778.3366917

Leinonen, A., Nygren, H., Pirttinen, N., Hellas, A., & Leinonen, J. (2019). Exploring the applicability of simple syntax writing practice for learning programming. In *Proceedings of the 50th ACM Technical Symposium on Computer Science Education* (pp. 84-90). ACM. DOI: 10.1145/3287324.3287378

Lennon, M., Pila, S., Flynn, R., & Wartella, E. A. (2022). Young children's social and independent behavior during play with a coding app: Digital game features matter in a 1:1 child to tablet setting. *Computers & Education*, 190, 104608. Advance online publication. DOI: 10.1016/j.compedu.2022.104608

Leung, S. K. Y., Wu, J., & Li, J. W. (2024). Children's knowledge construction of computational thinking in a play-based classroom. *Early Child Development and Care*, 194(2), 208–229. DOI: 10.1080/03004430.2023.2299405

Leung, S. K. Y., Wu, J., Li, J. W., Lam, Y., & Ng, O. L. (2024). Examining young children's computational thinking through animation art. *Early Childhood Education Journal*. Advance online publication. DOI: 10.1007/s10643-024-01694-w

Levent, F., & Yazıcı, E. (2015). Examination of Factors Affecting Success of Singapore Education System. *Marmara University Atatürk Education Faculty Journal of Educational Sciences*, 39(39), 121–143.

Levine, P. M. (2005). Metaphors and images of classrooms. *Kappa Delta Pi Record*, 41(4), 172–175. DOI: 10.1080/00228958.2005.10532066

Levinson, T., & Bers, M. (2024). Robotics in universal prekindergarten classrooms. *International Journal of Technology and Design Education*. Advance online publication. DOI: 10.1007/s10798-024-09905-6

Levy, R. B.-B., & Ben-Ari, M. M. (2015). Robotics Activities–Is the Investment Worthwhile? In Brodnik, A., & Vahrenhold, J. (Eds.), *Informatics in Schools. Curricula, Competences, and Competitions* (pp. 22–31). Springer. DOI: 10.1007/978-3-319-25396-1_3

Lewis, S. E. (2020). Chemistry assessments through the sudden implementation of online instruction. *Journal of Chemical Education*, 97(9), 3418–3422. DOI: 10.1021/acs.jchemed.0c00697

Lin, , H. CHwang, , G. J. (2019). Research trends of flipped classroom studies for medical courses: A review of journal publications from 2008 to 2017 based on the technology-enhanced learning model. *Interactive Learning Environments*, 27(8), 1011–1027. DOI: 10.1080/10494820.2018.1467462

Lindberg, S. (2019). Gamification for self-directed learning in higher education. In *EDULEARN19 Proceedings* (pp. 1764-1773). IATED. DOI: 10.21125/edulearn.2019.0507

Lindberg, R. S., Laine, T. H., & Haaranen, L. (2019). Gamifying programming education in K-12: A review of programming curricula in seven countries and programming games. *British Journal of Educational Technology*, 50(4), 1979–1995. DOI: 10.1111/bjet.12685

Linden, K., & González, P. (2021). Zoom invigilated exams: A protocol for rapid adoption to remote examinations. *British Journal of Educational Technology*, 52(4), 1323–1337. DOI: 10.1111/bjet.13109

Lin, P., Brummelen, J. V., Lukin, G., Williams, R., & Breazeal, C. (2020). Zhorai: Designing a Conversational Agent for Children to Explore Machine Learning Concepts. In *Proceedings of the AAArtificial Intelligence Conference on Artificial Intelligence*, New York, NY, USA, 7–12 February 2020, 34. DOI: 10.1609/aaai.v34i09.7061

Lin, Y., Liao, H., Weng, S., & Dong, W. (2023). Comparing the effects of plugged-in and unplugged activities on computational thinking development in young children. *Education and Information Technologies*, •••, 1–34. DOI: 10.1007/s10639-023-12181-x PMID: 37361760

Lin, Y., & Weintrop, D. (2021). The landscape of Block-based programming: Characteristics of block-based environments and how they support the transition to text-based programming. *Journal of Computer Languages*, 67, 101075. DOI: 10.1016/j.cola.2021.101075

Little, D. (2009). Language learner autonomy and the European language portfolio: Two L2 English examples. *Language Teaching*, 42(2), 222–233. DOI: 10.1017/S0261444808005636

Little, J. W. (1990). The Persistence of Privacy: Autonomy and Initiative in Teachers' Professional Relations. *Teachers College Record*, 91(4), 509–536. DOI: 10.1177/016146819009100403

Liu, R., Zenke, C., Liu, C., Holmes, A., Thornton, P., & Malan, D. J. (2024, March). Teaching CS50 with AI: leveraging generative artificial intelligence in computer science education. In *Proceedings of the 55th ACM Technical Symposium on Computer Science Education* V. 1 (pp. 750-756).

Liu, Y. Y., & Iversen, O. S. (2022). Computational Thinking through Tangible Play: Understanding Social Dialogues in Children's Learning. *Proceedings of Interaction Design and Children, IDC*, 2022, 596–603. DOI: 10.1145/3501712.3535288

Li, W., Huang, J. Y., Liu, C. Y., Tseng, J. C., & Wang, S. P. (2023). A study on the relationship between student' learning engagements and higher-order thinking skills in programming learning. *Thinking Skills and Creativity*, 49, 101369. DOI: 10.1016/j.tsc.2023.101369

Li, X. (2010). Conceptual metaphor theory and the teaching of English and Chinese idioms. *Journal of Language Teaching and Research*, 1(3), 206–210. https://doi.org/10.4304/jltr.1.3.206-210

Ljubic, S., Skoki, A., Hržić, F., & Salkanovic, A. (2023). Empowering Computer Engineering Education: Leveraging Cloud-Based Programming Platforms and Online Assessment Tools. *BOOKOF*, 43. https://www.researchgate.net/profile/Francesca-Finestrone/publication/378268879_HELMeTO_2023_Book-of-abstracts/links/65d08fd601325d4652114308/HELMeTO-2023-Book-of-abstracts.pdf

Locke, E. A., & Latham, G. P. (2002). Building a practically useful theory of goal setting and task motivation: A 35-year odyssey. *The American Psychologist*, 57(9), 705–717. https://psycnet.apa.org/doi/10.1037/0003-066X.57.9.705. DOI: 10.1037/0003-066X.57.9.705 PMID: 12237980

Lorenzo, G., & Ittelson, J. (2005). An overview of e-portfolios. EDUCAUSE Learning Initiative. ELI Paper, 1-28. Retrieved May 8, 2014, from https://net.educause.edu/ir/library/pdf/ELI3001.pdf

Low, G. (2008). Metaphor and education. In Gibbs, R. W. (Ed.), *The Cambridge handbook of metaphor and thought* (pp. 212–231). DOI: 10.1017/CBO9780511816802.014

Luckin, R., & Holmes, W. (2016). Intelligence unleashed: An argument for AI in education.

Ludi, S., & Reichlmayr, T. (2011). The use of robotics to promote computing to pre-college students with visual impairments. *ACM Transactions on Computing Education*, 11(3), 1–20. DOI: 10.1145/2037276.2037284

Lu, J. J., & Fletcher, G. H. L. (2009). Thinking about computational thinking. *SIGCSE Bulletin*, 41(1), 260–264. Advance online publication. DOI: 10.1145/1539024.1508959

Luo, F., Israel, M., & Gane, B. (2022). Elementary computational thinking instruction and assessment: A learning trajectory perspective. [TOCE]. *ACM Transactions on Computing Education*, 22(2), 1–26. DOI: 10.1145/3494579

Luo, Y., Liang, P., Wang, C., Shahin, M., & Zhan, J. (2021, October). Characteristics and challenges of low-code development: the practitioners' perspective. In *Proceedings of the 15th ACM/IEEE international symposium on empirical software engineering and measurement (ESEM)* (pp. 1-11). DOI: 10.1145/3475716.3475782

Lu, S., Eloanyi, C. B., & Olelewe, C. J. (2023). Computer educators' perception of the utilization of online assessment in the Covid-19 era. *Computer Applications in Engineering Education*, 31(4), 983–1000. DOI: 10.1002/cae.22618

Luxton-Reilly, A. (2016). Learning to program is easy. In *Proceedings of the 2016 ACM Conference on Innovation and Technology in Computer Science Education (ITiCSE '16)*. Association for Computing Machinery, USA, 284–289. DOI: 10.1145/2899415.2899432

Lye, S. Y., & Koh, J. H. L. (2014). Review on teaching and learning of computational thinking through programming: What is next for K-12? *Computers in Human Behavior*, 41, 51–61. DOI: 10.1016/j.chb.2014.09.012

Lynch, K., Hill, H., Gonzalez, K., & Pollard, C. (2019). Strengthening the research base that informs stem instructional improvement efforts: A meta-analysis. *Educational Evaluation and Policy Analysis*, 41(3), 260–293. DOI: 10.3102/0162373719849044

Machine Learning for Kids. (n.d.). Retrieved April 01, 2024, from

Mahara. (2024). https://demo.mahara.org/

Manches, A., McKenna, P. E., Rajendran, G., & Robertson, J. (2020). Identifying embodied metaphors for computing education. *Computers in Human Behavior*, 105(10585), 1–11. DOI: 10.1016/j.chb.2018.12.037

Manches, A., & Plowman, L. (2017). Computing education in children's early years: A call for debate. *British Journal of Educational Technology*, 48(1), 191–201. DOI: 10.1111/bjet.12355

Manzano-León, A., Camacho-Lazarraga, P., Guerrero, M. A., Guerrero-Puerta, L., Aguilar-Parra, J. M., Trigueros, R., & Alias, A. (2021). Between level up and game over: A systematic literature review of gamification in education. *Sustainability (Basel)*, 13(4), 2247. DOI: 10.3390/su13042247

Marden, N. Y., Ulman, L. G., Wilson, F., & Velan, G. M. (2013). Online feedback assessments in physiology: Effects on students' learning experiences and outcomes. *Advances in Physiology Education*, 37(2), 192–200. DOI: 10.1152/advan.00092.2012 PMID: 23728137

Marques, L. S., Gresse Von Wangenheim, C., & Hauck, J. C. R. (2020). Teaching Machine Learning in School: A Systematic Mapping of the State of the Art. *Inform. Educ.*, 19, 283–321. DOI: 10.15388/infedu.2020.14

Marr, B. (2018). What Is Industry 4.0? Here's a Super Easy Explanation for Anyone. [Retrieved from]. *Forbes*, •••, 4–7.

Marsh, J. A., Pane, J. F., & Hamilton, L. S. (2006). *Making sense of data-driven decision making in education*. RAND Corporation.

Martinez, E., & Pfister, L. (2023). Benefits and limitations of using low-code development to support digitalization in the construction industry. *Automation in Construction*, 152, 104909. DOI: 10.1016/j.autcon.2023.104909

Masarwa, B., Hel-Or, H., & Levy, S. T. (2024). Kindergarten children's learning of computational thinking with the "Sorting Like a Computer" learning unit. *Journal of Research in Childhood Education*, 38(2), 165–188. DOI: 10.1080/02568543.2023.2221319

Mataric, M. J., Koenig, N., & Feil-Seifer, D. (2007). Materials for enabling hands-on robotics and STEM education. In Proceedings of the AAArtificial Intelligence Spring Symposium: Semantic Scientific Knowledge Integration (pp. 99–102). Stanford University.

Mate, K. E., & Weidenhofer, J. (2021). Considerations and strategies for effective online assessment with a focus on the biomedical sciences. *FASEB bioAdvances*, 4(1), 9–21. DOI: 10.1096/fba.2021-00075 PMID: 35024569

Matook, S., Maggie Wang, Y., Koeppel, N., & Guerin, S. (2024). Metacognitive skills in low-code app development: Work-integrated learning in information systems development. *Journal of Information Technology*, 39(1), 41–70. DOI: 10.1177/02683962231170238

McMillan, J. H., & Hellsten, L. (2010). *Classroom assessment: Principles and practice for effective standards-based instruction*. Pearson Education. https://researchportal.murdoch.edu.au/esploro/outputs/book/Classroom-Assessment-Principles-and-Practice-for/991005631470107891

McMillan, J. H., & Hearn, J. (2008). Student Self-Assessment: The Key to Stronger Student Motivation and Higher Achievement. *Educational Horizons*, 87(1), 40–49.

Mealin, S., & Murphy-Hill, E. (2012). An exploratory study of blind software developers. *2012 IEEE Symposium on Visual Languages and Human-Centric Computing (VL/HCC)*, 71–74. https://doi.org/DOI: 10.1109/VLHCC.2012.6344485

Means, B., Chen, E., DeBarger, A., & Padilla, C. (2011). *Teachers' ability to use data to inform instruction: Challenges and supports*. US Department of Education.

Medoh, C., & Telukdarie, A. (2022). The future of cybersecurity: A system dynamics approach. *Procedia Computer Science*, 200, 318–326. DOI: 10.1016/j.procs.2022.01.230

Melchior, A., Cohen, F., Cutter, T., & Leavitt, T. (2005). *More than Robots: An Evaluation of the FIRST Robotics Competition Participant and Institutional Impacts*. Heller School for Social Policy and Management, Brandeis University.

Mellar, H., Peytcheva-Forsyth, R., Kocdar, S., Karadeniz, A., & Yovkova, B. (2018). Addressing cheating in e-assessment using student authentication and authorship checking systems: Teachers' perspectives. *International Journal for Educational Integrity*, 14(1), 1–21. DOI: 10.1007/s40979-018-0025-x

Méndez-Ortega, M. G., Herrera-Granda, E. P., Prado Malte, A. E., & Heredia Enríquez, R. B. (2021). 'Supervision and Control of Students during Online Assessments Applying Computer Vision Techniques: A Systematic Literature Review'. *Universal Journal of Educational Research*, 9(5), 1000–1013. DOI: 10.13189/ujer.2021.090513

Mensan, T., & Osman, K. (2018). Development of BIC-Science Module: An Interdisciplinary Approach of Computer Science and Primary Science Education. In Kong, S. C., Andone, D., Biswas, G., Crick, T., Hoppe, H. U., & Hsu, T. C.. ... (Ed.), *Proceedings of the International Conference on Computational Thinking Education* (pp. 93-96). The Education University of Hong Kong.

Mercer, N., & Littleton, K. (2007). *Dialogue and the development of children's thinking: A sociocultural approach*. Routledge. DOI: 10.4324/9780203946657

Merkouris, A., Chorianopoulos, K., & Kameas, A. (2017). Teaching programming in secondary education through embodied computing platforms: Robotics and wearables. [TOCE]. *ACM Transactions on Computing Education*, 17(2), 1–22. DOI: 10.1145/3025013

Metin, S. (2022). Activity-based unplugged coding during the preschool period. *International Journal of Technology and Design Education*, 32(1), 149–165. DOI: 10.1007/s10798-020-09616-8

Metin, Ş., Başaran, M., Seheryeli, M. Y., Relkin, E., & Kalyenci, D. (2024). Adaptation of the Computational Thinking Skills Assessment Tool (TechCheck-K) in Early Childhood. *Journal of Science Education and Technology*, 33(3), 365–382. DOI: 10.1007/s10956-023-10089-2

Metzger, M. J., & Flanagin, A. J. (2013). Credibility and trust of information in online environments: The use of cognitive heuristics. *Journal of Pragmatics*, 59, 210–220. DOI: 10.1016/j.pragma.2013.07.012

Meyer-Baron, L., Stieger, R., Waldvogel, B., Schumann, N., Ruedisueli, C., & Mayr, F. (2022). Observing Computational Thinking Skills of Kindergarten Children. *Proceedings of the 17th Workshop in Primary and Secondary Computing Education*, 1–4. DOI: 10.1145/3556787.3556867

Miani, P., Kille, T., Lee, S. Y., Zhang, Y., & Bates, P. R. (2021). The impact of the COVID-19 pandemic on current tertiary aviation education and future careers: Students' perspective. *Journal of Air Transport Management*, 94, 102081. DOI: 10.1016/j.jairtraman.2021.102081 PMID: 36569599

Microsoft Cooperation. (2023). *Microsoft Secure Development Documentation*, [Online]. Available: https://learn.microsoft.com/pdf?url=https%3A%2F%2Flearn.microsoft.com%2Fen-us%2Fazure%2Fsecurity%2Fdevelop%2Ftoc.json. Access Date: 23.07.2024

Miller, P. H. (2012). *Theories of developmental psychology* (5th ed.). Worth Publishers.

Milne, L. R., & Ladner, R. E. (2019). Position: Accessible block-based programming: Why and how. In *2019 IEEE Blocks and Beyond Workshop (B&B)* (pp. 19-22). IEEE.

Mindstorms Inventor Kit. (n.d.). Retrieved from

Ministry of Education of the People's Republic of China. (2022). *Compulsory Education Information Technology Curriculum Standards 2022 Edition*, [Online]. Available: http://www.moe.gov.cn/, https://www.ictr.edu.cn/download_center/ywjy.html, Access Date: 01.07.2024.

Ministry of Education Singapore. (2017). *O-Level Computing Syllabus - Upper Secondary*, [Online]. Available: https://www.moe.gov.sg/-/media/files/secondary/syllabuses/science/2021-o-level-computing-teaching-and-learning-syllabus.pdf Access Date: 01.08.2024.

Ministry of Education Singapore. (2024). *Computing Teaching and Learning Syllabus.* [Online]. Available: https://www.moe.gov.sg/-/media/files/secondary/fsbb/syllabus/2024-g3-computing-teaching-and-learning-syllabus.pdf Access Date: 01.08.2024.

Ministry of Education. Culture, Sports, Science and Technology (MEXT). (2020). *Developing Skills to Use Information.* Ministry of Education, Culture, Sports, Science and Technology, Elementary and Secondary Education Bureau, Information Education and Foreign Language Education Division, [Online]. Available: https://www.mext.go.jp/content/20201002-mxt_jogai01-100003163_1.pdf. Access Date: 04.08.2024

Mishra, P., Yadav, A., Henriksen, D., Kereluik, K., Terry, L., Fahnoe, C., & Terry, C. (2013). Rethinking Technology & Creativity in the 21st Century. In *TechTrends* (Vol. 57, Issue 3). DOI: 10.1007/s11528-013-0655-z

Mishra, P., & Koehler, M. J. (2006). Technological pedagogical content knowledge: A framework for teacher knowledge. *Teachers College Record*, 108(6), 1017–1054. DOI: 10.1111/j.1467-9620.2006.00684.x

Mishra, R., Bian, J., Fiszman, M., Weir, C. R., Jonnalagadda, S., Mostafa, J., & Del Fiol, G. (2014). 'Text Summarization in the Biomedical Domain: A Systematic Review of Recent Research'. *Journal of Biomedical Informatics*, 52, 457–467. DOI: 10.1016/j.jbi.2014.06.009 PMID: 25016293

Mistretta, S. (2022). Virtual robotics in hybrid teaching and learning. *New Updates in E-Learning*, 145-156.

Mizell, H. (2010). *Why professional development matters*. Learning Forward.

Mladenovic, S., Granic, A., Zaharija, G., & Krpan, D. (2023). LOW-CODE AND NO-CODE APPROACH TO TEACHING ARTIFICIAL INTELLIGENCE. In *17th International Technology,Education and Development Conference.*

Mladenović, M., Boljat, I., & Žanko, Ž. (2018). Comparing loops misconceptions in block-based and text-based programming languages at the K-12 level. *Education and Information Technologies*, 23(4), 1483–1500. DOI: 10.1007/s10639-017-9673-3

Mladenović, M., Žanko, Ž., & Aglić Čuvić, M. (2021). The impact of using program visualization techniques on learning basic programming concepts at the K-12 level. *Computer Applications in Engineering Education*, 29(1), 145–159. DOI: 10.1002/cae.22315

Moape, T., Ojo, S., & Van Wyk, E. (2018). A metaphor-driven interactive multimedia simulation for teaching and learning of programming concepts. In P. Cunningham & M. Cunningham (Eds.), *2018 IST-Africa Week Conference* (p. 1-25). IEEE.

Mohamad, S. N. H., Patel, A., Latih, R., Qassim, Q., Na, L., & Tew, Y. (2011, July). Block-based programming approach: challenges and benefits. In *Proceedings of the 2011 international conference on electrical engineering and informatics* (pp. 1-5). IEEE.

Mohiudddin, K., Islam, A., Mohd, S., & Shariff, M. (2019). Evaluation of an academic program: The case of computing accreditation commission framework in higher education. *International Journal of Emerging Technologies in Learning*, 14(11), 70. DOI: 10.3991/ijet.v14i11.10178

Mohorovicic, S., & Strcic, V. (2011). An overview of computer programming teaching methods. In *Proceedings of the 22nd Central European Conference on Information and Intelligent Systems* (pp. 47-52.). Faculty of Organization and Informatics Varazdin. Retrieved May 12, 2024, from https://www.proquest.com/conference-papers-proceedings/overview-computer-programming-teaching-methods/docview/1322999502/se-2?accountid=10699

Molenda, M. (2003). In search of the elusive ADDIE model. *Performance Improvement*, 42(5), 34–37. DOI: 10.1002/pfi.4930420508

Mondal, S., Das, S., & Vrana, V. G. (2023). 'How to Bell the Cat? A Theoretical Review of Generative Artificial Intelligence towards Digital Disruption in All Walks of Life'. *Technologies*, 11(2), 44. Advance online publication. DOI: 10.3390/technologies11020044

MoNE. (2015). MEB'ten görme engelli öğrencilere teknolojik destek. https://www.aa.com.tr/tr/bilim-teknoloji/mebten-gorme-engelli-ogrencilere-teknolojik-destek/73990

MoNE. (2020). Görme engelli öğrencilerimiz için metinleri braılle alfabesine çeviren program ücretsiz olarak kullanımda. https://www.meb.gov.tr/gorme-engelli-ogrencilerimiz-icin-metinleri-braille-alfabesine-ceviren-program-ucretsiz-olarak-kullanimda/haber/20630/tr

Montuori, C., Ronconi, L., Vardanega, T., & Arfé, B. (2022). Exploring Gender Differences in Coding at the Beginning of Primary School. *Frontiers in Psychology*, 13, 887280. Advance online publication. DOI: 10.3389/fpsyg.2022.887280 PMID: 36211854

Moosvi, F., Eddelbuettel, D., Zilles, C., Wolfman, S. A., Fund, F., Alford, L. K., & Schroeder, J. (2023, March). Creating Algorithmically Generated Questions Using a Modern, Open-sourced, Online Platform: PrairieLearn. In *Proceedings of the 54th ACM Technical Symposium on Computer Science Education* V. 2 (pp. 1177-1177). https://doi.org/DOI: 10.1145/3545947.3569634

Moraiti, I., Fotoglou, A., & Drigas, A. (2022). Coding with block programming languages in educational robotics and mobiles, improve problem solving, creativity & critical thinking skills. *International Journal of Interactive Mobile Technologies*, 16(20), 59–78. Advance online publication. DOI: 10.3991/ijim.v16i20.34247

Morgan, G. (2006). Images of Organization. *Sage (Atlanta, Ga.).*

Morrison, C., Villar, N., Hadwen-Bennett, A., Regan, T., Cletheroe, D., Thieme, A., & Sentance, S. (2019). Physical programming for blind and low vision children at scale. *Human-Computer Interaction*, 36(5-6), 535–569. DOI: 10.1080/07370024.2019.1621175

Morrison, G. R., Ross, S. M., Kalman, H. K., & Kemp, J. E. (2010). *Designing effective instruction* (6th ed.). Wiley.

Moussawi, S., Koufaris, M., & Benbunan-Fich, R. (2021). 'How Perceptions of Intelligence and Anthropomorphism Affect Adoption of Personal Intelligent Agents'. *Electronic Markets*, 31(2), 343–364. DOI: 10.1007/s12525-020-00411-w

Mukhirez, E. J., Asqule, M., & Hasan, M. S. (2022). Effectiveness of CS Unplugged Program in Developing Programming Skills for Eighth Grade Female Students. *IUG Journal of Educational & Psychological Studies,* 30(4).

Muldner, K., Jennings, J., & Chiarelli, V. (2022). A review of worked examples in programming activities. *ACM Transactions on Computing Education*, 23(1), 1–35. DOI: 10.1145/3560266

Mulyati, E. N., Sabatini, R., Nuraeni, I., & Fitriani, N. (2023). Development of Ict Learning Task Analysis about Microsoft Office Word on Jaws (Job Access with Speech) Application for Visually Impaired Students Class X At Slbn Pajajaran Bandung City. *resmilitaris, 13*(2), 2030-2039.

Munasinghe, B., Bell, T., & Robins, A. (2023). Unplugged activities as a catalyst when teaching introductory programming. *Journal of Pedagogical Research*, 7(2), 56–71. DOI: 10.33902/JPR.202318546

Munisamy, M., Osman, S. Z. M., & Sanmugam, M. (2024). Code, Click, Learn: A Systematic Review Of Online Assessment Tools In 21st Century Programming Education. *International Journal of Medical Education*, 6(20), 358–377. DOI: 10.35631/IJMOE.620027

Murad, D. F., Heryadi, Y., Wijanarko, B. D., Isa, S. M., & Budiharto, W. (2018, September). Recommendation system for smart LMS using machine learning: a literature review. In 2018 international conference on computing, engineering, and design (ICCED) (pp. 113-118). IEEE.

Muro, M., Whiton, J., & Maxim, R. (2019). *What Jobs Are Affected by Artificial Intelligence?* Better-Paid, Better-Educated Workers Face the Most Exposure. Brookings Institution.

Nacher, V., Garcia-Sanjuan, F., & Jaen, J. (2016). Evaluating the Usability of a Tangible-Mediated Robot for Kindergarten Children Instruction. *2016 IEEE 16th International Conference on Advanced Learning Technologies (ICALT)*, 130–132. DOI: 10.1109/ICALT.2016.59

Naps, T. L., Rößling, G., Almstrum, V., Dann, W., Fleischer, R., Hundhausen, C., . . . Velázquez-Iturbide, J. Á. (2002). Exploring the role of visualization and engagement in computer science education. In Working group reports from ITiCSE on Innovation and technology in computer science education (pp. 131-152).

Narahara, T., & Kobayashi, Y. (2018). Personalizing homemade bots with plug & play Artificial Intelligence for STEAM education. In *SIGGRAPH Asia 2018 Technical Briefs* (pp. 1–4). ACM. DOI: 10.1145/3283254.3283270

National Curriculum Information Center (NCIC). (2022*). Basic Curriculum, Utilization of Information and Communication, 408-428,* [Online]. Available: https://ncic.re.kr/mobile.brd.ntc.view.do;jsessionid=3988D6B62A20BF3282FBCE62F14F7E2B?articleNo=10000070, Access Date: 21.06.2024

National Professional Development Center on Inclusion. (2008). *What do we mean by Professional development in the early childhood field?* The University of North Carolina, FPG Child Development Institute, Author.

Navarro-Cota, C., Molina, A. I., Redondo, M. A., & Lacave, C. (2024). Individual differences in computer programming: A systematic review. *Behaviour & Information Technology*, •••, 1–19. DOI: 10.1080/0144929X.2024.2317377

Naya, M., Varela, G., Llamas, L., Bautista, M., Becerra, J. C., Bellas, F., Prieto, A., Deibe, A., & Duro, R. J. (2017). A versatile robotic platform for educational engagement. In Proceedings of the 2017 9th IEEE International Conference on Intelligent Data Acquisition and Advanced Computing Systems: Technology and Applications (IDAACS) (Vol. 1, pp. 138–144).

NCCE. (2023). National Centre for Computing Education. https://teachcomputing.org/curriculum

NCCE. (2023b). National Centre of Computing Education. https://teachcomputing.org/curriculum

NCCE. (2024). National Centre for Computing Education (NCCE). https://computingeducation.org.uk/

Negrini, L. (2020). Teachers' attitudes towards educational robotics in compulsory school. *Italian Journal of Educational Technology*, 28(1), 77–90. DOI: 10.17471/2499-4324/1136

Neumann, R., Parry, S., & Becher, T. (2002). Teaching and learning in their disciplinary contexts: A conceptual analysis. *Studies in Higher Education*, 27(4), 405–417. DOI: 10.1080/0307507022000011525

Ngugi, J. K., & Goosen, L. (2021). Innovation, Entrepreneurship, and Sustainability for ICT Students Towards the Post-COVID-19 Era. In Carvalho, L. C., Reis, L., & Silveira, C. (Eds.), *Handbook of Research on Entrepreneurship, Innovation, Sustainability, and ICTs in the Post-COVID-19 Era* (pp. 110–131). IGI Global., DOI: 10.4018/978-1-7998-6776-0.ch006

Nguyen, Q., Rienties, B., Toetenel, L., Ferguson, R., & Whitelock, D. (2017). Examining the designs of computer-based assessment and its impact on student engagement, satisfaction, and pass rates. *Computers in Human Behavior*, 76, 703–714. DOI: 10.1016/j.chb.2017.03.028

NICE K12 Cybersecurity Education Conference. (2024). [Online]. Available: https://www.nist.gov/itl/applied-cybersecurity/nice/events/nice-k12-cybersecurity-education-conference, Access Date: 16.07.2024.

Nishida, T., Kanemune, S., Idosaka, Y., Namiki, M., Bell, T., & Kuno, Y. (2009). A CS unplugged design pattern. *SIGCSE Bulletin*, 41(1), 231–235. DOI: 10.1145/1539024.1508951

Nixon, M., & Aguado, A. (2019). *Feature Extraction and Image Processing for Computer Vision*. Academic Press.

Noma, H., Sasamoto, H., Itoh, Y., Kitamura, Y., Kishino, F., & Tetsutani, N. (2003). Computer learning system for pre-school-age children based on a haptized model railway. *First Conference on Creating, Connecting and Collaborating Through Computing, 2003. C5 2003. Proceedings.*, 118–119. DOI: 10.1109/C5.2003.1222343

Noone, M., & Mooney, A. (2018). Visual and textual programming languages: A systematic review of the literature. *Journal of Computers in Education*, 5(2), 149–174. DOI: 10.1007/s40692-018-0101-5

Northrup, A., Borowczak, A., & Slater, T. (2022). K-12 teachers' perceptions and experiences in starting to teach computer science. *Education Sciences*, 12(11), 742. Advance online publication. DOI: 10.3390/educsci12110742

Nourbakhsh, I. R., Crowley, K., Bhave, A., Hamner, E., Hsiu, T., Perez-Bergquist, A., Richards, S., & Wilkinson, K. (2005). The Robotic Autonomy Mobile Robotics Course: Robot Design, Curriculum Design and Educational Assessment. *Autonomous Robots*, 18(1), 103–127. DOI: 10.1023/B:AURO.0000047303.20624.02

Nouri, J., Zhang, L., Mannila, L., & Norén, E. (2020). Development of computational thinking, digital competence and 21st century skills when learning programming in K-9. *Education Inquiry*, 11(1), 1–17. DOI: 10.1080/20004508.2019.1627844

Nuhu, K. M., Adedokun-Shittu, N. A., & Shittu, A. J. K. (2018). Assessment of Students' Comprehension of Binary Concept Using Computer-Science-Unplugged-Method in a Selected Secondary School in Ilorin, Kwara State. *Fountain Journal of National Ad Applied Sciences*, 7(2). Advance online publication. DOI: 10.53704/fujnas.v7i2.232

Numanoğlu, M., & Keser, H. (2017). Programlama öğretiminde robot kullanımı-Mbot örneği. *Bartın Üniversitesi Eğitim Fakültesi Dergisi*, 6(2), 497–515. DOI: 10.14686/buefad.306198

Odden, T. O. B., Marin, A., & Rudolph, J. L. (2021). How has Science Education changed over the last 100 years? An analysis using natural language processing. *Science Education*, 105(4), 653–680.

OECD. (2022). *OECD PISA Reports Volume 1*, [Online]. Available: https://www.oecd.org/en/publications/2023/12/pisa-2022-results-volume-i_76772a36/full-report/component-9.html#tablegrp-d1e2203-92e1015b90, Access Date: 12.07.2024.

Oh, J., Kim, J., & Kim, J. (2014). Development and Application of Primary Puzzle-Based Learning Program for Computer Science Education. *The Journal of Korean association of computer education, 17*(3), 11-23.

Okcu, B., Yazıcı, F., & Sozbilir, M. (2016). Ortaokul düzeyindeki görme engelli öğrencilerin okuldaki öğrenim sürecine dair görüşleri. *Amasya Üniversitesi Eğitim Fakültesi Dergisi*, 5(1), 51–83.

Oppenlaender, J. (2022, November). The creativity of text-to-image generation. In *Proceedings of the 25th international academic mindtrek conference* (pp. 192-202).

Osabutey, E. L., Senyo, P. K., & Bempong, B. F. (2022). Evaluating the potential impact of online assessment on students' academic performance. *Information Technology &Amp. Information Technology & People*, 37(1), 152–170. DOI: 10.1108/ITP-05-2021-0377

Osuji, S. (2017). The use of e-assessment in the Nigerian higher systems. *Turkish Online Journal of Distance Education*, 13(4), 140–152.

Osunde, J., Windall, G., Bacon, E. A., & Mackinnon, L. (2013, Sep). Female under-representation in Computer Science education and workplace-A survey of issues and interventions, moving towards a game-based learning solution. *Building new cultures of learning*. University of Nottingham. Retrieved from https://oro.open.ac.uk/54981/

Overflow, S. (2022). Stack Overflow Developer Survey 2022. https://survey.stackoverflow.co/2022/?utm_source=socialshare&utm_medium=social&utm_campaign=dev-survey-2022

Özcan, M., & Kert, S. (2020). Use of mobile applications in collocation teaching. *Cypriot Journal of Educational Sciences*, 15(5), 1176–1190. Advance online publication. DOI: 10.18844/cjes.v15i5.4629

Özdemır, İ. H., Kişla, T., & Tito, S. S. (2023, June). Mobile Programming with Kuika: A Course Design. In 2023 32nd Annual Conference of the European Association for Education in Electrical and Information Engineering (EAEEIE) (pp. 1-6). IEEE.

Özdener, N. (2008). A comparison of the misconceptions about the time-efficiency of algorithms by various profiles of computer-programming students. *Computers & Education*, 51(3), 1094–1102. DOI: 10.1016/j.compedu.2007.10.008

Özel, E. H. Y. (2018).. . *T.C. Resmi Gazete*, (30471), 22–77.

Özelmacı, Ş., & Çakır, U. (2017). Metaforlar ve benzerlileri ile ilgili söylenenler. In Kılcan, B. (Ed.), *Metafor ve Eğitimde Metaforik Çalışmalar İçin Bir Uygulama Rehberi* (pp. 1–14). Pegem Akademi. DOI: 10.14527/9786052410806.02

Paiva, J. C., Leal, J. P., & Figueira, Á. (2022). Automated assessment in computer science education: A state-of-the-art review. [TOCE]. *ACM Transactions on Computing Education*, 22(3), 1–40. DOI: 10.1145/3513140

Paleyes, A., Urma, R. G., & Lawrence, N. D. (2022). Challenges in deploying machine learning: A survey of case studies. *ACM Computing Surveys*, 55(6), 1–29.

Palominos, F. E., Palominos, S. K., Durán, C. A., Córdova, F. M., & Díaz, H. (2018). Challenges in the use of a support tool with automated review in student learning of programming courses. *Procedia Computer Science*, 139, 424–431. DOI: 10.1016/j.procs.2018.10.260

Pandiaraja, P., Boopesh, K. B., Deepthi, T., Laksmi Priya, M., & Noodhana, R. (2022). An Analysis of Document Summarization for Educational Data Classification Using NLP with Machine Learning Techniques. In Iyer, B., Crick, T., & Peng, S.-L. (Eds.), *Applied Computational Technologies, Smart Innovation, Systems and Technologies* (pp. 127–143). Springer Nature. DOI: 10.1007/978-981-19-2719-5_12

Papadakis, S., Kalogiannakis, M., Zaranis, N., & Orfanakis, V. (2016). Using Scratch and App Inventor for teaching introductory programming in secondary education. A case study. *International Journal of Technology Enhanced Learning*, 8(3-4), 217–233. DOI: 10.1504/IJTEL.2016.082317

Papadakis, S., & Orfanakis, V. (2017). The combined use of Lego Mindstorms NXT and App Inventor for teaching novice programmers. In Alimisis, D., Moro, M., & Menegatti, E. (Eds.), *Educational Robotics in the Makers Era. Edurobotics 2016 2016. Advances in Intelligent Systems and Computing* (Vol. 560). Springer., DOI: 10.1007/978-3-319-55553-9_15

Papert, S. (1980). Mindstorms Children, Computers, and Powerful Ideas (Second edition). In *BasicBooks* (Vol. 1).

Papert, S. (1980). *Mindstorms: Children, Computers, and Powerful Ideas* (Vol. 1). Basic Books.

Papert, S. (1980). *Mindstorms: Children, computers, and powerful ideas*. Basic Books.

Park, D., Ahn, J., Jang, J., Yu, W., Kim, W., Bae, Y., & Yoo, I. (2020). The Development of Software Teaching-Learning Model based on Machine Learning Platform. *Journal of The Korean Association of Information Education*, 24(1), 49–57. DOI: 10.14352/jkaie.2020.24.1.49

Parsons, P. C. (2018). Conceptual metaphor theory as a foundation for communicative visualization design. In *IEEE VIS Workshop on Visualization for Communication* (VisComm 2018). Retrieved June 15, 2024, from https://www.dvclab.net/wp-content/uploads/2019/02/Parsons-Conceptual-Metaphor-Theory-as-a-Foundation-for-Com.pdf

Passey, D. (2016). Computer science (cs) in the compulsory education curriculum: Implications for future research. *Education and Information Technologies*, 22(2), 421–443. DOI: 10.1007/s10639-016-9475-z

Passey, D. (2017). Computer science (CS) in the compulsory education curriculum: Implications for future research. *Education and Information Technologies*, 22, 421–443.

Patrick, M., Alexander, R., Oriol, M., & Clark, J. A. (2014). Probability-Based Semantic Interpretation of Mutants. *2014 IEEE Seventh International Conference on Software Testing, Verification and Validation Workshops*, 186–195. DOI: 10.1109/ICSTW.2014.18

Patterson, J., Collins, L., & Abbott, G. (2004). Effective Leadership in the Eye of the Storm. *NASSP Bulletin*, 88(638), 2–14.

Peel, A., Sadler, T. D., & Friedrichsen, P. (2022). Algorithmic explanations: An unplugged instructional approach to integrate science and computational thinking. *Journal of Science Education and Technology*, 31(4), 428–441. DOI: 10.1007/s10956-022-09965-0 PMID: 35535350

Peng, J., Wang, M., & Sampson, D. (2017). Scaffolding project-based learning of computer programming in an online learning environment. In *2017 IEEE 17th International Conference on Advanced Learning Technologies (ICALT)* (pp. 315-319). IEEE. DOI: 10.1109/ICALT.2017.17

Pérez-Marín, D., Hijon-Neira, R., Bacelo, A., & Pizarro, C. (2020). Can computational thinking be improved by using a methodology based on metaphors and scratch to teach computer programming to children? *Computers in Human Behavior*, 105849, 1–10. DOI: 10.1016/j.chb.2018.12.027

Pérez-Marín, D., Hijón-Neira, R., & Martín-Lope, M. (2018). A methodology proposal based on metaphors to teach programming to children. *IEEE Revista Iberoamericana de Technologias del Aprendizaje*, 13(1), 46–53. DOI: 10.1109/RITA.2018.2809944

Pérez-Marin, D., Hijón-Neira, R., & Pizarro, C. (2022). Coding in early years education: Which factors influence the skills of sequencing and plotting a route, and to what extent? *International Journal of Early Years Education*, 30(4), 969–985. DOI: 10.1080/09669760.2022.2037076

Peters, L. (2019). An Educational Programming Environment for Teaching the Principles of Machine Learning using Lego Mindstorms (Unpublished doctoral dissertation). University of Applied Sciences Leipzig.

Petre, M., & Price, B. (2004). Using Robotics to Motivate 'Back Door' Learning. *Education and Information Technologies*, 9(2), 147–158. DOI: 10.1023/B:EAIT.0000027927.78380.60

Peytcheva-Forsyth, R., Aleksieva, L., & Yovkova, B. (2018). The impact of prior experience of e-learning and e-assessment on students' and teachers' approaches to the use of a student authentication and authorship checking system. *EDULEARN18 Proceedings*, 2311-2321. https://bit.ly/3OCGK80

Pezoa, W. G., & Domínguez, M. J. (2017, October). Combined approach using artificial vision and neural networks for facial recognition. In *2017 CHILEAN Conference on Electrical, Electronics Engineering, Information and Communication Technologies (CHILECON)* (pp. 1-5). IEEE.

Pfeiffer, A., Bezzina, S., Koenig, N., & Kriglstein, S. (2020). Beyond classical gamification: In-and Around-Game gamification for education. In *Proceedings of the 19th European Conference on e-Learning ECEL 2020* (pp. 415-420). https://doi.org/DOI: 10.34190/EEL.20.007

Phishing Quiz, [Online]. Available: https://phishingquiz.withgoogle.com/ Access Date: 29.06.2024

Piaget, J. (1977). *The development of thought: Equilibrium of cognitive structures.*

Piaget, J. (1952). *The origins of intelligence in children.* International Universities Press. DOI: 10.1037/11494-000

Picture: https://www.freepik.com/free-vector/pirate-capitan-ship-cabin-wooden-room-interior_30701210.htm#fromView=search&page=2&position=2&uuid=b1e51d02-25ea-462a-91e3-b6aa708637a0

Pila, S., Aladé, F., Sheehan, K. J., Lauricella, A. R., & Wartella, E. A. (2019). Learning to code via tablet applications: An evaluation of Daisy the Dinosaur and Kodable as learning tools for young children. *Computers & Education*, 128, 52–62. DOI: 10.1016/j.compedu.2018.09.006

Pinho, D., Aguiar, A., & Amaral, V. (2023). What about the usability in low-code platforms? A systematic literature review. *Journal of Computer Languages*, 74, 101185. DOI: 10.1016/j.cola.2022.101185

Pinto, A., Barbot, A., Viegas, C., Silva, A. A., Santos, C. A., & Lopes, J. B. (2012). Teacher education using computer simulations—pre and in-service primary school teacher training to teach science. *Learning science in the society of computers, 6*, pp. 28-36. Retrieved from https://cidtff.web.ua.pt/producao/jorge_bernardino_oliveira/3_fromcblis-2012_proceedings_v6.pdf

Pinto, A., Barbot, A., Viegas, C., Silva, A. A., Santos, C. A., & Lopes, J. B. (2014). Teaching science with experimental work and computer simulations in a primary teacher education course: What challenges to promote epistemic practices? *Procedia Technology*, 13, 86–96. DOI: 10.1016/j.protcy.2014.02.012

Popat, S., & Starkey, L. (2019). Learning to code or coding to learn? A systematic review. *Computers & Education*, 128, 365–376. DOI: 10.1016/j.compedu.2018.10.005

PRCVI. (2024). Inclusive Coding for Students with Visual Impairments. https://www.prcvi.org/outreach/school-based-services/inclusive-coding-for-students-with-visual-impairments/

Presidency of the Republic of Türkiye Digital Transformation Office. (2024 Updated Version). Cybersecurity Vocational Schools Project. [Online]. Available: https://cbddo.gov.tr/projeler/siber-myo/, Access Date: 29.08.2024.

Prickett, T., Crick, T., Harvey, M., Walters, J., & Yang, L. (2020, April 1). Exploring resilience for effective learning in computer science education. *Cambridge Computing Education Research Symposium.* University of Cambridge. Retrieved from https://nrl.northumbria.ac.uk/id/eprint/42892/1/CCERS2020_abstract_FINAL.pdf

Prickett, T., Walters, J., Yang, L., Harvey, M., & Crick, T. (2020). Resilience and effective learning in first-year undergraduate computer science. *Proceedings of the 2020 ACM Conference on Innovation and Technology in Computer Science Education.* https://doi.org/DOI: 10.1145/3341525.3387372

Proctor, C., Bigman, M., & Blikstein, P. (2019, February). Defining and designing computer science education in a k12 public school district. In *Proceedings of the 50th ACM technical symposium on computer science education* (pp. 314-320).

Prokofyeva, N., Uhanova, M., Katalnikova, S., Synytsya, K., & Jurenoks, A. (2017). Introductory Programming Training of First Year Students. *Procedia Computer Science*, 104, 286–293. DOI: 10.1016/j.procs.2017.01.137

Psycharis, S., Theodorou, P., Spanidis, Y., & Kydonakis, P. (2022). Teaching Programming Skills to Blind and Visually Impaired Learners. In Guralnick, D., Auer, M. E., & Poce, A. (Eds.), *Innovations in Learning and Technology for the Workplace and Higher Education. TLIC 2021. Lecture Notes in Networks and Systems* (Vol. 349). Springer., DOI: 10.1007/978-3-030-90677-1_26

Puhala, J. (2018). Changing Classroom practice: Elementary teacher experiences of a professional development program. *Technology. Knowledge and Learning*, 25(1), 129–147. DOI: 10.1007/s10758-018-9370-3

Pu, S., & Xu, H. (2021). Examining changing assessment practices in online teaching: A multiple-case study of efl school teachers in china. *The Asia-Pacific Education Researcher*, 30(6), 553–561. DOI: 10.1007/s40299-021-00605-6

Qian, Y., Hambrusch, S., Yadav, A., & Gretter, S. (2018). Who needs what: Recommendations for designing effective online professional development for computer science teachers. *Journal of Research on Technology in Education*, 50(2), 164–181. DOI: 10.1080/15391523.2018.1433565

Qian, Y., & Lehman, J. (2017). Students' misconceptions and other difficulties in introductory programming: A literature review. *ACM Transactions on Computing Education*, 18(1), 1–24. DOI: 10.1145/3077618

Quayyum, F. (2023). Collaboration between parents and children to raise cybersecurity awareness. In Proceedings of the 2023 *European Interdisciplinary Cybersecurity Conference* (pp. 149-152). DOI: 10.1145/3590777.3590802

Quayyum, F., Cruzes, D. S., & Jaccheri, L. (2021). Cybersecurity awareness for children: A systematic literature review. *International Journal of Child-Computer Interaction*, 30, 100343. DOI: 10.1016/j.ijcci.2021.100343

Radden, G., & Kövecses, Z. (1999). Towards a theory of metonymy. In Panther, K.-U., & Radden, G. (Eds.), *Metonymy in Language and Thought* (pp. 17–59). John Benjamins., DOI: 10.1075/hcp.4.03rad

Randles, B. M., Pasquetto, I. V., Golshan, M. S., & Borgman, C. L. (2017, June). Using the Jupyter notebook as a tool for open science: An empirical study. In *2017 ACM/IEEE Joint Conference on Digital Libraries (JCDL)* (pp. 1-2). IEEE.

Randolph, J. (2008). A methodological review of the program evaluations in k-12 computer science education. *Informatics in Education*, 7(2), 237–258. DOI: 10.15388/infedu.2008.15

Ranjeeth, S., & Naidoo, R. (2011). An Investigation into the Relationship between the Level of Cognitive Maturity and the Types of Errors Made by Students in a Computer Programming Course. *The International College Teaching Methods & Styles Journal*, 3(2), 31–40. DOI: 10.19030/ctms.v3i2.5279

Rao, N., Tsay, J., Kate, K., Hellendoorn, V., & Hirzel, M. (2024, March). Low-Code for AI. In *Proceedings of the 29th International Conference on Intelligent User Interfaces* (pp. 837-852).

Raschka, S. (2015). *Python Machine Learning*. Packt Publishing Ltd.

Ray, L., Whitehead, C., Shamim, K., Summers, W., & Obando, R. (2011, March). School Level Computer Science Education and Computer Science Teacher Training in the US: An Overview and an Example Solution. *Society for Information Technology & Teacher Education International Conference* (pp. 3931-3938)). Association for the Advancement of Computing in Education (AACE). Retrieved from https://www.learntechlib.org/p/36946/

Reddy, S. (2023). Best Assessment Software for Schools- E-tutor. https://etutor.co/blog/assessment-software/

Reigeluth, C. M. (Ed.). (1999). *Instructional-design theories and models: A new paradigm of instructional theory* (Vol. II). Routledge.

Renkl, A. (2014). Toward an instructionally oriented theory of example-based learning. *Cognitive Science*, 38(1), 1–37. DOI: 10.1111/cogs.12086 PMID: 24070563

Repenning, A., Webb, D., & Ioannidou, A. (2010). Scalable game design and the evolution of a checklist for getting computational thinking into public schools. In *Proceedings of the 41st ACM Technical Symposium on Computer Science Education* (pp. 265–269). ACM. DOI: 10.1145/1734263.1734357

Republic of Türkiye Ministry of National Education. (2018*). Information Technologies and Software Course Curriculum,* (2018). Ankara, 2018.

Republic of Türkiye Ministry of National Education. (2018). *Information Technologies and Software Course Level 2 Activity Book*, [Online]. Available: https://tegm.meb.gov.tr/meb_iys_dosyalar/2019_04/15151914_BiliYim_Teknolojileri_ve_YazYlYm_Dersi_2._Seviye_Etkinlik_KitabY_Ylkokul_2018-2019.pdf, Access Date: 07.07.2024

Resnick, L. B. (2017). Toward a cognitive theory of instruction. In *Learning and motivation in the classroom* (pp. 5–38). Routledge. DOI: 10.4324/9781315188522-2

Resnick, M. (2007). Sowing the seeds for a more creative society. *Learning and Leading with Technology*, 35(4), 18–22.

Resnick, M., Maloney, J., Monroy-Hernández, A., Rusk, N., Eastmond, E., Brennan, K., Millner, A., Rosenbaum, E., Silver, J., Silverman, B., & Kafai, Y. (2009). Scratch: Programming for all. *Communications of the ACM*, 52(11), 60–67. DOI: 10.1145/1592761.1592779

Ribble, M. (2015). *Digital citizenship in schools: Nine elements all students should know*. International Society for Technology in Education.

Rich, K. M., Yadav, A., & Larimore, R. A. (2020). Teacher implementation profiles for integrating computational thinking into elementary mathematics and science instruction. *Education and Information Technologies*, 25(4), 3161–3188. DOI: 10.1007/s10639-020-10115-5

Rich, P. J., Browning, S. F., Perkins, M., Shoop, T., Yoshikawa, E., & Belikov, O. M. (2019). Coding in K-8: International trends in teaching elementary/primary computing. *TechTrends*, 63(3), 311–329. DOI: 10.1007/s11528-018-0295-4

Ridgway, J., McCusker, S., & Pead, D. (2004). Literature review of e-assessment. https://telearn.hal.science/hal-00190440

Rieck, K., Holz, T., Willems, C., Düssel, P., & Laskov, P. (2008, July). Learning and classification of malware behavior. In *International Conference on Detection of Intrusions and Malware, and Vulnerability Assessment* (pp. 108-125). Berlin, Heidelberg: Springer Berlin Heidelberg.

Robins, A. (2019). Novice programmers and introductory programming. *The Cambridge Handbook of Computing Education Research, Cambridge Handbooks in Psychology*, 327-376. Retrieved June 4, 2024, from https://www.otago.ac.nz/computer-science/otago706761.pdf

Robins, A., Rountree, J., & Rountree, N. (2003). Learning and teaching programming: A review and discussion. *Computer Science Education*, 13(2), 137–172. DOI: 10.1076/csed.13.2.137.14200

Robinson, P. E., & Carroll, J. (2016). An online system for monitoring and assessing the programming process. *Bulletin of the IEEE Technical Committee on Learning Technology*, 18(2/3), 2. https://www.webofscience.com/wos/woscc/full-record/WOS:000398346100002

Robomaster S1. (n.d.). Retrieved from

Rodrigo, M., Andallaza, T. C. S., Castro, F. E. V. G., Armenta, M. L. V., Dy, T. T., & Jadud, M. C. (2013). An Analysis of Java Programming Behaviors, Affect, Perceptions, and Syntax Errors among Low-Achieving, Average, and High-Achieving Novice Programmers. *Journal of Educational Computing Research*, 49(3), 293–325. DOI: 10.2190/EC.49.3.b

Rodrigues, L., Toda, A. M., Oliveira, W., Palomino, P. T., Avila-Santos, A. P., & Isotani, S. (2021, March). Gamification works, but how and to whom? an experimental study in the context of programming lessons. In *Proceedings of the 52nd ACM technical symposium on computer science education* (pp. 184-190). ACM. DOI: 10.1145/3408877.3432419

Rodríguez-García, J. D., Moreno-León, J., Román-González, M., & Robles, G. (2021). Introducing Artificial Intelligence Fundamentals with LearningMachine Learning: Artificial Intelligence made easy. In *Proceedings of the Eighth International Conference on Technological Ecosystems for Enhancing Multiculturality*, Barcelona, Spain, 26–29 October 2021, 18–20.

Román-González, M., Moreno-León, J., & Robles, G. (2019). Combining assessment tools for a comprehensive evaluation of computational thinking interventions. *Computational thinking education*, 79-98. https://library.oapen.org/bitstream/handle/20.500.12657/23182/1006971.pdf?sequenc#page=85

Román-González, M., Pérez-González, J. C., & Jiménez-Fernández, C. (2017). Which cognitive abilities underlie computational thinking? Criterion validity of the Computational Thinking Test. *Computers in Human Behavior*, 72, 678–691. DOI: 10.1016/j.chb.2016.08.047

Rombach, R., Blattmann, A., Lorenz, D., Esser, P., & Ommer, B. (2022). High-resolution image synthesis with latent diffusion models. In *Proceedings of the IEEE/CVF conference on computer vision and pattern recognition* (pp. 10684-10695).

Romeike, R. (2019). The role of computer science education for understanding and shaping the digital society. In Sustainable ICT, Education and Learning: IFIP WG 3.4 International Conference, SUZA 2019, Zanzibar, Tanzania, April 25–27, 2019, Revised Selected Papers 1 (pp. 167-176). Springer International Publishing. https://link.springer.com/chapter/10.1007/978-3-030-28764-1_19

Romero, M., Lepage, A., & Lille, B. (2017). Computational thinking development through creative programming in higher education. *International Journal of Educational Technology in Higher Education*, 14(1), 1–15. DOI: 10.1186/s41239-017-0080-z

Rosenshine, B. (1986). Synthesis of research on explicit teaching. *Educational Leadership*, 43(7), 60–69.

Roth, W.-M., Bowen, G. M., & McGinn, M. K. (1996). Interpretive scientific research methods. *Journal of Research in Science Teaching*, 33(3), 157–173.

Roumen, G. J., & Fernaeus, Y. (2021). Envisioning Arduino Action: A collaborative tool for physical computing in educational settings. *International Journal of Child-Computer Interaction*, 29, 100277. DOI: 10.1016/j.ijcci.2021.100277

Rousseau, V. (2022). Lego Mindstorms: One-Legged Robot Learning How to Crawl with q-Learning [Video]. YouTube. Retrieved from

Royal Society. (2017). *Machine Learning: The Power and Promise of Computer That Learn by Example* [Technical Report]. The Royal Society.

Rubinstein, A., & Chor, B. (2014). Computational thinking in life science education. *PLoS Computational Biology*, 10(11), e1003897. DOI: 10.1371/journal.pcbi.1003897 PMID: 25411839

Rudder, A., Bernard, M., & Mohammed, S. (2007). Teaching programming using visualization. In *Proceedings of the Sixth IASTED International Conference on Web-Based Education* (pp. 487-492). ACTA Press. Retrieved June 16, 2024, from https://uwispace.sta.uwi.edu/server/api/core/bitstreams/cf1424a5-dc26-4204-a864-72c7bd3161ac/content

Ruiz de Mendoza Ibáñez, F. J., & Pérez Hernández, L. (2011). The Contemporary Theory of Metaphor: Myths, Developments and Challenges. *Metaphor and Symbol*, 26(3), 161–185. DOI: 10.1080/10926488.2011.583189

Ruiz, P., Nestor, E., Mills, K., Coenraad, M., & Burke, Q. (2022, March). Designing Equity-Centered Formative Assessment Artifacts for Computing. In *Proceedings of the 53rd ACM Technical Symposium on Computer Science Education V. 2* (pp. 1121-1121). https://www.webofscience.com/wos/woscc/full-record/WOS:000947124200075

Rustamov, M. M., Khomidov, M. E., & Goipov, E. A. (2019). Teaching Computer Science in Higher Education: Problems and Solutions. *Экономика и социум, 11*(66), 105-108. Retrieved from https://elibrary.ru/item.asp?id=42200285

Saeki, E., Segool, N., Pendergast, L., & von der Embse, N. (2018). The influence of test-based accountability policies on early elementary teachers: School climate, environmental stress, and teacher stress. *Psychology in the Schools*, 55(4), 391–403. DOI: 10.1002/pits.22112

Sáez-López, J. M., Román-González, M., & Vázquez-Cano, E. (2016). Visual programming languages integrated across the curriculum in elementary school: A two year case study using "Scratch" in five schools. *Computers & Education*, 97, 129–141. DOI: 10.1016/j.compedu.2016.03.003

Sáez-López, J., Otero, R. B., & García-Cervigón, S. D. L. (2020). Introducing robotics and block programming in elementary education. *RIED.Revista Iberoamericana De Educación a Distancia*, 24(1), 95. DOI: 10.5944/ried.24.1.27649

Safak, P. (2017). Braille yazı sistemi, tarihçesi ve dünyada Braille. P. Şafak (Ed.), *Görenler için braille (kabartma) yazı rehberi içinde* (1. Baskı., ss. 2–23). Ankara: Pegem Akademi Yayınları

Sahin, M., & Yorek, N. (2009). Teaching Science to Visually Impaired Students: A Small-Scale Qualitative Study. *Online Submission*, 6(4), 19–26.

Sahranç, Ü. (2013). 'Bir Durumluk Akış Modeli: Stres Kontrolü, Genel Özyeterlik, Durumluk Kaygı, Yaşam Doyumu Ve Akış İlişkileri'. *Sakarya Üniversitesi Eğitim Fakültesi Dergisi*, (16), 122–144.

Saleem, A. (2022). 'Applications of Natural Language Processing I Data Science Dojo'. Retrieved 23 May 2024 (https://datasciencedojo.com/blog/natural-language-processing-applications/)

Sammut, C. (2010). Concept Learning. In Sammut, C., & Webb, G. I. (Eds.), *Encyclopedia of Machine Learning* (pp. 205–208). Springer. DOI: 10.1007/978-0-387-30164-8

Samuelsson, R. (2022). Cultural Heritage Through Educational Robots: Using a Ukrainian Folk Tale with a Programmable Robot in Early Childhood Education. *HCI International 2022–Late Breaking Posters: 24th International Conference on Human-Computer Interaction, HCII 2022, Virtual Event, June 26–July 1, 2022, Proceedings, Part I*, 336–343.

Sánchez, J., & Aguayo, F. 2006. APL: Audio programming language for blind learners. Computers Helping People with Special Needs, Springer, 1334–1341.

San, İ. (1990). Eğitimde Yaratıcı Drama. [JFES]. *Ankara University Journal of Faculty of Educational Sciences*, 23(2), 573–582.

Santo, A. D., Farah, J. C., Martínez, M. L., Moro, A., Bergram, K., Purohit, A. K., Gelber, P., Gillet, D., & Holzer, A. (2022). Promoting computational thinking skills in non-computer-science students: Gamifying computational notebooks to increase student engagement. *IEEE Transactions on Learning Technologies*, 15(3), 392–405. DOI: 10.1109/TLT.2022.3180588

Santos, S., Tedesco, P., Borba, M., & Brito, M. (2020). Innovative approaches in teaching programming: A systematic literature review. *In Proceedings of the 12th International Conference on Computer Supported Education (CSEDU 2020)*. Vol. 1, (pp. 205-214). Science and Technology Publications. DOI: 10.5220/0009190502050214

Sarı, U., Pektaş, H. M., Şen, Ö. F., & Çelik, H. (2022). Algorithmic thinking development through physical computing activities with Arduino in STEM education. *Education and Information Technologies*, 27(5), 6669–6689. DOI: 10.1007/s10639-022-10893-0

Sarpong, K. A. M., Arthur, J. K., & Amoako, P. Y. O. (2013). Causes of failure of students in computer programming courses: The teacher-learner perspective. *International Journal of Computer Applications*, 77(12), 27–32. DOI: 10.5120/13448-1311

Sat, M., & Kadirhan, Z. (2024). Unveiling competence in the classroom: A multidimensional assessment of computer science teachers' self-efficacy in coding education. *Education and Information Technologies*, 1–29. DOI: 10.1007/s10639-024-12503-7

Sawyer, R. K. (2006). *The Cambridge handbook of the learning sciences*. Cambridge University Press.

Saxena, A., Lo, C. K., Hew, K. F., & Wong, G. K. W. (2020). Designing unplugged and plugged activities to cultivate computational thinking: An exploratory study in early childhood education. *The Asia-Pacific Education Researcher*, 29(1), 55–66. DOI: 10.1007/s40299-019-00478-w

Saygıner, Ş., & Tüzün, H. (2017). İlköğretim düzeyinde programlama eğitimi: Yurt dışı ve yurt içi perspektifinden bir bakış. *Akademik Bilişim Konferansı*, 1-5.

Scaico, P. D., & Costa, T. K. L. (2014). Supervised internships and their lessons: Challenges and experiences with teaching degree in computer science in brazilian scenario. *CLEI Electronic Journal*, 17(3). Advance online publication. DOI: 10.19153/cleiej.17.3.11

Scher, L., & O'Reilly, F. (2009). Professional development for k–12 math and science teachers: What do we really know? *Journal of Research on Educational Effectiveness*, 2(3), 209–249. DOI: 10.1080/19345740802641527

Schmidt, S. M. P., Ralph, D. L., & Buskirk, B. (2009). Utilizing online exams: A case study. *Journal of College Teaching and Learning*, 6(8), 1. DOI: 10.19030/tlc.v6i8.1108

Schön, D. A. (1983). *The reflective practitioner: How professionals think in action.* Basic Books.

Schulte, C., Clear, T., Taherkhani, A., Busjahn, T., & Paterson, J. H. (2010). An introduction to program comprehension for computer science educators. *Proceedings of the 2010 ITiCSE working group reports*, 65-86. https://doi.org/DOI: 10.1145/1971681.1971687

Scratch Extensions. (n.d.). Retrieved from

Scratch Lab's Face Sensing. (n.d.). Retrieved from

Segal, G., Schuck, S., Brady, L., Deer, C. E., & Segal, G. (1999). Innovation in primary science teacher education: Taking responsibility for learning through computer-mediated communication and classroom interactions. *Challenge of Change in Education Symposium Proceedings*, (pp. 318-330).

Selby, C., & Woollard, J. (2013). Computational Thinking : The Developing Definition. *ITiCSE Conference 2013.*

Selvi, A. (2020). Prediction of Student Success in Transition from Primary to Secondary Education Exams in Bilecik Province Using Machine Learning Methods. (Unpublished Master's thesis). Bilecik Şeyh Edebali University, Institute of Natural Sciences, Bilecik.

Sentance, S., Barendsen, E., Howard, N. R., & Schulte, C. (2023). *Computer science education: Perspectives on teaching and learning in school.* Bloomsbury Publishing. DOI: 10.5040/9781350296947

Sentance, S., & Csizmadia, A. (2017). Computing in the curriculum: Challenges and strategies from a teacher's perspective. *Education and Information Technologies*, 22(2), 469–495. DOI: 10.1007/s10639-016-9482-0

Sentance, S., Dorling, M., McNicol, A., & Crick, T. (2012). Grand challenges for the UK: upskilling teachers to teach computer science within the secondary curriculum (Paper presentation). *7th Workshop in Primary and Secondary Computing Education (WiPCSE).* Hamburg, Germany. DOI: 10.1145/2481449.2481469

Sentance, S., & Waite, J. (2017). PRIMM: Exploring pedagogical approaches for teaching text-based programming in school. Barendsen, E., & Hubwieser, P. (Eds.), In *Proceedings of the 12th Workshop on Primary and Secondary Computing* Education (pp.113-114), Association for Computing Machinery. DOI: 10.1145/3137065.3137084

Seppi, M. (2024). Cyber Security Career Roadmap: Building a Secure Future. International University of Applied Science. [Online]. Available: https://www.iu.org/blog/career-paths/cyber-security-career/#:~:text=Exploring%20the%20Cybersecurity%20career%20landscape&text=According%20to%20the%20U.S.%20Bureau,the%20average%20for%20all%20occupations. Access Date: 31.08.2024

Seralidou, E. & Douligeris, C. (2022). Investigating the transition from block-based to text-based programming techniques in secondary education in greece. *European Journal of Engineering and Technology Research*, 21-27. https://doi.org/DOI: 10.24018/ejeng.2021.0.CIE.2753

Serrano Pérez, E., & Juárez López, F. (2019). An ultra-low cost line follower robot as educational tool for teaching programming and circuit's foundations. *Computer Applications in Engineering Education*, 27(2), 288–302. DOI: 10.1002/cae.22074

Seto, K. (1999). Distinguishing metonymy from synecdoche. In K. U. Panther ve G. Radden, (Eds.), *Metonymy in language and thought* (pp. 91-120). John Benjamins Publishing. DOI: 10.1075/hcp.4.06set

Shahid, M., Wajid, A., Haq, K. U., Saleem, I., & Shujja, A. H. (2019). A review of gamification for learning programming fundamental. In *2019 International Conference on Innovative Computing (ICIC)* (pp. 1-8). IEEE. DOI: 10.1109/ICIC48496.2019.8966685

Shana, Z., & Abulibdeh, E. S. (2020). 'Science Practical Work and Its Impact on High Students' Academic Achievement'. *JOTSE*, 10(2), 199–215. DOI: 10.3926/jotse.888

Shanley, N., Martin, F., Hite, N., Pérez-Quiñones, M. A., Ahlgrim-Delzell, L., Pugalee, D., & Hart, E. (2022). Teaching programming online: Design, facilitation and assessment strategies and recommendations for high school teachers. *TechTrends*, 66(3), 483–494. DOI: 10.1007/s11528-022-00724-x PMID: 35434728

Sharifi, M., Soleimani, H., & Jafarigohar, M. (2017). E-portfolio evaluation and vocabulary learning: Moving from pedagogy to andragogy. *British Journal of Educational Technology*, 48(6), 1441–1450. DOI: 10.1111/bjet.12479

Sharma, R., Joshi, S., Agarwal, A., & Kulkarni, V. (2020). UniAssist-Implementation of Machine Learning Based Higher Education University Recommendation System. [IJREAM]. *International Journal for Research in Engineering Application & Management*, 6(1), 262–266.

Sharma, V. K., & Holbah, W. A. (2022). Online Language Assessment the Exception, Not the Rule: For Inclusive Language Learning. *Arab World English Journal (AWEJ). Special Issue on CALL*, (8), 299–313. DOI: 10.24093/awej/call8.20

Shim, J., Kwon, D., & Lee, W. (2016). The effects of a robot game environment on computer programming education for elementary school students. *IEEE Transactions on Education*, 60(2), 164–172. DOI: 10.1109/TE.2016.2622227

Shrestha, N., Botta, C., Barik, T., & Parnin, C. (2020). Here we go again: Why is it difficult for developers to learn another programming language? In *Proceedings of the ACM/IEEE 42nd International Conference on Software Engineering* (pp. 691-701). IEEE. DOI: 10.1145/3377811.3380352

Shuell, T. J. (1990). Teaching and learning as problem solving. *Theory into Practice*, 29(2), 102–108. DOI: 10.1080/00405849009543439

Shuhidan, S. M. (2012). *Probing the minds of novice programmers through guided learning* (Publication No. 9921861240001341) [Doctoral dissertation, RMIT University]. RMIT Research Repository. https://researchrepository.rmit.edu.au/esploro/outputs/doctoral/Probing-the-minds-of-novice-programmers/9921861240001341

Shulman, L. S. (1987). Knowledge and Teaching: Foundations of the New Reform. *Harvard Educational Review*, 57(1), 1–22. DOI: 10.17763/haer.57.1.j463w79r56455411

Sierra, A. J., Ariza, T., Fernández-Jiménez, F. J., Bellido, S., & Martínez-Gotor, A. (2014). E-assessment tool within PBL in programming subjects at engineering. In *EDULEARN14 Proceedings* (pp. 7074–7080). IATED., https://library.iated.org/view/SIERRA2014EAS

Sietses, L. (2016). White Paper Online Proctoring. Questions and answers about remote proctoring. *SURFnet*. Retrieved from https://www.surf.nl/files/2019-04/whitepaper-online-proctoring_en.pdf

Silva, E. F., Dembogurski, B. J., & Semaan, G. S. (2023). A literature review of computational thinking in early ages. In *International Journal of Early Years Education* (Vol. 31, Issue 3). DOI: 10.1080/09669760.2022.2107491

Silvis, D., Lee, V. R., Clarke-Midura, J., & Shumway, J. F. (2022). The technical matters: young children debugging (with) tangible coding toys. *Information and Learning Sciences, ahead-of-print*.

Silvis, D., Clarke-Midura, J., Shumway, J. F., Lee, V. R., & Mullen, S. (2022). Children caring for robots: Expanding computational thinking frameworks to include a technological ethic of care. *International Journal of Child-Computer Interaction*, 33, 100491. DOI: 10.1016/j.ijcci.2022.100491

Sim, T. Y., & Lau, S. L. (2022, November). Review on challenges and solutions in novice programming education. In *2022 IEEE International Conference on Computing (ICOCO)* (pp. 55-61). IEEE. DOI: 10.1109/ICOCO56118.2022.10031657

Sitthisak, O., Gilbert, L., & Davis, H. C. (2008). An evaluation of pedagogically informed parameterised questions for self-assessment. *Learning, Media and Technology*, 33(3), 235–248. https://www.tandfonline.com/doi/abs/10.1080/17439880802324210. DOI: 10.1080/17439880802324210

Sitthiworachart, J., Joy, M., & Sutinen, E. (2008, November). Success factors for e-assessment in computer science education. *E-Learn: World Conference on E-Learning in Corporate, Government, Healthcare, and Higher Education* (pp. 2287-2293). Association for the Advancement of Computing in Education (AACE). Retrieved from https://www.learntechlib.org/p/29993/

Skinner, B. F. (1958). Teaching machines. *Science*, 128(3330), 969–977. https://app.nova.edu/toolbox/instructionalproducts/edd8124/fall11/1958-Skinner-TeachingMachines.pdf. DOI: 10.1126/science.128.3330.969 PMID: 13592277

Sklirou, T. S. (2017). Programming in secondary education: Applications, new trends and challenges. *2017 IEEE Global Engineering Education Conference (EDUCON)*, 580–585. DOI: 10.1109/EDUCON.2017.7942904

Slavin, R. E. (2002). Evidence-based education policies: Transforming educational practice and research. *Educational Researcher*, 31(7), 15–21. DOI: 10.3102/0013189X031007015

Smith, A., Mott, B., Taylor, S., Hubbard-Cheuoua, A., Minogue, J., Oliver, K., & Ringstaff, C. (2020). Toward a block-based programming approach to interactive storytelling for upper elementary students. In *Interactive Storytelling: 13th International Conference on Interactive Digital Storytelling, ICIDS 2020, Bournemouth, UK, November 3-6, 2020* [Springer International Publishing.]. *Proceedings*, 13, 111–119.

Smith, J., Tessler, J., Kramer, E., & Lin, C. (2012, September). Using peer review to teach software testing. In *Proceedings of the ninth annual international conference on International computing education research* (pp. 93-98). https://doi.org/DOI: 10.1145/2361276.2361295

Smith, K., & Hill, J. (2018). Defining the nature of blended learning through its depiction in current research. *Higher Education Research & Development*, 38(2), 383–397. DOI: 10.1080/07294360.2018.1517732

Sobnath, D., Kaduk, T., Rehman, I. U., & Issa, R. (2020). Feature Selection for UK Disabled Students Engagement Post Higher Education: A Machine Learning Approach for a Predictive Employment Model. *IEEE Access : Practical Innovations, Open Solutions*, 8, 159530–159541. DOI: 10.1109/ACCESS.2020.3018663

Sobral, S. R. (2021). Project based learning with peer assessment in an introductory programming course. *International Journal of Information and Education Technology (IJIET)*, 11(7), 337–341. DOI: 10.18178/ijiet.2021.11.7.1532

So, H. J., Jong, M. S., & Liu, C. (2019). Computational thinking education in the asian pacific region. *The Asia-Pacific Education Researcher*, 29(1), 1–8. DOI: 10.1007/s40299-019-00494-w

Somuncu, B., & Aslan, D. (2021). Effect of coding activities on preschool children's mathematical reasoning skills. *Education and Information Technologies*, 27(1), 877–890. DOI: 10.1007/s10639-021-10618-9 PMID: 34226819

Sońta, M., & Przegalinska, A. (2024). Say 'yes' to 'no-code'solutions: how to teach low-code and no-code competencies to non-IT students. In *Handbook of Social Computing* (pp. 330–342). Edward Elgar Publishing. DOI: 10.4337/9781803921259.00030

Sophokleous, A., Christodoulou, P., Doitsidis, L., & Chatzichristofis, S. A. (2021). 'Computer Vision Meets Educational Robotics'. *Electronics (Basel)*, 10(6), 730. DOI: 10.3390/electronics10060730

Sözeri, M. C., & Kert, S. B. (2021). Ineffectiveness of online interactive video content developed for programming education. *International Journal of Computer Science Education in Schools*, 4(3), 49–69. DOI: 10.21585/ijcses.v4i3.99

Sparks, D., & Loucks-Horsley, S. (1989). Development for Teachers. *Journal of Staff Development*, 10(4), 40–57.

Spivey, M. F., & McMillan, J. J. (2014). Classroom versus online assessment. *Journal of Education for Business*, 89(8), 450–456. DOI: 10.1080/08832323.2014.937676

Stanny, C. J. (2016). Reevaluating Bloom's Taxonomy: What measurable verbs can and cannot say about student learning. *Education Sciences*, 6(4), 37. DOI: 10.3390/educsci6040037

Stanojević, D., Rosić, A., Ranđelović, B., & Stanković, Ž. (2021). Micro: Bit as a tool for improvement of education. *The International Journal of Management Science and Business Administration*, 7(2), 14–19. DOI: 10.18775/ijmsba.1849-5664-5419.2014.72.1002

Stefik, A. M., Hundhausen, C., & Smith, D. (2011). On the design of an educational infrastructure for the blind and visually impaired in computer science. In *Proceedings of the 42nd ACM technical symposium on Computer science education* (pp. 571-576). DOI: 10.1145/1953163.1953323

Stefik, A., Allee, W., Contreras, G., Kluthe, T., Hoffman, A., Blaser, B., & Ladner, R. (2024, March). Accessible to whom? Bringing accessibility to blocks. In *Proceedings of the 55th ACM Technical Symposium on Computer Science Education* V. 1 (pp. 1286-1292). DOI: 10.1145/3626252.3630770

Stefik, A., & Siebert, S. (2013). An empirical investigation into programming language syntax. [TOCE]. *ACM Transactions on Computing Education*, 13(4), 1–40. DOI: 10.1145/2534973

Steinbach, P., Seibold, H., & Guhr, O. (2021). Teaching Machine Learning in 2020. In *Proceedings of the First Teaching Machine Learning and Artificial Intelligence Workshop* (pp. 1–6). [Accessed online:(41/steinbach21a.html)]

Steve, M. (2004). *Code complete: a practical handbook of software construction*. Microsoft Press.

Stockman, G., & Shapiro, L. G. (2001). *Computer Vision* (1st ed.). Prentice Hall PTR.

Storjak, I., Pushkar, L., Jagust, T., & Krzic, A. S. (2020). First steps into STEM for young pupils through informal workshops. *2020 IEEE Frontiers in Education Conference (FIE)*, 1–5. DOI: 10.1109/FIE44824.2020.9274139

Students Wellbeing Hub. (2024). [Online]. Available: https://studentwellbeinghub.edu.au/. Access Date: 30.08.2024

Sufi, F. (2023). Algorithms in low-code-no-code for research applications: A practical review. *Algorithms*, 16(2), 108. DOI: 10.3390/a16020108

Su, J., Yang, W., & Li, H. (2023). A scoping review of studies on coding curriculum in early childhood: Investigating its design, implementation, and evaluation. *Journal of Research in Childhood Education*, 37(2), 341–361. DOI: 10.1080/02568543.2022.2097349

Sulmont, E., Patitsas, E., & Cooperstock, J. R. (2019). What Is Hard about Teaching Machine Learning to Non-Majors? Insights from Classifying Instructors' Learning Goals. ACM Transactions on Computing Education, 19, 33:1–33:16.

Sun, D., Zhu, C., Xu, F., Li, Y., Ouyang, F., & Cheng, M. (2024). Transitioning From Introductory to Professional Programming in Secondary Education: Comparing Learners' Computational Thinking Skills, Behaviors, and Attitudes. *Journal of Educational Computing Research*, 62(3), 647–674. DOI: 10.1177/07356331231204653

Sung, J. (2022). Assessing young Korean children's computational thinking: A validation study of two measurements. *Education and Information Technologies*, 27(9), 1–29. DOI: 10.1007/s10639-022-11137-x

Sung, W., Ahn, J., & Black, J. B. (2017). Introducing computational thinking to young learners: Practicing computational perspectives through embodiment in mathematics education. *Technology. Knowledge and Learning*, 22(3), 443–463. DOI: 10.1007/s10758-017-9328-x

Sung, W., Ahn, J., & Black, J. B. (2022). Elementary Students' Performance and Perceptions of Robot Coding and Debugging: Embodied Approach in Practice. *Journal of Research in Childhood Education*, 36(4), 681–696. DOI: 10.1080/02568543.2022.2045399

Sun, J., Liao, Q. V., Muller, M., Agarwal, M., Houde, S., Talamadupula, K., & Weisz, J. D. (2022, March). Investigating explainability of generative AI for code through scenario-based design. In *Proceedings of the 27th International Conference on Intelligent User Interfaces* (pp. 212-228).

Sun, L., Guo, Z., & Zhou, D. (2022). Developing programming skills in K-12 students: A systematic literature review. *Education and Information Technologies*, 27(5), 7059–7097. DOI: 10.1007/s10639-022-10891-2

Sun, L., Hu, L., & Zhou, D. (2021). Which way of design programming activities is more effective to promote K-12 students' computational thinking skills? A meta-analysis. *Journal of Computer Assisted Learning*, 37(4), 1048–1062. DOI: 10.1111/jcal.12545

Sun, L., & Liu, J. (2024). Effects of Gamified Python Programming on Primary School Students' Computational Thinking Skills: A Differential Analysis of Gender. *Journal of Educational Computing Research*, 62(3), 846–874. DOI: 10.1177/07356331231225269

Sun, L., Liu, J., & Liu, Y. (2024). Comparative experiment of the effects of unplugged and plugged-in programming on computational thinking in primary school students: A perspective of multiple influential factors. *Thinking Skills and Creativity*, 52, 101542. DOI: 10.1016/j.tsc.2024.101542

Sun, L., & Zhou, L. (2023). Does text-based programming improve K-12 students' CT skills? Evidence from a meta-analysis and synthesis of qualitative data in educational contexts. *Thinking Skills and Creativity*, 49, 101340. DOI: 10.1016/j.tsc.2023.101340

Sun, R., Lei, T., Chen, Q., Wang, Z., Du, X., Zhao, W., & Nandi, A. K. (2022). 'Survey of Image Edge Detection'. *Frontiers in Signal Processing*, 2, 826967. Advance online publication. DOI: 10.3389/frsip.2022.826967

Supovitz, J., & Turner, H. (2000). The effects of professional development on science teaching practices and classroom culture. *Journal of Research in Science Teaching*, 37(9), 963–980. DOI: 10.1002/1098-2736(200011)37:9<963::AID-TEA6>3.0.CO;2-0

Susanto, S., & Nanda, D. S. (2018). Teaching and learning English for visually impaired students: An ethnographic case study. English Review. *Journal of English Education*, 7(1), 83–92.

Susilo, E., Liu, J., Rayo, Y. A., Peck, A. M., Montenegro, J., Gonyea, M., & Valdastri, P. (2016). Stormlab for stem education: An affordable modular robotic kit for integrated science, technology, engineering, and math education. *IEEE Robotics &Amp. IEEE Robotics & Automation Magazine*, 23(2), 47–55. DOI: 10.1109/MRA.2016.2546703

Su, Y.-S., Wang, S., & Liu, X. (2024). Using Epistemic Network Analysis to Explore Primary School Students' Computational Thinking in Pair Programming Learning. *Journal of Educational Computing Research*, 62(2), 559–593. DOI: 10.1177/07356331231210560

Sweeney, T., West, D., Groessler, A., Haynie, A., Higgs, B., Macaulay, J., Mercer-Mapstone, L., & Yeo, M. (2017). Where's the Transformation? Unlocking the Potential of Technology Enhanced Assessment. *Teaching & Learning Inquiry*, 5(1), 1–13. DOI: 10.20343/5.1.5

Szeliski, R. (2022). *Computer Vision: Algorithms and Applications*. Springer Nature. DOI: 10.1007/978-3-030-34372-9

Takacs, A., Eigner, G., Kovacs, L., Rudas, I. J., & Haidegger, T. (2016). Teacher's Kit: Development, Usability, and Communities of Modular Robotic Kits for Classroom Education. *IEEE Robotics & Automation Magazine*, 23(4), 30–39. DOI: 10.1109/MRA.2016.2548754

Talan, T., & Aktürk, C. (2021). *Bilgisayar Bilimlerinde Teorik Ve Uygulamalı Araştırmalar*. Efe Akademi Yayınları.

Tang, T., Smith, R., Rixner, S., & Warren, J. (2016, July). Data-driven test case generation for automated programming assessment. In *Proceedings of the 2016 ACM Conference on Innovation and Technology in Computer Science Education* (pp. 260-265).

Tank, K. M., Ottenbreit-Leftwich, A., Moore, T. J., Yang, S., Wafula, Z., Kim, J., ... & Chu, L. (2024). Investigating Sequencing as a Means to Computational Thinking in Young Learners.

Tareq, Z.-A., & Raja Yusof, R. J. (2024). Modeling a Problem-Solving Approach Through Computational Thinking for Teaching Programming. *IEEE Transactions on Education*, 67(2), 282–291. DOI: 10.1109/TE.2024.3354425

Taylor, E., Breed, M., Hauman, I., & Homann, A. (2013). *Choosing Learning Methods Suitable for Teaching and Learning in Computer Science*. International Association for Development of the Information Society.

Tedre, M., Toivonen, T., Kahila, J., Vartiainen, H., Valtonen, T., Jormanainen, I., & Pears, A. (2021). Teaching Machine Learning in K-12 Computing Education: Potential and Pitfalls. arXiv, arXiv:2106.11034.

TensorFlow Playground. (n.d.). Retrieved from

Terroba, M., Ribera, J. M., Lapresa, D., & Anguera, M. T. (2022). Observational analysis of the development of computational thinking in Early Childhood Education (5 years old) through an intervention proposal with a ground robot of programmed directionality. *European Early Childhood Education Research Journal*, 30(3), 437–455. DOI: 10.1080/1350293X.2022.2055102

Theodoropoulos, A., & Lepouras, G. (2020). Digital game-based learning and computational thinking in P-12 education: a systematic literature review on playing games for learning programming. Handbook of research on tools for teaching computational thinking in p-12 education, 159-183.

Thomas, J. W. (2000). *A review of research on project-based learning*. Autodesk Foundation.

Thomson, K., & Falchikov, N. (1998). 'Full on until the sun comes out': The effects of assessment on student approaches to studying. *Assessment & Evaluation in Higher Education*, 23(4), 379–390. DOI: 10.1080/0260293980230405

Thornton, D., & Turley, F. (2020). Dynamic Difficulty Adjustment in Cybersecurity Awareness Games: Analysis of Player Behavior and the Potential of Electroencephalography. *Innovations in Cybersecurity Education*, 3-17.

Tiantian, W., Xiaohong, S., Peijun, M., Yuying, W., & Kuanquan, W. (2009) Autolep: An automated learning and examination system for programming and its application in programming course. *InFirst International Workshop on Education Technology and Computer Science,* 43-46. IEEE. DOI: 10.1109/ETCS.2009.18

Tikva, C., & Tambouris, E. (2021). Mapping computational thinking through programming in K-12 education: A conceptual model based on a systematic literature review. *Computers & Education*, 162, 104083. DOI: 10.1016/j.compedu.2020.104083

Tim, T. (2022). Reinforcement Learning with Lego Mindstorms—Crawling Robot [Video]. YouTube. Retrieved from

Timur, S., Timur, B., Güvenç, E., Us, I., & Yalçinkaya-Önder, E. (2021). Pre-service pre-school teachers' opinions about using block-based coding/SCRATCH. *Acta Didactica Napocensia*, 14(2), 299–317. DOI: 10.24193/adn.14.2.22

Tirronen, V., Uusi-Mäkelä, S., & Isomöttönen, V. (2015). Understanding beginners' mistakes with Haskell. *Journal of Functional Programming*, 25, e11. DOI: 10.1017/S0956796815000179

Tokarska, O. A. (2021). Informal education as an effective form of development of professional competence of modern computer science teacher. *Zhytomyr Ivan Franko State University Journal Pedagogical Sciences*, 1(104), 40–49. DOI: 10.35433/pedagogy.1(104).2021.40-49

Tomlinson, C. A. (2001). *How to differentiate instruction in mixed-ability classrooms*. ASCD.

Tonbuloğlu, B., & Tonbuloğlu, I. (2019). The effect of unplugged coding activities on computational thinking skills of middle school students. *Informatics in Education*, 18(2), 403–426. DOI: 10.15388/infedu.2019.19

Topuz, A. C., Saka, E., Fatsa, Ö. F., & Kurşun, E. (2022). Emerging trends of online assessment systems in the emergency remote teaching period. *Smart Learning Environments*, 9(1), 17. Advance online publication. DOI: 10.1186/s40561-022-00199-6

Touretzky, D. S., Gardner-McCune, C., Martin, F., & Seehorn, D. (2019). K-12 Guidelines for Artificial Intelligence: What Students Should Know. In *Proceedings of the ISTE Conference*, 23–26 June 2019, Philadelphia, PA, USA.

Tsai, C. Y. (2019). Improving students' understanding of basic programming concepts through visual programming language: The role of self-efficacy. *Computers in Human Behavior*, 95, 224–232. DOI: 10.1016/j.chb.2018.11.038

Tsai, M. J., Chien, F. P., Wen-Yu Lee, S., Hsu, C. Y., & Liang, J. C. (2022). Development and validation of the computational thinking test for elementary school students (CTT-ES): Correlate CT competency with CT disposition. *Journal of Educational Computing Research*, 60(5), 1110–1129. DOI: 10.1177/07356331211051043

Tsarava, K., Leifheit, L., Ninaus, M., Román-González, M., Butz, M. V., Golle, J., & Moeller, K. (2019, October). Cognitive correlates of computational thinking: Evaluation of a blended unplugged/plugged-in course. In *Proceedings of the 14th Workshop in Primary and Secondary Computing Education*, 1-9. https://doi.org/ DOI: 10.1145/3361721.3361729

Tselegkaridis, S., & Sapounidis, T. (2022). Exploring the Features of Educational Robotics and STEM Research in Primary Education: A Systematic Literature Review. *Education Sciences*, 12(2), 305. DOI: 10.3390/educsci12050305

Tsung, S., Wei, H., Li, H., Wang, Y., Xia, M., & Qu, H. (2022, June). Blocklens: visual analytics of student coding behaviors in block-based programming environments. In *Proceedings of the Ninth ACM Conference on Learning@ Scale* (pp. 299-303). DOI: 10.1145/3491140.3528298

TTKB. (2018). Bilişim Teknolojileri ve Yazılım Öğretim Programı [Information Technologies and Software Curriculum]. https://mufredat.meb.gov.tr/ProgramDetay .aspx?PID=1383

TTKB. (2023). Ortaöğretim Bilişim Teknolojileri ve Yazılım Dersi Öğretim Programı. [Secondary Education Information Technologies and Software Course Curriculum]. https://mufredat.meb.gov.tr/ProgramDetay.aspx?PID=1353

TUBITAK 4008. (2024). Özel Gereksinimli Bireylere Yönelik Kapsayıcı Toplum Uygulamaları Destekleme Programı. https://tubitak.gov.tr/tr/destekler/bilim-toplum/ulusal-destek-programlari/4008-ozel-gereksinimli-bireylere-yonelik-kapsayici-toplum-uygulamalari-destekleme-programi

Turing. 2024. 'All You Need to Know about Computer Vision and How It Works'. Retrieved 23 May 2024 (https://www.turing.com/kb/all-you-need-to-know-about-computer-vision)

Turkish Penal Code. (2004). [Online]. Available: https://www.mevzuat.gov.tr/mevzuat?MevzuatNo=5237&MevzuatTur=1&MevzuatTertip=5. Access Date: 25.08.2024

U.S. Department of Homeland Security Cybersecurity and Infrastructure Security Agency. (2023, January) Report, [Online]. Available: https://www.cisa.gov/sites/default/files/2023-01/K-12report_FINAL_V2_508c_0.pdf, Access Date: 16.07.2024.

Ülgen, G. (2004). *Kavram Geliştirme: Kuramlar ve Uygulamalar* (3rd ed.). Pegema yayıncılık.

UNESCO. (2023). *Global Education Monitoring Report 2023: Technology in education– A tool on whose terms?* UNESCO.

Vaculík, K., Popelínský, L., Mráková, E., & Jurco, J. (2013, October). Tutoring and automatic evaluation of logic proofs. In European Conference on e-Learning (p. 495). Academic Conferences International Limited.

Van Brummelen, J., & Lin, P. (2020). Engaging Teachers to Co-Design Integrated Artificial Intelligence Curriculum for K-12 Classrooms. arXiv, arXiv:2009.11100.

Van Roy, P., & Haridi, S. (2004). *Concepts, techniques, and models of computer programming*. MIT Press.

Vanicek, J. (2015). Programming in Scratch using inquiry-based approach. Brodnik, A., & Vahrenhold, J. (Eds.), In *International Conference on Informatics in Schools: Situation, Evolution, and Perspectives* (pp. 82-93). Springer. DOI: 10.1007/978-3-319-25396-1_8

Vartiainen, H., Tedre, M., & Valtonen, T. (2020). Learning machine learning with very young children: Who is teaching whom? *International Journal of Child-Computer Interaction*, 25, 100182. DOI: 10.1016/j.ijcci.2020.100182

Vartic, V., & Oprisan, E. (2019). Use of Assistive Technologies in Accessibility of Information for Students with Visual Impairments. *eLearning & Software for Education, 2*.

Vasilopoulos, I. V., & Van Schaik, P. (2019). Koios: Design, Development, and Evaluation of an Educational Visual Tool for Greek Novice Programmers. *Journal of Educational Computing Research*, 57(5), 1227–1259. DOI: 10.1177/0735633118781776

Veerasamy, A. K., D'Souza, D., & Laakso, M.-J. (2016). Identifying Novice Student Programming Misconceptions and Errors From Summative Assessments. *Journal of Educational Technology Systems*, 45(1), 50–73. DOI: 10.1177/0047239515627263

Velan, G. M., Jones, P., McNeil, H. P., & Kumar, R. K. (2008). Integrated online formative assessments in the biomedical sciences for medical students: Benefits for learning. *BMC Medical Education*, 8(1), 52. Advance online publication. DOI: 10.1186/1472-6920-8-52 PMID: 19032738

Verma, G., Adhikari, S., Khanduri, V., Tandon, S., Rawat, S., & Singh, P. (2020). Machine Learning Model for Prediction of Stress Levels in Students of Technical Education. Artificial IntelligenceJR Proceedings, 45-52. DOI: 10.21467/proceedings.100.5

Vescio, V., Ross, D., & Adams, A. (2008). A review of research on the impact of professional learning communities on teaching practice and student learning. *Teaching and Teacher Education*, 24(1), 80–91. DOI: 10.1016/j.tate.2007.01.004

Veugen, M. J., Gulikers, J., & Brok, P. (2022). Secondary school teachers' use of online formative assessment during covid-19 lockdown: Experiences and lessons learned. *Journal of Computer Assisted Learning*, 38(5), 1465–1481. DOI: 10.1111/jcal.12699 PMID: 35942306

Villalobos-Roman-Cañizares, M., & Palacios-Pacheco, X. (2020). Improvement of an Online Education Model with the Integration of Machine Learning and Data Analysis in an LMS. *Applied Sciences (Basel, Switzerland)*, 10(15), 5371. DOI: 10.3390/app10155371

Villegas-Ch, W., García-Ortiz, J., & Sánchez-Viteri, S. (2021). Identification of the factors that influence university learning with low-code/no-code artificial intelligence techniques. *Electronics (Basel)*, 10(10), 1192. DOI: 10.3390/electronics10101192

Villegas-Reimers, E. (2003). *Teacher professional development: an international review of the literature*. International Institute for Educational Planning.

Vollstedt, A. M., Robinson, M., & Wang, E. (2007). Using robotics to enhance science, technological progress, engineering, and mathematics curricula. In *Proceedings of the American Society for Engineering Education Pacific Southwest Annual Conference* (pp. 1–9). University of Nevada.

Von Solms, R., & Van Niekerk, J. (2013). From information security to cyber security. *Computers & Security*, 38, 97–102. DOI: 10.1016/j.cose.2013.04.004

Vonderwell, S., Liang, X., & Alderman, K. (2007). Asynchronous discussions and assessment in online learning. *Journal of Research on Technology in Education*, 39(3), 309–328. DOI: 10.1080/15391523.2007.10782485

Voogt, J., Fisser, P., Good, J., Mishra, P., & Yadav, A. (2015). Computational thinking in compulsory education: Towards an agenda for research and practice. *Education and Information Technologies*, 20(4), 715–728. DOI: 10.1007/s10639-015-9412-6

Voronina, L. V., Sergeeva, N. N., & Utyumova, A. (2016). Development of algorithm skills in preschool children. *Procedia: Social and Behavioral Sciences*, 233, 155–159. DOI: 10.1016/j.sbspro.2016.10.176

Vygotsky, L. S. (1978). *Mind in society: The development of higher psychological processes*. Harvard University Press.

W3C (2024). https://www.w3.org/WAI/fundamentals/accessibility-intro/

Wahid, A. (2017) 'Big Data and Machine Learning for Businesses'. *SlideShare*. Retrieved 23 May 2024 (https://www.slideshare.net/slideshow/big-data-and-machine-learning-for-businesses/75413684)

Waldron, N. L., & McLeskey, J. (2010). Establishing a collaborative school culture through comprehensive school reform. *Journal of Educational & Psychological Consultation*, 20(1), 58–74. DOI: 10.1080/10474410903535364

Wallace, M. (2009). Making sense of the links: Professional development, teacher practices, and student achievement. teachers college record. *Teachers College Record*, 111(2), 573–596. DOI: 10.1177/016146810911100205

Wang, C. H., & Wu, K. C. (2022, December). A preliminary study on interdisciplinary programming learning based on cloud computing low-code development platform. In *2022 International Conference on Computer and Applications (ICCA)* (pp. 1-5). IEEE. DOI: 10.1109/ICCA56443.2022.10039663

Wang, J. (2021). Use hopscotch to develop positive attitudes toward programming for elementary school students. *International Journal of Computer Science Education in Schools*, 5(1), 48–58. DOI: 10.21585/ijcses.v5i1.122

Wang, T., Su, X., Ma, P., Wang, Y., & Wang, K. (2011). Ability-training-oriented automated assessment in introductory programming course. *Computers & Education*, 56(1), 220–226. DOI: 10.1016/j.compedu.2010.08.003

Wang, X. M., Hwang, G. J., Liang, Z. Y., & Wang, H. Y. (2017). Enhancing students' computer programming performances, critical thinking awareness and attitudes towards programming: An online peer-assessment attempt. *Journal of Educational Technology & Society*, 20(4), 58–68.

Wang, Y. (2010). On concept algebra for computing with words (CWW). *International Journal of Semantic Computing*, 4(03), 331–356. DOI: 10.1142/S1793351X10001061

Washbrooke, S., & Giacaman, N. (2024). Play, Code, Learn: Fostering Computational Thinking in Primary Aged Learners Through Interactive Play. In Papadakis, S. (Ed.), *IoT, AI, and ICT for Educational Applications. EAI/Springer Innovations in Communication and Computing*. Springer., DOI: 10.1007/978-3-031-50139-5_7

Watanabe, T., Nakayama Kagawa-Fujimigaoka, Y., Kanagawa, K., Yasunori, J., Digitalpocket, H., Kanagawa, L., Kuno, J. Y., Nakayama, Y., Harada, Y., & Kuno, Y. (2019). *How Can Children Express Their Intentions Through Coding?-Anal-ysis of Viscuit Programs in Kindergarten*. https://doi.org/DOI: 10.1145/3304221

Watanabe, T., Nakayama, Y., Harada, Y., & Kuno, Y. (2020). Analyzing Viscuit Programs Crafted by Kindergarten Children. *ICER 2020 - Proceedings of the 2020 ACM Conference on International Computing Education Research*, 238–247. DOI: 10.1145/3372782.3406253

Webb, M., Davis, N., Bell, T., Katz, Y. J., Reynolds, N., Chambers, D. P., & Sysło, M. M. (2017). Computer science in K-12 school curricula of the 2lst century: Why, what and when? *Education and Information Technologies*, 22(2), 445–468. DOI: 10.1007/s10639-016-9493-x

Weintrop, D. (2019). Block-based programming in computer science education. *Communications of the ACM*, 62(8), 22–25. DOI: 10.1145/3341221

Weintrop, D., & Wilensky, U. (2017). Comparing block-based and text-based programming in high school computer science classrooms. [TOCE]. *ACM Transactions on Computing Education*, 18(1), 1–25. DOI: 10.1145/3089799

Wei, X., Lin, L., Meng, N., Tan, W., Kong, S.-C., & Kinshuk, . (2021). The effectiveness of partial pair programming on elementary school students' computational thinking skills and self-efficacy. *Computers & Education*, 160, 104023. Advance online publication. DOI: 10.1016/j.compedu.2020.104023

Weng, X., Ng, O. L., Cui, Z., & Leung, S. (2023). Creativity development with problem-based digital making and block-based programming for science, technology, engineering, arts, and mathematics learning in middle school contexts. *Journal of Educational Computing Research*, 61(2), 304–328. DOI: 10.1177/07356331221115661

Wetherill, K., Burton, G., Calhoun, D., & Thomas, C. (2001). Redefining professional career development in the twenty-first century: A systemic approach. *High School Journal*, 85(2), 54–66. DOI: 10.1353/hsj.2001.0026

Whitehill, J., & Seltzer, M. 2017. 'A Crowdsourcing Approach to Collecting Tutorial Videos -- Toward Personalized Learning-at-Scale'. Pp. 157–60 in *Proceedings of the Fourth (2017) ACM Conference on Learning @ Scale, L@S '17*. New York, NY, USA: Association for Computing Machinery.

Whitelock, D., Reudel, C., & Mackenzie, D. (2006). *E-assessment : Case studies of effective and innovative practice a JISC*. Jt. Inf. Syst. Comm.

WHO. (2024). Assistive technology. https://www.who.int/news-room/fact-sheets/detail/assistive-technology

Wiering, M. A., & Van Otterlo, M. (2012). 'Reinforcement Learning'. *Adaptation, Learning, and Optimization*, 12(3), 729.

Williams, R., Park, H. W., & Breazeal, C. (2019). A is for Artificial Intelligence: The Impact of Artificial Intelligence Activities on Young Children's Perceptions of Robots. In *Proceedings of the 2019 CHI Conference on Human Factors in Computing Systems*, Glasgow, UK, 4–9 May 2019, 1–11. DOI: 10.1145/3290605.3300677

Williams, R., Park, H. W., Oh, L., & Breazeal, C. (2019). PopBots: Designing an Artificial Intelligence Curriculum for Early Childhood Education. In *Proceedings of the AAArtificial Intelligence Conference on Artificial Intelligence*, Honolulu, HI, USA, 27 January–1 February 2019, 33, 1. DOI: 10.1609/aaai.v33i01.33019729

Wilson, M., & Hash, J. (2003). Building an information technology security awareness and training program. *NIST Special publication*, 800(50), 1-39.

Wing, J. M. (2008). Computational thinking and thinking about computing. *Philosophical Transactions.Series A, Mathematical, Physical, and Engineering Sciences, 366*(1881), 3717–3725. [doi]DOI: 10.1098/rsta.2008.0118

Wing, J. M. (2010). Computational Thinking: What and Why? *Thelink - The Magaizne of the Varnegie Mellon University School of Computer Science, March 2006.*

Wing, J. M. (2006). Computational thinking. *Communications of the ACM*, 49(3), 33–35. DOI: 10.1145/1118178.1118215

Wójcik, J., & Rataj, M. (2022). The impact of covid-19 on online final exam scores among computer science students. *European Conference on Knowledge Management, 23(*2), 955-964. https://doi.org/DOI: 10.34190/eckm.23.2.644

Wolff, A., Gooch, D., Cavero Montaner, J. J., Rashid, U., & Kortuem, G. (2016). Creating an understanding of data literacy for a data-driven society. *The Journal of Community Informatics*, 12(3). Advance online publication. DOI: 10.15353/joci.v12i3.3275

Wong, G. K., Cheung, H. Y., Ching, E. C., & Huen, J. M. (2015, December). School perceptions of coding education in K-12: A large scale quantitative study to inform innovative practices. In *2015 IEEE international conference on teaching, Assessment, and learning for engineering (TALE)* (pp. 5-10). IEEE. DOI: 10.1109/TALE.2015.7386007

Wong, G. K. (2024). Amplifying children's computational problem-solving skills: A hybrid-based design for programming education. *Education and Information Technologies*, 29(2), 1761–1793. DOI: 10.1007/s10639-023-11880-9

Wood, D., Bruner, J. S., & Ross, G. (1976). The role of tutoring in problem solving. *Journal of Child Psychology and Psychiatry, and Allied Disciplines*, 17(2), 89–100. DOI: 10.1111/j.1469-7610.1976.tb00381.x PMID: 932126

Woolfolk, A. E. (1993). *Educational psychology*. Allyn and Bacon.

Wörister, F., & Knobelsdorf, M. (2023, November). A Block-Based Programming Environment for Teaching Low-Level Computing (Discussion Paper). In *Proceedings of the 23rd Koli Calling International Conference on Computing Education Research* (pp. 1-7).

Wu, X., Duan, R., & Ni, J. (2024). 'Unveiling Security, Privacy, and Ethical Concerns of ChatGPT'. *Journal of Information and Intelligence*, 2(2), 102–115. DOI: 10.1016/j.jiixd.2023.10.007

Wu, Z., Zheng, L., & Huang, L. (2024). Learning to code and coding to learn: A robotics curriculum integrating tangible programming and road safety education for young children. *Education and Information Technologies*. Advance online publication. DOI: 10.1007/s10639-024-12757-1

Wyeth, P., & Wyeth, G. (2008). Robot building for preschoolers. *RoboCup 2007. Robot Soccer World Cup XI*, 11, 124–135.

Xie, Y., Fang, M., & Shauman, K. (2015). STEM Education. *Annual Review of Sociology*, 41(1), 331–357. DOI: 10.1146/annurev-soc-071312-145659 PMID: 26778893

Xobin. (2024). What is an Online Assessment? Everything You Need to Know. https://xobin.com/blog/guide-to-online-assessment/

Xu, E., Wang, W., & Wang, Q. (2023). A meta-analysis of the effectiveness of programming teaching in promoting K-12 students' computational thinking. *Education and Information Technologies*, 28(6), 6619–6644. DOI: 10.1007/s10639-022-11445-2

Xu, Z., Ritzhaupt, A. D., Tian, F., & Umapathy, K. (2019). Block-based versus text-based programming environments on novice student learning outcomes: A meta-analysis study. *Computer Science Education*, 29(2-3), 177–204. DOI: 10.1080/08993408.2019.1565233

Yadav, A., Burkhart, D., Moix, D., Snow, E., Bandaru, P., & Clayborn, L. (2015). *Sowing the seeds: A landscape study on assessment in secondary computer science education. Comp. Sci. Teachers Assn., NY, NY.* Computer Science Teachers Association.

Yadav, A., Hong, H., & Stephenson, C. (2016). Computational thinking for all: Pedagogical approaches to embedding 21st century problem solving in K-12 classrooms. *TechTrends*, 60(6), 565–568. DOI: 10.1007/s11528-016-0087-7

Yadav, A., Stephenson, C., & Hai, H. (2017). Computational thinking for teacher education. *Communications of the ACM*, 60(4), 55–62. DOI: 10.1145/2994591

Yang, W. (2024). Coding With Robots or Tablets? Effects of Technology-Enhanced Embodied Learning on Preschoolers' Computational Thinking and Social-Emotional Competence. *Journal of Educational Computing Research, 62.0*(4.0), 938–960. DOI: 10.1177/07356331241226459

Yang, W. (2022). Artificial Intelligence education for young children: Why, what, and how in curriculum design and implementation. *Computer Education and Artificial Intelligence*, 3, 100061. DOI: 10.1016/j.caeai.2022.100061

Yang, W., Luo, H., & Su, J. (2022). Towards inclusiveness and sustainability of robot programming in early childhood: Child engagement, learning outcomes and teacher perception. *British Journal of Educational Technology*, 53(6), 1486–1510. DOI: 10.1111/bjet.13266

Yang, W., Ng, D. T. K., & Su, J. (2023). The impact of story-inspired programming on preschool children's computational thinking: A multi-group experiment. *Thinking Skills and Creativity*, 47, 101218. Advance online publication. DOI: 10.1016/j.tsc.2022.101218

Yazici, F., Gul, S., Sozbilir, M., Cakmak, S., & Aslan, C. (2021). Altıncı sınıfa devam eden görme engelli öğrencilerin Fen Bilimleri dersine yönelik öğrenme ihtiyaçlarının belirlenmesi. *Millî Eğitim Özel Eğitim ve Rehberlik Dergisi*, 1(1), 26–64.

Ye, H., Liang, B., Ng, O. L., & Chai, C. S. (2023). Integration of computational thinking in K-12 mathematics education: A systematic review on CT-based mathematics instruction and student learning. *International Journal of STEM Education*, 10(1), 3. DOI: 10.1186/s40594-023-00396-w

Yıldız Durak, H. (2018). Digital story design activities used for teaching programming effect on learning of programming concepts, programming self-efficacy, and participation and analysis of student experiences. *Journal of Computer Assisted Learning*, 34(6), 740–752. DOI: 10.1111/jcal.12281

Yildiz, E. P., & Çengel, M. (2022). An Experimental Study in Determining Basic Robotic Coding Skills of Pre-School Students with Intellectual Disabilities. [IJIM]. *International Journal of Interactive Mobile Technologies*, 16(23), 84–98. DOI: 10.3991/ijim.v16i23.36077

Yildiz, M., & Karal, H. (2021). A Computer Science Unplugged Activity: CityMap. *International Journal of Computer Science Education in Schools*, 5(2), 14–27. DOI: 10.21585/ijcses.v5i2.110

Yoon, K. S., Duncan, T., Lee, S. W. Y., Scarloss, B., & Shapley, K. L. (2007). Reviewing the evidence on how teacher professional development affects student achievement. *Issues & Answers*. REL 2007-No. 033.

York-Barr, J., & Duke, K. (2004). What do we know about teacher leadership? Findings from two decades of scholarship. *Review of Educational Research*, 74(3), 255–316. DOI: 10.3102/00346543074003255

Youngs, P. (2001). District and state policy influences on professional development and school capacity. *Educational Policy*, 15(2), 278–301. DOI: 10.1177/0895904801015002003

Yücel, C., & Acartürk, C. (2006). *Görme engelliler için web sayfalarına erişebilirliğin sağlanması*. Pamukkale Üniversitesi Akademik Bilişim Konferansı.

Yue, X., Di, G., Yu, Y., Wang, W., & Shi, H. (2012). 'Analysis of the Combination of Natural Language Processing and Search Engine Technology'. *Procedia Engineering*, 29, 1636–1639. DOI: 10.1016/j.proeng.2012.01.186

Yurdakök, E. A., & Kalelioğlu, F. (2024). The Effect of Teaching Physical Programming on Computational Thinking Skills and Self-Efficacy Perceptions Towards Computational Thinking. *Journal of Educational Computing Research*, 62(3), 785–815. DOI: 10.1177/07356331231220313

Yu, W. J., Jang, J. H., Ahn, J. M., Park, D. R., Yoo, I. H., Bae, Y. K., & Kim, W. Y. (2019). Design of Artificial Intelligence Education Program based on Design-based Research. *Int. J. Adv. Smart Converg.*, 8, 113–120.

Zapata-Cáceres, M., Martín-Barroso, E., & Román-González, M. (2020, April). Computational thinking test for beginners: Design and content validation. In *2020 IEEE Global Engineering Education Conference (EDUCON)*. pp. 1905-1914. IEEE. https://doi.org/DOI: 10.1109/EDUCON45650.2020.9125368

Zawacki-Richter, O., Kerres, M., Bedenlier, S., Bond, M., & Buntins, K. (2020). *Systematic reviews in educational research: Methodology, perspectives and application*. Springer Nature. DOI: 10.1007/978-3-658-27602-7

Zhang, X., Chen, Y., Hu, L., Bao, Y., Tu, Y.-F., & Hwang, G.-J. (2024). A metaphor-based robot programming approach to facilitating young children's computational thinking and positive learning behaviors. *Computers & Education*, 215, 215. DOI: 10.1016/j.compedu.2024.105039

Zhan, Z., Tong, Y., Lan, X., & Zhong, B. (2022). A systematic literature review of game-based learning in Artificial Intelligence education. *Interactive Learning Environments*, 32(3), 1137–1158. DOI: 10.1080/10494820.2022.2115077

Zheng, X. (2023). Robot translation based on computer vision for cultural psychology of english culture education. International journal of humanoid robotics, 20(02n03), 2250006.

Zhong, B., Liu, X., Xia, L., & Sun, W. (2022). A proposed taxonomy for instructional models in STEM education: The case of robotics. *SAGE Open*, 12(2), 21582440221099525. DOI: 10.1177/21582440221099525

Zhong, B., & Xia, L. (2020). A systematic review on exploring the potential of educational robotics in mathematics education. *International Journal of Science and Mathematics Education*, 18(1), 79–101. DOI: 10.1007/s10763-018-09939-y

Zhu, K. (2019). An Educational Approach to Machine Learning with Mobile Applications. (Unpublished doctoral dissertation). Massachusetts Institute of Technology.

Zhu, J., & Van Brummelen, J. (2021). Teaching students about conversational ai using convo, a conversational programming agent. In *2021 IEEE Symposium on Visual Languages and Human-Centric Computing* (pp. 1-5). IEEE. DOI: 10.1109/VL/HCC51201.2021.9576290

Zhu, M., & Wang, C. (2024). K-12 computer science teaching strategies, challenges, and teachers' professional development opportunities and needs. *Computers in the Schools*, 41(1), 1–22. DOI: 10.1080/07380569.2023.2178868

Zilinskiene, I. (2022). Insights from Empirical Results on Robotics in Early Childhood Education: Lithuanian Case. *TEM Journal*, 11(3), 1103–1107. DOI: 10.18421/TEM113-15

Zorluoglu, S. L., & Sozbilir, M. (2017). Teaching the concept of density through insoluble liquids to visually impaired students. *Journal of Theory and Practice in Education*, 13(2), 211–231.

Zumi. (n.d.). Retrieved from

Zurnacı, B., & Turan, Z. (2022). Türkiye'de okul öncesinde kodlama eğitimine ilişkin yapılan çalışmaların incelenmesi. *Kocaeli Üniversitesi Eğitim Dergisi*, 5(1), 258–286. DOI: 10.33400/kuje.1062803

About the Contributors

Serhat Bahadır Kert is professor of Computer Science education and Instructional Technologies at Yildiz Technical University. He is also the chair of the department of computer education and instructional technologies (CEIT). His research interests are computer science education for children, methodologies in programming language education, computational thinking, game-based education and development of e- learning environments. He teaches courses at both undergraduate and graduate levels and goes on to conduct national and international research on the pedagogical features of computer science education. One of his last projects on programming education for visually impaired children was founded by British Council in 2021.

* * *

Leonard Busuttil, PhD. (Sheffield), is an associate professor at the University of Malta, within the Faculty of Education, Department of Technology and Entrepreneurship Education. He is a resident academic and researcher with expertise in Learning Sciences, Computer Science (Digital Technologies) Education, Teacher Training, and Educational Technology. He applies learning sciences theory and mixed-methods research to investigate and improve learning and teaching in Computer Science and online learning. Additionally, he coordinates teacher training in Computing education at the Faculty of Education, University of Malta. His research interests include Computational Thinking, Game-Based Learning, and AI in Education.

Fatih Erdoğdu is an Associate Professor of Computer Technologies at Zonguldak Bülent Ecevit University in Türkiye. He graduated with a bachelor's degree from the Middle East Technical University. He graduated from Computer Education and Instructional Technology at Gazi University with the degree of master in 2015. Dr. Erdoğdu gained his PhD in Computer Education and Instructional Technology at Karadeniz Technical University. His academic interest areas are instructional technology, distance learning, teacher training and humorous learning. He conducted over 30 scientific studies. He also serves as head of the Department of Computer Technologies at Zonguldak Bülent Ecevit University.

Erkan Geçitli, Ph.D. has been working as an IT teacher in the Ministry of National Education in Türkiye since 2008. He received his Bachelor's from Hacettepe University, Department of Computer Education and Instructional Technology. He completed his Master's and Ph.D. at Ege University, Department of Curriculum and Instruction. He continues his research on curriculum studies, program evaluation, curriculum analysis and programming teaching methods. He gives programming courses in various fields and age groups.

Seyfullah Gökoğlu is a researcher and faculty member at Bartın University, Türkiye. With MA and PhD degrees in computer education and instructional technologies, Dr. Gökoğlu focuses on empirical studies in virtual reality, online learning, programming education, and educational technology. He applies critical theories like constructivism, experiential learning, and social learning to his research. Dr. Gökoğlu is also interested in emerging research paradigms, including topic modeling, sentiment analysis, and meta-analysis. Dr. Gökoğlu's studies also cover integrating artificial intelligence technologies into educational processes in the axis of human-computer interaction. His dedication to advancing the field is reflected in his publications in leading journals in the instructional technology field, such as Computers & Education, Journal of Educational Computing Research, The International Review of Research in Open and Distributed Learning, and Online Information Review.

Leila Goosen is a full professor in the Department of Science and Technology Education of the University of South Africa. She holds a C2 rating via the South African National Research Foundation. Prof. Goosen was an Associate Professor in the School of Computing, and the module leader and head designer of the fully online signature module for the College for Science, Engineering and Technology, rolled out to over 92,000 registered students since the first semester of 2013. She usually supervises around ten Masters and Doctoral students, and has successfully completed supervision of 43 students at postgraduate level. Previously, she was a Deputy Director at the South African national Department of Education. In this capacity, she was required to develop ICT strategies for implementation. Before that, she had been a lecturer of Information Technology (IT) in the Department for Science, Mathematics and Technology Education in the Faculty of Education of the University of Pretoria. Her research interests have included cooperative work in IT, effective teaching and learning of programming and teacher professional development.

Habibe (Kazez) Güneş has been working as a research assistant at Fırat University, Faculty of Education, Department of Computer Education and Instructional Technology since 2014. She continues her research on STEM education applications, distance education, visual and physical programming in higher education, instructional design, the use of educational technologies in mathematics teaching, human-computer interaction, programming education in early childhood, the use of social robots in education and the use of technology in special education. Dr. Güneş, who has worked as a consultant, researcher and trainer in various categories of TUBITAK Projects (1001, 2209-A, 4005, 4007 and 4008), continues her learning adventure with national and international presentations and articles. She is married and the mother of two little boys.

Tuba Kaynarca İdil, an expert in educational technology and electronic signature and certificate services, graduated with honors from Boğaziçi University Computer Education and Educational Technology undergraduate program. She completed MSc degree in Computer Education and Instructional Technology field at Yıldız Technical University and she continues PhD education at Anadolu University. She studies on instructional design and development of educational software and information security field. She works on electronic signature and electronic certificate services at a governmental institution.

Memnüne Kokoç is a Lecturer Dr. at Karadeniz Technical University, Turkey. She earned her Ph.D. degree from the Department of Computer Education and Instructional Technologies at Atatürk University, Turkey. Her academic interests are open and distance education, coding and robotics, technology addiction, educational technologies and instructional design.

Gamze Mercan completed her undergraduate degree in "biology education" at Hacettepe University. She pursued her master's degree at Hacettepe University in the field of "secondary education science and mathematics" with a focus on "the level of recognition of trees in the immediate surroundings of biology teacher candidates: the case of Ankara province." She completed her Ph.D. at Hacettepe University in the field of "mathematics and science education" on the topic of "the use of three-dimensional multi-user virtual environments in teaching tree species." She is currently continuing her research on biology education, nanotechnology, nanomedicine, out-of-school learning environments, and three-dimensional virtual environments.

İbrahim Halil Özdemir is currently pursuing his Ph.D. in the department of Computer Education and Instructional Technology at Ege University, where he also completed his Master's in 2023 with a GPA of 4.00/4.00. He earned his Bachelor's degree in the same field from Ege University in 2020, graduating with a GPA of 3.62/4.00. Özdemir began his professional career as an Instructional Technologist and Designer at Ege University, contributing to significant projects and developing instructional designs. Since 2022, he has been working as an Educational Specialist and Learning Experience Designer at Kuika Software. As of 2024, he also serves as a Visiting Lecturer at Bahçeşehir University and a Mentor at Junior Achievement Turkey. Özdemir has published articles in international journals, contributed to book chapters, and presented at international conferences. His expertise includes instructional design, online learning environment design, Adobe Photoshop, Adobe Illustrator, and social media management. He has also specialized in blended learning, online learning, cognitive load, low-code development, motivation, and instructional technologies in engineering education. Additionally, Özdemir has delivered various trainings for foundations and NGOs and currently holds the position of vice president of a local sports club. Recognized for his academic and professional achievements, he continues to make significant contributions to the field of educational technologies.

Firat Sarsar is an Associate Professor at Ege University, Department of Computer Education and Instructional Technology in Turkey. He earned his BA and MS degrees in the Department of Computer Education and Instructional Technology in Turkey. Dr. Sarsar graduated from Georgia State University in USA with his Ph.D. in Instructional Technology as a Fulbright scholar in 2014. His PhD was fully funded by Fulbright Scholarship. He was in many project related to technology integration and teacher education. He holds the Association for Educational Communications and Technology (AECT) Cochran Intern Award in 2013 which is given for recognition of young leaders of the field. Currently, He teaches "Social Media and Web2.0 tools in Education", "Internet for Educator", Technology Integration in Education" and "e-Learning Design" courses in undergrad and graduate levels in Ege University. His research interests are motivation, online learning, mobile technologies, e-learning and online feedback strategies. He is currently the Director of Distance Learning Application and Research Center and also Vice-Director of Ege University Continuing Education Center.

Patrick Schembri holds a PhD in Brian-Computer Interfaces from the University of Greenwich, London and acts as Senior Lecturer at the University of Malta. His research interests are in brain-computer interfaces and computing education.

Betül Tonbuloğlu is a faculty member at the Distance Education Application and Research Center of Yıldız Technical University. She holds a Master's degree in Computer and Instructional Technologies Education and a Ph.D. in Educational Programs and Instruction, with a focus on distance education programs. Her research interests include distance education, educational technologies, e-learning, e-assessment, usability evaluation, computer science education, quality standards and program evaluation.

İsmail Tonbuloğlu is an assistant professor at Marmara University, Department of Computer Education and Instructional Technologies. He completed his master's degree on usability evaluation of educational software and his PhD on pre-service teachers' acceptance of mobile technologies for instructional purposes. His research interests are computer science education, educational technology integration, distance education, e-learning, technology acceptance, usability evaluation.

Ayşin Gaye Üstün is an Asst. Prof. at Vocational School at Sinop University, Turkey. She earned her doctoral degree from the Department of Computer Education and Instructional Technology at Atatürk University, Turkey. Her academic interest areas are open and distance education environments, coding and robotics, educational technologies and instructional design.

Zümrüt Varol Selçuk completed her undergraduate degree in "biology education" at Hacettepe University. She completed her master's degree at Gazi University in the field of "gamification in biology education: a systematic review." Additionally, she completed her studies at Hacettepe University in the Master's Program in Educational Technology with the topic "A systematic review of research on digital storytelling (DS) in the context of information and communication technologies (ICT) (January 2018-October 2022)." She is currently pursuing her doctoral education (coursework stage) at Ordu University. She continues her research in the fields of biology education, educational technology, and advanced technologies.

Diane Vassallo, PhD. (Belfast), is an academic lecturer at the University of Malta, within the Faculty of Education, Department of Technology and Entrepreneurship Education. Prior to this engagement she worked as a Computing educator. She also served as a curriculum educational leader where she had the opportunity to lead various curriculum initiatives. As part of this tenure, she also served as a member of the committee for the development of the national syllabus in Computing. She is currently involved in a number of research initiatives and projects, including ERASMUS+ funded projects. Her areas of special interest include Computing Education, Computational Thinking, Curriculum Development and AI in education.

Bünyamin Yurdakul is an Associate Professor of Curriculum and Instruction at the Faculty of Education, Ege University, Türkiye. He received his bachelor's and master's degrees in Curriculum and Instruction from Ankara University and Ph.D. in Curriculum and Instruction from Hacettepe University. His research interests include curriculum studies, constructivism, teacher education, and program evaluation. He published various articles, papers, projects, and book chapters related to his research interests. He studied curriculum theories and qualitative inquiry as a visiting scholar in the School of Education at Indiana University, Bloomington in 2012. Since 2020, he has been working as an evaluator for the Association for Evaluation and Accreditation of Teacher Education.

Index

A

Abstraction 28, 29, 30, 37, 39, 42, 56, 119, 236, 237, 243, 350, 352
academic integrity 228, 234, 251
activity theory 1, 8, 14, 15, 18
Algorithm Design 28, 30, 40, 157, 243, 350
algorithmic thinking 2, 3, 6, 9, 10, 14, 18, 29, 30, 37, 38, 42, 43, 61, 238, 335, 368, 370
Artificial Intelligence (AI) 33, 49, 56, 58, 76, 111, 112, 115, 116, 117, 118, 124, 125, 126, 127, 128, 129, 130, 131, 132, 133, 134, 135, 136, 138, 139, 140, 151, 153, 154, 156, 160, 163, 166, 168, 174, 189, 203, 205, 213, 214, 234, 236, 239, 293, 295, 296, 297, 298, 300, 301, 303, 304, 308, 310, 311, 312, 313, 314, 315, 316, 317, 318, 322, 324, 347, 349, 350, 351, 356, 357, 364, 365, 366, 368, 369
automated assessment 60, 70, 128, 192, 224, 244, 245, 250, 253, 255

B

Blind Students 193, 208, 217, 218

C

Coding 1, 2, 3, 4, 5, 6, 7, 8, 9, 10, 11, 12, 13, 14, 15, 16, 17, 18, 19, 20, 21, 22, 23, 24, 25, 27, 30, 33, 34, 35, 36, 37, 38, 39, 42, 43, 44, 45, 46, 47, 49, 50, 51, 52, 53, 56, 57, 61, 67, 71, 145, 146, 150, 151, 163, 168, 171, 173, 174, 180, 185, 187, 189, 193, 196, 199, 200, 201, 202, 205, 206, 207, 209, 210, 211, 212, 213, 214, 217, 218, 219, 220, 223, 224, 228, 230, 233, 236, 238, 248, 250, 273, 339, 344, 352, 353, 355, 363, 364, 365, 366, 367, 371, 372
coding education 3, 4, 22, 37, 61, 71, 168, 193, 205, 212, 214
Computational Thinking 1, 2, 19, 20, 22, 24, 25, 27, 28, 30, 32, 33, 34, 35, 36, 40, 41, 42, 43, 44, 45, 46, 47, 48, 49, 50, 51, 52, 53, 54, 56, 57, 59, 64, 67, 69, 70, 83, 146, 147, 148, 156, 162, 163, 165, 168, 169, 173, 174, 175, 182, 187, 189, 190, 191, 192, 218, 224, 225, 242, 250, 253, 255, 256, 259, 261, 262, 296, 297, 298, 304, 309, 312, 314, 320, 322, 335, 337, 338, 343, 344, 347, 350, 351, 352, 353, 354, 355, 357, 358, 365, 366, 367, 368, 369, 370, 371, 372
Computer Programming 25, 47, 145, 163, 174, 188, 190, 193, 196, 198, 210, 227, 253, 337, 343, 344, 345, 346, 347
Computer Science 19, 28, 33, 45, 47, 48, 49, 53, 55, 56, 57, 58, 59, 60, 61, 62, 63, 64, 65, 66, 67, 68, 69, 70, 71, 72, 73, 81, 106, 107, 111, 112, 115, 119, 120, 122, 129, 130, 131, 132, 133, 134, 136, 138, 139, 140, 141, 142, 145, 146, 157, 160, 161, 162, 163, 164, 165, 168, 169, 172, 188, 189, 190, 191, 193, 194, 195, 196, 198, 201, 202, 206, 207, 214, 215, 216, 217, 218, 219, 223, 224, 225, 226, 227, 228, 230, 235, 237, 239, 241, 242, 244, 247, 248, 250, 251, 252, 254, 255, 256, 258, 259, 260, 261, 262, 270, 271, 272, 278, 287, 291, 300, 304, 311, 314, 319, 320, 336, 337, 338, 339, 341, 342, 344, 345, 347, 349, 350, 351, 352, 353, 354, 355, 356, 357, 358, 359, 360, 361, 362, 363, 364, 365, 366, 367, 368, 369, 371, 372
computer science education 45, 48, 49, 55, 56, 57, 58, 59, 60, 61, 62, 63, 64, 65, 66, 67, 68, 69, 70, 71, 72, 73, 106, 111, 112, 115, 129, 131, 132, 133, 134, 136, 139, 140, 141, 142, 145, 146, 160, 163, 164, 165, 168, 169, 188, 189, 191, 196, 198, 202, 214, 215, 216, 217, 218, 219, 223, 224,

225, 226, 227, 228, 230, 235, 237, 239, 241, 244, 247, 248, 250, 251, 252, 255, 258, 259, 260, 314, 336, 337, 338, 339, 341, 342, 345, 347, 349, 350, 351, 352, 354, 355, 356, 357, 358, 359, 360, 361, 362, 363, 364, 365, 368, 369, 371, 372
Computer Science Teachers Association (CSTA) 72, 304, 311, 349, 351, 357, 358, 361, 362, 367
Computer Vision 120, 121, 122, 123, 124, 131, 133, 136, 137, 138, 140, 141, 142, 143
Concept Learning 321, 345
Conceptual Metaphor 319, 325, 326, 330, 332, 339, 341, 343
Curriculum 4, 7, 19, 21, 24, 38, 45, 47, 53, 56, 57, 60, 62, 69, 70, 71, 81, 82, 83, 107, 108, 109, 111, 112, 131, 132, 133, 134, 138, 141, 146, 157, 158, 161, 162, 167, 173, 175, 191, 196, 197, 211, 217, 225, 236, 239, 258, 262, 271, 274, 277, 278, 279, 280, 281, 282, 284, 285, 288, 289, 295, 296, 298, 304, 308, 313, 315, 316, 318, 319, 320, 331, 334, 338, 344, 349, 350, 351, 358, 359, 361, 362, 363, 364, 369
Curriculum Integration 318
Cybersecurity 73, 74, 75, 76, 77, 78, 79, 80, 81, 82, 83, 84, 85, 87, 88, 89, 91, 93, 105, 106, 107, 108, 109, 236, 237, 238, 272, 363

D

data literacy 278, 279, 290, 292
Data Representation 28, 30
Data Science 112, 141, 145, 350, 364, 365, 367
Decomposition 28, 29, 30, 37, 39, 43, 56, 189, 350, 352
Deep Learning 114, 123, 124, 139, 189
digital literacy 20, 56, 77, 145, 211, 224, 225, 230, 241, 251, 263, 266, 280, 281, 282, 285, 287, 297, 323, 358, 359
digital rubrics 223, 224, 226, 248, 250

E

Educational Robotics (ER) 19, 23, 38, 45, 47, 48, 124, 141, 293, 296, 297, 303, 305, 308, 309, 310, 311, 315, 318, 343, 368, 372
e-portfolio 232, 247, 248

F

Feature Extraction 121, 122, 140
Further Education and Training 55, 58, 61, 65

G

Generative Artificial Intelligence 116, 124, 125, 126, 127, 128, 129, 131, 132, 133, 135, 136, 139, 140
Grade 10-12 Classrooms 55, 58, 61, 65, 66

I

Information Security 73, 74, 75, 76, 77, 79, 80, 81, 82, 83, 88, 105, 106, 107, 110, 238, 241
Information Technology (IT) 55, 58, 59, 61, 65, 68, 69, 70, 71, 74, 82, 94, 108, 110, 166, 189, 190, 196, 205, 237, 241, 255, 258, 338, 339, 357, 360, 362, 364, 367, 369
instructional design 1, 11, 12, 21, 57
International Society for Technology in Education 282, 290, 291, 349, 351, 357, 358, 369

J

Jupyter 114, 141

K

K12 Computer Science Education 73, 223, 224, 227, 235, 237, 239, 244, 250
K–12 Education 296, 297, 304, 318, 350, 357, 358
K12 Education 4

K-12 level 1, 2, 3, 4, 5, 6, 7, 8, 11, 17, 57, 58, 147, 148, 157, 158, 161, 162, 166, 173, 174, 175, 183, 184, 185, 224, 225, 324, 331, 342, 355, 363
KIBO 36, 37, 38, 40

L

Learning Programming 160, 168, 171, 172, 173, 175, 176, 178, 179, 183, 194, 319, 320, 321, 322, 323, 325, 329, 334, 338, 341, 343, 346, 353, 364
Low-code programming 145, 146, 150, 151, 152, 153, 154, 155, 156, 157, 158, 159, 160, 161, 162, 165

M

Machine Learning (ML) 76, 112, 113, 114, 115, 124, 129, 133, 135, 137, 139, 140, 141, 142, 165, 201, 272, 293, 294, 295, 296, 297, 298, 299, 300, 301, 302, 303, 304, 305, 306, 307, 308, 309, 310, 311, 312, 313, 314, 315, 316, 317, 318, 345, 371
mathematical thinking 2, 10

N

National Centre for Computing Education (NCCE) 349, 359, 362, 369, 370
Natural Language Processing 115, 116, 117, 118, 119, 125, 126, 127, 133, 137, 140, 141, 143, 339
novice programmer 187, 189

O

Online assessment 123, 223, 224, 225, 226, 227, 229, 230, 231, 232, 233, 235, 237, 238, 239, 244, 246, 250, 251, 252, 253, 255, 256, 257, 258, 261, 262
online exams 223, 224, 226, 232, 234, 239, 240, 250, 251, 260

P

Pattern Recognition 28, 30, 37, 42, 56, 141, 243, 318, 350, 352
peer review 60, 67, 248, 261
problem-solving 1, 2, 3, 4, 5, 6, 7, 8, 9, 10, 11, 14, 15, 21, 27, 29, 31, 33, 34, 35, 36, 37, 39, 40, 43, 49, 56, 61, 148, 156, 157, 160, 161, 172, 173, 175, 176, 178, 181, 182, 189, 192, 208, 211, 214, 225, 226, 271, 281, 295, 296, 297, 298, 318, 337, 352, 353, 355
professional development 2, 22, 40, 41, 44, 57, 59, 60, 62, 64, 65, 66, 67, 157, 158, 159, 161, 169, 171, 173, 263, 264, 265, 266, 267, 268, 269, 270, 271, 272, 273, 274, 275, 276, 277, 278, 281, 282, 283, 284, 285, 287, 288, 289, 290, 291, 292, 317, 319, 331, 344, 351, 358, 359, 360, 365, 368, 372
Programming Concepts 9, 13, 14, 17, 37, 160, 161, 166, 173, 176, 178, 180, 181, 204, 206, 208, 209, 319, 320, 321, 322, 324, 325, 329, 331, 332, 333, 334, 335, 339, 341, 342, 346, 347, 352, 353, 355, 368
Programming education 59, 61, 62, 72, 145, 146, 147, 155, 157, 158, 160, 163, 164, 166, 167, 172, 175, 181, 183, 184, 185, 186, 189, 192, 193, 198, 200, 207, 230, 258, 303, 324, 330, 338, 339, 346, 356
programming mistakes 163, 172, 173, 177, 178, 185, 186, 188
Python 9, 114, 121, 141, 172, 174, 175, 192, 200, 201, 210, 226, 236, 245, 301, 302, 305, 306, 353, 363, 365

R

robotic coding 3, 17, 39, 53, 236

S

Scratch Junior 34, 43
Seymour Papert 2, 296
standardized tests 223, 226, 242, 243, 250

STEM Education 19, 25, 169, 187, 272, 295, 296, 307, 308, 311, 312, 313, 316, 317, 318, 355, 356, 367, 370, 371

T

teacher leadership 282, 283, 288, 292
Teaching Programming 22, 146, 148, 156, 172, 173, 175, 176, 179, 191, 192, 204, 206, 207, 216, 218, 219, 260, 301, 319, 320, 321, 322, 323, 324, 325, 329, 331, 332, 333, 334, 335, 341, 342, 345, 347
Technological Advancements 267, 271, 294
Tensorflow 114, 137, 138, 301, 307, 315
TPACK model 1, 8, 10, 11, 13

U

Unplugged Computing 46

V

Visually Impaired 193, 194, 195, 196, 197, 198, 199, 200, 201, 202, 203, 204, 205, 206, 207, 209, 211, 212, 213, 214, 215, 217, 219, 220

www.ingramcontent.com/pod-product-compliance
Lightning Source LLC
LaVergne TN
LVHW080348011026
849161LV00009B/2230